Standard Lesson Com...

Customer Survey

As part of Standard Publishing's commitment to provide you excellent Christian education resources, we would appreciate your comments about this product: 2001-02 Standard Lesson Commentary. *Please take a moment and complete the survey below, detach and mail promptly. Your input is valuable as we develop products for your future use. Thank you for taking time to participate and for purchasing the Standard Lesson Commentary.*

User Profile (check one response for each item)

1. Gender: ❏ male ❏ female
2. Age: ❏ under 20 ❏ 20—39 ❏ 40—59 ❏ 60 +
3. Education: ❏ High School ❏ Some College ❏ College Graduate ❏ Graduate School
4. Residence: City _____ State _____
5. Church affiliation:
   ❏ Assembly of God
   ❏ Baptist
   ❏ Christian Churches / Churches of Christ
   ❏ Christian Church (Disciples)
   ❏ Church of God
   ❏ Churches of Christ (a cappella)
   ❏ Episcopal
   ❏ Lutheran
   ❏ Methodist
   ❏ Presbyterian
   ❏ Pentecostal
   ❏ Roman Catholic
   ❏ Other_____
6. Purchased by: ❏ Individual User ❏ Church ❏ As gift

7. What is the primary use for your Standard Lesson Commentary? (Check one.)
   ❏ Teacher resource for Sunday school lesson preparation
   ❏ Student resource for Sunday school
   ❏ Devotions
   ❏ Personal study
   ❏ Group Bible study
   ❏ Reference
   ❏ Other_____

8. Features. (Please circle the number that indicates your assessment of the feature indicated.)

   1 unacceptable   2 below average   3 average   4 above average   5 excellent

Lesson Development	1	2	3	4	5
Graphics	1	2	3	4	5
Ease of Use	1	2	3	4	5
CD Rom	1	2	3	4	5	NA
Index	1	2	3	4	5
Pronunciation Guide	1	2	3	4	5
Activities	1	2	3	4	5
Discussion Questions	1	2	3	4	5

(Continued on back.)

-------------------------------- FOLD HERE --------------------------------

9. Factors influencing purchase decision. (Circle the number that indicates the importance of each factor in the purchase decision.)

1 not at all   2 slightly   3 somewhat   4 very   5 extremely

	1	2	3	4	5
Price	1	2	3	4	5
Advertising	1	2	3	4	5
King James Version	1	2	3	4	5
New International Version	1	2	3	4	5
CD ROM availability	1	2	3	4	5
Companion to Standard Publishing Curriculum	1	2	3	4	5
Standard Publishing reputation	1	2	3	4	5
Recommended by church/friend	1	2	3	4	5
Product features	1	2	3	4	5

10. Which other Standard Publishing products do you use? (Check all that apply.)

❑ Christian Standard Magazine
❑ The Lookout Magazine
❑ Standard Publishing Sunday school Curriculum
❑ Vacation Bible School program

❑ Children's ministry resources
❑ Solid Foundation Bible Studies
❑ Other adult ministry resources

*Thank you for taking time to complete this survey
and for purchasing the **Standard Lesson Commentary**!*

PLEASE TAPE OR GLUE ENDS TOGETHER BEFORE MAILING.

The NIV®
STANDARD
LESSON
COMMENTARY
2001-2002

edited by

RONALD G. DAVIS, DOUGLAS REDFORD,
RONALD L. NICKELSON, AND JONATHAN UNDERWOOD

published by
Standard Publishing
Mark A. Taylor, Publisher
Jonathan Underwood, Senior Editor
Cheryl Frey, Office Editor

Eighth Annual Volume

CD-ROM AVAILABLE

The *Standard Lesson Commentary* is available in an electronic format in special editions of the *Standard Lesson Commentary* (King James edition) and *The NIV® Standard Lesson Commentary*. These editions (order # 20002 for KJV and 30002 for NIV®) contain a compact disk for use with Windows®-based computers.

The electronic version of *The Standard Lesson Commentary* and the *Logos Library System* search engine are contained on the CD-ROM so you can:
- Instantly search the complete text of the Commentary for any word, phrase, or Bible reference.
- Access related articles or information via hyperlinks within the text of each book.
- Access any reference in the King James Version of the Bible.
- Unlock the NIV® Bible to access references in it. (This is NOT a free unlock.)
- Print lessons directly from the *Logos Library System®*, export to *Logos Lesson Builder*, or customize in any Windows® word processor.

System Requirements: Windows 2000/ME/98/95; 32 Meg RAM; 25 Meg Available Hard Drive Space; 2x or better CD-ROM drive

If you have any questions regarding the use or content of this CD-ROM, please contact Technical Support by telephone at 800-446-5564 or 630-789-0710, by fax at 630-789-0997, or by email at techsup@isgrupe.com. Technical Support is available from 9:00 am to 5:00 pm (CST), Monday through Friday.

© 2001
STANDARD PUBLISHING
a division of STANDEX INTERNATIONAL Corporation
8121 Hamilton Avenue, Cincinnati, Ohio 45231
Printed in U.S.A.

In This Volume

Special Features

Fall Quarter, 2001
Jesus' Ministry

Writers

Lesson Development ....*Orrin Root*
Verbal Illustrations ....*Charles R. Boatman*
What Do You Think? ....*Kenton K. Smith*

Discovery Learning ....*Ronald L. Oakes*
Reproducible Activities ....*Ronald L. Oakes*

Winter Quarter, 2001-2002
Light for All People

Writers

Lesson Development...........*Dennis Gaertner (1-5),
David Reece (6-9), Lloyd Pelfrey (10-13)*
Verbal Illustrations................*Jeffrey Metzger (1-5),
Robert C. Shannon (6-13)*

What Do You Think? ....*Richard A. Koffarnus*
Discovery Learning ....*Alan Weber*
Reproducible Activities.........................*Alan Weber*

Spring Quarter, 2002
The Power of the Gospel

Writers

Lesson Development..............*John W. Wade (1-9),
Kenneth L. Boles (10-13)*
What Do You Think? ....*Kenneth Beck (1-5),
Phil Roberts (6-13)*

Verbal Illustrations ....*Charles R. Boatman*
Discovery Learning ....*Rick Shonkwiler*
Reproducible Activities.................*Rick Shonkwiler*

Summer Quarter, 2002
Worship and Wisdom for Living

Writers

Lesson Development........*Richard W. Baynes (1-5),
Terry A. Clark (6-9), John W. Wade (10-13)*
Verbal Illustrations ....*Jerran Jackson (1-5),
Richard W. Baynes (6-9), Jeffrey Metzger (6-13)*

What Do You Think?...............*Kenneth Goble (1-5)
Charles E. Cook (6-13)*
Discovery Learning ....*Everett Brewer*
Reproducible Activities....................*Everett Brewer*

Index of Printed Texts, 2001-2002

The printed texts for 2000-2001 are arranged here in the order in which they appear in the Bible. Opposite each reference is the page number on which the lesson that treats the passage begins in this volume.

Cumulative Index of Printed Texts

A cumulative index for the Scripture passages used in *The NIV Standard Lesson Commentary* for September, 1998—August, 2002 is presented here for your convenience.

Fall Quarter, 2001

Jesus' Ministry

(Miracles, Parables, the Sermon on the Mount)

Special Features

Lessons

Unit 1: Performing Miracles

Unit 2: Truth in Parables

Unit 3: The Sermon on the Mount

About These Lessons

These lessons will focus on the life of Jesus. Rather than examine texts from one Gospel, the lessons of the current quarter will draw from all four of the Gospel records. Together, these four witnesses will provide a unified composite of the life of our Lord, particularly in his wonderful miracles and his powerful teaching. May we follow in the path he has set.

Sep 2

Sep 9

Sep 16

Sep 23

Sep 30

Oct 7

Oct 14

Oct 21

Oct 28

Nov 4

Nov 11

Nov 18

Nov 25

Blessed to Bless Others

When God called Abram, he called him to be a blessing to "all peoples on earth" (Genesis 12:3). The lessons for the coming year call attention to our privilege and purpose as "Abraham's seed" (Galatians 3:29). The fall quarter focuses on Jesus' miracles, which distinguish him as the Son of God, and on his teachings, which define the way of life that should distinguish his followers.

The winter quarter features lessons drawn from the Old Testament, particularly Isaiah. These studies remind us that God has always had a heart for the nations—and so must his people.

The lessons for the spring quarter are taken from Romans and Galatians. These letters resonate with the themes of God's grace in Jesus Christ and the responsibility of his people to live by grace.

The summer quarter brings us back to the Old Testament with the theme, "Worship and Wisdom for Living." Using texts from Psalms and Proverbs, these studies will encourage us to see life the way God sees it.

May these lessons help us in fulfilling our mission as "children of Abraham"—blessed to bless others!

International Sunday School Lesson Cycle
September, 1998—August, 2004

YEAR	FALL QUARTER (Sept., Oct., Nov.)	WINTER QUARTER (Dec., Jan., Feb.)	SPRING QUARTER (Mar., Apr., May)	SUMMER QUARTER (June, July, Aug.)
1998-1999	God Calls a People to Faithful Living (Old Testament Survey)	God Calls Anew in Jesus Christ (New Testament Survey)	That You May Believe (John)	Genesis: Beginnings (Genesis)
1999-2000	From Slavery to Conquest (Exodus, Leviticus, Numbers, Deuteronomy, Joshua)	Immanuel: God With Us (Matthew)	Helping a Church Confront Crisis (1 and 2 Corinthians)	New Life in Christ (Ephesians, Philippians, Colossians, Philemon)
2000-2001	Rulers of Israel (Judges, 1 and 2 Samuel, 1 Kings 1-11)	Good News of Jesus (Luke)	Continuing Jesus' Work (Acts)	Division and Decline (1 Kings 12-22, 2 Kings 1-17, Isaiah 1-39, Hosea, Amos, Micah)
2001-2002	Jesus' Ministry (Parables, Miracles, Sermon on the Mount)	Light for All People (Isaiah 9:1-7; 11:1-9; 40-66; Ruth, Jonah, Nahum)	The Power of the Gospel (Romans, Galatians)	Worship and Wisdom for Living (Psalms, Proverbs)
2002-2003	Judgment and Exile (2 Kings 18-25, Jeremiah, Lamentations, Ezekiel, Habakkuk, Zephaniah)	Portraits of Faith (Personalities in the New Testament)	Jesus: God's Power in Action (Mark)	God Restores a Remnant (Ezra, Nehemiah, Daniel, Joel, Obadiah, Haggai, Zechariah, Malachi)
2003-2004	Faith Faces the World (James, 1 and 2 Peter, 1, 2, 3 John, Jude)	A Child Is Given (Samuel, John the Baptist, Jesus) Lessons From Life (Esther, Job, Ecclesiastes, Song of Solomon)	Jesus Fulfills His Mission (Death, Burial, and Resurrection Texts) Living Expectantly (1, 2 Thessalonians, Revelation)	Hold Fast to the Faith (Hebrews) Guidelines for the Church's Ministry (1, 2 Timothy, Titus)

Learning From Jesus

by Orrin Root

Jesus is our master teacher and our perfect example. More than that, he is our Lord and our King. It should be our duty and our pleasure to learn what he teaches and follow his example.

In our Sunday school studies, then, it is fitting to spend about a quarter of each year focusing on the life and teachings of Jesus. Within our current six-year cycle, one quarter is devoted to a study of each of the four Gospels—Matthew, Mark, Luke, and John. During the last year of the cycle (2003-2004), portions of two quarters will be devoted to studies from the Gospels. (See the chart on the opposite page.)

For the three months ahead (September, October, and November of 2001), we shall draw material from all four of the Gospels to form a series of lessons arranged by topics. In September we shall study some of Jesus' miracles, in October we shall consider some of his parables, and in November we shall examine four lessons from his Sermon on the Mount.

What follows are brief previews of the lessons to be covered during the next three months.

UNIT 1: PERFORMING MIRACLES

Lesson 1: Jesus Works His First Miracle. There was a small emergency at a wedding feast in Cana of Galilee: the wine was all gone. Compassionate Jesus solved the problem by turning approximately one hundred fifty gallons of water into superior wine. Thus he saved the host from embarrassment and, more important, he strengthened his earliest disciples' faith in him. It should strengthen the faith of modern disciples as well.

Lesson 2: Jesus Displays Power Over Nature. Only a preacher knows how exhausting it is to preach for hours, and only a doctor knows how wearying it is to care for the seriously ill. Jesus had been doing both—though no doctor or preacher is comparable to Jesus. Still, he was so exhausted that he went to sleep in a little boat as it crossed the Sea of Galilee. He continued to sleep, even when a terrific storm arose and threatened to overturn the boat. The frightened disciples awakened Jesus. At his rebuke the wind stopped blowing and the sea was calm. Thus the disciples' faith in Jesus was fortified yet more.

Lesson 3: Jesus Displays Power Over Disease. Jesus quickly became the most popular teacher in Galilee, making the established teachers wild with jealousy. They wanted to accuse him of breaking the law when he healed on the Sabbath, but his questions left them speechless. So they plotted to kill him.

The established teachers in Jerusalem were as envious as those in Galilee. When Jesus gave sight to a blind man on the Sabbath, they claimed that he was a sinner. But the man who received his sight resisted their harassment and declared his faith in Jesus.

Lesson 4: A Mother Persists in Faith. Jesus traveled north from Galilee to the area around Tyre and Sidon. Even in that foreign territory his reputation was known. Soon he was recognized by a woman who pleaded for help on behalf of her daughter, who was troubled by a demon. Jesus initially ignored the woman's request because, as he explained to the disciples, his personal mission was only to the people of Israel. When she kept on asking, Jesus told the woman the same thing, noting that it was not proper to give the children's food to the dogs. Humbly she replied that dogs eat crumbs that fall from the children's table. Jesus then praised the woman's faith and set her daughter free from the demon. This reminds us that Jesus' salvation is meant for all the people of the world.

Lesson 5: Lazarus Is Raised. Mary and Martha and their brother Lazarus were dear friends of Jesus. They lived in Bethany, just east of Jerusalem. When Lazarus became very sick, his sisters sent word to Jesus; but Jesus delayed his response to their message. He arrived in Bethany four days after Lazarus had died and had been entombed in a cave. Still, when Jesus called him, the dead man came forth! Jesus' power is stronger than death.

OCTOBER

UNIT 2: TRUTH IN PARABLES

Lesson 6: Jesus Teaches in Parables. When asked why he used parables in his teaching, Jesus replied that by parables he revealed the truth about his kingdom to those disciples who cared enough to seek it. His answer implied that the truth would remain hidden to hearers who cared only about seeing the miracles that Jesus could do.

One parable described a man who sowed good seed throughout his field, yet the harvest was different because the soil was different in various parts of the field. As Jesus explained the parable, he himself was the sower, the truth he taught was the seed, and the hearers were the field. The same truth produced different results because the hearers were different. Each of us must ask himself or herself, "What kind of soil am I?" All of us can be better soil than we are now.

Lesson 7: The Good Samaritan. "Who is my neighbor?" asked a lawyer. Jesus answered the question with the story of a good Samaritan who spent time and money to help a wounded stranger. That Samaritan showed himself to be a good neighbor, though he neither lived near the man he helped nor had any acquaintance with him. "Go and do likewise," said Jesus to the lawyer—and to you and me.

Lesson 8: Parables on Prayer. To teach us to be persistent in prayer, Jesus told of a widow who kept on presenting her plea until an unjust judge finally issued a just decision. To teach us to be humble in prayer, he contrasted two men: a proud Pharisee's prayer was devoted to bragging about himself; a humble tax collector's prayer was a fervent plea for mercy.

Lesson 9: The Sheep and the Goats. Jesus said that at the final judgment he will separate the people of all nations as a shepherd separates sheep from goats. Strictly speaking, this story is a simile rather than a parable; but it resembles a parable in that people are compared with lesser things. Some people will be invited to the kingdom long prepared for them, for they have been kind and helpful to Jesus. Others will be consigned to everlasting fire because they have ignored Jesus in his needs.

When were these people either kind or unkind to Jesus? The answer: when they were kind or unkind to some of his people. Thus, even now you and I are choosing our eternal destiny.

NOVEMBER

UNIT 3: THE SERMON ON THE MOUNT

Lesson 10: Blessed Are You. Jesus' Sermon on the Mount begins with a series of blessings pronounced on people in circumstances that would seem to produce only unhappiness. Thus are we encouraged to walk with Jesus day by day, trusting him to bless us in any situation. By doing this we become the salt of the earth, improving its flavor and preserving it. According to another metaphor, we become the light of the world, helping all its people to find the right way.

Lesson 11: Jesus Fulfills the Law. Before giving some teaching that appeared to be quite different from the law, Jesus announced that he had not come to destroy the law, but to fulfill it. His fuller teaching covers thoughts, motives, and emotions, as well as acts. He teaches us to be generous rather than merely just, to love even the enemies who hate us, and to do good to those who do only evil to us. Thus do we show ourselves to be children of our Father in Heaven, for he provides rain and sun for the evil people as well as the good.

Lesson 12: Storing Treasures in Heaven. Jesus advised his hearers to lay up treasures in Heaven rather than on earth. To do this, we must not be anxious about our physical needs such as food and clothing. God provides food for the birds; will he not provide for us as well? He provides clothing for the wildflowers; will he not do as much for us? Our first aim is to be ruled by God, to do his will, to be righteous in his sight. Then our physical needs will be supplied.

Lesson 13: Living by the Law of Love. The law said, "Love your neighbor as yourself" (Leviticus 19:18). Our text for this lesson presents the same truth in the form of the well-known Golden Rule: "In everything, do to others what you would have them do to you" (Matthew 7:12). Among other things, this means that we will not be harsh and merciless in judging others, but will first seek out and correct our own faults. We judge a tree correctly by observing what kind of fruit it bears, and we judge a person fairly when we see the results of what he or she says and does.

What will these thirteen lessons do for us? That depends on what we do with them. If we learn them well, they will increase our understanding of Jesus and his will. If we follow their teaching in our daily living, they will make us better people.

Lesson Planning Page

LESSON AIMS

List the aims here, either directly from the lesson or revised to suit your individual needs.

GETTING STARTED

Begin with an opening activity like the illustration from the beginning of the lesson, "Into the Lesson" from the Discovery Learning page, a discussion question, or some other appropriate opener.

LESSON DEVELOPMENT

I.

List in order the activities you will use. These include discussion questions, activities from the discovery learning page and the reproducible page—as well as key points from the commentary section.

II.

III.

CONCLUSION & APPLICATION

How will you bring the lesson to a climax, stressing the key point and desired action steps?

CLOSING ACTIVITY

Dismiss the class with an activity that reinforces the Bible lesson.

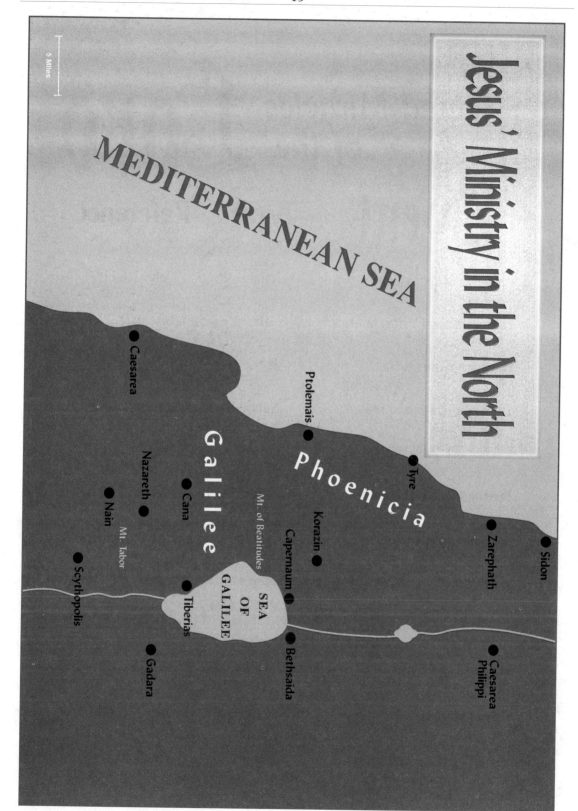

Selected Miracles of the Lord

Event	Type	Reference
Changing Water to Wine	Nature	John 2:1-11
Passing Through a Hostile Crowd	Nature	Luke 4:28-30
Healing a Withered Hand	People	Mark 3:1-6
Stilling the Storm and Sea	Nature	Matthew 8:23-27
Casting out Demons	Demons	Mark 5:1-20
Feeding the Five Thousand	Nature	Matthew 14:14-21
Walking on Water	Nature	John 6:15-21
Healing the Canaanite s Daughter	People	Matthew 15:21-31
Predicting a Coin in a Fish	Knowledge	Matthew 17:24-27
Healing a Blind Man	People	John 9:1-12
Raising Lazarus	People	John 11:38-44
Appearing in a Closed Room	Nature	John 20:19

Jesus' Ministry
Unit 1: Performing Miracles
(Lessons 1-5)

JESUS WORKS HIS FIRST MIRACLE

LESSON 1

WHY TEACH THIS LESSON?

Miracle is a word heard frequently today. People escape unharmed from a terrible car wreck and the TV reporter calls it "a miracle." A healthy baby is born after a difficult pregnancy, and the excited parents refer to the new child as their "miracle baby." Many religious broadcasts today seem to be centered around the idea of encouraging the audience to "expect a miracle" (often as a change in financial status, or some such). But as we shall see, the word *miracle* as used in the Gospels often has a meaning quite different from these modern understandings! Furthermore, the miracles that Jesus performed during his earthly ministry had a singular focus: to prove that he was indeed the Son of God, and that he is one with the Father (John 14:11). Since the truth of the Christian faith rests on the genuineness of Jesus' claims about himself, we should study these miracles carefully to discover what they prove.

INTRODUCTION

A. FEELING HELPLESS

One wintry night a carload of friends from another town dropped in to attend the evening service at our church. My wife and I greeted them with joy, but there was no time for us to talk. The prelude was already sounding, so we hurried to our seats. After the benediction, I urged our friends, "Come on over to the house. We'll have ice cream."

Ice cream was an ever-present delight at our house. Almost always there were two or three flavors in the freezer, ready to be served as a favorite bedtime snack, a ready dessert for any meal, or an impromptu refreshment for unexpected guests.

The guests that evening had eaten ice cream at our house before, and they happily followed us home. As we all trooped into the house, I told my wife, "I promised ice cream."

Her reply nearly floored me: "We don't have any." The unthinkable had happened. For the first time since we had obtained a home freezer, we were out of ice cream—and the house was full of expectant guests. I knew then how the host must have felt at that wedding celebration in Cana of Galilee when a servant whispered nervously, "We're running out of wine." I was speechless, helpless.

Fortunately, my wife was not so helpless. We had milk in the refrigerator, bread in the breadbox, and able helpers among the guests. In just a few minutes we had an ample supply of cinnamon toast and hot chocolate, which proved to be an even better treat than ice cream for that wintry night.

B. LESSON BACKGROUND

In our lesson text we read of "a wedding . . . at Cana"; however, at a first-century wedding the guests did not see the happy pair stand together and

DEVOTIONAL READING:
PSALM 77:11-15
BACKGROUND SCRIPTURE:
JOHN 2:1-11
PRINTED TEXT:
JOHN 2:1-11

LESSON AIMS

After participating in this lesson, a student should be able to:

1. Give the details and result of the miracle that Jesus performed at the wedding feast in Cana of Galilee.

2. Explain the role of Jesus' miracles in establishing his identity as the Son of God.

3. Give thanks for the many miracles that provide solid evidence for believing in Jesus as the Son of God.

KEY VERSE

This, the first of his miraculous signs, Jesus performed at Cana in Galilee. He thus revealed his glory, and his disciples put their faith in him.

—John 2:11

LESSON 1 NOTES

promise to love, cherish, and protect each other "till death do us part." The equivalent of such promises occurred at the "betrothal," when a man and a woman became engaged. The "wedding" was more similar to what we call a wedding reception—simply a glad celebration and a time to rejoice with the happy couple and wish them well in their life together.

More details about the marriage customs of the time are revealed in Jesus' parable of the ten virgins (Matthew 25:1-13). There the festivities began with a party for the groom and his friends at the groom's home, while the bride's girl-friends got together at her home. At a time not announced in advance, the groom went to get his bride and took her to his home. In Jesus' parable the bridegroom did not come until midnight. Probably the celebration then continued for some time, perhaps until dawn. It is not hard to imagine that such an extended party might easily consume more refreshments than the host had provided.

Yet note that there is no suggestion of drunkenness, either in the parable or in today's text. The wine used in such celebrations was usually so diluted with water that its alcoholic content was slight.

I. EMBARRASSING SITUATION (JOHN 2:1-5)

Our text begins by setting the stage for a crisis that must have made the host feel as I did when I had no ice cream for the guests I had invited to our home. We have no hint of how long the wedding feast had been going on before the crisis occurred. Perhaps it had continued for hours.

A. THE OCCASION (vv. 1, 2)

1. On the third day a wedding took place at Cana in Galilee. Jesus' mother was there.

The chapter before this had its setting by the Jordan River, where John the Baptist was preaching. John announced that Jesus was "the Lamb of God, who takes away the sin of the world!" (John 1:29). Several of John's disciples then accompanied Jesus when he left the Jordan to return to *Galilee* (John 1:43). (He may have led them to his boyhood home in Nazareth.) *The third day* in our text should be counted from the day Jesus left the Jordan.

This group of disciples probably included Peter and Andrew (John 1:40-42), John (most likely the other disciple mentioned in John 1:35-40), and Philip and Nathanael (John 1:43-51). Many students suggest that John's brother James was present as well at this point, making a total of six disciples who went to Galilee with Jesus.

Cana was a small town near Nazareth, though its exact location is uncertain. Most likely *Jesus' mother* was a relative or close friend of the bridegroom's family. Perhaps she was helping with some of the details of the gathering.

2. . . . and Jesus and his disciples had also been invited to the wedding.

Jesus had been away from home for nearly two months. During that time, he had been baptized by John the Baptist; he had spent forty days in the desert without human companionship, but tempted by the devil; and he had returned to the Jordan and recruited his first *disciples* from among the disciples of John (Matthew 3:13–4:11; John 1:29-51). Now he came home to Galilee just in time for *the wedding* in Cana, and a quick invitation was given to him and his six new disciples. Such an invitation is another reason for supposing that Jesus' family and the bridegroom's family were either relatives or close friends.

A CAUSE FOR CELEBRATION

You can find almost anything on the Internet these days: vitamins, automobiles, exercise equipment—even a wife! At least that's what Rod Barnett thought, when, in

VISUALS FOR THESE LESSONS

The visual pictured in each lesson (e.g., page 21) is a small reproduction of a large, full-color poster included in the Adult Visuals packet for the Fall Quarter. The packet is available from your supplier. Order No. 192.

WHAT DO YOU THINK?

Jesus' attendance at a wedding feast may surprise some people. Is it hard for you to imagine Jesus having fun at a party? Why or why not?

1998, he launched his World Wide Web site with an offer of ten thousand dollars to anyone who would introduce him to the woman whom he would eventually marry.

During the first year of his offer, Barnett received thousands of responses, ranging from children suggesting that he marry their single moms to proposals for immoral liaisons. After about a year had passed, Barnett's unique approach to searching for a wife had resulted in only one "serious relationship," and that lasted just a couple of months. Up to that point he had found nothing to celebrate.

The way one finds a spouse today is certainly different from the custom in Jesus' day. What hasn't changed is the expectation that one's wedding will be a cause for celebration. Jesus was probably invited to the wedding at Cana because he was the kind of person who enjoyed such occasions. He wasn't the dour, lonely, religiose person-who-never-had-much-fun whom some have associated with Jesus.

Perhaps Jesus chose to begin his ministry of miracles at a wedding feast in order to show us that piety shouldn't keep us from celebrating even the intimately physical delights that God has created us to enjoy. —C. R. B.

B. THE NEED (v. 3)

3. When the wine was gone, Jesus' mother said to him, "They have no more wine."

The host had a serious problem. *The wine* provided for the party *was* all *gone*, or nearly all gone, and the party was not nearly at an end. The reason for the lack is unknown and is not important. The lack itself was terribly embarrassing.

Why did *Jesus' mother* take this distressing news to him? Jesus had done no miracles to this point. Mary wouldn't have been expecting that, would she? On the other hand, Mary knew that her son was also God's Son, destined to rule forever (Luke 1:31-33). Now he was approximately thirty years old (Luke 3:23). He had been baptized. He had gathered a few disciples. All of these events might have been taken to indicate that Jesus was about to assert himself and begin the promised rule. Was Mary hoping he would do so by working a miracle in order to produce *more wine?* We can only wonder.

C. THE PLAN (vv. 4, 5)

4. "Dear woman, why do you involve me?" Jesus replied. "My time has not yet come."

In the Greek text, Jesus' address to Mary is simply *woman*. That may sound to us as though Jesus were being rude to his mother, but Mary would not have taken it that way. It is the same way Jesus spoke to Mary as he tenderly provided for her care while he was dying (John 19:26). Still, a son's addressing his mother in this way is not found in any Greek or Hebrew literature outside the Gospel of John. We wonder about the significance of the address, no matter how tender. Some have suggested that Jesus was asserting his independence from family ties, signaling that Mary's role as his mother was now to be considered less significant than her position as his disciple.

"What to me and to you?" is a literal translation of *why do you involve me?* The words seem to say that the shortage of wine was none of Jesus' business or of Mary's. The reason follows: *my time has not yet come.* References to Jesus' "time" occur elsewhere in John's Gospel (7:6, 8, 30; 8:20). It is clear from later usage of this language in John that Jesus' "time" described his crucifixion (12:23, 27; 13:1; 16:32; 17:1). Mary was mistaken if she thought this was the time for Jesus to fulfill his mission as the Son of God.

5. His mother said to the servants, "Do whatever he tells you."

Mary did not beg or plead with Jesus. She simply told *the servants* present to *do whatever* Jesus told them to do. She did not try to tell Jesus what to do, but it is clear that she hoped he would do something.

II. MIRACLE (JOHN 2:6-10)

Perhaps something in Jesus' manner told Mary that he was not flatly refusing to help. We can imagine how eagerly she waited to see what would happen.

A. THE MATERIAL (vv. 6, 7)

6. Nearby stood six stone water jars, the kind used by the Jews for ceremonial washing, each holding from twenty to thirty gallons.

The *six stone water jars* may have contained water that had been used for washing the guests' feet as they came in from the dusty street. The word for *ceremonial washing* literally means "cleansing." Thus, the water may have been provided for the traditional washing of the guests' hands before they ate (Matthew 15:1, 2). The *twenty to thirty gallons* of water in each jar suggest that there were many guests.

7. Jesus said to the servants, "Fill the jars with water"; so they filled them to the brim.

Easily we imagine that all available *servants* were summoned to help carry out Jesus' command. Perhaps some took a smaller jar and hurried to the town well or spring. Soon the six big jars were *filled . . . to the brim.*

B. THE PRODUCT (v. 8a)

8a. Then he told them, "Now draw some out and take it to the master of the banquet."

Dippers were at hand to fill cups from the big jars. At Jesus' word, the first cupful was taken to *the master of the banquet*, whom we would be more likely to call the master of ceremonies or the toastmaster.

C. THE RESULT (vv. 8b-10)

8b, 9. They did so, and the master of the banquet tasted the water that had been turned into wine. He did not realize where it had come from, though the servants who had drawn the water knew. Then he called the bridegroom aside.

At some point before *the master* of ceremonies *tasted it, the water . . . had been turned into wine.* In fact, it was such excellent wine that the taster thought it merited special praise. He *called the bridegroom* to hear the praise. Of course, he did not know where the wine came from, but *the servants who had drawn the water knew.*

10. . . . and said, "Everyone brings out the choice wine first and then the cheaper wine after the guests have had too much to drink; but you have saved the best till now."

Everyone brings out the choice wine first. So said the master of ceremonies. Then he serves a *cheaper wine*—an inferior wine—when those drinking are too drunk to know the difference. Whether this was true or false, whether it was spoken in earnest or in jest, the praise that followed was certainly sincere: *You have saved the best till now.*

Again, we see no evidence that anyone was drunk at this celebration. The master of ceremonies did not find his taste dulled. With his first sip, he knew that the wine from the water jar was the best he had tasted that evening. And we suppose that every guest agreed with him.

III. EPILOGUE (JOHN 2:11)

Three important statements concerning Jesus' ministry of miracles are evident in this short verse that concludes John's record of an amazing event.

A. THE BEGINNING OF MIRACLES (v. 11a)

11a. This, the first of his miraculous signs, Jesus performed at Cana in Galilee.

John notes that this was *the first* of Jesus' miracles. Thus he implies that others followed. Reading through Matthew, Mark, Luke, and John, we see miracles of four kinds.

WHAT DO YOU THINK?

The servants at the wedding feast did as Jesus instructed them. How important do you think their later testimony might be in the face of skepticism concerning this miracle? (Note verse 9: "the servants . . . knew.")

HOW TO SAY IT

Cana. KAY-nuh.
Gadarene. GAD-uh-reen.
Galilee. GAL-uh-lee.
Nathanael. Nuh-THAN-yull.
Nazareth. NAZ-uh-reth.

1. Miracles in nature. In today's lesson we have seen Jesus change water into wine. In another such miracle, he multiplied a boy's lunch to make a meal for five thousand men, plus some women and children (John 6:1-14). In another, He walked on the surface of the sea (John 6:16-21). In yet another, his command stopped a raging storm (Mark 4:35-41). In these miracles, objects with no sense of hearing obeyed Jesus' command, and objects without a mind obeyed his will.

2. Miracles with people. In countless cases, Jesus healed "every disease and sickness among the people" (Matthew 4:23, 24). He even restored life to some who had died (Luke 7:11-17; 8:41, 42, 49-56; John 11:38-44).

3. Miracles with demons. Evil spirits sometimes took control of people, causing them to suffer various physical and mental disorders. At Jesus' command, those demons had to release their victims (Luke 7:21; 8:26-39; 9:37-43).

4. Miracles of knowledge. Jesus knew what people were thinking (Luke 5:22; 6:8; 9:47; 11:17; John 2:24, 25). He knew what was happening far away (John 11:14). He did not know when he would come again (Mark 13:32), but he knew he would come (Mark 13:26, 27).

Like the first miracle, all of these miracles demonstrated the glory of Jesus and led others to believe in him (John 14:11; 20:30, 31).

Selected Miracles of the Lord		
Event	**Type**	**Reference**
Changing Water to Wine	Nature	John 2:1-11
Passing Through a Hostile Crowd	Nature	Luke 4:28-30
Healing a Withered Hand	People	Mark 3:1-6
Stilling the Storm and Sea	Nature	Matthew 8:23-27
Casting out Demons	Demons	Mark 5:1-20
Feeding the Five Thousand	Nature	Matthew 14:14-21
Walking on Water	Nature	John 6:15-21
Healing the Canaanite's Daughter	People	Matthew 15:21-31
Predicting a Coin in a Fish	Knowledge	Matthew 17:24-27
Healing a Blind Man	People	John 9:1-12
Raising Lazarus	People	John 11:38-44
Appearing in a Closed Room	Nature	John 20:19

This poster is a chart of Jesus' miracles. You will find it useful throughout the quarter.

B. THE GLORY OF JESUS (v. 11b)
11b. He thus revealed his glory.

Sometimes the word *glory* means praise or honor. That is its meaning when we say, "Give glory to God." But in this verse the word *glory* means those attributes of Jesus that are worthy of honor and praise. Several of them are shown clearly in his first miracle.

1. His creative power. Without so much as a word or a touch, Jesus transformed six jars of water into jars of excellent wine. Impossible as this would be for any human, it was not difficult at all for the Lord of creation (John 1:3). The heavens and the earth are the handiwork of the One who made six jars of wine at Cana.

2. His compassion. As noted above, Jesus first seemed to say that the shortage of wine was no concern of his. It was a concern of the host. He had made a mistake. He had not provided enough wine. He would be ashamed and embarrassed—but why should anyone else care?

But Mary did care, not because of any failure of her own, but because she shared the feelings of the host. And Jesus cared. He shared the feelings of his mother and his friend. So the creative power of the Almighty was used to supply refreshments for a wedding reception.

3. His flexibility. Jesus' time had not yet come (v. 4). But he was willing to adjust his schedule at the request of his mother in order to meet the need of a friend.

C. THE BELIEVING DISCIPLES (v. 11c)
11c. . . . and his disciples put their faith in him.

Jesus' *disciples put their faith in him* before they came to Cana. The first two of them had followed him because John the Baptist pointed him out as "the Lamb of God" (John 1:35-37). These men had been disciples of John. No doubt they had heard John say much more about the greater One who was to come (Luke 3:15-17; John 1:26-34). Philip was convinced that Jesus was the one foretold by the law and the prophets; Nathanael exclaimed, "Rabbi, you are the Son of God; you are the King of Israel" (John 1:43-49).

But the faith of these men grew stronger and deeper when they saw water poured into six jars and wine dipped out. They knew God's power was in what Jesus did; how could they ever doubt that God's truth was in what he said?

WHAT DO YOU THINK?

Jesus used his miracle-working power to save a family from embarrassment during a wedding banquet, overriding the fact that his time had "not yet come." What does that indicate about his compassion toward us?

PRAYER

Father, thank you for the solid foundation of facts that supports our faith. Thank you for sending Jesus with the kind of power that convinces us that he is more than human. Thank you for the inspired record that tells of him. May we have wisdom to understand that record and courage to follow it. In Jesus' name, amen.

THOUGHT TO REMEMBER

Jesus served with God's power and spoke with God's truth.

WHEN GOD SPEAKS

In Christian circles, one occasionally hears someone say, "The Lord told me . . ." or "The Lord showed me . . ." such-and-such. Some Christians wonder whether this kind of "message" is really God speaking or simply a feeling prompted by the person's own desires.

Other people hear "divine messages" that are clearly *not* from God. For example, Brandon Wilson claimed that God had told him to murder a nine-year-old boy in an Oceanside, California, beachfront rest room in 1998. Wilson, a drifter, said he began to have murderous thoughts as a result of hearing the "shock-rock" music of Marilyn Manson and reading the writings of the German philosopher, Nietzsche (*Nee-cheh*). After his arrest, Wilson said God had told him to start killing people so that the world would come to an end: "There was a part of me that was evil and God had put it there for a reason—to use me."

The incident at the wedding feast in Cana offers a striking contrast to such twisted thinking as Wilson's. At Cana those who obeyed the voice of Jesus found delight and satisfaction for themselves and others, rather than suffering and grief.

So how do *we* determine whether someone's words really represent the voice of God? First, we must measure any alleged "message" by what Scripture teaches. And second, we must examine the "fruits" of the people who claim to have heard from God. If chaos and destruction follow their words and actions, we do well to question the source of their message. —C. R. B.

CONCLUSION

Jesus' first miracle was followed by miracles innumerable and undeniable. Day after day Jesus "revealed his glory": he showed his divine power, his tender compassion, and his eagerness to help the needy. How could anyone in that time fail to believe in him? How can anyone in our time doubt that he is the Son of God?

A. ANCIENT UNBELIEVERS

The priests and Pharisees would not believe in Jesus because he was not one of them. They could not believe that God had chosen a carpenter of Galilee to be the Messiah. But they could not deny that Jesus' miracles were done by superhuman power, so they claimed that he did them by the power of Satan (Matthew 12:22-24).

B. MODERN UNBELIEVERS

Modern unbelievers are often vocal in denying Jesus' miracles. They say that every false religion is supported by myths and that Christianity is like all the rest.

But Christianity is supported by facts, not myths. Matthew and John reported what they saw and heard. According to ancient testimony, Mark was taught by Peter. Luke was a careful investigator. He learned from numerous witnesses (Luke 1:1-4). For example, he may have heard the nativity stories from Mary and learned of the plotting of the priests against Jesus from priests who later became Christians (Acts 6:7).

C. THE WORD OF GOD

Besides having a thorough knowledge of the facts they recorded, the Gospel writers were inspired by the Holy Spirit. Jesus promised that guidance to Matthew and John (John 14:26). There is no reason to deny that Mark and Luke had the same divine leading. Their accounts of Jesus are truly the Word of God, and they all serve the same purpose: "that you may believe that Jesus is the Christ, the Son of God, and that by believing you may have life in his name" (John 20:31).

Discovery Learning

This page contains an alternate lesson plan emphasizing learning activities. Classes desiring such student involvement will find these suggestions helpful. The next page is a reproducible activity page to further enhance discovery learning.

LEARNING GOALS

After participating in this lesson, each student will be able to:

1. Give the details and result of the miracle that Jesus did at the wedding in Cana of Galilee.

2. Explain the role of Jesus' miracles in establishing his identity as the Son of God.

3. Give thanks for the many miracles that provide solid evidence for believing in Jesus as the Son of God.

INTO THE LESSON

Begin this week's lesson by asking the class to think about the many miracles Jesus performed. State: "When you think of a specific miracle that Jesus performed, call it out, and we'll make a list." *Answers may include the following: feeding the five thousand (John 6:1-14), walking on the water (John 6:18-21), calming a raging storm (Mark 4:35-41), raising the widow of Nain's son (Luke 7:11-16), raising Jairus's daughter (Luke 8:49-56), casting out demons from the Gadarene demoniac (Luke 8:26-39), knowing that Nathanael was sitting under a fig tree (John 1:47, 48), and knowing that Lazarus was dead (John 11:14), and—of course—a variety of others.*

After a few minutes, state: "Jesus' miracles can be categorized into at least four different kinds: miracles in nature, miracles with people, miracles with demons, and miracles of knowledge." (The fourth category may not be as quickly identified as the others, but it is equally as evidential as the others. Be certain your class understands that.) Ask the class to identify an example of each kind of miracle from those listed on the board or others. State: "Jesus performed many kinds of miracles. But what was the purpose of his miracles? Why did he perform them? Today's lesson focuses upon his first miracle, and it helps us to answer these questions."

INTO THE WORD

Ask someone in the class to read aloud John 2:1-11. After the reading ask the following questions:

1. Who attended this wedding in Cana of Galilee? *(mother of Jesus, Jesus, his disciples, vv. 1, 2.)*

2. How did Jesus find out that the wine was gone? *(His mother told him, v. 3.)*

3. Since Jesus had not performed any miracle prior to this event, what do you suppose his mother expected him to do after being told there was no more wine?

Why? *(Perhaps she thought he would demonstrate his power. After all, she knew he was God's Son, Luke 1:31-33. He had been baptized, Luke 3:21-22, and had gathered six disciples, John 1. Jesus' response here, "My time has not yet come," v. 4, assumes she expected him to act in power.)*

4. What did Jesus tell the servants to do? *(Fill six water jars with water and take some to the master of the banquet, vv. 7, 8.)*

5. What is meant by the phrase, "the kind used by the Jews for ceremonial washing" in v. 6? *(Jewish custom and hospitality was to provide water for ceremonial cleansing of people's feet when they entered a house. The Jews also ceremonially washed their hands before eating—Matthew 15:1, 2.)*

6. How did the wine that Jesus created compare to the wine previously served? *(His wine was excellent; the wine served previously was mediocre by comparison, v. 10.)*

7. What was the result of this miracle of changing water into wine? *(It established his identity as the Son of God and promoted belief in the disciples, v. 11.)*

8. What is the meaning of the word *glory* in v. 11? *(It refers not to praise or honor, but to those attributes of Jesus that are worthy of praise.)*

9. What attributes of Jesus do you find in this first miracle? *(His power; his compassion—he cares and is concerned about people; his willingness to get involved in others' situations.)*

INTO LIFE

Divide the class into six groups, assigning each group one passage. (Or three groups may be used, assigning two passages to each group). State: "We've seen how Jesus' first miracle established his identity and promoted belief in his disciples. Using the 'Reactions to Jesus' Miracles' section on the reproducible page that follows, identify the miracle and discover the people's reaction to his miracle. Then, fill in the blank." After several minutes, ask each group to summarize the results. *(Matthew 9–glorified God; Matthew 20–followed Jesus; Mark 4–fear; Luke 8–amazement and fear; John 6–called him a prophet.)*

Direct the attention of your class to the lower section of the reproducible page, "Thanking God for His Miracles." Say: "The grand purposes for Jesus' miracles give us reason to thank God for revealing his Son in powerful signs and wonders. Express your thanksgiving to him in some specific ways."

Reactions to Jesus' Miracles

Jesus' first miracle resulted in establishing his identity as the Son of God and promoting belief in his disciples. Read the passages below and discover other reactions to his working of miracles.

Passage	Miracle	Reaction
Matthew 9:1-8		
Matthew 20:29-34		
Mark 4:35-41		
Luke 8:26-39		
Luke 8:49-56		
John 6:1-14		

Thanking God for His Miracles

When we reflect on the miracles of Jesus and how they give testimony to his identity as the Son of God, our natural response must be to thank him for making himself known to us. Write four reasons you are thankful for the miracles of Jesus.

1.

2.

3.

4.

JESUS DISPLAYS POWER OVER NATURE

LESSON 2

WHY TEACH THIS LESSON?

The letters *WWJD* are very popular in Christian circles. Bracelets, backpacks, and bumper stickers are just a few places where they appear. The letters—which stand for "What would Jesus do?"—are intended to inspire the reader to act in any given situation as Jesus himself would (and did) act. But Jesus solved certain problems by performing *miracles*—something we obviously cannot do! So *WWJD*, as well intentioned as it is, creates problems if taken literally for all situations.

You will recall from last week that the focus of the Gospel miracles was to prove Jesus to be the Son of God as they demonstrate the power that only such a One would have. Although this remains the primary purpose of his miracles, the two miracles considered in this week's lesson also highlight Jesus' *compassion*. When we learn to emulate this compassion—even without the ability to perform miracles—we minister in Jesus' place (Mark 9:41). In so doing, we practice *WWJWMTD*—or "What would Jesus want me to do?"

INTRODUCTION

A. WEATHER WATCHING

Weather forecasting is a sophisticated and technical science these days. With radar, satellite images, and computerized models, meteorologists are able to track approaching tornadoes, hurricanes, and other storms so that residents in a threatened area can take cover.

In spite of these advances, weather watchers—even the most capable—are by no means infallible. Sometimes a tornado will develop so fast that no one has an opportunity to be given sufficient warning. Or the strength of a particular snowstorm may be misjudged so that it produces much more snow than had been predicted.

There were no weather watchers with Doppler radar and computer models in Jesus' day. When a storm arose on the Sea of Galilee, it often came without warning. Descending from the surrounding hills, an intense storm might develop so swiftly that only boats near the shore could elude it. The water was whipped to a fury by the raging winds. Every boat was endangered; everyone caught in a boat became terrified.

B. LESSON BACKGROUND

During this month of September (the first unit of this quarter's lessons), all of our lessons deal with miracles of Jesus. Last week we considered the first one. Today (in the first portion of our printed text) we move ahead toward the middle of Jesus' three-and-a-half year ministry. Jesus had become the best-known person in Galilee. Crowds gathered wherever he went. They were attracted by his marvelous miracles and his astounding teaching (Matthew 4:23-25; 7:28, 29).

DEVOTIONAL READING:
JOHN 6:28-40

BACKGROUND SCRIPTURE:
MATTHEW 8:23-27; 14:1-21

PRINTED TEXT:
MATTHEW 8:23-27; 14:14-21

LESSON AIMS

After this lesson a student should be able to:

1. Describe how Jesus displayed his power over nature in the two miracles mentioned in today's texts.

2. Tell how these miracles demonstrate not only Jesus' power but also his compassion.

3. Suggest one way we can act with the same compassion Jesus demonstrated.

KEY VERSE

The men were amazed and asked, "What kind of man is this? Even the winds and the waves obey him!"

—Matthew 8:27

LESSON 2 NOTES

Use this visual to illustrate verses 26 and 27 of today's text.

WHAT DO YOU THINK?

*"Why are you so afraid?" Jesus asked his disciples. The point is often made that they should not have been fearful since Jesus was with them—and that we should not fear either. But how should we take that? Should we **never** have any fear for personal safety? If so, is this a blanket statement that Christians will never suffer harm? Then what of the many who do suffer harm by storms or other accidents—are they weak in faith? What does it mean to have no fear in a dangerous world?*

I. A TROUBLED SEA (MATTHEW 8:23-27)

Perhaps to escape the constant pressure of the crowds, Jesus planned to cross to the eastern side of the Sea of Galilee (Mark 4:35). He needed to rest after an especially strenuous day of teaching (Mark 4:1-34).

A. SUDDEN STORM (vv. 23, 24)

23. Then he got into the boat and his disciples followed him.

At least four of Jesus' *disciples* (Peter, Andrew, James, and John) had been fishermen on the Sea of Galilee. Probably they now *got into* one of the boats they had used in fishing. Apparently *the boat* was big enough to carry thirteen men without crowding them, but it was likely not much bigger than that.

With some disciples rowing, the boat moved out to the east. Unwilling to lose sight of Jesus, some of the crowd got into other boats and followed (Mark 4:36).

24. Without warning, a furious storm came up on the lake, so that the waves swept over the boat. But Jesus was sleeping.

Only minutes after the approaching *storm* could be seen, it was on them with a fury. High *waves* entered the boat, threatening to capsize it and throw the passengers into the turbulent *lake. But* while all this was taking place, *Jesus was sleeping. The boat* was tossing wildly, and the waves were splashing water on the sleeper; yet he slept on. How tired he must have been from his day of teaching!

B. GREAT CALM (vv. 25, 26)

25. The disciples went and woke him, saying, "Lord, save us! We're going to drown!"

Even seasoned fishermen were helpless against such a tempest as this. *The disciples* realized that they were in grave danger. Yet Jesus could turn water into wine; he could heal all kinds of diseases; he could banish demons from the individuals under their control. If anyone could *save* them from their predicament, surely Jesus could. Growing increasingly hopeless, they *woke him.*

26. He replied, "You of little faith, why are you so afraid?" Then he got up and rebuked the winds and the waves, and it was completely calm.

The disciples did have a *little faith*—enough to hope Jesus could save them, but not enough to keep them from being terrorized by the storm. Shouldn't they have known that Jesus was in control, whether awake or asleep? The frightened men soon learned that Jesus' mastery included *the winds and the waves.* At his rebuke the winds stopped blowing and the waves stopped rolling. The great storm that had threatened their lives just moments ago *was* now *completely calm.*

NATURE AND NATURE'S GOD

On a calm April 14, 1912, the *RMS Titanic* struck an iceberg on her maiden voyage and took two-thirds of her passengers and crew to an icy grave. Human vanity conspired with imperfect engineering in the building and outfitting of the ship in such a way as to court disaster. Watertight bulkheads rose only partway through the hull of the ship. Only half the necessary lifeboats were provided. Those in charge, hoping to make headlines by crossing the Atlantic Ocean in record time, pressed the ship forward at high speed through iceberg-filled waters.

In our text today, we see a picture quite the opposite of the *Titanic*'s final night. Just a few people in a small boat were in danger of drowning in a storm-tossed sea. On this occasion, those on board humbly recognized their frailty before the forces of nature; and the Captain of the vessel took control of those forces. As a result, all on board were saved.

Comparing these two events provides an insightful reminder of a fact of life: our vanity can lead us into foolish schemes that can destroy us and others, but yielding ourselves in trust to the power of God brings salvation.   —C. R. B.

C. DISCIPLES' RESPONSE (v. 27)

27. The men were amazed and asked, "What kind of man is this? Even the winds and the waves obey him!"

No ordinary *man* could command *the winds and the waves.* Only God can do that. The disciples' "little faith" (v. 26) was being guided into learning even greater truth about Jesus: this man was also God. Before him they were right to marvel.

II. A HUNGRY MULTITUDE (MATTHEW 14:14-21)

Some time after the tempest was stilled, Jesus gave his twelve disciples miraculous power like his own and sent them out in pairs to preach as he had been preaching (Matthew 10:1-8). The second part of our printed text takes up the account as the Twelve came together with their Teacher once again (Mark 6:30). By this time, approximately four months had passed since the stilling of the tempest.

The joy of this reunion was mixed with grief, however, for just at that time came news that John the Baptist had been put to death by Herod Antipas (Matthew 14:1-12). Jesus told the disciples to "come . . . to a quiet place," away from the clamoring crowds, perhaps for a time of mourning for John and certainly for a little rest after their strenuous preaching tour (Mark 6:31). So they boarded a boat (probably near Capernaum) and set out to go across to the eastern side of the Sea of Galilee. (This time no storm disturbed them as they crossed the sea.)

However, the only time the men had for rest was during their journey in the boat. A crowd of people saw them leave. Unwilling to miss any of Jesus' miracles or any of his teaching, many of that throng hurried around the north end of the sea. These were joined by people from the villages that they passed. Thus, by the time Jesus and the disciples reached the eastern shore, an even larger gathering was waiting for Jesus (Matthew 14:13; Mark 6:32, 33).

A. CHANGE OF PLAN (v. 14)

14. When Jesus landed and saw a large crowd, he had compassion on them and healed their sick.

Jesus went out from the boat, but not to a secluded area where he and his disciples could relax and talk together privately. He *saw a large crowd* eager for his attention. A less compassionate man might have climbed back into the boat and gone some place where he could rest. But Jesus *had compassion on them.* It must have been difficult for some of the sick people to come to that remote area far from their homes. In some cases, they would have required assistance from family members or friends. All had made the effort because they believed that Jesus could make them well, and they were not disappointed: he *healed their sick.*

Jesus also had compassion for the people who were not sick. They were in distress because they were without good spiritual leaders—"like sheep without a shepherd" (Mark 6:34). Abandoning his plan for a time of rest and mourning, Jesus led the multitude up the hill (John 6:3) and began to teach (Mark 6:34).

B. PUZZLING PROBLEM (v. 15)

15. As evening approached, the disciples came to him and said, "This is a remote place, and it's already getting late. Send the crowds away, so they can go to the villages and buy themselves some food."

If Jesus and his *disciples* started across the Sea of Galilee early in the morning, they must have arrived before noon. People who came on foot were there ahead of them. Now it was *already getting late.* Many must have been getting hungry.

Matthew, Mark, Luke, and John all record this incident, and they record different details. Perhaps Jesus himself was the first to mention the problem. He

WHAT DO YOU THINK?

When Jesus calmed the storm, the disciples marveled at his power. But according to an old proverb, "familiarity breeds contempt," and those who have read this account many times may no longer experience amazement. But shouldn't we still be "amazed" as the disciples were? How can we maintain a reverent sense of awe at the "amazing" power of Jesus?

WHAT DO YOU THINK?

Jesus was moved with compassion at the sight of the crowds, so he healed their sick and taught them. Without the ability to perform miracles, how can we show compassion?

interrupted his teaching for an aside to Philip: "Where shall we buy bread for these people to eat?" (John 6:5). Of course, Philip was stumped. "Eight months' wages" (v. 7) would hardly be enough to feed such a crowd.

Perhaps Jesus continued teaching while Philip quietly consulted the other disciples. To them, Jesus' suggestion seemed impractical. Even if they had enough money, any place where bread could be purchased was miles away. So the disciples came to Jesus with the suggestion we see here: Jesus should dismiss the *crowds* so that the people could *go* and *buy themselves some food*. That suggestion was not very practical either. The *place* where they were was *remote*, which implies no one lived there, though the region included splendid grazing land for sheep or cattle (note the reference to "plenty of grass" in John 6:10). There were *villages* a few miles away, but did all of them together have enough bread for sale to feed that hungry crowd? And how many in the crowd had come with no money?

C. MIRACULOUS SOLUTION (vv. 16-21)

16. Jesus replied, "They do not need to go away. You give them something to eat."

In response to Jesus' suggestion, the disciples could only shake their heads. Perhaps that was when Jesus sent them to see how much bread was available within the crowd (Mark 6:38). So the disciples searched, and Andrew found one boy who had "five small barley loaves and two small fish" (John 6:8, 9).

UNAWARE OF THE POWER AT HAND

The Yates Pool, an oil field in western Texas, got its name from a sheep rancher who owned the property when the Great Depression began. Mr. Yates could not pay his mortgage and was living on government relief. He was faced with foreclosure and with the loss of his land and livelihood.

One day, Yates gave an oil company crew permission to drill for oil on his ranch. Soon after drilling began, a large oil reserve was tapped. The first well started out producing eighty thousand barrels of crude oil a day. Some thirty years later, this huge reserve was yielding even more oil than it had at the beginning.

Before the oil was discovered, Mr. Yates was living in poverty, unaware of the source of wealth that lay so close at hand. He was much like the disciples when confronted with a hungry multitude. Unaware that Jesus himself was able to solve the dilemma, they were ready to send the crowd away with empty stomachs. Then Jesus gave them a command that caused them to examine their abilities and resources before he stepped in to meet the need.

God may lead us through a similar process. When we face difficulties, he may wait until we have tested our own strength and resources before he shows us the solution. But his power is always close at hand, waiting for us to tap into it.   —C. R. B.

17. "We have here only five loaves of bread and two fish," they answered.

No other food was found among the huge crowd. The *loaves* were flat and round, not at all like the loaves of bread we buy today. We might call them rolls or biscuits instead of loaves. That they were made of barley (John 6:9) indicates a cheaper kind of bread; the boy may have been from a poor family.

The Greek word for *fish* indicates "small fish" (John 6:9), possibly like the sardines that are available in little flat cans. Apparently the boy was willing to contribute the meal he had brought along, but he must have wondered, as Andrew did, "How far will they go among so many?" (John 6:9).

18. "Bring them here to me," he said.

In the hands of the boy who brought them, those loaves and fish could have satisfied one boy's hunger. In the hands of Jesus, they could do whatever Jesus wanted them to do. So Jesus called for them to be brought to him.

WHAT DO YOU THINK?

When Jesus told the disciples, "You give them something to eat," the disciples thought he had given them an impossible task. But Jesus had the situation in hand and, with his help, the disciples were indeed able to feed the crowd. Have you ever had an "impossible" task to do? How did you respond? How did you find God's strength sufficient for the task?

SOLUTION TO PUZZLE ON P. 32
DOWN
1. pieces
2. Heaven
4. Solitary
5. Compassion
6. Evening
10. Foot

ACROSS
3. Rebuked
7. Amazed
8. Sleeping
9. Storm
11. Drown
12. Little

19a. And he directed the people to sit down on the grass.

Mark and Luke tell us that Jesus told the disciples to have the *people to sit down* in groups of about fifty or a hundred (Mark 6:39, 40; Luke 9:14, 15). Most likely there would have been aisles between the groups, making it easy to distribute the food that soon would be available. This grouping would have made the people expectant; they would watch and listen intently when Jesus spoke again.

19b. Taking the five loaves and the two fish and looking up to heaven, he gave thanks and broke the loaves. Then he gave them to the disciples, and the disciples gave them to the people.

Having given *thanks* for the food, Jesus began to break the bread. How we would like to have a fuller description of that! Perhaps he broke a fragment from a loaf, and the fragment was as big as the loaf. Then both fragment and loaf could be broken and rebroken into pieces increasing in size and number. Jesus handed the pieces to his *disciples,* and the disciples carried them *to the people.*

20. They all ate and were satisfied, and the disciples picked up twelve basketfuls of broken pieces that were left over.

Anyone could have a second helping if he wanted it, or even a third. Any leftovers were not thrown away. Jesus had the disciples gather up uneaten fragments so that nothing would be wasted (John 6:12), and they gathered *twelve basketfuls.*

Where did the baskets come from? Those people had rushed after Jesus impulsively, without planning to go where he would eventually stop. Did some of them just happen to have baskets?

Perhaps they did. Those who read and know Greek tell us that the word used here for *basket* is *kophinos,* which *Young's Analytical Concordance* defines as "a wicker traveling basket." Wickerwork was much less expensive than leather. A traveler might use it for the equivalent of a backpack or valise.

Note that we are reading of a time when the Passover Feast was near (John 6:4). The crowd on this occasion may have included many people on the way from northern Galilee to Jerusalem for the feast. A person on that trip may well have carried a *kophinos* with some clean clothing or other items in it, and may have been eager to lay the contents out on the grass in order to lend the container to one of Jesus' disciples.

Another suggestion is that each of the twelve disciples had such a basket and carried it as he traveled with Jesus about the country. True, the Twelve had just finished a preaching tour during which they took no such item (Matthew 10:5-10); but if they usually carried traveling baskets, they could have left them in Capernaum and picked them up when they finished their tour.

21. The number of those who ate was about five thousand men, besides women and children.

We can only guess how many *women and children* ate along with the *five thousand men.* Regardless of the specific number, Jesus had worked yet another unforgettable miracle.

CONCLUSION

Both this lesson and the previous one have featured two important truths: the unlimited divine power of Jesus and the godly compassion that guided what he did with that power.

A. POWER

The power of Almighty God worked in Jesus, and still does. "Through him all things were made" (John 1:3). Even today, Jesus is "sustaining all things by his powerful word" (Hebrews 1:3). It would seem that Jesus needs no help from us.

WHAT DO YOU THINK?

It may surprise the first-time reader to note that Jesus commanded that the fragments of food be collected (John 6:12). Why is this surprising, and what should we learn from it?

HOW TO SAY IT

Antipas. AN-tih-pus.
Capernaum. Kuh-PER-nay-um.
Galilee. GAL-uh-lee.
kophinos (Greek). KAW-fin-awss.

DAILY BIBLE READINGS

Monday, Sept. 3—*Jesus Calms a Storm (Mark 4:35-41)*

Tuesday, Sept. 4—*Jesus Walks on Water (Matthew 14:22-27)*

Wednesday, Sept. 5—*Peter's Doubt (Matthew 14:28-33)*

Thursday, Sept. 6—*Feeding Four Thousand (Mark 8:1-13)*

Friday, Sept. 7—*"Do You Not Yet Understand?" (Mark 8:14-21)*

Saturday, Sept. 8—*Would-be Followers (Matthew 8:18-27)*

Sunday, Sept. 9—*Feeding Five Thousand (Matthew 14:14-21)*

PRAYER

Gracious Father, since we cannot emulate the miracles of Jesus, may we emulate the good-will and good sense of the boy who put what he had in Jesus' hands. Help us to see and use our opportunities to do good to all men, especially to those who are of the household of faith. In Jesus' name. Amen.

THOUGHT TO REMEMBER

Count your blessings—and share them.

Here, then, is a marvel that ranks with the greatest marvels of all time: Jesus wants our help. He values our help. He does marvelous things with our help. Last week we read that Jesus made six big jars of superior wine. He could have made it from nothing, but he chose to make it with water carried by household servants. This week we read that he made a meal for more than five thousand hungry people. That too he could have done from nothing, but he chose to do it with the food contributed by a willing boy.

Never think your tithe is unimportant. Never think the Lord does not appreciate the hours you spend teaching a Sunday school class, or practicing with the church choir, or encouraging the despondent, or cleaning up the kitchen after a fellowship dinner at church. Jesus is using you for the good of his people and the glory of his kingdom. That's wonderful!

And how the Lord multiplies the value of your small help! Through months or years you keep on telling your friend of the joy you find in Christ, and you demonstrate what you say by joyous Christian living. Then one happy day your friend is born again and destined to live forever. How much is that worth?

Regretfully you decide to keep the old car another year, or three years if necessary, so that you can make a large contribution to the fund to acquire property and double the size of the church parking lot. When the lot is ready, church attendance promptly begins to grow. In a few months, church membership also begins to grow. Nearly every week sees people responding to Christ's call and being baptized into him. See what the Lord has made of your contribution? Aren't you glad you decided to keep that old car?

B. COMPASSION

Jesus' compassion is scarcely less notable than his power. Why should he care if the host at a wedding was embarrassed? But he did care, as we saw last week. Why should he care if a crowd was hungry? But he did care, as we saw today.

"Being in very nature God" amid the glories of Heaven, why should Jesus care if people were dying on earth? It was their own fault. But he did care. He exchanged the wealth of Heaven for poverty on earth and for the agonizing death of the old rugged cross (Philippians 2:4-8).

Yes, Jesus cares, and his people care. Our hearts are wrenched when we see pictures of children starving because of tragic circumstances. But what can we do? We cannot feed everyone; should we therefore feed no one?

Paul outlines the activity of our compassion: "As we have opportunity, let us do good to all people, especially to them who belong to the family of believers" (Galatians 6:10).

1. AS WE HAVE OPPORTUNITY. Our opportunity is often limited by our ability and by our resources. It will make matters worse if we recklessly give all we have, and thus make ourselves dependent on the charity of others. We can give generously, even sacrificially, but we need to know when to stop giving.

2. LET US DO GOOD TO ALL PEOPLE. Yes, men and women and children, too! No one on earth should be outside the scope of Christian compassion. But we cannot end the distress of all who are in distress. To which appeals must we respond? To which must we say, regretfully, no?

3. ESPECIALLY TO THEM WHO BELONG TO THE FAMILY OF BELIEVERS. This sets our priority. We cannot feed all the starving orphans, but we can feed all those in our own church—and perhaps help with another church as well. In that way we show the kind of love that Jesus said must be our "trademark" to the world (John 13:35).

Are we really doing all we can for others?

Discovery Learning

This page contains an alternate lesson plan emphasizing learning activities. Classes desiring such student involvement will find these suggestions helpful. The next page is a reproducible activity page to further enhance discovery learning.

LEARNING GOALS

After participating in this lesson, each student will be able to:

1. Describe how Jesus displayed his power over nature in the two miracles mentioned in today's text.

2. Tell how these miracles demonstrate not only Jesus' power but also his compassion.

3. Suggest one way we can act with the same compassion Jesus demonstrated.

INTO THE LESSON

Prior to class prepare a poster with the scrambled word, "A C I M N O O P S S" on the top line and the following message "_ _ _ _ _ _ _ _ _ _ leads to action!" on the next line. Begin class by revealing the poster and stating, "Unscramble these letters and find the one word that reveals the message of today's lesson." (The answer is "Compassion leads to action!") When the answer is given correctly, write the word "Compassion" on the ten spaces for the letters. State: "Today we look at two of Jesus' miracles that demonstrate not only his power over nature but also the compassion that led him to get involved in people's lives."

INTO THE WORD

Make copies of the reproducible activity on page 32. Ask the class to move into groups of two or three. State: "Using the *New International Version*, read Matthew 8:23-27 to find the words going across and Matthew 14:13-21 to find the words going down to complete this crossword puzzle." Give the students about five minutes to work on this puzzle; then go over the answers with the class. (The solution is found on page 28.)

State: "Both of these miracles described Jesus' divine power over nature. He hushed the wind and stilled the raging sea in the one. He multiplied the bread and the fish in the other. But how did these miracles demonstrate his compassion?" (His compassion led him to respond to the need. His disciples were afraid for their lives, so they cried out to Jesus and he saved them. The crowd by the sea was hungry and needed food for strength.

Compassion always leads to action. It is active, not passive. If it is true, it will reveal itself. It gets involved in people's lives—seeking to meet them at their point of need.)

INTO LIFE

State: "Genuine compassion always leads to action. When Jesus recognized the two circumstances of fear and hunger, he got involved. Though we do not have the power to perform a miracle over nature, there is still much that our compassion for people can lead us to do. But first, we have to recognize people's needs."

Ask the following questions and list the answers on the board or overhead transparency.

1. What situations in people's lives today cause people to be fearful? (*Possible answers may include: facing a surgical procedure or terminal illness; taking a major examination; loss of a job; an opportunity to share one's faith; decisions during or after a divorce; awaiting medical test results.*)

2. What are some situations in which people today have an unmet physical need? (*Hunger; heating or cooling for comfort; shelter and clothing following a natural disaster such as fire or storm; protection from a situation involving an abusive family member; economic homelessness.*)

Say: "We've now identified a number of situations and circumstances that cause people to have emotional and physical needs. Whom do we know in our church or community who is facing one of these emotional or physical needs?" Use the "Compassion Leads to Action" section of the following reproducible page for this activity. Ask the class to move into groups of three. Under each column heading of the activity, ask each group to fill in the name of the person(s) needing help, the situation, and the action that would demonstrate compassion for the person. Allow several minutes to complete the worksheet. Then ask each small group to decide (either as a group or as individuals) how to respond to at least one individual listed on the worksheet. Share the decisions with the whole class and conclude the lesson with a prayer of commitment to act in a spirit of compassion for someone this week: "Father, there are many who need us to communicate your love to them this week. Help us from day to day to see them in our lives, to act wisely in offering the loving help they need, and never to embarrass or humiliate them by our actions. May the glory come to your Son as we do good deeds in his name. Amen."

Consider asking for class members to volunteer reports on their acts of compassion next Sunday in class and to solicit additional help from class members.

Crossword Puzzle

DOWN—MATTHEW 14:13-21
1. There were twelve basketfuls of broken ____.
2. Jesus looked to _____ and blessed the food.
4. They left the ship and went in to a ____ place.
5. When Jesus saw a great multitude, he was moved with _____.
6. When it was _____ the disciples suggested sending the people away.
10. The people came to Jesus from the cities on _____.

ACROSS—MATTHEW 8:23-27
3. Jesus _____ the winds and the waves.
7. The disciples were _____ when the sea was calm.
8. In spite of the tossing waves, Jesus was ____.
9. There arose a great _____ on the lake.
11. The disciples thought they were going to _____.
12. Jesus described the disciples' faith as ____.

Compassion Leads to Action

In the manner of Jesus each of us must let our compassion lead us to action on behalf of those needing tender, loving care. Fill in the following chart to identify some possibilities in your own life.

PERSON NEEDING HELP	THE SITUATION CALLING FOR HELP	MY PLAN OF ACTION

JESUS DISPLAYS POWER OVER DISEASE

LESSON 3

Sep
16

WHY TEACH THIS LESSON?

Witnessing to others about their need for Jesus can be disheartening at times, because not everyone accepts the gospel message. Today we learn that we are not alone in our disappointment. Jesus Christ himself performed miracles *right in front of people* who steadfastly refused to believe, and his own frustration showed. Today's lesson is important for understanding how the non-Christian thinks when confronted with the evidence of the gospel miracles. This understanding prepares us to respond in a Christ-honoring way.

INTRODUCTION

A. JUST IMAGINE

Can you imagine how hard it would be to eat a steak if you had only one hand? That piece of meat seems alive. It refuses to lie still under the knife unless you hold it down with a fork. Do you ask a friend to cut it for you, or do you order meat loaf?

But that is only the beginning of your troubles. A broom is designed for two hands. How can you sweep the autumn leaves from the deck of your house? If you call a motel to reserve a room, you had better ask if you can open the door with one hand. A lady I know who likes to travel and has only one hand said that in some motels you can't.

Perhaps the worst part is knowing that very little can be done about it. You can hide the condition with a costly prosthesis, but the result is not really a hand.

Jesus, the Great Physician, specialized in situations like this—severe cases of affliction that no one else could do anything about. This week's lesson calls attention to two examples.

B. LESSON BACKGROUND

Our printed text begins with an incident from Jesus' busy ministry in Galilee. It took place earlier than the calming of the storm at sea (at the beginning of last week's lesson), but already Jesus was famous for his miracles and his teaching. For the second incident in our text we go to a later time, when Jesus was in Jerusalem only a few months before his death.

I. SHRIVELED HAND MADE WHOLE (MARK 3:1-6)

Jesus' custom was to go to a synagogue meeting every Sabbath (Luke 4:16), and it was a Jewish custom to invite visiting teachers to speak at such meetings (Acts 13:15). However, the Pharisees (who were the regular teachers) were not pleased with Jesus. They resented the intrusion of a teacher who was not one of them, and they envied Jesus because he was more popular than they were. They watched him constantly and listened to him intently, not hoping to learn from him but hoping to find fault with him.

DEVOTIONAL READING:
JOHN 4:46-54
BACKGROUND SCRIPTURE:
MARK 3:1-6; JOHN 9
PRINTED TEXT:
MARK 3:1-6; JOHN 9:1-12, 35-38

LESSON AIMS

After this lesson a student should be able to:

1. Summarize the accounts of the miracles recorded in today's texts and the reaction of the Pharisees to them.

2. Contrast how Christians and non-Christians tend to view the evidence concerning Jesus found in the Gospels.

3. Prepare a presentation of the gospel (one that anticipates questions non-Christians may ask) and plan to share it soon with a friend.

KEY VERSE

(Jesus) said to the man, "Stretch out your hand." He stretched it out, and his hand was completely restored.
—Mark 3:5b

LESSON 3 NOTES

A. THE CRITICS (vv. 1, 2)

1. Another time he went into the synagogue, and a man with a shriveled hand was there.

There was nothing unusual in Jesus' presence at a *synagogue*, but the presence of *a man with a shriveled hand* made some especially watchful.

2. Some of them were looking for a reason to accuse Jesus, so they watched him closely to see if he would heal him on the Sabbath.

These careful watchers are identified as Pharisees in verse 6. Like nearly everyone in Galilee, they knew Jesus had been healing "every disease and sickness" (Matthew 4:23). If he healed this man's hand, they would *accuse* him of working *on the Sabbath*. On another Sabbath the Pharisees had criticized Jesus' disciples' actions in a grain field (Mark 2:23-28). Jesus defended the disciples then: he obeyed the divine law concerning the Sabbath, but not all the traditions of the Pharisees.

B. THE ISSUE (vv. 3, 4)

3. Jesus said to the man with the shriveled hand, "Stand up in front of everyone."

Matthew records an interesting piece of information that Mark omits. The Pharisees raised the Sabbath question by asking Jesus, "Is it lawful to heal on the Sabbath?" (Matthew 12:10). Jesus chose to face the issue squarely. He focused attention by asking *the man with the shriveled hand* to *stand up* and be seen by all. Here was a living visual aid that could be used to address the Pharisees' question.

4. Then Jesus asked them, "Which is lawful on the Sabbath: to do good or to do evil, to save life or to kill?" But they remained silent.

Instead of answering the Pharisees with a plain yes or no, Jesus chose a way that was more thoughtful and more challenging. Before them all stood a man with his right hand (Luke 6:6) hanging limp and useless. It certainly would be good to repair that hand, to make it strong and useful like the other. Therefore, wouldn't it be bad to leave that hand limp and useless when it could be repaired? Which would be better on a *Sabbath* Day—*to do good or to do evil*?

To the crowd it must have seemed that Jesus was expanding the principle to a more severe case than the one before them. Suppose this man were on the verge of death. To heal him would be *to save life*; to do nothing would be, in effect, *to kill* him. Should a man be killed simply because it was the Sabbath? But perhaps what Jesus really had in mind was the contrast between his doing good—as he would shortly heal the man's hand—and the Pharisees' doing evil—as they depart to plan Jesus' death (v. 6).

But they remained silent. The Pharisees could not deny that doing good was better than doing evil, saving life better than killing. But they stubbornly refused to concede that Jesus was right and they had been wrong. They remained silent.

C. THE MIRACLE (v. 5)

5. He looked around at them in anger and, deeply distressed at their stubborn hearts, said to the man, "Stretch out your hand." He stretched it out, and his hand was completely restored.

We wonder how long Jesus *looked around at them*—looking from one Pharisee to another. *Anger* showed on his face, but it was an anger mixed with grief at *their stubborn hearts*. Then Jesus put the truth into action: he did good and not evil, and the shriveled *hand was completely restored*.

D. THE REACTION (v. 6)

6. Then the Pharisees went out and began to plot with the Herodians how they might kill Jesus.

WHAT DO YOU THINK?

The Pharisees were very interested in what Jesus said and did, but their interest was for the purpose of finding fault. Bearing in mind that Jesus did not let public opinion determine his actions, how should we deal with people who continually find fault with us?

WHAT DO YOU THINK?

Seldom do we read of Jesus' being angry, but Mark 3:5 is one instance. Note that he was grieved at the Pharisees' stubborn hearts. What is it that grieves us when we get angry? What do you think we can learn from Jesus' anger here?

Consider Matthew 6:33 in your discussion.

The Pharisees proceeded to join forces with *the Herodians,* who were supporters of Herod Antipas, king of Galilee. The corruption in the Herod family made the Herodians unlikely allies with the Pharisees, who prided themselves on their avoidance of anything or anyone sinful. That the Pharisees were willing to seek such assistance shows the intensity of their desire to *kill Jesus.*

"THAT'S NOT HOW WE DO THINGS HERE"

Robert Pipes is an eighty-three-year-old preacher with an unconventional approach to evangelism. Every Saturday afternoon for twenty-five years he has driven his motor home through some of the most dangerous housing projects in Los Angeles. Wherever he sees a group of people, he stops and starts preaching through a loudspeaker on top of the vehicle.

Pipes can't say whether anyone has ever been converted by his unusual method, but he perseveres anyway. Drug dealers have thrown rocks at him, the police have given him tickets, and other ministers have criticized him. In essence each was saying, "That's not how we do things here."

Sometimes we object to those who do things differently because we fear that their success might make our methods look bad in comparison. Sometimes we're just stubborn: we don't like anyone to force change on us and upset the status quo.

Both of those reasons probably led to the Pharisees' objections to Jesus' healing ministry. Of course, they cloaked their jealousy and stubbornness in theological robes, claiming that it was not "lawful" to heal on the Sabbath. It's an ancient (but also very up-to-date) technique for avoiding a confrontation with some tough questions and issues that we would rather not face.   —C. R. B.

II. BLIND EYES GIVEN SIGHT (JOHN 9:1-12, 35-38)

The next portion of our text is set in Jerusalem, the capital of Judea, at a later time, only a few months before Jesus was crucified. The Pharisees there opposed Jesus as bitterly as did those of Galilee. So did the priests, who for the most part were Sadducees. The closing verses of John 8 record that those vindictive enemies, unable to debate with Jesus, picked up stones to kill him; but he slipped away.

A. DISCIPLES' QUESTION (vv. 1, 2)

1. As he went along, he saw a man blind from birth.

We are not told where this *man* was seen. He may have been begging in the street.

2. His disciples asked him, "Rabbi, who sinned, this man or his parents, that he was born blind?"

The disciples held the popular belief that such afflictions as blindness, deafness, and lameness were punishment for sin. The Pharisees likely held this belief, too (John 9:34). When one was *born blind,* that raised perplexing questions. Could he possibly have sinned before he was born? Could he be punished from birth for sins he would commit later? Or was he being punished for the sins of *his parents?* If so, where was the justice in that?

B. ANSWER BY WORDS (vv. 3-5)

3. "Neither this man nor his parents sinned," said Jesus, "but this happened so that the work of God might be displayed in his life.

This does not mean that the *man* and *his parents* had lived sinless lives; it means that his blindness was not caused by the sins of any of them. Neither should we think that God had caused the blindness in order to have a setting in which to show his *work.* Instead, Jesus turned the disciples' thinking from cause to effect. Because this man was blind, God's work was about to *be displayed in his life.*

WHAT DO YOU THINK?

The Pharisees were bent on destroying Jesus. How do Jesus' enemies attempt to destroy him in our times? What can we do about it?

JESUS saith unto the man, Stretch forth thine hand . . . and his hand was restored whole as the other.

Mark 3:5

This poster, illustrating Jesus' healing of the man with the shriveled hand, can be found in the Adult Visuals *packet.*

HOW TO SAY IT

Antipas. AN-tih-pus.
Herodians. Heh-ROE-dee-unz.
Judea. Joo-DEE-uh.
Pharisees. FAIR-ih-seez.
Sadducees. SAD-you-seez.
Siloam. Sigh-LO-um.
synagogue. SIN-uh-gog.

4. *"As long as it is day, we must do the work of him who sent me. Night is coming, when no one can work.*

Jesus' time on earth was growing short. In a few months he would be crucified. He would rise from the dead and go back to Heaven, but he would no longer do God's *work* on earth with his own hands and feet and voice. In those few months before his death, he must not be diverted from his Father's work.

5. *"While I am in the world, I am the light of the world."*

For nearly three years Jesus had been giving the *light* of truth to those around him. Now he was about to symbolize this work by bringing literal light to a man who had spent his entire life in darkness.

C. ANSWER BY ACTIONS (vv. 6, 7)

6, 7. *Having said this, he spit on the ground, made some mud with the saliva, and put it on the man's eyes. "Go," he told him, "wash in the Pool of Siloam" (this word means Sent). So the man went and washed, and came home seeing.*

The *Pool of Siloam* was located on the southeastern end of Jerusalem. While we are not told exactly how far the man had to go to reach it, the pool was not far from the temple area, where the incidents recorded in chapter 8 took place.

Jesus could give sight with a touch (Matthew 9:27-30) or a mere word (Mark 10:46-52), so why this elaborate ritual? Jesus did not give a reason, and neither does John. Perhaps it was to teach the man (and us) that some of God's blessings depend on the faith and obedience of the receiver as well as on the power and goodness of the Giver (compare 2 Kings 5:1-14). What we do know is that the man did as he was told, and for the first time in his life he could see.

D. STORM OF QUESTIONS (vv. 8-12)

8. *His neighbors and those who had formerly seen him begging asked, "Isn't this the same man who used to sit and beg?"*

Naturally enough, *his neighbors* were amazed. They took a second look and gasped, *"Isn't this the same man who used to sit and beg?"*

9. *Some claimed that he was.*

Others said, "No, he only looks like him."

But he himself insisted, "I am the man."

Immediately a difference of opinion developed: some said that this man was the one who "used to sit and beg." Others claimed that he was someone else who only looked like him. The man himself settled the question: *I am the man.*

10. *"How then were your eyes opened?" they demanded.*

When the first question was answered, the second followed naturally. How did a blind man become a seeing one?

11. *He replied, "The man they call Jesus made some mud and put it on my eyes. He told me to go to Siloam and wash. So I went and washed, and then I could see."*

Point by point the man told precisely what had happened. But he did not believe that the miracle had been done either by the *mud* on his *eyes* or by the water in the Pool of *Siloam.* He understood that *Jesus* had done it, and later he said, "He opened my eyes" (v. 30). He understood further that Jesus had done this miracle by divine power: "If this man were not from God, he could do nothing" (v. 33).

12. *"Where is this man?" they asked him.*

"I don't know," he said.

The man's answer in verse 11 had turned attention from the miracle to the one who had done it—"the man they call Jesus." Of course, the man did not know *where* Jesus was. He had never seen Jesus, and at this point he would not know him if he did see him.

WHAT DO YOU THINK?

The man whom Jesus had healed was questioned about his new condition. While he did not know all the answers, he told what he knew—he told what had happened to him. How can we use his example to encourage Christians of various levels of spiritual maturity to share the good news of Christ today?

The Pharisees "were divided" about Jesus (v. 16). Some were sure that Jesus was a sinner because he did such an act on the Sabbath. Others asked how a sinner could do such a miracle. So they tried to prove that no miracle had been done. But when the evidence proved undeniable, the Pharisees became angered by the man's firm stand; so they cast him out of the synagogue. To be thus "excommunicated" was a most shameful punishment. The Jews would not recognize the man as a Jew, but neither would the Gentiles recognize him as a Gentile. He was a man alone.

E. NO LONGER ALONE (vv. 35-38)

35. Jesus heard that they had thrown him out, and when he found him, he said, "Do you believe in the Son of Man?"

This outcast was not alone for long. Soon Jesus *found him.* We wonder if anything was spoken between the two before Jesus asked the momentous question recorded here: *Do you believe in the Son of Man?*

36. "Who is he, sir?" the man asked. "Tell me so that I may believe in him."

In the face of angry opposition by eminent scholars, this man already had declared Jesus to be a prophet and a man of God (vv. 17, 33). He would *believe* whatever that prophet said; but what did Jesus mean by "Son of Man"? Who was he?

37. Jesus said, "You have now seen him; in fact, he is the one speaking with you."

The title "Son of Man" (see Daniel 7:13) is the one Jesus most often uses when referring to himself in the Gospels. *You have now seen him* was a reminder that this man had seen nothing at all until the Son of Man had given him sight. *He is the one speaking with you* suggests that the man had much yet to learn.

38. Then the man said, "Lord, I believe," and he worshiped him.

At this point, the man could not have known all the significance in that phrase "Son of Man" (again, see Daniel 7:13) But he believed what Jesus said, and, appropriately, *he worshiped him.* Like any follower of Jesus, he could spend the rest of his life learning more and more about this One he now worships.

Isn't our experience like this man's? On the basis of ample evidence we believe that Jesus is "the Christ, the Son of the living God" (Matthew 16:16). We declare our faith in him; we worship him; we take our place in the fellowship of believers. As long as we live we keep on learning about his power, his goodness, his grace, his love, and his companionship in our daily walk.

WILLING TO FIND THE TRUTH

John Archibald Wheeler is the physicist who proved that "black holes" exist out in the far reaches of space. A more important fact about him is that he keeps asking questions that many of his fellow scientists are uncomfortable with—questions about creation, about meaning in life, and about why the universe exists.

Wheeler asks, "How could the universe exist and make sense unless it were guaranteed to give rise at some point to life and mind and meaning?" And again, "Is man an unimportant bit of dust on an unimportant planet in an unimportant galaxy somewhere in the vastness of space? No! The necessity to produce life lies at the center of the universe's whole machinery and design." These are really theological issues, but Wheeler raises them as a scientist who sees a logic in the creation with which some scientists are not willing to grapple.

The blind man at first had expressed ignorance of Jesus' identity. Later, when confronted by Jesus about his belief in the Son of Man, it became apparent that the man was not an agnostic. Far from it—he expressed an active interest in coming to faith.

John Wheeler and the blind man may be considered brothers in the quest for truth. There is no shame in being ignorant, if we also possess a desire to know the truth and a willingness to ask the right questions, no matter how difficult or unpopular they may be.   —C. R. B.

WHAT DO YOU THINK?

The man healed of his blindness thrills us with his question about the Son of Man: "Who is he, sir? . . . Tell me so that I may believe in him." How do we find people with a similar eagerness to believe the truth about Jesus Christ?

Monday, Sept. 10—Healed Because of Friends' Faith (Mark 2:1-12)

Tuesday, Sept. 11—Wanting to Be Healed (John 5:2-9a)

Wednesday, Sept. 12—Healing the Gerasene Demoniac (Mark 5:1-15)

Thursday, Sept. 13—Healing Jairus's Daughter (Mark 5:21-24a, 35-43)

Friday, Sept. 14—The Faith That Makes You Whole (Mark 5:24b-34)

Saturday, Sept. 15—"Help My Unbelief" (Mark 9:17-29)

Sunday, Sept. 16—Healing a Man with a Shriveled Hand (Mark 3:1-6)

PRAYER

Thank you, Father, for the clear record of your Son. We believe it, Lord, and we want to follow him faithfully. May we have the wisdom and courage to do so. In Jesus' name. Amen.

THOUGHT TO REMEMBER

Jesus Christ is Lord.

CONCLUSION

In the Scripture we have read today, we see two very different conclusions about Jesus. Let's summarize the conclusions along with the presuppositions and evidence on which they were based. Then let's consider some of the conclusions of people today.

A. CONCLUSION OF THE PHARISEES

1. *Presuppositions.* We are the best of God's people, the wisest and most obedient.

2. *Evidence.* Jesus is not a Pharisee. He does not honor our traditions. He does not respect our authority. He heals people on the Sabbath.

3. *Conclusion.* "We know this man is a sinner" (v. 24).

B. CONCLUSION OF THE MAN GIVEN SIGHT

1. *Presuppositions.* "If this man were not from God, he could do nothing" (v. 33).

2. *Evidence.* Jesus gave me my sight.

3. *Conclusion.* "He is a prophet" (v. 17).

C. CONCLUSION OF AN AGNOSTIC

1. *Presuppositions.* The laws of nature are changeless, and the working of nature is uniform. There are no miracles, and there never were.

2. *Evidence.* The Gospels tell of many miracles done by Jesus.

3. *Conclusion.* Those books are mythical, not factual. We don't know whether Jesus was a real person or just a mythical one.

D. CONCLUSION OF AN EGOTIST

1. *Presuppositions.* I am number one. What I like is good.

2. *Evidence.* Jesus taught his people to love their neighbors as themselves, even to make sacrifices for the good of others.

3. *Conclusion.* That's not for me.

E. CONCLUSION OF A MATERIALIST

1. *Presuppositions.* The "scientific method" is the only avenue for learning. We cannot know much about anything that we cannot see, hear, touch, taste, or smell.

2. *Evidence.* Jesus and his followers thought that "what is seen is temporary, but what is unseen is eternal" (2 Corinthians 4:18).

3. *Conclusion.* Jesus was a dreamer. I am awake. I give first attention to things I know are real, like money in the bank.

F. CONCLUSION OF A CHRISTIAN

1. *Presuppositions.* Some people who are now Christians held very different presuppositions before they looked at the evidence about Jesus. Those who grew up in devout Christian homes learned that the Bible is true and that Jesus is the Son of God. When they began to examine the evidence, they discovered that the facts supported their presuppositions. But those who were reared in non-Christian homes held the exact opposite presuppositions and, upon objective examination of the evidence, found that it disproved those presuppositions.

2. *Evidence.* The books of Matthew, Mark, Luke, and John have the earmarks of true records. They were written by Jesus' contemporaries. These credible books proclaim that Jesus is who he claims to be.

3. *Conclusion.* Jesus is all the Bible says he is: the Savior and Lord of those who believe him and follow him. He is worthy of full allegiance, and I will follow him today and always.

Discovery Learning

*This page contains an alternate lesson plan emphasizing learning activities. Classes
desiring such student involvement will find these suggestions helpful. The next page
is a reproducible activity page to further enhance discovery learning.*

LEARNING GOALS

After participating in this lesson, each student will be able to:

1. Summarize the accounts of the miracles recorded in today's texts and the reaction of the Pharisees to them.

2. Contrast how Christians and non-Christians tend to view the evidence concerning Jesus found in the Gospels.

3. Prepare a presentation of the gospel (one that anticipates questions non-Christians may ask) and plan to share it soon with a friend.

INTO THE LESSON

Prior to the lesson prepare a poster or an overhead transparency sheet with the following uncompleted simile: "Diseases are to Jesus as_____ are to _____." At the beginning of class, state: "The New Testament describes a number of diseases and conditions that Jesus healed: leprosy, fever, dropsy, paralysis, hearing and speech impairments, blindness, and lameness. Today, we want to start the lesson by completing a simile about Jesus and his power over diseases. [Show the simile.] Work with the person sitting next to you to complete this simile. You have two to three minutes." (Some possible answers: "grains of salt are to a mountain climber"; "toothpicks are to a lumberjack"; "simple addition problems are to a calculus major.") State: "All of these similes point out just how easy it is for Jesus to make people whole or well. Today, we find two such cases: Jesus healing a withered hand and restoring sight to the blind. Let's review these miracles."

INTO THE WORD

Prior to class prepare copies of the reproducible page that follows. Ask a student to read the text aloud. State: "One way to review these miracles is to take this true/false test. Without looking at the text, see how many of these you can get right." After about a minute, go over the answers with the class. (*Answers: 1. false; in the synagogue; 2. true; 3. false, the disciples asked; 4. false, with the Pharisees; 5. true; 6. false, Jesus spat on the ground; 7. true; 8. true; 9. false, the blind man was; 10. true.*)

Say, "Now I want us to notice the different reactions of people to these two miracles. Look at the worksheet and you'll find a chart to complete." There are two columns: the first column is labeled "Person/Group" and the second column is "Possible Reaction." See John 9:18-22. Then say, "Work with a person sitting next to you to complete the right-hand column. What are the revealed and/or possible reactions of these people to Jesus' miracles?" After a couple of minutes, go over the answers (*Some possibilities: 1. Thankfulness, 2. Anger, 3. Revenge, 4. Worship, 5. Doubt/Confusion, 6. Fear*).

INTO LIFE

Say: "Even as there were different reactions in the New Testament to Jesus' miracles, there are different reactions today. Non-Christians view the evidence concerning Jesus differently from the way Christians view it. Consider these three areas: Jesus' identity, miracles, and teaching. How do Christians and non-Christians view the evidence regarding these three?" Lead a class discussion on the contrasting points of view. (*Possible responses include the following: Jesus' Identity: Son of God or simply a prophet; a good moral man but not God; Jesus' Miracles: supernatural demonstration of God's power in human affairs, trickery and sleight of hand, or mythical stories in a non-credible Bible; Jesus' Teaching: God's truth for wholesome living in a divinely inspired book, good moral teaching especially for its time and place, or a mythical collection of human stories.*)

State: "Many of us know some non-Christians who have asked some very pointed questions about the identity of Jesus, the Bible, and biblical teaching. What are some of these questions that non-Christians ask?" Write these questions on the board or overhead transparency, as learners suggest and add them appropriately to the last activity on their reproducible page. (*Possible questions may include: Why is there evil in the world? If God is love, why doesn't he heal my friend's terminal illness? What kind of God would condemn people to an everlasting hell and torment? Is the devil real?*)

Draw the session to a close by saying, "For the remaining minutes of the class, I'd like you to work together in groups of three or four: Each group is to select one of the questions we have just listed and to prepare a presentation of the gospel in response to that question. Close the lesson with a prayer requesting an opportunity to share that presentation with someone. Make a short commitment statement to that effect at the bottom of your reproducible page."

Miracle Review

Read each sentence and circle "T" for True or "F" for False. Check the Scriptures to confirm.

T F 1. Jesus met a man with a shriveled hand in the temple.
T F 2. The Pharisees watched to see if Jesus would violate the Sabbath.
T F 3. The Pharisees asked Jesus, "Who sinned to cause the blind man's blindness?"
T F 4. The Herodians plotted together with the Sadducees as to how they might destroy Jesus.
T F 5. Jesus described himself as "the Son of Man."
T F 6. After spitting on the man's eyes, Jesus told the man to wash in the pool of Siloam.
T F 7. Some people thought the man that could see only looked like the blind man that begged.
T F 8. Jesus become angry with the hardness of the Pharisees' hearts.
T F 9. After the blind man was healed, Jesus was cast out of the synagogue.
T F 10. When Jesus revealed himself to the man who could now see, the man worshiped Jesus.

Miracle Reactions

What reactions do you see or suppose for each person/group involved in the healing of the man's hand?

PERSON/GROUP	POSSIBLE REACTIONS
1. Man with a shriveled hand	
2. Pharisees	
3. Herodians	
4. Man born blind	
5. Neighbors	
6. Blind man's parents	

Gospel Presentation Response

Peter clearly challenges us to "Always be prepared to give an answer to everyone who asks [us] to give the reason for the hope that [we] have" (1 Peter 3:15). What questions do you hear non-believers asking? How would you answer their questions?

Are your answers "with gentleness and respect" as Peter further challenged?

A MOTHER PERSISTS IN FAITH

LESSON 4

WHY TEACH THIS LESSON?

The Bible notes in many places the impact of persistence and perseverance, both for good (Luke 18:1-8; Romans 2:7; 5:3, 4; etc.) as well as for evil (2 Kings 17:34; Isaiah 1:5; etc.). When we think of persistence in a Christian context, we usually think of enduring or passively trusting God in the face of misfortune or demonic roadblocks. Job, of course, is a prime example (James 5:11).

In our lesson today we meet a woman who models persistence, undergirded by faith and humility. Her faithful persistence and humility are examples for us today as we bring our prayer requests before the throne of grace.

INTRODUCTION

Where did national pride and prejudice come from? Possibly their origin can be traced to that long-ago day when the builders of the tower of Babel found that they could not understand one another. The resulting confusion must have been extremely frustrating. It was reduced when the people were scattered over the earth, thus separating the different language groups from one another (Genesis 11:1-9). Perhaps, as time passed, the people of each group looked down on those who did not understand their language.

A. A PROUD PEOPLE

The ancient Israelites were called to be God's people—"a kingdom of priests and a holy nation" (Exodus 19:6). As such, they were commanded by God to destroy nations that were too wicked to live (Deuteronomy 7:1-5). And they were to obey God's laws so that other nations would witness their obedience and say, "Surely this great nation is a wise and understanding people" (Deuteronomy 4:6).

Though warned not to become proud or arrogant, the Israelites often forgot their God-given duties and responsibilities. They seemed to think that God would protect and bless them regardless of how they lived. The Old Testament records several occasions when they were either oppressed or taken captive by pagan foreigners because they failed to follow the Lord God faithfully.

By the time of Christ, God's people were but a tiny part of the Roman Empire. But they still had their pride as "Abraham's descendants" (John 8:33), and they despised their Roman masters. Many saw the promised Messiah as someone who would deliver Israel from its oppressors and restore its national, earthly greatness.

B. LESSON BACKGROUND

Soon after his miraculous feeding of the five thousand, Jesus withdrew from the crowded centers of Galilee. Perhaps he was trying to find time for some private teaching with his twelve disciples. He had desired such an occasion just before the feeding of the five thousand occurred (Mark 6:30-34). Perhaps Jesus also meant to

DEVOTIONAL READING:
LUKE 4:16-21

BACKGROUND SCRIPTURE:
MATTHEW 15:21-31

PRINTED TEXT:
MATTHEW 15:21-31

Sep
23

LESSON AIMS

After this lesson a student should be able to:

1. Tell how Jesus' love and power were manifested outside Jewish territory.

2. Explain why Jesus expanded his ministry beyond "the lost sheep of the house of Israel."

3. Suggest a specific way to reach beyond one's usual circle to share Christ's love.

KEY VERSE

Then Jesus answered, "Woman, you have great faith! Your request is granted." And her daughter was healed from that very hour.   —Matthew 15:28

frustrate the plotting of the Pharisees against his life (Mark 3:6). Whatever his reasons, he was clearly seeking to avoid public notice (Mark 7:24).

I. JESUS IN THE NORTH (MATTHEW 15:21-28)

A. Desperate Plea (vv. 21, 22)

21. Leaving that place, Jesus withdrew to the region of Tyre and Sidon.

Tyre and Sidon were the principal cities of Phoenicia, which was located to the north of Galilee. These two cities, situated on the Mediterranean coastline, are mentioned many times in the Old Testament. (For example, see Joel 3:4.)

22. A Canaanite woman from that vicinity came to him, crying out, "Lord, Son of David, have mercy on me! My daughter is suffering terribly from demon-possession."

Jesus had never been to this region before, but people from here were among the crowds that had followed him in Galilee (Mark 3:7, 8). Evidently they had filled Phoenicia with reports of the wonders Jesus had done. Thus, when he entered their country, some of them recognized him and spread the word that he was there. Apparently *a Canaanite woman* had heard that Jesus could subdue the demons that sometimes took control of people (see Matthew 4:23-25), so she came to ask him to help her afflicted *daughter.* Her use of the title *Son of David* indicates that she was aware of the Jews' messianic expectations and believed that Jesus was the fulfillment of those hopes. This was not the only time that a non-Jew exhibited more faith than many Jews (Matthew 8:10).

While the term *Canaan* is used many times in the Old Testament, this is the only time it is used in the Gospels. (It also appears twice in Acts.) Some believe that this was the Jewish manner of describing the people of this territory.

What Do You Think?

The lesson writer suggests the possibility that the disciples wanted Jesus to heal the woman just to get rid of her. If true, that would seem to be a case of doing the right thing with wrong motives. How can we today maintain a right attitude in ministry even when we are tired or frustrated?

B. First Response (vv. 23, 24)

23. Jesus did not answer a word. So his disciples came to him and urged him, "Send her away, for she keeps crying out after us."

Apparently this woman repeated her plea for help. Her cries would attract attention at a time when Jesus and *his disciples* wanted to avoid attention, so the disciples told him, *Send her away.* Did they mean that he should send her away with a refusal, or grant her request and send her away? Jewish prejudice might suggest the former, but Jesus' reply (in the next verse) seems to indicate the latter.

24. He answered, "I was sent only to the lost sheep of Israel."

Jesus came to seek and save *the lost* (Luke 19:10), but his personal mission was to *Israel* only. He gave similar instructions to his disciples when he sent them out to preach during his own ministry (Matthew 10:5, 6). Later they would be sent to all nations (Matthew 28:19, 20); but during the brief three-and-a-half years when Jesus was among them in visible form, it was better to center his attention on the people best prepared to hear his message and pass it on.

What Do You Think?

Jesus had a clear concept of who it was to whom he had been "sent." How can we have such an assurance, to know when to accept a ministry opportunity and when to defer?

When God Doesn't Hear Us

Teen-age suicide has been called the "unheard cry for help." We often don't like to talk about it, but it is the second leading cause of death among adolescents. The fifteen- to twenty-four-year-old age group is the only American age cohort whose death rate has not declined in the last twenty years. This is due primarily to suicide.

Many causes for this tragedy have been suggested: easy availability of alcohol and drugs; a society that glamorizes violence; high family mobility; the demise of the two-parent family; the availability of guns, etc. While these all play a part, a major factor may be that many young people have concluded that they are not important to anyone: no one cares about them or hears them when they cry for help.

The Canaanite woman in today's text may have wondered whether anyone—even God—cared about her plight. When she begged Jesus to heal her daughter, he at first seemed to ignore her; and then he gave an answer that seemed quite abrupt.

But what Jesus was doing was challenging this woman's faith: was she willing to trust him implicitly? When it seems that God isn't listening to our prayers, is it possible that he is challenging us to trust him regardless of what happens?

Are we willing to choose a life of faith rather than risk the death of faith? It is only by stretching our faith that we grow.   —C. R. B.

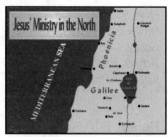

Use this map from the Adult Visuals *packet to locate the events of the lessons covered in this quarter.*

C. PERSISTENT PLEA (vv. 25-27)

25. The woman came and knelt before him. "Lord, help me!" she said.

Now the woman *came* closer to Jesus *and knelt before him* in humility and, possibly, worship. She repeated her plea simply as *"Lord, help me."*

26. He replied, "It is not right to take the children's bread and toss it to their dogs."

Jesus said it is not good *to take . . . bread* away from the children and give it to *dogs.* His comment startles us at first. Did Jesus share the Jewish national pride? Did he really think that only the Jews were God's children, and all other people were little better than dogs?

One possibility that would soften the seeming harshness of Jesus' statement is that the Greek word for *dogs* could be translated "puppies," to describe well-loved pets in the home rather than the half-wild dogs that roamed the streets and scrounged for food among the garbage. This possibility leads some to believe that Jesus spoke to this woman in a gentle tone that robbed the comment of its presumed sting. Whether this supposition is correct or not, the woman answered with humble persistence instead of taking offense.

27. "Yes, Lord," she said, "but even the dogs eat the crumbs that fall from their masters' table."

A woman with more pride and less wisdom and faith might have felt insulted by Jesus' comment or would have turned away with a curse. But this woman was content to be a "dog"—if only she might be given a scrap of the leftovers from the blessings Jesus had been distributing freely among the Jews. Perhaps some Phoenicians had been present when Jesus fed the five thousand and had reported that the leftovers from that miracle had filled twelve baskets. Certainly they had reported that Jesus had healed every illness and freed every person afflicted by a demon. Surely, the woman thought, surely there was more of that divine power than was needed by Jews alone. And how she needed a bit of that power—not for herself, but to set her daughter free from that demon!

WHAT DO YOU THINK?

A proud person might have been insulted by Jesus' remark about tossing food to dogs. We could say this woman's faith was greater than her pride. Using 1 Corinthians 13:5 and Philippians 1:15-18 as keys, what are some ways we today can overcome pride?

D. REQUEST GRANTED (v. 28)

28. Then Jesus answered, "Woman, you have great faith! Your request is granted." And her daughter was healed from that very hour.

Now the expression on Jesus' face and the tone of his voice must have emphasized the approval spoken by his words. Here was a woman with *faith* enough to be sure of the Master's ability, humility enough to accept a rebuff without anger or despair, and hope enough to keep on pressing her plea.

And her daughter was healed from that very hour. Mark's account (Mark 7:30) indicates that the daughter was not there with her mother when this miracle occurred. In some way beyond our understanding, Jesus' command reached the evil spirit. He got the message, and he left. The girl was set free.

WHOSE SIDE IS GOD ON?

The National Football Conference "wild card" playoff game between the San Francisco 49ers and the Green Bay Packers on January 3, 1999, was won by the

HOW TO SAY IT

Decapolis. Dee-CAP-uh-lis.
Galilee. GAL-uh-lee.
Hermes. HER-meez.
Judea. Joo-DEE-uh.
Mediterranean. MED-uh-tuh-
    RAY-nee-un.
Pharisees. FAIR-ih-seez.
Phoenicia. Fuh-NISH-uh.
Phoenicians. Fuh-NISH-unz.
Sidon. SIGH-dun.
Tyre. Tire.
Zeus. Zoose.

49ers, apparently because God liked the 49ers best. After all, the touchdown pass that won the game was caught by born-again Christian receiver Terrell Owens. After the touchdown, Owens yelled, "Thank you, Jesus!"

But wait a minute. Some of the five Packer defenders who surrounded Owens when he caught the pass were also Christians. And Green Bay defensive end Reggie White said that God had called him out of retirement to play one more season. But to end it like this?

During that same 1998–1999 National Football League season, Minnesota Vikings' quarterback Randall Cunningham, who won his conference's Most Valuable Player award, said, "I can't go out and win unless I do it through Christ. Does God care? Evidently he's cared, because of the success we've had this year." (The Vikings won fifteen of sixteen regular season games that year.)

It has been estimated that as many as forty percent of professional football players claim to be born-again Christians, which leads to the question in the title of this essay: *Whose side is God on?* Or is it possible that God doesn't really care much about who wins a football game?

The Jews in Jesus' day (including his disciples) thought that God was on the side of the "home team" (them) and could not possibly care about a Canaanite woman. But Jesus' words and actions show us that his concern is for all of any race or social class who trust him. Have we learned this lesson yet?   —C. R. B.

II. JESUS IN THE EAST (MATTHEW 15:29-31)

Jesus did not stay long in the region of Tyre and Sidon, but neither did he return quickly to Galilee. He went to another place where the population was largely Gentile. Again he found that even among foreigners his reputation was well known (Matthew 4:24, 25).

A. MORE MIRACLES (vv. 29, 30)

29. Jesus left there and went along the Sea of Galilee. Then he went up on a mountainside and sat down.

Jesus left Phoenicia, the region where Tyre and Sidon were located. He *went along the Sea of Galilee,* but not to the area called Galilee. He journeyed to the east side of the sea, to the area called the Decapolis (Mark 7:31). The name *Decapolis* means "ten cities." East and southeast of the Sea of Galilee, ten cities had banded together, along with the region surrounding them, to form what might be called a "league" of cities. Only one of the ten was located west of the Jordan River. Like Galilee and Judea, this territory was not independent, but was a part of the Roman Empire.

Mark tells us more about the beginning of Jesus' ministry in this area. It seems that he was recognized quickly, and people began to gather about him. Some of them brought a deaf man who had an impediment in his speech. Still trying to avoid publicity, Jesus took the man away from the gathering crowd and gave him normal hearing and speech. Jesus then asked the man and those present not to tell others about it; but they disregarded that request (Mark 7:32-37). No doubt the crowd grew rapidly.

Perhaps after a large crowd had gathered, Jesus *went up on a mountainside and sat down.* In today's English we would call this a hill rather than a mountain. We wonder if Jesus found a place where he could sit comfortably and teach such a crowd, as he had done in the famous Sermon on the Mount (Matthew 5:1, 2). The people of the Decapolis had not come to listen to a sermon, however. They had other concerns on their minds, as we see in the next verse.

30. Great crowds came to him, bringing the lame, the blind, the crippled, the mute and many others, and laid them at his feet; and he healed them.

Great crowds who had physical problems were brought to Jesus—*and he healed them*. No patient was told to stay in bed; no medicine was given; no one was told to come back in a week or a month. Healing was quick, complete, and permanent. That was plain to the witnesses.

B. MARVELING MULTITUDE (v. 31)

31. The people were amazed when they saw the mute speaking, the crippled made well, the lame walking and the blind seeing. And they praised the God of Israel.

The *people* in the Decapolis had never seen anything like this. They *were amazed*, as you and I would be if we could see the Lord in human form giving such a demonstration of his power and grace. Probably most of these people (being Gentiles) gave nominal worship to the mythical gods of the Greeks: Zeus, Hermes, and the rest. But they knew whom Jesus represented, *and they praised the God of Israel*. On an earlier occasion, Jesus said, "Let your light shine before men, that they may see your good deeds and praise your Father in heaven" (Matthew 5:16). Jesus practiced what he preached. He himself was honored, yes; but he managed his miracle working so that the observers also praised his Father in Heaven.

CONCLUSION

At the beginning of last week's lesson, we noted a problem with the popular "What would Jesus do?" slogan. While it often is an excellent question to ask (all Christians ought to be followers of Jesus, becoming more and more like him), this month's lessons remind us that in many cases the question of what Jesus would do is not pertinent. Jesus could turn water into wine, stop a raging wind from blowing, feed thousands with one boy's lunch, rebuild a shriveled hand, give sight to a blind man and hearing to a deaf one, and drive a demon away from an afflicted girl. We cannot do any of these. Rather than, "What would Jesus do?" we often need to ask, "What does Jesus want me to do?"

All of us want to obey Jesus' commands and follow his example, don't we? We want to conduct ourselves so that the people around us will not only see us doing good, but will give God credit for the good we do (Matthew 5:16). Here are some examples to think about.

A. SHINING LIGHTS

1. To pray or not to pray. While this lesson was being prepared, the TV news told of a Texas high school that had prayer before every game on its athletic schedule. But someone objected vigorously, and a court ordered the custom discontinued. That prayer violated the constitutional separation of church and state, said the court. If a majority of teachers, trustees, and students are Christians, how can they best let their lights shine for the glory of God in such a situation? Consider which of the following options would accomplish this goal most effectively.

a. Accept the ruling of the court and stop having prayer before games. Christians ought to obey the officials of their government (Romans 13:1, 2).

b. Defy the court and continue to have prayer before games. Christians ought to obey God rather than men (Acts 5:27-29).

c. Have a minute of silence in which anyone can pray as he or she sees fit. Christians ought to pray continually (1 Thessalonians 5:17), but while trying to live at peace with everyone (Romans 12:18).

d. Let the team have prayer in the locker room. Jesus told us to pray in private (Matthew 6:6).

2. Beer in the woods. In our suburb, "the woods" is a little patch of trees down by the railroad track. Underage boys sometimes hide there to drink beer illegally.

WHAT DO YOU THINK?

The crowds saw Jesus' miracles of healing, "and they praised the God of Israel." With help from 1 Corinthians 10:23, 31 and Colossians 3:17, how can we make the praise of God our aim?

DAILY BIBLE READINGS

Monday, Sept. 17—"Come to Me, All You Who Are Weary" (Matthew 11:25-30)

Tuesday, Sept. 18—A Son Raised From the Dead (Luke 7:11-17)

Wednesday, Sept. 19—Cured, But Don't Tell (Matthew 12:15-21)

Thursday, Sept. 20—Healing by What Authority? (Matthew 12:22-28)

Friday, Sept. 21—Breaking the Tradition of the Elders (Matthew 15:1-9)

Saturday, Sept. 22—Things That Defile (Matthew 15:10-20)

Sunday, Sept. 23—A Woman of Great Faith (Matthew 15:21-31)

Even Christian boys sometimes do this. After all, no Christian wants to seem too pious, does he?

Jim got an older cousin to buy some beer for him, and he was inviting some high school friends to share it. In the following scenario, which boys, if any, show a gleam of Christian light?

Jim: I've got a six-pack in my locker, and some of us are going to the woods after school. Want to come?

Tom: Sure, count me in.

Dick: Not me. You know that's against the law. Do you want us all to go to jail?

Harry: How many guys will be there?

Jim: I don't know. If more than six come, two or three can share a can.

Harry: OK, I'll be there, and I'll bring my own beer.

When the little group gathered in the woods, Harry's beer turned out to be root beer.

Tom: Hey, look what he's got. That's sissy stuff. You're chicken!

Harry: OK, I'm chicken, but I'm a legal chicken. Besides, this sissy stuff tastes better.

Tom: You've got a point there. In fact, you've got two points. It's legal, and it tastes better. How about sharing your sissy stuff with me?

B. Caution Without Compromise

Jesus spent much time in Galilee because leaders of the Jews in Judea were plotting to kill him (John 5:18). Then the Pharisees of Galilee began plotting to kill him (Mark 3:6). That may have been one reason for his leaving Galilee and going to Phoenicia and the Decapolis. Jesus intended to give his life, but not until the time chosen by his Father. He postponed this time by moving away from a dangerous place, but never by leaving the truth behind. Attacked in Galilee because he healed on the Sabbath, He exposed the hypocrisy of the Pharisees who would do a bit of work on the holy day for the comfort of a sheep, but would permit no work at all for the welfare of a human being (Matthew 12:9-14). Even more devastating was his denunciation of the hypocritical scribes and Pharisees of Jerusalem (Matthew 23:1-36) only days before they had him crucified.

If we are trying to be like Jesus, surely we must take a firm stand for truth. In places where these Sunday school lessons are used, opposition to truth is not often life-threatening. We have no need to flee our country to escape death. So is there anything we can do to dull the fury of opposition?

Consider our *manner* of telling the truth. We are Christian soldiers, told to "put on the full armor of God" (Ephesians 6:11) and to "fight the good fight of the faith" (1 Timothy 6:12). But that does not cancel our instruction to talk and act "completely humble and gentle" (Ephesians 4:2) and with "the humility that comes from wisdom" (James 3:13). Some faithful, earnest, and vigorous preachers of the Word sound as if they are egotistical, arrogant, and vindictive. Of one such preacher a listener said, "He sounds like he's glad some people are going to Hell."

Very plainly Jesus said, "How will you escape being condemned to hell?" (Matthew 23:33). But no hearer thought he was glad about that. In fact, Jesus was overcome with grief (Matthew 23:37-39). His grief is pictured poignantly in the record of his triumphal entry into Jerusalem. Multitudes were shouting his praises and calling, "Blessed is the King who comes in the name of the Lord!" (Luke 19:37, 38). But that King looked down on Jerusalem and wept (Luke 19:41-44).

"Speaking the truth in love," a beautiful little phrase from Ephesians 4:15, is a part of our growing into the likeness of Christ. When love shines through the truth we tell and the work we do, hateful opposition is put to shame.

What Do You Think?

How can we express to non-Christians God's disapproval of their sinful lifestyles without appearing to be harsh and judgmental?

Prayer

Thank you, Father, for the truth set forth so plainly in your Word. From him who verified it by divine power may we learn to speak it plainly; from him who wept because of its rejection may we learn to speak it in love. In his name we ask, amen.

Thought to Remember

Tell the truth, and tell it with love.

Discovery Learning

This page contains an alternate lesson plan emphasizing learning activities. Classes desiring such student involvement will find these suggestions helpful. The next page is a reproducible activity page to further enhance discovery learning.

LEARNING GOALS

After this lesson each student will be able to:

1. Tell how Jesus' love and power were manifested outside Jewish territory.

2. Explain why Jesus expanded his ministry beyond "the lost sheep of the house of Israel."

3. Suggest a specific way to reach beyond one's usual circle to share Christ's love.

INTO THE LESSON

Begin class today by writing the word *persistence* on the chalkboard or on an overhead transparency. State: "When you think of this word, you probably think of someone not giving up—sticking to a particular task. Think about a time in your life when you were the most persistent. Complete this sentence and share it with someone next to you: 'The time in my life when I was most persistent was when _____.'" After a few minutes of sentence completions, ask if there are any who will share their examples of persistence with the class. Then state: "In our text today, we have another example of persistence. Turn to Matthew 15:21-28 and read about a persistent woman said by Jesus to have great faith. Follow this by seeing the persistence of the crowds in verses 29-31."

INTO THE WORD

Prior to class, prepare six copies of the lesson text. Label the first copy "Jesus," and use a highlighter to mark all the words spoken by Jesus. Label the second copy "Woman," and highlight the woman's words. Label three copies "Disciples" and another copy "Narrator," and highlight the text accordingly. Select six students, and assign each one to read the part highlighted on his or her copy of the text. Ask the students to stand in front of the class to present this reading. After the reading, ask the following questions:

1. What did this woman of Canaan—outside of Jewish territory—believe about Jesus? (*He is the promised Son of David; the Lord; he could help her daughter.*)

2. Why did Jesus not give her an answer when she asked (v. 24)? (*He was sent to the lost sheep of Israel; he was testing the depth of her faith.*)

3. Why did Jesus expand his ministry beyond Israel? (*Because of the faith of this Canaanite woman; because he came to save all people.*)

4. When Jesus went up into the mountain near the Sea of Galilee, what miracles did he perform? (*He caused the lame to walk, the blind to see, the mute to speak, the crippled made well, and many others, vv. 30, 31.*)

5. How did the people react to Jesus' miracles? (*They were amazed and praised God, v. 31.*)

INTO LIFE

State: "Again we see Jesus' love and power reaching out to people in need. But there's a difference this time from other miracles we've studied. Here Jesus reaches beyond his circle of Israelites to share God's love."

Use the reproducible activity "Reaching Beyond Your Group," from page 48. Make a transparency of the page and project it. State: "Each of us has a circle of friends and family with whom we associate and where it is safe and comfortable. If we were to reach beyond our usual circle to share Christ's love, whom would we reach?" As answers are given, write them on the transparency.

Say: "We may not be able to perform miracles like Jesus to show Christ's love, but there are other ways Christ's love can be shown. Move into groups of three and make a list of ways we could show Christ's love to these people." After a few minutes, ask each group to share their suggestions. (*Answers may include: provide food for those who are hungry, donate clothes to those who need them, read to the blind, go shopping with/for the individual with a mobility impairment, spend time with children of single parents, pay for special events for disadvantaged children, and others.*) Write these for all to see.

Then say, "We can share Christ's love in many ways with those beyond our usual circle. Jesus expanded his ministry beyond the Jews. And we to expand our ministry beyond our own church family." Using the reproducible activity, "Planning to Reach Beyond," encourage each group to select a specific way for the group to reach beyond their usual circle this week. Each group should decide the individual or group they will reach, the need of the person or group, what they will do to show Christ's love, and when Christ's love will be shown. After several minutes, ask each group to write their plans on a sheet of newsprint. Tape these sheets to the wall as a public commitment to reach beyond the normal circle of friends. Ask each group to pray on behalf of the person or group who will be reached this week.

Reaching Beyond Your Group

If you were to reach beyond "your group" with the gospel, whom would you reach? What people are nearby, who need the gospel, but with whom you rarely if ever interact?

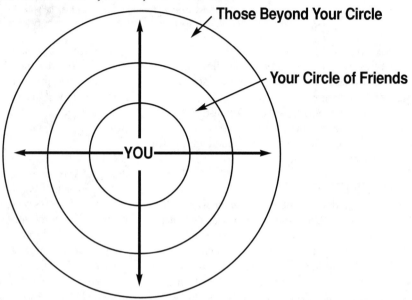

Those Beyond Your Circle

Your Circle of Friends

YOU

Planning to Reach Beyond

With a group of classmates, discuss the ones who are "beyond." Name several; identify needs each has; plan and resolve to meet one of the needs, either as a group or individually.

Person/Group	Need	What Will Your Group Do?	When Will Your Group Do It?

Jesus' Ministry
Unit 1: Performing Miracles
(Lessons 1-5)

LAZARUS IS RAISED

LESSON 5

WHY TEACH THIS LESSON?

With this fifth and final lesson in our unit on miracles, we come full circle: lesson 1 began by noting the importance of the Gospel miracles for establishing the genuineness of Jesus' claims about himself as the Son of God, and this final lesson ends the same way (John 11:42). Our five-lesson unit began with Jesus' changing water into wine. We finish with the most amazing type of miracle found in the four Gospels: resurrection from the dead. Both of these miracles—and all the others as well—prove that the Jesus of the Gospels is the same One who created the laws of nature in the first place (Colossians 1:16), as he is able to set them aside and transcend them whenever he chooses. This surely strengthens our faith that the Jesus of two thousand years ago truly was (and still is) the Son of God.

But the miracles can teach us even more. For one, we see the plans of God and the desires of humans come into conflict (see John 2:4 and 11:21, 32). For another, we see the Son of God asking for human help (see John 2:7, 8 and 11:39, 44). Today, our plans and desires still can and do conflict with God's. And even with the unique gift of the Holy Spirit since Jesus' ascension into Heaven, God still asks for human help in carrying out his eternal plans.

INTRODUCTION

A story worth repeating has come down to us from the troubled centuries in Palestine just before the time of Christ. During a portion of those centuries, Israel was under the barbarous rule of Syrians, who were determined to wipe out the Jewish religion. They defiled the temple in Jerusalem, using the sacred altar to sacrifice swine to pagan gods. Jews known for their devotion to God were summoned before the authorities and ordered to renounce their faith or die.

One of the Syrians' "tools" for persuading people was a man-sized frying pan under which a huge fire burned. Any Jew who refused to give up his faith was tossed into the pan, where he suffered horribly before he died.

One day three brothers were brought in for questioning. Their widowed mother was summoned as well. The Syrians hoped that she would plead with her sons to renounce their faith rather than leave her desolate. But the mother disappointed her captors. Passionately she urged her sons to cling to their faith regardless of the cost.

The oldest son then was thrown into the frying pan, where the others could watch him writhe until he died. White-faced but resolute, the second son reaffirmed his faith and was also thrown into the pan. The Syrians then urged the remaining son to think of his mother. Without him she would have no means of support. She would live in abject poverty—*if* she lived. She might starve to death. With that, the young man broke from his captors, ran swiftly, and leaped into the pan (4 Maccabees 12).

A. MISCONCEPTIONS

Two misconceptions about death have been held by thousands through the centuries and are held by thousands now.

DEVOTIONAL READING:
JOHN 11:17-27

BACKGROUND SCRIPTURE:
JOHN 11:1-44

PRINTED TEXT:
JOHN 11:1-7, 11b-15, 38-44

Sep
30

LESSON AIMS

After this lesson a student should be able to:

1. Relate the details surrounding Jesus' raising of Lazarus from the dead.

2. Describe some ways in which people worked with Jesus in doing his miracles, and some ways in which we can work with Jesus today.

3. Express a commitment to work with God in Jesus' life-giving ministry.

KEY VERSE

Jesus said . . . "I am the resurrection and the life. He who believes in me will live, even though he dies; and whoever lives and believes in me will never die."
—John 11:25, 26

One misconception is that death is the worst thing that can happen to someone. Many a person would lie, steal, kill, betray a friend, or even deny Christ if that would save his own life. What is left, he asks, if life is gone?

That misconception was courageously refuted by the Jewish heroes whose story is told above. They were convinced that giving up their faith in God was worse than dying. That conviction was strongly affirmed by Jesus: "Do not be afraid of those who kill the body but cannot kill the soul. Rather, be afraid of the One who can destroy both soul and body in hell" (Matthew 10:28).

A second misconception is the belief that death is final and irreversible—that dead people stay dead forever. The text of today's lesson records a time when Jesus disproved that fallacy. Not much later he disproved it again when he himself arose from the dead and ascended into Heaven. And one day all of us will see him disprove it again (John 5:28, 29).

What comes after death is far more important than death itself.

"Jesus said . . .
I am the resurrection,
and the life:
he that believeth in me,
though he were dead,
yet shall he live."

John 11:25

Use this attractive poster to illustrate today's Key Verse. You might also want to display it even after today's lesson is over.

B. LESSON BACKGROUND

John 7:1 notes that Jesus had purposely stayed away from Judea because the Jewish leaders there were plotting to kill him. However, verse 2 records that "the Jewish Feast of Tabernacles was near." Jesus proceeded to go to Jerusalem to observe that autumn feast (John 7:10). It seems that he stayed in that vicinity for more than two months, until the winter "Feast of Dedication" (John 10:22, 23).

Within the record of what occurred during these two months, we are introduced to two sisters from Bethany, a village near Jerusalem. Busy housekeepers can sympathize with practical Martha, who was overworked with "all the preparations" when she had to provide for a houseful of company. But Jesus said that Mary, who found her delight in sitting at his feet and listening to him, had made the better choice (Luke 10:38-42).

The hostility of Jesus' enemies in Jerusalem increased during the time that he was there. Twice they picked up stones to stone him, but he escaped (John 8:59; 10:31, 39). Following the second incident, Jesus went across the Jordan beyond their jurisdiction (John 10:40).

I. SICKNESS (JOHN 11:1-7)

While Jesus was staying east of the Jordan, the sisters from Bethany enter the story again. This time we also meet their brother, Lazarus.

A. NEWS OF LAZARUS (vv. 1-3)

1. Now a man named Lazarus was sick. He was from Bethany, the village of Mary and her sister Martha.

The nature of *Lazarus*'s sickness is not mentioned, but the rest of the account indicates that it was a very serious one. His life was in danger. *Bethany* is about two miles southeast of Jerusalem (v. 18).

2. This Mary, whose brother Lazarus now lay sick, was the same one who poured perfume on the Lord and wiped his feet with her hair.

This anointing was done some time later (John 12:1-8). John mentions it here to help the readers identify this particular *Mary* (there are at least five Marys in the New Testament). The anointing was already known to many readers, for Matthew and Mark recorded it long before John wrote this record (Matthew 26:6-13; Mark 14:3-9). Those earlier writers did not mention Mary's name, however. John now reveals that she was the one about whom the others wrote. In this verse he also reveals that the *sick* man *Lazarus* was a *brother* of Mary and Martha.

3. So the sisters sent word to Jesus, "Lord, the one you love is sick."

HOW TO SAY IT

Bethany. BETH-uh-nee.
Jairus. JYE-rus or JAY-ih-rus.
Judea. Joo-DEE-uh.
Lazarus. LAZ-uh-rus.
Nain. Nane.
Syrians. SEAR-ee-uns.

Lazarus's *sisters sent word* to Jesus of his illness, apparently dispatching a messenger to carry the news. It would be easy to find Jesus; most likely there would be a crowd with him. John 10:41 and 42 note that "many people came to him" and "believed in" him while he was residing east of the Jordan.

The message was simple: *Lord, the one you love is sick.* We do not know whether the messenger gave details as to the identity of the sick person and the seriousness of his illness. *The one you love* may have been enough to identify the person as Lazarus, indicating the close friendship that existed between him and Jesus.

The text does not report that the sisters asked Jesus to come and heal Lazarus. Perhaps they were afraid to ask, knowing Jesus' life would be in danger if he came near Jerusalem. Still, it seems obvious that they hoped he would come. Both of them almost chided Jesus for not being there when their brother died (vv. 21, 32).

B. JESUS' FIRST RESPONSE (v. 4)

4. When he heard this, Jesus said, "This sickness will not end in death. No, it is for God's glory so that God's Son may be glorified through it."

The disciples must also have counted Lazarus a friend. Jesus assured them that his *sickness* would *not end in death*. Note that "end in" is not the same as "bring" or "result in," as subsequent events will show. The sickness would instead bring *glory*, honor, and praise to God and to *God's Son*, Jesus. The disciples had seen many of Jesus' miracles and the praise that followed. They must have taken Jesus' statement to mean that he was going to receive more praise by healing Lazarus.

C. WAITING, THEN GOING (vv. 5-7)

5. Jesus loved Martha and her sister and Lazarus.

John wanted his readers to know that all of these three were dear friends of Jesus. Wouldn't such a fact prompt Jesus to get to Bethany as fast as he could to heal his friend? No, strange as it seems, it did not make him hurry to the rescue.

6. Yet when he heard that Lazarus was sick, he stayed where he was two more days.

We are not told what Jesus did during these *two . . . days*; we suppose that he continued the ministry that he had begun there (John 10:41, 42). It seemed that he was simply ignoring the urgent message from Bethany. That did not appear to be the action one would expect of a dear friend, so John prefaced it with the assurance we saw in verse 5.

7. Then he said to his disciples, "Let us go back to Judea."

The *disciples* were stunned. Jesus had almost been killed in *Judea* recently (v. 8). And if Jesus was going *back to Judea* in response to the message from Bethany, why hadn't he gone when the message first arrived? If the sickness was not going to be fatal, why go there at all? The disciples protested, reminding Jesus that some in Jerusalem were about to stone him before he had left. But Jesus insisted that he must go on with his work, regardless of any danger (vv. 9-11).

II. DEATH (JOHN 11:11b-15)

Between the time the messenger was sent to tell Jesus of Lazarus's condition and the time Jesus started toward Judea, Lazarus died. (Since the delay was only two days, but Lazarus had been dead four days when Jesus arrived [v. 39], Lazarus may already have been dead when the messenger reached him.) Jesus knew of his friend's death, but the disciples did not. So Jesus told them the sad news.

A. FIGURATIVE WORDS (vv. 11b-13)

11b. He went on to tell them, "Our friend Lazarus has fallen asleep; but I am going there to wake him up."

WHAT DO YOU THINK?

Lazarus could be identified to Jesus as "the one you love." What is the value of such endearing friendships among believers? How can we cultivate such relationships within the church today?

WHAT DO YOU THINK?

When we read John 11, we are initially puzzled by Jesus' slowness in responding to Mary and Martha's message regarding the illness of Lazarus. But later we see how perfect Jesus' timing was. What does this indicate to us about God's responses to our prayers?

Many speakers and writers, both ancient and modern, have referred to death figuratively as sleep. But no one else could use that metaphor as appropriately as Jesus did, for no one else could wake the dead as easily as we can wake a sleeper.

12. His disciples replied, "Lord, if he sleeps, he will get better."

A person who is seriously ill may be kept awake by pain through long days and sleepless nights. When he relaxes and goes to sleep, we breathe a sigh of relief. We know the crisis is past. The patient is getting better. That is what the *disciples* thought concerning Lazarus. If he were sleeping, he would be all right. There was no need to go back to Bethany—so close to Jerusalem, where vindictive enemies desired to kill Jesus (and perhaps his disciples as well).

13. Jesus had been speaking of his death, but his disciples thought he meant natural sleep.

Carefully John explained the misunderstanding for his readers. Jesus had spoken figuratively, using *sleep* to mean *death*. But the disciples had taken the Lord's words literally, thinking Lazarus had fallen into a restful *sleep*.

B. PLAIN WORDS (vv. 14, 15)

14, 15. So then he told them plainly, "Lazarus is dead, and for your sake I am glad I was not there, so that you may believe. But let us go to him."

Jesus knew not only that Lazarus was *dead*, but also that he was going to restore him to life. That resurrection would strengthen the disciples' belief more than a healing would have. For that Jesus was *glad*, because soon their belief would be severely tested by his own death.

Jesus had brought at least two persons back from death before this incident: the widow's son at Nain (Luke 7:11-17) and the daughter of Jairus (Luke 8:41-56). Perhaps the disciples should have realized that he intended to bring Lazarus back, but their minds were on something else when he spoke of going to Bethany. Verse 16 shows that Thomas, and possibly the other disciples as well, were afraid that Jesus and all of them would be killed if they returned to Bethany.

A DELAYED BLESSING

The Owens River runs along the eastern side of California's Sierra Nevada range. In 1903 Los Angeles diverted the river southward, enabling the growth of Los Angeles into what eventually became today's megalopolis. Population growth in the valley was stifled, and Owens Lake dried up, becoming a source of occasional dust storms.

In effect, the valley "died," becoming a relatively unpopulated area of America's most populous state. While recent court decisions have forced Los Angeles to give back some of the water to Owens Valley residents, there is still not much impetus for growth. And most of the valley residents are content with this situation. By causing the valley to "die," Los Angeles enabled it to stay isolated from the urban sprawl and pollution that characterizes much of southern California. In a sense, Owens Valley was given a new (and arguably better) life—pristine, scenic, and undeveloped.

Jesus' delay in going to Bethany might have seemed callous—a selfish refusal to respond when a friend needed him. However, it provided an opportunity for Lazarus and his family to enjoy the wonderful grace of his being brought back to life.

Sometimes, when God delays in answering our cries for help, the result can be blessings that we did not foresee—including the opportunity to grow into new levels of spiritual health. —C. R. B.

III. RESURRECTION (JOHN 11:38-44)

Verses 17-37 of this chapter record that Jesus arrived at Bethany and talked first with Martha, then with Mary. When Jesus asked where Lazarus was buried, Mary led him and a throng of friends to the place. There Jesus wept along with the others. Though he knew Lazarus soon would be alive again, he shared the grief of the mourners.

A. THE TOMB (v. 38)

38. Jesus, once more deeply moved, came to the tomb. It was a cave with a stone laid across the entrance.

Jesus felt a new surge of grief as he approached the burial place. *It was a cave with a stone* placed across the entrance. Among people who could afford it, the preferred burial place was not a grave dug in the ground and then filled with earth to cover the dead body. It was either a natural cave or a small chamber cut into solid limestone. Usually the stone around the entrance was cut to make a vertical face, resembling a wall. Then a large flat slab of stone was cut into a circular shape, like a wheel. This was rolled across the entrance to close the tomb (or rolled aside to open it). A groove wide enough to match the thickness of the wheel was cut in the ground to provide a track for the stone when it closed the entrance.

B. JESUS' REQUEST (vv. 39, 40)

39. "Take away the stone," he said.

"But, Lord," said Martha, the sister of the dead man, "by this time there is a bad odor, for he has been there four days."

There were many people present (vv. 19, 31), so there was no lack of manpower to move the heavy *stone*. However, practical *Martha* objected. After *four days* the body would be well into decay. The smell would be offensive. Wouldn't this cause a fresh outburst of grief from the mourners?

40. Then Jesus said, "Did I not tell you that if you believed, you would see the glory of God?"

This first instance of this saying is not recorded in the account of Jesus' talk with Martha a little earlier, but he may have said more than is recorded. It seems that Martha was having an inner struggle between the knowledge that dead people stay dead and the hope that Lazarus would rise that very day.

Her struggle is seen in verses 21-27. Martha believed that God could do anything Jesus asked (v. 22); but when Jesus promised that Lazarus would rise again, she thought he was speaking of the future day when all the dead will rise. She believed Jesus to be the Christ, the Son of God (v. 27); so she believed whatever he said. But since he did not specifically say Lazarus would rise that day, it was hard for her to believe that he would.

Thus, when Jesus spoke of opening the grave, Martha's first thought was of a rotting corpse. Jesus promised that faith and hope would be rewarded with a glimpse of *the glory of God*. Did Martha dare believe God would show his glory by bringing Lazarus back to life? No doubt her inner struggle persisted.

WHAT DOES THE FUTURE HOLD?

"The man who saw the future" was an accolade given to R. Buckminster Fuller (1895–1983). This American inventor, engineer, and architect was compared to Leonardo da Vinci, the fifteenth-century Italian genius. On one occasion, Albert Einstein—a genius in his own right—said to Fuller, "Young man, you amaze me!" In the 1920s Fuller conceived of a house that would have solar power, television, air-conditioning, "seeing eye" doors, and a vacuum-cleaning system—none of which had yet been invented!

In his early years, Fuller was thought by many people to be a "crackpot" because his ideas seemed so far-fetched. However, with his 1952 invention of the geodesic dome, this all changed. Today Fuller's domes have a wide range of uses, including housing businesses, radar facilities, and private homes.

WHAT DO YOU THINK?

When Jesus approached the tomb of Lazarus, he was "deeply moved." Since Jesus knew he would raise Lazarus to life, why was he so emotionally stirred?

WHAT DO YOU THINK?

With his divine power Jesus could have moved the stone from the entrance to the tomb before calling Lazarus back to life. Instead, he asked for men to remove the stone. Suggest some possible reasons why he did this.

Martha believed that when Jesus told her Lazarus would live again, he was referring to the final resurrection. But Jesus knew the future, both the long-term and the short-term as well. Others may speculate on what the future holds. Some, like da Vinci and Fuller, may do so quite well. But God alone holds the future in his hands. For those who believe in him, it will be a blessed one. —C. R. B.

C. CALLING TO GOD (vv. 41, 42)

41. So they took away the stone. Then Jesus looked up and said, "Father, I thank you that you have heard me.

The tomb was opened as Jesus had asked (v. 39). Then Jesus thanked his *Father* in Heaven that his prayer had been *heard*—which seems to mean both heard and answered. Jesus was certain of the miracle that was about to take place.

42. "I knew that you always hear me, but I said this for the benefit of the people standing here, that they may believe that you sent me."

Jesus expressed his thanks for answered prayer because of *the people* who were hearing him. Soon they would see the answer to Jesus' prayer, and they would witness new evidence that God had *sent* Jesus and that Jesus was doing God's work.

D. CALLING TO THE DEAD MAN (v. 43)

43. When he had said this, Jesus called in a loud voice, "Lazarus, come out!"

No doubt *Lazarus* would have responded to Jesus' call if it had been expressed in a whisper or only in a thought. Like the thanks for answered prayer (v. 41), the *loud voice* was for the benefit of the people standing by. They heard Jesus speak, and they would see Lazarus obey, though he had been dead for four days.

E. LAZARUS'S RESPONSE (v. 44)

44. The dead man came out, his hands and feet wrapped with strips of linen, and a cloth around his face.

Jesus said to them, "Take off the grave clothes and let him go."

At Jesus' command *the dead man came out*. Lazarus was bound hand and foot with *grave clothes* so that he could not walk, yet he *came out*. There was *a cloth around his face*, so that he could not see the door, yet he *came out*. Can you imagine the stunned silence among the onlookers? But then Jesus issued a command to them: *Take off the grave clothes and let him go*. So some of those near Lazarus stepped forward to remove the grave clothes. Perhaps one of them took off his own outer garment to clothe the man once dead—now alive!

CONCLUSION

Jesus could do anything he wanted to do, but he often asked humans to help him. He could open blind eyes with a touch or a word, but once he let a blind man stay blind until he found a pool and washed his sightless eyes. He could have given Lazarus clothing along with life, but he left that for bystanders to do.

It is not hard to think of modern examples of how God works with human helpers. God makes the wheat grow, but humans plant the seed, harvest the crop, grind the flour, and bake the bread. God puts stone in the mountains, trees in the forests, and iron in the ground; but a house does not stand until humans quarry the stone, cut the trees into lumber, make the iron into nails, and drive the nails with man-made hammers.

God made the wonders of this world, designing them to be used by mankind. How wise we are when we cherish his gifts, conserve them, and use them well! We are winners when we work with God, and losers when we work against him.

Discovery Learning

This page contains an alternate lesson plan emphasizing learning activities. Classes desiring such student involvement will find these suggestions helpful. The next page is a reproducible activity page to further enhance discovery learning.

LEARNING GOALS

After this lesson each student will be able to:

1. Relate the details surrounding Jesus' raising of Lazarus from the dead.

2. Describe some ways in which people worked with Jesus in doing his miracles, and some ways in which we can work with Jesus today.

3. Express a commitment to work with God in Jesus' life-giving ministry.

INTO THE LESSON

Prior to class prepare a large poster board with the following stimulus statement written on it: "Death is . . . ." Attach two markers on a string to the poster and place the poster where it will be easily seen near the door to the classroom. As students arrive, ask them to write a one- to three-word response to the phrase on the poster. *(Possible answers: "final," "permanent," "scary," "fearful," "unwelcome," "overcome by Jesus.")* When all the students arrive, move the poster to the front for all to see. Review the graffiti statements. Say: "Death does elicit many different reactions. Today we see several in our lesson text. Open your Bibles to John 11, and let's read about these reactions."

INTO THE WORD

Ask three students to read the three sections of the text, John 11:1-7, 11b-15, and 38-44. Then review this miracle by asking the following questions:

1. After hearing that Lazarus was sick, how long did Jesus delay? *(Two days, v. 6.)*

2. Who would be glorified through this illness? *(God; God's Son, v. 4.)*

3. Why did Martha resist the command to take away the stone from Lazarus's grave? *(By this time "there is a bad odor," v. 39.)*

4. How many days had Lazarus been dead when Jesus arrived? *(Four days, v. 39.)*

5. What effect was this miracle of raising Lazarus from the dead meant to have on the disciples? *(To increase their belief in Jesus, v. 15.)* What effect on those who witnessed this miracle? *(To lead them to believe that God sent Jesus to the world, v. 42.)*

Say: "This miracle involved more than Jesus' just speaking a word. Others were involved in working with Jesus to complete this miracle. How did Jesus involve others in this miracle?" *(Some removed the stone from the cave, v. 41; some removed the grave clothes, v. 44).* "Let's review four of the miracles we've studied and discover some other ways people worked with Jesus when he performed them."

Distribute copes of the reproducible page that follows. Then divide the class into four groups and assign each group one of the miracle passages: John 2:1-11, water into wine; Matthew 14:14-21, feeding of the five thousand; Mark 3:1-6, withered hand; John 9:1-12, man born blind. Allow several minutes for each group to read the passage and list the ways that others were involved in helping Jesus; then ask each group to report their findings to the class.

State: "Several Scriptures also illustrate this 'working with Jesus.'" Ask volunteers to read 1 Corinthians 3:9; 2 Corinthians 5:18-20; 6:1. Point out that we are God's fellow workers in a ministry of reconciliation.

INTO LIFE

Say, "We have the privilege of working with Jesus in his life-giving ministry. Let's take a few minutes to consider the many different ways that we can work with Jesus." Ask the class to brainstorm specific ways. As ideas are suggested, write them on the board or overhead transparency so that all can see the many ways available.*(Some possibilities: invite someone to church, conduct a Bible study, pray daily for someone who is outside of Christ, greet and get acquainted with visitors at church, share the message of salvation).*

State: "If you were to evaluate people in our church on the extent to which we work with Jesus in the ministry of reconciliation, where would you place us on a scale of 1 (no effort) to 10 (regular effort)?" Ask for suggested answers from the class. Then ask the class to evaluate themselves as God's fellow workers.

State: "As you can see, there is room for improvement in our working with Jesus. Now, I'd like you to look at the list of possible ways we placed on the board (or overhead) and select one way that you are not currently doing. Then I want to encourage you to complete a commitment worksheet expressing your decision to get involved in Jesus' life-giving ministry." Direct the class to the commitment section on the reproducible page. Ask your students to complete the statement, sign, and date it for personal reference later.

God's Fellow Workers

Look back at the four miracles we have studied in this series. How did Jesus rely on others for assistance in his performance of each? Note the person or group who helped; note the way in which each helped.

MIRACLE	PERSON/GROUP	TASK PERFORMED
Water into wine John 2:1-11		
Feeding of the 5000 Matthew 14:14-21		
Man with withered hand Mark 3:1-6		
Man born blind John 9:1-12		

Commitment to Work With God

Consider some of the ways God needs your help to see that ministries within your church and community are fulfilled. Select one and make a commitment to it in the following statement.

Dear Father,

In recognition of Jesus' desire that we work with him in his life-giving ministry, I now

commit myself to _____

during the next four weeks.

Signed _____

Date _____

Date accomplished _____

JESUS TEACHES IN PARABLES

WHY TEACH THIS LESSON?

Discovering truth in the Bible may be likened to digging in a mine: some gems lie close to the surface and are easily gathered, while others lie deep within the earth and require much effort to dig out. The parables of Jesus are like that. Some seem obvious; others confounded even Jesus' own disciples!

But our struggle to find meaning in these teachings will be well worth the effort, because the truths here can unlock the meaning and significance of God's eternal kingdom. Those who miss these truths may miss that kingdom as well—and nothing could be more tragic than that.

INTRODUCTION

As children, "Hide and Go Seek" was the name we gave to a favorite game at our country school. Shrubbery and outbuildings provided wonderful hiding places near "home base" and far away. To find a hidden child and then win the race to "home base" was a joyous triumph for the one who was designated "it."

A. HIDDEN TRUTH

Just as healthy, active children find joy in "Hide and Go Seek," adults of strong and healthy minds find joy in seeking after truth; they value truth all the more when they have searched diligently for it. To make the truth more interesting, more effective, and more memorable, Jesus often hid it in a parable.

The degree of "seeking" necessary to find the truth in Jesus' parables varies. Matthew 13:31-33 presents the short parables of the mustard seed and of the leaven. The hidden truth in these is not hard to find, and Jesus left us to seek it without any help. Next week we shall consider a longer parable—the parable of the Good Samaritan (Luke 10:25-37). Jesus followed it with a simple question that led one of his adversaries to acknowledge the lesson Jesus wanted to teach.

In today's lesson we consider the parable of the sower (Matthew 13:3-9). Its message was well hidden, but Jesus unveiled it plainly to seekers who cared enough to ask (Matthew 13:18-23; Mark 4:10).

B. LESSON BACKGROUND

Matthew 13 describes an incident that took place a little past the midpoint of Jesus' three-and-a-half-year ministry. In it the word *parables* appears for the first time in Matthew's Gospel. This does not mean that Jesus had never used a parable before, but it seems that he increased his use of parables at this time. Matthew and Mark both note that on this occasion Jesus taught only in parables (Matthew 13:34; Mark 4:34). The parable of the sower so caught the disciples' attention that they asked Jesus why he was using parables in his teaching (Matthew 13:10).

"Repent, for the kingdom of heaven is near" (Matthew 4:17). Thus did Matthew summarize Jesus' early teaching in Galilee. Jesus, in his Sermon on the Mount, spoke plainly about the attitudes, the thinking, and the conduct appropriate for people who belong to God's kingdom. Sincere disciples drew closer to Jesus as they tried to follow his instructions, but it appears that more of the hearers liked their

DEVOTIONAL READING:
MATTHEW 13:18-23
BACKGROUND SCRIPTURE:
MATTHEW 13:1-35
PRINTED TEXT:
MATTHEW 13:1-13, 16, 34, 35

LESSON AIMS

After this lesson a student should be able to:

1. Give the important details of the parable of the sower, and tell what Jesus said about why he taught in parables.

2. Explain the significance of the different kinds of soil in the parable of the sower.

3. Suggest one way he or she can be a better "hearer."

Oct
7

KEY VERSE

This is why I speak to them in parables: "Though seeing, they do not see; though hearing, they do not hear or understand."
—Matthew 13:13

selfish way of living and saw no need to repent. Many of them thronged about Jesus solely to be entertained and amazed by his miracles (compare John 6:26). Many of them seem to have followed Jesus in the hope that he would organize an armed rebellion and throw off the rule of Rome (compare John 6:15); but they too had no thought of repenting and changing their way of living.

As we shall see in today's study, Jesus used parables as a means of separating true seekers from those interested only in the excitement created by his miracles. Sadly, most of those in the multitudes that thronged about Jesus were not interested in doing his will, but in getting him to do their will. They missed the real message of his parables. Genuine seekers after truth did not.

I. PARABLE OF THE SOWER (MATTHEW 13:1-9)

For about a year Jesus had been teaching in Galilee. He was by far the most popular teacher there. People gathered about him by the thousands, but they came with different attitudes, different intentions, and different hopes.

A. THE SETTING (vv. 1, 2)
1. *That same day Jesus went out of the house and sat by the lake.*

That same day ties this account in to the events of Matthew 12 and Mark 3. Mark's account notes that Jesus had first gone into a *house* (Mark 3:20). However, the people who were gathering about him were so numerous that both he and they needed more space. So Jesus moved outside to the shore *by the* Sea of Galilee.
2. *Such large crowds gathered around him that he got into a boat and sat in it, while all the people stood on the shore.*

Even on the open shore *the people* pressed so closely about Jesus that only those very near him could see him. Jesus solved that problem by getting *into a boat* and pushing out from *the shore*. Thus separated from the crowd, he could be seen by most of the people. Contrary to modern custom, this preacher *sat* down while the audience remained standing. We wonder if some or all of the twelve disciples were in the boat with Jesus, but we are not told.

B. THE PARABLE (vv. 3-9)
3. *Then he told them many things in parables, saying: "A farmer went out to sow his seed.*

Most of Matthew 13 is filled with some of the *parables* Jesus used in teaching *many things* that day. The first parable—about a *farmer* sowing *seed*—is the subject of our study. Probably most of Jesus' hearers knew how sowing seed was done. Holding a bag or basket of seed in front of him, the *farmer* would walk across a field, taking handful after handful of the *seed* and scattering (or "broadcasting") it on the earth. Some suggest that a farmer in the distance may have been doing this as Jesus began to speak, thus giving the Master Teacher a visual aid.
4. *"As he was scattering the seed, some fell along the path, and the birds came and ate it up.*

The path was a footpath through the fields. In the process of a farmer's random sowing, *some seeds fell* on this ground, which was trodden hard by many passing feet. On it the seeds lay exposed, and *the birds* soon *ate* them.

Jesus' explanation of this parable is omitted from our printed text in order to make room for a discussion of why Jesus used parables; but we can read it in verses 18-23 of this chapter. The hard path represented an individual who heard Jesus' message with his ears, but did not take it into his mind and heart. As birds soon took seed from the path, so also "the evil one" (the devil) quickly snatched Jesus' teaching from the memory of a hearer and it was forgotten (v. 19).

5, 6. "Some fell on rocky places, where it did not have much soil. It sprang up quickly, because the soil was shallow. But when the sun came up, the plants were scorched, and they withered because they had no root.

The *rocky places* were not places with scattered stones on or near the surface; they were places with solid rock just a few inches below the surface. The shallow *soil* was warm and—in the first few weeks after the rainy season had ended—moist. The seed sprouted quickly and tiny green plants soon appeared. But days of sunshine soon dried all the moisture out of that shallow soil, and the plants *withered*. This soil represented a person who responded enthusiastically to Jesus' call to repent and began a new and better way of living. But when he found that the better way was not always easy or convenient, his shallow devotion withered (vv. 20, 21).

7. "Other seed fell among thorns, which grew up and choked the plants.

The seed that *fell among thorns* was not sown among thorn bushes, but among thorns that were only seeds hidden in the ground. When the seed started to sprout and grow, so did the thorns. They grew faster, thicker, and stronger than whatever was sown, and soon the desired growth was *choked* and crowded out.

This represented a person in whom Jesus' preaching was unfruitful because that individual was preoccupied by "the worries of this life and the deceitfulness of wealth" (v. 22).

8. "Still other seed fell on good soil, where it produced a crop—a hundred, sixty or thirty times what was sown.

The *good soil* was not all alike. The more fertile soil *produced* a hundred times as much as was sown; some less fertile soil produced only *thirty* times as much. But all the good soil produced as much as it could. This soil represented the people who heard Jesus' message, took it to heart, and lived by it. The fact that some did more good than others reflects the different abilities that different individuals possess, but all of them did what they could (v. 23; compare Matthew 25:15).

9. "He who has ears, let him hear."

Thus Jesus challenged the people to *hear*, and the context requires that this hearing also include understanding and obedience so that they would produce the fruit of godly living. James, the Lord's half-brother, will make this same point later (James 1:22).

SPIRITUAL GARDENS

Henry Beard and Roy McKie wrote a book entitled, *Gardening: A Gardener's Dictionary*. To anyone who has battled bugs and dreaded drought in hopes of getting some homegrown vegetables, their tongue-in-cheek definitions have a certain ring of truth.

Here are some of them. *Garden:* "A free outdoor restaurant operated by the charity-minded to provide meals for insects, birds, and animals." *Annual:* "Any plant that dies before blooming." *Perennial:* "Any plant which, had it lived, would have bloomed year after year." *Nursery:* "The only known place where money grows on trees." *Seed:* "Highly nutritious form of bird food sold in handsome packets."

Jesus' listeners knew about such matters as these. Many or most of them "gardened," but not as a pastime or an amusement. It was their primary means of putting food on their tables. They had no difficulty understanding the vital importance of good soil. They knew how birds, weeds, and hard ground could severely limit an anticipated harvest.

Even if we aren't farmers or gardeners, Jesus' words are clear enough that we should have no difficulty applying them to our circumstances. We should be moved to ask, "What kind of soil and growing conditions does my soul offer for God's Word?"
—C. R. B.

WHAT DO YOU THINK?

The hearers represented by the rocky places are prone to hearing only part of what is being taught. They love to hear messages on love, peace, and joy, but not about commitment, sacrificial service, or perseverance in the face of trial. How can we be sure we are not acting like the "rocky" hearers? How can such hearers be challenged to listen to the more "difficult" messages?

WHAT DO YOU THINK?

The hearers represented by the thorny soil are people who need to do some weeding in their spiritual gardens. How can we do this?

Use Philippians 4:8 as a guide for this discussion.

Use this poster to discuss the potential of each seedling—each disciple. Note that a good beginning is not enough.

II. PURPOSE OF PARABLES (MATTHEW 13:10-13, 16)

Both Matthew and Mark tell of this occasion when Jesus used a number of parables in teaching a multitude, and "he did not say anything to them without using a parable" (Matthew 13:34; Mark 4:33, 34). The twelve disciples did not interrupt that continued teaching, but saved their questions until Jesus was alone with them and some others (Mark 4:10).

A. DISCIPLES' QUESTION (v. 10)

10. The disciples came to him and asked, "Why do you speak to the people in parables?"

The *disciples* were puzzled. With a huge crowd listening, Jesus did not teach as he had done in the Sermon on the Mount. All he did was tell a lot of simple little stories about ordinary happenings. Even his closest followers did not understand the lessons that those stories were intended to teach. It looked to them as if a great opportunity was being wasted. *Why* did Jesus teach this way?

B. JESUS' ANSWER (vv. 11-13, 16)

11. He replied, "The knowledge of the secrets of the kingdom of heaven has been given to you, but not to them.

These *secrets* involve matters that can be known only by God's revealing them. These cannot be sought out and discovered by human effort; unless one is told, he or she will never know. Jesus was revealing great truths about the *kingdom of heaven* to his disciples, but not to the multitudes of people who cared little or nothing about those truths. *Knowledge* of the kingdom's secrets was *given* to the disciples because they wanted it, not because they were Jesus' "favorites." It was *not* given to most of the people in the crowds because they were not interested in it.

12. "Whoever has will be given more, and he will have an abundance. Whoever does not have, even what he has will be taken from him.

The disciples had a genuine interest in Jesus' teaching; thus they had a growing knowledge of matters pertaining to the kingdom of Heaven. The parables would add to that knowledge, and the disciples would *have an abundance*. Most of the people who heard Jesus were more impressed with his manner of teaching (Matthew 7:28, 29) than with his message. Since they cared little about the truth he taught, whatever they heard was soon *taken* away, or forgotten.

13. "This is why I speak to them in parables:

'Though seeing, they do not see; though hearing, they do not hear or understand.'

These words describe those who were part of the careless, curious crowd that came to Jesus to see the miracles he did rather than to learn the truth he taught. They were like the hard-packed soil "along the path" (v. 4). The priceless truth of Jesus fell on their ears, but did not sink into their minds and hearts; so it was soon forgotten.

16. "But blessed are your eyes because they see, and your ears because they hear."

The disciples resembled the good soil in Jesus' parable (v. 8). They received Jesus' example and his teachings into their minds and hearts. They shaped their lives by what they learned, and they became fruitful in their service to the Master. They did not understand all that Jesus meant by the parable of the sower; but they were willing to ask him about it (Luke 8:9), and he explained it to them (Matthew 13:18-23).

Such a blessing was not given to the twelve disciples alone; others were with them to ask and receive the explanation of the parable of the sower (Mark 4:10). It seems, then, that anyone who cared enough to seek further instruction from Jesus could share the blessing of understanding the truth of his message.

WHAT DO YOU THINK?

Compare Jesus' reason for using parables (v. 13) with the idea of preaching so-called "seeker-sensitive" sermons—messages aimed especially at those who do not have a church background and know little about the Bible.

III. PROPHECY OF PARABLES (MATTHEW 13:34, 35)

Jesus' use of parables was not an afterthought. The Spirit of God foretold it in the words of Psalm 78:2. This is a psalm of Asaph, one of David's chief musicians (1 Chronicles 16:4, 5; 2 Chronicles 5:12), and thus was penned about a thousand years before Christ.

A. SERMON IN PARABLES (v. 34)

34. Jesus spoke all these things to the crowd in parables; he did not say anything to them without using a parable.

Again we are reminded that on this occasion Jesus' teaching was solely *in parables*. Overall, about one-third of Jesus' teaching recorded in the New Testament is in parable form. Mark ends this part of his account by saying, "With many similar parables Jesus spoke the word to them" (Mark 4:33). Thus Jesus used more parables than are recorded in the Scriptures.

B. PREDICTION FROM PSALMS (v. 35)

35. So was fulfilled what was spoken through the prophet:
"I will open my mouth in parables, I will utter things hidden since the creation of the world."

The lines quoted from Psalm 78:2 are Asaph's promise of what he was going to do in that psalm. But at this point Asaph was a *prophet* inspired by God: these lines were also a prophecy of what Jesus would do centuries later by teaching *in parables*. In the chapter we are reading this week, Matthew gives a partial record of how this prophecy *was fulfilled*.

MORE THAN A FAD

Tamagotchis (Tam-uh-*got*-cheez) were a short-lived fad among the younger generation during the late 1990s. You may have missed them if you didn't have children or grandchildren in the right age group at the time. A Tamagotchi was one of several forms of electronic "pets" that needed "feeding" and other forms of attention lest it "die" a "virtual" death (in computer talk).

When the fad itself died, a Web site opened on the Internet, offering white satin-lined caskets in which to bury the "virtual pets." For a total of twenty dollars, one could also add a tiny tombstone with the "animal's" name on it! Included with the casket and tombstone was a suggested eulogy for an appropriate burial ceremony.

Some of us may find that the meaning of this phenomenon was (and remains) a mystery to us. If there is a meaning there, it seems to be a very obscure one!

Matthew explains Jesus' use of parables as more than just a "fad" that distinguished his teaching style. By using parables, Jesus was fulfilling a prophecy in the Psalms. Although the meaning of his parables was hidden from the spiritually blind, it was available to those who were sincere seekers after spiritual truth.

Two millennia separate us from Jesus' earthly ministry, but his message is still clear to those who seek, not just "virtual" life, but *eternal* life. —C. R. B.

CONCLUSION

Many students have noted that the parable of the sower might fittingly be called the parable of the soils. The sower did his work well, but the results depended on the ground that received the seed. This means little to us unless we take it personally. What kind of soil are you?

A. THE HARD-PACKED PATH

George has been going to church regularly ever since he was a baby. He enjoys it. Sunday is his favorite day of the week. He never would have guessed that he

HOW TO SAY IT

Asaph. AY-saff.
Galilee. GAL-uh-lee.
Samaritan. Suh-MARE-uh-tun.

DAILY BIBLE READINGS

Monday, Oct. 1—Parable of Weeds Among Wheat (Matthew 13:24-30)

Tuesday, Oct. 2—Parable of Wheat and Weeds Explained (Matthew 13:36-43)

Wednesday, Oct. 3—Kingdom of Heaven is Like . . . (Matthew 13:31-33, 44-46)

Thursday, Oct. 4—More Kingdom Parables (Matthew 13:47-53)

Friday, Oct. 5—Ears to Hear (Mark 4:21-29)

Saturday, Oct. 6—Parable of the Sower Explained (Matthew 13:18-23)

Sunday, Oct. 7—So He Told a Parable (Luke 15:1-10)

was not a good listener. But then his wife was seriously injured in an accident and was unable to leave the house for a month.

When George came home from church one Sunday, his wife asked what the sermon had been about. To his surprise, George did not know. He remembered a joke the preacher told, but that was all. "I guess I wasn't listening," he confessed. "I'm like that hard-packed dirt in the parable. The message just didn't sink in."

The next week, George took a pocket notebook to church. He wrote the sermon title, the main points, and a summary of what the preacher said about each point. He even recorded the joke. When he went home, his report to his wife was nearly as long as the preacher's sermon.

Only three weeks later, George gave the same kind of report without even looking at his notebook. Better than that, he thought of the sermon every day that week. Often it helped him decide what to do. George had become good soil.

B. THE ROCKY GROUND

A Sunday school class of young couples without children decided they had more leisure time than most parents had, so they ought to be helping other people. They announced in some of the other adult classes that they were available for baby-sitting, for visiting the sick (to help with housework and yard work), and for maintenance work with the church house and grounds. Soon calls for help were coming to the class secretary, and she was passing them on to class members. They were delighted. They were helping people, and it felt good!

Six months later, the secretary complained in a class meeting. Too often the members found it inconvenient to answer calls for help. Too often the secretary and her husband had to respond themselves. They were becoming overburdened. Upon hearing this, class members were ashamed. They knew they had been refusing many calls for help. Their helpfulness was like the seed on rocky ground. After a glorious start, it had withered.

The project had been great fun in the beginning, so, they reasoned, the thing to do was to begin again every week. They did, and the project became fun again.

C. THE THORNS

"Is that a thorn?" When John and Mary became Christians, they asked that question about some of their activities. Their weekly evening at the tavern was a thorn, they decided. The more they learned of Christian activities, the more that evening disgusted them. So they eliminated it from their lives.

Tennis did not appear to be a thorn. It provided clean fun, good exercise, and pleasant companionship. But John and Mary's tennis club became a thorn when it began to meet on Sunday morning. So they rooted it out of their lives. When they began to play tennis with Christian friends, they found the same fun and exercise and even more pleasant companionship.

D. THE GOOD SOIL

John and Mary were delighted to find themselves surrounded by Christians who were growing and producing the fruit of Christian service. Mary soon found her field of service in the nursery. John was a construction worker, and his expertise helped maintain the large church building. They both applied themselves to Bible study, and, in a few years, they became joint teachers of a class of young people.

E. THE CRUCIAL QUESTION

Now comes the crucial question, and it is a personal one: *what kind of soil are you?* You can be good soil if you want to.

Discovery Learning

This page contains an alternate lesson plan emphasizing learning activities. Classes desiring such student involvement will find these suggestions helpful. The next page is a reproducible activity page to further enhance discovery learning.

LEARNING GOALS

After participating in this lesson, each student will be able to:

1. Give the important details of the parable of the sower and tell what Jesus said about why he taught in parables.

2. Explain the significance of the different kinds of soil in the parable of the sower.

3. Suggest one way he or she can be a better "hearer."

INTO THE LESSON

The reproducible page that follows has a word find puzzle titled "Parable Puzzle." Use this with your class to begin. Having a transparency of the puzzle will allow you to mark words as class members find them. Words to be found: birds, Jesus, parables, rocks, seeds, sower, teaches, thorns. State: "Many people like puzzles and the challenge of solving them. Today's lesson is entitled, 'Jesus Teaches in Parables.' In a sense, Jesus' use of parables was a kind of a puzzle. Let's turn to Matthew 13 and read the 'puzzle' of the sower."

INTO THE WORD

Ask a class member to read the lesson text to the class, Matthew 13:1-13, 16, 34, 35. Then ask these questions to make certain the parable is understood:

1. What were the four types of ground where the seed fell? (*Path; Rocky; Thorny; Good*)

2. What happened to the seed in each of these four types of ground? (*Path—birds ate the seed; rocky—scorched and withered away; thorny—choked out; good—bore fruit.*)

3. There were differences in the four soils, but were there differences within the good soil? Why do you say that? (*Yes. The same seed produced more in some good soil than in other good soil.*)

4. Why did Jesus teach in parables? (*Fulfillment of prophecy, v. 35; secrets of the kingdom were given to the disciples, not to the crowds, v. 11*)

Say: "Now let's read Jesus' interpretation of the meaning of this parable in Matthew 13:18-23." Ask for a volunteer to read the passage and discuss the following questions.

5. What are the points of similarity among the four soils in Jesus' interpretation? (*All hear the word; the word and kingdom are the same; the word is sown.*)

6. What role does a person's understanding of the word have to do with the kingdom? (*Understanding is necessary for faith, v. 19, and for bearing fruit, v. 23. See also Romans 10:17.*) Say: "Using the 'puzzle' of the four soils, Jesus communicated the importance of understanding the Word of God."

7. What factors hindered or eliminated the possibility of the seed-bearing fruit? (*Failure to understand the Word; trouble or persecution; worries of this life and the deceitfulness of wealth.*)

8. Why did the seed in the good soil produce "a hundred, sixty, or thirty times what was sown"? (*Understanding of the word.*)

INTO LIFE

For this next activity, ask the class to move into groups of three. Say: "Now that we have studied the text and understood what Jesus was teaching, we need to think about its application to Christian lives today. Without giving any names, think of someone you know, perhaps from another congregation, who seems to identify with one of the four soils indicated here. Share with your group of three the circumstances of that person and why you see a similarity with a particular type of ground." After several minutes, ask the following questions:

1. What types of "trouble or persecution" arise today because of the Word? (*Possible answers may include: lawsuits prohibiting prayer or religious symbols in school; rejection from peers; ridicule of a person's faith.*)

2. How do the "worries of this life" and the "deceitfulness of wealth" choke the word? (*Distraction to hearing and understanding.*)

3. What different results did hearing the word produce? (*Understanding; depth of faith; fruit-bearing.*)

State: "As you can clearly see, hearing the word of the kingdom is only the first step. Yet, it is a vital step to bearing fruit. The question we want to reflect upon is: How can people become better hearers of the Word today?" As answers are suggested, write them on the board or overhead transparency sheet. Ask the class, "What do you need to do to improve your hearing of the Word. Spend the next few minutes reflecting upon this question, and then share your decision with someone sitting next to you." Close the lesson with a prayer to be a better listener, both to God and to others.

Parable Puzzle

In a sense, Jesus' use of parables was a kind of a puzzle for people to solve. Hidden in this puzzle are eight words of at least five letters from today's parable in Matthew 13. Draw a line around each of the words. Write the words to the right.

```
S   D   R   I   B   T   A   L
I   E   Z   S   E   S   E   U
G   P   L   A   F   O   D   S
U   J   N   B   K   W   E   K
S   E   H   C   A   E   T   C
O   S   Q   D   D   R   E   O
Q   U   I   S   R   H   A   R
M   S   N   R   O   H   T   P
```

Becoming a Better Hearer

In our media-focused world, people tend to depend more on pictures that they see than words that they hear. Unfortunately, the skill of hearing that was so important in the first century has diminished today. Yet there are ways to improve this skill. Use the three questions below to complete this chart to identify what you can do to improve your hearing of the Word today.

What helps people become better hearers today? Record your thoughts under "Objective Report."
Do I follow this way to become a better hearer? Record your thoughts under "Self-Analysis."
What will I do to become a better hearer? Record your thoughts under "Subjective Response."

OBJECTIVE REPORT	SELF-ANALYSIS	SUBJECTIVE RESPONSE

THE GOOD SAMARITAN

LESSON 7

WHY TEACH THIS LESSON?

Today, people will chat with a stranger a continent away over the Internet, but never get to know someone who lives right next door. If we see a car broken down by the highway, we assure ourselves the driver probably has a cell phone and can call for help as we speed on by. More and more it seems that we expect human needs to be met by someone else—rarely do we take another's needs upon ourselves as burdens we should personally lift. There are now six billion people in the world, two-thirds of whom have serious needs regarding their physical safety and survival.

In this second lesson from Jesus' parables, we meet someone who tried to excuse himself from helping those in need and, at the same time, establish own eligibility for eternal life. But what started out as an attempt to test Jesus' authority and knowledge of Scripture resulted instead in that individual's finding himself confronted by a trap of his own making. As we probe this man's encounter with the Master, we may see a little more of ourselves than we expected.

INTRODUCTION

When at last the county paved the dirt road by our farm, that road had to be closed for a long time. When we wanted to leave the farm, we had to drive to the end of our lane and then half a mile across the fields to a neighbor's drive that led us to another road.

That was the route my brother and I took early one evening when we started out to a young people's party at church. Carefully we had kept the irrigating water off the field that we would cross, but our neighbor had not been so careful. Not long after reaching his field, we found our wheels spinning in deep mud.

We broke branches from the cottonwood trees and pushed them under the wheels, hoping for traction enough to get us to solid ground; but progress was very slow. Soon it was apparent that we were going to miss the party. My brother was expected to direct some of the activities there, so he hiked half a mile back home to make his excuses by telephone.

I was still working to no avail with the branches when my brother returned. Close behind him came a neighbor with a team of horses to pull our car out of the mud. How did he know about our predicament? His wife had been eavesdropping on the party line. She had heard my brother's telephoned excuse. Just at that moment her husband had come in from the field, his team still harnessed after the day's work. Without hesitation, he had hurried to help us.

A. A REAL NEIGHBOR

That man who helped my brother and me out of the mud lived up to the Old Testament meaning of *neighbor*. In New Testament Greek, as in English, the word *neighbor* is related to the word *near*. A neighbor is one who lives nigh, or nearby. But in Old Testament Hebrew, the word *neighbor* is related to the verb that describes what a shepherd does for his sheep. Our English version often translates that verb *feed*, but a shepherd does far more than feed his sheep. He leads them

DEVOTIONAL READING:
DEUTERONOMY 15:7-11
BACKGROUND SCRIPTURE:
LUKE 10:25-37
PRINTED TEXT:
LUKE 10:25-37

LESSON AIMS

After participating in this lesson, a student should be able to:

1. Describe the occasion for the parable of the Good Samaritan and retell the parable.

2. Contrast the expert in the law's desire to identify his neighbor with Jesus' command to be a neighbor.

3. Identify one person to whom he or she can be a neighbor, and state one specific act of kindness that will be done this week.

Oct 14

KEY VERSE

[Jesus asked,] "Which of these three do you think was a neighbor to the man who fell into the hands of robbers?" The expert in the law replied, "The one who had mercy on him."

—Luke 10:36, 37

to still waters as well as green pastures. He gives them periods of rest after feeding (Psalm 23:1, 2). He carries lambs too young to keep up with the flock; he takes care to keep pregnant ewes from overexertion (Isaiah 40:11). If necessary, he risks his life to protect the sheep from predators such as lions and bears (1 Samuel 17:34-36). From that same verb comes the name of one who gives similar care to people. That is the word that we usually translate *neighbor.*

The farmer who was neighbor to our family lived up to that name, and he lived near us as well. In the text of today's lesson Jesus tells a story about a man who lived up to that Hebrew name, though he did not live near the man he helped.

B. LESSON BACKGROUND

Jesus spoke the parable of the good Samaritan in or near Jerusalem. For a long time he had avoided that area because the opposition of scholars and politicians was most fierce there (John 7:1). But about six months before he was to be crucified, Jesus came boldly into that hotbed of hostility to attend the autumn Feast of Tabernacles (John 7:2, 14). It seems that he stayed in that vicinity for more than two months, observing the winter Feast of Dedication (John 10:22, 23). During those months, Jesus evaded attempts to arrest him (John 7:32, 45, 46; 10:39) and to stone him (John 8:59; 10:31). But there was no evasion when some of the nation's most skilled debaters stood up to challenge him. Jesus met each challenge and won each debate. One of those challenges is recorded in our text.

I. OPENING QUESTION (LUKE 10:25-28)

A. "WHAT ABOUT ETERNAL LIFE?" (v. 25)

25. On one occasion an expert in the law stood up to test Jesus. "Teacher," he asked, "what must I do to inherit eternal life?"

The designation "expert in the law" is a favorite of Luke's, who uses the phrase (or its plural) seven times in his gospel. (By contrast, this phrase occurs elsewhere in the New Testament only in Matthew 22:35.) Our text indicates that the motive behind his question was *to test Jesus.* This expert was probably hoping to catch Jesus saying something erroneous or questionable so he could accuse him of ignorance or untruth; if this was indeed the expert's motive, then his address of Jesus as *teacher* would be sarcastic.

What must I do to inherit eternal life? was the expert's question. The Old Testament is not very clear about this matter, with indications that the dead will rise being comparatively rare. From passages such as Job 14:13-15; 19:25, 26; Isaiah 26:19; and Daniel 12:2, 3 arose a belief in resurrection and eternal life. Resurrection was denied, on the one hand, by much of Greek philosophy then in vogue, as well as by the Sadducees (Acts 17:32; 23:8); on the other hand, resurrection was affirmed by the common people and the Pharisees (John 11:24; Acts 23:8).

B. JESUS' QUESTION (v. 26)

26. "What is written in the Law?" he replied. "How do you read it?"

Jesus answered the expert's question by asking a question in return. It was reasonable to ask such a question, for the expert prided himself on his knowledge of *the Law.* What answer did he find *written* there for the question he himself had asked?

C. CORRECT ANSWER (vv. 27, 28)

27 He answered: "'Love the Lord your God with all your heart and with all your soul and with all your strength and with all your mind'; and, 'Love your neighbor as yourself.'"

HOW TO SAY IT

*denarii (Greek). dih-NAIR-ee or
     dih-NAIR-eye.*
Galilee. GAL-uh-lee.
Jericho. JAIR-ih-ko.
Judea. Joo-DEE-uh.
Levite. LEE-vite.
Pharisees. FAIR-ih-seez.
Sadducees. SAD-you-seez.
Samaritan. Suh-MARE-uh-tun.

Eternal life depended on keeping God's commandments—all of them. Apparently this expert in the law and his fellow "lawyers" had concluded that all the commandments could be summed up in the two commandments he quoted—from Deuteronomy 6:5 and Leviticus 19:18. In other words, one who fully kept those two commandments would keep all the others as well. That was a valid conclusion. Jesus himself affirmed it a little later (Matthew 22:34-40).

28. "You have answered correctly," Jesus replied. "Do this and you will live."

Regardless of the answer the expert in the law expected or hoped for, he must have been surprised to hear a reply so brief, so approving, so conclusive. All he had to do to inherit eternal life was what he himself knew and believed—what he had learned from the law he cherished. All he had to *do* was to keep God's commandments.

We Christians may be just as surprised by Jesus' reply. Don't we come to eternal life by God's grace and our faith rather than by what we do (Ephesians 2:8, 9)? Isn't it true that no one is justified by keeping God's commandments (Romans 3:20)? Haven't we all failed in keeping his commandments (Romans 3:23)?

Yes, that is true. But Jesus and the expert in the law were talking during a time before that truth was revealed—before Jesus died in our place. Before offering the gift of eternal life through the death of Jesus, God gave his law, and perfect obedience to that law would lead to life (Romans 2:13). But no one who has ever lived has kept God's law well enough to earn eternal life (Romans 3:10; 5:12; James 2:10). In this way, the law demonstrated our need for a Savior (Galatians 3:23, 24). We all deserve to die because of our sin (lawbreaking), but God sent Jesus to die in our place; in taking our punishment upon himself, Jesus offers us life as a gift (Romans 3:21-24).

That plan, however, was yet to be carried out. This expert correctly described the offer that was in effect at that time, and Jesus agreed with him.

RIGHTNESS OR RELATIONSHIP?

The legal profession is one of several about which people enjoy telling jokes. One of the reasons for this is the tendency of lawyers to complicate issues with careful definitions of terms that often confuse the person who is untrained in "legalese."

You may have heard the story about a doctor, an engineer, and a lawyer who were arguing over whose profession was oldest. "God took one of Adam's ribs and created Eve," said the doctor. "That makes him a surgeon first." The engineer said, "Before that, God created the world from chaos and confusion, so he was first an engineer." "Interesting," said the lawyer smugly, "but who do you think created the chaos and confusion?"

Apparently the lawyer who questioned Jesus was trying to create confusion or to discredit Jesus (as a lawyer today might discredit a witness testifying in court). Of course, we need those who can define certain terms carefully. At times, having such information may be crucial. However, the person who tries to define his or her relationship to God and fellow human beings legalistically is missing the point. That is what Jesus wanted the lawyer to see, both through leading him to quote the Law of Moses (Luke 10:27) and telling him the parable of the Good Samaritan.

Goodness, as well as eternal life, is about more than rightness; it is also about relationships—with God and others.

—C. R. B.

WHAT DO YOU THINK?

The two great commandments quoted in Luke 10:27 instruct us to love God wholeheartedly and to love our neighbors as ourselves. Realizing that keeping these commandments is not our means of gaining eternal life, how are they still applicable to Christians today?

II. HARDER QUESTION (LUKE 10:29-35)

A. "WHO IS MY NEIGHBOR?" (v. 29)

29. But he wanted to justify himself, so he asked Jesus, "And who is my neighbor?"

The Law of Moses did not provide an exact definition of *neighbor*. Perhaps the expert in the law was thinking of Deuteronomy 23:19, 20, which allowed a Jew to

WHAT DO YOU THINK?

The expert in the law wanted more to "justify himself" than to do what was right. How do people today use the concept of "no absolutes" to justify their behavior? Can you think of instances when someone used Matthew 7:1 to excuse their questionable conduct?

charge interest to a foreigner, but not to a fellow Jew. If so, the expert would be able to consider only his fellow Jews to be his "neighbors." Better yet, if his "neighbors" were only his fellow scribes and Pharisees who supported and helped one another, then perhaps he could claim that he loved them as himself. Then he could *justify himself*, or claim to be just according to the law he had quoted.

B. ANSWER IN A PARABLE (vv. 30-35)

30. In reply Jesus said: "A man was going down from Jerusalem to Jericho, when he fell into the hands of robbers. They stripped him of his clothes, beat him and went away, leaving him half dead.

Jesus answered this next question of the expert in the law with an illustration rather than a definition. The journey *from Jerusalem to Jericho* covered approximately seventeen miles. It literally went *down* through mountainous country that provided ideal terrain for bandits waiting in ambush for an unwary traveler. Along that road *a certain man* was attacked by *robbers*. They took all he had, including the *clothes* he was wearing. Viciously they *beat him* half to death, leaving him naked, bleeding, and semi-conscious by the road.

31. "A priest happened to be going down the same road, and when he saw the man, he passed by on the other side.

Like many of us when confronted with someone else's trouble, the *priest* did not want to get involved. We can imagine the excuses he may have made:

- The robbers might still be close at hand; he had better leave right away.
- He had no first-aid material or expertise, so what could he do?
- It looked as if the man were dead or dying, and probably beyond help.
- The priest had an appointment in Jericho; there was no time to delay.
- The wounded man was none of his business anyway.

Any of these would be excuse enough for someone who did not want to get involved in the first place.

32. "So too, a Levite, when he came to the place and saw him, passed by on the other side.

A Levite was an assistant to priests. He was more accustomed to getting his hands dirty with unpleasant menial tasks. Perhaps he would be more likely to help a man lying in his own blood. But no, he too just looked and went on by. He did not want to get involved either.

33. "But a Samaritan, as he traveled, came where the man was; and when he saw him, he took pity on him.

The Samaritans lived in an area between two Jewish regions, north of Judea and south of Galilee. They were the descendants of those people who had been displaced by Assyrian deportations in the eighth century B.C., people of mixed blood and—worse—mixed religion. There had been ill will between the Jews (Judeans) and Samaritans since the return from Babylonian captivity (see Ezra 4; Nehemiah 4:1, 2), and it had not cooled in Jesus' day. John 4:9 notes, "Jews do not associate with the Samaritans." One Samaritan village refused to let Jesus and his disciples pass through (Luke 9:51-53). *A Samaritan* would hardly be expected to help a Jew in trouble. But this Samaritan was different; unlike the Jews who had preceded him down the road, he *took pity*. He *saw* a fellow human being in trouble, and he wanted to help.

34. "He went to him and bandaged his wounds, pouring on oil and wine. Then he put the man on his own donkey, took him to an inn and took care of him.

Gladly the Samaritan used whatever he had for the welfare of the man in need. *Wine* (or any alcoholic drink) is a time-honored antiseptic for emergency use. The *oil*—most likely olive oil—was soothing to the man's *wounds*. We suppose

WHAT DO YOU THINK?

To hear a story with a Samaritan playing the role of hero, morally superior to Jewish leaders, must have been repugnant to the Pharisees. What group or class is hard for us to love? Why? How can we be better neighbors?

the Samaritan must have torn up a portion of his own clothing to use as bandages. He probably used some of it to cover the man's nakedness.

After treating the man's injuries, this kind Samaritan placed him *on his own donkey*. Thus he would have walked beside the donkey to the nearest *inn*, where he saw that the man had a comfortable place to sleep.

35. *"The next day he took out two silver coins and gave them to the innkeeper. 'Look after him,' he said, 'and when I return, I will reimburse you for any extra expense you may have.'*

The next day the Samaritan went on his way, but he did not ignore the continuing need of the wounded man. *Two silver coins* is literally "two denarii," which would have been two days' pay for a working man (Matthew 20:2). If the wounded man's needs required *any extra expense*, the Samaritan promised to *reimburse* the *innkeeper* on his *return* trip.

III. CLOSING QUESTION (LUKE 10:36, 37)

The Master Teacher was finished with his illustration. Now it must be translated into application in order to answer the question that had been raised (v. 29).

A. "WHO WAS THE NEIGHBOR?" (v. 36)

36. *"Which of these three do you think was a neighbor to the man who fell into the hands of robbers?"*

Sometimes a parable hid the truth, as we saw in the lesson last week. A hearer had to search for the truth or wait until the one who gave the parable revealed it. But in this case, the parable made the truth so plain that no one could miss it; and that, too, is one of the purposes of parables.

B. CORRECT ANSWER (v. 37a)

37a. *The expert in the law replied, "The one who had mercy on him."*

The *expert in the law* gave the right answer, as any thoughtful person could have done. It was the only possible answer to the question Jesus asked. The Samaritan showed himself to be a neighbor in the more profound sense of the Hebrew word noted earlier in the Introduction. He took care of the wounded man as a shepherd takes care of sheep, providing whatever kind of care is needed.

C. APPLICATION (v. 37b)

37b. *Jesus told him, "Go and do likewise."*

Then swiftly came the application: *Go and do likewise.* Notice that the expert in the law was still one step short of an answer to the question he had raised. He had asked, "Who is my neighbor?" Jesus had answered with a parable picturing a Samaritan being a neighbor, a helper, and a caregiver. Who was the Samaritan's neighbor? Obviously he was the wounded man, the man who needed care.

Then Jesus told the expert to do as the Samaritan had done—in effect, to "raise his standard" to that of the despised Samaritan. Who, then, was the expert's neighbor? Obviously he was anyone who needed care—care that this expert could give, care that he would be glad to give if he really loved his neighbor as himself.

AND THEN CAME THE HARD PART

At the end of 1999, as the world was gearing up for giant "Y2K" celebrations, the nation of Israel was carefully watching several groups of what were termed "millennial Christian" extremists. Late in October, Israeli police had arrested twenty foreigners—thirteen of them Americans—who were members of two Christian groups suspected of plotting violence in order to "hasten the return of Christ"!

WHAT DO YOU THINK?

We marvel at the Samaritan's instructions to the innkeeper. He accepted the risk that the innkeeper or the injured man might take advantage of his benevolence. What kinds of risks do we take in being "good Samaritans" today, and how should we view these risks?

Visual for lessons 7 and 9. See the Adult Visuals *packet*.

WHAT DO YOU THINK?

Jesus' words "Go, and do likewise" have powerful implications. What are some practical ways we can "do likewise"? Use the visual shown above to stimulate discussion. Discuss how the class can be involved in such "neighborly" ministries as helping in the situations pictured there.

DAILY BIBLE READINGS

Monday, Oct. 8—*Your Neighbor in Need (Deuteronomy 15:7-11)*

Tuesday, Oct. 9—*Sad, for He Was Rich (Luke 18:18-25)*

Wednesday, Oct. 10—*Follow Now; Don't Look Back (Luke 9:57-62)*

Thursday, Oct. 11—*Hidden From the Wise (Luke 10:17-24)*

Friday, Oct. 12—*Love God (Deuteronomy 6:4-9)*

Saturday, Oct. 13—*Love Your Neighbor (Leviticus 19:13-18)*

Sunday, Oct. 14—*Who Is My Neighbor? (Luke 10:25-37)*

PRAYER

Dear Father, we are shamed by our failure to follow the example of your Son, Jesus. Responding to the call of our need, he left Heaven's glory to die on the cross. Help us, we pray, to see and seize every glorious opportunity to answer the call of need and thus to serve our Savior. In his name, amen.

THOUGHT TO REMEMBER

"Go and do likewise."

All of the people arrested on this occasion were in Israel illegally, either with expired visas or without passports. The Israelis suspected that they might bomb the mosques on the Temple Mount or commit mass suicide to stir up trouble.

It always seems easier to do some "great thing" than it is to live by the gospel day in and day out. Jesus' call to love your neighbor is rather tame stuff when your theology tells you to create chaos in hopes of hastening the Lord's return.

The expert in the law gave the right answer to Jesus' question, "Which man was the neighbor to the victim of the thieves?" But the hard part came when Jesus said to him (and to us), "Now, *you* go and be a neighbor."   —C. R. B.

CONCLUSION

A. THE BROADENING FIELD

Who is my neighbor? The expert in the law who questioned Jesus was trying to "narrow the field," to designate only a few people as neighbors whom he was required to love. Jesus challenged that thinking. An unnamed man waylaid on the Jericho road was considered a neighbor by a despised Samaritan after a priest and a Levite had passed on by. That implied that this expert had to "broaden the field," to include anyone whom he had the ability and opportunity to help.

How that broad field is multiplied before us today! Daily we learn of people impoverished by hurricanes and earthquakes or of the pitiful starving children orphaned by civil war or ethnic cleansing. The vastness of the needs tends to paralyze us. We cannot help them all—but does that mean we can ignore them all?

B. SELECTIVITY

Recently, during a single week, the mail brought me more than twenty appeals for money. I thought every one of them came from a reputable enterprise—well managed and doing a great work for needy people. And there may be twenty more such appeals next week, and the next. If I were to send a mere ten dollars to each of them, I couldn't pay my rent.

How do I choose among so many good and helpful enterprises? First, I look for enterprises that are definitely Christian, that give glory to God rather than to human beings. (See Galatians 6:10.) Among the definitely Christian enterprises, I favor those involving people I know. I favor a Christian college where some members of the faculty and staff are my long-time friends. I favor missionaries who used to be members of my home church. I favor an orphans' home and school that I visited when my niece was its school nurse. Why do I favor those enterprises? It is not just because I like the people involved in them. It is because I know those people to be loyal to the Lord, capable in their service, and unfailing in their devotion.

C. ANOTHER KIND OF CHOICE

A multiplicity of needs confronts us. We cannot meet them all. Which one or ones shall we choose? They are so many and so urgent! The easy way is to mind our own business, to go on our way and ignore them all.

The parable in our text presents a different kind of choice. A suffering man, lying in his blood by the roadside, offered that choice to every passerby. The priest and the Levite did not want to get involved. The Samaritan did.

An injured man is trapped in his crumpled car, from which a hit-and-run driver has fled. By another road, an elderly lady stands alone, looking helplessly at her flat tire. In the mall, a terrified child is separated from his parents. A well-groomed dog, complete with license tag, follows your children home. Will you get involved?

In the brief encounter recorded in our text, Jesus twice issued the imperative *do* (vv. 28, 37). Are we listening? Are we *doing*?

Discovery Learning

This page contains an alternate lesson plan emphasizing learning activities. Classes desiring such student involvement will find these suggestions helpful. The next page is a reproducible activity page to further enhance discovery learning.

LEARNING GOALS

After participating in this lesson, each student will be able to:

1. Describe the occasion for the parable of the good Samaritan and retell the parable.

2. Contrast the lawyer's desire to identify his neighbor with Jesus' command to be a neighbor.

3. Identify one person to whom he or she can be a neighbor and state one specific act of kindness that will be done this week.

INTO THE LESSON

Display this statement as class begins: "God gives eternal life to those who love him with all their heart, soul, strength, and mind!" Prepare also four signs: "Strongly Agree," "Mildly Agree," "Mildly Disagree," and "Strongly Disagree." Place these signs in the four corners of the classroom with "Strongly Agree" and "Strongly Disagree" diagonally across the room. Begin class by asking the learners to focus their attention on the statement you reveal. Say: "Within fifteen seconds of seeing the statement, make a decision as to how much you agree or disagree. Then go to the corner of the room under the sign that best represents your opinion." After the class relocates, ask each group to discuss the reasons for their opinion. (Have them make their notes on the top section of the reproducible page that follows.) After about two minutes ask each group to relate its opinion. After hearing each group, ask the learners to return to their seats.

Say: "In Luke 10:25-37, Jesus stated how important love for God is to inheriting eternal life. Then he gave the parable of the good Samaritan. Let's read the text and look for the setting."

INTO THE WORD

Ask a member of the class to read aloud the text. Explain how easy it is to miss the contextual setting. Then ask the following questions to the class:

1. What was the setting in which Jesus gave this parable? (*An expert in the law asked Jesus a question about inheriting eternal life, v. 25.*)

2. What was the lawyer seeking to accomplish in asking Jesus this? (*He wanted to test Jesus' knowledge of the Scripture and Jewish tradition, v. 25; he wanted to justify himself, v. 29.*)

3. What happened to the man who traveled from Jerusalem to Jericho? (*He was robbed, stripped, beaten, and left to die, v. 30.*)

4. Why did the priest and the Levite who saw the injured man pass by on the other side? (*Possible answers: didn't want to get involved; had no compassion; feared robbers may be near; had no first-aid experience; didn't have time; did not want to become "unclean."*)

5. Why did the Samaritan help the injured man? (*He had compassion for the needy, v. 33.*)

6. What did the Samaritan do for the injured man? (*He bound up his wounds, pouring oil and wine on them; put him on his donkey; took him to an inn to care for him overnight; paid for his continued care, vv. 34, 35.*)

7. Why would Jesus answered the question, "Who is my neighbor?" with this parable and command to "Go and do likewise"? (*The question, "Who is my neighbor?" implies that an expression of compassion should be given only to those who are our neighbors. It assumes that compassionate care would not need to be given to some people. Jesus simply commands, "Be a neighbor."*)

8. According to Jesus, who is our neighbor? (*Anyone in need of help.*)

INTO LIFE

Say: "The message of this parable has yet to penetrate many Christians' hearts and lives. What are situations today where Christians have 'passed by on the other side'?" (*Passing a car broken down along the highway; ignoring news of great disasters around the world, not responding to needs in church ministries.*)

Ask the class to turn to Matthew 22:36-40; read it. Then say: "Jesus said here that all the law and the prophets hang on loving God and loving your neighbor as yourself." Needs are all around the world: major catastrophes strike; people are homeless and hungry; mission projects need funds.

Say: "Sending money to projects is a worthy demonstration of being a neighbor. But we may lose the personal element of helping someone in need. What about the people near you? What are their needs? If we ignore them, aren't we 'passing by on the other side'?" Ask the class to fill in the pledge card at the bottom of the reproducible page. State: "By loving God and your neighbor as yourself, you'll demonstrate God's love anew! You'll answer Jesus' question, 'Who is my neighbor?'"

Is It True?

Poll your class or group to see how they feel about the statement below. Cite reasons some might strongly agree, mildly agree, mildly disagree, or strongly disagree.

God gives eternal life to those who love him
with all their heart, soul, strength, and mind!

Loving My Neighbor
Pledge Response Card

Dear Father,

How easy it is for me to "pass by on the other side" like the priest and Levite in this parable of the Good Samaritan! My pace of life and hectic schedules drain my energy and lead me to ignore those around me who are in need. This parable teaches me to be a neighbor and act with compassion toward anyone who is in need.

Lord, I make this commitment to you today. With the compassion you have shown me, I

will extend an act of kindness to_____ in the following way:

Father, create within me this compassion of the Samaritan so that I can freely respond to people in need with genuine care and concern for their well-being.

In Jesus' name I make this commitment,

_____
(Signature)

PARABLES ON PRAYER

LESSON 8

WHY TEACH THIS LESSON?

The humorist Zig Ziglar once noted that *conceit* is the weirdest disease—it makes everyone sick except the one who has it! The opposite of conceit is humility, and the two parables considered today offer insight into how humility and effective prayer are closely linked. But a constant challenge to humility is our own *expectations*. Based on our past experiences with the modern conveniences we enjoy, we come to expect things always to operate a certain way. Our microwave ovens, remote controls, and Internet connections provide us with nearly instantaneous results, so we expect them to do so all the time. But what is our reaction when one of these conveniences fails to live up to expectations? If the reaction is one of annoyance (or, worse, anger), then conceit is beginning to rear its ugly head: "Why isn't this stupid thing working? My time is valuable, and I'm in a hurry!" If such an attitude "leaks over" into our prayer life, the result will be spiritual disaster.

INTRODUCTION

A last-minute change had been made in the order of worship. In the original plan the choir was to sing immediately after the minister had offered the morning prayer, but for some reason that had been dropped. Feeling a need to alert the minister of the change, the worship leader leaned over and whispered, "After the prayer there will be no response."

Do you ever feel like, after the prayer, there is no response? Are you impatient for an answer, like Phillips Brooks—noted preacher and hymn writer of an earlier generation? A friend once found him pacing irritably in his study, so he asked him what was the trouble. "I have been praying for weeks," Brooks replied, "and nothing happened. 'The trouble' is, I am in a hurry, but God isn't."

A. WHY?

Why are God's answers often so long in coming? We pray for a loved one who is suffering from some illness. We pray for healing, or we pray for release from pain—and yet our loved one finds neither healing nor release for weeks.

Sometimes it may be for the witness the suffering one has. When pain is endured patiently, it is a testimony to the sustaining power of faith and of Jesus, who is the "author and perfecter of our faith" (Hebrews 12:2). It testifies to medical staff and visitors, to the saints and to the lost. In Job's case it even testified to Satan!

Sometimes it may be for the growth of the sufferer. "Consider it pure joy," wrote James of our trials, because "the testing of your faith develops perseverance . . . that you may be mature and complete, not lacking anything" (James 1:2-4).

B. PERPLEXED ABOUT PRAYER

More than one observer has remarked that God has three answers for our prayers. One is *Yes*. Another is *No*. A third is *Wait a while*. Most of us have been perplexed by a firm *No* in answer to a fervent prayer. *Wait a while* is not much less perplexing. Not until the *while* of waiting is over can we distinguish it from a *No*.

DEVOTIONAL READING:
GENESIS 32:22-30

BACKGROUND SCRIPTURE:
LUKE 18:1-14

PRINTED TEXT:
LUKE 18:1-14

LESSON AIMS

After completing this lesson, a student should be able to:

1. Summarize the two parables in today's Scripture and the lesson Jesus drew from each.

2. Tell why the attitudes of persistence and humility are so important in one's prayer life.

3. Evaluate one's own prayer life to see whether persistence and humility have their proper place, and suggest one way to improve it.

Oct 21

KEY VERSE

Jesus told his disciples a parable to show them that they should always pray and not give up.
—Luke 18:1

In the meantime, we may wonder if our faith is deficient, for Jesus promised to grant the prayer of a believer (Mark 11:24). Or perhaps we may realize that we have prayed a selfish prayer and tried to disguise it by saying, "In Jesus' name." But the Lord is not fooled. He knows when a prayer is really in our own name. And most of us must admit that at times we do not know what to pray for. We can only trust the Holy Spirit to carry the proper request to the Father with an urgency beyond words (Romans 8:26, 27).

Today's lesson brings us two parables on prayer, and in these there is not much perplexity. In each case, Luke lets us know clearly what the parable is designed to teach. Let's learn it.

C. LESSON BACKGROUND

In last week's lesson we saw Jesus teaching in and around Jerusalem during the two months between the autumn Feast of Tabernacles and the winter Feast of Dedication. Then, when the opposition of the Jewish rulers grew more determined and severe, Jesus withdrew to Perea, located "across the Jordan," or, east of the Jordan River (John 10:39, 40). That area was not subject to the Jerusalem rulers. It belonged to the realm of Herod Antipas, king of Galilee. Jesus stayed away from Jerusalem for most of the next three months, until he returned for the springtime Feast of Passover, during which he was crucified. The two parables of our text were given during the few months Jesus spent in Perea.

I. PERSISTENT PRAYER (LUKE 18:1-8)

A. A PARABLE'S MESSAGE (v. 1)

1. Then Jesus told his disciples a parable to show them that they should always pray and not give up.

This *parable* was addressed primarily to Jesus' *disciples*, not to the Pharisees or to the larger crowd (compare Luke 14:25). Luke tells us at the outset what the parable is intended to teach: people *should always pray and not give up.*

B. A BAD JUDGE (v. 2)

2. He said: "In a certain town there was a judge who neither feared God nor cared about men.

Having no regard for *God* or *men*, this *judge* cared nothing for either God's law or a person's rights. On what basis would such a judge render his verdict in a particular case? He would probably rule in favor of the highest bidder for his services. The bigger bribe would buy his decision.

C. A WIDOW'S PLEA (v. 3)

3. "And there was a widow in that town who kept coming to him with the plea, 'Grant me justice against my adversary.'

The plea of this *widow* was a cry for justice. We do not know the nature of her complaint against her *adversary*. Widows were a particularly helpless group in Jesus' day and were often the targets of unscrupulous men—some of them from among the religious leaders (Mark 12:38-40).

D. A JUDGE'S DECISION (vv. 4, 5)

4, 5. "For some time he refused. But finally he said to himself, 'Even though I don't fear God or care about men, yet because this widow keeps bothering me, I will see that she gets justice, so that she won't eventually wear me out with her coming!'"

This widow had no money for a bribe; thus this corrupt judge had no interest in her case. He simply dismissed it and sent her away. But this woman would not

WHAT DO YOU THINK?

What factors are most likely to make us doubt the value of our prayers and cause us to give up praying? How can we resist such a temptation?

WHAT DO YOU THINK?

Jesus said that the judge in his story "neither feared God nor cared about men." How commonly do these two traits occur in our own attitude toward other people? How can either or both traits be corrected?

Use 1 John 4:20 as a guide to this discussion.

take no for an answer; repeatedly she came back and made the same plea for justice, in spite of the judge's refusal to help her. Her continual *coming* began to irritate the judge. Finally, just to get this persistent woman "off his back," the judge decided to help her.

E. APPLICATION (vv. 6-8)

6. And the Lord said, "Listen to what the unjust judge says.

Jesus wanted the disciples who were with him (and the disciples considering this lesson today) to give some thought to the just decision of that *unjust judge*—and then to consider what is said in the next verse.

7. "And will not God bring about justice for his chosen ones, who cry out to him day and night? Will he keep putting them off?

It may seem inappropriate for *God* to be represented by an unjust judge. But the main point of this comparison is not the similarity between God and the judge; it is the differences. The judge was bad; God is good. The judge cared nothing for truth or right or justice; God is greatly concerned about all of these. The judge cared nothing for the people who came seeking his help; God loves his people (*his chosen ones*) with a deep and everlasting love. So if repeated requests can move even a bad judge to do what is right, is it not much more certain that persistent prayer can move the good God to give what is good to those he loves?

Still, we need to remember that the stated purpose of this parable is to teach us to keep on praying when an answer seems slow in coming (v. 1). While God will not *keep putting* us *off*, there may still be a period of waiting before he replies to our prayers by giving us what we seek. As suggested in the Introduction to this lesson, waiting gives us time to rethink our prayer. Has our request been selfish or otherwise mistaken? If we are certain that our request is right and if the time of waiting becomes distressing, then we need to reflect upon how that distress can make us better servants of the Lord (James 1:2-4).

8. "I tell you, he will see that they get justice, and quickly. However, when the Son of Man comes, will he find faith on the earth?"

Jesus proceeded to answer the question he had just raised. *Quickly* the Lord will bring *justice* to his people who pray to him night and day. Does that imply that our waiting will not be long? Consider how the latter part of the verse turns our thinking to the longest wait of all for Christians. "I am coming soon," said Jesus nearly two thousand years ago. And for all those years Jesus' people have been praying with John the apostle, "Amen. Come, Lord Jesus" (Revelation 22:20). This shows us that *quickly* does not necessarily mean "very soon." Rather, it means that when Jesus does come, that event will occur "suddenly" (2 Peter 3:10).

Remember why Jesus gave this parable. It was to teach that we "should always pray and not give up" (v. 1). The important thing is not the waiting; it is the praying. Jesus' people must keep on praying through every time of waiting, short or long, through all the weeks and years until he comes again. In addition, they must live daily in a way that keeps them prepared for his return. Jesus' question *"when the Son of Man comes, will he find faith on the earth?"* expresses his concern that if people do not have enough faith and perseverance to pray continually, will they have enough to keep them spiritually alert and prepared for his return?

"THE WORLD'S MOST IMPORTANT SHORTCUT"

These words have been used to describe the Panama Canal, although the history of this "shortcut" has been rather long and involved. In 1534 King Charles V of Spain ordered a survey of a possible canal route across Panama. But it was not until 1881 that a French company made the first attempt to construct a canal, only

We "ought always to **Pray**, and not to faint."
Luke 18:1

This poster provides a powerful contemporary illustration of the Key Verse. It is found in the Adult Visuals packet.

WHAT DO YOU THINK?

In Luke 18:8, Jesus asks whether or not he will find faith on earth at the time of his return. What can we do to be sure that he does?

to be frustrated by bankruptcy and by the deaths of twenty thousand workers. In 1904, the United States took over the project, and by 1914 the Panama Canal was completed. Thus, a fifty-one-mile trip through the canal made the ten-thousand-mile sea voyage around South America unnecessary.

For Panama's citizens, however, patience was still in order: the canal (controlled by the United States) had cut their nation in half. Many Panamanians were restive about this state of affairs and eventually initiated a campaign to have their nation's sovereignty over the Canal Zone restored. In 1977, U.S. President Jimmy Carter signed a treaty agreeing to turn over control of the Canal to Panama on December 31, 1999. When that date finally arrived, there was great jubilation in Panama.

Regardless of what one thinks about the political, economic, or strategic wisdom of yielding control of the canal, its history is an illustration of enduring patience. This is the primary point of Jesus' parable of the unjust judge: patient supplication, anchored by a trust in God's power to work for good, is a vital part of faith in God.

Prayer may well be "the world's most important shortcut" in bringing our concerns to the Heavenly Father. We must remember, however, that in some situations it may take time to discern his hand at work. —C. R. B.

II. HUMBLE PRAYER (LUKE 18:9-14)

A. TARGET AUDIENCE (v. 9)

9. To some who were confident of their own righteousness and looked down on everybody else, Jesus told this parable:

Luke helped us with the first parable of our text by telling us in advance what the parable was meant to teach (v. 1). He helps us with *this parable* by telling us to whom it was directed—people who were too proud *of their own righteousness* and contemptuous of others who did not "measure up" to their standard. We can be sure that this parable is meant to rebuke pride and teach humility in prayer.

B. TWO PRAYING MEN (v. 10)

10. "Two men went up to the temple to pray, one a Pharisee and the other a tax collector.

Almost any *Pharisee* would be an example of the kind of person described in verse 9. The Pharisees were proud of knowing the law, and they were meticulous about obeying it in small matters that were often easily observed by others. Yet, as Jesus told them, they "neglected the more important matters of the law—justice, mercy and faithfulness" (Matthew 23:23). Their proud prayers were intended for the ears of men rather than the mind of God. They wanted to be seen and heard and praised for their piety (Matthew 6:5).

Almost any *tax collector* would be an example of the kind of people whom the proud Pharisees despised. They took money from their fellow Jews on behalf of the Romans, so patriotic Jews considered tax collectors as the vilest of sinners.

C. THE PHARISEE'S PRAYER (vv. 11, 12)

11. "The Pharisee stood up and prayed about himself: 'God, I thank you that I am not like other men—robbers, evildoers, adulterers—or even like this tax collector.

The Pharisee's prayer was *about himself*, mainly bragging about how good he was, but it also showed his contempt of others. The prayer was spoken to *God*, but it gave him thanks for nothing but the Pharisee's self-perceived goodness. It expressed no sense of dependence on God for material or spiritual needs.

12. 'I fast twice a week and give a tenth of all I get.'

This was the kind of Pharisee upon whom Jesus pronounced "woe" (Matthew 23:23). Such a man carefully obeyed visible matters of the law in such as fasting and giving tithes. The Pharisees usually fasted *twice a week*—on Mondays and

WHAT DO YOU THINK?

Arrogance and selfishness characterized the Pharisee's prayer. What are some similar prayer practices that we need to be careful to avoid?

Thursdays. But there was no concern for qualities such as faithfulness and mercy (this Pharisee showed no mercy at all to the tax collector). He obeyed, not because he loved God, but because he loved the praise of men (Matthew 23:5-7).

D. THE PUBLICAN'S PRAYER (v. 13)

13. *"But the tax collector stood at a distance. He would not even look up to heaven, but beat his breast and said, 'God, have mercy on me, a sinner.'*

Instead of boasting about his goodness, the *tax collector* confessed his sin and begged for *mercy*. Phrase after phrase describes his sense of humility and shame before God. He stood *at a distance*, perhaps at the side of the courtyard farthest from the Holy Place, because he felt unworthy to approach God's sanctuary. He bowed his head and lowered his eyes, ashamed to show his face before God's dwelling place in *heaven*. He *beat his breast* with his fists—the traditional expression of deep grief. He expected his voice would somehow reach God's throne beyond the sky—but only with a humble plea, not a selfish demand.

E. THE RESULT (v. 14)

14. *"I tell you that this man, rather than the other, went home justified before God. For everyone who exalts himself will be humbled, and he who humbles himself will be exalted."*

The tax collector begged for mercy and received it. He was forgiven, which is the meaning of the word *justified*. In contrast, the Pharisee asked for no mercy and received none. He went home with the same sins he came with, and without even recognizing that he had them. His pride and arrogance were sins, but he thought they were only an objective evaluation of his goodness. No doubt he was covetous, as other Pharisees were (Luke 16:14); but he thought his greed was only a recognition of what was due to one of the best of God's people. His hatred of Jesus was a sin, but he thought it was demanded by loyalty to the ancient faith of his people. Even his hatred of sinners (such as the tax collector) was a sin, but he thought it was an echo of God's own hatred.

In contrast, the tax collector knew his sins for what they were. In agony he pleaded to be free from them, and Jesus declared him justified before God.

Jesus ended this parable with a statement that seems to contradict itself. It also challenges the thinking so prevalent in our self-centered age. *Everyone who exalts himself will be humbled, and he who humbles himself will be exalted.*

NO MATTER HOW YOU SAY IT

Learning to talk is one of the most difficult things anyone will ever do. The process of sorting out various sounds, the combination of those sounds into words, and the eventual organization of those words into meaningful speech is a highly complex task. The process must wait until a baby's brain and muscle control are sufficiently developed to make speech possible.

Researchers have demonstrated that deaf children who have been exposed to American Sign Language go through the same developmental process as hearing children. The hand motions mimicking those of their "signing" parents go through a "babbling" stage and finally reach meaningful speech patterns at generally the same age that hearing children reach theirs. In either case, the child's brain develops its speech capabilities according to a predictable pattern and time schedule, regardless of the language the child is learning to "speak."

The point (as it applies to this part of our lesson today) is that, both in speech and action, we reveal what is going on deep within us. In the case of children learning to speak, it is their neurological development. In the case of the Pharisee and the publican in Jesus' parable, it was their spiritual development.

WHAT DO YOU THINK?

The tax collector demonstrated by his posture and physical action that he was approaching God in reverence and humility. Jesus also adopted a physical posture of humility when praying (Matthew 26:39; Luke 22:41). How important in our prayers are our posture and physical actions?

HOW TO SAY IT

Antipas. AN-tih-pus.
Herod. HAIR-ud.
Perea. Peh-REE-uh.
Pharisees. FAIR-ih-seez.

PRAYER

Forgive us, Father, if our talking with you has become less constant than your providing of daily bread. Forgive us if we have overvalued ourselves and despised others. Help us daily to follow our Savior, who leads us in his faultless way. In his name, amen.

THOUGHT TO REMEMBER

Be persistent in a humble way.

What do our own words and actions tell the world about how our souls are "developing"?

—C. R. B.

CONCLUSION

Our two parables on prayer teach two different principles: persistence in prayer and humility in prayer. Are the two compatible or contradictory?

A. HOW WE PERSIST HUMBLY

1. No matter how many times we come to our Father with some request that is dear to our heart, each time we must also present the request that is most important of all: "Not my will, but yours be done." In doing so, we follow the example of our Savior himself (Luke 22:42).

2. When God's answer seems to be *No*, it may be only *Wait a while*. So we must wait humbly, without resentment and without giving up, while we renew our plea as persistently as the widow in the first parable of our text renewed hers.

3. When God's answer is *No* or *Wait a while*, we must humbly restudy our request. Perhaps we can change it to make it more in tune with our Father's will.

B. CAN HUMILITY BE A SIN?

Humility is not so admirable when it is a mask for laziness. A successful school teacher with years of experience says, "Oh no! I'm sorry. I can't teach in Sunday school. I don't know enough about the Bible." A salesman who has set new records for his company declines a place in the Outreach and Evangelism ministry. "I wouldn't know how to persuade people to accept Christ," he says. The best cook in town doesn't want to get involved in preparing church dinners. "I'm just a family cook," she says modestly. "I don't know anything about cooking for a crowd."

C. PERSISTENCE IN HUMAN RELATIONS

The first parable that we studied teaches us to be persistent in prayer to God. Maybe that offers some hints for human relations. Maybe you should ask that good teacher again about working in the Sunday school. Maybe you will show her what fine helps you have for teachers. When she sees how Sunday school teaching is done, maybe she will decide that it is for her after all.

Maybe you should keep after that salesman. Maybe he will go with the preacher on some calls. If you have a visiting evangelist, perhaps the salesman will go with him to help him find addresses. Maybe that salesman will decide that persuading people of their need for the Lord is no harder than selling monkey wrenches.

Maybe you should enlist that family cook for a minor role in preparing a big church dinner. When she sees what a ministry this provides, perhaps she will welcome a more involved role.

D. HUMILITY IN HUMAN RELATIONS

What we learn about humility in today's study can also be extended into human relations. The Pharisee of our second parable was one who despised others (vv. 9, 11) and exalted himself (v. 14). Christian teaching urges us not to think of ourselves too highly, but to have an objective opinion (Romans 12:3). We are also told, "In humility consider others better than yourselves" (Philippians 2:3).

How can you esteem another better than yourself, if obviously he is not better? Instead of noting his faults and weaknesses, you can focus on his virtues and strengths. You can encourage him to do what he can do, and you can appreciate his efforts. Thus your esteem will help him become better than he is now.

Discovery Learning

This page contains an alternate lesson plan emphasizing learning activities. Classes desiring such student involvement will find these suggestions helpful. The next page is a reproducible activity page to further enhance discovery learning.

LEARNING GOALS

After this lesson each student will be able to:

1. Summarize the two parables in today's Scripture and the lesson Jesus drew from each.

2. Tell why the attitudes of persistence and humility are so important in one's prayer life.

3. Evaluate one's own prayer life to see whether persistence and humility have their proper place, and suggest one way to improve it.

INTO THE LESSON

Begin this lesson with a role-play activity. Ask the class to move into groups of three and to think about a situation in which "persistence" can be illustrated. Possible ideas: a child's asking for a toy, an employee's demanding a raise, a spouse's nagging regarding doing a household chore, or a pet's demanding to be taken for a walk. Ask each group to select a situation and create a one- to two-minute role play that illustrates this principle. Give approximately five minutes to develop their role plays. Then ask for groups to give their role plays in front of the class. Following the last situation, say: "From the looks of these role plays we certainly understand persistence. Sometimes, persistence may have got us into trouble. Other times, it was the key to fulfilling a dream or a task. The Bible clearly teaches the importance of persistence in our spiritual lives, and in particular, in our prayers. Open your Bibles to Luke 18 and let's read two parables Jesus told regarding prayer."

INTO THE WORD

Divide the class into two groups and assign the first parable of the unjust judge (Luke 18:1-8) to one group and the second parable of the Pharisee and the publican (Luke 18:9-14) to the other group. Ask one person from each group to read the Scripture text aloud to the whole class. Prior to class prepare a handout for each group listing the following questions, and ask each group to provide answers to give to the class.

QUESTIONS FROM LUKE 18:1-8:

1. What indications of the judge's character did Jesus give? (*Neither feared God nor cared about men, v. 2.*)

2. How would his character affect the decisions he made? (*Probably not concerned about justice, integrity, or fairness; his decisions may have been based upon bribery.*)

3. What did Jesus say of the widow's character? (*Concerned for justice; persistence, v. 3.*)

4. What was the judge's motivation in granting the request? (*Selfish desire to be rid of her.*)

5. Why did Jesus present this parable of the unjust judge? (*To teach his disciples to pray persistently.*)

QUESTIONS FROM LUKE 18:9-14:

1. How would you describe the attitude of the Pharisee when he prayed? (*Self-righteous; thankful for his own character; proud of his spiritual efforts, vv. 11, 12.*)

2. How would you describe the the publican when he stood afar off and prayed? (*Humble recognition of personal sin; a sense of personal grief for his sinfulness.*)

3. How did the attitudes of these two individuals influence God's response? (*Pharisee: not justified for he did not even know he was prideful and arrogant; publican: justified, forgiven, because God exalts the humble.*)

4. Why did Jesus present this parable? (*To rebuke pride and to teach humility.*)

After about five minutes, ask each group to read their questions and give their answers to the class.

INTO LIFE

State: "In these texts, Jesus teaches about our persistence and humility when we pray. Let's consider how these principles influence us today." Tell your students to turn to someone next to them and answer these questions: "Why is this attitude of persistence so important in one's prayer life today?" and "Why is this attitude of humility so important in one's prayer life today?"

Allow time for each person to share answers with another. Then distribute copies of the reproducible page that follows. Direct each learner to record both positive and negative motives and attitudes in the top section.

Next, ask the learners to evaluate their own personal persistence and humility, using the lower section of the page. Suggest they consider the presence or absence of some of the attitudes and motives they listed above.

Allow a few minutes for reflection; then say: "Jesus wants us to follow his teaching. Look at the numbers you circled for persistence and humility. What specific ways can Christians improve their rating on persistence and humility?" As answers are given, write them on the board. Ask each student to select one way to practice and develop; then close with a prayer of commitment.

Principles for Effective Prayers

From today's text, Luke 18:1-14, list in the left column all those motivations and attitudes displayed in both the judge and the Pharisee. List in the right column all those motivations and attitudes displayed in both the woman and the tax collector.

MOTIVATIONS/ATTITUDES TO AVOID	MOTIVATIONS/ATTITUDES TO FOLLOW
1.	1.
2.	2.
3	3.
4.	4.
5.	5.
6.	6.

Evaluation of Personal Prayers

Evaluate your own prayer life on the following scales. Consider the factors noted above as well as other indications from the class discussion and your own self-evaluation.

PERSISTENCE in my own prayer life is . . . .

Never Followed   Always Followed

    1   2   3   4   5   6   7   8   9   10

HUMILITY in my own prayer life is . . . .

Never Followed   Always Followed

    1   2   3   4   5   6   7   8   9   10

In order to raise the level of persistence and humility in my personal prayers, I will . . .

THE SHEEP AND THE GOATS

LESSON 9

WHY TEACH THIS LESSON?

The most well-known and oft-quoted passage of the Bible used to be John 3:16. In today's climate of "tolerance," however, Matthew 7:1 seems more popular: "Do not judge, or you too will be judged." Non-believers like to quote this verse to Christians whenever those Christians point out immoral behavior.

But whether the non-believers appreciate the concept of judgment or not, a day is coming when the One we serve will return to judge all humanity (Acts 17:31). The Lord delays that judgment for a period of time so that all might come to repentance (2 Peter 3:9). While we wait for that day, we continue our good deeds and works of human benevolence in anticipation of his return and final judgment, and out of love for the One who has already purchased our salvation. As your learners will be reminded today, the consequences of a "do nothing" attitude are most dire!

INTRODUCTION

A. JESUS IS COMING AGAIN

Nearly ninety years ago some newspapers reported a would-be prophet's confident announcement that Jesus would return to earth in 1914. When that year had passed, the prophet conceded that he had been wrong about the event; but he still held that he was right about the date. The year 1914 saw the start of the war (World War I) that would culminate, the prophet claimed, in the battle of Armageddon and the end of the world. Failure of that prediction did not deter other would-be prophets of the twentieth century. Different ones predicted the return of Jesus in 1927, 1948, 1972, and 1988. More cautious students of Jesus' promise to return have called attention to his words: "No one knows about that day or hour, not even the angels in heaven, nor the Son, but only the Father" (Matthew 24:36). We do not know *when* Jesus will come again, but that must never blind us to the promise that he will.

B. LESSON BACKGROUND

Today's lesson brings us to the week when Jesus died. On the first day of that week he rode into Jerusalem on a donkey, while uncounted thousands hailed him as one coming in the name of the Lord (Matthew 21:1-9). Many in the crowd thought that Jesus was the long-expected Messiah of the Jews, but they thought of his rule only in political terms. Many were hoping he would overthrow the Romans that very week and free Israel from its oppression.

Daily Jesus taught in the temple, and the people listened eagerly to him. The men in authority desperately wanted to stop him, but they feared the attentive crowds (Luke 19:47, 48; 21:37, 38). They knew that if anyone tried to arrest Jesus, a riot might result (Matthew 26:3-5).

From what we can piece together about Jesus' final week, Tuesday appears to have been a particularly busy day of teaching. It was also a day during which some of Jesus' most hostile enemies tried to trap him with difficult questions (Luke 20:1-47). As Jesus left the temple on this day, the disciples called his attention to

DEVOTIONAL READING:
1 JOHN 4:7-21
BACKGROUND SCRIPTURE:
MATTHEW 24, 25
PRINTED TEXT:
MATTHEW 25:31-46

LESSON AIMS

After this lesson a student should be able to:

1. Briefly retell what our text says about Jesus' prophecy of the final judgment.

2. Tell how this description encourages us to serve Jesus and prepare for his return.

3. Develop a project, either for the class or the church, that will seek to minister to some of the people described in the text.

Oct
28

KEY VERSE

Whatever you did for one of the least of these brothers of mine, you did for me.
—Matthew 25:40

the buildings of the temple. How impressive and beautiful they were! But Jesus replied that one day all of those buildings would be destroyed (Matthew 24:1, 2).

Later, when the disciples were alone with Jesus, they asked him to tell them more about that destruction, as well as his second coming and the end of the world (Matthew 24:3). In Jesus' lengthy answer (Matthew 24:4–25:46), some find it difficult to distinguish when he was covering one of these concerns and when he was addressing another. We suggest the following approach.

First, Jesus spoke about the destruction of the temple and what would lead up to it (Matthew 24:4-27). Many troubles would come (vv. 4-14). Then the followers of Jesus would see "the abomination that causes desolation" (v. 15; compare Daniel 9:27; 11:31; 12:11). Luke describes this "desolation" as enemy armies surrounding Jerusalem (Luke 21:20). That would be the signal for Jesus' followers to leave Jerusalem in order to avoid the massacre that would accompany the destruction (Matthew 24:15-22). But that disturbance would not bring about Jesus' second coming (Matthew 24:23-28). He would come later—after that period of tribulation (Matthew 24:29-31; Mark 13:24-27; Luke 21:24-28).

The destruction of the temple and of Jerusalem would occur while some people of that generation were still living (Matthew 24:32-34). (It happened in A.D. 70, about forty years after Jesus foretold it.) But only God knew (and knows) when Jesus will come again. He will come at a time when he is not expected. Therefore, his people should be ready to welcome him at any time (Matthew 24:36-44).

Jesus then added a series of parables to emphasize preparation for his return (Matthew 24:45–25:46). Our printed text includes the last of these parables. It tells about the judgment Jesus will administer when he comes again.

I. THE DAY OF JUDGMENT (MATTHEW 25:31-33)

When Jesus comes, he will send his angels to gather his people from all parts of the earth (Matthew 24:30, 31). Those followers of Jesus who have died will be restored to life and gathered along with those who have not died (1 Thessalonians 4:16, 17). Our text for today reminds us that the people who do not belong to Jesus will be gathered as well, whether they have died or not—gathered for the great Judgment Day (John 5:28, 29). This is an appointment that all must keep (Hebrews 9:27).

A. THE JUDGE (v. 31)

31. "When the Son of Man comes in his glory, and all the angels with him, he will sit on his throne in heavenly glory.

Jesus' most frequently used title for himself was *Son of Man*, emphasizing his humanity. He was "made in human likeness" (Philippians 2:7), and he knew (and knows) our needs, weaknesses, and temptations. But the Son of Man is also the Son of God, and God has made him the judge of all humanity (Acts 17:31).

B. THOSE TO BE JUDGED (v. 32)

32. "All the nations will be gathered before him, and he will separate the people one from another as a shepherd separates the sheep from the goats.

All the people of *all the nations* and all times will be gathered *before* Jesus on this day. Can you imagine the countless billions of people? Yet the Judge will evaluate each one individually, separating them *one from another*—and it will not be difficult for him to do. A shepherd does not need a series of tests to tell a sheep from a goat; a mere glance is enough. In the same way, the all-knowing Judge recognizes instantly whether a person is his or not. The identity of an individual is apparent in what he has done or failed to do.

WHAT DO YOU THINK?

Verse 32 tells us the Lord will separate the righteous from the unrighteous at the judgment. How "separate" should the righteous try to be from the unrighteous today?

Consider these Scriptures in your discussion: Matthew 5:13-16; 1 Corinthians 7:16; 15:33; 2 Corinthians 6:14-18; Philippians 2:15; Hebrews 7:26; James 1:27; 1 John 2:15.

C. THE SEPARATION (v. 33)

33. "He will put the sheep on his right and the goats on his left."

Throughout history the *right* hand of a ruler has been considered a place of honor. Jesus' own people will be placed there in recognition of what their actions have shown them to be.

THE GREAT DIVIDE

The Berlin Wall stood for twenty-eight years as a concrete symbol of the Cold War—"concrete" in more ways than one. First, it was made of steel-reinforced slabs of concrete that sliced through the heart of Berlin, Germany. It was also concrete—not abstract—as a tangible and visible symbol of the philosophical chasm that separated the free world from the Communist bloc of nations.

The West offered freedom and increasing prosperity. The East's only appeal was the drabness of a collective society where the possibility for economic success was as limited as the opportunity for political self-determination. The difference between the two sectors created a kind of "sheep and goats" scenario: on the one side, the blessings of a free society; on the other, the confining restrictions of a repressive system. When the crumbling foundations of Communism finally caused the Berlin Wall to fall on November 9, 1989, Germans on both sides of the border rejoiced at the reunification now made possible—and the world rejoiced with them.

While the strict separation represented by the Berlin Wall eventually ceased, the "sheep and goats" separation on Judgment Day will be eternally permanent. And it will be based, not on the caprice of political fortune, but on the decision each of us has made as to which side we have given allegiance. —C. R. B.

II. THE SHEEP (MATTHEW 25:34-40)

A. THE BLESSING (v. 34)

34. "Then the King will say to those on his right, 'Come, you who are blessed by my Father; take your inheritance, the kingdom prepared for you since the creation of the world.

What an invitation! To inherit *the kingdom* is not merely to have a place in it; it is to inherit the kingship—to be a king. Thus, amid the magnificent visions of Revelation, the apostle John heard these words addressed to Jesus the Lamb: "You were slain, and with your blood you purchased men for God from every tribe and language and people and nation. You have made them to be a kingdom and priests to serve our God, and they will reign on the earth" (Revelation 5:9, 10).

If we stand with the redeemed at Jesus' *right* hand, shall we be equal to Jesus himself? No; we shall be kings, but he will be King of kings (Revelation 17:14). "His servants will serve him" (Revelation 22:3), but "they will reign for ever and ever" (Revelation 22:5).

If we rule with Christ forever, who will be our subjects? Whom shall we rule? Shall we not rule each other and ourselves? Every king will be a subject, and every subject will be a king, for no one will be ruled against his will. Can you imagine yourself so well attuned to everything true and right that every desire of your heart will also be a desire of God's heart? What heavenly harmony!

That *kingdom* eternal—that land of perfect harmony—will be neither an accident nor an afterthought in the mind of God. *Since the creation of the world* it has been *prepared* for those who will align themselves with God's Son (compare 1 Peter 1:18-20).

B. THE REASON (vv. 35, 36)

35, 36. "'For I was hungry and you gave me something to eat, I was thirsty and you gave me something to drink, I was a stranger and you invited me in, I needed

HOW TO SAY IT
Armageddon. Ar-muh-GED-dun.

Visual for lessons 7 and 9. Note how activities formerly described as neighborly are also acts of serving Jesus himself.

clothes and you clothed me, I was sick and you looked after me, I was in prison and you came to visit me.'

On his royal throne the Judge describes, one by one, some of the most common needs and distresses of humanity: hunger, thirst, loneliness in a strange place, lack of clothing, illness, and imprisonment. The Judge has experienced all of these situations, he says, and those people who are now at his right hand have helped him bear the burden of them. That is the reason they are receiving the blessing described in verse 34.

C. A QUESTION (vv. 37-39)

37-39. *"Then the righteous will answer him, 'Lord, when did we see you hungry and feed you, or thirsty and give you something to drink? When did we see you a stranger and invite you in, or needing clothes and clothe you? When did we see you sick or in prison and go to visit you?'*

Remember who these *righteous* are: they are followers of Jesus who have been gathered from all nations of the world (v. 32) and throughout all centuries of history. Very few of them have seen Jesus before; here they view him enthroned in glory. When did they ever have the opportunity to help him in a time of need?

D. AN EXPLANATION (v. 40)

40. *"The King will reply, 'I tell you the truth, whatever you did for one of the least of these brothers of mine, you did for me.'*

Most of the righteous (v. 37) have not seen Jesus in person before his appearance on the judgment throne, but they have seen others in need. They have seen some of the righteous in distress and have helped them. Jesus calls these righteous people *brothers of mine*. Of course, Jesus is God's "one and only Son" (John 3:16), but those who believe in him are given the right to become children of God in a different way. They, too, in a different way, are born of God (John 1:12, 13). Therefore he "is not ashamed to call them brothers" (Hebrews 2:11). And all the help given to those "brothers" he counts as help given to him personally.

This does not mean that we have the freedom to ignore the needs of any who are not followers of Jesus. Jesus did not do this during his earthly ministry, and neither should his people. Paul's words in Galatians 6:10 are instructive on this matter: "As we have opportunity, let us do good to all people, especially to those who belong to the family of believers."

III. THE GOATS (MATTHEW 25:41-45)

After the wonderful invitation extended to the "sheep" at his right, Jesus turns to the "goats" on his left. In light of his words recorded in Matthew 7:13, 14, we suppose that the throng on the left is much larger than the one on the right.

A. THE CURSE (v. 41)

41. *"Then he will say to those on his left, 'Depart from me, you who are cursed, into the eternal fire prepared for the devil and his angels.*

Notice how precisely the command to this group is the opposite of that given to the group on Jesus' right. One group is invited to come; the other is ordered to *depart*. One is called blessed; the other is called *cursed*. One is called to a kingdom; the other is sent to *eternal fire*. Those in one group inherit a kingdom prepared for them. Those in the other have no place prepared for them; they can only share the place *prepared for the devil and his angels*. There is nowhere else to go. Notice that Hell is not a place "prepared" for human beings. God wants no one to go there (2 Peter 3:9).

B. THE REASON (vv. 42, 43)

42, 43. "'For I was hungry and you gave me nothing to eat, I was thirsty and you gave me nothing to drink, I was a stranger and you did not invite me in, I needed clothes and you did not clothe me, I was sick and in prison and you did not look after me.'

Observe that these people condemned to eternal fire are not accused of doing anything maliciously evil: no murder, mayhem, assault, adultery, arson, or theft. They are condemned for doing nothing. They had opportunities to do good, just as the people on the right; but they chose to do nothing. The heavenly kingdom is prepared for doers; the "do-nothings" are left out.

C. A QUESTION (v. 44)

44. "They also will answer, 'Lord, when did we see you hungry or thirsty or a stranger or needing clothes or sick or in prison, and did not help you?'

Like those on the right, most of these on Jesus' left had never seen him. Seeing him now "on his throne in heavenly glory" (v. 31), they could hardly believe that he had ever been a victim of poverty or imprisonment. Were they being condemned unjustly? They asked for an explanation.

D. AN EXPLANATION (v. 45)

45. "He will reply, 'I tell you the truth, whatever you did not do for one of the least of these, you did not do for me.'

These, too, have seen many of the Lord's people in need. They have seen them and have neglected to help them. Jesus takes that neglect personally, as if he himself were neglected. For that neglect, the people on the left are sent from the presence of Jesus into eternal fire.

SINS OF OMISSION?

Thomas Rossi claimed that he had been a faithful husband for twenty-five years. So it came as no small shock when "out of the blue" his wife told him that she wanted a divorce. It was not until three years later that Rossi learned the reason for his wife's sudden request.

Three weeks before Denise Rossi filed for the divorce, she had won $1.3 million in the California State Lottery. She wanted to divorce Mr. Rossi to keep him from finding out about her winnings and to avoid having to share the money with him. Eventually, the truth caught up with Mrs. Rossi, and the matter was taken to court. The judge found her guilty of violating state asset disclosure laws and gave all of the money to her ex-husband!

It could be argued that Mrs. Rossi was guilty of a sin of omission—a failure to tell her husband about her money or to share it with him. However, like many (perhaps most?) sins of omission, her failure was really a sin of *commission*—a willful decision to commit an act that she knew was wrong.

That is the reason Jesus' condemnation is so strong against those who "did not do for one of the least of these." A failure to do a good act is all too often a willful decision not to act.

           —C. R. B.

IV. SUMMATION (MATTHEW 25:46)

46. "Then they will go away to eternal punishment, but the righteous to eternal life."

The invitation in verse 34 and the rejection in verse 41 are not idle words. The people placed at Jesus' right hand in the final judgment really will inherit the kingdom prepared for them from the foundation of the world. Those placed at his left really will be banished to everlasting fire prepared for the devil and his angels.

WHAT DO YOU THINK?

The lesson writer notes that the "goats" were not necessarily the murderers, adulterers, arsonists, and the like. "They had opportunities to do good . . . but they chose to do nothing." In what situations are we tempted to "do nothing"? How can we avoid being like these "goats"?

DAILY BIBLE READINGS

Monday, Oct. 22—Signs of the End (Matthew 24:1-8)

Tuesday, Oct. 23—Those Who Endure Will Be Saved (Matthew 24:9-14)

Wednesday, Oct. 24—No One Knows the Hour (Matthew 24:36-44)

Thursday, Oct. 25—The Faithful Servant; the Wicked Servant (Matthew 24:45-51)

Friday, Oct. 26—Parable of the Ten Virgins (Matthew 25:1-13)

Saturday, Oct. 27—Parable of the Talents (Matthew 25:14-29)

Sunday, Oct. 28—"When Did We See You?" (Matthew 25:31-46)

Now that our advanced means of communication can give us daily news of the needy around the world, we are appalled by the number of them. Unable to help them all, we ignore them all—but that is the way to everlasting fire. So we struggle with the decision: which of the needy shall I help, and how much shall I help them? Each person makes his own choice, and no two choices are alike. But let each person remember that he is choosing more than where he will spend his or her money. That person is choosing where he or she will spend eternity.

CONCLUSION

In some Bibles the words spoken by Jesus are printed in red. If we read those words only, we might conclude that we earn eternal life by what we do. Two weeks ago we considered how a lawyer cited the two all-inclusive commands as the way to eternal life, and Jesus said, "Do this and you will live" (Luke 10:25-28). This week's text seems to indicate that eternal life is the reward of those who are diligent in helping the needy. But we know that this is not the whole story.

A. THE REST OF THE STORY

The law did say that those who keep the law will live by it (Leviticus 18:5; Romans 10:5); however, that was not good enough, for no one has kept the law well enough to earn eternal life (Romans 3:23). We get eternal life as a gift (Romans 6:23) or not at all; however, that gift is not given to everyone. God did not retract the law that sin brings death. Instead, he sent his Son to die the death that we deserved. So the gift of life is free to us, but very expensive to God and to Jesus. Such a costly gift is offered only to those who believe in the Savior who died for the undeserving (John 3:16).

There is yet more to the rest of the story. Eternal life is not offered to all who believe in Jesus. Through the centuries, many have taught that we are saved by faith alone—but the Bible does not say that. In fact, the Bible specifically denies it (James 2:24). On the other hand, many have continued to teach that we can "win" Heaven by doing good works and by doing penance to atone for our sins. The Bible does not say that either. Rather, it belittles the role of works (or lawkeeping) as a means of salvation (Romans 3:20; Galatians 2:16). We are not saved *by* works (Ephesians 2:9), but *for* works (Ephesians 2:10).

B. SALVATION BY COOPERATION

If you have been taking part in the debate about how we are saved, here is a suggestion: read the entire New Testament. Read it slowly, thoughtfully. If you read only a little while each day, it may take weeks or months to finish; but read all of it. As you read, make a list of things which are "connected" to our salvation (our justification). If your list consists of more than one item, can you ever again say that your salvation involves that one thing *only*?

To encourage this search, here is some of what you will find:

1. We are saved by what God has done—his grace, or undeserved favor (Ephesians 2:8).

2. We are saved by what we do—namely, by putting our faith in Jesus as our Savior (Galatians 3:26), by repentance from sin (2 Corinthians 7:10), by confession of Christ (Romans 10:9), and by baptism (1 Peter 3:21).

3. We are justified by what we do (James 2:24). This means that the good things we do are done, not as a means of salvation, but because we have accepted Jesus as Lord and Savior and want to obey him.

To summarize, God has done all he can do to provide the gift of salvation; we must do all he commands to "open" this gift.

Discovery Learning

This page contains an alternate lesson plan emphasizing learning activities. Classes desiring such student involvement will find these suggestions helpful. The next page is a reproducible activity page to further enhance discovery learning.

LEARNING GOALS

After participating in this lesson, each student will be able to:

1. Briefly retell what our text tells about Jesus' prophecy of the final judgment.

2. Tell how this description encourages us to serve Jesus and prepare for his return.

3. Develop a project, either for the class or the church, that will seek to minister to some of the people described in the text.

INTO THE LESSON

Begin this week's lesson with a word-association activity. Write the words "Final Judgment" where everyone in the class can see them. State: "What words, thoughts, or emotions flood into your minds when you think of the final judgment?" As ideas are shared, write them on the board or an overhead transparency under the two words. *(Possible suggestions include: glory, eternal, justice, punishment, fear, separation, salvation, Heaven, Hell).* Say: "People have different reactions to the idea of a final judgment. Some look on it favorably; others express fear and dread. Today's lesson in Matthew 25:31-46 presents the separation that occurs in the final judgment and encourages us to prepare for Christ's return."

INTO THE WORD

Ask a class member to read the lesson Scripture to the class. Say: "To make certain that we understand what the text tells about Jesus' prophecy of the final judgment, let's briefly retell the facts of this passage." Write the basic facts of the passage on the board or overhead transparency. Make certain the following truths are included: (1) Jesus, the Son of Man, is coming again; (2) He will sit on the throne of judgment; (3) All people will stand before him to be judged; (4) He will divide all people into two groups; (5) The "sheep" on his right will inherit the kingdom on the basis of their compassionate service to the Christ; (6) Ministry to members of his family is accepted as equal to ministry to Jesus personally (vv. 37-40); (7) The "goats" on his left will go into everlasting punishment because neglect of "the least of these" is equal to neglect of the Lord. Say: "Ministry to people's basic needs truly reflects the heart of God. So important is this practice that God accepts it as if it were service done directly to Jesus. Based on Jesus'

description of ministry to the 'least of these,' what are these basic human needs that the righteous in his teaching met?" *(Basic needs include food, water, friendship, clothing, shelter, health, and freedom; which of these are used as examples in Jesus' teaching?)*

Use the reproducible activity titled "Contrasting Judgments" from the following page. Separate the class into groups and give a copy of this worksheet to each person. Appoint a leader for each group and ask the leaders to assign a specific row to each person. After a few minutes, ask for the answers to be shared before the whole class. *(For the consecutive lines, these are the desired responses, left then right respectively. Group Called: Cursed/Blessed; Command Given: Depart/Come; Inheritance Received: Everlasting fire/Kingdom; Prepared for: Devil and his angels/Sheep; Ministry Performed: No/Yes).*

INTO LIFE

Make the transition to application by saying something like this: "Jesus identifies in this passage the principle that by ministering to others we minister to him. One way we can prepare for his return is to get involved in ministry to some of the 'least of these.' Let's consider how this principle can be applied to our class, to our congregation, or to ourselves personally."

Direct the attention of your class to the reproducible activity, "Serving Christ by Serving Others." Say: "During the remainder of the class, let's develop a project that we can do as a class or as individuals in preparation for Jesus' return. He wants us to be involved in ministry to the 'least of these.' Let's start by suggesting some possible projects that we could do."

Write these suggested projects on the chalkboard. Once there appears to be a general agreement about which project to develop, turn on the overhead projector and state: "Now let's develop our plans to serve Christ by serving others." Work through each category to complete the worksheet. If your chosen project involves the need for financial support, plan how the funding will be obtained. If the class has an account, suggest they designate a significant portion to the plan.

Conclude by having the students stand together in a prayer circle, holding hands, and committing this project to the Lord. Ask individuals to pray voluntarily for specific individuals or groups you have included in your discussion.

Contrasting Judgments

Fill in the following chart based on the two basic groups of Jesus' story in Matthew 25.

JUDGMENT CONTRASTS		
THOSE ON THE LEFT		THOSE ON THE RIGHT
	← Group is Called →	
	← Command Given →	
	← Inheritance Received →	
	← Prepared for Whom →	
	← Ministry Performed →	

Serving Christ by Serving Others: Project Development

On your own or in a small group your teacher appoints, fill in the following chart to help you decide an appropriate service opportunity in which you serve Christ by serving another.

AREAS OF BASIC HUMAN NEEDS						
What	Food	Thirst	Friendship	Clothing	Health	Freedom
Where						
When						
Who						
How						
A Group or Personal Project:						

BLESSED ARE YOU

LESSON 10

WHY TEACH THIS LESSON?

Society seems always to put people into classes. On the evening news, one can hear references to "the rich," "the middle class," and "the disadvantaged" almost nightly. But where one is placed in this spectrum always seems to come down to one thing: how much money or material wealth that person has.

But God looks at this issue very differently. For him, true riches concern that which is inward, spiritual, and eternal, not outward, material, and temporary. Today's lesson will help your students to focus on those things that God values. "The Lord does not look at the things man looks at. Man looks at the outward appearance, but the Lord looks at the heart" (1 Samuel 16:7).

INTRODUCTION

A. HAPPINESS IS . . .

What makes you happy? An evening out with friends, or solitude in your easy chair after a hard day's work? Taking a journey to faraway places, or coming back home? A big holiday celebration with the entire town, or a quiet evening with a good book? No matter where your happiness comes from, it's important to you!

Happiness is a rare word in the New Testament. There we more often read of "blessing" or "joy." The reason for that is our word *happiness* comes from the word *hap*, which implies luck or chance. When the New Testament tells of blessings, it is describing something more than "happiness"; it is a blessing bestowed by the heavenly Father. It does not depend on "happenings," but on a relationship with God that sustains us regardless of what "happens."

B. LESSON BACKGROUND

In September, our lessons dealt with some of Jesus' miracles. In October, they called attention to some of his parables. Now, during November, each lesson will be taken from a portion of what we call Jesus' Sermon on the Mount. This Sermon, extending from Matthew 5:1 to 7:29, is the first (and longest) of five major discourses in the book of Matthew.

In his record of Jesus' life, Matthew does not always arrange events in chronological order. It is difficult, then, to determine exactly when Jesus gave the Sermon on the Mount. Many Bible students estimate that it was delivered during the first half of the second year of Jesus' ministry, and probably soon after he chose twelve men out of a larger group of disciples (Luke 6:12-16). He called these men *apostles*, which means "those who are sent." Jesus wanted these men to be "with him" to learn from him; then he planned to "send them out to preach" (Mark 3:14). The Sermon on the Mount was a part of the teaching they received, though it was given also to the larger group of disciples and to multitudes of other listeners.

I. OUTDOOR SETTING (MATTHEW 5:1, 2)

Jesus often chose wide-open spaces in which to teach because the crowds that gathered around him were too big to be contained in the narrow streets of a town (Mark 1:45).

DEVOTIONAL READING:
PSALM 24

BACKGROUND SCRIPTURE:
MATTHEW 5:1-16

PRINTED TEXT:
MATTHEW 5:1-16

LESSON AIMS

After participating in this lesson, each student will be able to:

1. Tell what the primary theme of the Beatitudes is and how Jesus described the impact Christians should have in the world.

2. Tell how practicing the Beatitudes can make Christians "salt" and "light" in their community.

3. Choose one of the Beatitudes and seek to apply its message to his or her responsibility as salt and light.

Nov
4

KEY VERSE

Let your light shine before men, that they may see your good deeds and praise your Father in heaven.   —Matthew 5:16

A. PEOPLE AND PLACE (v. 1a)

1a. Now when he saw the crowds, he went up on a mountainside.

Jesus *went up on a mountainside* to find a place to teach. In today's English we would call where he went a *hill* rather than a *mountain*, for the area around the Sea of Galilee is full of hills. Probably Jesus chose a hillside that provided a natural amphitheater where the *crowds* could both see and hear him as he taught.

B. TEACHER AND STUDENTS (vv. 1b, 2)

1b. . . . and sat down. His disciples came to him.

It was customary for a teacher to be seated as he taught. Here, Jesus *sat down*, probably on the ground or on a rock. *His disciples*, as soon as they saw the spot he had chosen, took their places in front of him, getting as close as they could.

The word *disciples* suggests learners. Sometimes in the Gospels it is used of the twelve apostles; sometimes it is used of the larger group of learners. No doubt the Twelve and the larger group were both present on this occasion.

2. . . . and he began to teach them, saying:

Usually I attend Sunday school with a class of about fifty members. A public-address system allows everyone to hear the teacher. Day after day Jesus taught uncounted thousands of people in the open air. What a magnificent voice he must have had! And his message was even more magnificent than his voice!

II. THE BEATITUDES (MATTHEW 5:3-12)

The New Testament was originally written in Greek, and we read it in English. But for a long time Rome was considered the center of Christianity, so Latin, the language of Rome, was used by Christian scholars all over Europe. Each verse of our text that begins with the word *blessed* was viewed as describing a source of blessedness or happiness. The Latin word for that is *beatitudo*. This has come over into English as *beatitude*, and so these statements of Jesus beginning with the word *blessed* are called the Beatitudes.

A. THE POOR IN SPIRIT (v. 3)

3. "Blessed are the poor in spirit,
  for theirs is the kingdom of heaven.

One who is *poor in spirit* feels that spiritual poverty deep within, and knows that it is a need that cannot be met by personal effort. *The kingdom of heaven* belongs to these poor in spirit, because their very spiritual poverty makes them aware of their need to receive it. They are willing, even eager, to be ruled by Jesus the King. They exert themselves in doing his will, and they find joy in doing it.

B. THE MOURNERS (v. 4)

4. "Blessed are those who mourn,
  for they will be comforted.

The tax collector in one of Jesus' parables (which we studied two weeks ago) offers a perfect example of what this Beatitude means. He mourned over his sins; beating his breast (Luke 18:13) was the traditional expression of deep sorrow. He went home "justified," or forgiven (Luke 18:14). What blessed comfort!

C. THE MEEK (v. 5)

5. "Blessed are the meek,
  for they will inherit the earth.

Who are the *meek*? Words similar in meaning are "mild," "gentle," and "patient." Meek people prefer to avoid conflict, but that does not mean that they are

WHAT DO YOU THINK?

Jesus' commendation of "the poor in spirit" seems out of step with much popular thinking today. "Be assertive!" "Win through intimidation!" "Don't let anything stand in your way!" Even Christians can get caught up in this kind of thinking. How can we encourage people to be poor in spirit and not "run after" the necessities of life (Matthew 6:32)?

weak or cowardly. Students of Greek tell us that the Greek word for *meek* was used of a horse that was trained to pull a plow or carry a rider. A meek horse does not waste his strength in conflict, as a wild horse does when he is captured. His strength is channeled toward the accomplishment of a useful purpose. Likewise, a meek person uses his or her energy in God-pleasing tasks rather than in combat.

In what way will the meek *inherit the earth*? Perhaps we should think of it as more than just the enjoyment of material wealth. There is also the sense of fulfillment and contentment that comes when one uses the earth's resources as the Creator intended them to be used. This is a blessing that those who use the earth's resources selfishly can never call their own. And when this old earth is replaced by a new one, the meek will enjoy that one even more (2 Peter 3:10-13).

D. The Hungry (v. 6)

6. *"Blessed are those who hunger and thirst for righteousness,*
   for they will be filled.

A greater blessing than *hunger* for food is hunger *for righteousness*. Hunger for food compels us to get some food; hunger for righteousness compels us to get some righteousness.

There are two ways to obtain righteousness. One is by simply doing right. We can try to keep that up every day, but it is not enough. So God has provided a second way to obtain righteousness—a way by which our righteousness can be made complete. Speaking of this better way, Paul wrote that he desired to "be found in him, not having a righteousness of my own that comes from the law, but that which is through faith in Christ—the righteousness that comes from God and is by faith" (Philippians 3:9). So by God's gracious forgiveness, we can be *filled* with the righteousness of Christ. But that will not take place unless we are hungry and thirsty—unless we really want to be righteous.

E. The Merciful (v. 7)

7. *"Blessed are the merciful,*
   for they will be shown mercy.

Merciful people are grieved by the grief or pain of others, and they do what they can to end it. Often, when those who have been merciful are in trouble, they will *be shown mercy* from others who are aware of their kindness. Best of all, God will bless them and show mercy to them.

F. The Pure in Heart (v. 8)

8. *"Blessed are the pure in heart,*
   for they will see God.

Pure gold is solid gold all the way through; it is not mixed with anything cheaper. The pure *in heart* have hearts of solid good: their tastes, their thoughts, their desires, their motives are good. They do not value or desire anything evil.

G. The Peacemakers (v. 9)

9. *"Blessed are the peacemakers,*
   for they will be called sons of God.

God is the greatest peacemaker of all. Our sins made us his enemies (Colossians 1:21); but instead of destroying us, he loved us and sent his only begotten Son to die in our place (Romans 5:8). When we believe in Jesus and obey him, our sins are forgiven and we have peace with God (Romans 5:1). We then find a blessing in making and keeping peace with our Christian brothers and sisters and, if possible, with everyone (Romans 12:18).

WHAT DO YOU THINK?

How would you describe the characteristics and mannerisms of one who has a "hunger and thirst for righteousness"?

WHAT DO YOU THINK?

How can we be "pure in heart" while living in a society where there is much impurity? Consider such texts as Job 31:1 and Psalm 101:3 in your discussion.

H. The Persecuted (vv. 10-12)

10. "Blessed are those who are persecuted because of righteousness,
    for theirs is the kingdom of heaven.

Jesus' life was faultless, yet evildoers were constantly plotting to kill him (Matthew 26:3, 4; John 5:18; 7:1). He warned his disciples that they would be *persecuted*, too (John 15:20; 16:2).

11. "Blessed are you when people insult you, persecute you and falsely say all kinds of evil against you because of me.

Here the general promise of verse 10 is applied to the disciples whom Jesus was teaching (vv. 1, 2). Is it not applicable to us as well? Notice, however, that there is no promise of blessing unless the persecution comes for Jesus' sake. If we suffer because we have done wrong, or because we have not been poor in spirit (v. 3) or meek (v. 5) or merciful (v. 7), then we have no blessing (see 1 Peter 4:15). The *evil* spoken *against* us must be false, not accurate.

12. "Rejoice and be glad, because great is your reward in heaven, for in the same way they persecuted the prophets who were before you."

Persecuting God's people did not begin with Jesus and his disciples. God's *prophets* had been mistreated long before this. Examples include Elijah (1 Kings 19:2, 13, 14), Micaiah (1 Kings 22:26, 27), and Jeremiah (Jeremiah 37:15; 38:6).

The book of Acts tells how disciples of Jesus were beaten and imprisoned (Acts 5:17, 18, 40; 8:3), killed (Acts 7:59, 60), and driven out of Jerusalem (Acts 8:1). But they were not to wail or complain. Jesus said, *Rejoice and be glad, because great is your reward in heaven*. Acts tells of this happening as well (Acts 5:41).

"Say It Ain't So!"

Joe Jackson, who maintained a .400 batting average for the Chicago White Sox, was accused of throwing the 1919 World Series. According to baseball legend, when the charge against Jackson was made, a little boy who was a devoted fan said, "Say it ain't so, Joe."

But times have changed. Nowadays, when we hear of the antics (or even criminal activity) of professional athletes, we are supposed to look the other way if their athletic performance is noteworthy. When a "star" is suspended for illegal or questionable conduct, many fans respond, "So what? Look what a great player he is!"

Perhaps all of this would be irrelevant if sports stars were not held in such high regard by young people who see these athletes as enjoying the kind of life worth emulating. Success seems to be the only standard by which we are to measure success! But Jesus says, "Say it ain't so!" He calls us to a different standard. In the Beatitudes, he tells us that a life worth living—a happy life—is measured neither by selfish indulgence nor by disregard for how one's actions affect others, but by one's character, service to others, and the pursuit of godliness.   —C. R. B.

III. THE SALT (MATTHEW 5:13)

The rest of our text describes the impact Jesus' disciples are to have on the rest of the world.

A. Good Salt (v. 13a)

13a. "You are the salt of the earth.

As commonly used, *salt* has two purposes. First, it makes foods taste better. Almost any meat or vegetable dish is bland if the cook forgets to salt it. Only a little salt is needed, but it makes a big difference. Likewise Christians may be only a minority of the world's population, but they improve the flavor of the whole.

Salt is also used to preserve foods. (Such use was much more common before there were refrigerators and freezers in homes and stores.) Seeing how much evil

"Seeing the multitudes, he went up into a mountain . . . and he opened his mouth, and taught them." Matthew 5:1, 2

This hillside by the shore of the Sea of Galilee is believed to be the site where Jesus preached the Sermon on the Mount.

How to Say It

Beatitudes. Be-AT-ih-tudes.
beatitudo (Latin). be-AT-ih-TOO-doe.
Elijah. Ee-LYE-juh.
Jeremiah. Jair-uh-MY-uh.
Micaiah. My-KAY-uh.

there is in the world, do you ever wonder why God hasn't destroyed it before now? Perhaps this old world is being preserved by the *salt of the earth*. God is giving you and me and the other Christians time to win yet more people to Christ and to eternal life (2 Peter 3:9). This brings to mind yet another application of the salt metaphor that some have suggested: just as salt makes us thirsty, Christians are meant to have such an impact that they make others thirsty for Christ.

B. BAD SALT (v. 13b)

13b. *"But if the salt loses its saltiness, how can it be made salty again? It is no longer good for anything, except to be thrown out and trampled by men."*

In ancient Israel, *salt* was often gathered from the shores of the Dead Sea. During the dry, hot summer, the shallow water at the edge of the Dead Sea would evaporate rapidly, leaving its salt on the beach to be picked up. This was not pure salt, of course; it was mixed with other minerals that had been suspended in the water. Salt is easily dissolved; so if any rain fell while the salt lay on the beach with other minerals, much of the salt was washed back into the sea. Anyone who picked up what was left would have salt that had lost *its saltiness*. Such inferior salt could not improve the flavor of a piece of meat or keep it from spoiling.

What a disappointment for someone to discover that his salt had lost its saltiness! He would not have wanted to throw it on a field or a garden; that would make the soil less productive. Most likely he would dump it on an often trodden path, where nothing would grow anyway.

WHEN SALT KEEPS ITS SAVOR

Chris Lapel fled from Cambodia in 1979. While in a refugee camp, he became a Christian. Later he came to America and eventually graduated from Pacific Christian College. Today Lapel ministers to the Golden West Cambodian Christian Church in Los Angeles. And he regularly goes back to his homeland to tell his people of Christ.

Two small churches that Lapel started in a refugee camp have become more than a hundred churches with approximately eleven thousand members—"the closest thing [I've seen] to what is depicted in the Book of Acts," said an elder from an American church who visited the area.

During Lapel's trip back to Cambodia in 1993, he met Duch *(Dook)*, the director of a Communist prison where thousands were murdered between 1974 and 1979. Lapel told Duch about Christ and Duch became a Christian. Duch has admitted his responsibility for the deaths of those thousands of prisoners. He says he is willing to face justice and wants only to "serve God by doing God's work to help people." Duch now understands that work to include preaching the gospel to others of his people.

Both Lapel and Duch are living demonstrations of what happens when Christian salt *keeps* its saltiness: lives are changed through the influence of people who take the words of Jesus seriously. These two men are modern-day examples of the amazing power that characterized first-century Christianity and is meant to characterize it in every century.   —C. R. B.

IV. THE LIGHT (MATTHEW 5:14-16)

We cannot see the salt in our soup, but with the first spoonful we know it is there. It makes the soup taste much better. Jesus' people are like that: not flamboyant, not noisy, but quietly at work to make the world better.

Now we turn to another symbol of Jesus' people: light. Like salt, light works silently yet effectively. It comes quietly with the dawn, but its impact is far-reaching. Christians are like that too. They do not brag about their goodness, yet it cannot be hidden.

WHAT DO YOU THINK?

Most Christians feel the moral state of society is in decline. How valid is the preservative figure of the "salt of the earth" metaphor for today? What implications does it have for us?

DAILY BIBLE READINGS

Monday, Oct. 29—Called to Holy Living (1 Peter 1:10-16)

Tuesday, Oct. 30—What Truly Endures (1 Peter 1:18-25)

Wednesday, Oct. 31—A Spiritual House (1 Peter 2:1-8)

Thursday, Nov. 1—Called to Inherit a Blessing (1 Peter 3:8-15a)

Friday, Nov. 2—Suffer for God, Not for Evil (1 Peter 3:17-22)

Saturday, Nov. 3—Add to Your Faith (2 Peter 1:3-11)

Sunday, Nov. 4—"Blessed Are You When . . . " (Matthew 5:1-11)

A. THAT OTHERS MAY SEE (vv. 14, 15)

14. *"You are the light of the world. A city on a hill cannot be hidden.*

On another occasion Jesus said, "I am the *light of the world*" (John 8:12). Here he describes his disciples in the same way. Could we say that Jesus is like the sun? (See Psalm 84:11.) His light is his own: it shines from his own person. His people, then, are like the moon that reflects the light of the sun; in other words, Christians shine with the light of Jesus. Just as a *city* on a hilltop can be seen for miles and just as the moon can be seen all over the world, the light of a sincere Christian is seen by all who know him.

15. *"Neither do people light a lamp and put it under a bowl. Instead they put it on its stand, and it gives light to everyone in the house.*

The ordinary household light in New Testament times was provided by a small *lamp* fueled by olive oil. Yet, Jesus' words are true, whether we think of a candle, an oil-burning lamp, or an electric light bulb. The purpose of any light would be frustrated if we hid it *under a bowl.* We leave the lamp uncovered and place it where it will best fill the room with *light.*

B. THAT GOD MAY BE GLORIFIED (v. 16)

16. *"In the same way, let your light shine before men, that they may see your good deeds and praise your Father in heaven."*

This instruction seems plain and straightforward, but it calls for some serious thinking. Jesus was sharply critical of people who did good "for *men* to see" (Matthew 23:5). He advised his people to do good secretly (Matthew 6:1-4). Now we find him telling them to let others *see* their *good deeds.*

Perhaps the key to understanding this seeming contradiction is in the last phrase of our text: *praise your Father in heaven.* God's people ought to be doing good, of course, but doing it in such a way that grateful people will praise God more than they praise his people.

CONCLUSION

Millie was a fragile widow in her nineties. She had no family except her son Ben, who had tuberculosis. The doctor said that Ben needed to live in a desert climate; it would be better for someone in his condition. So Millie fixed a bed for him in their old car and drove west.

At the edge of the desert one Saturday morning, she spent the last of her money for groceries. On a desert road that evening she ran out of gas and steered the car off the road before it stopped rolling. She slept on a cot beside the car, and in the morning she walked a mile to the church in a little town.

Millie declined invitations to lunch, explaining where her son was and what had happened to them. People took her back to her car, and others followed quickly with a hot dinner, a folding table, and some chairs. "The Lord gave us more than we needed," they said. "We think he meant it for you."

Millie said, "Praise the Lord."

There was only one vacant house in town, and its roof leaked badly. Before sunset the men of the church covered it with a new roof while the women cleaned the inside, got the water and electricity turned on, and stocked the refrigerator. Someone took some gas to Millie's car and escorted her to her new house. "Nobody's using it," the owner explained. "I think God wants you to live here."

Millie said, "Praise the Lord."

Of course, Millie was grateful to the Lord's people; but she said, "Praise the Lord."

WHAT DO YOU THINK?

Contrast the behavior of those who do good deeds "for men to see" with those who follow Jesus' instruction to let their light shine "before men" so that they will praise God.

PRAYER

Thank you, Lord. Almost daily you give us opportunities to do good. May we have eyes to see each one, strength to make use of it, and wisdom to give you the glory. In Jesus' name, amen.

THOUGHT TO REMEMBER

Do good, and praise the Lord.

Discovery Learning

*This page contains an alternate lesson plan emphasizing learning activities. Classes
desiring such student involvement will find these suggestions helpful. The next page
is a reproducible activity page to further enhance discovery learning.*

LEARNING GOALS

After participating in this lesson, each student will be able to:

1. Tell what the primary theme of the Beatitudes is and how Jesus described the impact Christians should have in the world.

2. Tell how practicing the Beatitudes can make Christians "salt" and "light" in their community.

3. Choose one of the Beatitudes and seek to apply its message to his or her responsibility as salt and light.

INTO THE LESSON

Prior to class, prepare an overhead transparency from the upper half of the reproducible page that follows. Prepare a handout for the learners' use from the same activity. When it is time for class to begin, turn on the overhead projector to show this chart to the class. Direct learners' attention to the handout and state: "Today we want to contrast the worldly and the Christian perspectives of happiness. Starting with the worldly perspective, what does the world think makes people happy? Call out your ideas and I'll write them as you do." *(Ideas could include: money, possessions, power, position, prestige, sin, selfish indulgence.)* After writing down their answers, ask, "Now, what makes Christians happy?" *(Worship, singing, giving, sharing, helping others, serving others, Christ, salvation, hope.)* After ideas have been generated, say: "The worldly perspective is radically different from the Christian perspective. Let's open our Bibles to Matthew 5:1-16 and read what Jesus says makes us not only happy, but blessed."

INTO THE WORD

Ask a class member to read the lesson text to the class. Then ask the question, "What is the primary theme of these Beatitudes that Jesus gave?" *(Personal qualities that make people truly happy or blessed.)* Briefly go over the meaning of these eight Beatitudes as described in the lesson commentary. Prior to class, prepare a handout with the following questions. Move the class into groups of three and distribute a copy of the handout with these questions:

1. How did Jesus describe the impact Christians should have in this world? *(As salt and light.)*

2. Describe what Jesus meant when he said we are to be "salt" of the earth? *(Salt cleanses, purifies, protects, and enhances flavor. We are to do the same things for our world spiritually.)*

3. Describe what Jesus meant when he said we are the "light" of the world? *(Light attracts attention; shows the path to walk; dispels darkness. We are to do the same spiritually for those who are lost.)*

4. What is the relationship between practicing these Beatitudes and Jesus' teaching his disciples to be salt and light in this world? *(These "beatitude qualities" are so uncommon in this world that they become as noticeable as light in a dark room and salt on a bite of food.)*

5. What attitudes or behaviors hinder the cultivation of these Beatitudes in a person's life? *(Possible answers include: selfishness, pride, greed, and anger.)*

Give about ten minutes for the groups to work on these questions. Then go over the questions and their answers with the class. Say: "Jesus sets before us in this passage the obligation and the responsibility of being visible witnesses for him in this dark world. Not only does such behavior on our part bring happiness to us, it also brings glory and praise to God (v. 16). Let's apply these principles to our lives today."

INTO LIFE

Distribute copies of the reproducible activity "Applying the Beatitudes to Life" from the next page. Point out that the left column lists the eight Beatitudes: poor in Spirit, mourn, meek, hunger and thirst for righteousness, merciful, pure in heart, peacemakers, persecuted for righteousness sake. Tell the class to use the right column, "Specific Application," for writing life applications of each Beatitude. Ask, "What are specific ways Christians can apply these Beatitudes to their responsibility as 'light' and 'salt' in the world?" This time divide the class into four groups and assign each group to work on two of these Beatitudes. Allow ten minutes for the groups to generate ideas. Ask for each group to report its answers to the class.

Say: "We've now looked at some ways Christians can apply these Beatitudes to their responsibility of being salt and light. Now, however, I want you to select one Beatitude and one specific suggested application to apply in your life. Pair up with one other person in the room now; I'll give you a few minutes to share the Beatitude and application together. Then pray for each other to keep this commitment to God."

Contrasting Perspectives of Happiness

Contrast the Christian and worldly views of what makes people happy. Write your suggestions in the spaces provided.

WORLDLY PERSPECTIVES OF HAPPINESS   CHRISTIAN PERSPECTIVES OF HAPPINESS

Applying the Beatitudes to Life

How do you see the Beatitudes to be applicable to your daily life?

BEATITUDES OF JESUS	SPECIFIC APPLICATION TO MY LIFE
The Poor in Spirit	
Those Who Mourn	
The Meek	
Those Who Hunger and Thirst for Righteousness	
The Pure in Heart	
The Peacemakers	
Those Persecuted for Righteousness Sake	

Jesus' Ministry

Unit 3: The Sermon on the Mount
(Lessons 10-13)

JESUS FULFILLS THE LAW

LESSON 11

WHY TEACH THIS LESSON?

Perhaps you remember the line "Love means never having to say you're sorry" from Erich Segal's *Love Story,* the 1970 novel that spent forty-one weeks in the number-one position on the *New York Times* bestseller list. The enduring popularity of this line and this novel demonstrates the type of "sound bite moralizing" that many find so captivating today. But when placed alongside Jesus' profound teaching on love, the shallowness of this phrase becomes clear. And with eternity at stake, it is Jesus' teaching on love, not man's, that requires our attention.

When Jesus walked the earth, he lived a life characterized by love. It was love that compelled him to come to earth and to die for sins, thus fulfilling a requirement of God's law that sin must be punished. More is yet to be accomplished in God's eternal plan, both by God and by us. Today our text reminds us of Jesus' authority in matters regarding that plan as it relates to God's law. For our own part in that eternal plan, we also learn about something Jesus expects of us as we interact with a world that is frequently hostile to his message.

INTRODUCTION

In a class of Junior boys, the teacher laid his Bible on the table. With his right hand he held the pages of the New Testament between thumb and forefinger. With his left hand he held the Old Testament pages. Then he asked, "Which of these would you rather learn and live by?"

Unanimously the boys chose the New Testament. It was smaller, so they thought it would be easier to learn and live by. The Old Testament looked three times as thick.

A. THE NEW TESTAMENT HELPS US

There are better reasons to choose the New Testament, but there is no better choice. In the Old Testament, obedience to God and his law was linked to receiving eternal life (Leviticus 18:5; Romans 10:5). That way did not work, because no one has ever obeyed well enough (Romans 3:23). God then sent his sinless Son to suffer the death earned by sinners. Now sins can be forgiven and eternal life can be received as a gift (Romans 6:23). That offer is presented in the New Testament.

B. THE OLD TESTAMENT HELPS US

This does not mean that the Old Testament is no longer useful. All things recorded there, though they happened long ago, serve as "examples" for us and are recorded "as warnings for us" (1 Corinthians 10:6, 11). Bad examples warn us not to repeat ancient mistakes (1 Corinthians 10:6-13). Good examples encourage us to follow them (Hebrews 11:4–12:2).

Last week we considered the first part of Jesus' Sermon on the Mount. This week we turn to the next part of it. In this section Jesus speaks of the Old Testament. He encourages us to have a high regard for it.

DEVOTIONAL READING:
AMOS 5:4-15

BACKGROUND SCRIPTURE:
MATTHEW 5:17-48

PRINTED TEXT:
MATTHEW 5:17-20, 38-48

LESSON AIMS

After this lesson a student should be able to:

1. Tell how Jesus fulfilled the law with love and taught his disciples to do the same.

2. Compare some wrong contemporary ideas about human relationships with those of which Jesus said the people had "heard it said," but that he replaced.

3. List the names of two or three people whom he or she can love this week with **agape**, as Jesus commands us to do.

Nov
11

KEY VERSE

Do not think that I have come to abolish the Law or the Prophets; I have not come to abolish them but to fulfill them.
—Matthew 5:17

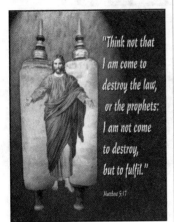

This poster illustrates the truth that Jesus is the fulfillment of the Old Testament Scriptures.

WHAT DO YOU THINK?

Like Jesus, we should aim to fulfill the demands of the law through love. What are some practical ways we can do that?

C. LESSON BACKGROUND

Jesus had been teaching in Judea and Galilee for more than a year. Most likely many of the religious leaders in Jerusalem considered him a lawless rebel, because he had driven from the temple those who were selling oxen, sheep, and doves to be used for sacrifices in the temple (John 2:13-21). In Galilee some Pharisees had accused Jesus and his disciples of violating the law of the Sabbath (Mark 2:23–3:6). Perhaps the accusation that Jesus was out to destroy the law of Moses was becoming more widespread.

In the Sermon on the Mount, Jesus contrasted some of his teachings with the Old Testament (Matthew 5:21-48). He prefixed those contrasts with a declaration of his respect for the Old Testament.

I. JESUS AND THE LAW (MATTHEW 5:17-20)

A. FULFILLING THE LAW (vv. 17, 18)

17. "Do not think that I have come to abolish the Law or the Prophets; I have not come to abolish them but to fulfill them.

Jesus did not intend to *abolish*, destroy, or disobey anything in God's Word. He and his disciples had not broken God's *law* regarding the Sabbath, as the Pharisees had charged (Mark 2:23, 24); they had ignored some mistaken interpretations of it.

Jesus' teaching in Matthew 5:21-48 does not contradict or condemn the law; it fulfills it—or fills it full. Consider four ways Jesus fulfilled *the Law and the Prophets.*

1. He fulfilled the Old Testament by calling attention to its true meaning and to the need to keep its laws inwardly as well as in action (Matthew 5:21-48).

2. He fulfilled the laws by obeying them fully, applying them as God intended. Driving the sellers and the moneychangers out of the temple is one example.

3. He fulfilled Old Testament prophecies by doing what they foretold. (Compare Isaiah 53:4 with Matthew 8:16, 17; Psalm 78:2 with Matthew 13:34, 35; and Zechariah 9:9 with Matthew 21:4, 5. Many other examples could also be cited.)

4. The most significant way Jesus fulfilled the law was to complete its purpose. The law told what was right and what was wrong before God. It let people know that they were sinners, not good enough to receive eternal life (Romans 3:19, 20). It was "put in charge to lead us to Christ" (Galatians 3:24) by whom our sins are forgiven. When we come to Christ and are forgiven, the law is fulfilled. Its purpose is accomplished, and we are no longer under its tutelage (Galatians 3:25).

Consider one example of how to apply this principle. The law required a sinner to sacrifice an animal to atone for his sin. But the sacrifice of an animal is not enough to take away the sins of anyone. Such sacrifices were offered repeatedly until Jesus' death on the cross, through which sins really are taken away. Thus the law is fulfilled, and animal sacrifices are no longer necessary (Hebrews 10:1-18).

18. "I tell you the truth, until heaven and earth disappear, not the smallest letter, not the least stroke of a pen, will by any means disappear from the Law until everything is accomplished.

Jesus said that not even the tiniest part of the law—*not the smallest letter, not the least stroke of a pen*—would be removed until it was *accomplished.* This happened when Jesus declared on the cross, "It is finished" (John 19:30).

B. KEEPING THE LAW (vv. 19, 20)

19. "Anyone who breaks one of the least of these commandments and teaches others to do the same will be called least in the kingdom of heaven, but whoever practices and teaches these commands will be called great in the kingdom of heaven.

When Jesus said this, he had not yet died to fulfill the Old Testament law; so it was still in effect. All of God's people needed to obey it. To break even the *least*

significant of God's *commandments* and to teach *others* to treat his law that way was unacceptable for anyone who would claim interest in *the kingdom of heaven.*
20. For I tell you that unless your righteousness surpasses that of the Pharisees and the teachers of the law, you will certainly not enter the kingdom of heaven."

The *Pharisees and the teachers of the law* claimed to be the most obedient of God's people, but they were not. They made a show of obeying in ways that could be seen and admired, but they neglected to obey in more important ways (Matthew 23:23).

In the remainder of Matthew 5, Jesus contrasts the Old Testament law as understood and applied by the religious leaders of his day with his own teaching on a variety of subjects. In every instance, Jesus taught that sin and righteousness are found in one's thoughts and motives as well as in one's actions. To recognize this is to follow after the kind of righteousness that will surpass that of the Pharisees and teachers of the law.

II. JESUS AND HUMAN RELATIONS (MATTHEW 5:38-42)

One way to fulfill the law was to call attention to the need to keep God's laws inwardly as well as by one's actions. Jesus knew that if people's thoughts and motives were what they ought to be, proper actions would follow. The next part of our text focuses on a portion of Jesus' teaching that deals with person-to-person relations.

A. NONRESISTANCE (vv. 38, 39)
38. "You have heard that it was said, 'Eye for eye, and tooth for tooth.'

The *eye for eye, and tooth for tooth* prescription is clearly stated in the law (Exodus 21:23-25; Leviticus 24:19, 20). It establishes the principle of justice in the punishment of evildoers. It also served to limit acts of vengeance and thus to prevent bitter feuds from escalating into something worse. Without this law, a person who lost an eye might go so far as to seek the offender's life.
39. "But I tell you, Do not resist an evil person. If someone strikes you on the right cheek, turn to him the other also.

A slap on the cheek in Jesus' day was done to insult someone more than to injure him. Some have compared it with spitting in someone's face. In such an instance, Jesus taught that the offended person should act in humility rather than seek justice or retaliation. He should even be willing to *turn . . . the other* cheek and accept an additional insult!

B. GENEROSITY (vv. 40-42)
40. "And if someone wants to sue you and take your tunic, let him have your cloak as well.

The quickest way to settle a lawsuit is simply give the plaintiff more than he asks, but do it cheerfully, not resentfully or grudgingly. Such generosity is costly, of course—costly to the one who gives up both his *tunic* (the shirt-like "inner garment" that a person usually wore) and his *cloak* (the heavier "outer garment"). That may be a part of the point Jesus was making. The generous giver gains peace, approval, and goodwill. Aren't these worth the price being paid here?

Jesus' instruction here does not mean that Christians are to be "doormats," allowing people to take advantage of them. It means that Christians are to be concerned about more than just their "rights." Such an attitude will set them apart from those who are continually demanding their rights and are quick to sue anyone who stands in their way. Jesus wants his people to be more concerned about relations with others than with personal rights.
41. "If someone forces you to go one mile, go with him two miles.

WHAT DO YOU THINK?

Even for a committed Christian the challenge of "turning the other cheek" is a difficult one. What are some biblical helps we can use in meeting this challenge?

Refer to Proverbs 15:1; 16:32; Romans 12:17-21 to aid in the discussion.

In Jesus' day Israel was annexed to the Roman Empire. The Romans kept an occupation army there to keep the peace and prevent uprisings. Jews resented these foreigners' presence, especially because each Roman soldier on duty was authorized to draft a civilian to carry his pack for a *mile*. (This was the Roman *mile*—about a kilometer and a half, or nine-tenths of a mile as we measure it today.) Imagine the angry grumbling that the soldier heard throughout that mile!

But what if a draftee would take up the pack with a cheerful smile? What if the mile was filled with friendly conversation instead of grumbling? What if the draftee then volunteered to go another happy mile? Enmity would be swallowed up by goodwill. From this teaching of Jesus comes the familiar phrase, "going the second mile." A follower of Jesus should go above and beyond "duty" to render service.

42. "Give to the one who asks you, and do not turn away from the one who wants to borrow from you."

This verse may get our attention more quickly than those before it because those who ask us for help are probably more than those who hit us in the face, file lawsuits against us, or compel us to go a mile. Since the news media keep us constantly aware of millions in desperate need, it is literally impossible for us to *give* meaningful help to all of them. We can recognize at least two limitations.

First, Jesus does not want us to neglect our own families in order to help needy people (1 Timothy 5:8). Second, Jesus does not want us to give to literally everyone who asks. Years ago a friend who works downtown told me of a day when he left the office and went out for a late lunch. On the street a poorly dressed man asked him for "some money to get a bit of lunch." My friend was on his way to lunch and invited the man to come along as his guest. But rather than accept the gracious offer, the man turned away, snarling a curse. It was easy to guess that he wanted money, not for lunch, but only for cigarettes or booze or some illegal drug. Should a follower of Jesus give to him just because he asked?

Paul encouraged Christians to be among the most generous of people (Galatians 6:10). But he also instructed that if an able-bodied person would not work, then neither should he eat (2 Thessalonians 3:10).

THE "OTHER CHEEK" APPROACH

Some folks don't think much of Jesus' "other cheek" approach to interpersonal problems. Consider Sam Horrell, self-appointed "governor, mayor, sheriff, postmaster, clerk, and banker" of Sammyville (unincorporated, population about forty), located in the northeastern corner of the state of Oregon. "No trespassing" signs abound around Sammyville, and some have the added message that "trespassers will be shot." Sam owns one hundred and fifty registered firearms and has a concealed weapon permit. No one knows how many other guns exist in Sammyville.

Sam is a devout churchgoer, but he seems to follow Teddy Roosevelt's dictum, "Speak softly and carry a big stick," more than Jesus' plea to "turn the other cheek." He is reputed to be a kind and generous man, but he has also been known to pull his guns—triggers cocked—on anyone who threatens him.

Living out Jesus' teaching on how to respond to evil has always been difficult, but that's no reason for us not to make the attempt. Jesus applies the principle to dealing with insults, fending off lawsuits, and responding to a simple request for help. In each case, Jesus says, "Take the initiative and be proactive in doing good, even to those who might do otherwise to you."

—C. R. B.

III. JESUS AND LOVE (MATTHEW 5:43-48)

It is fitting that some teaching about love follows the teaching about generosity, for love is the motive of our generous help; and lack of love limits our willingness to be of help.

WHAT DO YOU THINK?

Jesus said, "Give to the one who asks you." Yet Jesus himself once declined to help a man who expressed a concern with material things (Luke 12:13-21). When is it better not to give to someone? What should we do instead?

A. WELL-KNOWN SAYING (v. 43)

43. "You have heard that it was said, 'Love your neighbor and hate your enemy.'

Love your neighbor was written plainly in the law (Leviticus 19:18). In contrast, hate your enemy was not in the law at all. However, at times Israel was commanded to exterminate certain enemies (Deuteronomy 7:1, 2; 20:16, 17; 1 Samuel 15:3). It is not surprising that later teachers added "hate your enemy" to the popular teaching that was heard in the synagogues.

B. BETTER SAYING (v. 44)

44. "But I tell you: Love your enemies and pray for those who persecute you.

Love your enemies. That must have surprised all who heard it! Not only did it seem contrary to popular teaching; it seemed contrary to human nature. But Jesus intended to change human nature. His way answers cursing with caring, hatred with helpfulness, persecution with prayer.

C. FOLLOW YOUR FATHER (vv. 45-48)

45. " . . . that you may be sons of your Father in heaven. He causes his sun to rise on the evil and the good, and sends rain on the righteous and the unrighteous.

Don't say you can't love your enemies or do good to those who hate you. Your Father in heaven provides for people who are evil and unrighteous with the same sun and rain that he gives to his sons. Children are expected to be like their Father—to love all those he loves, to do good to all those who enjoy his goodness.

46. "If you love those who love you, what reward will you get? Are not even the tax collectors doing that?

Of course you love your family and friends—the people who love you. So what? Those tax collectors, those people the ancient Jew thought to be among the very worst—also love their families and friends who love them. Are you content to be like the worst of people, or do you want to be like your Father in Heaven?

47. "And if you greet only your brothers, what are you doing more than others? Do not even pagans do that?

Of course you greet . . . your brothers affectionately, but that does not mark you as a Christian. If you are a child of God, you ought to be helping a wider circle of people, for your Father in Heaven is "kind to the ungrateful and wicked" (Luke 6:35).

48. "Be perfect, therefore, as your heavenly Father is perfect."

Too readily we excuse our imperfections by saying, "nobody's perfect" or "I'm only human." Yet in some ways and within human limits, we can and ought to be perfect, as perfect as God himself.

The Greek New Testament has several words that are translated into English as perfect. The word that is used here also means "complete" or "mature." In what ways can we be as complete as our heavenly Father? We can in no way match his omnipotent power, obviously, or his unlimited knowledge and wisdom. But this text is talking about loving our enemies (v. 44). We can and ought to love all those whom God loves, and we ought to do good to them as we have opportunity (Galatians 6:10). Instead of trying to excuse our imperfections, let's try to improve our loving and helping.

LOST IN TRANSLATION

Excitement mounted among personnel at the National Aeronautics and Space Administration (NASA) as the Mars Climate Orbiter approached the "red planet" in the fall of 1999. The excitement turned to dejection, however, when the orbiter flew too close to Mars and was destroyed.

WHAT DO YOU THINK?

Jesus said "pray for those who persecute you." How is that a very practical way of loving our enemies?

WHAT DO YOU THINK?

Some people believe that if they love and take care of their families, such love should put them in good standing with God. What did Jesus say about that viewpoint?

HOW TO SAY IT

Agape (Greek). Uh-GAH-pay.
Eros (Greek). AIR-oss.
Galilee. GAL-uh-lee.
Judea. Joo-DEE-uh.
Pharisees. FAIR-ih-seez.
Phileo (Greek). Fih-LEH-oh.
Storge (Greek). STORE-gay.

PRAYER

Father, we thank you that Jesus has fulfilled the law, and that we are under grace. By your grace and our effort may our love become complete so that we might do our own part in fulfilling the law. In our Master's name, amen.

THOUGHT TO REMEMBER

"Love is the fulfillment of the law" (Romans 13:10).

As the data were analyzed to discover what had gone wrong, the answer was found to be embarrassingly simple: the navigation team at Jet Propulsion Laboratories had used the metric system of millimeters and meters in its calculations, while the builders at Lockheed-Martin Astronautics had provided their data in the English system of feet and inches! Years of work by hundreds of people and an expenditure of 125 million dollars were lost because the data were "lost in translation" from one form of measurement to another—and no one caught the error.

Far too often, Jesus' instructions about loving our enemies have been "lost in translation" from the pages of Scripture to the pages of our lives. This isn't a matter of spoken or written languages; it's the difference between the language of godliness and the language of this world.
      —C. R. B.

CONCLUSION

We English-speaking people are terribly unkind to that small word *love*. We load it with so many meanings that we hardly know what it means when we hear it.

The ancient Greeks were kinder. They took the many meanings we have attached to love and distributed them among at least four words, each of which can describe a specific kind of love (although context will ultimately determine the meaning).

A. KINDS OF LOVE

Eros refers to sexual love. That kind is proper between husband and wife, and in no other setting. In its place it ought to be strong and lasting, but it has no place in this lesson. In fact, *eros* is not found in the New Testament.

Storge is family love, especially the love of parents for children and children for parents. That word appears in the New Testament with a negative prefix and is translated "heartless" and "without love" (Romans 1:31; 2 Timothy 3:3).

Phileo is friendly love. The noun form is translated *friend* in James 4:4, but the verb form of the same word appears many times and is translated *love*.

Agape is the kind of love mentioned most often in the New Testament. Its noun form appears more than a hundred times and is translated *love* or *charity*. God loves the whole world with *agape* (John 3:16), and this is the kind of love we are commanded to have for our enemies (Matthew 5:44).

B. WHAT IS AGAPE?

Someone has defined *agape* as active, intelligent goodwill without regard for a response. It is active: it does good to the loved one (Matthew 5:44). It is intelligent: thoughtfully, it does nothing but good, and it gives the loved one what he needs rather than what he wants. It is goodwill: earnestly it desires what is best for the loved one. And it is selfless, loving not because it is loved, but whether or not it is loved in return.

Some claim that love cannot be commanded or chosen—that it is an emotion that arises unbidden, sometimes even against our will. That may be true of *eros* or *storge*, or even to some extent of *phileo*, but it certainly is not true of *agape*. Deliberately, thoughtfully, by an act of our own mind and will, we choose to love our enemies and do good to them as Jesus commands (Matthew 5:44). Thus do we demonstrate that we are children of our Father in Heaven.

"Jesus Fulfills the Law." So says the title of this lesson. As Jesus' people, we are "not under the law" (Romans 6:14) as those who lived in Old Testament times were. As Jesus' people we rejoice that he has fulfilled the law; we also fulfill the law, in a different way, by living under the control of *agape* (Romans 13:8-10).

Discovery Learning

This page contains an alternate lesson plan emphasizing learning activities. Classes desiring such student involvement will find these suggestions helpful. The next page is a reproducible activity page to further enhance discovery learning.

LEARNING GOALS

After this lesson each student will be able to:

1. Tell how Jesus fulfilled the law with love and taught his disciples to do the same.

2. Compare some wrong contemporary ideas about human relationships with those of which Jesus said the people had "heard it said," but that he replaced.

3. List two or three people whom he or she can love this week with *agape*, as Jesus commands us to do.

INTO THE LESSON

Distribute copies of the first activity on the reproducible page that follows. Give these instructions: "Pretend that you are sitting at your computer. You have just connected to the Internet. Using a search engine to locate specific articles, you type in the phrase, 'responding to God's laws.' Within a few seconds you have a number of 'hits.' Each 'hit' has a two-word title that ends with the word 'it.' Each title describes one way that people can respond to God's laws. The first one is 'Obey it.' As you skim the list, what other titles do you see? Write them down on your handout." Allow just a few minutes; then ask for volunteers to tell what they wrote.

Titles may include "disobey it, deny it, reject it, ignore it, rebuke it, follow it, forget it, avoid it, overlook it." Summarize the suggested "article titles" and state: "People respond to God's laws in a variety of ways. In our lesson text today, Jesus gives another response to God's law: 'fulfill it.' Let's read Matthew 5:17-20, 38-48 and see how Jesus fulfills the Law."

INTO THE WORD

Ask two class members to read Matthew 5:17-20, 38-48. Say: "With someone next to you, discuss the answer to this question: What did Jesus mean when he used the term 'fulfill' in verse 17?" (*Possible answers: He fulfilled the law by perfectly obeying it to become the perfect sacrificial lamb without blemish; he fulfilled the prophets by doing what the prophecies foretold [see Isaiah 53:4 and Matthew 8:16, 17 as examples]; he fulfilled by adding a person's thoughts and motives to the concept of obedience to the law, Matthew 5:21-37.*) Make certain the class understands these answers. Then ask the following questions:

1. What did Jesus say would not "disappear from the Law until everything is accomplished? (*the smallest letter or the least stroke of a pen, v. 18.*)

2. What did Jesus say determines whether a person is great or least in the kingdom of heaven? (*The response to God's law and teaching others to do the same, v. 19.*)

3. What kind of righteousness did Jesus say was needed to enter the kingdom of Heaven? (*Righteousness that exceeded the righteousness of the Pharisees and teachers of the law.*)

4. Describe the righteousness of the Pharisees and teachers of the law. (*Diligent but hypocritical followers of the law; very legalistic; concerned about appearing righteous, Matthew 6:5, 16.*)

5. How could a person's righteousness exceed that of the scribes and Pharisees? (*Obedience from the heart; a recognition that salvation is undeserved and is by grace through faith.*)

6. In your own words, what is the principle of the law in verse 38? (*Pay back evil for evil; retribution.*)

INTO LIFE

Note that in verses 38-44 Jesus presents teaching that goes beyond the law in the way that we respond no matter how people treat us. Then discuss these questions:

1. What is the principle underlying Jesus' teaching in vv. 39-42 on how we should respond? (*Non-retaliation; generosity.*)

2. What unnatural principle does Jesus encourage us to follow when we respond to those who curse us, hate us, or persecute us? (*Love, v. 44.*)

3. What does Jesus say we become when we respond to the way he instructs? (*Children of our Father.*)

4. Describe how God the Father models these principles. (*The Father treats the evil and the good, the just and the unjust, the same, v. 45.*)

State: "Loving, non-retaliatory behavior is what Jesus expects from his servants: We bless those who curse us, we do good to those who hate us, and we pray for those who persecute us. Such a response is totally unexpected and goes counter to our culture. Yet, it truly reflects our heavenly Father." Distribute copies of the reproducible activity, "But I Say . . . Love Them!" from the next page. Say: "Think of some people who need you to respond to them in loving non-retaliation. They may curse you, hate you, or persecute you. Write down the names of two or three. Beside each name write the specific action you will do this week to show that you love the person and that you are a child of your Father."

Responding to God's Law

When people encounter God's law, they respond in a number of different ways. On the lines below, write specific ways that people respond to God's law. Each answer should be only one word, and the word "it" refers to God's law. An example is suggested.

When people encounter God's law, they . . .

_____Obey_____ it.   _____ it.

_____ it.   _____ it.

_____ it.   _____ it.

"But I Say . . .

Love Them!"

Jesus wants us to respond to people with love, regardless of how they treat us. Think of those with whom you have difficulty getting along. Have you always responded to them in love? Or have you reacted as inappropriately as they have acted toward you? Write their names; then write a loving response that you should make toward them. Commit yourself to being the loving, generous, non-retaliating person Jesus desires.

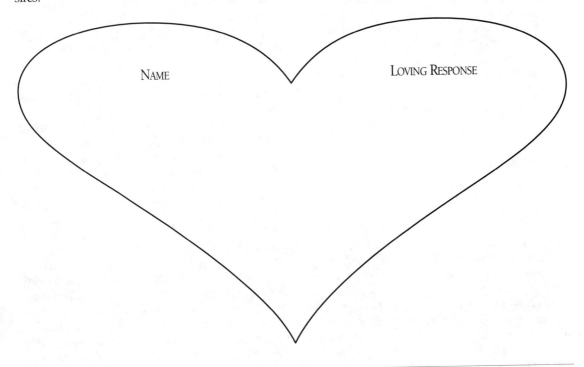

NAME   LOVING RESPONSE

STORING TREASURES IN HEAVEN

LESSON 12

WHY TEACH THIS LESSON?

Are you living in a "transition home"? It's not the house you really want to live in for the rest of your life, it's just what you're settling for right now until you are finally able to afford what you *really* want.

We see this attitude all around us today, not only as it concerns the homes we live in, but also with regard to the cars we drive, the furnishings we surround ourselves with, and the vacations we take. Those who "don't have" want to "have," while those who "have" want to "have more." Rich Mullins's song "My One Thing" describes the condition well: "Everybody I know says they need just one thing. And what they really mean is they need just one thing more." If you are living in a transition home or driving a transition car—if you "need just one thing more"—Jesus has something important to say to you today!

INTRODUCTION

One of the most memorable events of my childhood was our rural community's bank failure. In the language of the townspeople, the bank "went broke." Most of the farmers had recently deposited their returns from the wheat and barley harvests, and now they couldn't get a cent of their money. They had to survive the rest of the summer on the produce of their own farms. They all had chickens for eggs and cows for milk, and most had some fruits and vegetables as well.

Ultimately the farmers were able to get back most of what they had deposited in the bank. Until then there was considerable discussion of what to do with one's money if and when it became available. Put it in the other bank? That one might go broke, too. Keep it at home? You couldn't sit there all day with a shotgun to guard it. Some of the farmers devised hiding places under floors or in walls where thieves would never find their savings. But what if the house burned down?

A. MANY MONEY PROBLEMS

Money problems have been around as long as money has. If you have no money, your problem is how to get some. If you have more than you can use immediately, your problem is how to keep it safe. A servant in one of Jesus' parables buried his money in the ground, but his master called him a "wicked, lazy servant" (Matthew 25:25, 26). Other servants put their money to work and managed to double it. That was great, but the prospect of such a return must have involved a certain amount of risk. Today's investment counselors all warn us that there is no investment without risk, and that a big return requires a big risk.

This week's lesson brings us an exception to that rule. Just invest your treasures in Heaven. There is no risk involved, and the return is far greater than you can ever imagine.

DEVOTIONAL READING:
PHILIPPIANS 4:4-9
BACKGROUND SCRIPTURE:
MATTHEW 6
PRINTED TEXT:
MATTHEW 6:19-34

LESSON AIMS

After this lesson students should be able to:

1. Tell what Jesus said in this portion of the Sermon on the Mount about our treasures and our priorities.

2. Contrast Jesus' teaching about these matters with the world's perspective on material wealth.

3. Pinpoint an area of their lives where trust in God needs to replace worry, and commit that area to him.

KEY VERSE

Seek first his kingdom and his righteousness, and all these things will be given to you as well. Therefore do not worry about tomorrow.

—Matthew 6:33, 34

Nov
18

LESSON 12 NOTES

B. LESSON BACKGROUND

Today's study is the third of our lessons from Jesus' Sermon on the Mount. Jesus was teaching on a hill in Galilee, and a large crowd was listening (Matthew 5:1, 2).

I. CHOOSE THE BEST (MATTHEW 6:19-24)

Jesus' disciples must have been aware of the financial risk involved in choosing to follow him. Some of them left their jobs to become disciples of One who had no place to lay his head (Matthew 8:20). We are told of certain individuals who "were helping to support them out of their own means," apparently meaning that they provided material assistance to Jesus and the Twelve (Luke 8:1-3).

In the portion of the Sermon on the Mount we are studying today, Jesus confirms that those who have chosen to follow him have made the best choice.

A. THE BEST TREASURE (vv. 19-21)

19. *"Do not store up for yourselves treasures on earth, where moth and rust destroy, and where thieves break in and steal.*

Jesus' words are not a prohibition against efforts to provide the necessities of life for oneself or family. Such work is commended in Scripture (2 Thessalonians 3:12; 1 Timothy 5:8). Jesus is warning us not to consider material wealth (the things of this *earth*) our *treasures*. Material wealth is subject to decay and corrosion. And (like the farmers who were mentioned in the Introduction to this lesson) anyone with material wealth must guard against *thieves* who are more than eager for him to "share" his wealth. It was not very hard to *break in* through the walls of most houses in Jesus' day, which were made of mud bricks.

20. *"But store up for yourselves treasures in heaven, where moth and rust do not destroy, and where thieves do not break in and steal.*

It is hard to argue with the fact that *treasures in heaven* are eternally secure, but how can you *store up* your treasures there? One way is to help Jesus' brothers who are in need, thereby identifying with Jesus himself (Matthew 25:31-40). With that thought in mind, you can probably think of specific treasures that are suited to your particular circumstances.

For example, the money you send to a missionary who is holding forth the word of life on the other side of the world or is planting a new church on the other side of your hometown—don't you know it is credited to your account beyond the skies? The sacrificial gift you give to a college that is preparing preachers of the gospel—aren't you certain that it has been deposited in your heavenly treasure with interest beyond your imagining? And don't think that your treasure is all in money. Each precious hour you spend in unpaid Christian service will be waiting with interest when you "take your inheritance, the kingdom prepared for you since the creation of the world" (Matthew 25:34).

There are so many ways to lay up treasures in Heaven! So choose the way that is best for you and most suited to your abilities and opportunities. Just be sure that you don't leave all your treasures on earth and end up a pauper where heavenly treasures are concerned.

21. *"For where your treasure is, there your heart will be also.*

Often we notice that one's *treasure* follows his *heart*. For instance, if you visit an orphans' home and really fall in love with it, some of your money will go there. But Jesus reminds us of the other side of the picture. One's *heart* follows his *treasure*. If you really aren't interested at all in what your church's favorite missionary is doing, try doubling your contribution to that mission. Of course, you won't want your money to be wasted, so you will learn all you can about the work of the mission—and you will soon find that your heart is in that mission.

WHAT DO YOU THINK?

"Do not store up for yourselves treasures on earth," Jesus said. Some have taken this to mean that Christians should not have savings accounts or insurance policies. What do you think about that?

Perhaps you will then double your contribution again. Or, if you have not been very interested in the local work of your church, try putting twice as much time into it. You'll be surprised to see how dear to your heart that work becomes.

B. The Best Light (vv. 22, 23)

22. "The eye is the lamp of the body. If your eyes are good, your whole body will be full of light.

The eye is the lamp of the body. It is through our eyes that we become conscious of light, and with light comes a vast amount of information, understanding, and guidance. It is with our eyes that we find our way. Thus does Paul pray that "the eyes of your heart may be enlightened" (Ephesians 1:18) to express his desire that the Ephesian Christians grow in their knowledge of the Lord.

If your eyes (your attention and thinking) *are good* (focused only on treasure in Heaven and what produces it), then *your whole body will be full of light.* You will be thoroughly enlightened with truth and goodness. Your motives, your thinking, your talking, and your doing will be guided in ways pleasing to the Lord. You will be laying up treasure in Heaven.

23. "But if your eyes are bad, your whole body will be full of darkness. If then the light within you is darkness, how great is that darkness!

On the other hand, if your attention and thinking are focused on earthly treasure without any regard for what God says is right and wrong, then you shut out the light of truth and goodness. Instead you become filled with the *darkness* of selfishness and greed. The eye is the only way you have to receive light. If it brings you darkness instead, *how great is that darkness!*

C. The Best Master (v. 24)

24. "No one can serve two masters. Either he will hate the one and love the other, or he will be devoted to the one and despise the other. You cannot serve both God and Money.

It is true that a man can have two jobs with two different employers. But he cannot serve both employers with equal devotion. If both want his service at the same time, he has to make a choice. One job will be his principal job; the other will get whatever leftover time is available.

It is true that most of us who serve God work for money as well. But serving God is a full-time job. Even when we are working at the job that provides our living, God's directions are to guide every area of life. If the employer who pays us money wants us to do something contrary to God's teaching, we have to make a choice. It is better to serve God and starve than to serve *Money* and disobey God.

II. TRUST THE BEST (MATTHEW 6:25-30)

When we choose the best Master, God, we are relieved of the responsibility of making some other choices that might be difficult. When God tells us plainly to do something, we do it and trust him for the outcome. When he tells us not to do something, we refuse to do it, no matter how enticing the other master— "Money"—makes it seem. Either way, we trust God, and we don't worry.

A. Do Not Worry (v. 25)

25. "Therefore I tell you, do not worry about your life, what you will eat or drink; or about your body, what you will wear. Is not life more important than food, and the body more important than clothes?

The conclusion *therefore . . . do not worry* follows from the three choices we are called to make from verses 19-24. The point here is not to be overly concerned

What Do You Think?

Jesus said, "Where your treasure is, there your heart will be also." What are some means we can use to make sure our treasure and our heart are in Heaven? Specifically, what are you doing in this regard?

What Do You Think?

Few people would admit that money is their master, but it surely is in many cases. What are some tests we can apply to determine if money is our master?

about physical necessities; excessive fretting about such things would reveal that our treasure is in the wrong place, our eyes are focused on the wrong things, and that we serve the wrong master. "Do not worry," is not, of course, an excuse for laziness (2 Thessalonians 3:10).

B. CONSIDER THE BIRDS (v. 26)

26. *"Look at the birds of the air; they do not sow or reap or store away in barns, and yet your heavenly Father feeds them. Are you not much more valuable than they?*

Perhaps some *birds* could be seen near the hillside where Jesus and his audience were. These birds are not idle, but neither are they anxious about their daily food. They do the work they are created to do, and the *heavenly Father* provides for them. Any human being is *much more valuable than* many such birds. How can anyone doubt that God will feed him if he does the work the Creator designed him to do?

C. WORRY IS WORTHLESS (v. 27)

27. *"Who of you by worrying can add a single hour to his life?*

Worry can cause stress and ulcers. Rather than adding hours to *life,* worry can result in quite the opposite!

D. CONSIDER THE FLOWERS (vv. 28-30)

28. *"And why do you worry about clothes? See how the lilies of the field grow. They do not labor or spin."*

We might paraphrase Jesus' words this way: "Why *worry* about clothing? Look at the wildflowers that bloom every spring. They *do not labor* long hours, as people do, to *spin* wool into yarn, weave yarn into fabric, and sew fabric into garments."

29. *"Yet I tell you that not even Solomon in all his splendor was dressed like one of these.*

Solomon was king of Israel at the peak of that nation's power and glory. Surely he wore the very best clothing that could be made at that time. Even so, he was not *dressed* as beautifully as one of those common wildflowers on the hillside.

30. *"If that is how God clothes the grass of the field, which is here today and tomorrow is thrown into the fire, will he not much more clothe you, O you of little faith?*

The wildflowers may be prettier than you are, but not for long. Quickly they wither, and soon they and other sun-dried plants are raked up and used as fuel to bake the bread in someone's backyard oven. You can see how God clothes them beautifully in spite of their short life; don't you know he will *clothe you* adequately if you faithfully do the work he designed you to do? How can you be so lacking in *faith* and trust that you worry about where your next set of clothes will come from?

III. SUMMARY (MATTHEW 6:31-34)

Many people have been amused by the way one preacher described his method of constructing a sermon: "First I tell them what I'm going to tell them. Then I tell them. Then I tell them what I've told them." Jesus did not exactly follow that procedure in the text we have before us, but he did make two points emphatic by repeating them: "Trust God" and "Don't worry."

A. TRUST GOD (vv. 31, 32)

31. *"So do not worry, saying, 'What shall we eat?' or 'What shall we drink?' or 'What shall we wear?'*

Jesus' counsel *not to worry* is especially appropriate today when so many worry about *what* to *eat* and *drink* and *what* to *wear.*

WHAT DO YOU THINK?

When speaking of how the Father provides for his creation, Jesus observed that birds do not "store away." However, other animals, such as the squirrel, do indeed store food for later use. If one of Jesus' disciples had pointed this out to him, how do you think he would have responded?

WHAT DO YOU THINK?

The birds of the air and the lilies of the field provided illustrations in Jesus' message. What other illustrations from nature demonstrate God's care for us?

32. For the pagans run after all these things, and your heavenly Father knows that you need them.

Pagans are idol worshipers. When they *run after all these things,* they demonstrate that they know nothing of a *heavenly Father* who rules the universe and who cares for his people. They become desperate and stingy when they are hungry or when they experience hard times. Children of God, on the other hand, know their Father—or they ought to. They know that he lives, he rules, he knows, and he cares.

B. Put God First (v. 33)

33. "But seek first his kingdom and his righteousness, and all these things will be given to you as well.

To *seek first* God's *kingdom* is to seek above everything else to be ruled by him. It means desiring to know his will and to do it. When you live by God's priorities, you can be assured that he will not leave you without the food and clothing about which so many fret and worry.

Forsaking All for the Kingdom

H. L. Mencken called it "the greatest news story since the Resurrection." He was talking about King Edward VIII's abdication of the British throne. Edward announced that he was stepping down for the sake of "the woman he loved." The woman was Wallis Simpson, a commoner and an American, once divorced and involved in an affair with the king (although still married to her second husband). Her divorce was a major problem, since in those days it was thought scandalous for the head of the Church of England (the king) to marry such a woman. British papers kept the matter quiet as long as they could.

Edward's abdication avoided what could have been a major constitutional crisis in England. But he was willing to lose his claim to a kingdom for the sake of "the woman he loved."

In contrast, Jesus calls us to seek *first* the kingdom of God. He challenges us to give up all other allegiances for the sake of "the God we love." While this appears to be a foolish risk in the eyes of many, we who know and serve our heavenly Father realize that we are always in his care. The real risk—one with eternal consequences—is taken by the individual who tries to live as if he himself were king.

—C. R. B.

C. Don't Worry (v. 34)

34. "Therefore do not worry about tomorrow, for tomorrow will worry about itself. Each day has enough trouble of its own."

Like every good teacher, Jesus knew the value of repeating. He capped this section of his teaching by saying once again, *Do not worry.* Don't spoil today by worrying about *tomorrow.* Tomorrow will bring its own problems. Spend today dealing with today's problems, not worrying about what has not yet happened. Live one day at a time—and live it acknowledging God as the Giver of that day and of all that he allows you to enjoy that day.

Borrowing From Tomorrow's Troubles

There was once a time when business executives could leave all their cares at the office. But now, thanks to all of our "labor-saving" devices, it is getting harder and harder to do that. Cell phones, laptop computers, and e-mail make it increasingly difficult to "disconnect."

A recent survey of five thousand executives revealed that 82 percent of them worked during their vacations. More than a fourth of them called the office on their

What Do You Think?

What is involved—mentally, physically, and spiritually—in heeding Jesus' exhortation to "seek first [God's] kingdom"?

Use this poster to encourage your students to put the Lord's kingdom first on their priority list.

PRAYER

Dear Father, gracious Father, loving Father, we do want to please you in all our thinking and talking and doing. Help us, we pray, in our efforts to do so. In Jesus' name, amen.

THOUGHT TO REMEMBER

My mind is made up.

days off, and 13 percent checked their e-mail when away from work. Cutting a vacation short because of work was admitted to by 13 percent of the executives. "If you don't stay in touch," the surveyors concluded, "you'll fall behind."

Of course, people in many occupations seldom have "days off." Farmers whose livestock need daily feeding and/or milking and stay-at-home mothers of small children are two groups of people who would love to get a day off, even if they had to "stay in touch."

Whatever our occupation, excessive involvement in our work can lead to mental burnout, poor health, disrupted family life, and decreased involvement in spirit-nurturing activities such as church attendance. Trying to get ahead of tomorrow's troubles can actually increase the trials tomorrow may bring. Our experience should tell us that Jesus was right when he said, "Do not worry about tomorrow, for tomorrow will worry about itself."

—C. R. B.

CONCLUSION

A. WHEN TO "TAKE SOME THOUGHT"

The *King James Version* uses the phrase "take no thought" rather than "do not worry." It would be easy (but wrong) to interpret either phrase to mean that we are to be totally oblivious to all that is around us. Sometimes without thinking we slip into the mistake of worrying about material concerns such as food and clothing and other treasures on earth.

We are not to worry about treasure in Heaven, either. But we do need to take thought of certain matters. Here are examples of things of which the Bible says that we are indeed to take *some* thought.

Think about good things. Fill your mind with them (Philippians 4:8).

Think about Jesus. Think of what a glorious Savior he is (Hebrews 3:1-3). Think how much he endured for you (Hebrews 12:3, 4).

Think about yourself. Don't be conceited, but make a fair estimate (Romans 12:3). Watch yourself lest you be tempted (Galatians 6:1).

Think about your fellow Christians. Consider ways to stir them up to love one another and to do good (Hebrews 10:24).

Think about your Christian leaders. Think about the outcome of their way of life, and imitate their faith (Hebrews 13:7).

B. MAKE UP YOUR MIND

Worry flourishes in a divided mind. Perhaps you have chosen the best Master and the best treasure; yet there is something you really need, like a new car or an extended vacation or an addition to the house. So just this once you decide to take orders from "Money." You overcharge a customer, or misrepresent your merchandise, or cheat on your income tax. It's just this once, but next year you may "really need" something else, and that will be "just this once," too. Soon "Money" has you in its grip, and your worries begin to increase.

So make up your mind. Give first place to God's kingdom and his righteousness. Refuse to do anything dishonest, deceitful, or greedy—no matter what "Money" offers. Make the old car last another year, or maybe two or three. Go camping in the nearest state park instead of taking a cruise. Put a cheaper partition in that basement bedroom instead of building an addition to the house. See if a lower cost detergent will work as well as the highly advertised one. God will bless your full allegiance, and you will stop lying awake at night with worry.

Make up your mind. God is your Master; seek to please him day by day. Treasure in Heaven is your objective; store it up hour by hour. God's peace will be a by-product of your commitment; enjoy it moment by moment (Philippians 4:7).

Discovery Learning

This page contains an alternate lesson plan emphasizing learning activities. Classes desiring such student involvement will find these suggestions helpful. The next page is a reproducible activity page to further enhance discovery learning.

LEARNING GOALS

After this lesson students will be able to:

1. Tell what Jesus said in this portion of the Sermon on the Mount about our treasures and our priorities.

2. Contrast Jesus' teaching about these matters with the world's perspective on material wealth.

3. Pinpoint an area of their lives where trust in God needs to replace worry, and commit that area to him.

INTO THE LESSON

Begin by asking the class to move into groups of three. Make sure each group of three has paper and pencil. State: "This morning I'm going to ask you a question, and I'd like you to generate a list of answers. You will have about three minutes." Then ask this question: "What do people use to keep their valuables and possessions safe and secure?" (*Possible answers: locks, security systems, alarms, computer passwords, safety deposit boxes, safes, and others.*) After sufficient time has been given, ask the group with the most answers to read them to the class. Then ask if the other groups have additional answers. Say: "People use many different ways to protect their valuables and possessions. Yet even with all these different devices, security of our valuables is not guaranteed. Even very complex security systems have not always prevented the theft of valuable merchandise. Today's lesson focuses upon Jesus' words about our treasures and our priorities. Turn to Matthew 6:19-34; let's read what Jesus said about storing our treasures."

INTO THE WORD

Ask a class member to read Matthew 6:19-23 aloud to the class. Then ask these questions:

1. What did Jesus say happens to treasures stored upon the earth? (*Moths eat the woolen fabric; rust destroys metal; and thieves steal the treasures, v. 19.*)

2. What is the connection between a person's treasure and a person's heart? (*Your heart follows, or is directed toward, that which you value, v. 21.*) State: "Jesus stated that treasures stored in Heaven are secure: they will not be eaten, they will not rust, nor will they be stolen by thieves."

3. What does Jesus mean by "laying up treasures in Heaven"? (*He is talking about what we value, about our priorities.*) Observe that Jesus illustrates this in verses 22, 23. If we are focused upon the light of truth and that is what we value, our whole body will characterize the light of truth.

Ask another class member to read aloud Matthew 6:24-34. Then ask the following questions to the class:

1. What contrast does Jesus make in this passage of Scripture? (*Between two life ambitions: secular and godly. The secular focus is accumulating possessions, gaining more and more wealth. The godly focus is on serving God, seeking his kingdom, and trusting him to provide the basics of food and clothing.*)

2. What was the point of Jesus' illustrations about birds (v. 26) and flowers (v. 28)? (*God will provide our needs, so we have no need to worry.*)

3. What does Jesus say should be the first priority of every person? (*Seeking the kingdom of God and his righteousness, v. 33.*)

INTO LIFE

Jesus presents in this passage a common characteristic of people today: worry. Distribute copies of the reproducible activity "The World of Worry" from the next page. Ask the class to move back into the groups of three as they were earlier in the lesson. State: "In each of your groups, have someone write down for the respective headings the worries that concern the non-Christian and the areas of life that concern the Christian." Give several minutes for the groups to generate answers. Then ask for the answers to be reported to the class. As answers are given, write them on an overhead transparency so the class can see the answers. (*Possible answers: money, clothes, paying bills, possessions, safety, personal appearance, health, travel safety, broken relationships.*) Say: "As you can see, non-Christians and Christians worry about many of the same things. But what does Jesus teach in this passage about worry?" (*Worry does not change anything, v. 27; worry indicates little faith, v. 30; worry is unnecessary, v. 32.*) So if worry is something that Jesus does not want us to do, then what does he teach we should do? We should seek first the kingdom of God and his righteousness and trust him to provide those things that we need.

Some of us worry about many of these same elements. Select one wherein trust in God needs to replace worry. After you select it, fill in the prayer to God on the reproducible page committing yourself to trust him to take care of you.

The World of Worry

First, identify the subjects of worry that plague people today. Then place a check mark (✔) in the non-Christians' column if this item is something non-Christians worry about. Place a check mark (✔) in the Christians' column if they also worry about that element of life.

SUBJECTS OF WORRY	NON-CHRISTIANS	CHRISTIANS

What differences do you see? What differences **should** you see?

Prayer of Release and Commitment

Dear Father,

    I am spending too much time worrying about _____.
Today's lesson helps me to see how important I am to you. You already know what I need, and you want me to seek your kingdom and your righteousness first. You want me to trust you in this element of life. So, Father, I release this worry to you. Help me trust you to provide what I need. And I will give you all the glory.

In Jesus' name I pray,

_____
      (Sign your name here)

Date _____

LIVING BY THE LAW OF LOVE

LESSON 13

WHY TEACH THIS LESSON?

To modern culture a "loving person" is someone who is "broad minded" and "tolerant" of all behavior in others. Upholding an absolute standard of morality is considered "mean spirited" and bigoted. The Christian, trying to live by the law of love, may become confused and be tempted to compromise the unchanging standard of the Word of God. His or her motives may be honorable, but the result is, in fact, the very opposite of what was desired.

For the Christian, an important part of loving one's neighbor involves helping that person get on (or stay on) the narrow road that leads to life. That neighbor may not at first realize the need or appreciate the Christian's efforts in this regard. Today's message equips the learner to expect and be ready to respond to the opposition that may come so that he or she can continue to practice the law of love.

INTRODUCTION

"Living by the Law of Love." What a noble title for the closing lesson of this series from the life of Christ! What a ringing statement of what all of us should want to be doing! We are puzzled, then, when we read the lesson text from beginning to end, and the word *love* is not there. Have we forgotten the substance of the lesson in our search for a catchy title?

No, the title aptly states what the lesson is all about. The word *love* is not in the text, but the Golden Rule is there (Matthew 7:12). And the Golden Rule is closely related to the law of love.

A. THE LAW OF LOVE AND THE GOLDEN RULE

Jesus clearly stated what we might call "the twofold law of love" in Matthew 22:37-40: "'Love the Lord your God with all your heart and with all your soul and with all your mind' This is the first and greatest commandment. And the second is like it: 'Love your neighbor as yourself.' All the Law and the Prophets hang on these two commandments."

The Golden Rule appears in verse 12 of our text: "So in everything, do to others what you would have them do to you, for this sums up the Law and the Prophets." More often we hear the shorter paraphrase: "Do unto others as you would have them do unto you," and that is not a bad summation. But the relationship between the twofold law of love and the Golden Rule is seen in what follows: "for this sums up the Law and the Prophets."

Thus all the law and the prophets "hang on" the twofold law of love. And the Golden Rule sums up the law and the prophets. It is the law and the prophets in action; it is their teaching applied. The Golden Rule tells briefly what you do when you are guided by the law and the prophets. So, in effect, the law of love and the Golden Rule are the same. Living by the Golden Rule is living by the law of love.

DEVOTIONAL READING:
ROMANS 13:8-14
BACKGROUND SCRIPTURE:
MATTHEW 7
PRINTED TEXT:
MATTHEW 7:1-5, 12-20

LESSON AIMS

After completing this lesson, a student should be able to:

1. Tell what Jesus said about judging, not judging, and loving others in the way one wants to be loved.

2. Explain why Jesus' teaching about the narrow way and the examination of the fruits of others does not contradict living by the law of love.

3. Suggest a specific way to implement the Golden Rule this week, perhaps to the benefit of one he or she might be tempted to "judge" in the manner Jesus disallowed.

KEY VERSE

So in everything, do to others what you would have them do to you, for this sums up the Law and the Prophets.
—Matthew 7:12

Nov
25

LESSON 13 NOTES

B. LESSON BACKGROUND

The Sermon on the Mount is drawing to its close. Jesus has taught us how to be blessed (lesson 10). He has explained that he does not destroy the law, but fulfills it (lesson 11). He has reminded us that treasures in Heaven are vastly more precious than treasures on earth (lesson 12). He has given other important teachings, too—bright gems of truth that are not included in this short series of lessons.

Now the sermon soars toward its climax in the call to live by the law of love.

I. PROPER JUDGING (MATTHEW 7:1-5)

Good judgment is what we need when we choose a grocer to supply food for our table, a mechanic to repair our car, a trade to earn our living, a college to prepare us for a trade, and a husband or wife to fill life with joy. Yet our text begins by bluntly saying, "Do not judge." Does that mean we should stop trying to distinguish between good and bad, or between good and better? Of course not! Judging and choosing are necessary parts of intelligent living.

A. JUDGE NOT (v. 1)

1. *"Do not judge, or you too will be judged.*

Often the command *Do not judge* is quoted as if it were followed by a period. Faced by the most incriminating proof of his wrongdoing, someone will say, "Well, the Bible says we're not to judge." And this text is not the only one that warns against judging. Consider Romans 2:1; 14:4; and James 4:12, among others.

On the other hand, other Scriptures call us (just as clearly) to engage in judging. Matthew 7:6 warns against giving "what is sacred" to "dogs" or throwing "pearls" to "pigs." No careful student of the Bible thinks that Jesus is referring to literal dogs or pigs here. And while there is some debate about just what Jesus meant by "what is sacred" and the "pearls," it is clear that some type of judgment must be made about who it is who should not receive them. This is consistent with what Jesus said, when, upon sending his disciples out to preach, he told them not to linger with hostile hearers, but to go on to another city (Matthew 10:23). An event in the lives of Paul and Barnabas offers a similar illustration: when a Jewish audience "talked abusively against" their efforts, they turned to the Gentiles with the holy "pearls" of the gospel (Acts 13:45-47).

Or consider verse 15 of our printed text: "Watch out for false prophets." How can we do that unless we judge some so-called prophets to be false? Jesus warned against hasty judging "by mere appearances," but he encouraged "right judgment" (John 7:24). Paul told the Corinthians to "judge" even what he himself was saying (1 Corinthians 10:15). The whole church is given the responsibility of judging unrepentant sinners, even of expelling them if they refuse to turn from their sinful ways (Matthew 18:15-17; 1 Corinthians 5).

Thus, according to Scripture, the necessity of judging is as clear as the warnings against it. Is the Bible contradicting itself? Certainly not. God's Word is always in harmony with itself, but at times our understanding may be faulty.

Then how should we understand *do not judge* in our text? We must read the whole sentence: *Do not judge, or you too will be judged.* Jesus not only gives a command; he provides the reason for the command. He says that people are less likely to judge us if we do not judge them. The next verse expands on that thinking.

B. JUDGE CAREFULLY (v. 2)

2. *"For in the same way you judge others, you will be judged, and with the measure you use, it will be measured to you.*

WHAT DO YOU THINK?

Many believers appear to be hypersensitive to this matter of judging. How should you respond when a brother or sister, upon a fair critique of improper behavior, quotes, "Do not judge"?

HOW TO SAY IT

*Barnabas. BAR-nuh-bus.
Calvary. CAL-vuh-ree.
hypocrite. HIP-uh-krit.*

Some frequent critics seem almost gleeful in pronouncing judgment on others. Then they become indignant when someone points out any wrongdoing in their own lives. Jesus' counsel may be summarized as follows: if I am harsh, insensitive, and insulting in judging *others*, I can expect others to retaliate in the same way. And not only will the one I insult respond in kind; his friends will likely join in. If I am loud and long in my judgment of others, heaping a full *measure* of condemnation on wrongdoers, I can expect a similar measure of condemnation from others.

On the other hand, if I speak out in judgment only when absolutely necessary and if I do it with regret (more in sorrow than in anger or self-righteousness), then I can hope for an equally sympathetic judgment of my own misdeeds.

It is the "flip side," if you will, to the Golden Rule. Do *not* do to others (judge them harshly) what you would not have them do to you (judge you thus). We are not surprised, then, when the "Golden Rule" shows up in this context (v. 12).

C. LOOK AT YOURSELF (vv. 3-5)

3, 4. "Why do you look at the speck of sawdust in your brother's eye and pay no attention to the plank in your own eye? How can you say to your brother, 'Let me take the speck out of your eye,' when all the time there is a plank in your own eye?

Imagine someone concerned about a *speck* in his *brother's eye*, while a large object (*a plank*) is lodged in his *own eye*! As we try to help a Christian brother rid his life of sin, how often are we handicapped by sin in our own lives? And is our sin far more serious than his? Or perhaps it is made so by our presumption of innocence in picking at our brother's sin!

5. "You hypocrite, first take the plank out of your own eye, and then you will see clearly to remove the speck from your brother's eye."

We need to judge ourselves *first*. With honesty, humility, and clear thinking guided by God's Word, we can be made aware of our own sins. With the help of God's gracious forgiveness and with earnest repentance, we can get rid of those sins. At that point the battle is not over, for we must guard against the sin of pride in our own goodness. If we can do that, we will be better prepared to discern the sins of our brothers and sisters—not to condemn them, but to help them get rid of those sins. Galatians 6:1 has a word about that: "Brothers, if someone is caught in a sin, you who are spiritual should restore him gently. But watch yourself, or you also may be tempted."

WHAT DO YOU THINK?

Jesus used the term hypocrite to condemn certain attitudes and behavior. What cautions would you suggest about using that term today?

PLAYING WITH FIRE

There seems to be no end to the production of "action" movies and television programs. These often feature special effects in which the "bad guy" gets blown to bits or the hero escapes dramatically from an exploding vehicle or building.

Pyrotechnic specialists (or "pyros" as they are called in the entertainment business) have developed to a fine science the art of fooling an audience into thinking that all the destruction they see is real. However, "pyros" recognize that they are literally "playing with fire." And on the rare occasion when something goes wrong, it can go *very* wrong. Such was the case several years ago when a special-effects explosion blew the tail rotor off a helicopter, resulting in a crash that killed an adult actor and two children.

The act of judging another requires similar caution. It is absolutely necessary for us to make judgments about the rightness or wrongness of many things; however, as Jesus clearly warns, we are playing with fire if we judge others without first judging ourselves and putting our own lives in order. Only then can we keep from getting burned when our angry spirits and stinging judgments are turned back upon us by those who see through our hypocrisy.   —C. R. B.

II. PRACTICAL GUIDANCE (MATTHEW 7:12-14)

The law of Moses fills large portions of Exodus, Leviticus, Numbers, and Deuteronomy. The lawyers and scribes of Jesus' day knew the laws recorded in those books, as well the countless interpretations and court precedents that had been made authoritative; but no one else knew them. An ordinary farmer or merchant or carpenter did not even have the Scriptures at home, nor could he refer to them in a public library. Yet in the Sermon on the Mount (particularly in the Golden Rule), Jesus gave some simple helps for people who wanted to live according to the Law and the Prophets.

A. THE GOLDEN RULE (v. 12)

12. "So in everything, do to others what you would have them do to you, for this sums up the Law and the Prophets.

For generations this has been known as the Golden Rule, and indeed it is more precious than gold. How quickly it can be remembered! How readily it can be applied to almost anything you think of saying or doing to someone! How easily it can be passed on to children or grandchildren!

Jokesters like to have fun with the Golden Rule. One story tells of a husband who wanted a costly set of golf clubs. So, in obedience to the Golden Rule, he gave his wife such a set for Christmas, though she never played golf. A similar story tells of a wife who gave her husband a sewing machine because that is what she wanted him to give her. But Jesus' teaching is not meant to be used to further one's selfish interests; it is designed to help relationships between people be the kind that God wants them to be.

B. THE TWO WAYS (vv. 13, 14)

13. "Enter through the narrow gate. For wide is the gate and broad is the road that leads to destruction, and many enter through it.

Who wants to be *narrow*, especially in today's society? Most of us like to go along with the crowd, to be congenial, to do what "everyone" is doing. Who wants to be labeled narrow-minded? But Jesus taught that the crowded expressway *leads to destruction*. If that is not where we want our lives to go, we had better not choose the *wide* road. We don't like to think that the majority is wrong more often than right, but what else can we think if we believe Jesus?

THE DANGERS OF THE BROAD WAY

During the last half of the twentieth century, many nations went on a road-building spree. In the United States, the Interstate system brought travelers new freeways and expressways of up to ten lanes in width. Europe developed a similar system of highways; perhaps the most familiar is the *autobahn* in Germany.

One of the attractions of such highways anywhere in the world is the apparent safety with which one can travel at high speed. As hills were leveled and dangerous curves straightened to construct the highways, the accident and fatality rates on these roads plummeted in spite of increasing traffic and higher velocities. Nevertheless, serious trouble still awaits the unwary. Just a couple of years ago, a crash on a German *autobahn* involved one hundred ten cars and caused one million dollars in damages. Amazingly, only two people were killed. Authorities said that fog had cut visibility to just thirty feet, and people were simply going too fast for the conditions.

These popular, broad highways almost beg drivers to travel too fast. The same is true of the "broad way" described by Jesus, where "fast living" can lead to destruction—with eternal consequences. Conditions on the broad way are much like those were on the German *autobahn* when the terrible crash described above occurred: too many people paying too little attention to matters involving life and death.—C. R. B.

The Golden Rule, as this visual demonstrates, is a fulfillment of the law's entire code of how to treat one another.

WHAT DO YOU THINK?

Occasionally we may hear someone say, "My religion is the Golden Rule." Using passages such as Acts 4:12 and 1 John 2:2, how should we respond to such a declaration?

14. "But small is the gate and narrow the road that leads to life, and only a few find it.

If *life* is our chosen destination, then we have to be content to travel with the minority. But let's not oversimplify the matter. In the choices that face us day by day, we cannot choose a position or a way just by counting the people who are in favor of it. The majority may be wrong more often than right, but it is not always wrong. In some cases, parting company with the majority might mean forsaking the truth. Therefore, day by day we must chart our course solely by God's Word, regardless of those who share the road with us.

III. JUDGING BY RESULTS (MATTHEW 7:15-20)

We have been warned against judging others and against judging our own course by anything but the Word of God. In the remainder of our printed text, Jesus tells us a dependable way to conduct the kind of judging that is acceptable to God.

A. TESTING FRUIT (vv. 15, 16)

15. "Watch out for false prophets. They come to you in sheep's clothing, but inwardly they are ferocious wolves.

Sheep are peaceful animals, with little means to defend themselves. They depend on a shepherd for protection as well as direction. What could be more disastrous to a peaceful flock than a hungry wolf disguised as a sheep? Beware! Be alert! Don't let him fool you!

16. "By their fruit you will recognize them. Do people pick grapes from thornbushes, or figs from thistles?

Perhaps you don't know the difference between a fig tree and a sycamore tree—until the *fruit* appears. Then anyone can identify the fig tree. Perhaps you can't tell a wild grapevine from a good one until you see what grows on it. Then the good vine becomes apparent.

B. DEPENDABLE STANDARDS (vv. 17, 18)

17. "Likewise every good tree bears good fruit, but a bad tree bears bad fruit.

Here is a test that is always reliable: the nature of the *fruit* reveals the nature of the *tree*.

18. "A good tree cannot bear bad fruit, and a bad tree cannot bear good fruit.

This statement is essentially a restatement of the previous principle. A tree simply *cannot* bring forth any kind of *fruit* but its own.

C. UNFRUITFUL TREE'S END (v. 19)

19. "Every tree that does not bear good fruit is cut down and thrown into the fire.

Fuel was scarce in the land where Jesus lived. A *tree* that was useless in bearing *fruit* still had some value in heating the oven where bread was baked. A man who does nothing *good* in this world does not even have that secondary use. The *fire* where he will be cast will not benefit anyone (Matthew 25:41-46).

D. WHEN WE ARE TO DISCERN (v. 20)

20. "Thus, by their fruit you will recognize them."

The fruitless tree may have green leaves and even bright flowers, but the harvest season reveals that it is worthless. The fire is its destiny. Likewise, the false prophet (v. 15) or the do-nothing person (Matthew 25:42, 43) may have a handsome face and an eloquent tongue, but time will reveal his worthlessness. Judgment by one's *fruit*, or results, is an accurate judgment.

WHAT DO YOU THINK?

Jesus declared that the road to life is a "narrow" one. In this age of "tolerance," the conventional wisdom is that being narrow is a thing to be shunned. How can we be "narrow" and still have a credible witness to the world?

WHAT DO YOU THINK?

What are some of the fruits of a person's life that enable us to discern the genuineness of that person's faith in God? How should we respond to the absence of good spiritual fruits?

Prayer

   Heavenly Father, we give you thanks for the blessed privilege of living by the law of love, of growing daily in love and fruitfulness, and of serving you even in small ways. Even more, we give you thanks for the greatness of your grace by which we shall dwell forever in your kingdom. In Jesus' name, amen.

Thought to Remember

   "The gift of God is eternal life" (Romans 6:23).

CONCLUSION

   "Living by the Law of Love" is the challenge in the title of this lesson. Have we wandered far from our subject in thinking so much about judging and not judging? No, for if we live by the law of love, we must constantly be judging and choosing. The wide road looks easy and inviting, but we are to judge rightly, not by appearance (John 7:24). We must look beyond the attractiveness of that easy road and judge it by its destination. It leads to destruction (Matthew 7:13). We must turn away from it and take the narrow, climbing road that leads to life (v. 14). In doing so, we will see that the law of love directs us to that same narrow way.

   The law of love given through Moses directs our love in two paths: toward God and toward neighbors (Matthew 22:37-40). As expanded upon by Jesus, it also prescribes a third direction—toward our enemies (Matthew 5:43-45). That compels us again to think about the nature of love. Obviously the love we give our enemies is not the kind of love that fills many fictional love stories. It is not a mutual attraction between a man and woman—a feeling that arises unbidden and sometimes becomes a consuming passion.

   So what is this love—the kind of love we have for God and neighbors and even for enemies? In lesson 11 we defined it as "active, intelligent goodwill." This love does not arise unbidden and dominate us against our will. We choose it because it is right. We cultivate it with difficulty, but we cultivate it persistently because it is the way of God's children.

A. Difficult Love

   It is not easy to "love your enemies." It is not natural to "love your enemies and pray for those who persecute you" (Matthew 5:44). If you were coasting easily down the road that leads to destruction, you would do none of these. But you have chosen the narrow way that leads to life. This is not a road for coasting, but a road for climbing. So keep on climbing.

   How can you love your enemies? How can you speak well of those who speak evil of you? Your first battle may be with yourself—a battle for self-control. Bite your tongue to stop the curse that comes to mind when someone curses you. That scowl that would take possession of your face when someone puts you down—arrest it before it is fully formed. Replace it with a smile. Tell your enemy, "You may have a point. I know I'm not all I ought to be." Such an answer may struggle with your angry inclination at first; but if you make a habit of answering softly, you will find yourself happily turning away wrath instead of stirring up anger (Proverbs 15:1). You will learn to enjoy doing a favor for someone who does only evil to you. Can any joy on earth be more delightful than the joy of being and living like a child of your Father who is in Heaven? (Matthew 5:44, 45).

B. God's Love Is Enough

   Though we may grow in love year by year, our love alone can never be enough to get us to Heaven. Even if it becomes as faultless as our Father's own (Matthew 5:48), our perfected love today cannot atone for our love's failures in the past. There is no atonement but one: Jesus' sacrifice of his life at Calvary. We cannot earn our way to Heaven, not even by perfected love and by years of doing good. Only God's love is enough. In his love he sent his Son to provide the atonement for our sins (John 3:16). For our survival we depend on his grace, his favor that we do not deserve, his forgiveness of our every sin. "For it is by grace you have been saved, through faith—and this not from yourselves, it is the gift of God" (Ephesians 2:8). Praise the Lord!

Discovery Learning

This page contains an alternate lesson plan emphasizing learning activities. Classes desiring such student involvement will find these suggestions helpful. The next page is a reproducible activity page to further enhance discovery learning.

LEARNING GOALS

After this lesson each student will be able to:

1. Tell what Jesus said about judging, not judging, and loving others in the way one wants to be loved.

2. Explain why Jesus' teaching about the narrow way and the examination of the fruits of others does not contradict living by the law of love.

3. Suggest a specific way to implement the "Golden Rule" this week, perhaps to the benefit of one he or she might be tempted to "judge" in the manner Jesus disallowed.

INTO THE LESSON

Begin class by writing the word *hypocrite* on the board or overhead transparency. Say: "We probably know what a hypocrite is. But to make certain that we agree, let's define it. If you have a definition, share it with the class." As suggested definitions are given, write them on the chalkboard or transparency. State: "Perhaps you have known some individuals who fit this description. They give an appearance of being something they are not. They say one thing but do something else. In today's text, Jesus warns us against becoming hypocrites in the way we judge others. Later he gives us a useful alternative: 'the Golden Rule.' Turn to Matthew 7 and let's read what Jesus said."

INTO THE WORD

Ask a class member to read Matthew 7:1-5, 12-20 aloud. Prior to class, prepare either a handout or a transparency with the following questions. Divide the class into groups of three. Show the transparency to reveal the questions or distribute the handout. Say: "This passage of Scripture provides some of Jesus' key teaching about judging, getting along with other people, and human nature. Answer these questions for a better view."

1. Describe the circumstances that led Jesus to call someone a hypocrite. (*Jesus rejects judging another person—even pointing out the other person's flaws—without first evaluating one's self.*)

2. What is the standard Jesus gave by which we should treat other people? (*Treat others the way we want to be treated.*)

3. Contrast the two ways Jesus described in verses 13 and 14 for each of the following: the gate, the way, the direction, and the number of people who travel. (*Gate:*

wide/straight; way: broad/narrow; direction: destruction/life; number: many/few.)

4. What is the standard by which false prophets are clearly distinguished from true prophets? (*Their fruit reveals their nature.*)

5. What is the relationship between fruit and the nature of the tree? (*Good fruit comes from good trees; bad fruit comes from bad trees.*)

6. What is the relationship between the law of love in Matthew 22:37-40 and the Golden Rule in Matthew 7:12? (*Both express "the Law and the Prophets." Living by the law of love and living by the Golden Rule are the same.*)

7. Why does Jesus expect us to evaluate the fruits of others? (*To recognize false prophets, so that we don't find ourselves in the broad way that leads to destruction.*)

After several minutes, review the questions and answers with the class.

INTO LIFE

Say: "Now we need to consider the principles and how they may be applied to our lives today. In your groups, draw a principle from the lesson text, and after several minutes, we'll discuss those principles with the class." (*Possible principles: "Self-examination precedes the correction of self and others"; "Treat others the way you want to be treated"; "Words and actions reveal true character."*)

This lesson focuses specifically on living by the law of love—or the Golden Rule, "Treat others the way you want to be treated." Distribute copies of the reproducible page that follows, and ask the learners to focus on the activity "Living Daily by the Golden Rule." This self-examination activity evaluates the extent to which the Golden Rule is consistently practiced toward a variety of people. Give a few minutes for each learner to rate her or his own practice of the Golden Rule toward the people listed.

Then ask each learner to select the one area that ranked the lowest on the handout and to identify a specific person treated improperly. Write this person's name in the appropriate space on the lower part of the handout. Next, ask each to write a specific way to implement the Golden Rule this week with this person. Ask all to share their suggestions with other class members. Suggest that class members post the handout prominently in their homes for the next week as a constant reminder. Conclude the class session with a prayer that commits the class to living by the law of love.

Living Daily by the Golden Rule

Treating others the way you want to be treated is a daily challenge. Every day we encounter people who "got up on the wrong side of the bed." Sometimes we respond to them in less than a Christian manner. Jesus instructs us that we need to treat others the way we want to be treated—living by the law of love. Evaluate yourself. How consistently do you follow the Golden Rule when you deal with the following groups of people? Circle the number under each group that best represents your present level of living by the law of love.

1. FAMILY
Inconsistent   Consistent

1   2   3   4   5   6   7   8   9   10

2. NEXT DOOR NEIGHBORS
Inconsistent   Consistent

1   2   3   4   5   6   7   8   9   10

3. STORE CLERKS AND CASHIERS
Inconsistent   Consistent

1   2   3   4   5   6   7   8   9   10

4. PHONE SOLICITORS
Inconsistent   Consistent

1   2   3   4   5   6   7   8   9   10

5. WORK ASSOCIATES
Inconsistent   Consistent

1   2   3   4   5   6   7   8   9   10

Commitment to Live by the Golden Rule

Father,

I thank you for this teaching on the Golden Rule. Living by the law of love requires that I treat other people the way I want to be treated. Yet, as I have evaluated myself today, I find that I have not consistently practiced this rule in my life. I frequently stumble in my relationships with _____ _____, and so I ask for your forgiveness for my harsh judging and failure to love as I should. Father, I ask you to give me the ability this week to demonstrate the Golden Rule with him/her by

I commit myself to practice this principle and through it to give you the praise.

In Jesus' name I pray,

Amen.

Winter Quarter, 2001-2002

Light for All People
(*Isaiah, Ruth, Jonah*)

Special Features

Lessons

Unit 1: The Mission of God's Servant

Unit 2: The Response of God's People

Unit 3: All People May Share God's Grace

About These Lessons

The lessons of the present quarter interrupt our chronological study of Old Testament texts to remind us that God always has been interested in all people, not just the members of the Jewish race. His calling of Israel was a means of conferring blessing on all people, not just the Jews. Through the prophecies of Isaiah, through the life of Ruth, and through the experience of Jonah, that truth is clear. May we share his concern—for everyone.

Dec 2
Dec 9
Dec 16
Dec 23
Dec 30
Jan 6
Jan 13
Jan 20
Jan 27
Feb 3
Feb 10
Feb 17
Feb 24

Light for the World

by David Reece

The coming of Jesus, the Servant of the Lord, into our world might be likened to the appearance of a brilliant comet. However, unlike the flare of such a passing astral guest, the light of our Christ never fades.

Occasionally the arrival of a comet surprises us. It may be that the comet is traveling on such a huge orbit that it has not passed by us since records of such phenomena began to be kept. More likely, we are simply not aware of the comet's course. But when Halley's comet appeared in 1986, everyone knew it was coming. In fact, we know when this comet will reappear because we know it travels in an orbit that takes it past the earth every seventy-six years.

Like the passing of Halley's comet, the coming of Jesus and the miraculous nature of his darkness-ending ministry were no accidents. Jesus told his disciples, "Everything must be fulfilled that is written about me in the Law of Moses, the Prophets and the Psalms" (Luke 24:44). Today Christians can read both the prophecies in the Old Testament and their fulfillments as cited in the New Testament. The result will be a greater confidence in the trustworthiness of their faith.

Isaiah prophesied at the end of the eighth century and the beginning of the seventh century before Christ. No other prophet had more to say about the light of the world than he. This is not to say that everything that Isaiah preached or wrote related to the ministry of our Lord. He had much to say about his own day as well. He was particularly concerned with God's displeasure with his people because of their repeated failures to live as people of the covenant should. But it is also clear that Isaiah's prophetic insight (guided by the Holy Spirit) looked beyond his own day. Isaiah looked to the inclusion of "every nation, tribe, people and language" (Revelation 7:9) into God's kingdom. God wants all people to come to his light! And Jesus was, is, and always will be the means by which they must do that (John 14:6).

The theme of the coming quarter is "Light for All People." The thirteen lessons will focus on God's concern for all people as expressed in part of the Old Testament. The first two units will be drawn from the book of Isaiah. We will see in unit one the different facets of the ministry of God's Servant. Unit two will consider various responses to the Servant and his mission. In unit three we will illustrate the "Light for All People" theme through the examples of Ruth and Jonah. It is clear that God always has wanted all people to receive the blessings and benefits of his mercy.

DECEMBER

UNIT 1: THE MISSION OF GOD'S SERVANT

Lesson 1: God's Servant Brings Light. God intended that Israel, through faithful obedience to him, would demonstrate their "wisdom and understanding to the nations" (Deuteronomy 4:6). However, the Old Testament is painfully honest about the many failures of Israel to be God's "servant" in this manner. Clearly another Servant was needed who would succeed in fulfilling God's purposes, and Jesus was that Servant.

Lesson 2: God's Servant Brings Peace. Here the Servant of God is described as one empowered by the Spirit of God to make judgments with righteous insight and universal fairness. The peace established by the Servant is pictured in language that portrays "natural" enemies in the animal kingdom living in harmony.

Lesson 3: God's Servant Brings Comfort. Isaiah lived through tumultuous times, including Assyria's destruction of Samaria, the capital of the northern kingdom. Although Jerusalem was spared for some 135 years, Isaiah's prophetic vision saw that her future would be the same as Samaria's. However, it was Babylon (not Assyria) that would carry out the impending destruction. To those future exiles, Isaiah wrote the words of hope and comfort found in chapter 40. But those words spoke of much more than just deliverance from captivity in Babylon. John the Baptist used them to describe his ministry of preparing for the Messiah, who would offer the ultimate comfort (Luke 3:3-6).

Lesson 4: God's Servant Brings Hope. In another prophecy, Isaiah called attention to some of the names by which this Servant would be known. This lesson, which will be taught on the Sunday before Christmas, includes Isaiah's stirring prophecy that begins, "For to us a child is born, to us a son is given" (Isaiah 9:6).

Lesson 5: God's Servant Brings Justice. It is a striking paradox that justice can come from One who was unjustly treated and who did not cry out for justice when he himself was unfairly condemned. But because God's Servant follows the Lord's plan to establish justice by suffering injustice himself, he will be the one, says the Lord, "in whom I delight" (Isaiah 42:1; cf. Matthew 3:16, 17).

UNIT 2: THE RESPONSE OF GOD'S PEOPLE

Lesson 6: Hear the Good News. To be in spiritual darkness is frightening. But the focus of Isaiah's message was not just the gloom and darkness of sin. He also described the life-giving light that God has provided to dispel that darkness. Isaiah does more than point out the problem: he also announces the solution! It is found only in Jesus, "the true light that gives light to every man was coming into the world" (John 1:9).

Lesson 7: Seek the Lord. The pervasive darkness of sin cannot be ended by anything other than divine light. Of course, people may try to form their own light; but their efforts are no more effective than birthday candles lit in a violent windstorm. Isaiah proclaimed that deep and enduring satisfaction cannot be attained unless a person seeks the Lord.

Lesson 8: Worship in Truth. The forms of public worship do not please God unless the daily actions of faithful living accompany them. In the text to be studied for this lesson, Isaiah describes the kind of fast that is most pleasing to God. Such a fast means much more than abstaining from food; it means helping those in both physical and spiritual need.

Lesson 9: Anticipate God's New Creation. The return of a remnant to Jerusalem means, in effect, God's return to his beloved city. That return is itself prophetic of the ultimate reunion of God with his people in the "new Jerusalem" (Revelation 21:2).

UNIT 3: ALL PEOPLE MAY SHARE GOD'S GRACE

Lesson 10: Ruth Chooses Naomi's God. A series of tragedies, culminating in the deaths of her husband and her two sons, shattered the life of aged Naomi. But her daughter-in-law Ruth, a Moabite woman of exceptional integrity, refused to abandon Naomi to find security in Moab. In an especially moving scene, Ruth made what amounted to a "Good Confession" (Ruth 1:16, 17) and accompanied Naomi to the promised land to live as a servant of the true God.

Lesson 11: God Blesses Ruth. Ruth's exemplary devotion to Naomi and Naomi's God is especially striking when one considers that these events took

JANUARY

FEBRUARY

place in a time when, in the picturesque language of the *King James Version*, "every man did that which was right in his own eyes" (Judges 21:25). God blessed Ruth's faithfulness through his merciful and providential care. It is clear that God was the "matchmaker" who brought Boaz and Ruth together. Boaz, a God-fearing "man of standing," and Ruth, a vulnerable new resident of Bethlehem (and a Moabite at that), married and became the parents of Obed. Obed became the grandfather of David, Israel's greatest king.

Lesson 12: Jonah Rejects God's Call. When God sent Jonah to those in Nineveh who needed to be warned of his impending judgment, Jonah promptly deemed the Ninevites unworthy of such treatment. Instead of obeying, Jonah fled from God. God then sent his own special brand of discipline in the form of a large fish that swallowed Jonah. After the fish spit the contrite preacher onto the beach, he who had run *from* God began to run *with* God.

Lesson 13: God Shows Mercy to Nineveh. Jonah had received a powerful demonstration of God's grace: he had been delivered from death! Now he was ready (at least in outward obedience) to extend the Lord's grace to Nineveh. In what may be the most successful evangelistic campaign in all history, thousands of violent, unrighteous people repented and received the same amazing grace that Jonah had taken for granted.

One would think that a preacher would be elated at such results. However, as the book of Jonah concludes, Jonah is pouting from his booth east of Nineveh, where he has been awaiting the hoped-for destruction of the city. He confesses what is evident from the very beginning of the book (and what is still true today): "You are a gracious and compassionate God, slow to anger and abounding in love" (Jonah 4:2).

God still wants to demonstrate that grace to those who are lost and groping in the darkness of sin. If his people fail to communicate that message, who will? May we never become so self-righteous or self-centered that we forget the "amazing grace" that has been shown to us.

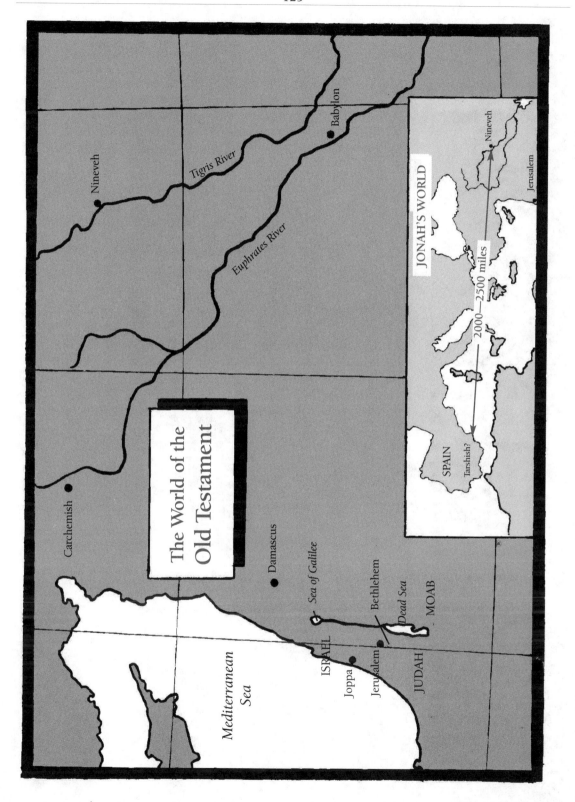

God's Light for All People

Jonah (Lessons 10, 11)
Jonah delivered God's message to Nineveh, the capital of Assyria, Israel's enemy.

Captivity
586-538 B.C.

Kingdom of Israel
930-722 B.C.

United Kingdom
1050-930 B.C.

Kingdom of Judah
930-586 B.C.

Return From
Exile
538 B.C.

Period of the Judges
1380-1050 B.C.

Ruth (Lessons 12, 13)
Ruth was a Gentile whom God used to prepare the world for the Messiah. She was an ancestor of David and of Christ.

Isaiah (Lessons 1-9)
Isaiah prophesied to Judah, warning them the same thing would happen there as had happened to Israel if they did not repent. He also prophesied the coming Messiah.

GOD'S SERVANT BRINGS LIGHT

LESSON 1

WHY TEACH THIS LESSON?

Stop and think about the phases of the moon for a minute. The moon goes through a regular cycle of "waxing and waning"—getting progressively brighter over a period of several days, then dimmer, then starting the cycle all over again. But the moon actually has no light of its own; its light is always and only reflected light. And the amount of light the moon appears to cast at any given time is purely dependent on its position relative to the sun.

This is the relationship the church has to Jesus Christ. Christians are the light of the world (Matthew 5:14-16), yet all the light we have comes from Jesus (John 1:4-9). And the amount of light we cast in the world—light that we reflect from him—depends on how we have chosen to place ourselves relative to him and his light. (Unfortunately, some who claim the name of Christ today are actually blocking his light as the moon occasionally eclipses the sun.) Remember that Jesus does not do all the work of reaching the lost by himself. Through the power of his Holy Spirit, we are his hands, his feet, and his light for this task. Today's lesson is for those who need encouragement and direction about the importance of this task as fellow servants of God.

INTRODUCTION

A. GOLDEN OR YELLOW?

An old adage says, "Silence is golden." Any parent of a preschooler, anyone who works in a noisy factory or operates loud machinery, or any resident who lives near an elementary school playground will surely agree. When the little ones are in bed, when the workday comes to an end, or when the children leave the playground—what a welcome relief is the ensuing silence!

There are times, however, when silence is not "golden." There are times when a person must take a stand and express the truth, for to keep silent would be taken as acceptance of falsehood. It's not easy; it takes courage. That is the reason someone has taken issue with the old saying. "Silence is not always 'golden'; sometimes it's just yellow!"

In today's text, the prophet Isaiah describes a Servant chosen and called by God to bring his light to the people of the world. The Servant expresses both his discouragement and his delight in the service of the Lord. Anyone who has faced resistance to the work of Christ appreciates the courage it takes to keep speaking up when it would be much easier to remain silent. Are we ready to speak up? Or are we yellow?

B. LESSON BACKGROUND

By the time the prophet Isaiah comes on the scene of world history, the Jewish people had been divided into two kingdoms for at least 140 years: the southern

---

DEVOTIONAL READING:
ISAIAH 49:8-13

BACKGROUND SCRIPTURE:
ISAIAH 49:1-7

PRINTED TEXT:
ISAIAH 49:1-6

LESSON AIMS

After this lesson, each student will be able to:

1. Summarize the call of God's "Servant" and the scope of his mission.

2. Tell how Jesus fulfilled Isaiah's prophecy of the Servant and how the church does so today.

3. Suggest specific ways to follow the Lord's Servant in loving service today.

KEY VERSE

I will also make you a light for the Gentiles, that you may bring my salvation to the ends of the earth.   —Isaiah 49:6

kingdom of Judah and the northern kingdom of Israel. (Sometimes, however, the text might use the word "Israel" to refer collectively to all the Jewish people of both kingdoms.) Isaiah conducted a lengthy ministry to the nation of Judah, serving during the reigns of four of its kings—Uzziah, Jotham, Ahaz, and Hezekiah (Isaiah 1:1). As such, his ministry probably covered well over fifty years.

During Isaiah's ministry, the Assyrian Empire, which had regained strength under Tiglath-pileser III, began moving westward with the aim of conquering new territory. Syria, Israel, and Judah were among the lands affected by the Assyrian threat. When the kings of Syria and Israel tried to persuade King Ahaz of Judah to join them in an alliance to stand up to Assyria, he refused and instead requested help from Tiglath-pileser. The Assyrians responded by conquering Syria in 732 b.c. and Israel in 722 b.c.

Although Judah had averted the Assyrians' wrath for a short time, approximately twenty years later Judah was besieged by their forces during the reign of Hezekiah. When Hezekiah prayed earnestly to God on behalf of his people, God brought about a miraculous deliverance. The account in Isaiah 37:36, 37 reports that the angel of the Lord put to death 185,000 Assyrian soldiers.

That, however, did not end the threat of foreign domination. Isaiah predicted that another captivity would overtake Jerusalem because of her sins—a punishment that came about in 586 b.c. at the hands of the Babylonians. Isaiah also foretold the eventual return of captives through the decree of King Cyrus of Persia (2 Chronicles 36:22, 23; Ezra 1:1-4; Isaiah 45:1). That return took place in 538 b.c.

Isaiah 40–66 (which follows the record of events from Hezekiah's reign in chapters 36–39) moves forward in time from the threat of the Assyrian siege of Jerusalem to the destruction of Jerusalem and the Babylonian captivity over one hundred years later. Of course, Isaiah would be long dead by the time those events occurred; yet these chapters describe the conditions and the fears of God's people that were sure to come about during that time of exile. In fact, the chapters so convincingly portray the Babylonian captivity that many scholars have assumed that they must have been written by a later author—someone who had experienced firsthand the exile in Babylon. They believe that this "someone" could not be Isaiah, since he would have died years before the Babylonian captivity of 586 b.c. However, Bible students who believe in predictive prophecy have no trouble seeing these chapters as a divinely-inspired description—in advance—of the Babylonian captivity and of the promise that the Lord would one day deliver his people from their misery.

Isaiah 49, from which today's text is taken, contains the second of what are often termed the four "Servant Songs" of Isaiah. (The others are found in Isaiah 42:1-7; 50:4-9; and 52:13–53:12, though in some cases Bible students differ in exactly how many verses of a passage should be included in each "Song.")

One of the larger issues for the Bible student in the Servant Songs is the exact identity of the servant. Is this servant to be identified as national Israel itself? Is he a portion of national Israel? Or is he perhaps an individual from within the nation, specifically the promised Messiah?

Clearly there are places in Isaiah where the "servant" language refers to the nation of Israel (Isaiah 44:21; 48:20) and others where an individual is being described (Isaiah 42:1-4; 52:13–53:12). Some students have suggested that the servant passages be understood as a kind of pyramid. At the base of this pyramid is the nation of Israel, in the center is the righteous core of faithful servants of the Lord, and at the top is the true servant of the Lord—Jesus the Messiah. Perhaps one could say that Isaiah's Servant Songs point to one person (Jesus) who will fulfill God's plan and serve him in a way that the servant/nation of Israel never could because of its sins. And while some passages in the Songs may appear to describe what occurs to Israel following the captivity in Babylon, the language is such that it points to a much greater fulfillment—in Jesus and in the work of the church.

A good illustration of this fulfillment is seen in how the New Testament describes the fulfillment of one of the Servant Songs (Isaiah 42:1-7) in both personal terms (Jesus, in Matthew 12:15-21) and corporate terms (the church, in Acts 13:47; 26:23). In God's plan the church is now the "Israel of God" (Galatians 6:16), continuing the servant's ministry by taking his gospel to the world.

I. GOD'S SERVANT DESCRIBED (ISAIAH 49:1-3)
A. HIS CALL (v. 1)
1. Listen to me, you islands;
   hear this, you distant nations:
  Before I was born the LORD called me;
   from my birth he has made mention of my name.

This Servant Song begins with the servant addressing the *islands*. These islands represent the *distant* pagan *nations* who do not know the Lord. In Isaiah 66:19 the islands are described as "distant . . . that have not heard of my fame or seen my glory." In this verse, God declares that these "nations" will indeed hear of his glory. (See also Isaiah 11:11; 24:15; 42:4, 10, 12; 51:5; and 60:9.)The servant's words in the verse before us today prepare us for the description of his expanded mission in verse 6: bringing God's salvation "to the ends of the earth."

The servant, describing himself as being called by the Lord *before I was born* and *from my birth*, brings to mind Jeremiah's description of his prophetic call (Jeremiah 1:5). Paul considered his call to apostolic ministry as "from birth" (Galatians 1:15).

The personal nature of the servant's call is also clear from the solemn announcement of the servant's *name* and its mention by the Lord, which brings to mind a father's post-birth announcement of the name of his child. Recall that Isaiah has already predicted that a virgin would bear a son and that he would be called "Immanuel" (Isaiah 7:14).

THE ATTITUDE OF THE EFFECTIVE

The earthquake that struck Los Angeles in 1994 left dozens dead and thousands homeless. One of the most impressive stories during the extensive news coverage included an interview with a lady who survived all the uncertainty and damage of the quake. She said, "We don't like this, but we won't move. We are Californians and Angelinos. We will handle anything that comes our way."

The resolve displayed by this woman was admirable. Her attitude and actions embody the words etched over the entrance to the California state capital building in Sacramento: "Give us men to match our mountains." History is shaped by people possessed with a passion, a resolve, and a purpose to conquer mountains. Their sense of identity and calling are unmistakable.

Consider other examples of resolve and purpose. At the age of seventeen, Alexander Hamilton was writing political pamphlets. At twenty-one George Washington was a colonel in the Virginia militia—and he had driven the French from the borders of Virginia. At twenty-six Napoleon conquered Italy and began a quest to rule the world. In approximately twelve years, Paul traveled over much of the Mediterranean world and saw the gospel of Christ penetrate new lands.

Effective people often describe a deep conviction that God has called them to a special task. Like the servant of the Lord, who declared that he was "called . . . from my birth," they experience an early sense of God's call and purpose.

Are you living with a sense of God's direction and purpose? Are you his servant?
          —J. A. M.

WHAT DO YOU THINK?

The lesson writer has noted that the identity of the servant is on some levels "national Israel," on some levels "the Messiah," plus also some valid application to those of us who continue Christ's ministry today as the church. What are we doing as servants to take the gospel to the distant "islands" and "distant nations"? What more can we do?

WHAT DO YOU THINK?

The church continues the battle suggested by the weapons imagery in verse 2, fighting against the forces of evil. Where in our community do we especially see this battle being waged? What can we do—individually or together—to participate in this battle?

B. HIS PREPARATION (v. 2)

2. He has made my mouth like a sharpened sword,
  in the shadow of his hand he hid me;
he made me into a polished arrow
  and concealed me in his quiver.

The servant realizes that God has prepared him with a powerful message—a message that pierces *like a sharpened sword.* Isaiah 11:4 portrays the Messiah as One who will "strike the earth with the rod of his *mouth."* Elsewhere the Bible paints a picture of the Word of God as a sword, penetrating and powerful (Ephesians 6:17; Hebrews 4:12; Revelation 1:16; 2:12, 16). In the case of the servant, God has prepared him as any soldier in an ancient army would prepare his spear for battle. The servant knows that he is *a polished arrow* in the hand of the Lord. He stands ready in his Master's *quiver* for the spiritual warfare in which he will take part. Today, Christians have also been equipped with the powerful truth of God. This truth is the weapon that Paul, in his description of the Christian's armor, called "the sword of the Spirit, which is the word of God" (Ephesians 6:17).

In addition, the servant is aware of God's protection over him as he carries out his ministry. The Lord hides him *in the shadow of his hand* as if to protect him from the blazing sun of tribulation. In this way, the servant can entrust himself to the will of the Lord and never fear. Hostility often rises against today's servants of the Lord who seek to bear witness of their faith. Our society continues to look for ways to ridicule the values that Christians hold dear. But believers need not fear. The God who placed the servant in the shadow of his hand will also place soldiers of the cross under his protection and care. When Jesus commissioned his apostles to go and make disciples of all nations, he provided this assurance: "And surely I am with you always, to the very end of the age" (Matthew 28:20).

C. HIS IDENTITY (v. 3)

3. He said to me, "You are my servant,
  Israel, in whom I will display my splendor."

Here it would seem that, since the *servant* is addressed as *Israel,* the term must represent the nation of Israel. However, *Israel* designated an individual (formerly called Jacob; Genesis 32:28) before it designated a nation. The passage thus far has focused on an individual, so it seems unwise to abandon that identity too easily. Here is a good illustration of the dynamic described earlier, where the identity of the servant must be understood at more than one level. The servant's work is to bring the Lord's salvation "to the ends of the earth" (v. 6; cf. Isaiah 66:19). That applies to Israel in its role of ushering in the Messiah. It also applies to the church. As servants of the Servant, may we continue to carry out that grand mission!

II. THE SERVANT'S RESPONSE (ISAIAH 49:4)

A. FRUSTRATION (v. 4a)

4a. But I said, "I have labored to no purpose;
  I have spent my strength in vain and for nothing.

How difficult is it to speak God's truth when people close their minds to it? The servant knows the frustration of holding out to people the word of truth—and seeing no results except rejection. The phrases *in vain* and *for nothing* underscore this disappointment. Consider how Jesus wept as he agonized over Jerusalem's rejection of its only hope of deliverance (Luke 19:41-44).

The servant's frustration stands in sharp contrast to his sense of purpose expressed in verses 1-3. The servant senses God's calling, but also knows firsthand the resistance of people to the truth. Such is the frequent experience of the servant

WHAT DO YOU THINK?

The servant said he had "labored to no purpose." Have you ever felt that way about your efforts for the Lord? Why? What encouragement can you offer to one who feels similarly frustrated?

of Christ who understands the call that he or she has answered, yet experiences the heartaches that trying to witness for Christ in a sinful world produce. Sometimes we may be at fault; perhaps we fail to speak the truth in love. Keep in mind, however, that we are speaking a message that asks people to surrender themselves to the Lord—and that message may not always be welcomed. In many cases the opposition may not be aimed at us as much as at the truth we proclaim.

B. ASSURANCE (v. 4b)

4b. "Yet what is due me is in the LORD's hand,
    and my reward is with my God."

During periods of discouragement in the Lord's work, we do well to remember that even the apostles of Christ experienced frustrations in holding forth the light of Jesus. Often they were driven out of cities because of their message (see Acts 13:50, 51; 14:5, 6; 17:13, 14). Our confidence should remain in the One who calls us. He will see to it that our testimony for him will not go forth in vain.

LIFE ON PURPOSE

The Servant of the Lord was frustrated, but he remained faithful. He was uncertain of his fruitfulness, but very sure of his reward, because he served God's purpose.

In his book *The Death of Ivan Ilych* (Ill-itch) Leo Tolstoy describes the anguish of a man who discovers on his deathbed that he has wasted his life. Ilych had always done the right things. He took the right job, married the right woman, and had the proper number of children. But he lived without passion, conviction, love, or purpose.

Dying, Ilych realizes that he has never known real happiness. He has been so busy doing what was expected—living only in the survival mode—that he never did the things he truly wanted to do, the purpose-driven things that he believed he was meant to do. It occurs to him that the entire arrangement of his life, of his family, and of all his social and professional interests has been false. He has lived for the wrong reason. He tries to defend himself and suddenly finds that there is nothing to defend. He comes to a bitter end.

Frustration is common in life, but no one has to die like Ivan Ilych. The servant of the Lord lived free from regret because he lived his life on purpose. Are you? Determine that, even when you are frustrated, you will be faithful to the Lord.   —J. A. M.

III. THE SERVANT'S MISSION (ISAIAH 49:5, 6)

At the moment when the Servant of the Lord needed a word of encouragement, he was reminded of the glorious task to which he had been called.

A. TO ISRAEL (v. 5)

5. And now the LORD says—
    he who formed me in the womb to be his servant
to bring Jacob back to him
    and gather Israel to himself,
for I am honored in the eyes of the Lord,
    and my God has been my strength—

The precise mission of the *servant* is described in this verse and the next one. Part of the servant's task is *to bring Jacob back to him*. The name *Jacob* here represents the nation of Israel. As noted in the Lesson Background, some portions of the Servant Songs appear to describe the return from Babylonian captivity, and this is one of them.

The context, however, points to something far more noteworthy. It is common in Old Testament prophecy to describe blessings of the messianic age by using Old Testament people, places, or events. The New Testament helps us to see

WHAT DO YOU THINK?

Part of the servant's task was the spiritual restoration of Israel. What can we do to minister to members of our church who are in need of spiritual restoration?

This poster illustrates the truth of today's Key Verse: Jesus is the light for "salvation to the ends of the earth."

WHAT DO YOU THINK?

References to the "distant nations" (v. 1) and "ends of the earth" (v. 6) remind us that we, too, have a Commission to reach the whole world with the gospel. How well are we communicating the imperative of this Commission to the next generation? How can we impress on young people the need to pursue evangelism aggressively?

PRAYER

Father, keep my light burning brightly so that the path to salvation may be seen through me. May people find Jesus, the Light of the world, through my testimony. In Jesus' name. Amen.

THOUGHT TO REMEMBER

Jesus is the Light of the world; I must be a reflection of his light.

these fulfillments. For example, the resurrection of Jesus is described as fulfilling a promise concerning the "sure blessings promised to David" (Acts 13:34; Isaiah 55:3). Including Gentiles in the church is said to fulfill a prophecy that the fallen tabernacle of David would be restored (Acts 15:14-17; Amos 9:11, 12). Romans 11:25, 26 links turning "godlessness away from Jacob" with a covenant "when I take away their sins." Thus the phrase *bring Jacob back to him* can be taken to refer to the proclamation of the gospel "first for the Jew" (Romans 1:16).

B. TO THE GENTILES (v. 6)

6. . . . he says:

> "It is too small a thing for you to be my servant
> to restore the tribes of Jacob
> and bring back those of Israel I have kept.
> I will also make you a light for the Gentiles,
> that you may bring my salvation to the ends of the earth."

While the task described in verse 5 would seem significant enough, now the servant is told that *it is too small a thing* for him to be called *to restore the tribes of Jacob, and bring back those of Israel I have kept.* The Lord has more than that in mind; the servant's mission will extend beyond the chosen nation, reaching *the Gentiles* and extending *to the ends of the earth.* This verse should call to mind the commission of Jesus in Acts 1:8, plus the fact that his gospel "is the power of God for the salvation of everyone who believes: first for the Jew, then for the Gentile" (Romans 1:16).

The New Testament alludes to the final part of Isaiah 49:6 at least twice. The first time occurs when Joseph and Mary take Jesus to the temple to fulfill the requirements of the Law of Moses. There they were approached by godly Simeon, who took the child in his arms and spoke of him as "a light for revelation to the Gentiles" (Luke 2:32). This was the same child whose birth was announced by angels: "I bring you good news of great joy that will be for all the people" (Luke 2:10).

The second incident is recorded in Acts 13. Part of this passage relates how Paul and Barnabas encountered opposition from the Jews when they tried to preach the gospel in Antioch of Pisidia. Paul and Barnabas responded by turning their focus to the Gentiles. They supported their actions by quoting the words of our text: "I have made you a light for the Gentiles, that you may bring salvation to the ends of the earth" (Acts 13:47).

The gospel of Jesus Christ is still intended to go worldwide. It is still the church's mission to see that that happens. After all, Jesus is "the light of the world" (John 8:12)—and so are his people (Matthew 5:14).

CONCLUSION

In responding to a Gentile woman, the Servant of the Lord (Jesus) declared that he was initially "sent only to the lost sheep of Israel" (Matthew 15:24). But the impact of his ministry ultimately included many "other sheep . . . not of this sheep pen" (John 10:16). He died for the sins of the entire world so that all nations may turn from darkness to light.

Today, Christians are the "light-bearers" who have answered the call of the gospel and whose task it is to "declare the praises of him who called you out of darkness into his wonderful light" (1 Peter 2:9). Like the servant of the Lord, we must give all of our strength to our task. Yes, there will be enemies and hardships as we labor, but these must not be allowed to stand in the way of the Lord's work. Even as the servant took comfort in the encouragement and the protection provided by the Lord, so must we. We must continue to labor faithfully until the servant of the Lord returns.

Discovery Learning

This page contains an alternate lesson plan emphasizing learning activities. Classes desiring such student involvement will find these suggestions helpful. The next page is a reproducible activity page to further enhance discovery learning.

LEARNING GOALS

After this lesson each student will be able to:

1. Summarize the call of God's "Servant" and the scope of his mission.

2. Tell how Jesus fulfilled Isaiah's prophecy of the Servant and how the church does so today.

3. Suggest specific ways to follow the Lord's Servant in loving service today.

INTO THE LESSON

Give groups of four or five people a piece of poster board and a marker. Ask them to draw a line down the middle of the board, creating two columns. At the top of column one they should write "Darkness/Evil." At the top of column two write "Light/Good."

Ask the teams to quickly list every word, phrase, or illustration often used to equate good with light or darkness with evil. They may cite Scriptures, movie lines, movie sets, or other sources. For example, which character in old movies was likely to have the dark, unshaved look? Give them only about three or four minutes to list these and tape the poster board to the wall.

Make the transition to Bible study by telling them the use of light and darkness as imagery for "good vs. evil" is as old as Scripture and is the core of today's lesson. In today's study we can sense frustration and find help in being the light God wants us to be in this world.

INTO THE WORD

Deliver a brief lecture on the background of today's text. Be sure to focus on the meaning of the word *servant* and the mission to bring light to the world. Then distribute a handout that has been divided into two columns. Put this list of questions in the first column, using the heading "Plunging Into God's Word." Questions for column 2 will be listed later. (These questions are also included in the student book, *NIV Bible Student.*) Ask the groups formed earlier to discuss these questions together.

1. What do you think is the significance of the imagery of the words *islands* and *distant nations* in verse 1? What is God emphasizing in this verse?

2. Explain the following word images in verse 2: *sharpened sword, the shadow of his hand, a polished arrow,* and *quiver.* What is the main thought in this verse?

3. Verses 3 and 4 are key to understanding this prophecy. Why would Israel express the frustration

found in verse 4a? Give illustrations from Israel's history that the people could use to justify their frustration.

4. Write a three- or four-word phrase that describes the attitude of the "servant" in verse 4b, or write a slogan that summarizes verse 4.

Give the groups about ten minutes to complete this task. After hearing a few of their answers, give another brief lecture about the servant's expanded mission. Focus on the mission to become a light to the Gentiles. Use the lesson commentary and other study sources to help you prepare this lecture.

INTO LIFE

Have the groups proceed to column 2, which has the heading, "Becoming God's Light," and these questions:

1. Isaiah 49:6; Matthew 28:19, 20; and Luke 2:10, 14 have a common thread. In these passages, what message does God make clear about the scope of his offer of salvation? (*It is to all people.*)

2: Today's believer may want to echo the frustration of Isaiah 49:4a as he or she tries to be the light God desires. Why? What frustrations or challenges to becoming God's light would you put on a list?

3. How does verse 4b teach trust and perseverance?

To conclude the lesson, display another poster you have prepared before class. (This exercise is also in the student's book.) The poster board will have three columns. Each column will be separated by a solid line. The large heading of the poster board should read "Darkness vs. Light." Column 1 will have the heading "Men Loved Darkness" (John 3:19). Column 2 will have the heading "Walk in the Light" (1 John 1:7). Column 3 will read "Let Your Light Shine Before Men" (Matthew 5:16). Tell the class that sometimes it is helpful, as we struggle to be God's light in a dark world, to revisit basic concepts in God's Word. Ask the students to share what these concepts mean and give illustrations of each. Emphasize, in column three, practical ways to be God's light in a world that seems to love darkness. List the students' answers and illustrations on the poster board.

Option: Use the reproducible activity page that follows to direct your learners to application of this passage. Use the handout in groups or individually.

Ask someone in the group to pray on behalf of the group, seeking God's help in being a faithful and consistent reflection of his light.

Send the Light

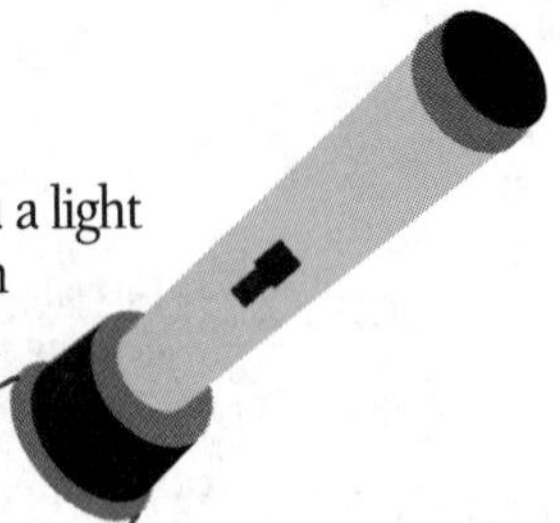

God makes his mission very clear to the Jews as he says, "I will also make you a light for the Gentiles, that you may bring my salvation to the ends of the earth" (Isaiah 49:6). Read the following Scriptures and jot a note about what each teaches today's believer about becoming a "light."

John 12:35, 36

Romans 13:12-14

1 Corinthians 4:4, 5

Ephesians 5:8-14

1 Thessalonians 5:4, 5

1 Peter 2:9

1 John 1:5-7

1 John 2:9-11

Killing Light Killers!

As we try to share the "light," we may sometimes feel like the servant who said, "I have labored in vain." Read the following Scriptures. Then, using Peter as a model, find encouragement for your own testimony as you note the discouraging circumstance and how Peter handled it. Write the details on the chart below.

SCRIPTURE	CIRCUMSTANCE/FRUSTRATION	PETER'S RESPONSE
Acts 4:1-22		
Acts 5:1-11		
Acts 7:54–8:3		
Acts 12:1-17		

Spend a few moments reflecting on your performance as God's "light." Be thankful for your opportunities and celebrate those moments when you have reflected the Christ who is in you. Jot one of those circumstances below as you also determine to be an even more faithful "light of the world."

GOD'S SERVANT BRINGS PEACE

LESSON 2

WHY TEACH THIS LESSON?

C. S. Lewis's *The Screwtape Letters* is a fascinating work of fiction that describes the efforts of an experienced demon named Screwtape to instruct a younger demon named Wormwood in the fine art of tempting humans to sin. In his first letter, the wiser Screwtape counsels his young charge on the importance of focusing a human's attention on "the stream of immediate sense experiences" and away from "universal issues." In this way, the human will be enslaved to "the pressure of the ordinary." Today's lesson is about reversing this procedure. The people of Isaiah's time were indeed enslaved—as many are today—by what they could experience through their own senses; they trusted earthly things rather than God. This "enslavement of outlook" eventually led to an "enslavement of body" in the form of the Babylonian Exile.

In trying to redirect his readers' attention, Isaiah reminds us that a radically different world order is on its way. And if the people can only lift their thoughts to anticipate this coming new creation, they will change their motives and behavior *now* to prepare to be admitted to it. This lesson is for those today who are caught up—occasionally or usually—in "the pressure of the ordinary" and need such a lift. In other words, this lesson is for everyone!

INTRODUCTION

A. NAMED FOR PEACE

Bob Shannon tells of a member of a church in Queensland, Australia, whose name is Pax Young. It is not unusual to encounter the surname Young, but one wonders how he got his unusual first name. The answer is that he was born on the very day World War I ended. The midwife who took care of his delivery asked for the privilege of naming him. She named him *Pax*, which means "peace."

While the name Pax may seem uncommon, a common name in Slavic lands is *Vladimir*. Like *Pax*, it means "peace." And sometimes one hears the name *Olivera*, which also means "peace." But there was only person whose very *life* meant "peace." That was Jesus Christ, the Prince of peace. Only he can give "the peace . . . which transcends all understanding" (Philippians 4:7).

The prophet Isaiah—during a period of great uncertainty for God's people—foretold a coming era of peace. God grants that peace to all who trust in and obey Jesus. By knowing him as Savior and Lord, his followers can come to know the peace of being made right with God—a peace that can sustain them during the times of uncertainty in their lives.

B. LESSON BACKGROUND

The first half of the eighth century B.C. appeared quite promising for both Israel (the northern kingdom) and Judah (the southern kingdom). During the reign of

---

DEVOTIONAL READING:
ISAIAH 12

BACKGROUND SCRIPTURE:
ISAIAH 11

PRINTED TEXT:
ISAIAH 11:1-9

LESSON AIMS

After participating in this lesson, each student will be able to:

1. Describe the characteristics of the "Branch" and the unique way his ministry is pictured.

2. List some current conditions that challenge the peace and security envisioned by Isaiah.

3. Identify and pray for a person who needs Christ's peace.

KEY VERSE

The wolf will live with the lamb, the leopard will lie down with the goat, the calf and the lion and the yearling together; and a little child will lead them.
—Isaiah 11:6

Jeroboam II in Israel (793–753 B.C.), a prosperity enveloped the country that reminded people of Israel's glory days. In Judah the same economic boom was felt during the reign of Uzziah (792–740 B.C.). But the outward prosperity of these times masked an inner sinfulness that eighth-century prophets such as Isaiah, Amos, and Hosea could not overlook.

After Uzziah's death, Judah's condition began to deteriorate swiftly. While Uzziah's son Jotham "did what was right in the eyes of the Lord" (2 Kings 15:34), Jotham's son Ahaz was an extremely wicked king who engaged in many practices forbidden by God (2 Kings 16:2-4).

As noted last week, it was during Ahaz's reign that Israel and Syria joined forces to counter the rising aggression of Tiglath-pileser III of Assyria. When Judah refused to join this coalition, Syria and Israel attacked Judah in an effort to force Ahaz to join the alliance. Ahaz responded to this pressure by calling on Tiglath-pileser for assistance, in spite of Isaiah's counsel to trust in the Lord instead (Isaiah 7:3-9). The result was the Assyrian conquest of Damascus in 732 B.C. and of Samaria (capital of Israel) in 722.

It was during this crisis in Judah that Isaiah uttered some of his most significant messianic prophecies (Isaiah 7:14; 9:1-7; and today's text in 11:1-9). Following the majestic description of a special child in 9:1-7, the prophet returned to the crisis facing God's people. It is important to note that his prophecy of a "Branch" (11:1) is the climax to a series of messages using trees (or similar plants) to symbolize nations. For example, in 9:18 we read of his words concerning Israel's impending judgment: "Surely wickedness burns like a fire; it consumes briers and thorns, and it sets the forest thickets ablaze, so that it rolls upward in a column of smoke."

Isaiah 10 then focuses on Assyria as the instrument that God will use to administer his judgment. Assyria itself, however, is filled with "the willful pride of his heart and the haughty look in his eyes" (Isaiah 10:12), and God will judge this nation, too. Note the imagery used in verse 19 to describe the outcome of this judgment: "And the remaining trees of his forests will be so few that a child could write them down."

Chapter 10 concludes with a description of the Assyrian army's march toward Jerusalem (vv. 28-34). The Assyrians reach Jerusalem (v. 32) but go no farther because the Lord intervenes, cutting down the proud Assyrian tree. ("Lebanon" in verse 34 is probably a reference to Assyria; see Ezekiel 31:3.) However, whereas the Assyrian tree is completely cut down, the Israelite tree, though reduced to a stump, is still alive. It indicates that God is not yet finished with his people.

I. THE PROMISED BRANCH (ISAIAH 11:1, 2)

In Isaiah 10:13, the Assyrian king is pictured as arrogantly reflecting on his conquests (cf. Daniel 4:29-30). Isaiah now declares that another (and better) king is coming who will reign in a manner directly opposite that of the Assyrian.

A. HIS HUMBLE ORIGINS (v. 1)

1. A shoot will come up from the stump of Jesse;
    from his roots a Branch will bear fruit.

After Assyria overran Israel (and later Judah), the once great nation ruled by David and Solomon was reduced to a *stump*. Even so, *a shoot* would *come up* from that stump of David's father *Jesse*. The word *Branch* (the Hebrew term is *netzer*) is similar in meaning to *shoot*. This Hebrew term is most likely the basis for Matthew's reference to the fulfillment of this passage in Jesus: "He will be called a Nazarene" (Matthew 2:23).

How to Say It

Ahaz. AY-haz.
Assyrians. Uh-SEAR-ee-uns.
Damascus. Duh-MASS-cus.
Hosea. Ho-ZAY-uh.
Isaiah. Eye-ZAY-uh.
Jeroboam. Jair-uh-BO-um.
Jotham. JO-thum.
messianic. mess-ee-AN-ick.
Nazarene. NAZ-uh-reen.
netzer (Hebrew). NET-zer.
Samaria. Suh-MARE-ee-uh.
Tiglath-pileser. TIG-lath-pih-
   LEE-zer.
Uzziah. Uh-ZYE-uh.

Note that the state of the nation is so pitiful that it is not even referred to by the name of its greatest king (David) but by the name of his father. This calls attention to the humble origins of the Branch, as well as to the fact that another "David" would be raised up by the Lord to be a righteous ruler and to provide the blessings described in the remainder of our text (cf. Ezekiel 34:23, 24).

B. HIS GODLY CHARACTER (v. 2)

2. *The Spirit of the LORD will rest on him—*
     the Spirit of wisdom and of understanding,
     the Spirit of counsel and of power,
     the Spirit of knowledge and of the fear of the LORD.

Different leaders throughout the Old Testament (such as the judges) were given God's Spirit for specific tasks. However, the Spirit would *rest on* the Branch. This indicates the continual guidance that the Spirit would provide (cf. John 3:34).

The Spirit's provisions are then listed in terms of the qualities necessary for godly leadership. Some students have found significance in the fact that there are six qualities listed, so that adding the gift of the Spirit himself yields seven. If they are right, the symbolism implies that the Branch will be perfectly endowed by the Spirit with everything needed to carry out his mission (cf. Revelation 5:6).

II. HIS REIGN OF RIGHTEOUSNESS (ISAIAH 11:3-5)

A. SPIRITUAL PRIORITIES (v. 3)

3. *. . . and he will delight in the fear of the LORD.*
   He will not judge by what he sees with his eyes,
     or decide by what he hears with his ears.

The reign of this coming ruler will demonstrate all of the best in what a ruler should be. He will possess ideal royal insight to *judge*—that is, to administer justice based on a higher standard than the earthly concerns that occupy most kings. Because *he will delight in the fear of the Lord*, he will judge with correct motives. His judgment will not be limited to a surface judgment based only on *what he sees with his eyes* or *what he hears with his ears*. Recall that Jesus "did not need man's testimony about man, for he knew what was in a man" (John 2:25).

This description does not mean that true judgment ignores evidence presented to the senses. Rather, the point is that the coming Ruler will place a much higher priority on God's law than he will on human standards that might influence his judgments in a negative manner.

TRUE COLORS

As he was leaving the Disney World theme park, a man noticed an elderly couple in some distress. The wife was in a wheelchair, and the man pushing it looked exhausted. All around them, people were being rude and inconsiderate. The large crowds heading for the exit had forced them to the side, and no one would allow this couple to move through.

As the man noticed the couple's plight, he also happened to notice that the older man was wearing a Cincinnati Reds baseball cap. When he reached the exit, he played the part of a friendly traffic cop and helped the weary couple pass through the exit.

Outside, the couple expressed their thanks, and then the man asked, "Why did you do that? Why did you help?"

Their new friend replied, "For two reasons. First, because it was the right thing to do. And second, I noticed your Reds cap. I'm a Reds fan, too—and we Reds fans have to stick together!"

"Well, I have to be honest," said the man. "I'm not a Reds fans; I'm a New York Mets fan. I wore this hat only because it matches my shirt." The helpful man was

WHAT DO YOU THINK?

The "Branch" from Jesse's "roots" is certainly the Messiah—Jesus Christ. How are the traits ascribed to him important for leaders in his church?

WHAT DO YOU THINK?

Isaiah said the Messiah would judge by standards other than what he saw or heard. How can we encourage believers today to value the things that cannot be seen with the eye or heard with the ear, but instead are spiritually discerned?

still glad to have assisted the couple, but he realized anew how easy it is to be deceived. Many people don't always show their true colors. You can't always judge them by their appearance.

Isaiah's coming King would not be deceived by pretense. He himself always displays his true colors, and his judgments are always true and just; for he sees and judges the heart. Is your heart right before him? —J. A. M.

B. IMPARTIAL JUSTICE (vv. 4, 5)

4. But with righteousness he will judge the needy,
    with justice he will give decisions for the poor of the earth.
He will strike the earth with the rod of his mouth;
    with the breath of his lips he will slay the wicked.

Many rulers in Isaiah's day did not treat the *needy* and the *poor* in the way described here. Previously Isaiah had voiced disapproval of the national leaders, telling them to "seek justice, encourage the oppressed. Defend the cause of the fatherless, plead the case of the widow" (Isaiah 1:17). Justice was often corrupted, sold to the highest bidder. Under such conditions, it is usually the needy and the poor who suffer most.

In refreshing contrast, the coming messianic ruler will not permit the corruption of God's law. The wicked who oppress the needy and the poor will be smitten with *the rod of his mouth*. Earlier (Isaiah 10:5, 24) the prophet had described Assyria as the rod of the Lord's anger, used by him to punish Israel. But when the messianic ruler comes, he himself will possess this rod. He will administer true justice; all the *wicked* will be slain by *the breath of his lips*. On the Day of Judgment, the words of Jesus will seal the eternal destiny of all nations (Matthew 25:31-46).

The words *needy* and *poor* call to mind Jesus' teachings in The Beatitudes about the poor in spirit and the meek (Matthew 5:3, 5). He has taught us that we are to value inner qualities that are pleasing to God instead of focusing on the outward, material concerns that occupy so many individuals' time and attention. Isaiah's words can also be taken as a challenge to Christians to treat others with impartiality (in other words, as Jesus would treat them).

5. Righteousness will be his belt
    and faithfulness the sash around his waist.

The words *belt* and *sash* are understood by considering the style of clothing worn in the ancient world. A man who was about to engage in an activity that required physical exertion and freedom of movement would gather up his loose outer garment and tuck it under his belt so his garment would not hinder him (see also 1 Kings 18:46 and 2 Kings 4:29). First Peter 1:13 applies this imagery to one's spiritual preparation, although the idea is clearer in the *King James Version* which renders part of that verse as "gird up the loins of your mind."

The words of Isaiah highlight the fact that the Branch will be prepared for action with regard to his pronouncements of judgment. But his actions will not be motivated by a quest for political advantage or personal gain. Instead, he will act according to *righteousness* and *faithfulness*.

It is important to notice the parallels between the messianic rule outlined here and those occasions in Jesus' earthly ministry when his power served the purpose of healing the brokenhearted, encouraging the weak, and lifting up the oppressed. Jesus' ministry was characterized by the sense of impartiality described here.

III. HIS KINGDOM OF PEACE (ISAIAH 11:6-9)

The reign of the righteous messianic ruler will usher in a period of peace that is described in the highly poetic lines in the remainder of our printed text.

WHAT DO YOU THINK?

Jesus rendered the kind of impartial justice that Isaiah predicted of the Messiah. He freely associated with sinners and outcasts because they desperately needed to find salvation (Luke 5:30-32). At the same time, Jesus openly criticized the powerful scribes and Pharisees for their self-righteous hypocrisy (Luke 11). How can the church demonstrate that same kind of impartiality?

WHAT DO YOU THINK?

In verse 5 the qualities of righteousness and faithfulness are parallel. How are these two concepts similar? How can the pursuit of one help in attaining the other?

A. WILD CREATURES TAMED (vv. 6-8)

6. *The wolf will live with the lamb,*
    the leopard will lie down with the goat,
  the calf and the lion and the yearling together;
    and a little child will lead them.

In the reign of the Branch ferocious animals that are normally natural enemies will live at peace with one another—even with animals that they normally hunt as prey. The *wolf* will no longer harm the *lamb*. The *leopard* will not hunt the *goat* for food. The *lion* will not disturb the young *calf*. Peace and safety will characterize this era—so much so that a *little child* shall *lead* these former rivals.

7. *The cow will feed with the bear,*
    their young will lie down together,
    and the lion will eat straw like the ox.

To emphasize further the safety in this era, Isaiah describes how fierce animals will be tamed and will behave like domesticated cattle. Rather than attack and kill to satisfy their hunger for meat, they will content themselves with vegetation—straw. The entire animal kingdom will become an ideal world of security.

8. *The infant will play near the hole of the cobra,*
    and the young child put his hand into the viper's nest.

Both an *infant* and a toddler (a *young child*) are at an especially innocent and vulnerable stage of life. They do not know when they are in dangerous situations, for they do not have the experiences that teach older children what they should avoid. Normally a parent would panic to see his or her small child playing near the *hole* of a deadly snake. But the new era of peace will be blessed with such harmony that even defenseless children will face no threat to their safety.

B. WORLDWIDE KNOWLEDGE OF GOD (v. 9)

9. *They will neither harm nor destroy*
    on all my holy mountain,
  for the earth will be full of the knowledge of the LORD
    as the waters cover the sea.

This verse summarizes life in this new era of peace. In the prophet's own time this seemed an impossible dream. There appeared to be no peace in sight—either from a national standpoint (because of the Assyrian menace) or from a spiritual standpoint (because of the nation's sinfulness, encouraged by King Ahaz).

The Messiah, however, will usher in a kingdom of peace that will fulfill the longings of all who have placed their hope in the Lord. His kingdom will take on a character like none the world has ever seen. The result of his righteous reign will be the spread of *the knowledge of the Lord* throughout the *earth*.

Some Christians take Isaiah's language in verses 6-9 literally. They believe that the effects of sin on the animal kingdom will be erased when Jesus returns, and that animals will behave in just the way described by Isaiah. Such an interpretation is possible, in light of Paul's description of how "the creation waits in eager expectation for the sons of God to be revealed" and how "the creation itself will be liberated from its bondage to decay" (Romans 8:19, 21).

Other Bible students understand Isaiah's language to be symbolic, just as the "stump," "shoot," and "Branch" in verse 1 must be symbolic. They see Isaiah using vivid, poetic language to portray the glory of the messianic kingdom, drawing on scenes from the natural world. Very similar is the prophet's earlier description of the peace that will come when "the mountain of the Lord's temple" is established as a place where all nations would go to hear the word of the Lord (Isaiah 2:2, 3). As a result of that event ,the nations will "beat their swords into plowshares, and

This poster beautifully illus-trates the Key Verse for today's lesson, Isaiah 11:6.

WHAT DO YOU THINK?

Isaiah 11:6-9 gives a mar-velous description of the Mes-siah's reign. How do we see that fulfilled even now in the church?

DAILY BIBLE READINGS

Monday, Dec. 3—*God's Children Have Rebelled (Isaiah 1:1-9)*

Tuesday, Dec. 4—*Do Justice, Not Empty Rituals (Isaiah 1:10-20)*

Wednesday, Dec. 5—*An Age of Peace (Isaiah 2:1-5)*

Thursday, Dec. 6—*Give Thanks to the Lord (Isaiah 12:1-6)*

Friday, Dec. 7—*Compassion for God's People (Isaiah 14:1-7)*

Saturday, Dec. 8—*Hope for the Remnant (Isaiah 11:1-9)*

Sunday, Dec. 9—*The Remnant's Second Chance (Isaiah 11:10-16)*

PRAYER

We anticipate with joy, O Lord, the return of Jesus and the establishment of his heavenly kingdom. While we wait for that day, we pledge our faithfulness to the King of kings. Through him we pray, amen.

THOUGHT TO REMEMBER

"Therefore, since we have been justified through faith, we have peace with God through our Lord Jesus Christ" (Romans 5:1).

their spears into pruning hooks" (Isaiah 2:4). These figures of speech are believed to paint a vivid picture of people at peace with one another because of the righteous reign of the Lord. The fact that this is pictured as occurring "in the last days" (v. 2) is considered as pointing to the messianic age as the time when Isaiah's prophecy reaches fulfillment. Christians always have lived in the "last days" (Hebrews 1:1, 2), during which those who know the Lord are to make him known to the world.

Whatever their position may be on this matter, all believers anticipate the consummation of Christ's kingdom, which will take place when he returns. They share the hope of New Testament believers regarding that glorious day. They pray, as did the apostle John, "Come, Lord Jesus" (Revelation 22:20).

In addition, all believers can enjoy the peace of God in this present world. This is the "peace . . . which transcends all understanding" (Philippians 4:7). Christians today can be sustained by that same peace, no matter where they live or what their circumstances may be. (Paul wrote the verse cited above from prison!)

A BABY BRINGS PEACE

One of the most intriguing individuals who fought during the Civil War was Confederate General George E. Pickett. He was a flamboyant character, romantic and brave. He led the famous "Pickett's Charge" at the Battle of Gettysburg.

At Gettysburg, Pickett's army was drawn up for battle, prepared to face Ulysses S. Grant, when Pickett's first baby, a son, was born. All along the two-mile Confederate front, cheers were shouted and bonfires were built in celebration of the event. It was a beautiful sight, as the bonfires illuminated the thick darkness.

General Grant, curious to know what was happening in the Confederate Army, sent out scouts to investigate. They reported that General Pickett had a son, his first child. General Grant replied, "Have we any kindling wood on this side of the line? Why don't we strike up a row of lights?"

Soon bonfires were blazing all along the Union line. Not a shot was fired that night; not a gun was aimed at an enemy. Bright lights and peace reigned because a baby was born. A few days later, a baby's silver service, engraved to George E. Pickett, Jr., was sent through the lines—a gift from General Grant and two other Union generals. A baby's birth produced peace, if only temporarily.

Such is the impact, and even more, of the Christmas baby—Jesus, the Prince of peace. His birth resulted in the announcement of "glory to God in the highest, and on earth *peace*" (Luke 2:14). And his peace is eternal!   —J. A. M.

CONCLUSION

To Isaiah's audience in the eighth century before Christ, the promise of peace may have given hope for a time when Assyria would be removed from power and would no longer be the enemy of God's people. In time, that did happen. However, when the "big picture" of the entire Bible is considered, Isaiah's words had a far more sweeping impact. They predicted a time when what was lost in the Garden of Eden through sin would be regained through the reconciliation accomplished by the sinless One, Jesus.

The peace described by Isaiah can never be destroyed by anything in this world, because this peace is not "as the world gives" (John 14:27). Isaiah's description of peace will reach its ultimate fulfillment when we are welcomed into a "new heaven and a new earth" where there will be "no more death or mourning or crying or pain, for the old order of things has passed away" (Revelation 21:1, 4).

That new creation begins the moment a person's life is changed through the gospel of Jesus Christ. "If anyone is in Christ, he is a new creation; the old has gone, the new has come!" (2 Corinthians 5:17). Thus in one sense Isaiah's words are fulfilled when we become Christians. In another sense, the best is yet to come!

Discovery Learning

This page contains an alternate lesson plan emphasizing learning activities. Classes desiring such student involvement will find these suggestions helpful. The next page is a reproducible activity page to further enhance discovery learning.

LEARNING GOALS

After this lesson each student will be able to:

1. Describe the characteristics of the "Branch" and the unique way in which his ministry is pictured.

2. List some current conditions that challenge the peace and security envisioned by Isaiah.

3. Identify and pray for a person who needs Christ's peace.

INTO THE LESSON

Write on a chalkboard or poster, "Peace is not usually so easily made as we have done it. Not in a life nor in a nation." Ask students whether they agree or disagree with this statement, and ask them to tell why.

Ask, "What are some different ways people interpret and apply the word *peace?*" List the responses on a transparency or chalkboard. *Ideas may include: an absence of war, relationship situations, justice, relationships with God.* State, "People have many different ideas about what *peace* means. Today we will see how Isaiah describes peace in a most beautiful manner."

Option: Use the first activity on the reproducible page that follows to introduce today's theme.

INTO THE WORD

Use the lesson commentary to prepare and deliver a brief lecture about the significance of the words *shoot, stump of Jesse,* and *Branch.*

Assign small groups one of the following three assignments. The groups will answer the basic questions of "Who? What? and Why?" Give each group photocopies of the appropriate lesson commentary pages, the following assignments, a piece of poster board, and a marker.

Group 1. Read Isaiah 11:1-9. Your task is to help the class understand the "Who" of this prophecy. Answer the following questions to share with the class.

1. Who is the subject of this passage, and what does Isaiah mean by saying "the Spirit of the Lord will rest on him"? Second Kings 2:15 may be helpful.

2. List on a poster board the character qualities of the "Branch" as cited in verses 2 and 3a. Locate other Scriptures that support or fulfill this prophecy. The lesson commentary will be helpful.

Group 2. You will help the class see "What" the Branch is to do, his mission. Read Isaiah 11:1-9 and prepare answers to the following questions:

1. What mission of the Branch is emphasized in verses 3 and 4? What is his purpose?

2. Read the commentary on verses 3-5 and be prepared to explain the meaning of "will not judge by what he sees with his eyes" and will not "decide by what he hears with his ears." Explain verses 4 and 5 to the class.

3. If the ultimate goal is peace, verses 6-9, why are the previous verses loaded with harsh, violent words like *strike, slay,* and *judge*? How will these relate to peace?

Group 3. Your task is exploring the "Why" of this prophecy. Read Isaiah 11:1-9 and be ready to help the class know why the Lord was sending the "Branch."

1. Verses 6-9 figuratively portray the peaceable kingdom. List on poster board the words and imagery used.

2. Read the lesson commentary and be ready to explain the significance of the imagery.

3. Do you believe the kingdom of righteousness and peace is present or future? Why? See also Luke 2:14.

Allow each group to report their findings to the class.

INTO LIFE

Use the visual from the beginning of the lesson to remind the class that the word *peace* has many meanings and applications. Ask the groups to apply their understanding of peace to life today.

Group 1: Peace with God. Read Romans 5:1-11 and summarize this peace for the class. Comment on the impact this peace makes on the lives of believers.

Group 2: Peace in Church Leadership. Every church should experience a sense of peace and harmony in itself and its leadership. What are some Christlike qualities we should expect of our leaders? Isaiah 11:2, 3 and 1 Timothy 3:1-7 may be helpful.

Group 3: Peace at Home. Proverbs 17:1 highlights the importance of peace in the home. Discuss and share basic principles that help to keep this peace.

Option: If there is time to do so, expand on this theme by using the second activity on the reproducible page that follows.

Ask class members to identify in their minds a person who needs Christ's peace. Ask them to bow and pray this prayer as you say it: "Father of peace and love,\We thank you that we are no longer your enemies but your children through Jesus Christ.\Help my friend to find the peace of Christ in his or her life.\Through the name of the Prince of Peace we pray. Amen.

Finding Peace

Isaiah drew a wonderful word picture of peace in chapter 11. He also told us the source of this peace: "A shoot will come up from the stump of Jesse" (Isaiah 11:1). Remove the letters of that prophecy—in order—from the letters below. The remaining letters will share a wonderful promise echoed in Romans 5:1.

ASHOWOTEWHILLACOVM

EEUPPFROEMATHCEEST

UWMPOIFTJHEGSOSDE

Write the promise and solution to the puzzle below.

Hymn Study

Through the centuries music has been used to express our hearts and teach our minds. Look up the following hymns and note what they teach us about peace.

PEACE WITH GOD
Hark the Herald Angels Sing (especially stanza 1)

Nothing but the Blood

PERSONAL PEACE
Wonderful Peace

It Is Well

PEACEFUL RELATIONSHIPS
Dear Lord and Father of Mankind

Blest Be the Tie That Binds

A PEACEFUL FUTURE
Sweet By and By

We're Marching to Zion

"Peace I leave with you; my peace I give you."
—Jesus (John 14:27)

GOD'S SERVANT
BRINGS COMFORT

WHY TEACH THIS LESSON?

As Christmas approaches, perhaps you will have an opportunity to hear a live or recorded rendition of Handel's *Messiah*. After the opening instrumental, the very first lyrics that you will hear are also the first words of today's lesson text: "Comfort ye, comfort ye my people" (*King James Version*). What will be your response?

You might find yourself thanking God for the general comfort he has provided his people in the past. Perhaps, however, your prayer of thanks will be more specific as you give thanks for some particular help he has given you in an especially difficult time. Or you might cling to these words for hope, eagerly anticipating his deliverance from some situation you are currently experiencing.

In the same way, your learners will have different reactions to these words today, depending on their own individual life situations. Some will find themselves not feeling much need for "comfort" at the present time; but this lesson is still valuable to them as a reminder of God's faithfulness when those tough times do come, as they surely will. Some, having just come through some problems, will experience a special gratitude to God. Others, perhaps feeling themselves caught right now in some type of struggle or bondage, will desperately need to hear these words to maintain a sense of hope.

Whatever their situation, and whatever is yours, today's lesson will address it in some way with the marvelous message of God's grace.

INTRODUCTION

A. SAFE IN GOD'S ARMS

Catherine Marshall, in her book *The Helper*, tells how the Holy Spirit brought her comfort in a time of emotional turmoil. Her husband, Peter (who served for several years as chaplain of the United States Senate), began to experience heart problems and had to be taken to the hospital. After the ambulance sped him away, she was left at home, feeling helpless and overwhelmed by worry. She describes in detail what followed: "My knees no sooner touched the floor than I experienced God's comfort . . . the feeling of the everlasting arms around me. . . . It was the infinite gentleness of the loving heart of God, more all-pervading than any human being's love could ever be."

All of us face discouragement or heartache at times. During such circumstances it is reassuring to know that we have a God who is both willing and able to reach out to us with everlasting arms of comfort.

The prophet Isaiah ministered at a time when God's people desperately needed a message of comfort. Today's text includes some of the words he used to convey that message. Those words have not lost their power, for the God who spoke them has not lost his.

DEVOTIONAL READING:
ISAIAH 40:25-31
BACKGROUND SCRIPTURE:
ISAIAH 40
PRINTED TEXT:
ISAIAH 40:1-11, 28-31

LESSON AIMS

After participating in this lesson, each student will be able to:

1. Summarize the message of comfort given in Isaiah 40.

2. Explain how this message comforted the Israelites and comforts believers today.

3. Identify someone going through a difficult time and share God's comfort with that person.

KEY VERSE

The grass withers and the flowers fall, but the word of our God stands forever.—Isaiah 40:8

LESSON 3 NOTES

B. LESSON BACKGROUND

In lesson 1 we observed that Isaiah 40–66 has produced much debate among Bible students. Those who believe that Isaiah was predicting the Babylonian captivity and the return home explain the detailed account as an example of a prophecy inspired by the Holy Spirit. Those who reject predictive prophecy have to invent some unknown author for these chapters, one who lived and wrote during (or not long after) the captivity and the return. These students allege that the material was later attached to the book of Isaiah. However, the Lord who is described in these chapters needs no assistance in speaking about things to come. That fact is emphasized several times! (See 41:21-29; 44:7, 8, 24-28; 45:20, 21; 46:8-11; 48:6, 7.)

I. GOD'S WORDS OF COMFORT (ISAIAH 40:1-5)

Isaiah 40 begins with words of comfort addressed to the (future) exiles in Babylon. The message is one of pardon and promise.

A. HIS PARDON OFFERED (vv. 1, 2)

1. Comfort, comfort my people, says your God.

This message begins with God's command to *comfort* his *people*, as Isaiah looks more than 140 years into the future to the eventual end of the Babylonian captivity. The repetition of *comfort* gives added emphasis to the command. Similar double commands are found in later chapters of Isaiah (51:9, 17; 52:1, 11; 57:14; 62:10). Note the personal terms *my people* and *your God*, reflecting the covenant relationship between Israel and the Lord.

2. Speak tenderly to Jerusalem,
and proclaim to her
that her hard service has been completed,
that her sin has been paid for,
that she has received from the Lord's hand
double for all her sins.

The phrase *speak tenderly to Jerusalem* is literally "speak to the heart of Jerusalem." From Isaiah's perspective, Jerusalem's exile and captivity will not even begin for at least a hundred years, yet God gives him a message foreseeing the end of that *hard service*.

God's message is one of pardon: Jerusalem's punishment is sufficient. *Double for all her sins* does not necessarily mean that Jerusalem is to be punished with twice the severity she deserved. Rather, the phrase is likely a hyperbole, a vivid way of saying that Jerusalem's punishment was sufficient.

Consider what is later written of the Suffering Servant, on whom the Lord will lay "the iniquity of us all" (Isaiah 53:6). Christians have the assurance that their *iniquity is pardoned* through what Jesus Christ accomplished at the cross. There is comfort in knowing that, although we have sinned against God and deserve condemnation, our debt has been paid. Although Jerusalem will suffer for her own misdeeds, Jesus took the condemnation that should have been ours.

WHAT DO YOU THINK?

What are some reasons that God's people need comfort today? How does God meet those needs?

TOO MUCH PROBING

James A. Garfield was a remarkable man. He was a lay preacher, a classics professor, the president of Hiram College (located near Cleveland, Ohio), a general in the United States Army, and a congressman. He was so ambidextrous that he could simultaneously write in Greek with one hand and in Latin with the other!

In 1880 Garfield was elected the twentieth president of the United States. After only six months in office, he was shot in the back by a man who was angry that Garfield had not appointed him to a government position.

The president never lost consciousness. Eventually teams of doctors tried to locate the bullet, probing the wound over and over. In desperation they even asked Alexander Graham Bell to see if he could locate the bullet using an electrical device. But his efforts also failed.

Garfield lasted through July and August, but on September 9, 1881, he died. Ironically, the cause of death was not the gunshot wound. The repeated probing, by which the physicians hoped to help the president, caused a fatal blood infection.

There comes a time when too much probing of a wound is not good. That is also true in the spiritual realm. Isaiah announced to God's people that it was time to stop probing the past and move into the tomorrow of God's mercy and grace. "Comfort, comfort my people, . . . her hard service has been completed" was his message.

That message speaks to us today. Let's put away the past and accept the comfort of God's forgiveness.   —J. A. M.

B. HIS WAY PREPARED (vv. 3-5)

3. A voice of one calling:
   "In the desert prepare
      the way for the Lord;
   make straight in the wilderness
      a highway for our God.

Here the first of three voices is heard (see also vv. 6 and 9). The first announces, *prepare the way for the Lord*. The language of this and the next verse reflects a standard practice in the ancient Near East. When a dignitary visited a territory, a messenger preceded his visit by announcing his coming. Necessary preparations were made, often including repairing, or even building, roadways. Especially important in the pagan world was the construction of "processional roads" on which supposed gods were carried to the temple sanctuaries. Many of these roads were constructed with smooth pavement (using flat stones), proper drainage, and curbing.

The Lord's people, however, are not asked to initiate a massive earthmoving project. Their preparations are to be spiritual: the exiles should prepare their hearts, repenting of sin, to clear the way for the Lord's arrival among his people. And unlike pagan idols, he will not need to be carried, but will come under his own power. If anyone is to do the carrying, it will be the Lord (Isaiah 46:3, 4)!

The New Testament links this *voice* with John the Baptist and his efforts to prepare the way for the Messiah (Luke 3:1-6; John 1:23). John declared that repentance was the pathway that prepared for the Messiah's coming (Matthew 3:1, 8).

4. "Every valley shall be raised up,
      every mountain and hill made low;
   the rough ground shall become level,
      the rugged places a plain.

Building the highway on which God would travel was to be no small undertaking! Again, the application to the situation described by Isaiah was spiritual. If God were to lead his people back home and dwell in their midst, they would need to make some changes. John the Baptist preached the same message, offering specific suggestions of how people could demonstrate repentance (Luke 3:10-14).

5. "And the glory of the LORD will be revealed,
      and all mankind together will see it.
         For the mouth of the Lord has spoken."

When all of the preparations were completed, *the glory of the Lord* would be *revealed*. Judah's release from captivity, fulfilling the promise of God, would demonstrate God's ability to keep his word and to overrule earthly powers in doing so. *All mankind together will see it* implies that this will be done openly and without challenge from the enemies of God and his people.

DAILY BIBLE READINGS

Monday, Dec. 10—*Turn to God and Be Saved (Isaiah 45:18-25)*

Tuesday, Dec. 11—*God Promises Better Days (Isaiah 44:1-8)*

Wednesday, Dec. 12—*The Folly of Idols (Isaiah 44:9-20)*

Thursday, Dec. 13—*God Who Redeems (Isaiah 44:21-28)*

Friday, Dec. 14—*Nothing Compares With God (Isaiah 40:12-17)*

Saturday, Dec. 15—*Human Made Idols vs. Almighty God (Isaiah 40:18-24)*

Sunday, Dec. 16—*Everlasting Creator God (Isaiah 40:25-31)*

WHAT DO YOU THINK?

Isaiah 40:3-5 predicts the future ministry of John the Baptist (Matthew 3:3), who came to prepare the way for the Messiah. What can we do today to prepare the way for Christ's second coming?

However, *all mankind* suggests a work of God that goes far beyond anything accomplished by his people's return from captivity. The glory of God is most fully seen in Jesus Christ. Of him, John writes, "The Word became flesh and made his dwelling among us. We have seen his glory, the glory of the One and Only, who came from the Father, full of grace and truth" (John 1:14). Paul states that God has given us "the light of the knowledge of the glory of God in the face of Christ" (2 Corinthians 4:6). This "revealing" will be completed when Jesus "comes in his glory" (Matthew 25:31), when "every eye will see him" (Revelation 1:7).

For the mouth of the Lord has spoken emphasizes the certainty of this promise. Isaiah uses similar language elsewhere (see Isaiah 1:20; 9:7; 37:32; 58:14).

II. CERTAINTY OF GOD'S COMFORT (ISAIAH 40:6-11)

A. HIS ETERNAL WORD (vv. 6-8)

Now the second voice urges the prophet to cry out.

6. A voice says, "Cry out."
    And I said, "What shall I cry?"
"All men are like grass,
    and their glory is like the flowers of the field.

The source of the *voice* is not identified; it simply tells Isaiah to *cry out*, leaving the prophet puzzled about what to say. However, a message is provided. *All men are like grass* is a statement of the temporary nature of human beings. Blades of grass or *flowers* are fragile and easily destroyed; so are human beings (cf. James 4:14). By contrast, the word of God is powerful and permanent (v. 8).

Their glory describes outward appearances. Outwardly, both the Assyrian and Babylonian empires had seemed invincible. But these empires, part of "all men," in time passed from the stage of world history. God is not subject to such limitations.

7, 8. "The grass withers and the flowers fall,
    because the breath of the Lord blows on them.
    Surely the people are grass.
The grass withers and the flowers fall,
    but the word of our God stands forever."

The logic Isaiah is using goes something like this: (1) the Lord has power over his creation, (2) *people* are part of that creation, so (3) the Lord has power over people. And that power comes through his *word*. Peter uses Isaiah 40:6-8 to remind us that our new birth in Jesus has come about "through the living and enduring word of God" rather than by any "perishable seed" (1 Peter 1:23-25). Whenever we need reassurance, we can recall the words of Jesus: "Heaven and earth will pass away, but my words will never pass away" (Mark 13:31).

B. HIS STRONG ARM (vv. 9-11)

The third voice in our text seems to be addressed to those who would later return from exile to Jerusalem. It encourages them to herald the arrival of their God, so that all the towns and villages of Judah will hear the good news.

9. You who bring good tidings to Zion,
    go up on a high mountain.
You who bring good tidings to Jerusalem,
    lift up your voice with a shout,
lift it up, do not be afraid;
    say to the towns of Judah,
    "Here is your God!"

Once the Lord arrives in *Jerusalem* and has made his home with his people again, they are to climb to the mountaintops and shout the news. Everyone in

---

Today's visual illustrates verse 8. Its message is a good reminder to have on display at any time, not just with today's lesson.

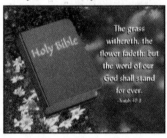

The grass withereth, the flower fadeth: but the word of our God shall stand for ever.
—Isaiah 40:8

WHAT DO YOU THINK?

How significant to you personally is Isaiah's statement, "all men are like grass"? How does it help you to know that, unlike the grass, the Word of God will stand forever?

Judah needs to hear it. Though Jerusalem had once sat in ruins, her people wearied with sorrow and grief, her situation is now different. This is a time to celebrate!

The announcement *Here is your God!* is similar to that of John the Baptist, who proclaimed, "Look, the Lamb of God" (John 1:29). In a larger sense, they also apply to the truly *good tidings* to which Christians bear witness. If being released from captivity in a foreign land produces the celebration described in these verses, how much more should the release from the captivity of sin!

10. See, the Sovereign LORD comes with power,
and his arm rules for him.
See, his reward is with him,
and his recompense accompanies him.

Remember that this promise was meant to comfort God's people exiled in Babylon. The descriptions of God's *power* and *arm* indicate that he has lost none of his ability to deliver. Jesus' return will fulfill the second part of this verse, as he comes to *reward* "everyone according to what he has done" (Revelation 22:12).

11. He tends his flock like a shepherd:
He gathers the lambs in his arms
and carries them close to his heart;
he gently leads those that have young.

While the previous verse emphasized the Lord's strength and might, this verse notes the gentle manner in which he cares for his people. (The same arm by which God rules [v. 10] now tenderly caresses his flock.) The *lambs* and *those that have young* are individuals who need more care; the Lord recognizes this and provides it.

The picture of God as a *shepherd* is used by other prophets to provide encouragement to the exiles in Babylon (Jeremiah 31:10; Ezekiel 34:11-16). This is how God cares today for his people as well. Christians can take genuine comfort from knowing that we are under the care of Jesus, our "good shepherd" (John 10:11).

III. GOD'S ABILITY TO COMFORT (ISAIAH 40:28-31)

In Isaiah 40:12 Isaiah begins a series of questions that challenge the people to think about the greatness of God. Now he brings the series to a climax and calls attention to the strength God provides to the discouraged and the weary.

A. THE STRENGTH HE HAS (v. 28)

28. Do you not know?
Have you not heard?
The Lord is the everlasting God,
the Creator of the ends of the earth.
He will not grow tired or weary,
and his understanding no one can fathom.

During the years in exile yet to come, the prophet anticipates that the people will forget or doubt what they had heard of God's power. Perhaps they will start to entertain doubts as to whether he is able to keep his promises. Yet, just as his power was demonstrated in the creation, so it will be in the "re-creation" of his people in their homeland. He will not grow tired in the middle of the project and walk away from the job.

B. THE STRENGTH HE GIVES (vv. 29-31)

29. He gives strength to the weary and increases the power of the weak.

To anyone who is weakening from personal struggles—whether an ancient exile journeying homeward or a Christian today battling temptation—the Lord provides the necessary *power* and *strength*.

WHAT DO YOU THINK?

Isaiah 40:11 likens God to a shepherd. Identify some ways in which Jesus is a shepherd to Christians today.

[Consider passages such as John 10:11 and 1 Peter 2:25 in your discussion.]

WHAT DO YOU THINK?

What do you find most significant about Isaiah's statement that God will not grow weary?

HOW TO SAY IT

Assyrian. Uh-SEAR-ee-un.
Babylon. BAB-uh-lun.
Babylonian. Bab-uh-LOW-nee-un.
Isaiah. Eye-ZAY-uh.

HE'S BEEN WHERE YOU ARE

In the *Chicago Tribune* Bob Greene told the story of Doug Maurer, age fifteen, of Creve Coeur, Missouri. Doug had been feeling bad for several days. Eventually his temperature rose to 105 degrees, and he exhibited severe flu-like symptoms. Doug's mother took him to a hospital in St. Louis, where he was diagnosed with leukemia.

Upon learning the details of how his condition would be treated, including three years of chemotherapy and side effects such as baldness and bloating, Doug Maurer went into a deep depression. His aunt called to have an arrangement of flowers delivered to him. She told the clerk it was for her teenage nephew who had leukemia.

When the beautiful flowers, Doug read the card from his aunt. Then he saw a second card. It said: "Doug, I took your order at the florist's. I had leukemia when I was seven years old. I'm twenty-two years old now. Good luck. My heart goes out to you. Sincerely, Laura Bradley." Doug's face lit up and his spirit soared.

Doug Maurer was in a hospital filled with sophisticated medical equipment. He received treatment from expert doctors and nurses. But it was a salesclerk in a flower shop, *a woman who had been where he was*, that gave him comfort, hope, and the will to keep going.

"He gives strength to the weary and increases the power of the weak" (Isaiah 40:29). We Christians can take special comfort from these words because we know God's Suffering Servant "has been tempted in every way, just as we are—yet without sin" (Hebrews 4:15). Let his encouragement cause your spirit to soar.   —J. A. M.

30, 31. Even youths grow tired and weary,
*   and young men stumble and fall;*
but those who hope in the Lord
*   will renew their strength.*
They will soar on wings like eagles;
*   they will run and not grow weary,*
*   they will walk and not be faint.*

Those returning to Jerusalem would be of all ages. If the *young men stumble and fall*, imagine how the elderly would fare! The solution is to *hope in the Lord* rather than to depend on one's own strength. This is something the Israelites had proven very deficient at in the past.

Eagles are notable for their strength (Psalm 103:5) and speed (2 Samuel 1:23; Jeremiah 4:13). To paraphrase Jesus' words in the Sermon on the Mount, if God thus strengthens and equips the eagles, how much more will he strengthen and equip us when we begin to grow weary and faint!

PRAYER

O Lord, may I find in You the comfort that not only satisfies my soul, but enables me to be a source of comfort to those around me. Make me a channel of your comfort so that others will know that you are "the God of all comfort." In Jesus' name I pray. Amen.

CONCLUSION

Isaiah's words of comfort encourage Christians today to keep on serving the Lord and living for him. When we become weary from our efforts, these words help us find renewed vigor. So does the testimony of the apostle Paul, who expressed his personal need for "the God of all comfort" (2 Corinthians 1:3). Paul told the Corinthians that God comforts individuals "so that we can comfort those in any trouble with the comfort we ourselves have received from God" (v. 4). Thus the comfort God provides *to* his people is often provided *through* his people. Later in that same letter Paul notes how God had comforted him "by the coming of Titus" (2 Corinthians 7:6).

The Lord promises to give strength and comfort to those who trust him during the difficult stages of their walk with him. Never forget that he often uses people to do that. If he has done that for you, why not express your gratitude to the person he used? And always be prepared for the times God may use you as an instrument of comfort to someone else.

THOUGHT TO REMEMBER

God comforts us, not just so we can be comforted, but so that someone else can be comforted through us.

Discovery Learning

This page contains an alternate lesson plan emphasizing learning activities. Classes desiring such student involvement will find these suggestions helpful. The next page is a reproducible activity page to further enhance discovery learning.

LEARNING GOALS

After participating in this lesson, each student will be able to:

1. Summarize the message of comfort given in Isaiah 40.

2. Explain how this message comforted the Israelites and comforts believers today.

3. Identify someone going through a difficult time and share God's comfort with that person.

INTO THE LESSON

As students enter the classroom, direct them to one of several pieces of poster board you have placed on the wall. Each poster board should have this heading written on it: "Circumstances for which someone may need a word of comfort include. . . ." Ask each person to write two or three circumstances from the lives of individuals, families, or groups of people who may need encouragement. You may write an example on each poster board such as "a Sunday School class whose teacher has suddenly become unfaithful to God" or "a friend whose unmarried daughter became pregnant."

Briefly review the lists and circumstances. Tell the class that the word *comfort* has different meanings and applications to people. People will define *comfort* based on their need or circumstances. Individuals, families, groups, churches, and even nations need comfort at times. Today's study shows God's offer of compassion and comfort to a nation. But we also glimpse his love and offer of comfort to individuals who need him.

INTO THE WORD

Give a brief lecture about the exile of the Jews in Babylon. Emphasize their sense of despair as expressed in Psalm 137. Also highlight the sense of hope they must have experienced from Isaiah's prophecy.

Give pairs of class members a photocopy of today's scripture text and a highlighter pen (or refer them to the appropriate page in the student book, *NIV Bible Student*). One couple should be given a copy of the text on a transparency. Ask the pairs to read the text and highlight every word or phrase of comfort and encouragement they discover. *Some possible answers include "her hard service has been completed"(v. 2), "sin has been paid for" (v. 2), "the glory of the Lord will be revealed" (v. 5), "the word of our God stands forever" (v. 8), "do not be afraid"* (v. 9), *"Here is your God" (v. 9), "the Sovereign Lord comes with power" (v. 10), "He tends his flock" (v. 11), "He gathers the lambs . . . carries them . . . gently leads" (v. 11), "the everlasting God . . . will not grow tired" (v. 28), "He gives strength to the weary" (v. 29), "the Lord will renew their strength" (v. 31).*

Give the teams about five minutes. Then project the transparency of Scripture that has been highlighted by one of the teams, emphasizing the many words of comfort and encouragement God offered to these Jewish exiles. Direct the learners' attention to the "Isaiah 40 Word Search" activity on the reproducible page following.

INTO LIFE

Give another handout to each team. This handout should have three columns. The left column should be headed "God's Comfort to Jewish Exiles." You should also list below this heading every word or phrase included in the highlighter exercise completed in the Bible study portion of this lesson. The second column should have the heading "A Parent Whose Child Has Died." The third column's heading will read "A Friend Overcoming an Addiction." First, ask the teams to find two or three words or concepts from the left column that may be helpful in comforting the persons in the circumstances described in columns 2 or 3. Ask them to place a check mark in the corresponding columns to identify the appropriate word or concept. Second, remind them that different circumstances or crises require comforting words appropriate to that situation. Ask the teams to add and write a few other scriptural words or teachings that may be comforting or encouraging in these two circumstances.

Finally, ask each class member to identify a friend, neighbor, or fellow Christian who may need a word of comfort or encouragement. Use the case studies in the reproducible page activity "Creating Comfort" to get started. For the personalization of the activity say, "The person may be experiencing serious illness, trying to overcome a sinful habit, struggling with a personal relationship, looking for work, grieving a death, or going through some other situation of stress and distress." Ask each learner to make a personal commitment to contact that person this week by telephone, note, or personal visit. They should identify at least one scriptural thought to use in this word of comfort.

Isaiah 40 Word Search

In the blanks below write God's words of comfort to a very discouraged people (from Isaiah 40:1-11, 28-31). Then locate the words in the grid below.

"_____ my people. Speak _____. Her hard service has been _____. Her _____ has been paid for. The _____ of the _____ will be revealed. The _____ of our God stands _____. Do not be _____. The _____ Lord comes with _____. His _____ rules for him. His _____ is with him. His _____ accompanies him. He tends his _____ like a _____: . . . and carries them close to his _____; he _____ _____ those that have young.

The Lord is the _____ God. The _____ of the ends of the earth. He will not grow _____ or _____. His _____ no one can fathom. He gives _____ to the weary and increases the power of the _____. Those who _____ in the Lord will _____ their strength. They will soar on _____ like _____."

```
E V E R L A S T I N G R Z W I L T
A R M E T M V A V A H Y O J X K Q
G E F C E I D I Y L V R L B K F P
L W H O K X T L R O V K R B S O S
E A O M U L R W S G N I W E A R Y
S R P P L E S Q J A E E V Y W L I
N D E E D L Z D D E T E L P M O C
I D U N D E R S T A N D I N G O P
S E E S E O Q T E H Q O L Q M E L
H T P E W W G E N T L Y A F E P W
E E R E L E F L O C K Y O B X P H
P A A E Q E A O O O C R E A T O R
H K F R N C A R R R T U T I U U N
E D R Q T G B D Y E Y T R Y Y T X
R X A R Q C T C S O V E R E I G N
D C I Q E H T H R D D E L E C G K
W M D T W H W R Y R Z Z R M E N P
```

Creating Comfort

Consider the circumstances below and—on the back of this sheet—write words of comfort from God's wonderful model.

1. Your neighbor is a thirty-year-old father of two young children. As you visit with him and his wife, they tell you the doctor has just told the husband he has lung cancer. You might offer comfort by saying . . . .

2. You have been called to be the teacher in a Bible class whose teacher has just confessed an addiction to pornography. He resigned last week after confessing, asking prayerful support. The class has been devastated and disappointed. Your first lesson to the class might offer these thoughts: . . . .

Light for All People
The Mission of God's Servant
(Lessons 1-5)

GOD'S SERVANT
BRINGS HOPE

LESSON 4

WHY TEACH THIS LESSON?

Christmastime presents us with something of a paradox: what is supposed to the happiest, most joy-filled time of year turns out, for many, to be the saddest. The world of secular psychology has observed a larger problem it calls "the winter blues," or, more technically, "Seasonal Affective Disorder" (SAD). But the sadness we're talking about here seems specifically related to Christmastime itself.

Perhaps you've seen this mood in yourself or others. The holiday trimmings are all about us, travel plans are made, stores bustle with shoppers. But you or someone you know just doesn't have that sense of happiness that everyone else seems to be enjoying. Winter seems to rage on the *inside* as well as out; loneliness grips the soul even when—maybe *especially* when—in the company of loved ones.

One possible explanation is that we sometimes make wrong comparisons. We analyze our own life situations in comparison to that of others—others who seem to be happier. Such comparisons are bound to be painful. There will always be someone else who has more or better earthly things than we do—nicer material possessions, more quality relationships, or better health. Profound, lasting happiness comes ultimately from knowing that God is with us, no matter what our circumstances. This is the meaning of "Immanuel" (Isaiah 7:14; Matthew 1:23). The people of Isaiah's day were to take comfort in the yet-to-be-kept promise of a child who would reign on David's throne. How much greater should our own faith be now that that promise *has* been kept!

INTRODUCTION

A. WHAT WE DO MATTERS

Today's lesson is about hope—not the kind that voices a vague wish for better times, but the kind of trust in God's plans and purposes that always has sustained his people. Such hope delivers us from the despair of thinking that nothing we do matters; in fact, it enables us to tackle even the most menial job with vigor.

Elmer Bendiner tells the story of a B-17 bomber that was flown in bombing missions over Germany during the latter days of World War II. The plane was hit several times by shells and flak, and some of the hits struck the compartment where bombs were stored. Miraculously, however, the bomber did not explode.

Later, when the plane landed, eleven unexploded twenty-millimeter shells were removed from it. The shells were dismantled, and, to the amazement of everyone, they contained no explosives! Inside one shell was a note written in the Czech language. Translated, it read, "This is all we can do for you now." A member of the Czech underground, working in a German munitions factory, had not added the explosives to at least eleven of the twenty-millimeter shells on his assembly line. Perhaps that worker often wondered whether the quiet work he had done to subvert the Nazi war effort was going to make any difference during the conflict.

DEVOTIONAL READING:
LUKE 2:8-20

BACKGROUND SCRIPTURE:
ISAIAH 9:1-7; LUKE 2:1-20

PRINTED TEXT:
ISAIAH 9:2-7

Dec
23

LESSON AIMS

After participating in this lesson each student will be able to:

1. Cite several images Isaiah uses to tell how God's Servant, the Messiah, brings hope to his people.

2. Tell why hope was needed in Isaiah's time and is needed today.

3. Praise God for the hope we have in Jesus.

KEY VERSE

For to us a child is born, to us a son is given, and the government will be on his shoulders. And he will be called Wonderful Counselor, Mighty God, Everlasting Father, Prince of Peace.
—Isaiah 9:6

How discouraging can our circumstances get? The answer: never discouraging enough to quit doing what God commands us to do. On this Sunday before Christmas, Isaiah's words challenge us to reflect on the hope we possess because Jesus came into our world. When Isaiah considered the terrible destruction that was facing God's people and the fact that few people were going to listen to his pleas (Isaiah 6:10-13), he might have concluded that nothing he said really mattered. But Isaiah's message also included a word of hope—the promise of a "great light" that would dispel the darkness of sin. That hope, which God offered to Isaiah's dark times, is the same hope that inspires our celebrations during this season of Christmas.

B. LESSON BACKGROUND

The message of hope found in today's lesson text must be considered against the backdrop of the dark and discouraging conditions that were present in Judah when Isaiah spoke this message. We have noted in previous lessons that when Tiglath-pileser III came to the throne of Assyria in 745 B.C., he led in a resurgence that restored Assyria's prominence as a world power. His intentions to move westward and conquer territories made Assyria a force with which to be reckoned. This placed immediate pressure on the kingdoms of Syria, Israel, and Judah.

Syria and Israel joined forces to counter this threat. They tried to get King Ahaz of Judah to become part of their alliance, but he refused. So the allied forces invaded Judah to place their own king on Judah's throne and make Judah part of their alliance. Both Ahaz and the people of Judah became terrified (Isaiah 7:1, 2).

The prophet Isaiah went to Ahaz and told him not to fear the alliance, for it would not stand. He urged the king to trust God for deliverance. Judah's problems were spiritual in nature, not political (Isaiah 7:3-7). But instead of turning to God, Ahaz appealed to Assyria for help. So Isaiah warned Ahaz that the Assyrian military machine would eventually turn on Judah and leave behind extensive damage (7:18-25). In effect, the Lord would hide his face from his people (8:17).

The final verses of chapter 8 describe conditions that would exist in Judah as a consequence of the Assyrian invasion. The people would actually go to mediums and spiritists for help rather than to "the law and to the testimony" (vv. 19, 20). They would be engulfed in spiritual darkness, and their land would be turned into a curse. But God would not be finished with them; he had other, grander plans.

Isaiah 9 begins this change in tone with the word "nevertheless." It then refers to the troubles that afflicted the areas of Zebulun and Naphtali—two tribes located at the northernmost part of the nation of Israel. Armies invading Israel tended to come from the north (rather than east, because of the extensive desert there). This meant that areas such as Zebulun and Naphtali would be among the first to experience any hardship that occurred. During Isaiah's time, these tribes in particular suffered during the invasion of Tiglath-pileser III (2 Kings 15:29).

Thus, perhaps the last place in Israel where one might have expected to find any reason for hope would have been the territories of Zebulun and Naphtali. Yet it is to these very people, "in . . . the shadow of death" (Isaiah 9:2; Matthew 4:16), that Isaiah addresses his message of hope.

I. HOPE AMID DARKNESS (ISAIAH 9:2, 3)

A. LIGHT SHINES (v. 2)

2. *The people walking in darkness*
have seen a great light;
on those living in the land of the shadow of death
a light has dawned.

Ahaz. AY-haz.

Assyria. Uh-SEAR-ee-uh.

Babylonian. Bab-uh-LOW-nee-un.

Capernaum. Kuh-PER-nay-um.

Davidic. Duh-VID-ick.

Gabriel. GAY-bree-ul.

Gideon. GID-ee-un.

Hezekiah. Hez-ih-KYE-uh.

Immanuel. Ih-MAN-you-el.

Isaiah. Eye-ZAY-uh.

Manasseh. Muh-NASS-uh.

messianic. mess-ee-AN-ick.

Midian. MID-ee-un.

Midianites. MID-ee-un-ites.

Naphtali. NAF-tuh-lye.

Tiglath-pileser. TIG-lath-pih-LEE-zer .

Zebulun. ZEB-you-lun.

The tense of the verbs *have seen* and *has dawned* normally indicate an event that already has happened. Here, however, they describe an event that is yet to take place. This is a way of emphasizing the certainty that the prophet's words will come true; he pictures a future event as if it already has occurred.

How were these afflicted regions of Zebulun and Naphtali (v. 1) to become so enlightened? The answer is given by Matthew, who quotes Isaiah 9:1, 2 (Matthew 4:15, 16) after noting that Jesus settled in Capernaum, a town located in the territory of Naphtali. Later in the book of Isaiah, the prophet will describe a special Servant whom God will call to extend light to Gentiles as well as Jews (Isaiah 42:6; 49:6). These prophecies are likewise fulfilled in Jesus, "the light of the world" (John 8:12) who comes "to shine on those living in darkness and in the shadow of death" (Luke 1:79). Wherever the darkness of sin has enslaved people, the light of the gospel can set them free.

A HOPELESS TOWN

You've probably never heard of Flagstaff, Maine. That's not surprising—since it no longer exists! But once upon a time Flagstaff was a thriving New England community. It remained so until the Army Corps of Engineers erected a dam in the vicinity, and Flagstaff, Maine, was slowly but surely buried in water. The residents were forced to find new places to call home.

One resident of Flagstaff said that the most painful part of the experience of relocation was watching his hometown die. All improvements and all repairs ceased immediately. Why bother to paint a house when it is going to be flooded? Why repair a building when the whole village is going to be wiped out? Why repair potholes in streets soon to be abandoned? Why remove graffiti only fish will read?

As the weeks until the inevitable destruction passed by, the townspeople became more and more despondent. Another resident made this comment: "When there's no hope for the future, there's no power in the present." Effort diminishes, then ceases altogether when hope is absent. The book of Proverbs declares, "Hope deferred makes the heart sick" (Proverbs 13:12).

To people for whom oppression and suffering had become commonplace, Isaiah brought a word of hope: "The people walking in darkness have seen a great light" (Isaiah 9:2). Only Heaven's light can dispel the darkness of a sinful world. —J. A. M.

B. JOY IS MULTIPLIED (v. 3)

3. *You have enlarged the nation*
      and increased their joy;
   they rejoice before you
      as people rejoice at the harvest,
   as men rejoice
      when dividing the plunder.

Because of the Assyrian invasion, many of Israel's citizens had been torn from their homeland and taken captive. God promises, however, that this decline will be reversed in the future: the *nation* will be *enlarged*. Isaiah 49:19-23 and 54:1-3 provide similar words of hope and encouragement for the time when the people will find themselves in despair during the Babylonian captivity.

The multiplication of the nation is seen as a blessing from the Lord just as a plentiful *harvest* is a blessing from the Lord. Likewise, the celebration can be associated with the *dividing* of the spoil of war because it implies victories in battle that have been granted by the Lord. The *joy* of Isaiah's prophecy is a blessing of God.

Implied in these words is the truth that the hope of God's people can never be based on the changing circumstances of life. Our hope is not built on the belief that our country is strong and that no enemy can harm our land. Our hope is

WHAT DO YOU THINK?

Where are some places and what are some ways in which the world walks in darkness? How can we bring light to those situations?

WHAT DO YOU THINK?

How can we share in the joy of "harvest" that Isaiah describes? Consider both personal and corporate activities.

not built on the strength of the economy, the upward trend of the stock market, or the lower numbers of unemployment. Our hope is built on the One who is not limited by the variable winds and shifting sands of contemporary events. His enduring power gives us reason to have an enduring hope.

II. HOPE BECAUSE GOD ACTS (ISAIAH 9:4, 5)

When what we see seems to be falling apart, how can we place our trust in an unseen God and his purposes? Isaiah assured his listeners that the God who acted powerfully in the past has lost none of his power.

A. DELIVERANCE PROVIDED (v. 4)

4. For as in the day of Midian's defeat,
   you have shattered
the yoke that burdens them,
   the bar across their shoulders,
   the rod of their oppressor.

The mention of the *day of Midian's defeat* brought to mind the victory that the Lord gave Israel over the Midianites during the days of Gideon over four hundred years previously (Judges 7:19-25). In that campaign Gideon defeated the Midianites, whose soldiers were like a swarm of "locusts," with camels as numerous as "the sand on the seashore" (Judges 7:12). Through the power of God, Gideon's "army" of three hundred men won the victory. This incident would have had special meaning for the tribes of Zebulun and Naphtali (Isaiah 9:1), because it occurred in the vicinity of that portion of Israel.

Again, speaking as if a future event is a fact already accomplished, Isaiah predicts that God will destroy those who are oppressing Israel and will relieve her from their oppression. *The yoke, the bar,* and *the rod* were all items used to control animals. Israel was reduced to such an enslaved condition during the Assyrian invasion and would have welcomed the promise of an end to such oppression.

However, the removal of the Assyrian menace could deal with only part of the reason for Israel's misery, and not the main part at that. Another menace lay at the root of Israel's woes. That was the menace of sin. Sin was the yoke, bar, and rod that was degrading the nation and leading it toward destruction (Isaiah 1:2-8). Israel could never be truly free until it was rid of this far more deadly menace.

Thus Isaiah's prediction points to a much more dramatic and comprehensive event. It is linked with the coming of a Ruler who will reign on the throne of David in such a way that his kingdom will be everlasting (Isaiah 9:7). It describes a hope that speaks to the hearts of all who are weighed down by the oppression of sin. Only God can provide such a deliverance as this; it is as impossible for man to do it as it was for Gideon to conquer Midian in his own strength.

B. WEAPONS DESTROYED (v. 5)

5. Every warrior's boot used in battle
   and every garment rolled in blood
will be destined for burning,
   will be fuel for the fire.

Continuing his message of hope, Isaiah now focuses on some of the essentials of war that will no longer be needed after the Lord's deliverance. These items will become so useless that they might as well be used as *fuel* for a *fire.* The picture is one of peace—but, as the next verse clearly points out, not the kind of peace that the world seeks to achieve. It is a peace that only the Lord could provide. And his primary "weapon" for bringing about this peace would be a child.

WHAT DO YOU THINK?

When have you seen God break the yoke of some oppressor and give a victory "as in the day of Midian's defeat"?

WHAT DO YOU THINK?

The lesson writer notes that Isaiah pictures "a peace that only the Lord could provide." Describe a time in your life when God's peace sustained you—a peace that only God could have provided.

III. HOPE THROUGH A CHILD (ISAIAH 9:6, 7)
A. HIS TITLES (v. 6)

6. For to us a child is born,
    to us a son is given,
    and the government will be on his shoulders.
  And he will be called
    Wonderful Counselor, Mighty God,
    Everlasting Father, Prince of Peace.

Display this poster as you begin to discuss verse 6. It is found in the Adult Visuals packet.

Here is the glorious climax of Isaiah's picture of future deliverance and joy: a *child.* The phrase *to us a child is born* is similar to the words of the angel announcing Jesus' birth: "Today . . . a Savior has been born to you; he is Christ the Lord." (Luke 2:11). Not only is this child *born,* he is also *given.* Jesus was God's greatest gift to mankind—a truth perhaps most memorably expressed in the words of John 3:16.

The government shall be upon his shoulder. The child will be entrusted with the responsibilities of ruling. Earlier Isaiah had spoken negatively of child rulers, in a context of judgment (Isaiah 3:1-5). This child, however, is refreshingly different.

This is the second prophecy in which Isaiah has mentioned a special child. The first was the virgin birth prophecy of Isaiah 7:14. According to Matthew 1:23, that statement looked ahead to Jesus. It is obvious that this second child-prophecy must refer to Jesus as well.

The titles given in this verse reflect the unique characteristics that we would expect to be associated with this unique One. First, he is called *Wonderful Coun-selor.* Some Bible students see *Wonderful* and *Counselor* as two traits, but the two-word designation is consistent with the other descriptions in this passage. He is, of course, wonderful by nature, and people would express a sense of wonder not only at his counsel, but at himself. Still, *Wonderful Counselor* is an apt description for someone who will possess "the Spirit of counsel" (Isaiah 11:2). Whereas most ancient kings surrounded themselves with counselors for guidance in making difficult decisions, this promised Ruler will possess "all the treasures of wisdom and knowledge" (Colossians 2:3).

In addition, he will be called *Mighty God*—a name that highlights the child's divine character. It is interesting that immediately following the phrase "Spirit of counsel" in Isaiah 11:2 come the words "and of power." No mere earthly power will be able to withstand the power of this child. Being One with God (John 14:9), this ruler will also be called *Everlasting Father.*

The title *Prince of Peace* is perhaps the most familiar of these accolades during the Christmas season, primarily because at Jesus' birth the Heavenly host announced "on earth peace" (Luke 2:14). This is peace between God and humanity. It became a reality through Jesus' death on the cross, where he triumphed over "powers and authorities" (Colossians 2:15) and destroyed the devil (Hebrews 2:14, 15). There the Prince of Peace paid the price of peace between us and God—his own blood (Colossians 1:20). That peace is the only true and lasting peace, for it is peace with God.

WHAT DO YOU THINK?

What do you find most significant about each of the titles for Christ used by Isaiah in verse 6?

Isaiah's prophecy of a special child gave hope to the oppressed of Israel at a time when the nation desperately needed such a message. For followers of Jesus, this same word of hope helps us to keep the challenges of life in perspective. Those who remember what life was like when they were enslaved by sin rejoice in the coming of the Mighty God who has set them free from sin. Those who recall moments when they despaired of life praise God that the Prince of Peace has given them reason to live! It is no wonder that Christians everywhere sing Christmas carols with a true spirit of joy and celebration. "To us a child is born"—a child who grew to manhood to become our Savior.

PRAYER

O God, who makes all things possible, thank you for the hope that we possess through Jesus Christ. During this season, we celebrate not only his birth but also his life, his death, and his resurrection. We honor him as King of kings and Lord of lords, and we anticipate his return. In his name we pray. Amen.

THOUGHT TO REMEMBER

The world cannot steal our hope, because the world did not give it to us—God did.

B. HIS KINGDOM (v. 7)

7. *Of the increase of his government and peace*
    there will be no end.
He will reign on David's throne
    and over his kingdom,
establishing and upholding it
    with justice and righteousness
    from that time on and forever.
The zeal of the Lord Almighty
    will accomplish this.

The line of Davidic kings certainly had its share of disappointments. Kings such as Ahaz and Manasseh (2 Kings 16:1-20; 21:1-18; Matthew 1:9, 10) darken the record of the rulers of Judah. But Isaiah looks ahead to another king who will sit on the *David's throne*. He will establish a kingdom that will never fail. His rule will be characterized by *righteousness* and *justice* (cf. Isaiah 11:4-9; Jeremiah 33:15, 16). The *peace* he will bring is peace between humanity and God, not necessarily peace between people and nations (Isaiah 11:4b; Matthew 10:34-36). His government and peace will increase as people "from every tribe and language and people and nation" submit to his lordship (Revelation 5:9). All of this leads to the conclusion that Isaiah's words do not describe a particularly great king of Judah (such as Hezekiah, for example). The magnificent description of this King and his kingdom requires us to look beyond these earthly kings to the Messiah himself.

The mention of the *throne* of David is another signpost marking this passage as messianic. David had been promised an everlasting kingdom (2 Samuel 7:12-16). When the angel Gabriel announced to Mary that she would become the mother of the Messiah, he told her, "The Lord God will give him the throne of his father David, and he will reign over the house of Jacob forever; his kingdom will never end" (Luke 1:32, 33). Today Jesus Christ has indeed taken up a position of authority over his kingdom. Paul notes that God has "placed all things under [Jesus'] feet and appointed him to be head over everything for the church" (Ephesians 1:22). The church is part of the kingdom that "will never be destroyed" and that "will itself endure forever" (Daniel 2:44).

When Isaiah wrote these words, to think that such a dramatic turn of events could be possible for the ravaged regions of Zebulun and Naphtali would have appeared to be asking the impossible. The devastating power of Assyria looked insurmountable. It would take a miracle just to get Israel back on her feet, let alone find a king who could establish the kingdom described in Isaiah 9:6, 7. But it was to be *the zeal of the Lord Almighty* that guaranteed that these events would come to pass. God's jealous love for people and his zeal that the entire world should come to know him is the certain assurance!

CONCLUSION

Amid the gloom of despair and death, Isaiah offered Israel the hope that comes from knowing that God has not abandoned his people. Isaiah assured them that Israel will see a glorious future because a child will come—born to sit on David's throne and to rule a government that far transcends any political boundaries. Unfolding events would demonstrate that his kingdom would be a spiritual one; he rules not only as a son of David, but also as the Son of God.

As we celebrate the birth of this King whom Isaiah foretold, our hearts are filled with the hope that we will one day see his kingdom in its fullness. There may be "scoffers" who question our hope (2 Peter 3:3, 4), but let us not be swayed by their unbelief. In God's own time, "the zeal of the Lord Almighty will accomplish this."

Discovery Learning

This page contains an alternate lesson plan emphasizing learning activities. Classes desiring such student involvement will find these suggestions helpful. The next page is a reproducible activity page to further enhance discovery learning.

LEARNING GOALS

After this lesson each student will be able to:

1. Cite several images Isaiah uses to tell how God's Servant, the Messiah, brings hope to his people.

2. Tell why hope was needed in Isaiah's time and is needed today.

3. Praise God for the hope we have in Jesus Christ.

INTO THE LESSON

Make a large baby announcement on poster board. It should have the heading "It's a Boy!" Do not include a name nor the parents' names on the announcement. You may, however, include a length and a birth weight (for example, 21"; 7 lbs., 13 ounces.)

Pointing to the announcement, ask the class to consider this scenario: "Imagine you are an invisible observer in a home that is having an open house for their newborn. What words to describe the baby might you hear?" Write their answers on a chalkboard or marker board. After the list is complete, point out that most of these descriptive words or adjectives deal with the baby's physical condition or appearance. None seriously describe his or her future job, career, impact on the world, or the like. Why? (*He or she has not yet experienced these nor made an impression on the world.*)

Say, "A birth announcement for Jesus would have been very different. As a matter of fact, a 'we are expecting' announcement would have been different. These could have included descriptions of his work, his mission, and his character. Several announcements made in the Old and New Testaments so describe Jesus."

Ask the students to call out some of these characteristics, and have one class member write them beside the list of descriptions of a baby. As a hint, ask the class to remember the angels' announcement of Jesus' birth to the shepherds.

Make the transition to Bible study by telling the class the announcement of what was expected of the Savior's coming was more wonderful than the Jewish hearers could have imagined. The word pictures of the coming Savior were colorful, predictive, and able to give hope to those who had lost hope.

INTO THE WORD

Mix lecture and question/answer by using the following outline:

A. Lecture on the political and spiritual circumstances before reading the text.

B. Ask the following questions:

1. Why does Isaiah use the past tense in verse 2, when the event he describes has not yet happened?

2. What are the phrases in verses 2-4 that describe wonderful changes coming for these afflicted people? (*Ask a class member to write these on a visual*). What is the significance or meaning of these descriptions? (*Be sure to use the lesson commentary to clarify verse 5 for the class.*)

C. Tell the class that verses 6 and 7 could be Israel's "We're expecting" announcement. Have two poster boards available. One will be headed, "What will he be like?" The second will say, "What will he do?" Using verses 6 and 7, allow class members to find words and phrases that answer each question. Ask a "scribe" to note these answers on the appropriate board. After this is complete, review these descriptions by asking questions like, "What does this mean?" and, "How will this come to pass?"

D. Remind the class of the joy this hope brought to a hopeless people. (Use the activities on the reproducible page that follows to assist in this.)

INTO LIFE

Ask and discuss the question "Why do we need hope in today's world? What kind of hope do we need?" If you need to help get the discussion started, you might remind them that one of the problems the people of Judah experienced was doubting God's faithfulness. And they began to be unfaithful to him and his word. Is there any similarity to today's believer or to our nation?

Ask groups of three or four people to work together. Tell the groups that Christmas carols are more than mere sentiment and tradition. They share messages about Christ's coming. Give each group several hymn books and ask them to look for lines that imply hope for today. They can note these lines on a piece of paper. After a few minutes, ask the groups to share those lines.

Then ask the groups to form prayer circles. Ask the group to hold hands and give each person the chance to pray, thanking or praising God for one of the characteristics or purposes of the Savior mentioned in today's text.

Post the words to the last stanza of "O Little Town of Bethlehem." Lead the class in singing or reciting this verse and in prayer.

Images of Hope . . . Then and Now!

Isaiah's prophecy to the exiled Jews held wonderful hope. But, after the coming of Christ, we know there is more hope packed in that prophecy than the Jews knew.

Read the images of hope from Isaiah 9 printed below. Then make a few notes about the significance of the prophetic lines to the Jews (Then) and to us (Now).

PROPHECY	THEN	NOW
People walking in darkness have seen a great light (v. 2).		
You have shattered the yoke that burdens them (v. 4).		
For to us a child is born, to us a son is given (v. 6).		
No end to the increase of his government and peace (v. 7).		
He will reign on David's throne (v. 7).		
Establishing and upholding his Kingdom with justice and righteousness (v. 7).		

High on Hope

The words "to us a child is born, to us a son is given" (Isaiah 9:6) brought wonderful hope to the Jews hearing Isaiah's prophecy—and hope to our world today (Luke 2:11). So, how can you help to spread this hope to people close to you as you celebrate Christmas day? Use the letters of the word HOPE to start four words or phrases that describe an action you can take in your Christmas celebration to share Christ's hope.

H _____

O _____

P _____

E _____

Light for All People
The Mission of God's Servant
(Lessons 1-5)

GOD'S SERVANT
BRINGS JUSTICE

LESSON 5

WHY TEACH THIS LESSON?

"And justice for all" are familiar words to anyone who has memorized the United States of America's "Pledge of Allegiance." Yet often these words seem to describe more of an unfulfilled dream than a reality. The ancient prophets also observed a lack of justice in their day (e.g., Isaiah 59:1-15). Most of human history is stained with the indignity of injustice.

And yet justice is to be a defining characteristic of God's kingdom! Those calling themselves "Christian" today seem to approach this fact in two ways. At one extreme are churches that focus solely on the evangelizing imperative of the Great Commission (Matthew 28:19). Such churches are content to know that issues of justice will be fulfilled when God's kingdom reaches its ultimate fullness at Jesus' second coming; at that time the One who was himself deprived of justice will bring final justice to all (Acts 8:33; 17:31).

At the other extreme are churches that focus solely on bringing about justice in the here-and-now, on curing the social inequities of the present world. Both extremes are wrong. God expects his church to maintain a Great Commission focus while not neglecting its responsibility to be the conscience of the community on issues of justice. Today's lesson demonstrates God's concern for justice and how his servant will bring it about.

INTRODUCTION

A. WITH JUSTICE FOR ALL

A class of third-graders in Maryland was studying the justice system of the United States. They were asked to form a "jury" and to stage a mock trial of Goldilocks, the little girl in the well-known children's story, "The Three Bears." As a result of the jury's "deliberations," Goldilocks was convicted on two breaking-and-entering charges. The jury deadlocked, however, on theft charges brought in connection with the disappearance of the bears' porridge.

Questions about justice are common in today's confused world, where many desire to live as if they were a law to themselves. Today's lesson challenges us to consider the justice established by the servant of the Lord. We shall see that it is a different kind of justice, because the servant of the Lord is a different kind of leader.

B. LESSON BACKGROUND

In the Background to lesson 1 (pages 127-129), we noted that Isaiah 40–66 (which follows the record of events from Hezekiah's reign in chapters 36–39) moves forward in time from the threat of the Assyrian siege of Jerusalem to the destruction of the city and to the Babylonian captivity over one hundred years later. Within that section of Isaiah are the passages usually referred to as the Servant Songs. The first of these is found in Isaiah 42, from which today's lesson is taken.

DEVOTIONAL READING:
ISAIAH 43:1-7

BACKGROUND SCRIPTURE:
ISAIAH 42

PRINTED TEXT:
ISAIAH 42:1-9

Dec
30

LESSON AIMS

After participating in this lesson, each student will be able to:

1. Describe the manner by which the Lord's servant brings justice.

2. Contrast the gentle ways of the servant with the typical, and often unjust, ways of political rulers.

3. Consider an issue involving injustice in his or her community and suggest one specific way a Christian can address that issue in the gentle style of the "servant."

KEY VERSE

Here is my servant, whom I uphold, my chosen one in whom I delight; I will put my Spirit on him and he will bring justice to the nations.   —Isaiah 42:1

The identity of the servant was also considered in lesson 1. There it was noted that some passages in Isaiah that mention the servant must refer to Old Testament Israel (e.g., Isaiah 41:8, 9). But Israel had failed in its task because of its disobedience: "They would not follow his ways; they did not obey his law" (Isaiah 42:24).

Clearly there was a need for another servant of the Lord. The focus of Isaiah 42:1-9 is on an individual servant who "will not falter" (v. 4) in carrying out the Lord's purposes. This "individual emphasis" is especially clear from the New Testament references to this passage. For example, Matthew 12:18-21 cites Isaiah 42:1-4 and points to its fulfillment in the ministry of Jesus. In addition Isaiah 42:6 may be the source of terminology found in Luke 2:32; Acts 13:47; and Acts 26:23 (though Isaiah 49:6 contains similar language).

Isaiah's Servant Songs are not called "songs" because they were sung, but because they present psalm-like descriptions, using poetic language and structure, of the celebration associated with the coming of the servant of the Lord. The emphasis in Isaiah 42:1-9 is on the justice that he will promote and provide.

I. THE SERVANT COMMISSIONED (ISAIAH 42:1)

Isaiah 41:29 invited the reader to "see" the false gods whose "deeds amount to nothing." That image is a direct contrast to the servant of chapter 42.

A. ELECT OF GOD (v. 1a)

1a. "Here is my servant, whom I uphold,
　　my chosen one in whom I delight;

The difference between the powerless idols and God's *servant* is dramatic: God upholds his servant by his power. This stark contrast makes it clear that God is far superior and that his people should trust and obey him.

The Hebrew word that is translated here as *servant* often took on a royal and political meaning in the world of Isaiah (as in 2 Kings 22:12, where the same word is translated as *attendant*). This word could describe a trusted envoy or representative. It implied both the honor in holding such a title and the responsibility to obey whatever the king commanded. Remember that in the previous chapter Isaiah had spoken of Israel as God's servant (see 41:8-10, where the same Hebrew word is used). Here in chapter 42 we see an emphasis on an individual. Thus, while we should consider Jesus to be the ultimate fulfillment of these servant prophecies (for this is clear from the New Testament's use of them), we should also recognize the close association of the servant with the nation of Israel. He will succeed in carrying out the Lord's purpose, in contrast to Israel's failure. Some believe that a concept of the Messiah as the embodiment of Israel or as the epitome of Israel's mission may be the best way to explain the connection.

God also refers to the servant as *my chosen one* in order to make clear the close, personal relationship between the two. The phrase *in whom I delight* emphasizes the Lord's approval of the servant's efforts. These words highlight the contrast between faithless Israel and the servant, who "was faithful to the one who appointed him" (Hebrews 3:2). At both Jesus' baptism and the transfiguration, God spoke approvingly of his Son (Matthew 3:17; 17:5).

B. EMPOWERED BY GOD (v. 1b)

1b. " . . . I will put my Spirit on him
　　and he will bring justice to the nations.

In the Bible *justice* implies the kind of reign associated with the wisdom of a divinely led ruler. It depicts what might be called the *righteousness* of God's judgment. It is this concern for righteousness and truth that ultimately lies at the heart

Behold my servant, whom I uphold; mine elect, in whom my soul delighteth; I have put my Spirit upon him; he shall bring forth judgment to the Gentiles.
—Isaiah 42:1

This poster illustrates the connection between verse 1 and God's declaration at Jesus' baptism.

of the servant's ministry (cf. Jeremiah 23:5, 6). That truth embraces the gospel message, which declares how all people, including Gentiles (i.e., non-Jews, or *the nations*), can be forgiven of sins through the servant's atoning death on the cross.

The word *justice* also carries the traditional sense of treating people in a fair, or "just," manner. Today, the corruption of justice is frequently in the news. Even when it is not, the believer may experience the corruption of justice firsthand. Those with money and influence often manipulate the system and pervert justice to their own ends. God issued strong warnings against such corruption (Deuteronomy 16:19). The promise of God is that his servant will establish a justice that is pleasing to our righteous God.

THE BEATEN KING

In the movie *The Last Emperor*, the young child anointed as the last emperor of China lives a magical life of luxury. Among other privileges, he has a thousand servants at his command. Amazed at his surroundings, his brother asks, "What happens when you do wrong?"

"When I do wrong, someone else is punished," the young emperor replies. To demonstrate he breaks a jar, and one of the servants is immediately beaten. I would have loved a deal like that when I was growing up!

You and I, however, have a better "deal." Jesus loved us so much that he reversed the pattern described in the movie. When we servants erred, the King took the punishment. When we messed up, Jesus was beaten up.

God's justice would not allow him to ignore our sin. But God's mercy would not allow him to leave us hopeless and lost. So when we sinned, Jesus paid the price: he died for us. He is the suffering servant in whom the Father delights.

Because of his "elect," God does not treat me as I deserve to be treated. Instead, I can be treated the way Jesus deserves to be treated. That is possible only because Jesus took my punishment on himself at the cross. Thus God can be both "just and the one who justifies those who have faith in Jesus" (Romans 3:26). Paul describes it this way: "God made him who had no sin to be sin for us, so that in him we might become the righteousness of God" (2 Corinthians 5:21).   —J. A. M.

II. THE SERVANT DESCRIBED (ISAIAH 42:2-4)

Now Isaiah begins a description of the personal qualities of the servant who will bring about the Lord's justice.

A. GENTLE MINISTRY (vv. 2, 3)

2. "He will not shout or cry out,
    or raise his voice in the streets.

The servant of the Lord will be known, not for the volume of his words, but for his humble, quiet, gentle spirit. As Isaiah has earlier described him, he will be called the Prince of Peace (9:6). Jesus described himself as "gentle and humble in heart" (Matthew 11:29). Such an attitude reflects the spirit of servant leadership, to which Jesus calls all who would be great in his kingdom (Mark 10:42-45).

3. *"A bruised reed he will not break,*
    and a smoldering wick he will not snuff out.
  In faithfulness he will bring forth justice.

A *bruised reed* is one with a cracked, perhaps partially broken, stem. It is something fragile that must be handled carefully. Here it represents someone who is weak and struggling spiritually—one who has been bruised by sin or by difficult circumstances. A *smoldering wick* has a flame that is burning dimly. It represents those whose lives are nearly ruined; the flame of life is nearly gone. The servant of the Lord will conduct his ministry in such a way that the helpless and hopeless

WHAT DO YOU THINK?

What is the role of the church in addressing what the lesson writer calls "corruption of justice" in society? How well are we doing in fulfilling that role? What more can or should we do?

DAILY BIBLE READINGS

Monday, Dec. 24—"Good News of Great Joy" (Luke 2:8-14)

Tuesday, Dec. 25—All Who Heard Were Amazed (Luke 2:15-20)

Wednesday, Dec. 26—Light for Revelation to the Gentiles (Luke 2:25-35)

Thursday, Dec. 27—Sing a New Song (Isaiah 42:10-17)

Friday, Dec. 28—Israel's Blindness (Isaiah 42:18-25)

Saturday, Dec. 29—God Has Called You by Name (Isaiah 43:1-7)

Sunday, Dec. 30—The Lord Is the Only Savior (Isaiah 43:8-15)

will be saved from destruction. In contrast to the corrupt rulers of Isaiah's day, the prophet foretold a day when God's people will be blessed with a Messiah who will bring forth *justice* unto truth. This message of God's kingdom of justice should both thrill our hearts and challenge our own business practices. We should ask ourselves whether we conduct our own affairs in a way that reflects the justice of the Lord.

B. DETERMINED MINISTRY (v. 4)

4. " . . . he will not falter or be discouraged
   till he establishes justice on earth.
   In his law the islands will put their hope."

Here the theme of the servant's suffering is subtly introduced. Later it will be developed more fully, becoming especially clear in the Servant Song of Isaiah 52:13–53:12. In spite of the pressures to fail or become discouraged, the servant will not waver from the fulfillment of the Lord's task. Thus he is exactly like the God who has called him, who does not faint or grow weary (Isaiah 40:28).

The repeated use of *justice* (three times within these first four verses) indicates its prominence in the servant's ministry. Also highlighted is the impact of his ministry on the *islands*—another way of describing the servant's desire that faraway peoples (Gentiles) hear of his law and be instructed by him (cf. Isaiah 49:1). The involvement of Gentiles in God's plan is emphasized throughout Isaiah. It appears as early as Isaiah 2:2-4, where "all nations" are pictured as flowing like streams to Mount Zion in order to learn of the ways of the Lord. (See also Zechariah 2:11.)

TENDER STRENGTH

Isaiah describes the servant of the Lord as one characterized by gentle strength. He will not harm the weak (Isaiah 42:3), but at the same time he is fiercely committed to fulfilling the Lord's purpose (v. 4).

An article in *National Geographic* several years ago provided a penetrating picture of gentle yet tenacious strength. After a forest fire in Yellowstone National Park, rangers began their trek up a mountain to assess the damage. One ranger found a bird literally petrified in ashes, perched upright on the ground at the base of a tree. Somewhat sickened by the eerie sight, he knocked the bird over with a stick. Immediately three tiny chicks scurried from under their dead mother's wings. The loving mother, keenly aware of impending disaster, had carried her offspring to the base of the tree and had gathered them under her wings, protecting them from smoke and fire.

This mother bird could easily have flown to safety, but she refused to abandon her babies. When the blaze arrived and the heat scorched her small body, the mother remained steadfast. The gentle strength of her love compelled her to make the ultimate sacrifice. Because she was willing to die, those under the shelter of her wings could live.

The psalmist describes God's care in this manner: "He will cover you with his feathers, and under his wings you will find refuge" (Psalm 91:4; cf. Matthew 23:37). Isaiah affirms that God's servant will not be deterred from his purpose of bringing justice and hope to the world. Jesus did not run from the fiery wrath of God's judgment; he gave his life so that we could find shelter "under his wings."

—J. A. M.

III. THE SERVANT ASSURED (ISAIAH 42:5-9)

Isaiah declares that the servant will be empowered by God to accomplish his mission.

A. GOD'S POWER (v. 5)

5. *This is what God the LORD says—*
    he who created the heavens and stretched them out,
        who spread out the earth and all that comes out of it,
    who gives breath to its people,
        and life to those who walk on it:

The power of the One *who created the heavens* and *the earth* will be the power that undergirds the servant's ministry. The creation of the heavens as an act in which God *stretched them out* is an image already used in Isaiah 40:22. Also pictured is the creation of the earth, and that which *comes out of it,* probably a reference to animal life (cf. Genesis 1:24).

Next, Isaiah mentions the *people* to whom God has given *breath,* most likely "the breath of life" (Genesis 2:7) that each person possesses. The term *life* probably means the same as breath and provides an example of parallelism in Hebrew poetry.

B. GOD'S PURPOSES (vv. 6, 7)

6. *"I, the LORD, have called you in righteousness;*
        I will take hold of your hand.
    I will keep you and will make you
        to be a covenant for the people,
        and a light for the Gentiles.

Here the Lord speaks a message of encouragement and reassurance to the servant. (The language of this verse clearly identifies the servant in terms of an individual.) When the Lord declares that he *will make* the servant *to be a covenant for the people,* some students believe that *people* describes all the peoples of the world (as in v. 5). The phrase would thus be parallel in meaning to *a light for the Gentiles.*

Others say, however, that *people* refers to the Jews, and that light for the Gentiles points to the expanded mission of the servant beyond the scope of the chosen people. It is interesting to note a portion of Jesus' words to Paul on the road to Damascus: "I will rescue you from your own people and from the Gentiles. I am sending you to them to open their eyes and turn them from darkness to light" (Acts 26:17, 18). This would seem to favor the view that *people* describes the Jews.

If, then, the servant is offered as a covenant for the benefit of the people of Israel, the servant must be someone other than Israel. It is best to see the servant as an individual—specifically, the Messiah. The concept of a new covenant will be spelled out in greater detail by Jeremiah, who comes on the scene about sixty years after Isaiah concludes his ministry (Jeremiah 31:31-34; cf. Hebrews 8:8-13).

7. *" . . . to open eyes that are blind,*
        to free captives from prison,
        and to release from the dungeon those who sit in darkness.

The reference in Acts 26:17, 18 to opening *eyes* and turning individuals from *darkness* to light demonstrates once again an application to the ministry of Jesus and the impact of his gospel. In fact, these words are similar to those found in Isaiah 61:1, 2, which begin another Servant Song that Jesus specifically applied to himself. He read from those verses when he went to Nazareth and spoke in the synagogue there. After finishing his reading, "he rolled up the scroll, gave it back to the attendant," and said, "'Today this scripture is fulfilled in your hearing'" (Luke 4:20, 21). The kind of justice that the servant would bring is thus associated with relieving the oppression of those are who are spiritually helpless—blindly groping in the darkness of sin (cf. Matthew 4:16; 6:23; 23:16-19; John 1:5; 8:12; 2 Corinthians 4:6; 1 Peter 2:9). At the same time, we dare not ignore our responsibility to meet physical needs (cf. Matthew 25:31-46).

WHAT DO YOU THINK?

Some Christians believe the focus of the church should be on the Great Commission. Others think the emphasis should be on social justice for the poor and the oppressed. How can the church strike a scriptural balance between the two views?

[Use texts such as Matthew 28:19, 20; Acts 4:34; 6:1-7; Galatians 6:10; James 2:13-16; and 1 John 3:17 to guide your discussion.]

C. GOD'S SUPREMACY (vv. 8, 9)

8. "I am the LORD; that is my name!
> I will not give my glory to another
> or my praise to idols.

This declaration of the Lord's supreme position above all gods is the foundation of the law of Moses, and specifically of the Ten Commandments (Exodus 20:1, 2). There also comes a strict warning against all forms of idolatry. God is a jealous God (Exodus 20:5), and he will permit no rival to be worshiped by his people. To do so would be to endorse a hoax, since the other gods are not really gods at all (an emphasis found at the conclusion of Isaiah 41). This verse thus summarizes the message of the first two of the Ten Commandments (Exodus 20:3, 4).

This verse implies that what God does through the faithful work of his servant contributes to the *glory* of the Lord. Paul exhibits much the same emphasis in Ephesians 1, where he acknowledges "every spiritual blessing" (v. 3) that Christians have received from God through Christ. These include adoption by God, redemption, forgiveness of sins, and the gift of the Holy Spirit (vv. 3-14). Three times in this passage Paul affirms that all of these blessings have been given by God the Father to "the praise of his glorious grace" or to "the praise of his glory" (vv. 6, 12, 14). Likewise, Philippians 2:5-11 declares that Jesus' act of humbling himself and going to the cross was followed by his exaltation so that "every knee should bow" and "every tongue confess that Jesus Christ is Lord, to the glory of God the Father." Everything the servant (Jesus) does calls attention to the supremacy of his Father.

9. "See, the former things have taken place,
> and new things I declare;
> before they spring into being
> I announce them to you."

The former things may refer to earlier prophecies (by Isaiah or the Lord's prophets in general) of events that had come to pass. Perhaps included in the *new things* are the future rise of Cyrus and the release of the captives from Babylon (Isaiah 45:1-7). Although from Isaiah's perspective this was yet to come, it was to take place before the glorious new things that would be associated with the coming of the servant.

Isaiah's words should bring to mind the book of Revelation, which closes with a description of the eternal city built by the hands of God. The apostle John records seeing "the new Jerusalem, coming down out of heaven from God, prepared as a bride beautifully dressed for her husband" (Revelation 21:2). Then John hears the voice of God declaring, "I am making everything new" (v. 5). Both Jews and Gentiles, who have become part of the covenant predicted by Isaiah, will be blessed by knowing that God's word will indeed *spring into being*—for eternity.

CONCLUSION

The servant of the Lord is described in today's text as One who possesses the Lord's full support in the fulfillment of the Lord's mission and in the establishment of his truth. No one will escape the impact of the servant's efforts. The New Testament makes it clear that the servant thus described is Jesus Christ. Jesus' ministry fulfilled the hopes and dreams of Isaiah, who spoke the word of the Lord during especially trying circumstances in Judah.

The kingdom that Jesus established (which includes the church) is characterized by a devotion to the righteous standards of a holy God. It will be perfected only when we join Jesus himself in the eternal kingdom where righteousness dwells. In the meantime, we must live and labor so that the servant's mission continues to be carried out. Like Jesus, we must seek to bring others out of darkness into light and tell prisoners how they can be set free.

Discovery Learning

This page contains an alternate lesson plan emphasizing learning activities. Classes desiring such student involvement will find these suggestions helpful. The next page is a reproducible activity page to further enhance discovery learning.

LEARNING GOALS

After participating in this lesson, each student will be able to:

1. Describe the manner by which the Lord's servant brings justice.

2. Contrast the gentle ways of the servant with the typical, and often unjust, ways of political rulers.

3. Identify an issue involving injustice in the community and suggest a way the Christian may address the issue in the gentle style of the "servant."

INTO THE LESSON

Bring to class several daily newspaper clippings that speak of injustice or unfairness in nations around the world. These may focus on wartime atrocities, ethnic suppression or conflict, religious persecutions, foreign aggression, or other such evils. After you read the headlines and brief segments of each, tape it to the wall. Over the cluster of articles tape a small sign that reads "Injustice." Remind the class that many people throughout history have been forced to suffer at the hands of an unjust, ineffective government or an oppressive culture. These people have yearned for justice and compassion. God has hope for people in these circumstances, just as he offered hope for the chosen people to whom Isaiah spoke.

INTO THE WORD

With your lesson commentary as a resource, give a brief lecture on the background to this prophecy. Explain and define the words *servant* and *justice* as used in today's text. Read the printed text to the class.

Give groups of four or five people one of the following tasks. Also give groups 1 and 2 photocopies of the appropriate pages of the lesson commentary. In larger classes, several groups may work on the same task.

Group 1: Read Isaiah 42:2-4 and the attached notes from the lesson commentary. Identify and be ready to explain the colorful imageries of this passage to the class.

Group 2: Read Isaiah 42:1, 5-7 and the attached lesson commentary. Explain how these prophecies may be fulfilled through Israel and in Jesus.

Group 3: Read Isaiah 42:1-9. Find every phrase or line that gives a clue to the character or nature of the servant. List these characteristics on a piece of poster board.

Give the groups eight to ten minutes to complete their tasks. Ask each group to report its findings.

INTO LIFE

After the reports, ask the following questions:

1. As you view the list by group 3, what do you see about this servant's character and nature that is different from today's leaders of the world's unjust nations?

2. How does this prophecy offer hope to people suffering under suppressive national leaders today?

3. Believers may suffer injustice or suppression in free nations. Is this happening in our community? How?

Remind the class that the term *servant* refers to Israel, but also points to the Messiah. Then tell them that 2 Timothy 2:24 extends this image to apply to all believers. Give each of the groups a photocopy of 2 Timothy 2:14-26. Ask them to do two things: (1) Find and highlight the verse that best expresses our mission as believers (v. 15) and (2) underline every word or phrase that describes the kind of character or behavior God is wanting each of us to develop. After the exercise, tell the class, "It is apparent God wants his workmen to have that same gentle, faithful, and persistent character that he prophesied in Isaiah."

Direct the learners to the activity "A Hard Look at Myself" on the reproducible page that follows. Suggest that they use it as their personal follow-up of today's study.

Remind the class these are qualities God wants in us even as we address injustices in our community. Ask the class, "What are some of the injustices we see in our community? What groups of people may feel as though they are socially suppressed?" List answers and circumstances on a chalkboard.

Then ask, "Understanding how God wants us to work, what are some gentle and yet practical ways of fighting these injustices?" Note their suggestions by each of the circumstances listed on the chalkboard. Copy and distribute the reproducible page. Have the class suggest responses to the issues identified in the first activity on the reproducible page following.

Close the session by asking two people to pray. The first person is to thank God for the Savior who offers hope and peace to persons experiencing injustices or oppression in their lives. The other will ask for opportunities and God's help for class members to be the servants God calls us to be in ways discussed together in class.

Life's Not Fair, but God Is Good!

The heading of this section is also the title of a book that Robert Schuller wrote several years ago. It speaks to some of the frustrations experienced by many of God's followers as they struggle to live through the injustices of existence. Jot a few ideas about how you could give an encouraging word to believers experiencing some of the situations below.

LIFE'S NOT FAIR	BUT	GOD IS GOOD
Severe economic hardship		
A family death caused by a drunk driver		
Drug dealers and prostitutes taking over your section of town		
A couple is unable to have children while others kill their unborn babies		

A Hard Look at Myself

In 2 Timothy 2:24 Paul extends the image of the "servant" to apply to all believers. Read this passage in 2 Timothy (vv. 14-26), looking for qualities God would like in your life as you seek justice in our world. Then read the following statements and mark each with an A for always, U for usually, O for often, S for sometimes, and N for never. This exercise may give you a glimpse of how you are doing as God's servant.

_____I have godly pride in my daily behavior.

_____I try to be an effective and contributing part of my church.

_____I handle God's word of truth respectfully and correctly.

_____My speech reflects my faith and does not insult God.

_____I am effective at fleeing evil desires.

_____I avoid foolish and godless arguments.

_____I am kind to everyone.

_____I share my faith and gently teach others.

_____I am committed to being God's servant . . . no matter what!

Identify and circle one statement above that reflects an area of life you would like to improve in 2002.

Light for All People
Unit 2: The Response of God's People
(Lessons 6-9)

HEAR THE GOOD NEWS

LESSON 6

WHY TEACH THIS LESSON?

This is the time of year for "emotional letdown." Christmas is over, and by now most people have packed up all the trimmings to await next year's celebration. Today's lesson will help your learners grapple with the question "What's next?" as we consider the *light* that Jesus brings. Now that we have celebrated Jesus' arrival as the manger child of Bethlehem, we must make sure we don't "leave" him there! Although the birth of Jesus was indeed *good news*, that news was very much incomplete apart from the even better news that was yet to come.

INTRODUCTION

A. GOOD NEWS ALL YEAR

With the celebration and merriment of the holidays now past, many now find themselves back in the "daily grind" with little to make them feel cheerful. Once again the headlines seem to be dominated by all the "bad news" taking place. Occasionally we hear the desire expressed that somehow the "spirit of Christmas"—the sense of joy and goodwill that permeates the season—could last all year.

As Christians we know that such a wish can come true. The message of Christmas is about more than just a season or a spirit; it is about a Person. It is the message that God himself put on human flesh and came to live among us. He came to make a difference—not just for a month or a day—but for all time. The "good tidings of great joy" of which the angel spoke to the shepherds (Luke 2:10) is a message that all Christians can tell to those whose lives are being spent in the gloom and darkness of sin. Just as Isaiah brought the message of God's light and salvation to his dark times, so may we, as God's people today, bear witness faithfully to Jesus, the "light of the world."

B. THE MESSIANIC AGE

Isaiah 60 and 61, from which today's texts are taken, describe the future glory that God's people will experience. Chapter 60 uses highly poetic language to prophesy that God's people, whose sins have brought the Lord's condemnation (see chapters 57–59), will become a center of attraction for peoples throughout the world. Chapter 61 describes one whom the Lord has "anointed," who will initiate an "everlasting covenant" that will spread from Israel to all nations (61:8, 9). Isaiah 62 also continues this promise of hope with a prophecy that God will be like a bridegroom to Israel. Her former shame as an adulterous wife will be replaced by God's acknowledgment that he delights in her (62:4, 5).

The relevance of this text to Christians is seen in Jesus' appearance at the synagogue in Nazareth. Having read from Isaiah 61:1 and 2, Jesus declared its fulfillment "today" (Luke 4:21). Portions of these chapters are quoted in Revelation to describe the future glories of Heaven. Revelation 21:25, 26 alludes to Isaiah 60:11, and Isaiah 60:19 is undoubtedly a backdrop for Revelation 21:23; 22:5.

The glory promised by Isaiah in these verses was therefore not for national Israel, but rather for what we might term "spiritual Israel." This spiritual Israel includes the faithful remnant within Israel who would accept the Lord's anointed one, as

DEVOTIONAL READING:
ISAIAH 60:17-22
BACKGROUND SCRIPTURE:
ISAIAH 60, 61
PRINTED TEXT:
ISAIAH 60:1-3; 61:1-4, 10, 11

LESSON AIMS

After participating in this lesson each student will be able to:

Jan 6

1. List several of the blessings that the Lord's "anointed" brings to a world plagued by darkness.

2. Tell how this description also characterizes the mission of the church in the world today.

3. Give a specific example of how an individual or the church can carry out one of the tasks described in the text.

KEY VERSE

Arise, shine, for your light has come, and the glory of the LORD rises upon you. —Isaiah 60:1

LESSON 6 NOTES

well as Gentiles who accepted Christ (cf. Galatians 3:29). The early Christians, at first only Jewish, were used of God as the "light to the Gentiles" (Acts 10:34, 35, 44-48; 11:15-20). The church, then, consisting of both Jews and Gentiles, makes up the "household of God" (Ephesians 2:19; cf. Romans 11:11-24). The church continues to spread the good news of Jesus throughout the world, and in so doing it continues the mission begun by the Lord's anointed one.

C. LESSON BACKGROUND

We have noted in previous studies that Isaiah's prophetic messages touched on the threats of two world powers. The first was Assyria, who dominated the world during Isaiah's lifetime. Isaiah condemned Assyria's brutality and pride in the first part of his writings (chapters 1–39; see, for example, Isaiah 10:1-19, 24-27).

But Isaiah also looked toward the future and saw that the minor power Babylon (which was of little significance at the time) would grow to become the real threat to Judah. His yet-to-be-born countrymen would be enslaved in that foreign empire. Beyond the heartache of captivity, however, Isaiah saw the return of God's people to their homeland.

Then Isaiah looked still further into the future and saw the coming of God's servant who would loose the chains of sin. Jesus came as that servant; his message could be summarized by the title of today's lesson: "Hear the Good News!"

I. THE COMING LIGHT (ISAIAH 60:1-3)

Isaiah had earlier described the pitiful condition that God's people would find themselves in (Isaiah 59:9). But now the waiting is over.

A. PROMISE OF LIGHT (v. 1)

1. *"Arise, shine, for your light has come,*
    and the glory of the LORD rises upon you.

The coming of this *light* is connected with *the glory of the Lord*. Recall a previous lesson, in which Isaiah predicted a time when the glory of God would be "revealed" to all mankind (Isaiah 40:5). Such language finds its fulfillment in the grand event recorded in John 1:14: "The Word became flesh."

B. POWER OF LIGHT (v. 2)

2. *"See, darkness covers the earth*
    and thick darkness is over the peoples,
  but the LORD rises upon you,
    and his glory appears over you.

The picture of *darkness* covering *the earth* reminds us of the situation early in God's creative activity as recorded in Genesis 1:2. God's creative word "Let there be light" (v. 3) shattered that darkness. In parallel imagery, the light provided by the coming of the Word-made-flesh has dispelled the darkness caused by sin. This is the message of the opening verses of John's Gospel (John 1:1-9) and of Paul's words in 2 Corinthians 4:6: "For God, who said, 'Let light shine out of darkness,' made his light shine in our hearts to give us the light of the knowledge of the glory of God in the face of Christ."

C. PRODUCT OF LIGHT (v. 3)

3. *"Nations will come to your light,*
    and kings to the brightness of your dawn.

We already have seen that the ministry of the servant of the Lord is to have a dramatic impact on the *nations* (i.e., the *Gentiles*; Isaiah 42:1, 6; 49:6). The pas-

Arise, shine; for thy light is come, and the glory of the LORD is risen upon thee. —Isaiah 60:1

Display this poster as you begin the lesson. It is a beautiful illustration of today's Key Text.

WHAT DO YOU THINK?

What are some different kinds of "darkness" that threaten the world today? Cite specific examples.

sage before us also includes such an emphasis. While it is true that Jesus is the *light* of the world, his people are also called "the light of the world" (Matthew 5:14). God's people in every age are called "out of darkness into his wonderful light" (1 Peter 2:9) in order to let their light shine before others (Matthew 5:16).

Among those turning to the light of the Lord are *kings*. In Old Testament times, kings (even those who ruled God's people) often corrupted or openly opposed the worship of the Lord, turning instead to pagan gods and practices (cf. Psalm 2:2). Isaiah predicted a radical turnaround in their attitude. John, in his vision of the New Jerusalem, also foresaw evidence of this (Revelation 21:24).

TURNING ON THE LIGHT

Perhaps no inventor ever created more useful devices than Thomas Alva Edison. One that we often take for granted is the electric light bulb—and it may well be the most useful of all his inventions. Edison labored tirelessly over a period of two years, trying some six thousand different fibers to find just the right filament, until he had made his light bulb. More than 120 years later, Edison's invention still brings light to the world. When Edison died, Herbert Hoover, the President of the United States at the time, asked that lights all over America be dimmed in his honor.

In contrast, Jesus is honored, not by the dimming of light, but by the turning on of light—the light that he brought to dispel the darkness caused by sin. That light still "shines in the darkness" (John 1:5), even though the times in which we live seem to grow increasingly dark. Thus we can sing such great gospel songs as "Walking in Sunlight," "The Light of the World Is Jesus," and "Stepping in the Light." Comparing Jesus to light is an illustration that people can easily understand, no matter where or when they live.

It is always dangerous to walk in the darkness—particularly in spiritual darkness. And everyone knows that we live in a dark world. We have only to read the newspaper or watch television to know that. We should rejoice that the Light of the world has given us the possibility of "stepping in the light" and of reflecting that light before others. —R. C. S.

II. THE COMING LIGHT BEARER (ISAIAH 61:1-4)

Not long after Jesus' baptism (Matthew 3:13-17; cf. 4:1-11), he returned to his hometown of Nazareth and announced to those gathered in the synagogue there that he had come to fulfill the words of Isaiah 61:1, 2. (See Luke 4:16-21.) Up to that point, Jesus' miracles and teachings had caused his fame to spread throughout Galilee (Luke 4:14). In Nazareth, Jesus added the witness of Scripture to his messianic credentials. He knew that Isaiah, speaking some seven hundred years earlier, had been describing him and the beginning of the messianic age.

This prophecy has two primary applications. First, it spoke a message of comfort to those who would later become captives in Babylon. Second, it was fulfilled by Jesus in his messianic ministry; this fulfillment includes his ministry while he was in the flesh as well as certain elements that will not be fully realized until his second coming. That climactic event will give all Christians the ultimate "liberty" (Isaiah 61:1), when they are welcomed into Heaven. We have noted that the book of Revelation often uses imagery and vocabulary from this section of isaiah. (Compare Isaiah 60:11 with Revelation 21:25, 26, and Isaiah 60:19 with Revelation 21:23 and 22:5). The central theme of these levels of application is the joyous freedom (found only in the Lord) from all forms of darkness. It is a message of genuine hope!

A. ANOINTED BY GOD (v. 1a)

1a. The Spirit of the Sovereign LORD is on me, because the LORD has anointed me.

WHAT DO YOU THINK?
Identify some ways that the church can be a source of light in this world of darkness.

DAILY BIBLE READINGS
Monday, Dec. 31—Messianic Mission (Luke 4:14-21)
Tuesday, Jan. 1—God's People Will Prosper (Isaiah 60:4-9)
Wednesday, Jan. 2—Nation's Gates Will Stay Open (Isaiah 60:10-14)
Thursday, Jan. 3—God Will be Your Light (Isaiah 60:15-22)
Friday, Jan. 4—Anointed to Bring Good News (Isaiah 61:1-7)
Saturday, Jan. 5—Righteousness Before All Nations (Isaiah 61:8-11)
Sunday, Jan. 6—Worshipers From Afar (Matthew 2:1-12)

WHAT DO YOU THINK?

Jesus appropriated Isaiah 61:1, 2 to himself to describe his ministry (Luke 4:18, 19). To what extent, if at all, do you think it describes the church's ministry now? How can we apply this to ourselves?

[Think of ways in which new methods might be used while the central importance of proclaiming the gospel remains unchanged.]

WHAT DO YOU THINK?

What does the connection between the Old Testament concept of the Jubilee year with the ministry of Christ and his church suggest to you about what the church should be and do, in addressing both physical and spiritual needs?

To be *anointed* is to be separated, dedicated, and consecrated for a divine task. The act of anointing included pouring oil over the head of a person as he was set aside for a specific function or role. Kings were thus consecrated (1 Samuel 16:1, 13) as were priests (Leviticus 8:12). There is one case of the anointing of a prophet (1 Kings 19:16). From the Hebrew word for *anoint* comes the word *Messiah*, which means the same as the Greek word *christos*, from which we get *Christ*. Whether one says "Messiah," "Christ," or "anointed one," the meaning is the same. Isaiah says that God has set aside one to carry out these tasks. Jesus claimed to be that individual, proving that claim with both words and deeds.

B. BRINGING GOOD NEWS (vv. 1b-3)

1b. . . . to preach good news to the poor.
   He has sent me to bind up the brokenhearted,
     to proclaim freedom for the captives
     and release from darkness for the prisoners.

The anointed one will carry out a series of tasks, beginning with preaching *good news to the poor* and binding up *the brokenhearted*. (See Isaiah 42:3.) The references to *freedom* and *release* would have given those exiled in Babylon a sense of hope for better times. But the grandeur of this entire passage (along with Jesus' declaration that he came to fulfill it) indicates something much more wonderful and inclusive than physical liberation.

2. . . . to proclaim the year of the LORD's favor
     and the day of vengeance of our God,
   to comfort all who mourn.

The phrase *the year of the Lord's favor* suggests a link with the Old Testament Year of Jubilee.(See Leviticus 25.) This special year occurred once every fifty years, at which time land was to be returned to the family that had originally owned it and those in bondage set free. The Hebrew words for "proclaim freedom" in Isaiah 61:1 and "proclaim liberty" in the Jubilee regulations of Leviticus 25:10 are the same.

When Jesus quoted Isaiah 61:1 and 2 in the synagogue at Nazareth and applied it to himself, he was declaring his ministry to be the beginning of a new kind of Jubilee. Just as the New Covenant is superior to the Old, so is the New Jubilee superior to the Old. The Jubilee inaugurated by Jesus accomplished goals similar to those of the old one, but on a much grander scale. Jesus made it possible for all humanity to return to its original owner—namely, God himself. He came to bring freedom from sin to those held captive in its tyranny.

In the midst of such a glowing portrayal of the future, Isaiah adds the phrase *the day of vengeance of our God.* These words sound a somber warning to those who will not hear the good news described in the previous verse. God's justice demands that those who reject his grace must experience his justice.

3. . . . and provide for those who grieve in Zion—
   to bestow on them a crown of beauty
     instead of ashes,
   the oil of gladness
     instead of mourning,
   and a garment of praise
     instead of the spirit of despair.
   They will be called oaks of righteousness,
     a planting of the Lord
     for the display of his splendor.

With poetic imagery Isaiah continues to describe the transformations that the Messiah will initiate. Those who grieve in repentance for their sins will see their *ashes* (a symbol of mourning; see Ezekiel 27:30, 31) will give way to *a crown of beauty* (cf. 62:3). This phrase refers to an ornamental head covering signifying joy and gladness—perhaps even eternal reward (cf. Revelation 2:10). Parallel in significance is the phrase *the oil of gladness.* The pouring of oil on someone was associated with times of celebration (cf. Psalms 23:5; 45:7).

The expression *a garment of praise instead of the spirit of mourning* calls to mind other passages in Isaiah that feature clothing as symbolic of one's characteristics or attitudes (cf. 11:5; 59:16, 17). Verse 10 of our text today provides another example.

Finally, Isaiah describes those who feel the impact of the ministry of the Messiah as *oaks of righteousness* and as *a planting of the Lord . . . for the display of his splendor,* which echoes Isaiah 60:21. Romans 3:22 indicates that righteousness is credited to us through faith in Jesus Christ. It is a gift (Romans 5:17). As trees thus planted by the Lord, we are to bring forth fruit that brings glory to the Planter.

C. REBUILDING RUINS (v. 4)

4. *They will rebuild the ancient ruins*
    and restore the places long devastated;
they will renew the ruined cities
    that have been devastated for generations.

The emphasis now shifts to a consideration of the work to be done by God's "oaks of righteousness." Although originally intended for the exiles to return from Babylon, Acts 15:13-17 offers an extended application. There James, addressing the well-known Jerusalem Conference, spoke to the matter of including Gentiles in the church, observing that the prophets were in agreement with this action. While he quotes from Amos 9:11, 12 to support his position, that passage uses language similar to our text here, especially Acts 15:16: "After this I will return and rebuild David's fallen tent. Its ruins I will rebuild, and I will restore it." The rebuilding of *ancient ruins* and *places long devastated* thus finds reexpression in the church's activity in expanding its outreach and bringing the gospel to others. That rebuilding still goes on through the faithful witness of today's "oaks of righteousness."

III. THE COMING JOY (ISAIAH 61:10, 11)

A. LIKE NEW GARMENTS (v. 10)

10. *I delight greatly in the LORD;*
    my soul rejoices in my God.
For he has clothed me with garments of salvation
    and arrayed me in a robe of righteousness,
as a bridegroom adorns his head like a priest,
    and as a bride adorns herself with her jewels.

Here Isaiah again uses poetic imagery to describe what the Lord has done for his people. To be *clothed . . . with garments of salvation* and *arrayed . . . in a robe of righteousness* is his answer to our "filthy rags" (64:6). To have access to such a wardrobe should bring true joy to those who avail themselves of this privilege. See also the clothing imagery of Zechariah 3:3, 4; Revelation 3:4, 5; 6:11; and 21:2.

WEDDING WARDROBES

One of the items most noticed at a wedding ceremony is the attire of those in the wedding party, particularly the bride. Many in our culture today still follow the old rule that a bride must wear "something old, something new, something borrowed, something blue." With the passing of the years, the garments considered suitable for a wedding often change; and they change in different cultures. In the Western world the bride often wears white. In Pakistan the bride wears red. And if

HOW TO SAY IT

Assyria. Uh-SEAR-ee-uh.
Babylon. BAB-uh-lun.
Christos (Greek). KRIS-taws.
Isaiah. Eye-ZAY-uh.
Judea. Joo-DEE-uh.
messianic. mess-ee-AN-ick.

WHAT DO YOU THINK?

Isaiah compares his relationship to God to that of a bride being adorned with jewels (61:10). Similarly, the New Testament likens the church to a bride. What practical application of that analogy can you suggest for us today?

[Ephesians 5:22-33 may provide a good start.]

PRAYER

Father, as we learn more about your plans for our future, we become more grateful and excited. Thank you for Jesus, our anointed One, who is preparing a place for us. Empower us to proclaim boldly his good news. In his name, amen.

you have attended a wedding recently, you know that there can be considerable variety in the garments of the bridegroom.

It is not surprising that wedding customs should be an illustration of salvation. The church is the bride of Christ (Ephesians 5:25-27; Revelation 21:2, 9). Christians are preparing for the coming "wedding supper of the Lamb" (Revelation 19:9) that will forever unite them with their Lord. We cannot be prepared for this occasion as we are: "our righteous acts," says Isaiah, "are like filthy rags" (Isaiah 64:6). We must be clothed with "garments of salvation" and covered by the "robe of righteousness." And only God can provide that "wardrobe." There is no room for change or variety; to try to enter his presence with any attire other than what he supplies is to assure that we will be cast "outside, into the darkness" (Matthew 22:11-14).   —R. C. S.

B. LIKE NEW GROWTH (v. 11)

11. For as the soil makes the sprout come up
    and a garden causes seeds to grow,
so the Sovereign Lord will make righteousness and praise
    spring up before all nations.

Finally, the prophet depicts the worldwide acceptance of the Messiah's "good news." Using the imagery of *seeds* growing in a *garden,* he describes the impact of Jesus' Great Commission (Acts 1:8)—that through the faithful efforts of the church, *all nations* will hear and respond to the gospel. Isaiah's words continue to be fulfilled as thousands of new Christians are born into the family of God daily.

CONCLUSION

Prophecy in the Bible can be, in some respects, like looking into the night sky—first with the naked eye, then with a pair of binoculars, and finally with an extremely powerful telescope. At each of these "levels," new and thrilling sights expand our knowledge. In much the same way, in today's lesson three "horizons" are telescoped: ancient Israel returning from exile, the messianic community (the church), and the yet-to-be realized eternal fellowship of all believers in Heaven.

A. GOOD NEWS FOR EXILES

The first people to find hope in Isaiah's message were the ones who endured the bitterness of the Babylonian captivity. The prophecy let them know that God had not forsaken them. God's concern was not limited by national boundaries; he cared for his people just as much when they were in Babylon as when they were in Jerusalem. But they must "seek the Lord" (Isaiah 55:6).

B. GOOD NEWS FOR JESUS' DISCIPLES

Like Isaiah, Jesus also spoke a message of hope and deliverance. That is what he was doing in the Nazareth synagogue when he quoted from Isaiah 61. And when the residents there rejected him, he was not deterred; he simply spoke elsewhere (Luke 4:43, 44). But Jesus not only spoke the good news, he was and still is the good news. He is still "the way and the truth and the life" (John 14:6).

C. GOOD NEWS FOR US

As Christians, we are living in the messianic age, although not in the fullest form of it. What that fullest form will be, "No eye has seen, no ear has heard, no mind has conceived what God has prepared for those who love him" (1 Corinthians 2:9; cf. Isaiah 64:4). In this life, we experience only a foretaste of what God has in store for believers. We wait expectantly for Heaven and, in the meantime, we testify of our good news to as many as we can.

THOUGHT TO REMEMBER

Jesus is the Good News!

Discovery Learning

This page contains an alternate lesson plan emphasizing learning activities. Classes desiring such student involvement will find these suggestions helpful. The next page is a reproducible activity page to further enhance discovery learning.

LEARNING GOALS

After this lesson, each student will be able to:

1. List several of the blessings that the Lord's "anointed" brings to a world plagued by darkness.

2. Tell how this description also characterizes the mission of the church in the world today.

3. Give an example of how an individual or church can carry out one of the tasks described in the text.

INTO THE LESSON

Early in the week ask a student to prepare a brief report about "the year of the Lord" (Isaiah 61:3) for this lesson. Give the student a Bible dictionary for research.

Duplicate the puzzle below and ask pairs of students to work together to solve it. Provide these instructions: "The key verse of today's text is Isaiah 60:1. 'Arise, shine, for your light has come, and the glory of the Lord rises upon you.' Remove the letters of that statement—in order—from the grid below. The remaining letters will reveal the key concept for today's lesson."

ARISGESOHINOEFDORYNOULERIGWHT
HASCOSMEAHNDTHAEGLSORYOFT
HCELORODRISEMSNUPOENYOU

(Answer: "Good news has come.")

After the students solve the puzzle, tell the class that today's prophecy brought good news to the Israelites, brings good news to us, and promises good news for the future. Use the illustration from the conclusion of the lesson commentary on the naked eye/binoculars/powerful telescope (page 172) to illustrate this concept.

INTO THE WORD

Give a brief lecture about the background for today's prophecy. Then read Isaiah 60:1-3. Explain that darkness probably was more significant and threatening to the ancients than to us who have so many sources of light. To illustrate, turn out the lights and ask how we can proceed with the lesson. It's nearly impossible in some classrooms. Turn the lights back on, asking the class what the imagery of darkness implies in this text.

Provide a chart for the students as follows: The chart should have four columns. The first and largest column should be headed "Prophecy." The second should have the heading "Jews' Return From Captivity." Column 3 is "The Life of Jesus," and Column 4 is "Christ's Return."

Under column 1 write the following prophecies from this text; divide ideas further, as you see fit:

"The Lord rises upon you and his glory appears over you" (60:2).

"Nations will come to your light, and kings to the brightness of your dawn" (60:3).

"The Spirit of the Sovereign Lord is on me, because the Lord has anointed me to preach good news to the poor" (61:1).

"He has sent me to bind up the brokenhearted, to proclaim freedom for the captives and release from darkness for the prisoners" (61:1).

"To proclaim the year of the Lord's favor and the day of vengeance of our God" (61:2).

"To comfort all who mourn, and provide for those who grieve in Zion—to bestow on them a crown of beauty instead of ashes, the oil of gladness instead of mourning, and a garment of praise instead of a spirit of despair" (61:2, 3).

"They will be called oaks of righteousness, a planting of the Lord" (61:3).

"They will rebuild the ancient ruins and restore the places long devastated" (61:4).

"He has clothed me with garments of salvation and arrayed me in a robe of righteousness" (61:10).

"The Sovereign Lord will make righteousness and praise spring up before all nations" (61:11).

Ask the students to read each prophecy printed and to place a check mark (✔) in the appropriate column to indicate how the prophecy would be fulfilled. (Remind the class that a prophecy may have more than one fulfillment.) After the task is completed, review each prophecy and ask how or why the groups applied it in the chart. When you get to the prophecy about the "year of the Lord," ask the student who did the research to give his or her report.

Use the reproducible activity "Dressing Up!" from the page that follows to expand on the clothing imagery in some of these prophecies. The class may do this activity together or you may assign some students to work on it while others complete the chart described above.

INTO LIFE

Use the reproducible activity "Function and Action" from the page that follows to discuss with the class how the roles of the Messiah as God's Servant match that of God's church. Ask, "How does it need to do more? How can we individually help?"

Dressing Up!

Today's text contains some wonderful imagery of how God will work in the lives of his followers. Here is how God would like to dress you. Read the texts indicated. Then answer the questions and rediscover a beautiful glimpse of God's goodness to you. (Write your answers on the "garments" pictured below.)

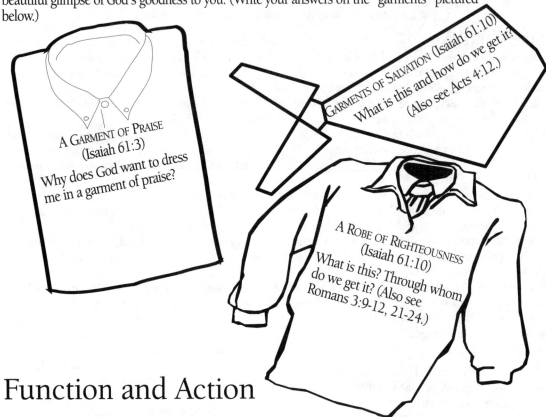

A GARMENT OF PRAISE
(Isaiah 61:3)
Why does God want to dress me in a garment of praise?

GARMENTS OF SALVATION (Isaiah 61:10)
What is this and how do we get it?
(Also see Acts 4:12.)

A ROBE OF RIGHTEOUSNESS
(Isaiah 61:10)
What is this? Through whom do we get it? (Also see Romans 3:9-12, 21-24.)

Function and Action

Isaiah 61:1-3 tells us the anointed one (Messiah) will perform at least six functions. List these six functions in the first column below. Remember that, as Christ's body, we also have a responsibility to carry out these functions as well as we can. In the second column give one or two ideas of how the church or individual Christians can help accomplish these tasks.

SIX FUNCTIONS OF THE MESSIAH	CHRIST'S CHURCH IN ACTION
v. 1 _____	_____
v. 1 _____	_____
v. 1 _____	_____
v. 2 _____	_____
v. 2 _____	_____
v. 3 _____	_____

SEEK THE LORD

LESSON 7

WHY TEACH THIS LESSON?

Blaise Pascal was a famous French mathematician who lived from 1623 to 1662. "Pascal's wager" is one of his more interesting contributions to human thought. In this "wager," Pascal proposed that if a person were to follow Christ and live a Christian life, then such a believer would lose nothing important in this life if the belief turned out to be false, but would gain eternal happiness in the next life if the belief turned out to be true. On the other hand, if a person were to reject Christ and the Christian life, then such an unbeliever would gain nothing important in this life if the unbelief turned out to be true, but would lose everything in the next life if the unbelief turned out to be false. Thus, Pascal concluded, logic favors embracing the Christian faith.

The Scripture tells us that God has set eternity in the human heart (Ecclesiastes 3:11). There is a basic yearning or thirst for that which is eternal in everyone. Today's lesson is about how to satisfy that thirst; it is about the blessings that God promises us if we make the right choice. And, like "Pascal's wager," this lesson demonstrates the foolhardiness of pursing earthly things that will ultimately fail to satisfy or amount to anything important. Today's lesson reassures the believer that he or she has indeed made the right choice. It also helps equip the believer for witnessing to unbelievers.

INTRODUCTION

A. PRIORITIES AND PROSPERITY

The boat salesman loved this customer! Every year the customer would stop by the salesman's showroom because he always wanted to buy the newest gadget or piece of equipment. These innovations intrigued the man for about a month or so; then he began to search the catalogs and to think about what his next purchase ought to be. It seemed that nothing—not the latest instruments, the biggest motor, or the sleekest design—could satisfy him for very long.

If only this man could have stepped back for a moment and taken a good look at himself! His passion for boat buying reflected how unfulfilled his life had become. His zeal for new boats reflected his ambition for other new items—a new house, a new car, new sports "toys," new lawn equipment, new clothing, and eventually (and most tragic of all) a new wife. But what were his real needs? What was he really longing for? Why had his life become so empty? And why did it seem to be getting emptier in spite of his efforts to fill it with more and more "things"?

Rather than recognizing that their deepest needs are spiritual, many people prefer to act like hummingbirds, who flit from flower to flower to satisfy their insatiable appetites. These spiritually empty people go from boat to boat, partner to partner, in search of fulfillment. But all too quickly their infatuation with newness wears off and the excitement with novelty dissolves into dullness. Many a parent has been annoyed by a child who spent thirty-five dollars for a popular T-shirt that faded after the first wash and soon ended up in the rag box. Yet many parents act like such children; they simply do so on a larger scale.

DEVOTIONAL READING:
PSALM 85:4-9

BACKGROUND SCRIPTURE:
ISAIAH 55

PRINTED TEXT:
ISAIAH 55:1-9

LESSON AIMS

After participating in this lesson, each student will be able to:

1. Summarize the invitation of Isaiah 55 and the blessings promised to those who respond.

2. Contrast those things that truly satisfy with the poor substitutes people too often crave and acquire.

3. Commit himself or herself to answering God's invitation at whatever level is needed in his or her life.

Jan
13

KEY VERSE

Seek the LORD while he may be found; call on him while he is near. —Isaiah 55:6

LESSON 7 NOTES

Such people view life through a very narrow lens. Their highest priority is to experience all that this life "under the sun" has to offer—even if their experiences are short-lived. Sadly, their lives become as shallow as that of the customer in the boat showroom. Not until we learn to look at life through the broad lens of eternity will our view become clear. Only then will we set priorities that replace a feeling of frustration and futility with a genuine sense of fulfillment.

B. LESSON BACKGROUND

The prophet Isaiah began his ministry to Judah in approximately 740 B.C.—"the year that King Uzziah died" (Isaiah 6:1). The first half of the eighth century B.C. had been prosperous for both Israel and Judah. To put the situation in today's terms, the national economy was strong, housing starts were up, chariot sales were at an all-time high—in short, the gross national product was higher than at any time since David and Solomon's golden age (see 2 Chronicles 26:1-15).

But beneath the external affluence, Isaiah saw spiritual problems that the material prosperity only disguised. He observed fragmented families, corrupt business practices, political kickbacks, and faithless religious leaders. And what Isaiah saw among the wealthy citizens he saw in the rest of the population as well. All were caught up in the delusion that a person's life consists in the abundance of possessions (cf. Luke 12:15). Such thinking is quite prevalent in our materialistic age, which makes Isaiah's message as timely for us as it was for his original hearers.

I. BECOMING SATISFIED (ISAIAH 55:1, 2)

We have noted that Isaiah 40–66 was written from the perspective of addressing (future) Jewish captives in Babylon and comforting them with the assurance that they would one day return home. But there are portions of these chapters that extend the Lord's appeal beyond Israel to include the entire world. "'Turn to me and be saved, all you ends of the earth; for I am God, and there is no other,'" declares the Lord through the prophet (45:22). In previous studies we have examined passages from Isaiah that indicate God's desire for the Gentiles to hear his truth and be blessed by his light (42:1, 6; 49:6; 60:3). That emphasis appears in today's text as well, beginning with an invitation to "all you who are thirsty."

A. GOD'S GRACIOUS OFFER (v. 1)

1. *"Come, all you who are thirsty,*
    come to the waters;
 and you who have no money,
    come, buy and eat!
 Come, buy wine and milk
    without money and without cost.

Waters, wine, and *milk* represent the essentials of a contented life. A similar "trinity of drinks" is used in Joel 3:18 to describe future blessings promised to Judah. Bible writers sometimes express completeness by using groups of three. For example, the aliens, the fatherless, and the widow represent helpless people (Deuteronomy 14:29; Psalm 94:6; Jeremiah 7:6); sword, famine, and plague stand for disaster (Jeremiah 29:17; 32:24; Ezekiel 6:11); and to wear sackcloth, to lament (mourn), and to wail are ways to express grief (Jeremiah 4:8; Joel 1:13).

Notice that Isaiah invites *all* to obtain what he offers—without paying. All who thirst for happiness, contentment, and satisfaction can have them *without money and without cost.* In God's sight, poverty is not a handicap and wealth is not an advantage. All the wealth in the world cannot buy God's favor. In fact, it must be accepted as a gift or not at all.

DAILY BIBLE READINGS

Monday, Jan. 7—I Sought; the Lord Answered (Psalm 34: 1-10)

Tuesday, Jan. 8—My Soul Thirsts for God (Psalm 63:1-8)

Wednesday, Jan. 9—Seek the Lord's Strength (Psalm 105:1-7)

Thursday, Jan. 10—The Holy One Redeems You (Isaiah 54:4-8)

Friday, Jan. 11—Heritage of the Lord's Servants (Isaiah 54: 9-17)

Saturday, Jan. 12—Accept the Lord's Free Grace (Isaiah 55:1-5)

Sunday, Jan. 13—Return to the Lord (Isaiah 55:6-13)

B. MAN'S FUTILE EFFORTS (v. 2)

2. *"Why spend money on what is not bread,*
  and your labor on what does not satisfy?
 Listen, listen to me, and eat what is good,
  and your soul will delight in the richest of fare.

Given the fact that contentment in life is free, Isaiah marvels that people *labor* so hard *on what does not satisfy.* Genuine satisfaction and fulfillment in life come not by laboring but by listening. They come only to those who *listen* to what God himself says. The phrase *richest of fare* signifies the joy of the spiritual blessings that come when we hear and obey the Word of God and find the *"bread* of life" available only in Jesus (John 6:35, 68).

THIRST

We can better appreciate Isaiah's invitation to "all you who are thirsty" if we consider the land in which he lived. Palestine has always been characterized by a scarcity of water. Most of the rivers there are small and have little if any water during the summer. As a result, rain becomes particularly critical; and in the dry summers, any vegetation is dependent on the heavy dews for moisture. Irrigation is practiced where necessary. Thus Isaiah's hearers knew how dangerous—how deadly—thirst could be. Most of us, who can obtain water simply at the turn of a tap, have not experienced that.

It is said that a person can live for sixty days without food, but only six days without water. In fact, the body is sixty percent water. For that reason, thirst is a good metaphor to picture a deep spiritual longing or need. Jesus used the same language in his Sermon on the Mount: "Blessed are those who hunger and thirst for righteousness, for they will be filled" (Matthew 5:6).

When you are really thirsty, only water will truly satisfy your thirst. You can drink coffee, tea, or soft drinks, but nothing quenches thirst like water. Just as the body must have water to live, so the soul must receive the kind of water offered by Isaiah in his great invitation. We are spiritual beings. We need to acknowledge our spiritual thirst—a thirst for God—and recognize that he has supplied what is needed to satisfy it. How tragic that many try to satisfy a longing for God without God's gracious provisions!
—R. C. S.

II. ENTERING A COVENANT (ISAIAH 55:3-5)

Isaiah goes on to specify what is in store for those who will heed God's voice.

A. AN EVERLASTING COVENANT (v. 3)

3. *"Give ear and come to me;*
  hear me, that your soul may live.
 I will make an everlasting covenant with you,
  my faithful love promised to David.

A *covenant* is an agreement or contract. God had made a covenant with Israel at Mount Sinai more than seven hundred years previously (Exodus 19:5, 6). This covenant was meant to govern the lives of God's people, though frequently it had been disregarded and was largely ignored in Isaiah's time. Centuries after this covenant, God made a covenant with an individual—*David*, whom God declared to be "a man after his own heart" (1 Samuel 13:14). He promised that David's kingdom would be established forever and that David's house would rule forever (2 Samuel 7:12-29). This covenant with David was to be the basis for a "new covenant" with God's people (Jeremiah 31:31). This covenant would not be like the old one, written on stone, but would be written on the people's hearts (Jeremiah 31:33).

WHAT DO YOU THINK?

The average person today labors for a nice home, financial security, a good education, and a host of other things. Why do these things not satisfy one's true need?

Other prophets called attention to the importance of this covenant with David and its *everlasting* nature. Jeremiah, who predicted the downfall of Jerusalem and then saw that sad event come to pass, nevertheless preached that God's covenant with David was as unchangeable as the laws of nature (Jeremiah 33:20-22). Ezekiel predicted the day when God's people would be established in their land with David as their king, shepherd, and prince (Ezekiel 37:24-28). It is clear from the New Testament that Jesus, the Son of David, came to fulfill the words of the prophets and to receive "the throne of his father David" (Luke 1:32). Of special note is the fact that Isaiah's words in the verse before us are quoted by Paul in Acts 13:34, where that which was *promised* to David is linked with the resurrection of Jesus. Christians are the beneficiaries of the everlasting covenant—the New Covenant—by which sins are forgiven and forgotten (cf. Hebrews 8:6-13).

B. A SPECIAL INDIVIDUAL (v. 4)
4. "*See, I have made him a witness to the peoples,*
    a leader and commander of the peoples.

It would appear at first glance that the pronoun *him* in this verse must refer to David, mentioned in verse 3. Certainly David fulfilled the roles of *witness, leader,* and *commander* listed here. However, given the role of David in prophecy (see the comments under the previous verse), these words are most likely describing Jesus, the King who was to inherit David's throne. Jesus is God's *witness* to the world (John 18:37). As King of kings and Lord of lords (Revelation 17:14; 19:16), he is the supreme *leader* and *commander.* The prophets looked back to David and saw the future Messiah. The apostles looked back to David and declared that the Messiah had come—in Jesus.

C. A WORLDWIDE APPEAL (v. 5)
5. "*Surely you will summon nations you know not,*
    and nations that do not know you will hasten to you,
  because of the LORD your God,
    the Holy One of Israel,
    for he has endowed you with splendor."

This verse raises a question about another pronoun, *you,* and to whom or what it refers. One possibility is that it refers to *Israel.* The first Christians were Jews (Israelites), and from them the gospel went forth to other *nations*—a scene vividly depicted in Isaiah 2:2-4. But these nations would not be attracted to Israel; they would be drawn to *the Holy One of Israel.* He *endowed* Israel *with splendor* by sending Jesus as part of that nation and giving its people the honor of heralding the good news of salvation to other nations.

On the other hand, *you* may refer to Jesus, who is the one to *summon* all *nations* to come to God through him (Matthew 28:19, 20; John 14:6). Certainly God glorified Jesus by raising him from the dead and giving him a place at his right hand. Either way, the focus is on Jesus as the One through whom the nations come to know the Lord. He thus becomes not only the Holy One of Israel, but also the Holy One of all peoples.

III. SEEKING GOD (ISAIAH 55:6-9)
The parables in Luke 15 picture two sides of what it means to seek God. The parables of the lost sheep (vv. 3-7) and the lost coin (vv. 8-10) picture God seeking a lost sinner. The parable of the prodigal son (vv. 11-24) pictures the sinner seeking God. The lost son was not found until he said, "I will set out and go

back to my father" (v. 18). Then he took action: "he got up and went to his father" (v. 20). No sinner is saved against his or her will; there must be a mutual seeking. The final section of our text tells us what is involved in seeking the Lord.

A. HIS NEARNESS (v. 6)

6. Seek the LORD while he may be found;
*   call on him while he is near.*

The phrases *while he may be found* and *while he is near* carry with them a solemn warning. A time will come when the Lord will not be found—when it will be too late to seek him. Such was the sad plight of the foolish virgins described in one of Jesus' parables (Matthew 25:11, 12). The Bible also describes instances where God "gives up" or "gives over" individuals to their sinful behavior (Romans 1:24, 26, 28). In spiritual matters, to delay or hesitate is to invite peril. The Scripture is clear: "I tell you, now is the time of God's favor, now is the day of salvation" (2 Corinthians 6:2).

B. HIS DEMANDS (v. 7)

7. Let the wicked forsake his way,
*   and the evil man his thoughts.*
* Let him turn to the Lord, and he will have mercy on him,*
*   and to our God, for he will freely pardon.*

While salvation is free (v. 1), it does require repentance. The *wicked* must *forsake his way*; the one who desires God's *mercy* must sever ties with the world and its pleasures and leave the sinful lifestyle behind. Further, repentance must go deeper than mere actions and words: even sinful *thoughts* must become a thing of the past (cf. Matthew 5:28). In short, the individual must change the direction of his or her life and *turn* (or return) to the Lord. Then, as he did with the people of Nineveh in Jonah's day (Jonah 3:10), God *will have mercy* and *will freely pardon* those who give evidence of such repentance.

PARDON ME

It has been said that the English language has more words than any other language on earth. (Some have estimated that there are around two million of them.) Yet, in spite of this remarkable number, many words can have more than one meaning. Such is the case with the word *pardon*. At the lower end of the scale, it means that an individual wants to be excused from some harmless discourtesy or minor infraction of the rules of decorum. After committing such an act, the individual will say, "Pardon me." At the opposite end of the scale, the word means that someone is granted a reprieve from punishment for a serious crime against the laws of the state or nation.

As *pardon* is used in today's lesson (Isaiah 55:7), it is on the high end of the scale. It does not describe being excused from a harmless mistake done accidentally. It means being forgiven for serious and deliberate acts of disobedience against the laws of Heaven.

We know from experience that only a high official (a governor, president, or prime minister, for example) can issue a pardon. In the spiritual realm, the same is true: only God can pardon us of our sins. No one else can do it.

In the situations we hear or read about, a pardon is usually issued because of some extenuating circumstances on the part of the offender. But that is not the case with spiritual pardon. It is issued solely because of grace on God's part; it is in no way linked to whether our circumstances mean that we somehow merit his forgiveness. We do not. Augustus M. Toplady, in the beautiful hymn "Rock of Ages," captures the futility of trying to earn God's favor:

WHAT DO YOU THINK?

The lesson writer tells how important it is for the *unbeliever* to seek the Lord. In what sense do you think the *believer* also needs to submit to Isaiah's command, "Seek the Lord while he may be found"?

[Draw on passages such as Ecclesiastes 12:1 and Matthew 6:33 in your discussion.]

WHAT DO YOU THINK?

Do you think unbelievers today think of themselves as "wicked"? Why or why not? How can we help people see the need to apply the message of Isaiah 55:7 to themselves?

HOW TO SAY IT

Babylon. BAB-uh-lun.
Ezekiel. Ee-ZEEK-yul or Ee-ZEEK-ee-yul.
Isaiah. Eye-ZAY-uh.
Jeremiah. Jair-uh-MY-uh.
Nineveh. NIN-uh-vuh.
Samaritan. Suh-MARE-uh-tun.
Uzziah. Uh-ZYE-uh.

PRAYER

Father, every time we drink deeply of your "living water," we find honest satisfaction in life. We find a contentment and a fulfillment greater than anything the world can and offer. Thank you that your "fountain of youth" never runs dry. May we drink deeply, and may we constantly seek to lead others to drink as well. In Jesus' name, amen.

WHAT DO YOU THINK?

How can we relate to a God who is infinitely greater than we are in every way?

[Consider passages such as Leviticus 11:44; Isaiah 55:8, 9; John 14:9; 1 Timothy 6:16; Hebrews 4:15; and 2 Peter 1:17-21 in your discussion.]

THOUGHT TO REMEMBER

No God, no peace;
Know God, know peace.

Could my tears forever flow,
    Could my zeal no languor know,
These for sin could not atone;
    Thou must save, and Thou alone:
In my hand no price I bring,
    Simply to Thy cross I cling.

—R. C. S.

C. HIS WAYS (vv. 8, 9)

8, 9. *"For my thoughts are not your thoughts,*
    neither are your ways my ways," declares the LORD.
As the heavens are higher than the earth,
    so are my ways higher than your ways,
    and my thoughts than your thoughts."

The word *for* should cause us to link this verse with the preceding one and to examine our own thoughts and ways. Too often they are not what God would have them to be. Like Jonah, perhaps we are unmerciful and unwilling to pardon when God is (Jonah 4:1-11). Perhaps we resemble the elder brother in Jesus' parable of the prodigal son—sour and bitter when we should be celebrating (Luke 15:25-32).

Isaiah's description of God in this passage is in line with others that we have already observed in our study of Isaiah (40:28-31; 42:5). He is all powerful, all knowing, all present, all in all. Is that the kind of God we worship and serve? Or is our view of God too limited? Have we allowed circumstances to dictate the size of our faith and to dim our vision of God's majesty and power?

On a recent preaching tour, I stayed in the home of some faithful church members. In the bedroom was a beautiful aquarium complete with ceramic castle, seaweed, colored gravel, aerator, and a happy little goldfish named Biff. Biff simply swam around his glass-encased world, totally ignorant of the greater reality beyond his experiences. He knew nothing of the music playing on the radio, nothing of the high-powered, fuel-injected pickup truck in the driveway, nothing of the angel food cake baking in the oven, nothing of the algebra that one of the boys was studying nearby. In fact, Biff knew almost nothing about anything. His experiences were limited to his own little ceramic castle, the wavy seaweed, and the bubbles from the aerator.

Humbling though it may be to us, we are, in a way, like Biff. We are in our own little world, limited by our physical experiences and unable to grasp the greater spiritual reality that lies beyond our senses. Unlike Biff, we are created in the image of God and are thus able to receive the revelation of God that he has provided. He has spoken to us through the witness of his creation (Romans 1:18-20) and through the greater witness of his Son (Hebrews 1:1, 2). Yet how often do we spend our days focused on and preoccupied with only our immediate surroundings. We do not see the magnitude of God. He has shown us what can give satisfaction in life: it is a relationship with him! To seek contentment in life apart from seeking the Lord is only an exercise in futility.

CONCLUSION

Isaiah extended the Lord's offer of an "everlasting covenant" (55:3). Today every Christian lives under this New Covenant, through which sins are forgiven and forgotten (Hebrews 8:8-12). It is in that covenant, accepted in faith, that we find our ultimate contentment. Life on earth is filled with many good things, and we know that "every good and perfect gift is from above" (James 1:17). But we must never be drawn away from the eternal good that comes when we seek God.

Discovery Learning

This page contains an alternate lesson plan emphasizing learning activities. Classes desiring such student involvement will find these suggestions helpful. The next page is a reproducible activity page to further enhance discovery learning.

LEARNING GOALS

After participating in this lesson each student will be able to:

1. Summarize the invitation of Isaiah 55 and the blessings promised to those who respond.

2. Contrast those things that truly satisfy with the poor substitutes people too often crave and acquire.

3. Commit himself or herself to answering God's invitation at whatever level is needed in his or her life.

INTO THE LESSON

Before class prepare two posters. One should resemble the popular bumper sticker: "No God, no peace. Know God, know peace!"

On the second poster have the following three sentences: "I wanted one very much, so I . . . "; "I know it was too expensive, but I bought it anyway"; "I was honored to be recognized for. . . . "

Begin this lesson by asking each class member to find a partner (other than his or her own spouse). Ask each person to begin with one of the above sentences to tell his or her partner about a personal experience. Allow a few minutes; then ask volunteers to tell about their partners' experiences. Take about five minutes for these reports. Then remind the class that people always seem to be looking for satisfaction and fulfillment in life. Unfortunately, real contentment usually does not come through accumulating possessions, power, or recognition. Point to the "Know God" poster saying, "This bumper sticker gets to the heart of today's Bible lesson."

INTO THE WORD

Use the introduction and historical background in the lesson commentary (pages 175, 176) to set the scene for this Bible study. Then choose some or all of the following activities.

Dramatization. Early in the week ask three persons to be ready to dramatize the encounter of a Samaritan woman with Jesus (John 4:1-18, 25, 26). The characters needed include a narrator, Jesus, and the woman. The team may feel free to paraphrase all or part of the text and to insert some of the problems with this encounter (such as a Jew talking to a Samaritan—and a woman, at that). After the drama, highlight the dialogue about the water that completely satisfies. Use this as an introduction to Isaiah 55:1.

Bible Paraphrase. Write the following Scripture references on a chalkboard: Isaiah 55:1, 2; Isaiah 55:3-5; Isaiah 55:6; Isaiah 55:7; Isaiah 55:8, 9. In pairs or small teams, class members should write one- or two-sentence paraphrases or interpretations of each section of Scripture. After a few minutes, allow groups to report. If you have too many groups to hear all the reports, choose a representative group for each passage. Other groups can add to each reporting group's insights.

Echoes of Ecclesiastes. This activity may be done with the entire class or in small groups. Give each student a copy of the reproducible page that follows. Ask the students to complete the first activity on the page. Allow a few minutes for them to work; then review their findings. (*Their responses may be similar to the following: 1:12-14: earthly wisdom is meaningless; 2:1, 10, 11: pleasure is meaningless; 2:17, 26: work is meaningless; 4:13-16: advancement is meaningless; 5:10: wealth is meaningless; 6:1-7: life itself is meaningless.*)

Note that, "under the sun," or from a purely human perspective, these things are meaningless. But, dedicated to God, each of these activities can be significant!

INTO LIFE

Make two columns on the chalkboard. Write over the first column "Unsatisfying Priorities." Ask the class to give practical illustrations of things people crave or pursue to find satisfaction—pursuits that do not fulfill our deepest yearnings. Write their ideas on the list. After that exercise, write "Seek the Lord—Practical Steps" over the second column. Ask learners to scan today's text, looking for clues on how to accomplish this task, and then brainstorm other practical steps to accomplish this goal.

Ask the class to share examples, good and bad, of these three Scriptures: (1) "Come, all you who are thirsty, come to the waters" (55:1). (2) "Why spend money on what is not bread?" (3) "Seek the Lord." This exercise is in the student book, *NIV Bible Student.*

Option. Refer students to the reproducible activity "Picking Priorities" on the page that follows. Ask the students to consider seriously their current priorities, as reflected in the criteria cited. Then have them write some revised priorities that will help them seek the Lord.

In small groups, each person who is willing is to offer a personal prayer, making a commitment to keep focused on seeking the Lord.

Echoes of Ecclesiastes!

Like Isaiah in Chapter 55:1-9, the writer of Ecclesiastes points us toward evaluating life's priorities. Much of Ecclesiastes spells out the foolish and meaningless goals some people have for life. Read a sampling of these teachings and jot these meaningless goals in the blanks below. Then read the key truth of the book and discover the conclusion of the matter.

Ecclesiastes 1:12, 14: What is meaningless?	Ecclesiastes 4:13-16: What is meaningless?
Ecclesiastes 2:1, 10, 11: What is meaningless?	Ecclesiastes 5:10: What is meaningless?
Ecclesiastes 2:17, 26: What is meaningless?	Ecclesiastes 6:1-7: What is meaningless?
Ecclesiastes 12:13: What is the conclusion of the matter?	

Picking Priorities

If an objective auditor were to use the following criteria to evaluate your priorities, what would he or she list as the top three priorities of your life? List them in the first column. After reading Isaiah 55:1-9, list the items you think God wants to be priorities for your life.

Criteria: How you use your money.
Where you spend your free time.
Where, how much, and when you volunteer.
What you think about.

MY PRIORITIES NOW   WHAT THEY SHOULD BE

1.

2.

3.

WORSHIP IN TRUTH

WHY TEACH THIS LESSON?

At least four modern pop songs carry the title "Going Through the Motions." Have you ever felt that way about the worship services you attend? That after you had sung the songs, broken the bread, and offered your offering, all you were left with was that empty feeling of just having "gone through the motions"? (Then, after the service was over, perhaps you said to someone "Boy, I sure didn't get much out of that service today!")

Maybe the problem isn't with the Sunday morning worship service itself—maybe the problem is with how God views you as a part of that service. Before worship can truly "mean something" to you, it must "mean something" to God. And he is very clear in his Word that he expects our various acts of worship to result in *action*. Perhaps the real problem with those Sunday worship services that seem so meaningless and "flat" is that we have disconnected them from that which we do the other six days of the week. If you think yourself guilty of this, you're not alone. The Jews of Isaiah's time made similar mistakes. Today, let us use their "bad example" to spur us on to more meaningful worship.

INTRODUCTION

A. FACTS ABOUT FASTING

Some form of the word *fasting* occurs seven times in today's text. Fasting is usually defined as going without food for the purpose of (1) seeking to draw closer to God, (2) seeking God's will in a particularly important matter, or (3) showing contrition and expressing a desire to repent of a particular sin or sins. Fasting is one of many acts of worship and is intended to be a deeply spiritual exercise. We see several individuals fasting in the Bible, including Moses (Exodus 34:28), David (2 Samuel 12:22), Ezra (Ezra 10:6), Daniel (Daniel 9:3, 4), Jesus (Matthew 4:2), and the leaders of the church in Antioch including Barnabas and Saul (Acts 13:1-3).

The law of Moses prescribed fasting only on the Day of Atonement (Leviticus 16:29, 31), though the practice was not limited to that. There are many occasions in which someone fasted as a response to specific circumstances or needs.

In some cases fasting was an expression of grief (1 Samuel 31:13; 2 Samuel 1:12; Nehemiah 1:4). In other instances it reflected individual and national repentance (1 Samuel 7:6; 1 Kings 21:27; Nehemiah 9:1, 2; Jonah 3:5-8). Note that 1 Kings 21:27 mentions the fasting of wicked King Ahab, and Jonah 3:5-8 describes how even the pagan Ninevites (Assyrians) fasted in response to Jonah's message of divine judgment.

As with all forms of worship, fasting can be reduced to a mere outward performance, intended to impress others or to try to put God in one's debt. In that sense fasting runs the same risk as singing special music, attending church and Sunday school regularly, having daily devotions, offering a Communion meditation, and participating in various other religious activities. In the Sermon on the Mount, Jesus warns us not to be like the "hypocrites," who "disfigure their faces to show men they are fasting" (Matthew 6:16). True fasting is a private act of worship, springing from a heart that desires to know God more fully.

DEVOTIONAL READING:
ISAIAH 58:9b-14
BACKGROUND SCRIPTURE:
ISAIAH 58
PRINTED TEXT:
ISAIAH 58:1-9a

LESSON AIMS

After this lesson students will be able to:

1. Tell the significant points Isaiah makes about the futility of empty worship.

2. Compare the useless worship of Isaiah's day with equally futile practices of some today.

3. Identify a specific way to practice a true fast and make a commitment to do it.

Jan
20

KEY VERSE

Is not this the kind of fasting I have chosen: to loose the chains of injustice and untie the cords of the yoke, to set the oppressed free and break every yoke?
—Isaiah 58:6

B. LESSON BACKGROUND

Many of God's people in Isaiah's day had lost sight of the true meaning of worship (cf. Isaiah 1:11-17; 43:22-24). Their attitude toward fasting was one example. To them, the practice of abstaining from food for a particular time had degenerated into nothing more than a mindless ritual. No doubt some people actually believed that their observance of the ritual impressed God, as though he needed to see evidence of their self-abasement. What a total misunderstanding (and staggering arrogance) they demonstrated by performing such empty actions!

The real issue of today's lesson text is not the act of fasting itself. Isaiah mentions fasting to make the point that God's people really have no heart for him and that their forms of worship have become mere outward expressions and evidence that love has grown cold. Thus, our lesson goes to "the heart of the matter" in worship: no religious expression has any validity unless the daily life of the worshiper is characterized by godliness. For Christians, this means that we must honor God *between* Sundays as well as *on* them. Otherwise, we cannot truly honor him on Sundays.

I. INEFFECTIVE WORSHIP (ISAIAH 58:1-5)

A. COMMAND TO ISAIAH (v. 1)

1. *"Shout it aloud, do not hold back.*
   Raise your voice like a trumpet.
Declare to my people their rebellion
   and to the house of Jacob their sins.

The first item mentioned in this passage is not the people's worship; it is their *sins* against God. Isaiah is commissioned to expose these sins (Isaiah 6), for they are the reason that the people's worship has become an abomination to God. The same indictment is applicable to anyone today who would try to "play church."

B. INDICTMENT OF THE PEOPLE (v. 2)

2. *"For day after day they seek me out;*
   they seem eager to know my ways,
as if they were a nation that does what is right
   and has not forsaken the commands of its God.
They ask me for just decisions
   and seem eager for God to come near them.

Using satire, Isaiah describes his countrymen as people who appear to want, above all else, to *know* God. If we look beneath the satire, we can get an idea of what truly characterizes a spiritual person: one who seeks God *day after day,* is *eager to know* his *ways,* lives by the standards of *what is right,* asks God for justice, and is *eager* to have *God . . . come near.* All of this is what God's people wanted to appear to be doing; however, the way they lived their lives told a different story.

C. THE PEOPLE'S QUESTIONS (v. 3a)

3a. *"'Why have we fasted,' they say,*
   'and you have not seen it?
Why have we humbled ourselves
   and you have not noticed?'

The people of Judah *fasted* and were regular in performing many other religious duties. They professed to be concerned about instruction from the Lord. They complained that God was not taking any note of them and they wanted to know why. Their words reflect their self-centered "me first" approach to God. They assumed that doing God's will carried with it certain benefits and rewards. Where were those benefits and rewards? What good was all this piety doing them?

D. GOD'S RESPONSE (vv. 3b-5)

Through his prophet, the Lord probed the real motivation behind the people's fasting. To these careless worshipers, this day was just like any other—a time to make a profit, a time to serve themselves. While going through the rigors of self-imposed hunger, they intended to manipulate God and to impress him with their "spirituality" so that he would become their servant! Instead of reporting for duty, they were giving orders to the one in charge! The people's daily conduct— their lack of concern for the things that mattered to God—revealed that fasting was not a genuine act of worship for them.

3b. "Yet on the day of your fasting, you do as you please
and exploit all your workers.

The *day of . . . fasting* had become a day of pleasure. Instead of pleasing God, the people were pleasing their own desires. Here they are accused of dishonesty in business practices, though the exact nature of the exploitation is not stated.

4. "Your fasting ends in quarreling and strife,
and in striking each other with wicked fists.
You cannot fast as you do today
and expect your voice to be heard on high.

Will God heed the requests of those who abuse the sacredness of fasting as these people have? If they *expect* their *voice to be heard on high,* they must change their entire outlook on fasting (and on worship in general).

5. "Is this the kind of fast I have chosen,
only a day for a man to humble himself?
Is it only for bowing one's head like a reed
and for lying on sackcloth and ashes?
Is that what you call a fast,
a day acceptable to the Lord?

The implied answer to all three questions is obvious. What the people were doing had no meaning as an act of genuine worship. They were merely abstaining from food. A time of fasting should be a time to focus on the Lord in a special way, a time for a person to humble himself or herself before God, a time to examine one's life in order to discard whatever is displeasing to our Creator. But God's people were "going through the motions" in a way that only appeared to indicate true worship. To put on an outward show of *bowing one's head like a reed* or to lie in *sackcloth and ashes* might fool one's fellow worshipers, but it won't fool God.

Consistency—that is what God expects from his people. One's piety should be the same every day, whether the day is sacred or not. It is deceptive and dangerous to hold that certain days are "sacred," while others are labeled as "secular" and therefore not subject to God's authority. All our lives should belong to the Lord and should be lived under the direction of his standards. As Paul later stated, "And whatever you do, whether in word or deed, do it all in the name of the Lord Jesus, giving thanks to God the Father through him" (Colossians 3:17).

II. TRUE WORSHIP (ISAIAH 58:6, 7)

Isaiah could have illustrated true worship with actions other than fasting. We are familiar with worship activities such as singing hymns, bowing our heads in prayer, reading the Scriptures, taking the Lord's Supper, giving an offering, and listening to a sermon. When we participate in such activities, we say we are in a "worship service." But is this the "service" that God seeks from his people?

Fasting is part of what we might call personal worship. It goes beyond the corporate "worship service" to engage the believer in a daily worship experience. Added to that can be private prayers, Scripture reading, and meditating on the

---

HOW TO SAY IT

Ahab. AY-hab.
Antioch. AN-tee-ock.
Assyrians. Uh-SEAR-ee-uns.
Barnabas. BAR-nuh-bus.
Isaiah. Eye-ZAY-uh.

WHAT DO YOU THINK?

Identify some church practices that can become "meaningless motions" if not observed properly. How can the church as a whole, and individuals separately, keep these from becoming meaningless?

Word. But Isaiah goes further. He challenges God's people to see that true fasting (true worship) results in joining the struggle for justice and being actively compassionate toward those in need.

A. FASTING AS JUSTICE (v. 6)

6. "Is not this the kind of fasting I have chosen:
    to loose the chains of injustice
        and untie the cords of the yoke,
    to set the oppressed free
        and break every yoke?

The people of Isaiah's day thought of fasting primarily in negative terms—not eating food or engaging in other actions that were part of one's daily routine. But according to Isaiah, true fasting is also expressed in positive, specific actions that are done to bless and encourage others. True fasting (the kind *chosen* by God and pleasing to him) is not an end in itself, but is the means to an end. It will have a positive impact on those who suffer injustice.

"Real" worship—whether the particular act of worship under consideration is fasting or something else—should develop within us a sensitivity to injustice and the desire to make a difference in Jesus' name. *The oppressed* we are called to help could be subject to various kinds of hardship—physical, economic, social, or spiritual—and these oppressed are all around us. Wherever we see their plight, we are to use our talents and abilities to help bring about a correction. This does not mean that we embrace a brand of "social gospel" that abandons the priority of evangelism. It means, rather, that if we do not show the kind of love and concern for the oppressed that Jesus did, then whatever acts of worship we perform on Sunday morning will be pointless and unacceptable to God. We must see people as Jesus saw them if we want people to see Jesus in us.

B. FASTING AS COMPASSION (v. 7)

7. "Is it not to share your food with the hungry
        and to provide the poor wanderer with shelter—
    when you see the naked, to clothe him,
        and not to turn away from your own flesh and blood?

A person who truly worships God is one who also has compassion on the needy and helpless. To go through religious exercises and then display a callous attitude toward disadvantaged people is worthless. It is sheer hypocrisy.

Isaiah mentions four specific groups: *the hungry, the poor wanderer, the naked,* and *your own flesh and blood.* The last phrase may refer to one's own family or to humanity in general. The message is similar to Paul's teaching that "as we have opportunity, let us do good to all people, especially to those who belong to the family of believers" (Galatians 6:10; cf. 1 Timothy 5:8).

Mere sympathy for the needy is not enough; we must take action. The hungry are to be fed, the poor are to be given refuge, and the naked are to be clothed. We cannot *turn away from* our responsibility to care for others. James challenges us to show our faith by our works. Simply wishing a needy person well without addressing the need reveals dead faith (James 2:15-17). If one is going to abstain from *food* by fasting, perhaps one should *share* that saved food with the hungry!

HELPS ON HELPING

True followers of Jesus should always want to share their blessings with those who have less than they. One minister, whose church was located on a busy highway, received frequent requests for help. If those seeking help were local residents,

---

WHAT DO YOU THINK?

Do you think the church today would benefit from a greater emphasis on and practice of fasting?

[Consider New Testament precedents such as Acts 13:3; also Acts 6:6; 14:23; 1 Timothy 4:14 in your discussion. See also Joel 2:12, Matthew 6:16-18, and Colossians 2:16-23.]

WHAT DO YOU THINK?

Isaiah reminds the people of Judah of their responsibility to care for the needy. Today, what groups of people can our church minister to in a special way?

there was usually a positive response. Often, however, the requests came from people who claimed to be "just passing through town." Such individuals would often claim to be a member of that church in another town. In fact, some would visit every congregation in town, affirming at each stop that that church was the same kind of church they belonged to back home!

Naturally, the minister became selective in how he extended the church's benevolence. He explained his policy this way: "I help everyone who comes to me and asks for assistance. Some I help by saying, 'Yes,' and some I help by saying, 'No.'"

We would be naive to respond to every request for help without considering the kind of help an individual really needs. On the other hand, we would be very cynical if we refused to help anyone, no matter the circumstances. We need a balanced perspective. And, while common sense may dictate that we not help someone in a particular case, we should never refuse out of selfishness or from a hard heart. —R. C. S.

III. RESULTS OF TRUE WORSHIP (ISAIAH 58:8, 9a)

What happens when people worship in truth, fasting with pure motivation, taking a stand for righteousness, and caring for the defenseless? Isaiah describes such faithful worshipers, using the metaphor of a sunrise.

While hiking in the High Sierras, I began my trek early one morning before the sun had come up. Walking in the wide shadows of the surrounding peaks, I celebrated a gorgeous sunrise. Overwhelmed by the beauty and warmth of the sight, I ran ahead, moving into the shadow of another peak so I could watch the sun rise again. In fact, before the hour had passed I had watched the sun come up over the mountain seven times—an entire week's worth of astounding beauty in one morning! Such magnificence is the basis for Isaiah's description of people who truly worship: they are like the exploding light of a glorious sunrise.

A. WITH GOD'S PEOPLE (v. 8a)

8a. *"Then your light will break forth like the dawn,*
    and your healing will quickly appear.

The technique of poetic parallelism presents itself again, with the concepts of *your light* and *your healing* to be understood as synonyms that reinforce and explain one another. The person who is spiritually whole (one who worships the Lord in truth) shines brilliantly for all to see.

B. WITH GOD (vv. 8b, 9a)

8b. *" . . . then your righteousness will go before you,*
    and the glory of the LORD will be your rear guard.

When God's people worship in truth (when they engage in true fasting), God blesses them. It is not that a person should try to manipulate God by performing religious acts. Trying to finagle blessings from God is a sure sign that one is *not* spiritual. The true worshiper of the Lord is rewarded by the wonder of his presence. A sense of awe and adoration raises such a one above trivialities.

Here the promise is that *your righteousness will go before you*. This *righteousness* may describe the spiritual condition of the people once they come to understand and practice true worship. However, Jeremiah refers to One called "the Lord Our Righteousness" (Jeremiah 23:6; 33:16)—obviously a messianic reference. So *your righteousness* may instead (or also) refer to the presence of the Lord going before the people. (See the footnote in the *New International Version*.) This latter explanation fits the promise in the next phrase: *the glory of the Lord will be your rear guard* (cf. Isaiah 52:12; Joshua 6:13). God's people are thus surrounded by the Lord's protective presence, front and rear. This promise looks forward to the righteousness and glory of the Lord provided through the coming of Jesus (Philippians 3:9).

The poster you used for last week's lesson will make an excellent illustration for today's lesson also.

9a. *"Then you will call, and the LORD will answer;*
you will cry for help, and he will say: Here am I."

We have noted that the people of Isaiah's day saw fasting (as well as other acts of worship) as a means of securing God's favor. But only when God's people begin to make his priorities and concerns their own will they have the assurance of his *answer*. Isaiah had responded to the Lord's call by saying, *"Here am I"* (Isaiah 6:8); now the Lord responds in a similar manner to the *cry* of his people.

WHEN GOD SAYS NO

Some years ago in a midwestern city, a small boy set fire to a church building. When he was caught, he gave this explanation: he had prayed for something but had not received it, so he decided to get even with God!

Most of us do not react to a *no* from God that radically, but sometimes we are disappointed by the results of our prayers. We call on God, and it seems to us that he does not answer. And yet, if we would keep careful records, we would discover that most of the time we do get what we pray for. What we tend to do is to forget the times our prayers were answered and focus more on the times we were disappointed by prayer.

When we receive a *no* answer to prayer, it usually is of little help to be reminded that God always answers prayer, but sometimes he says *no*. We want to know *why* God says *no*. It may even seem to us that the requests that are refused are the ones most logical for God to grant. We must recognize that we are children of God, and that no father gives a child everything he asks for.

From 1954 to 1963 one of the most popular programs on television was *Father Knows Best*. The show's subject was an earthly father, but the truth in that title can be applied to the spiritual realm. We pray best when we come to God acknowledging that our *Father Knows Best*.   —R. C. S.

CONCLUSION

A. ISAIAH'S WORDS AND JESUS' TEACHING

When we read Jesus' instructions on personal piety in Matthew 6:1-18, it sounds as if our Lord is teaching this same message from Isaiah. Both he and Isaiah declare fasting (or any form of worship) to be an intensely spiritual and personal matter. Both recognize fasting as a legitimate expression of worship; and while neither commands it, each appears to assume that some fasting will take place (note that Jesus says *"when* you fast" in Matthew 6:16).

B. ISAIAH, JESUS, AND US

Some practice fasting today as an expression of their deep regret for their sins, as a part of their efforts to discern the Lord's will in a particular situation, or as an aspect of their sincerity and intensity in prayer. Their intent is to elevate spiritual awareness above physical needs and to give up physical pleasures for spiritual gain. To achieve this spiritual gain, we must keep in mind that more is involved with fasting (or any act of worship) than just the act itself. First, we must recognize that God is not impressed with any act of worship where the worshiper's heart is not participating in the act (cf. 1 Samuel 16:7; Luke 6:45). Anything done from a self-serving motive—whether it be fasting, singing, making hospital visits, teaching, etc.—are as offensive to God today as were the hypocritical "performances" of God's people in Isaiah's day or of the Pharisees in Jesus' time.

Second, true worship is not given to God only on Sunday morning. Caring for the helpless results in "religion that God our Father accepts as pure and faultless" (James 1:27; cf. Matthew 25:31-46; 1 John 3:17, 18). Who will perform "true worship" this week by taking Isaiah, Jesus, and James seriously?

Discovery Learning

This page contains an alternate lesson plan emphasizing learning activities. Classes desiring such student involvement will find these suggestions helpful. The next page is a reproducible activity page to further enhance discovery learning.

LEARNING GOALS

After participating in this lesson, students will be able to:

1. Tell the significant points Isaiah makes about the futility of empty worship.

2. Compare the useless worship of Isaiah's day with equally futile practices of some today.

3. Identify a specific way to practice a true fast and make a commitment to do it.

INTO THE LESSON

Before class begins, write these two open-ended sentences on the chalkboard or a large poster: "When I hear of religious fasting, I often think . . ." and "I have or have not tried religious fasting because . . . ." As students arrive, encourage them to think about and be ready to complete these two statements. To begin class, put students in groups of three to five people. Ask them to share with the others in their groups how they would complete these statements.

Option: You may wish to do a brief interview of someone who has practiced fasting. Questions for the interview could include: "What is religious fasting?"; "Why do you fast?"; "How has fasting been a blessing to you?"; and "How does fasting honor or bless the Lord?"

Move to Bible study by telling the class that fasting is still legitimate and beneficial for Christians. However, as we will discover in today's lesson, fasting can become as ritualistic or meaningless as other religious practices.

INTO THE WORD

Give the following tasks or assignments to groups of 3-5 people. The first task should be given to only one group. The remaining two tasks may be given to several groups of class members. Each of these tasks should be given as written instructions as follows.

Task 1: Your group is to prepare and give a dramatization of an interview with Isaiah. The goal of the interview is to get a clearer understanding of his preaching in Isaiah 58:1-9a. Examples of questions you might use include these: "Why did God ask you to speak these words about fasting to his people?"; "How did the Israelites go wrong in this practice?"; and "What is the connection between fasting and social justice?"

Task 2: Read Isaiah 58:1-9a and discuss the following questions. Be prepared to share your answers.

1. What was wrong with the fasting practiced by the hearers of Isaiah's message?

2. What does God expect of those who fast? Why? (See vv. 6, 7.)

3. Explain the wonderful results of fasting God's way.

4. The real issue of Isaiah 58 is not fasting. The prophet cites fasting to make a point; what is the point?

Task 3. The other groups in the class are reading Isaiah's preaching about how fasting had become a mere empty and ritualistic form of worship. Jesus offered similar teachings (see Matthew 6:16). Find and read those teachings, summarize them, and then explain the message you see for today's godly person.

Ask Group 1 to give its interview with Isaiah for the class. Then have Groups 2 and 3 report their answers and feelings.

INTO LIFE

Encourage students to apply this Scripture to their own worship practices by asking these discussion questions:

(1) How may fasting still be an appropriate expression of worship?

(2) God calls the empty practice of fasting a "transgression" or sin. What other expressions of worship may become empty and meaningless rituals? Why or how?

(3) What have you learned about worship as it relates to everyday life?

Direct the attention of your learners to the activities on the reproducible page. Consider using the "Isaiah, Jesus, and Us" small group activity to highlight practical ways of demonstrating love and care for those who have true needs. Recommend that students take the "Honoring God . . ." activity home for a time of personal meditation and devotion some time during the next week.

Also consider another worksheet as a "homework assignment" by giving each student one with the heading "What Should I Do?" Under the heading include these questions and incomplete sentences:

1. Should I fast? How and when? For what purposes?

2. What social action could I do that expresses God's sense of justice?

3. I will prepare better for our weekly corporate worship by . . . .

4. The area of my life that I will clean up so that my worship will bring honor to God is . . . .

Honoring God in Worship and in Life

God is not impressed with any act of worship unless our hearts motivate us so that our lives reflect his principles. This is true for fasting, feasting at the Lord's Supper, giving tithes and offerings, singing praise, offering prayers, or any other act. Look at each statement below and decide whether the statement is always, sometimes, or never true of you. The secondary statement will help you evaluate your life practices that affect your worship.

1. My singing in church accurately reflects my heart, my life, and my relationship with the Lord. I am Christlike in speech, honesty, and fairness.
   ☐ Always True   ☐ Sometimes True   ☐ Never True

2. I give my tithes and offerings with a sense of joy and no sense of guilt. I am also willing to help people with material or financial needs.
   ☐ Always True   ☐ Sometimes True   ☐ Never True

3. I offer silent prayers in worship and allow them to express my heart, my life, and my love for God. I also pray daily to praise, to seek help, and to bless God.
   ☐ Always True   ☐ Sometimes True   ☐ Never True

4. I approach the Lord's supper with gratitude for God's grace and a sense of sorrow for my sin. I am willing to apologize to another believer when I have said or done something to hurt him or her.
   ☐ Always True   ☐ Sometimes True   ☐ Never True

5. I allow my heart to be open to the preaching of God's Word. I let the words of the sermon affect my everyday life.
   ☐ Always True   ☐ Sometimes True   ☐ Never True

6. I honestly want every day of my life to bring honor to my Heavenly Father.
   ☐ Always True   ☐ Sometimes True   ☐ Never True

Isaiah, Jesus, and Us

True worship of God is not given only on Sunday morning. Jesus and James echo Isaiah's theme that "Religion that God our Father accepts as pure and faultless" is caring for the helpless (Matthew 25:31-46; James 1:27).

As your class works in small groups, list over this heart a few practical ways your class might give care to someone today. If possible, ask the class to select a project from these ideas.

ANTICIPATE GOD'S NEW CREATION

LESSON 9

WHY TEACH THIS LESSON?

There is probably no better picture of *anticipation* than that of a child a few days before Christmas. The presents are *right there*, close enough to be held and shaken. Oh the sweet agony, as the arrival of that "big day" seems to come so slowly, with time just dragging by. But when the day does indeed come, no time is lost in ripping away the wrapping paper to get at the contents.

As Christians, the era in which we live can (and should) invoke similar longings. Christ has indeed come to die and pay the price for our sins. We have the gift of salvation—we hold it right in our hands—but we do not fully unwrap that gift and enjoy it in its fullness until the new heavens and earth are finally revealed on the last day. This lesson is for everyone who needs to reawaken that sense of anticipation that may have gone stale. This anticipation of our ultimate heavenly home lifts our vision and keeps us focused on the God who will bring it about.

INTRODUCTION

A. RADICALLY NEW

Some time ago I had a student in one of my college classes who made quite an impression on me and many others. Not only was she very bright and highly motivated, but she also displayed a singular refusal to be restricted by her limitations —including the impaired mobility and speech brought on by her cerebral palsy. She was determined to live every day to its absolute fullest. It didn't surprise anyone who knew her to learn that she had even tried skydiving! From that thrilling experience, this student came to know the heavens and the earth from a radically new perspective. She had seen them from a vantage point not appreciated by those who stay on the ground. Such acts of faith as these have transformed this student, convincing her that nothing can hold her back!

In this, our final study from Isaiah during this quarter, we see the prophet challenging God's people to let their faith go "skydiving" and to anticipate the radically new life that God has in store for them. He wrote to encourage all future believers, both Jews and Gentiles, to view the future by faith and to seize God's promise of the new heavens and new earth.

B. REVIEW OF GUIDELINES

A review of the principles that guided our study in lesson 6 will help us to interpret this passage. There (page 169) we noted that Isaiah 61 may be viewed as having two levels of application or fulfillment: (1) the return of the Judean exiles from Babylonian captivity in the sixth century B.C.; and (2) the messianic/church age, climaxed by the eternal state of Heaven, which will be ushered in at Jesus' return.

Isaiah 65 may be interpreted in a similar manner. First, it offered hope to those who were exiles in a foreign land, far from the land that God had given to his

DEVOTIONAL READING:
REVELATION 21:1-8
BACKGROUND SCRIPTURE:
ISAIAH 65:17-25
PRINTED TEXT:
ISAIAH 65:17-25

LESSON AIMS

After this lesson each student will be able to:

1. Recount the key points of Isaiah's description of the new heavens and earth.

2. Explain the fulfillment of this prophecy in the Jewish return from exile and in the messianic age, climaxed by the return of Christ.

3. Thank God for the promise of a "new heavens and a new earth" yet to be enjoyed by God's people.

Jan 27

KEY VERSE

Behold, I will create new heavens and a new earth. The former things will not be remembered, nor will they come to mind.

—Isaiah 65:17

people. Second, it describes the blessings provided through Jesus' messianic ministry, with a particular emphasis on the blessings awaiting God's people in Heaven.

In the predictions found in today's text, Isaiah employed highly poetic language that reminds us of the descriptions of the heavenly realm in Revelation. When John tried to put into words what he was privileged to see, he often used the words *like* or *as* (Revelation 4:7; 5:6; 6:1; 10:1; 15:2; 21:11). This is the language of someone trying to describe the indescribable. It is man's finite efforts to depict something that is infinite. Such language should whet our appetites for what the Lord has in store for all who "have longed for his appearing" (2 Timothy 4:8).

C. LESSON BACKGROUND

Isaiah foresees a time when many of the people of Judah had lived in exile in Babylon for seventy years (cf. Jeremiah 25:11; Daniel 9:2). Some had risen to positions of power and prestige (e.g., Daniel and his friends). Others, such as Ezekiel, had lived in outlying communities, where they tried to keep alive the promise of a return home. In 538 B.C. the time finally arrived for that promise to be fulfilled. Joyful anticipation grew as a remnant of Judeans headed west (cf. Ezra 1, 2).

Isaiah, writing about one hundred fifty years earlier, had helped encourage those who would eventually return to their homeland. His predictions described a life of radical newness: a new heavens and earth, a new people, a new city, and a new time of unprecedented productivity and prosperity.

I. GOD'S PROMISE (ISAIAH 65:17-19)

Going home to Judah after seventy years must have raised certain doubts and misgivings among the aged. Would this trip really be worth the effort? Wouldn't it be wiser to live out the rest of one's days in Babylon? On the other hand, the younger exiles had been born in Babylon and thus had no personal memories of Jerusalem. Returning to Judah did not have as much appeal to them. Thus, for both old and young, there must have been certain anxieties accompanying the kind of drastic move required in going home. However, balancing those apprehensions was the excitement of participating in a new beginning.

So it is with followers of Jesus, who see themselves as "aliens and strangers" (1 Peter 2:11) preparing to go to their real home—Heaven. Death (the process of moving to that new home) does raise certain genuine concerns, but the promise offsets our fears and gives us a wonderful sense of excitement and anticipation.

A. NEW HEAVENS AND EARTH (v. 17)

17. "Behold, I will create
    new heavens and a new earth.
  The former things will not be remembered,
    nor will they come to mind.

The people who heard these words in Isaiah's day, one hundred fifty years or so before they were to be fulfilled, must have found the prophet's message almost impossible to fathom; similarly, young Christians today may think the promises of Heaven to be a long way off. But among the elderly captives who lived as exiles in Babylon, Isaiah's promises of *new heavens and a new earth* could have caused intense excitement. The ability to envision their current bondage as becoming their *former* bondage would have been wonderful to anticipate!

The same anticipation of the future can capture the thoughts of contemporary elderly Christians who realize that they are nearing the time to "go home." The new heaven and new earth mentioned in Revelation 21:1 is described as a place where "the old order of things has passed away" (v. 4) and where "he who was

Have this poster on display as students arrive. It is sure to pique their interest and prepare them for Isaiah's exciting message.

seated on the throne said, 'I am making everything new!'" (v. 5). Peter describes this realm as "the home of righteousness" (2 Peter 3:13). There God and redeemed humanity will live in perfect, loving harmony.

B. Place of Joy (v. 18)

18. "But be glad and rejoice forever
    in what I will create,
 for I will create Jerusalem to be a delight
    and its people a joy.

Jerusalem had been destroyed so completely by the Babylonians in 586 B.C. (2 Kings 25:8-10) that its rebuilding could well have been considered a new creation. The people rejoiced when the temple was completed (Ezra 6:16) and later when the city wall was finished (Nehemiah 12:27, 43).

We must also think in terms of the blessings provided under the New Covenant. Hebrews 12:22 and 23 tells us that we "have come to the heavenly Jerusalem, . . . the church of the firstborn." Since this is stated as a present reality for the church, this prophecy at one level has already been fulfilled. Even so, we yet look forward to the "New Jerusalem" of Revelation 21. That will be a place of never-ending joy!

C. Place Without Tears (v. 19)

19. "I will rejoice over Jerusalem
    and take delight in my people;
 the sound of weeping and of crying
    will be heard in it no more.

The fall of Jerusalem in 586 B.C. signaled the sobering reality of God's judgment on his rebellious people. At that time, Jeremiah wrote the book of Lamentations to express his grief over the tragedy that had befallen a sinful nation. But when the period of judgment ends, sorrow gives way to joy.

Again, these lines from Isaiah apply in a special way to the eternal New Jerusalem, where God "will wipe every tear from their eyes" and where there will be "no more death or mourning" (Revelation 21:4). Weeping and crying will have no place in that land of pure joy.

II. GOD'S PROVISIONS (ISAIAH 65:20-25)

Isaiah now turns to more specific statements about God's new creation.

A. Long Life (v. 20)

20. "Never again will there be in it
    an infant who lives but a few days,
    or an old man who does not live out his years;
 he who dies at a hundred
    will be thought a mere youth;
 he who fails to reach a hundred
    will be considered accursed.

"The length of our days is seventy years," wrote Moses in Psalm 90:10. During a time of hardship (such as those in captivity in Babylon had experienced), the average life span would have been somewhat less than that. But Isaiah promised that life in God's new Jerusalem will be such that a hundred years will be the new standard. No person, whether an infant or an old man, will be "cheated" of a full life.

Applying this prophecy to any particular time is difficult. One-hundred-year life spans did not become the norm for the people of Judah after their release from

WHAT DO YOU THINK?

When Isaiah says "the former things will not be remembered," does that mean we will not be able to remember our earthly lives when we get to Heaven? What do you think people in Heaven will remember about their lives on earth?

[Consider Luke 16:19-31 and John 16:21 in your discussion.]

WHAT DO YOU THINK?

What is it about Heaven that you anticipate the most? Why is that a source of joy for you?

DAILY BIBLE READINGS

Monday, Jan. 21—"While You Are Waiting . . ." (2 Peter 3:11-18)

Tuesday, Jan. 22—Making All Things New (Revelation 21: 1-8)

Wednesday, Jan. 23—A New Spirit Within (Ezekiel 11:14-20)

Thursday, Jan. 24—Cleansed People; New Heart (Ezekiel 36:22-28)

Friday, Jan. 25—God Has Redeemed Jerusalem (Isaiah 52:7-12)

Saturday, Jan. 26—Nations Will See God's Glory (Isaiah 66:18-23)

Sunday, Jan. 27—New Heavens and New Earth (Isaiah 65:17-25)

WHAT DO YOU THINK?

*In commenting on verse 20 we noted that an important part of eternal life will be the quality of the relationship we will have with God. What does that suggest to you about the nature of the Christian life **this** side of Heaven?*

Babylon. But death at any age has no place in the new heavens and earth of which John wrote. Thus, the figure must be more symbolic than literal. Perhaps its basic message is that age will not be a factor in the new order of things that God will establish. It becomes a picture, then, of the better quality of life the Jews would experience as free people in their own homeland. Under the New Covenant "eternal life" is not viewed so much in terms of quantity of years as it is in terms of a relationship with God (John 17:3). Thus, Isaiah's picture of long life portrays the eternal life that all Christians possess by virtue of their relationship with Jesus.

B. PRODUCTIVE LABOR (vv. 21-23)

21. *"They will build houses and dwell in them;*
    they will plant vineyards and eat their fruit.

These words about *houses* and *vineyards* lead one to think of what the returning exiles would do when they resettled in Judah. Life is pictured as very good for them indeed. The Bible speaks of Israel's living in peace and prosperity by saying the people "lived in safety, each man under his own vine and fig tree" (1 Kings 4:25).

Can these words also apply to the Christian age? Probably not in the sense of literally building of *houses* and planting vineyards. Jesus told His disciples He would go to prepare a place in His Father's house for them (John 14:2). He did not say they would have to build their own houses. However, if we take the figure for a picture of security and safety, then certainly it applies. Just as living a hundred years can picture the eternal life we will enjoy in Heaven, building homes and enjoying the fruit of one's own vineyard can picture the blessing of being in Heaven.

22. *"No longer will they build houses and others live in them,*
    or plant and others eat.
    For as the days of a tree,
    so will be the days of my people;
    my chosen ones will long enjoy
    the works of their hands.

The Babylonians had laid siege to Jerusalem for a year and a half before it finally fell to them (2 Kings 25:1-3). Prior to and during that time, they no doubt ravaged the land, eating what the people of Judah had planted. And when the people of the land were seized and taken captive to Babylon, others moved into whatever houses remained. Isaiah declared that in the new heavens and earth no looters or spoilers would enter and steal the wealth of the residents. God's people would *long enjoy* the prosperity that the *works of their hands* had brought them. No one would take it from them.

Isaiah adds another word picture to describe the long life of God's people in their new home: *as the days of a tree, so will be the days of my people.* Perhaps Isaiah had in mind one of the majestic cedars of Lebanon, or a mighty oak tree (Isaiah 2:13). Either of these could stand for centuries, symbolizing the lengthy period of blessing and prosperity that God's people would enjoy.

GOING HOME

A group of tourists was visiting a country well known for its history of tension, war, and displaced persons. At one point, a woman ran out of a rundown shack and began speaking to them in English. "See this?" she said. "See how I live in this one room with my children? I had a lovely home in a northern city. But it was taken from me, and now I have to live here." This woman's story is similar to that of thousands upon thousands of refugees throughout the world. They built homes—now someone else lives in them.

Some time ago the newspapers carried the story of such a refugee. She had found safety in America, but she had to leave everything she owned behind—

HOW TO SAY IT

Babylon. BAB-uh-lun.

Babylonian. Bab-uh-LOW-nee-un.

Cyrus. SIGH-russ.

Ezekiel. Ee-ZEEK-yul or Ee-ZEEK-ee-yul.

Haggai. HAG-eye or HAG-ay-eye.

Isaiah. Eye-ZAY-uh.

Jeremiah. Jair-uh-MY-uh.

Judean. Joo-DEE-un.

Malachi. MAL-uh-kye.

messianic. mess-ee-AN-ick.

Nehemiah. Nee-huh-MY-uh.

Zechariah. Zek-uh-RYE-uh.

except for the key to her old house! She still had the key to a house that she had once owned but would never see again and in which someone else was living.

God gave his people in the Old Testament the promise of security in their homes as long as they were faithful to him. Followers of Jesus have been promised a home that no one can take away from them as long as they, too, are faithful. The Christian's sense of security is far greater than any the world can offer. It is the assurance that God is faithful to those who do not forsake him.   —R. C. S.

23. *"They will not toil in vain*
    or bear children doomed to misfortune;
for they will be a people blessed by the Lord,
    they and their descendants with them.

The people's *toil* was *in vain* when invaders such as the Babylonians stole their harvest. In the new heavens and earth, God's people would be able to enjoy the fruit of their efforts. This prophecy is also fulfilled in the church. Paul says, "You know that your labor in the Lord is not in vain" (1 Corinthians 15:58).

Isaiah describes God's new heavens and earth as a place where his people will not have to rear their families with the cloud of impending *misfortune* of tribulation or affliction hanging over them. In the new heavens and earth, just the opposite is true. The future will be bright with promise and hope.

This promise concerning bearing children in hope applies to *a people blessed by the Lord, they and their descendants with them.* Surely the remnant who returned from exile considered themselves *blessed by the Lord.* Even so, this prophecy finds even greater fulfillment in the church, where the blessed are "born not of natural descent, nor of human decision or a husband's will, but born of God" (John 1:13).

C. ANSWERED PRAYER (v. 24)

24. *"Before they call I will answer;*
    while they are speaking I will hear.

An essential part of all prayer is the ready, waiting presence of God to *hear* and *answer* his people. Jesus taught that "your Father knows what you need before you ask him" (Matthew 6:8). Jesus promised access to the Father in his (Jesus') name (John 14:13; 15:16). That bond will be perfected in the New Jerusalem, where God himself will dwell with his people (Revelation 21:3).

D. SUPERIOR SECURITY (v. 25)

25. *"The wolf and the lamb will feed together,*
    and the lion will eat straw like the ox,
    but dust will be the serpent's food.
They will neither harm nor destroy
    on all my holy mountain," says the Lord.

This description is very similar to one studied in lesson 2 (Isaiah 11:6-9, page 139). Taken literally, God's new heavens and earth (here called his *holy mountain*) will be free from the terrors of any creatures that would normally *harm or destroy* others. Taken symbolically, on the other hand, the picture is that of the gospel message bringing together people of different backgrounds, temperaments, and cultures. The Lord's mountain in this case likely signifies that which it does in Isaiah 2:2-4: a place from which the Lord's Word goes forth to all the nations.

Perhaps the phrase *dust will be the serpent's food* refers to no more than venomous snakes who, like the other wild animals mentioned in the passage, will no longer pose a threat to human safety. But who can read this without recalling God's words to the serpent in Eden: "You will crawl on your belly and you will eat

WHAT DO YOU THINK?

If God promises that our labor is not in vain, then why doesn't all Christian work result in a successful harvest of souls?

[Use passages such as Matthew 13:3-9, 18-23 and 1 Corinthians 3:6 to assist in your discussion.]

WHAT DO YOU THINK?

Specifically, what do you think would happen if we took more seriously the Bible's promises about prayer? How can we become more of a praying church?

dust all the days of your life" (Genesis 3:14)? Perhaps the real intent here is to picture the complete fulfillment of the curse of the serpent—that is, of Satan. Christ did come "to destroy the devil's work" (1 John 3:8; cf. Hebrews 2:14, 15), a destruction that will be completed on the day of judgment (Revelation 20:7-10).

THE WOLF AND THE LAMB

In children's stories, the wolf often represents danger. In the tale of "Little Red Riding Hood" it is the wolf who poses a threat to Red Riding Hood and her Grandma. In "The Three Little Pigs" it is the wolf who wants to huff and puff and blow the pigs' houses down. The proverbial expression for hunger or poverty (dating back at least to the sixteenth century) is that "the wolf is at the door." The wolf is almost always a symbol of danger. In contrast, the lamb often symbolizes innocence.

Long before these children's tales were written, the prophet Isaiah employed similar symbolism in his striking description of the peaceful conditions to be found in God's holy mountain. (He used similar language in a previous description of life in the messianic era; Isaiah 11:1-9.) For such natural enemies as the wolf and the lamb to lie down together, two changes must occur: the wolf must no longer attack, and the lamb must no longer be afraid. It is a beautifully poetic word picture of peace— the peace that God provides for his people.

The Bible has much to say about this peace. It tells us that we can be kept in God's perfect peace when our minds are fixed on him (Isaiah 26:3). Writing from his confinement in Rome, Paul described this peace as one "which transcends all understanding" (Philippians 4:7). Jesus said that his peace is unlike that which the world offers (John 14:27). Such "peace on earth" is a foretaste of the perfect, eternal peace we shall enjoy in Heaven.   —R. C. S.

CONCLUSION

A. WHAT MIGHT HAVE BEEN

Imagine the ancient Jew, languishing in Babylon, hearing King Cyrus's decree that all Judeans who want to return to Jerusalem may do so (Ezra 1:3). But this trip demanded a grueling trek of almost a thousand miles on a highway of uncertainty. Many were doubtful and fearful. Should they pull up stakes for an unknown future, or should they remain in the now-familiar surroundings of the foreign land? In the midst of this "valley of decision," perhaps someone recalled the ancient words of Isaiah: "Behold, I will create new heavens and a new earth."

Isaiah's predictions may well have fired the enthusiasm of the approximately fifty thousand who chose to return to Judah in 538 B.C. (Ezra 2:64-67). However, their faith was apparently a shallow and short-lived one. They did indeed make it to Jerusalem, but soon slipped back into spiritual darkness. The records of Ezra, Nehemiah, Haggai, Zechariah, and Malachi, make clear that the returning exiles did not hold true to the faith. They finally completed a new temple some twenty-two years after the first exiles returned (Ezra 6:15); but by the time of Nehemiah's governorship almost one hundred years later, the city walls were still in deplorable ruins. Faith faltered, and the promises of God went unclaimed. To use the terminology from our opening illustration, the Judeans refused to go "skydiving."

B. WHAT CAME TO PASS

Jesus initiated the fulfillment of Isaiah's prophecy, and Paul informs us that each Christian is a new creation as a result (2 Corinthians 5:17). Revelation 21 excites each of us with its description of a place where God is "making everything new" (v. 5). Every person who is a new creation in Christ is preparing to live in the place that is the new creation of God. How shall we live each day in anticipation of that future reality?

Discovery Learning

This page contains an alternate lesson plan emphasizing learning activities. Classes desiring such student involvement will find these suggestions helpful. The next page is a reproducible activity page to further enhance discovery learning.

LEARNING GOALS

After participating in this lesson, each student will be able to:

1. Recount the key points of Isaiah's description of the new heavens and earth.

2. Explain the dual fulfillment of this prophecy in the Jewish return from exile and in the return of Jesus Christ.

3. Thank God for the promise of a "new heavens and a new earth" that will be enjoyed by God's people.

INTO THE LESSON

Divide the class into two groups for the opening activity, giving each group a large poster board. Also, assign one of the following activities to each of the groups.

Group 1: Give these instructions: "Poetic and figurative language was used in both the Old and New Testaments to describe the indescribable—Heaven! Your task is to do the same, without using Scriptural word pictures like 'streets of gold.' Create your own word pictures."

Group 2: Say, "Imagine a perfect city in which you would love to live. Let your imagination run wild; list qualities or features of these perfect living conditions."

Tell the groups you will not ask for them to share their work until later in the class.

INTO THE WORD

Using the lesson commentary for preparation, give a brief picture of the lesson background and setting for Isaiah 65:17-25. Be sure to explain the dual levels of fulfillment of this prophecy.

Activity #1: Give teams of two or more people a copy of the reproducible activity "New Jerusalem" (from the next page) and two different colored pencils or highlighter pens. As team members read the text, they should highlight in one color all prophecies that speak only of the new Jerusalem Jews were anticipating. All prophecies that may be applied to both Heaven and the new Jerusalem are to be highlighted in the other color.

Activity #2: (The following is also in the student book.) This activity may be done in small groups with a worksheet or as a whole class with a large visual. The worksheet or visual should be divided into three columns. The heading of Column 1 should be blank; the heading for Column 2 will be "New Jerusalem"; the heading for Column 3 will be "Heaven." List the following words or phrases in Column 1: "Anticipation,"

"Anxieties," "Memories Erased," "A Delightful Place" (v. 18), "Intimacy With God," and "Peace/Security."

Tell the groups or the class that they will examine each of the emotions, feelings, or hopes listed. Ask them not to work ahead of you. You will ask questions or give instructions for each of these emotions or feelings listed. Answers may be simply noted in Columns 2 and 3. The questions and instructions follow:

Anticipation. "What hopes and dreams may the Jews have had for their new Jerusalem? What good things do Christians anticipate or look forward to in Heaven?"

Anxieties. "What may have been some of the fears or anxieties the Jews had about making the trip and returning to Jerusalem? What anxieties may Christians have about making the trip to Heaven?"

Memories Erased (v. 17). "What do you think the exiled Jews would like to forget?" After listing answers ask, "What personal memories do you look forward to having erased from your mind?" (Do not ask people to share specific personal examples, unless they wish to do so.)

A Delightful Place. Allow the two groups from the opening activity to share their thoughts now. After the reports, remind them that even our wildest dreams cannot match what God has in store for us in Heaven.

Intimacy With God. Use your commentary notes entitled "Unfulfilled Prophecy" to explain what happened in Jerusalem. Explain this is not what will happen in Heaven. Ask the class to share how they hope to experience intimacy with God in Heaven.

Peace and Security. Re-read verse 25 and ask, "Is this a literal or figurative prophecy? How may it be interpreted and applied to the New Jerusalem the Jews were expecting? To Heaven?"

INTO LIFE

Remind the class that this dual prophecy was a message of hope for the Jews and for all followers of the one true God. As believers, we look forward to the fulfillment of the prophecy about Heaven. The verse in 2 Corinthians 5:17 should become the theme for our hope: "Therefore, if anyone is in Christ, he is a new creation; the old has gone, the new has come!"

Refer learners to the "New Life—My Gratitude" section of the reproducible page. Ask them to write their personal prayer of thanksgiving there next to the butterfly image.

New Jerusalem

Highlight in one color all prophecies in the text below that speak only of the new Jerusalem that the Jews were anticipating when they returned to Judah from Babylon. All prophecies that may be applied to both Heaven and the new Jerusalem are to be highlighted in the another color.

ISAIAH 65:17-25

17. "Behold, I will create new heavens and a new earth.
    The former things will not be remembered, nor will they come to mind.
18. "But be glad and rejoice forever in what I will create, for I will create Jerusalem to be a delight and its people a joy.
19. "I will rejoice over Jerusalem and take delight in my people; the sound of weeping and crying will be heard in it no more.
20. "Never again will there be in it an infant who lives but a few days, or an old man who does not live out his years;
    he who dies at a hundred will be thought a mere youth; he who fails to reach a hundred will be considered accursed.
21. "They will build houses and dwell in them; they will plant vineyards and eat their fruit.
22. "No longer will they build houses and others live in them, or plant and others eat.
    For as the days of a tree, so will be the days of my people; my chosen ones will long enjoy the works of their hands.
23. "They will not toil in vain or bear children doomed to misfortune;
    for they will be a people blessed by the LORD, they and their descendants with them.
24. "Before they call I will answer; while they are speaking I will hear.
25. "The wolf and the lamb will feed together, and the lion will eat straw like the ox, but dust will be the serpent's food.
    They will neither harm nor destroy on all my holy mountain," says the LORD.

New Life—My Gratitude

The butterfly has long been a symbol of new life. God promises "The old has gone, the new has come!" (2 Corinthians 5:17). You are a new creation with a new hope. In the space next to this butterfly, please write your prayer of thanksgiving for the promise of a new life in Heaven. Then cut it out and put it someplace where you will see it as you prepare for each day—perhaps on a mirror in the bedroom or bathroom.

RUTH CHOOSES NAOMI'S GOD

LESSON 10

WHY TEACH THIS LESSON?

Life is full of choices. We tend to put choices into "categories," recognizing that some are relatively minor ("What shall I have for dinner?"), some are moderately important ("Should I buy a new car?"), and some can change the course of a person's life forever ("Should I ask her to marry me?"). What we don't often realize is that some seemingly minor choices can have untold consequences—for good or for ill—even many years hence. Such is the case with Ruth, whose answer to the question of "Where should I now live?" following personal tragedy resulted in her becoming an ancestor of both King David and Jesus Christ (Matthew 1:5). Because of her choice, she is also an eternal witness of faithfulness to any who would read the account of her life.

The example of Ruth should give pause to those of us caught up in the seemingly humdrum choices of everyday life. Tomorrow, will that little act of kindness (or that "insignificant" theft) at the office have any lasting influence on those who may have seen it? Will it go unnoticed—or will it end up rippling through the years, decades, and centuries ahead to influence many others for (or against) Christ? As we consider the life of Ruth today, perhaps we should assume the latter!

INTRODUCTION

A. UPROOTING ONE'S ROOTS

Many people have undertaken the challenge of putting together a family tree. In order to discover their roots, they have scoured genealogical records and other historical data. Such searches have yielded varied results: fascination, joy, frustration, disappointment—and occasionally some embarrassment.

Sometimes these investigations have revealed that someone among the ancestors made a momentous decision to uproot his family and to move to a distant location. In such cases, the final farewells to other family members must have been touching and emotional.

The lesson for today highlights two of the factors that often have motivated people to move: famine and faith. Famine will cause a person to take drastic measures to obtain food. The Great Depression in the U.S. during the 1930s resulted in some families leaving relatives and friends behind in order to seek employment in other places. Many men felt a keen responsibility to care for their families, and this motivated them to uproot their families in search of a better life elsewhere.

The faith factor is illustrated by different situations described in the Bible, including Abram's departure from Ur, the exodus from Egypt by the nation of Israel, and the return of God's people from exile in Babylon. Great faith may cause an individual to do things that seem strange and unrealistic to those who prefer

DEVOTIONAL READING:
PSALM 8
BACKGROUND SCRIPTURE:
RUTH 1
PRINTED TEXT:
RUTH 1:1-8, 16-19a

LESSON AIMS

After participating in this lesson, each student will be able to:

1. Tell how Ruth came to be associated with Naomi and the God of Israel.

2. Explain how the choice that Ruth made to stay with Naomi reflected great faith.

3. Suggest one or two specific ways a believer can share his or her faith with a non-Christian family member.

Feb
3

KEY VERSE

Where you go I will go, and where you stay I will stay. Your people will be my people and your God my God. —Ruth 1:16

to stay in their "comfort zones." No doubt it took significant faith when almost fifty thousand people departed from Babylon in 538 B.C. to return to Jerusalem. Many of those who returned had never seen Jerusalem, for they were born in captivity. They made the journey because their faith compelled them to do so.

We see a similar motivation when men and women determine to go to the mission field. With today's modes of travel, the time factor in making long trips is not as crucial as in times past. Cultural differences, however, must still be confronted. At first such differences are simply fascinating, but over a period of time that perspective can change. One person testified that only the conviction that she was doing God's will enabled her to withstand the discomforts she experienced daily. Even for those who do not go to a foreign mission field, job transfers often compel people to move to different cultural settings within their own country. May it be that wherever they go, they will take their faith with them!

B. LESSON BACKGROUND

Two books of the Bible are designated by the names of women—Ruth and Esther. The book of Ruth is the focus for today's and next week's lessons.

Over the last two months, our studies have come from the book of Isaiah. The events recorded in the book of Ruth took place approximately four hundred years before the time of Isaiah. Whereas Isaiah's writings provide many specific prophecies about the Messiah, the book of Ruth tells of the courageous faith of an ancestress of the Messiah (Matthew 1:5). She was also the great-grandmother of David, the second king of Israel.

The author of the book of Ruth is not named. A Jewish tradition proposes that it was Samuel, but this cannot be supported from Scripture.

I. NAOMI'S SITUATION (RUTH 1:1-3)

A. FAMINE (v. 1a)

1a. In the days when the judges ruled, there was a famine in the land.

The first verse of the book of Ruth reveals some important points. The first phrase implies that the book was written after the era of the *judges* had ended, having lasted approximately three hundred years (from about 1375 to 1075 B.C.). The additional judgeship of Samuel included the coronation of Saul as the first king of Israel in approximately 1050 B.C.

The generality of the statement *when the judges ruled* makes it difficult to determine which particular judges were ruling when the *famine* occurred *in the land* (or if, perhaps, it occurred between certain judges). The primary function of the judges was to deliver Israel from oppressors. Perhaps this famine was not caused by a lack of rain but by oppressors who robbed the people of their grain after the harvest (cf. Judges 6:1-4). The terminology "the Lord had come to the aid of his people" (v. 6) may suggest that the Lord had raised up a new judge to deliver Israel from the raiders.

B. RELOCATION (vv. 1b, 2)

1b. . . . and a man from Bethlehem in Judah, together with his wife and two sons, went to live for a while in the country of Moab.

Bethlehem in Judah, the future birthplace of Jesus, is located about six miles south of Jerusalem. (There was another Bethlehem in northern Israel [Joshua 19:15]; thus the reference to Judah helped clarify which Bethlehem was meant.) The word *Bethlehem* means "house of bread." It is an interesting irony that this family felt compelled to leave the "house of bread" because there was no bread!

This poster will help your students place the events of the lessons of this quarter in chronological order.

To go *to live* in *Moab* was no small matter. The move involved a trip of about fifty miles to an area east of the Dead Sea. It also meant that the family's land in Judah would be abandoned, at least temporarily. Besides that, the law of Moses excluded Moabite men from the assembly of the Lord, "even down to the tenth generation" (Deuteronomy 23:3-6). Since the number ten sometimes symbolizes completeness in the Bible, this may have indicated a permanent exclusion. While this may have caused some Israelites to harbor feelings of animosity toward the Moabites, it appears that this was not true of Elimelech. The presence of food in Moab may be attributed to conquest, trade, or the possibility that the famine was confined to Judah.

2. The man's name was Elimelech, his wife's name Naomi, and the names of his two sons were Mahlon and Kilion. They were Ephrathites from Bethlehem, Judah. And they went to Moab and lived there.

Personal names in the Bible often have great significance attached to them. *Elimelech* means "my God is king." *Naomi* means "pleasant." The significance of names is seen later in Naomi's return to Judah without her husband and *two sons*. At that time she told the women of Bethlehem that they should call her *Mara* (meaning "bitter"), and not *Naomi* (Ruth 1:20).

The names of the two sons (1:5) are also interesting: *Mahlon* means "weak," and *Kilion* means "pining." Both names suggest physical weakness, and this trait may have been a factor in Elimelech's decision to move to a place where food was more attainable. Loving parents will do whatever they can to help their children.

The family is designated as *Ephrathites from Bethlehem*. *Ephrath* ("fruitful") was a former name for Bethlehem (Genesis 35:16, 19), though it also could have designated the clan within the tribe of Judah to which this family belonged.

C. GRIEF (v. 3)

3. Now Elimelech, Naomi's husband, died, and she was left with her two sons.

Already Naomi had experienced the turmoil of being uprooted from her home, her family, and her friends. Now, in a foreign land, *her husband died*; and her sense of loss was compounded by the grief of losing a mate.

TAKE MY HAND

On one occasion Thomas A. Dorsey, who became known as the "Father of Gospel Music," was away from home leading the music for a revival in another town. His wife had stayed home because she was pregnant. While he was away, he received a telegram informing him that his wife had died.

Dorsey was so distraught at the news that he decided he would not continue in the field of gospel music. Instead, he would go into secular music. But he found he could not. One day, while still grieving deeply, he wrote a song that included these words: "Precious Lord, take my hand, Lead me on, help me stand; I am tired, I am weak, I am worn; Through the storm, through the night, Lead me on to the light, Take my hand, precious Lord, Lead me home." Dorsey's words have given hope and encouragement to many during times of grief and heartache. Mahalia Jackson sang his song at the funeral of Dr. Martin Luther King, Jr.

Faith in God is still the primary factor that sustains people during times of grief. It is what sustained Naomi during the loss of her husband and her two sons. Note that Naomi lived long before the Lord Jesus came to earth. She lived before the words of John 14:1 were spoken: "Do not let your hearts be troubled." She lived before the resurrection of Jesus gave a firm basis to the hope of eternal life.

Naomi did not stop believing in God when her husband and two sons died. She even had enough faith to express her frustrations about God, as Ruth 1:13, 20, 21 indicate. But she kept on believing in him, and so must all of us.   —R. C. S.

WHAT DO YOU THINK?

Naomi, whose name meant "pleasant," said her name should be "Mara," which means "bitter." If you were to change your name to reflect your current circumstances or the way God has dealt with you, what would you call yourself? Why?

DAILY BIBLE READINGS

Monday, Jan. 28—*You Were Strangers in Egypt* (Deuteronomy 10:12-22)

Tuesday, Jan. 29—*Tithe for Aliens, Orphans, and Widows* (Deuteronomy 26:1-15)

Wednesday, Jan. 30—*Act Justly; Do Not Oppress* (Jeremiah 7:1-7)

Thursday, Jan. 31—*Do Not Wrong Widows, Aliens* (Jeremiah 22:1-9)

Friday, Feb. 1—*Provide for Widows and Aliens* (Deuteronomy 24:14-22)

Saturday, Feb. 2—*Three Widows in Moab* (Ruth 1:1-14)

Sunday, Feb. 3—*Your God, My God* (Ruth 1:15-22)

II. NAOMI'S SONS (RUTH 1:4, 5)

A. MARRIED (v. 4)

4. They married Moabite women, one named Orpah and the other Ruth. After they had lived there about ten years,

For Israelite men to marry *Moabite women* was not forbidden by the Mosaic law, but, as noted above, Moabite males were prevented from being a part of the assembly of the Lord. It is not until Ruth 4:10 that we learn that Mahlon was the son of Naomi who married *Ruth*. No mention is made of any children, so it is likely that these marriages were childless.

The statement that the family dwelled in Moab *about ten years* seems to indicate that there was no thought of returning to Bethlehem. Apparently the sons were putting down their roots in Moab. Naomi continued to live there as well.

B. DECEASED (v. 5)

5. . . . both Mahlon and Kilion also died, and Naomi was left without her two sons and her husband.

Naomi's burdens increased with the death of *her two sons*. A woman without a *husband*, son, or relative to provide for her was in desperate straits. That was especially so in ancient times, but it also can be true in today's world as well.

Thus, although Naomi and her family had moved to Moab to better themselves, the results, tragically, did not fulfill their expectations. Perhaps Naomi debated with herself about the wisdom of that decision to move. Her thoughts may have started with those well-known words, "If only we had . . . " or, "If only we had not . . . ." The trials of life, however, can, in time, become a blessing and a source of rejoicing (James 1:2-4). God's plan was at work, but at this time only he knew where that plan was going.

Ancient Jewish interpretations of these events suggest that the deaths of Elimelech and his sons were a punishment for their lack of faith when they decided to leave their ancestral home, but this is purely speculative. And it is dangerous to state that every tribulation is a direct result of a previous sin. Recall that this was the error that the friends of Job made as they attempted to explain his sufferings.

III. NAOMI'S RETURN (RUTH 1:6-8, 16-19a)

A. JOURNEY BEGUN (vv. 6, 7)

6. When she heard in Moab that the LORD had come to the aid of his people by providing food for them, Naomi and her daughters-in-law prepared to return home from there.

At some point, good news from Bethlehem reached Naomi: the famine was over. The word for *come to the aid* (often rendered as "visit"), when used of God, highlights some specific action on his part. Sometimes it is a visitation of judgment (Exodus 20:5; Jeremiah 5:7-9); at other times, such as here, it is a visitation to bless (Exodus 4:31). This news prompted her to go home. Of course, there was really nothing in *Moab* to make her want to stay there any longer.

7. With her two daughters-in-law she left the place where she had been living and set out on the road that would take them back to the land of Judah.

Perhaps these three women felt such a common bond (as a result of their shared grief in losing their husbands) that they desired to stay together.

B. DAUGHTERS-IN-LAW DISMISSED (v. 8)

8. Then Naomi said to her two daughters-in-law, "Go back, each of you, to your mother's home. May the LORD show kindness to you, as you have shown to your dead and to me."

WHAT DO YOU THINK?

What responsibility does the church have to care for widows and widowers today? [See James 1:27 and 1 Timothy 5:3-16.]

WHAT DO YOU THINK?

What kinds of trials offer the greatest challenge to your relationship to God? How can these "become a blessing and a source of rejoicing" for you? [See 2 Corinthians 12:9, 10; James 1:2-4; 1 Peter 1:6, 7.]

WHAT DO YOU THINK?

What experiences provide "common bonds" for people today? How can we use such connections to share the gospel with people?

Naomi was genuinely grateful to her *daughters-in-law* for exhibiting such loyalty to her, but she also knew that it would be in their best interests to marry again (v. 9). This would be more likely to occur if they remained in their native Moab than if they accompanied her to Judah. Naomi's request that each of these younger women *go back* to her *mother's home* seems unusual, especially since Ruth's father was probably still alive (Ruth 2:11). We would expect a reference to the "father's house," which is where widows usually returned (Genesis 38:11; Leviticus 22:13). However, Genesis 24:28 tells how Rebekah went to "her mother's household" after speaking with Abraham's servant, who had been sent to find a wife for Isaac. Possibly Naomi knew that her daughters-in-law would find greater solace and understanding with their mothers.

Naomi then pronounced a blessing upon Ruth and Orpah, expressing her appreciation for their kindness to the *dead*. By this Naomi probably referred to the respect they had shown to Naomi's husband and sons by their treatment of her. After speaking these words, Naomi probably assumed that she would continue the journey back to Bethlehem alone.

The Mothers-in-Law Club

It may surprise some to learn that there is such an organization as the Mothers-in-Law Club International, Inc. With headquarters on Long Island, New York, the club publishes a newsletter and holds regular meetings. It was started in 1971 with the intent "to provide aid to every family throughout the country and the world and to dispel the hackneyed concept of the mother-in-law myth."

Certainly something needs to be said on behalf of mothers-in-law. Why are there so many negative jokes about them? Why are there so few expressions of appreciation for those who fill the role well? And why are there very few books, seminars, or discussion groups to help mothers-in-law with what can be a very difficult task?

It is obvious that Naomi filled the role of mother-in-law superbly. She was respected and loved by both her daughters-in-law. Every married person should treat his or her mother-in-law with respect. And every mother-in-law should act in such a way that she earns and deserves that respect. It is not easy to see the affection of your child transferred to someone else. It is not easy to be quiet when you think you know what your son or daughter (or son-in-law or daughter-in-law) ought to do. But it is necessary!

Every mother-in-law should see Naomi as a model and ask, "Is my attitude going to lead the one who married my child to a deep and lasting faith in God?" And everyone who has a mother-in-law should say, "This is the person who gave life to the one I love. I will treat her with the respect her position deserves." —R. C. S.

C. Steadfast Devotion (vv. 16, 17)

16. But Ruth replied, "Don't urge me to leave you or to turn back from you. Where you go I will go, and where you stay I will stay. Your people will be my people and your God my God.

Ruth's expression of devotion is considered to be one of the most beautiful statements, not only in Scripture, but in all of literature. The phrase *don't urge me to leave you* responded to Naomi's fourfold urging to her daughters-in-law to return to Moab (vv. 8, 11, 12, 15).

The sentiments expressed here are frequently heard at weddings. Some think they ought not to be because, in their context, the words are spoken by a daughter-in-law to her mother-in-law. However, there is nothing inappropriate about a bride or groom repeating these thoughts and making them their own.

Ruth had evidently come to esteem her mother-in-law very highly. The jesting (but often insulting) comments that are made about such relationships find no

How to Say It

Babylon. BAB-uh-lun.
Chemosh. KEE-mosh.
Elimelech. Ee-LIM-eh-leck.
Ephrath. EF-rath.
Ephrathites. EF-ruh-thites.
Isaiah. Eye-ZAY-uh.
Kilion. KIL-ee-on.
Mahlon. MAH-lon.
Mara. MAH-ruh.
Moab. MO-ab.
Moabite. MO-ub-ite.
Naomi. Nay-OH-me.
Orpah. OR-pah.

Solution to Puzzle on p. 206

Across	Down
1. Famine	2. Afflicted
3. Moabite	4. Orpah
7. Four	5. Two
8. Old	6. Judges
9. Husband	10. God
11. Clung	12. Food
13. Determined	14. Ten
16. Wept	15. Mahlon
18. Misfortune	17. Ephrathites
20. People	18. Moabitess
21. Mara	19. Elimelech
23. Bethlehem	22. Almighty
25. Stirred	24. Bitter
26. Barley	

expression here. Ruth had shared grief with her mother-in-law, and had observed Naomi as she experienced terrible loss. It is important to remember that how the Christian handles the trials of life is noticed by others. During such trials, the value and the strength of Christian faith become especially clear.

With this commitment, Ruth was declaring her decision to leave her *people* and her god (cf. v. 15). The worship of Chemosh, the chief god of Moab, included child sacrifice (2 Kings 3:26, 27; 23:13). Now a young woman with a pagan heritage had found the true God, and she wanted to walk in his way instead. To see faith such as this makes the book of Ruth a breath of fresh air in the midst of the chaotic time of the judges (Judges 17:6; 21:25). And amazingly, this statement of faith came from a Moabite—not from one of the Israelites!

17. *"Where you die I will die, and there I will be buried. May the LORD deal with me, be it ever so severely, if anything but death separates you and me."*

This affirmation by Ruth was not a violation of the commandment against taking the Lord's name in vain (Exodus 20:7). Ruth was so certain that only *death* would separate her from Naomi that she called on *the Lord* to take her life if she did not keep her word. The three words *ever so severely* should not be overlooked. In her vow, Ruth invites the Lord himself to punish her in the most severe way if she did not keep her promise.

D. COMPANIONSHIP ACCEPTED (vv. 18, 19a)

18. *When Naomi realized that Ruth was determined to go with her, she stopped urging her.*

Naomi realized that Ruth's statements were not just polite expressions. For Naomi to continue to encourage Ruth to return to Moab would have been disrespectful, not only to Ruth but to the Lord as well. Naomi therefore *stopped urging her,* surrendering to the sincere vow of her daughter-in-law.

Nothing is said about the subsequent reactions of the two women. This, however, must have been an emotional moment for both of them. It is easy to imagine tears, a joyful embrace, and a great joy that both of them were now genuine followers of the one, true, and living God. They were mother-in-law and daughter-in-law, but they were also sisters in the faith!

19a. *So the two women went on until they came to Bethlehem.*

Perhaps along the way, Naomi tried to describe to Ruth what they would find when they reached *Bethlehem*—the place where Naomi had lived with Elimelech and where she had reared her two sons. The two women must have shared much as they made their fifty-mile trek together. This journey was more than a long walk. It became a journey of faith that would be recounted through the ages.

CONCLUSION

It is usually an emotional experience to go home. Part of that emotion involves the fact that "home" never can stay the same as it was when we grew up there. Changes occur—both gradual and dramatic. Children become adults. Death removes familiar faces. Former buildings are gone, and new ones stand in their places. Yet those facts do not constitute reasons to stay away. We still look forward to going home.

The follower of Jesus Christ also anticipates "going home," understanding that he or she is only a temporary resident of this earth. The ultimate destination is Heaven, where Christians will dwell eternally with all the saints of all the ages. In many cases this will include family members and friends who have done what the lesson title suggests: they have chosen "Naomi's God." May we live in such a way that others will choose "Naomi's God," because they have seen that he is our God!

Discovery Learning

This page contains an alternate lesson plan emphasizing learning activities. Classes desiring such student involvement will find these suggestions helpful. The next page is a reproducible activity page to further enhance discovery learning.

LEARNING GOALS

After this lesson each student will be able to:

1. Tell how Ruth came to be associated with Naomi and the God of Israel.

2. Explain how the choice that Ruth made to stay with Naomi reflected great faith.

3. Suggest one or two specific ways a believer can share his or her faith with a non-Christian family member.

INTO THE LESSON

Display a picture of a family tree. Ask if anyone in the class has researched his or her family history. If so, ask, "Did you find anything unusual about religious beliefs in your ancestors?"

Tell the class that many who explore the religious history of their families find that one of their ancestors made a momentous decision to turn his or her back on family beliefs to accept Christian beliefs. Such a one may become an ancestor of many generations of Christians. Such courage is modeled in a widow's life pictured in today's text.

INTO THE WORD

From the commentary section of this book, use the Lesson Background and notes on verse 1 to prepare a brief lecture to introduce today's study of Ruth's adventure in faith. Write the following words on the chalkboard as you talk about each item: *Books Named for Women, Functions of Judges, Famine, Life in Moab.*

Have a volunteer read aloud Ruth 1:1-8, 16-19a. Then use as many of the following activities as time allows.

Activity 1: Crossword Puzzle. Distribute copies of the reproducible page that follows and give the students time to complete the puzzle. Review to provide the solution (see page 203) and answer questions.

Activity 2: Outline the Story Events. In small groups or as a class, have students outline the story included in today's printed text. Subtopics are to be filled in as they happen.

Activity 3: Question and Answer. Allow the class or small groups to discuss the following questions about the text:

1. What may have been some of the crises facing the widowed Naomi when her sons died?

2. When Naomi decided to go home to Judah, she tried to send her daughters-in-law back to their childhood homes. Why? Why was Naomi pessimistic about their marriageability?

3. Ruth's commitment to Naomi is considered to be one of literature's classic statements. For Ruth, this was a monumental and courageous decision. How do you see her life changing because of this statement?

Activity 4. What's in a Name? Explain that names for people in this culture often reflected an individual's personal characteristics or circumstances at birth. Use a poster or some other visual aid to display the names from today's text and their meanings. Ask pairs of people to select two names and discuss why each may have been chosen or why it was appropriate. See the lesson commentary for ideas about the significance of each.

List the following names: *Elimelech* ("my God is king"), *Mahlon* ("weak"), *Kilion* ("pining"), *Naomi* ("my delight" or "pleasant"), *Ruth* ("a female friend"), *Mara* ("bitter"). See Ruth 1:20, 21.

INTO LIFE

Tell the class there are tremendous lessons to be learned from the women of today's text.

From Ruth. Mention that Ruth's commitment to Naomi is a lesson in courageous decisions of faith. Ask class members to share testimonies of acquaintances or family members who have made courageous religious decisions.

From Naomi. Remind the class that Naomi provides a lesson of faith in the family. It was apparent that her faith carried a great deal of influence in Ruth's life. Discuss these questions:

1. Why do you think that some Christian families find it difficult to speak openly of their faith?

2. What are some ways to share our faith effectively with our children? With our parents or siblings? (Remind the class that there is a wonderful sense of satisfaction in seeing the family tree filled with the names of family members who follow Christ.)

Print the following on a commitment card for class members to sign and carry.

"Like Naomi, I want my faith in Jesus to be contagious to my family. To the best of my ability, I will. . . .

• *Demonstrate my faith through speech and behavior;*

• *Speak gently about God's plan and his love;*

• *Pray frequently for my family's relationship with the Lord."*

(Signature)

Models in Courage

The story of Ruth and Naomi is filled with adventure, trials, persistence, courage, love, and faith. Read the entire first chapter of Ruth to discover the exciting and touching adventure of faith of these two women. Then review the chapter to discover the answers to this crossword puzzle.

ACROSS

1. Motivation for Elimelech's family to move to Moab.
3. Nationality of women Elimelech's sons married.
7. Number of times Naomi told Ruth to go back to her own people.
8. Why Naomi thought she would never have another husband.
9. Naomi invited her daughters-in-law to return to their home to find another one of these.
11. What Ruth did to Naomi while Orpah kissed her.
13. Naomi realized Ruth was this kind of woman.
16. Orpah and Ruth's reaction to Naomi's kiss and request.
18. Naomi said the Almighty had brought this upon her.
20. Ruth made a commitment to Naomi that "your people will be my _____."
21. Naomi requested this as her new name.
23. Naomi and Elimelech's hometown.
25. The reaction of Bethlehem when Ruth and Naomi arrived.
26. What harvest was just beginning when Ruth and Naomi arrived?

DOWN

2. Naomi said the Lord had _____ her.
4. Ruth's sister-in-law.
5. The number of daughters-in-law of Elimelech and Naomi.
6. A ruling group who helped deliver Israel militarily from oppressors and who served as magistrates.
10. Ruth told Naomi that "Your God will be my _____."
12. Naomi heard that the Lord had come to the aid of his people by providing this blessing for them.
14. Number of years between death of Elimelech and his sons.
15. Kilion's brother.
17. Naomi and Elimelech's family were _____ from Bethlehem.
18. Ruth was a _____ by nationality.
19. The name of Naomi's husband.
22. Even though Naomi thought life was bitter, she still acknowledged God by calling him by this title.
24. Naomi's description of her plight because she felt the Lord had put his hand out against her.

GOD BLESSES RUTH

LESSON 11

WHY TEACH THIS LESSON?

Redeem is a word that seems to have very different uses in "secular" and "religious" English. In everyday, non-Christian parlance, this word seems mainly to be used to refer to what a shopper does with coupons or gift certificates. The savvy shopper perhaps clips out of a magazine a coupon that is worth a dollar off the price of a certain box of cereal. At the grocery store, our shopper selects the correct product and takes it to the checkout counter where the coupon can be "redeemed" to make the cost lower.

That is certainly smart shopping, but how much more profound is Christianity's use of this word! Of all the world's religions, only Christianity has a *redeemer* who comes to reclaim humanity from sin (Luke 1:68). And he does it by paying the price God demands for that sin (Ephesians 1:7).

But this powerful concept does not simply burst upon the stage of world history with the advent of Christ. *Redeem* as a "religious" concept actually reaches far back into the earliest history of God's Old Testament people (cf. Exodus 6:6). Today we continue with the account of an individual who experienced a redemption in terms of food, marriage, and children because of the intervention of a *kinsman-redeemer*. But this redemption only came about after she had made a resolute decision to leave everything behind—including blood relatives, native land, and the gods she had worshiped—for a new and uncertain path in life. Her decision inspires us also to make a resolute decision because of the intervention by our eternal Redeemer. The cost of this decision may be very high (Luke 14:26), but the ultimate reward will make any earthly loss worthwhile (Luke 18:30).

INTRODUCTION

A. TRY A LITTLE KINDNESS

It was one of those paradoxical statements—an apparent contradiction, yet the expression of something true. The person who was using it may have borrowed the statement from someone else, or perhaps it was an original analysis. The remark was this: "He's so right that he's wrong!" The person being described was always right, rigidly right, and sometimes obnoxiously right. A small amount of kindness or compassionate understanding would have gone a long way in encouraging others to see his side of an issue.

The attribute of kindness is to be a part of every Christian's life. It appears in Galatians 5:22 as the fifth aspect of the fruit of the Spirit. Some people seem to have this quality naturally, while others have to work to overcome backgrounds where kindness was the exception rather than the rule.

Today's church demonstrates kindness in very tangible ways. In recent years church-affiliated relief organizations have been called upon repeatedly to help during times of tragedy around the world. Such groups need financial support, and giving to meet their needs can be an opportunity for kindness that should not be overlooked. At the same time, it must be admitted that the actions of some Christians (particularly church leaders) have been so offensive as to drive people away.

DEVOTIONAL READING:
PSALM 126

BACKGROUND SCRIPTURE:
RUTH 2–4

PRINTED TEXT:
RUTH 2:1-3, 8-12; 4:13-17

LESSON AIMS

After participating in this lesson, each student will be able to:

1. Describe how God blessed Ruth through the kindness of Boaz.

2. Tell how God's providence worked with human effort to accomplish his purpose in the lives of Ruth and Naomi.

3. Keep a record this week of how God provides for him or her by working through people and circumstances.

Feb
10

KEY VERSE

May the LORD repay you for what you have done. May you be richly rewarded by the LORD, the God of Israel, under whose wings you have come to take refuge.
—Ruth 2:12

In Titus 3:4, 5 Paul writes, "But when the kindness and love of God our Savior appeared, he saved us." We are the recipients of God's marvelous kindness. Are we demonstrating kindness to others?

B. LESSON BACKGROUND

Last week's lesson was taken from the first chapter of the book of Ruth. It followed the family of Elimelech during a time of famine, a move to a foreign land, and the deaths of Elimelech and his two sons in that land. Then the focus turned to the women who were left: Naomi and her two daughters-in-law, Ruth and Orpah. Of special significance was Ruth's decision to remain with Naomi and to follow Naomi's God (Ruth 1:16, 17).

These two women, Naomi and Ruth, proceeded to Bethlehem, arriving in early spring just as the barley harvest was beginning (Ruth 1:22). In this second of our two studies from the book of Ruth, we consider the happy ending of this beautiful account.

I. RUTH'S REQUEST (RUTH 2:1-3)

A. BOAZ INTRODUCED (v. 1)

1. Now Naomi had a relative on her husband's side, from the clan of Elimelech, a man of standing, whose name was Boaz.

Boaz is the fourth *man* introduced in the book of Ruth. (The first three, Elimelech and his two sons, died in Moab.) The description of Boaz indicates that he was respected, wealthy, and a *relative* of Naomi through her husband *Elimelech*. Another Hebrew term for *relative*, used more frequently in the book of Ruth to describe Boaz, is translated "kinsman" or "near kinsman." In Israelite society such a person had the responsibility to care for his extended family, particularly the poor, the widows, and the orphans. In addition, he was responsible for buying back any land that had passed from the family's possession (Leviticus 25:25-28). Boaz's duty toward Naomi and Ruth will become more significant as the account unfolds.

B. REQUEST MADE (v. 2)

2. And Ruth the Moabitess said to Naomi, "Let me go to the fields and pick up the leftover grain behind anyone in whose eyes I find favor."

Naomi said to her, "Go ahead, my daughter."

The Lord's economic plan for the poor in Israel did not involve giving handouts, like the modern "welfare" system in the U.S., but more like what some have dubbed "workfare." Reapers were to leave the corners of the fields unharvested, and they could not pick up any grain they had dropped. These were to be left so that the poor and the sojourner could have something to gather (Leviticus 19:9, 10; 23:22). Ruth fit both of these categories, and she apparently knew about this special arrangement (perhaps as a result of conversations with Naomi as they traveled to Bethlehem). The reminder that Ruth was a *Moabitess* serves to emphasize her status as a foreigner and also puts Boaz in a favorable light. He showed kindness to Ruth, in spite of the fact that she was not a native Israelite.

That Ruth took the initiative in going into the fields is commendable. She was willing to work in order to put food on the table for her mother-in-law and herself. Before going, however, she respectfully asked permission for what she proposed to do.

The *leftover grain* was barley (1:22), a common crop in this area (Deuteronomy 8:8) and a dietary staple (2 Kings 4:42; John 6:9, 13). It was harvested during the months we call March and April.

WHAT DO YOU THINK?

Gleaning in the fields was a way provided by the law to help the poor without humiliating them. How can the church today help its poorer members while preserving their dignity?

GOD'S POVERTY PROGRAM

In his book *The Tragedy of American Compassion*, author Marvin Olasky speaks of the earliest efforts to help the poor in the New World. He writes, "Human needs were answered by other human beings, not by bureaucracies." That was the case with God's plan found in Leviticus and demonstrated in today's lesson. Assisting the poor required some effort on their own part, thus helping to preserve their dignity. It also required the active participation of a caring individual such as Boaz.

While designed for an agricultural society, the basic principles of God's poverty program are good for any society. No caring person should be indifferent to human suffering and human need. No person who claims to love God can close his heart to such situations (1 John 3:17). It can be difficult, however, to help the poor in a way that does not make them lifetime clients of welfare. It also can be difficult to help the poor in a way that requires their participation.

God's "poverty program" worked well during the time of Boaz and Ruth. Can we adapt that plan to today's urban, industrialized society? To do so will require a balance of compassion and wisdom. Compassion led Boaz to tell Ruth to stay in his fields. Compassion led him to tell the workers to leave a little more grain than they would have otherwise. Wisdom prevented him from sending Ruth to sit in the shade and letting others do her work.   —R. C. S.

C. GLEANING BEGINS (v. 3)

3. So she went out and began to glean in the fields behind the harvesters. As it turned out, she found herself working in a field belonging to Boaz, who was from the clan of Elimelech.

Sometimes the Lord takes direct control of the "happenings" in our lives. Certainly the fact that *it turned out* that Ruth *found herself working in a field belonging to Boaz* falls into that category. The previous introduction of *Boaz* indicates that the event was occurring within the providence of God. It was not mere luck.

All of us would do well to reflect upon events of the past that seemed coincidental at the time, but were used of God in a special way to provide the people or the circumstances that became a pivotal part of our lives. Often a certain amount of time must pass (in some cases, even years) until we become aware, like Joseph, that "God intended it for good" (Genesis 50:20).

A reminder is provided that Boaz was related to Ruth's deceased father-in-law, *Elimelech*. As noted in the comments under verse 1, this will have important implications as the account unfolds.

II. RUTH'S RECOGNITION (RUTH 2:8-12)

A. BOAZ'S KINDNESS (vv. 8, 9)

8. So Boaz said to Ruth, "My daughter, listen to me. Don't go and glean in another field and don't go away from here. Stay here with my servant girls.

A part of God's providence in this account is that *Boaz* came out from Bethlehem that very day to speak kindly to his reapers and to ask the Lord's blessing upon them (Ruth 2:4). While doing so, he saw *Ruth* and inquired about her identity. She was described to him as "the Moabitess" (Ruth 2:6).

Boaz's kindness was then extended to this woman (a foreigner) who had come to his field to glean. He addressed her as *my daughter,* which is usually understood to mean that Boaz was older than Ruth. His kindness compelled him to give special considerations to her in order to make her situation easier: she was not to *go* to *another field;* she was to *stay* close to his *servant girls.*

Some have suggested that the women in a harvest crew were the ones who tied the stalks of grain that the men had cut. Those who gleaned would follow the harvesting crew as it moved from field to field.

HOW TO SAY IT
Boaz. BO-az.
Elimelech. Ee-LIM-eh-leck.
Jericho. JAIR-ih-co.
Mara. MAH-ruh.
Moab. MO-ab.
Moabite. MO-ub-ite.
Moabitess. MO-ub-ite-ess.
Naomi. Nay-OH-me.
Obed. OH-bed.
Orpah. OR-pah.

WHAT DO YOU THINK?

The lesson writer suggests we all ought to reflect on how God's providence has been at work in our lives. Tell about some apparent coincidence or chance event in your life that you now believe to have been God's providence.

THE WORTH OF WORK

An old Greek proverb says "Work is no disgrace; the disgrace is idleness." D. W. Jerrold wrote, "The ugliest of trades have their moments of pleasure." Honest work always has been honorable. While we may call this the Protestant work ethic, the fact is that the dignity of work goes back to the creation. God is introduced to us as a God of work. He gave the first man work to do in the garden (Genesis 2:15). Jesus said, "My Father is always at his work to this very day, and I, too, am working" (John 5:17). Paul said that the one who would not work should not eat (2 Thessalonians 3:10). Thus Ruth did not need to feel humiliated or demeaned in any way by the work that she did gleaning grain.

A man retired after many years with the same firm. The company gave him a dinner and presented him with a plaque and a gold watch. Seated next to him was a young employee who said, "I envy you." The man who was retiring said, "Don't envy me. The greatest privilege you will ever have is to work."

Certainly Ruth was well rewarded for her willingness to work, and her reward went far beyond the harvest of the day's labor. All of us will find that work blesses us, not just in the wages we receive but in better physical and mental health. Our spiritual health will improve as well, when we seek to do our work "in the name of the Lord Jesus, giving thanks to God the Father through him" (Colossians 3:17).

—R. C. S.

WHAT DO YOU THINK?

Boaz went the "second mile" to help and encourage a stranger, a woman of a different race and religion from his own. What does this suggest to you about how Christians should treat people of other religions?

[Consider also John 14:6, Ephesians 4:15, and James 2:12, 13 to enlighten your discussion.]

9. *"Watch the field where the men are harvesting, and follow along after the girls. I have told the men not to touch you. And whenever you are thirsty, go and get a drink from the water jars the men have filled."*

Boaz expanded his gracious provisions. He encouraged Ruth not to go to any other fields except those where his servants were working. The *men* would be charged not to *touch* Ruth; that is, they should not harm her in any way. The fact that she was a foreigner and had no husband made this more likely. Finally, Ruth was allowed to satisfy her thirst from the *water jars* that the other workers had brought with them. She would not have to bring her own supply of water.

Thus Boaz was practicing what his descendant, Jesus, would later advocate: going the second mile or doing more than is required (Matthew 5:41). The Mosaic law required only that the corners of the field be left unharvested and that dropped stalks of grain not be picked up by the reapers. A deed of kindness may not be the most convenient for a person to do, but it can have eternal consequences.

B. RUTH'S GRATITUDE (v. 10)

10. *At this, she bowed down with her face to the ground. She exclaimed, "Why have I found such favor in your eyes that you notice me—a foreigner?"*

When Ruth left Naomi that morning, there was probably some uncertainty in her mind about how the events of the day would unfold. Now the kindness of Boaz overwhelmed her: a place to glean, water, and the promise of safety. She responded in a manner that is still typical for that region, bowing on her knees.

Not only was Ruth moved by this unexpected kindness, she also wanted to know *why* she was the object of this *favor.* Such treatment was not what she expected, for she was aware that she was a *foreigner* in Judah.

C. BOAZ'S COMPLIMENT (v. 11)

11. *Boaz replied, "I've been told all about what you have done for your mother-in-law since the death of your husband—how you left your father and mother and your homeland and came to live with a people you did not know before.*

Boaz was aware of recent events. He knew that it takes a special courage to leave behind the things and people that are a part of one's identity in order to take on what amounts to a new identity. Ruth's commitment is reminiscent of that of Abram (later called Abraham) when God called him to leave his homeland and his father's house to go to a new land (Genesis 12:1).

D. BOAZ'S BLESSING (v. 12)

12. *"May the LORD repay you for what you have done. May you be richly rewarded by the LORD, the God of Israel, under whose wings you have come to take refuge."*

Boaz then included a formal blessing that he pronounced in the name of *the Lord*—the God whom Ruth had chosen to accept as her own (Ruth 1:16). The final phrase in this verse emphasizes Ruth's decision to leave behind the god of her Moabite upbringing and to cast herself upon the Lord. Boaz used a particularly striking word picture: a young bird's taking refuge *under* the *wings* of its mother. This symbol is also found in the book of Psalms (36:7; 63:7; 91:4), and it was used by Jesus when he wept over the city of Jerusalem not long before his crucifixion (Matthew 23:37).

III. RUTH'S REWARD (RUTH 4:13-17)

A. MARRIAGE AND A SON (v. 13)

13. *So Boaz took Ruth and she became his wife. Then he went to her, and the LORD enabled her to conceive, and she gave birth to a son.*

Much transpired between the two sections of Scripture that make up our printed text. Ruth's gleaning continued through barley harvest and into wheat harvest, which occurred during our months of May and June (2:23). Naomi then re-entered the drama as a "matchmaker." She intended to find "a home" (meaning a husband) for Ruth (3:1), giving instructions to Ruth on how she should propose to Boaz, whom she described as "a kinsman of ours" (3:2).

Behind this plan for marriage was a command of God in the law of Moses that the brother of a man who had died childless was to marry the deceased man's widow and raise up children for him (Deuteronomy 25:5-10; Mark 12:19-23). Since there was no brother of the deceased for Ruth to marry, it was a kinsman's duty to take over this responsibility.

Ruth did propose to Boaz, and Boaz responded in an appropriate way. He was aware that there was a "kinsman-redeemer" who was more closely related than he (3:12), and that that person should be given first choice concerning Ruth. (Thus Boaz is to be commended and admired for his tact and consideration in this sensitive matter.) The closer relative, however, chose not to marry Ruth (4:5, 6). Boaz was then free to purchase all that belonged to Elimelech (Naomi's late husband), which included his land and the responsibility to marry Ruth, the widow of one of Elimelech's sons.

The verse before us is very austere. Left unmentioned are the emotions that must have been experienced by Naomi, Ruth (who apparently had no children from her former marriage), and Boaz. Most important is the statement that the conception of Boaz and Ruth's *son* was of *the Lord*.

B. THE WOMEN'S BLESSING (vv. 14, 15)

14. *The women said to Naomi: "Praise be to the LORD, who this day has not left you without a kinsman-redeemer. May he become famous throughout Israel!*

Perhaps *the women* of Bethlehem recalled that Naomi had requested to be called *Mara* (meaning "bitter"), not *Naomi* (meaning "pleasant"), upon her return from Moab. She added that she had left Bethlehem "full," but the Lord had brought her back "empty" (Ruth 1:20, 21). This praise to God from the women noted that he had made Naomi's life full yet again.

The visual for today's lesson illustrates verse 12 of the lesson text.

WHAT DO YOU THINK?

Boaz praised Ruth for trusting in God. How can we demonstrate our trust in God? How can we encourage others to do the same?

WHAT DO YOU THINK?

The women gave God the credit for what some might call Naomi's "good fortune." How can we be more mindful of God's working to bless our lives in everyday events?

PRAYER

Almighty God, may we become ever more resolute in living for Christ during the tough times and in exercising kindness to others who are experiencing their own tough times. In the name of your Son, Jesus. Amen.

THOUGHT TO REMEMBER

We have been blessed to bless others.

Bible students debate the identity of the *kinsman-redeemer* in this verse. Does it refer to Boaz or to the son of Boaz and Ruth? A good case may be made for either position. The special kindness of Boaz highlighted in this book seems to suggest that he is the one being described; on the other hand, the next verse calls attention to the son. Both Boaz and his son Obed became *famous throughout Israel,* as both are included in the ancestry of the long royal line leading down to Jesus (Matthew 1:5).

15. "He will renew your life and sustain you in your old age. For your daughter-in-law, who loves you and who is better to you than seven sons, has given him birth."

The women's pronouncements of blessing upon Naomi continued. They provided her with a confidence that the days ahead would be much brighter. Her *old age* would be a time of joy.

The person who helped make these blessings possible for Naomi was her *daughter-in-law,* Ruth, and the women praised her highly. They had observed her love for Naomi. The number *seven* is frequently used in the Bible to represent completeness. Thus the reference to *seven sons* highlights the superiority of Ruth's love for Naomi (cf. Jeremiah 15:9).

C. NAOMI'S CARE (v. 16)

16. Then Naomi took the child, laid him in her lap and cared for him.

Naomi had the privilege of caring for *the child,* who continued the line of her husband and son and thus would be considered her grandson.

D. A SPECIAL GENEALOGY (v. 17)

17. The women living there said, "Naomi has a son." And they named him Obed. He was the father of Jesse, the father of David.

Parents usually name their children, so the procedure in this verse seems a bit unusual. Even so, the fact that *the women* named the child may simply reflect the unusual circumstances behind the marriage of Boaz and Ruth. The name *Obed* means "servant"; perhaps he is so named because his birth served to ensure the survival of Naomi's family line. The reference to his being Naomi's *son* should be understood according to the word's Biblical usage, for *son* may describe any male descendant or successor (cf. Matthew 22:42). Again, it highlighted the fact that Naomi was no longer "empty."

Obed became the grandfather of *David,* Israel's second king. The mention of David indicates that the book of Ruth was written after David had become king over Israel. It also helps to give one reason why the book of Ruth was written: to give more details of the genealogy of Israel's most famous king.

CONCLUSION

The title for this lesson is "God Blesses Ruth," and he most certainly did. But while Ruth experienced many blessings, she also had many burdens. But sometimes blessings are appreciated more if they have been preceded by trials; for example, water means much to one who is experiencing great thirst! In addition, we must not overlook how Ruth, who was blessed so richly, became a channel of blessing to others. These "others" clearly included Naomi and Boaz; however, because of Ruth's place in the ancestry of Jesus, she also became a part of God's plan to redeem lost humanity through the death and resurrection of his Son.

Just as Ruth's example shone brightly in the spiritual darkness of her day, so must we shine the light of Jesus in times that are "crooked and depraved" (Philippians 2:15). True, we cannot erase all the darkness in our world, but we can, in the words of the old gospel song, "brighten the corner" where we are.

Discovery Learning

This page contains an alternate lesson plan emphasizing learning activities. Classes desiring such student involvement will find these suggestions helpful. The next page is a reproducible activity page to further enhance discovery learning.

LEARNING GOALS

After this lesson each student will be able to:

1. Describe how God blessed Ruth through the kindness of Boaz.

2. Tell how God's providence worked with human effort to accomplish his purpose in the lives of Ruth and Naomi.

3. Keep a record this week of how God provides for him or her by working through people and circumstances.

INTO THE LESSON

As class members arrive, give each person a sheet of paper on which the word *Providence* is printed vertically. Also have these instructions written on the paper:

"Providence is defined as guidance or care that comes from God. Please complete the acrostic using words that describe God's providential care. You may work in teams if you wish." (This activity is also included in the activity page of the student book.)

After a few minutes, ask each one of ten class members to share one of the words he or she used for one of the letters. Write these responses on a master acrostic to fill in all ten letters. Make the transition to Bible study by explaining that God's providential care often comes through everyday crises and circumstances of life—as illustrated in the story of Ruth and Boaz.

INTO THE WORD

Tell the class that the story of Ruth's second marriage is filled with tenderness and romance, but it is also a story of God's providence at work to bless all mankind. Write the name *Boaz* at the top of a poster and the name *Ruth* at the top of another poster. As you read Ruth 2:1-12, ask students to note clues to the character and faith of these two people. (Chapter 4 will be explored in another activity.) Appoint a "scribe" to write these characteristics on the posters while you conduct the discussion. *Characteristics of Boaz might include powerful (v. 1), wealthy (v. 1), considerate (vv. 4, 8), protective (v. 9), compassionate and kind (v. 11), and godly (vv. 4, 12).* After discovering the qualities of Boaz, mention another intriguing factor: according to Matthew 1:5, his mother was Rahab, the harlot of Jericho who helped the Israelite spies.

Characteristics of Ruth include willing to work (v. 2), respectful (v. 2), diligent (v. 7), appreciative (v. 10), and godly

(v. 12). After discovering Ruth's qualities, explain "leftover grain" and "glean" from verses 2 and 3. Be sure to thank your "scribe" for the assistance.

Summarize the many things that happened between this portion of the text and the marriage of Ruth and Boaz. Mention Boaz's continued kindness, Naomi's matchmaking, and Ruth's unique proposal.

Next, write at the top of a blackboard or marker board "Blessings of This Marriage." Read chapter 4:13-17, asking students to note good things that happened as a result of the marriage of Boaz and Ruth. Write these blessings as students cite them. *They may include a kinsman-redeemer for Naomi (v. 14), a provider for Naomi's old age (v. 15), a son, Obed (vv. 16, 17), Naomi's opportunity to care for her grandson (v. 16), and a lineage to David (v. 17)—and thus to Christ.*

INTO LIFE

Point out that God was working through very ordinary circumstances to bring about extraordinary results in Ruth's day. The loss of a husband for women in Ruth's culture was a traumatic event. But God used everyday cultural practices, such as gleaning grain, to accomplish a great thing in bringing Ruth and Boaz together. However, even this couple did not know God was blessing them in an even greater way than they could imagine. They did not know their great-grandson, David, would be chosen by God to become king of their nation. And they did not know the names of Ruth and Boaz would be tied to the lineage of Jesus, the Son of God. This couple illustrates how God may work through everyday circumstances to do grand things.

Distribute copies of the reproducible activity page that follows. Allow a few minutes for learners to complete the activity; then call for a few volunteers to tell some of the lessons they learned. Ask class members to share testimonies of how God has worked through circumstances in their own lives or in the lives of their acquaintances. While they are thinking, you might offer an example from your own life.

Conclude by reminding students that God often works in this way. Challenge students to keep a brief diary for at least this week, noting how God works through everyday circumstances in their lives. End with prayer, asking God for patience as you wait for his plan to work in your lives.

Lessons in Rich Relationships From Ruth

Read Ruth 2:1-23 and 4:13-17. To discover wonderful examples in human relationships, answer the questions below.

LESSONS FROM BOAZ

What lessons do you learn from Boaz concerning the following?

1. Responsible management of material wealth?

2. Sensitivity to need and circumstances of life?

3. Chivalry?

4. Kindness to others?

LESSONS FROM RUTH

How does Ruth teach you about the following?

1. Work ethics or work habits?

2. Courtesy and respect?

3. Trust in God's care?

LESSONS FROM NAOMI

What lessons does Naomi's example teach you concerning the following?

1. Giving advice and counsel to family members?

2. How God works in mysterious ways?

LESSONS FOR ME

Review the illustrations and lessons listed above. Select one or two of life's qualities listed above that you would like to develop more in your own life. Write them on a slip of paper to carry with you this week.

JONAH REJECTS GOD'S CALL

WHY TEACH THIS LESSON?

More than twenty-seven centuries ago, the prophet Jonah ran from God. He was not the last to do so, of course; Christians still run away from service that God expects of them. They excuse their flight in various ways. Some claim that they haven't had a "call." In fact, the Bible has issued a general call for God's laborers to go to the fields of service (Luke 10:2). Some may claim that they are too busy with work or other responsibilities, but people always seem to *make time* for the things they value most. Some beg off because they do not feel talented enough. But God has bestowed on each one of us *some* kind of talent or spiritual gift. Finally, there are those who use family obligations or expectations as an excuse. Jesus, however, said the believer must choose between Christ and family (Luke 9:61, 62; 14:26).

So although our "flights" from God may be less obvious than that of Jonah, they are no less real. Today's lesson provides a mirror for you and your students. Use it to see whether you, too, might be running from God.

INTRODUCTION

A. PRIDE AND PREJUDICE

"I have sinned." A theology professor once said that these are the three most difficult words for a person to say. Usually pride prevents one from saying them. It takes courage to tell the injured party, "I have sinned."

Marriages have been torn apart because of pride, as the husband or wife (or both) refused to admit to being guilty of certain actions or attitudes. Relationships between parents and children have remained fractured for years because of the stubborn refusal of one party or the other to say, "I was wrong." It is emotionally moving to read the accounts when such relationships have been restored to what they should be in the sight of God. Sadly, it often takes a tragedy, an illness, or a death before the people involved realize how immaturely they have acted.

Churches also have been torn apart because of struggles between personalities. Often pride is a key factor in creating and perpetuating the divisions, because no one will admit to being wrong.

A second *"p word"* that has caused immeasurable suffering is *prejudice*. This, too, has reared its ugly head among the people of God. Prejudice kept the Jewish Christians from taking any initiative to expand their outreach to the Gentiles. When Peter presented the gospel for the first time to Gentiles, he was compelled to make some revolutionary admissions on that occasion: "God has shown me that I should not call any man impure or unclean. . . . I now realize how true it is that God does not show favoritism" (Acts 10:28, 34).

Today's study comes from the book of Jonah. It tells of a prophet who had serious problems with both pride and prejudice. The attitudes that he exhibited

DEVOTIONAL READING:
PSALM 40:1-8
BACKGROUND SCRIPTURE:
JONAH 1, 2; NAHUM 3
PRINTED TEXT:
JONAH 1:1-7, 11-17; 2:1, 10

LESSON AIMS

After this lesson each student will be able to:

1. Tell the story of Jonah's rebellion against God's call and how he was brought to repentance.

2. Tell what factors may have made Jonah reluctant to obey God's call, and why people today are similarly reluctant.

3. Confront a situation where he or she is being challenged to carry out a task for the Lord and determine to obey him, not run from him.

Feb
17

KEY VERSE

But Jonah ran away from the LORD and headed for Tarshish.
—Jonah 1:3

should cause all of us to take a hard look at our own lives and attitudes. Is there any of Jonah in us?

B. LESSON BACKGROUND

The account of Jonah is one of the most familiar in the entire Bible. Personal information about him is found in 2 Kings 14:25. That verse tells us that Jonah's father was named Amittai (also mentioned in Jonah 1:1). Second, it says that Jonah's hometown was Gath-hepher, which was located about three miles northeast of Nazareth. Thus Jonah's prophetic ministry was apparently to the northern kingdom (Israel). Third, it cites a prophecy of Jonah that came to pass during the reign of Jeroboam II (who ruled Israel from 793 to 753 B.C.): the northern kingdom would expand its borders.

The specific date of God's command to Jonah to go to Nineveh (capital of Assyria) is not given in the Bible. Jonah's prophecy of the conquests of Jeroboam II probably occurred either at the end of the reign of Jeroboam's predecessor or at the beginning of Jeroboam's reign. Jonah's entire prophetic ministry would thus have included part of the first half of the eighth century before Christ. During these years, there was a power vacuum in the Near East. Assyria was weak and ineffective, and it was having difficulty controlling rebellions by outlying groups. (That is one reason Israel was able to expand its territory as it did.) Sixty or seventy years after Jonah's ministry, however, Assyria was strong enough to carry the ten northern tribes of Israel into captivity in 722 B.C.

The Assyrians had a reputation for extreme cruelty to those whom they captured. In addition, the northern kingdom had been forced to pay tribute to Assyria during the reign of Jeroboam's great-grandfather, Jehu. (This is not mentioned in the biblical account but has been found in Assyrian records.) Jonah must have been aware of all of this, and that probably influenced how he reacted to the call to go preach there.

IN THE PRESENCE OF OUR ENEMIES

The girl was engaged to be married when her fiancé went off to fight in World War II. But he never returned, for he was killed in the Pacific theater of the war by the Japanese. So the young woman enrolled in Bible college, with plans to become a missionary. After completing her studies, she set out for her mission field. Can you guess where she went? That's right—Japan.

This woman's actions were the very opposite of Jonah's. Jesus taught us to love our enemies and pray for them. It goes without saying that we ought to try to evangelize them. Jonah could not see that the best way to treat an enemy nation is to lead that nation to the true God.

What we learn from Jonah concerning nations applies equally to individuals. Every person needs Christ, including people we do not necessarily like and people who treat us badly. The Bible is a very practical book. It never presumes that we will get through life without making enemies. What it does teach us is how to deal with them. Those lessons are seen in the experiences of Jonah, and they are reinforced in the teachings and example of both Jesus and the apostles. No nation or individual should be considered "off limits" to the good news of salvation.   —R. C. S.

I. JONAH'S FLIGHT (JONAH 1:1-3)

A. GOD'S DESIRE (vv. 1, 2)

1, 2. The word of the LORD came to Jonah son of Amittai: "Go to the great city of Nineveh and preach against it, because its wickedness has come up before me."

Several of God's prophets delivered messages about other lands besides Israel and Judah, but no prophet but *Jonah* was sent on a lengthy preaching ministry to

WHAT DO YOU THINK?

God recruited Jonah as a "missionary" to a foreign land. What can the church do to recruit missionaries to serve in foreign lands today?

a foreign land. In one instance Elisha went to Damascus, but only to tell Hazael that he would be the next king of Syria (2 Kings 8:7-15). Both Daniel and Ezekiel lived in Babylon, but they ministered primarily to God's people who were in exile. Jonah's commission was unique.

The Lord described *Nineveh* as a *great city*. It was great because of its influence and its size. Located on the banks of the Tigris River, it was over five hundred miles from Jonah's hometown of Gath-hepher. The reference in Jonah 4:11 to one hundred twenty thousand persons "who cannot tell their right hand from their left" is considered by some as a description of small children. If so, the entire population of the city could have been as many as six hundred thousand. Nineveh was also great in a less impressive sense: its *wickedness* was great. The phrase *has come up before me* does not imply that God had only recently become aware of conditions in Nineveh. The language implies that God is about to act to address a particular situation. Exodus 2:23 notes, just prior to the account of the call of Moses, that the cry of the Israelites in bondage in Egypt "went up to God."

One truth seen in this account may be easily overlooked. Every nation's actions are known to God, and every nation is accountable to him. Even if a nation's leaders refuse to recognize the Lord as God, that does not eliminate the accountability.

B. JONAH'S DEFIANCE (v. 3)

3. But Jonah ran away from the LORD and headed for Tarshish. He went down to Joppa, where he found a ship bound for that port. After paying the fare, he went aboard and sailed for Tarshish to flee from the LORD.

The location of *Tarshish* is not known for certain; it may be the city of Tartessus, a city on the southern coast of Spain roughly two thousand miles west of Israel. It has been facetiously observed that Jonah was subscribing to the philosophy, "Go west, young man!" when God had said, "Go east!"

Approximately two hundred years before Jonah's time, David had written a psalm that expressed the futility of attempting to flee from the presence of the Lord. "Where can I go from your Spirit?" he wrote. "Where can I flee from your presence? . . . If I rise on the wings of the dawn, if I settle on the far side of the sea, even there your hand will guide me, your right hand will hold me fast" (Psalm 139:7, 9, 10).

The resulting contrast is worth noting: Jonah wanted to escape from God, while David was grateful that he could not do so.

Jonah *went down to Joppa*, a city on the Mediterranean seacoast that was fifty to sixty miles from his hometown. He determined to board a *ship* and to leave not only Israel, but also his responsibilities to God. He paid his fare and was on his way.

II. THE SAILORS' FRIGHT (JONAH 1:4-7, 11-16)

A. DANGEROUS STORM (v. 4)

4. Then the LORD sent a great wind on the sea, and such a violent storm arose that the ship threatened to break up.

The book of Jonah is unique among the twelve minor prophets in that it depicts the occurrence of mighty works of God. The first of these is the *great wind*, which created *a violent storm*. Apparently *the ship* on which Jonah traveled was a cargo ship (see the next verse). Besides the "sailors" (v. 5), Jonah seems to have been the only passenger. The raging waves crashed against the ship, so much so that it was in danger of breaking apart.

Display today's visual as you discuss verse 3. Note how we must choose from the same options.

WHAT DO YOU THINK?

Jonah resisted God's call. What are some ways Christians today try to avoid God's call to service?

B. DESPERATE MEASURES (vv. 5, 6)

5a. All the sailors were afraid and each cried out to his own god. And they threw the cargo into the sea to lighten the ship.

Three responses of the sailors are mentioned: they were *afraid*; they prayed, each man *to his own god*; and they took action to *lighten the ship* so that it would not sink amid the raging waves. That these seasoned *sailors* responded to this storm by praying reminds us that "there are no atheists in foxholes." The genuine believer, of course, does not wait for an emergency to pray. He or she prays "continually" (1 Thessalonians 5:17).

BELIEVING IN PRAYER

The comic strip *Family Circus*, drawn by Bill Keane, once pictured a little girl kneeling by her bed. She is saying to her mother, "I couldn't remember the Lord's Prayer, so I said the Pledge of Allegiance." In a sense, of course, every prayer is a pledge of our allegiance to God and of our dependence upon him for blessings both material and spiritual.

People often speak of believing in prayer, but that is not enough. We must also believe in the God who answers prayer. Pagans believe in prayer, and in times of danger almost everyone prays. (Witness the sailors on board ship with Jonah.) But merely believing in prayer can become similar to believing that there are magic words that, if you say them correctly, will cause certain things to happen. True prayer, however, is not the recitation of magic words. We are not spiritual magicians who say, "Hocus-pocus" and then witness an immediate and dramatic change. We are children who come to a loving Father, confident that he will answer our prayers if they are in accordance with his will. —R. C. S.

5b, 6. But Jonah had gone below deck, where he lay down and fell into a deep sleep. The captain went to him and said, "How can you sleep? Get up and call on your god! Maybe he will take notice of us, and we will not perish."

Jonah's ability to sleep amid such chaotic circumstances is amazing. Some have suggested the stress and weariness resulting from the journey to Joppa enabled him to sleep. Others believe his sleep was an attempt to escape from the uneasiness of his disobedience toward God.

The *captain* probably found Jonah while looking for items to be discarded. He awakened the sleeping prophet and, with great urgency, urged him to *call on* his *god*. The captain wanted to make certain that all the gods were being petitioned during this crisis in the hope that the prayers would somehow reach the right one. However, the one true God—the one responsible for the storm—was fully aware of what was taking place.

The contrast between the pagan captain's concern for all on board his ship with the callousness of Jonah toward the people of Nineveh is interesting. It is sad, indeed, when people who do not believe in or claim to follow the Lord appear to show more kindness and consideration for others than God's people do.

C. DETERMINATION OF BLAME (v. 7)

7. Then the sailors said to each other, "Come, let us cast lots to find out who is responsible for this calamity." They cast lots and the lot fell on Jonah.

Many peoples in the ancient Near East used casting *lots* to determine the will of their gods, including God's people. (See Joshua 14:2; Acts 1:26.) When pagan gods were involved, this practice was nothing more than blind superstition, but when it was done according to the providence of the one true God, it was reliable. There is nothing in the Bible that suggests we today should continue this practice, however.

WHAT DO YOU THINK?

For some people, prayer is merely a "spare tire," to be used only in emergencies. How can we avoid this danger?

DAILY BIBLE READINGS

Monday, Feb. 11—*Good News for an Ethiopian Eunuch (Acts 8:26-40)*

Tuesday, Feb. 12—*"What God Has Made Clean . . . " (Acts 10:1-18)*

Wednesday, Feb. 13—*Peter Greets Cornelius (Acts 10:19-33)*

Thursday, Feb. 14—*"God Shows No Partiality" (Acts 10:34-48)*

Friday, Feb. 15—*Jonah Flees From God's Call (Jonah 1:1-10)*

Saturday, Feb. 16—*Jonah Overboard; the Storm Calms (Jonah 1:11-17)*

Sunday, Feb. 17—*Jonah Prays From the Fish's Belly (Jonah 2:1-10)*

The exact procedure used by these sailors is not known; it may have been as simple as having one object marked, then the one considered guilty would draw the marked item. But whatever the procedure, the one true God saw to it that *the lot fell on Jonah.*

D. DEFINITIVE SOLUTION (vv. 11-13)

11. The sea was getting rougher and rougher. So they asked him, "What should we do to you to make the sea calm down for us?"

In the verses not included in our printed text (8-10), Jonah had identified himself as a Hebrew. He stated that he feared "the God of heaven, who made the sea and the land" (v. 9). Yet, at some point, he also had admitted to the sailors that he was trying to run away from this God (v. 10)! The sailors then made a logical assumption—that Jonah would know what should be done *to make the sea calm down.*

12. "Pick me up and throw me into the sea," he replied, "and it will become calm. I know that it is my fault that this great storm has come upon you."

Jonah's offer certainly appears courageous, but his motives are open to specu-lation. Was he sincerely penitent for what he had done and for what his actions had caused the sailors? Did he think that he would drown as punishment for having attempted to run from God? At any rate, Jonah was very emphatic that the *sea* would *become calm* if he were thrown overboard and that it was his fault that the *storm* had come up.

13. Instead, the men did their best to row back to land. But they could not, for the sea grew even wilder than before.

The sailors were reluctant to comply with Jonah's offer. We don't know whether they hesitated out of concern for Jonah's welfare or out of fear that caus-ing Jonah's death would further antagonize Jonah's God. Thus, *instead* of com-plying with Jonah's suggestion, they tried even harder *to row back to land.*

E. DIVINE APPEASEMENT (vv. 14-16)

14. Then they cried to the LORD, "O LORD, please do not let us die for taking this man's life. Do not hold us accountable for killing an innocent man, for you, O LORD, have done as you pleased."

The sailors seem to have been convinced of the power of Jonah's God. They did not want to do something that would anger such a God. So they went to him in prayer and asked in advance for forgiveness for what they were about to do.

15. Then they took Jonah and threw him overboard, and the raging sea grew calm.

The situation had become desperate, and the sailors seemed to have but two choices: they and Jonah could all die in the storm, or they could throw Jonah *over-board.* Hesitantly, they chose the latter. In wonder the men beheld the hand of God at work again—this time in the calming of the turbulent sea (cf. Mark 4:41).

16. At this the men greatly feared the LORD, and they offered a sacrifice to the LORD and made vows to him.

That the *men greatly feared the Lord* does not necessarily mean that they re-nounced their pagan gods. Ancient pagans believed in many gods. At the present moment, however, it was clear that the God of Jonah was supreme, for he had been in control of the events that occurred.

The men expressed their reverence by what they considered to be the appro-priate actions: they *offered a sacrifice* and *made vows.* We can only wonder at the contents of the vows that were made. We also wonder where the sacrifice was made. Were the sailors near land and thus able to proceed to shore, or did they offer their sacrifice on the ship? We are not told.

WHAT DO YOU THINK?

The sailors' vain rowing for shore illustrates the futility of doing the opposite of God's will. What are some contemporary il-lustrations of this principle? How can we convince people of the fu-tility of resisting God's will?

WHAT DO YOU THINK?

This verse tells us that the pagan sailors "feared the Lord." This reminds us of the disciples' reaction to Jesus' stilling the storm. How can we lead people today to appreciate God's awe-some power and to fear the Lord?

HOW TO SAY IT

Amittai. Uh-MIT-eye.

Assyria. Uh-SEAR-ee-uh.

Elisha. Ee-LYE-shuh.

Ezekiel. Ee-ZEEK-ee-yul or Ee-ZEEK-yul.

Gath Hepher. Gath HE-fer.

Hazael. HAZ-zay-el.

Jehu. JAY-hew.

Jeroboam. Jair-uh-BO-um.

Joppa. JOP-uh.

Mediterranean. MED-uh-tuh-RAY-nee-un.

Nazareth. NAZ-uh-reth.

Nineveh. NIN-uh-vuh.

Syria. SEAR-ee-uh.

Tarshish. TAR-shish.

Tartessus. Tar-TESS-us.

Tigris. TIE-griss.

PRAYER

Lord, give us courage, so that when you give us a task to do we will not run from the task or from you. Rather, may we walk with you in accomplishing that task. Lord, please bless our ministries for you. In Jesus' name, amen.

THOUGHT TO REMEMBER

Running from God always complicates our lives; obeying him simplifies our lives.

III. GOD'S MIGHT (JONAH 1:17; 2:1, 10)

A. SPECIAL FISH (v. 17)

17. But the LORD provided a great fish to swallow Jonah, and Jonah was inside the fish three days and three nights.

Again the *Lord* went to work. This time he arranged for *a great fish* to be at the right place at the right time *to swallow* up *Jonah.* Both the Hebrew word used here and the Greek word used in Matthew 12:40 are general terms meaning a large fish, not necessarily a whale (which many have come to associate with Jonah).

Several stories have been told concerning men who were swallowed by sea creatures, usually whales, and lived through the ordeals. One involves a man named James Bartley, who allegedly was part of a whaling crew working near the Falkland Islands (east of southern Argentina) in February, 1891. According to the account, Bartley spent a day and a night in a sperm whale, having been swallowed when the whale attacked one of the crew's small boats. The whale was caught, and Bartley was discovered the next day while the whale was being processed. He was alive, but parts of his skin were bleached white by the whale's gastric juices. Some conjecture that Jonah's appearance likewise changed as a result of his being inside the fish. They believe that this may have given added credibility to the message that Jonah would eventually preach in Nineveh.

Many people doubt the truth of the Bartley account. It may be true, and it may be legend. Either way, there is no good reason to discredit what the Bible says. God is clearly at work throughout the book of Jonah. He could prepare a fish to do what he wanted it to do as easily as he prepared the storm and, in chapter 4, the gourd, the worm, and the hot east wind.

Jonah is one of only two minor prophets mentioned by Jesus (Matthew 12:39-41; 16:4; Luke 11:29-32; the other is Zechariah, Matthew 23:35). The Matthew 12 passage is especially significant. There Jesus compared Jonah's time in the fish to his time "in the heart of the earth" (in the tomb), thereby predicting his resurrection.

B. SUBMISSIVE PROPHET (2:1)

1. From inside the fish Jonah prayed to the LORD his God.

The contents of Jonah's prayer (vv. 2-9) indicate that Jonah was expressing gratitude for his deliverance from what appeared to be certain drowning in the sea. It is interesting that he concluded his prayer with references to sacrifice and vows (v. 9), similar to how the sailors had responded on the ship (Jonah 1:16).

C. SAFE LANDING (v. 10)

10. And the LORD commanded the fish, and it vomited Jonah onto dry land.

The Lord responded to Jonah's prayer by initiating another special action by *the fish.* (Someone noted that a fish can stomach a backslider for only three days, and then it makes him sick!) Interestingly, the fish obeyed the Lord's command where Jonah had not.

CONCLUSION

Grasping the big picture in the book of Jonah need not involve the fish, though that is a noteworthy event. It need not involve the repentance of the people of Nineveh, even though that is also noteworthy. The big picture does include the fact that Jonah's stay inside the fish became a type of the burial of Jesus prior to his resurrection (Matthew 12:40). Jesus' resurrection is the greatest event in all of history, for by it he broke the stranglehold of sin and death on all mankind. Now those who believe and obey him have the promise of eternal life with him in Heaven.

Discovery Learning

This page contains an alternate lesson plan emphasizing learning activities. Classes desiring such student involvement will find these suggestions helpful. The next page is a reproducible activity page to further enhance discovery learning.

LEARNING GOALS

After this lesson each student will be able to:

1. Tell the story of Jonah's rebellion against God's call and how he was brought to repentance.

2. Tell what factors may have made Jonah reluctant to obey God's call, and why people today are similarly reluctant.

3. Confront a situation where he or she is being challenged to carry out a task for the Lord and determine to obey him, not run from him.

INTO THE LESSON

Before class, prepare and display this poster: "We are not looking for members; we are looking for servants!"

Also prepare a handout with the heading "Help Wanted" with the following instructions: "Read the want ads below and mark the box that best represents your response to each." List several ads from the newspaper from various fields. Include ads for laborers, nurses, truck drivers, and a variety of careers. Also include homemade ads for Sunday school teachers, missionaries, church cleaning teams, and others. After each ad, place these choices with a box by each for students to mark: would consider this job; would consider this job with adequate training; would never do this job.

After the students complete the handout, ask volunteers to report a few responses. Ask the students to look at their list again, at the "never do" list. Ask, "If God called you to do this job, would you change your answer? Why?" Remind the class, "God's call should not be ignored." But many still run from God as Jonah did.

INTO THE WORD

Use the commentary to prepare and give a brief lecture on the lesson background. Note especially the fact that Nineveh had a reputation for cruelty to its prisoners of war.

Read the printed text. Put two headings at the top of two columns on a chalkboard. The first heading will read "Reasons to Run." The second will read "Reasons to Obey." Then ask the following discussion questions.

1. Verse 2 gives two clues about why Jonah ran. What are they? Why would these make Jonah want to run?

2. The lesson commentary also says, "Jonah definitely had a problem with prejudice." Why would the author think that this may be another reason for Jonah to run?

3. When you consider Jonah's flight from God's call, what adjectives would you use to describe his undesirable personality traits? (See the notes on verse 3.)

4. What would you say should be reasons for Jonah to obey God's call? (Column two.) Mention that Jonah did change his mind and complete the mission God gave him. The result of his work is next week's study.

Option: Distribute copies of the reproducible activity "Lessons From Amateur Athletes" from the next page. Use it to guide your Bible study.

INTO LIFE

Use the reproducible activity "Exercise for the Mind and Heart" at the bottom of the page for application. Or do the following activity.

Point to the poster " . . . we are looking for servants," and ask what it means. What is this poster implying? Then read 1 Peter 4:10. Emphasize Peter's assumption that every believer has something God wants him to do. To respond properly, we must be objective and honest. Give each learner a copy of the following evaluation questions to use the next time a ministry opportunity arises.

1. Who in our congregation is better able and more available to do this than I?

2. How would doing this task help me develop the fruit of the Spirit? How would it hinder me?

3. How would my doing this task interfere with other church tasks for which I am responsible?

4. Does the Lord have something more important he wants me to do now or very soon? What?

5. Can I do this without damaging church and family relationships? If not, what negative impact do I foresee?

6. What non-essential activities in my life are consuming the time I would need to do this task well?

7. What opportunities that I do not now have would this service provide for me to be an evangelist?

8. What specifically do I need to pray about before saying yes or no to this Christian service?

Give each student a note card. Ask each to: (1) Write one or two things he or she has been asked to do by another church member recently and to which the answer was "no." (2) Ask each to look again at the opportunity for service that was not taken. Does he or she believe God would like the response to have been "yes"? Close with a quiet prayer that students will more readily answer yes to God's call.

Lessons From Amateur Athletes

Read Jonah 1-7, 11-17, 2:1-10 and answer the following questions from these athletic adventures.

RUNNING

Jonah was the runner. He "ran away from the Lord." Contrast that with David's confidence in God's omnipresence in Psalm 139:7-10.

One time when I behaved like Jonah and ran from God's will was . . .

One time, like David, that I rejoiced in God's everlasting presence was . . .

ROWING

The sailors were the rowing team. They were skilled seamen who turned to the Lord when in trouble.

Why did they turned to the Lord? Was it a valid motivation? Why or why not?

What do you learn from their response to the Lord's intervention?

FISHING

Jonah was also the fisherman . . . and the bait! Read his prayer given so fervently from the belly of the fish (2:2-9).

What flood of emotions do you see pouring out through Jonah's prayer?

What line of Jonah's prayer best expresses your present circumstances in life? Why?

Exercise for the Mind and Heart

Pieces of Jonah's prayer may be helpful and give strength when we are facing tough tests. Write the words from Jonah 2:5, 6 (or any other portion you may select) in this box. Tear it off, carry it with you, and memorize its rich words.

GOD SHOWS MERCY TO NINEVEH

WHY TEACH THIS LESSON?

There are many tasks or jobs that involve stepping outside of our "comfort zones"—tasks that most of us would rather not do. The Twelve thought that washing each other's feet was beneath them, but Jesus showed them they ought to do the job anyway (John 13). Today we may need to care for an elderly or sick person, clean a dirty bathroom, show love to a rude and rebellious teenager, or take on any number unpleasant of tasks. Such tasks may soil not only our hands and knees, but also our pride.

The unpleasant tasks may be not only in the physical realm, but in the spiritual as well. Today, we see Jonah abhorring the thought of taking God's word to an unworthy people. Peter also reacted with abhorrence when first confronted with his task of extending the gospel to Gentiles (cf. Acts 10:14). He had to learn, as did Jonah, that God is not one to show favoritism (Acts 10:34, 35; cf. James 2:1).

We have an advantage today that Jonah did not have: we have the historical facts of Jesus' death and resurrection that secure eternal life for all Christians. Considering all that God has done for us (1 Peter 3:18), what valid reason could we possibly have for resisting God's leading—wherever that leading may take us?

INTRODUCTION

A. SECOND CHANCES

In the 1929 Rose Bowl game, California played Georgia Tech. One incident in that game has been related many times. During the first half, California player Roy Riegels recovered a fumble, became disoriented in the resulting confusion, and ran sixty-five yards in the wrong direction. A teammate was able to catch him and tackle him just before he reached the wrong end zone. Later, when California attempted to punt from that spot, the kick was blocked and Georgia Tech scored a safety (worth two points). That play turned out to be critical, as Georgia Tech won the game by a score of eight to seven.

Something else happened that day in the California locker room, which overshadowed the wrong-way run. The California coach ended his halftime comments by announcing that the players who had started the first half would also start the second half. Everyone started to leave the locker room but Riegels. He was overcome with dejection and did not want to play. But his coach proved that he had not lost faith in his player: he encouraged Riegels, who went out to play an inspired second half. He received a second chance, and he gave it his all.

God in his wisdom saw fit to record the sins of many individuals in both the Old and New Testaments. But those failures are there for a purpose; as Paul stated in Romans 15:4: "Everything that was written in the past was written to teach us, so that through endurance and the encouragement of the Scriptures we might have hope." They teach us (among other things) that failure does not

DEVOTIONAL READING:
PSALM 113
BACKGROUND SCRIPTURE:
JONAH 3, 4
PRINTED TEXT:
JONAH 3:1-5, 10; 4:1-5, 11

LESSON AIMS

After this lesson each student will be able to:

1. Retell the story of Jonah's mission to Nineveh, including the people's repentance and Jonah's displeasure.

2. Contrast Jonah's anger at Nineveh's repentance with God's steadfast love for all people.

3. Suggest a specific means to demonstrate the mercy of God through some ministry of the church or in his or her relationship with another person.

KEY VERSE

You are a gracious and compassionate God, slow to anger and abounding in love, a God who relents from sending calamity.
—*Jonah 4:2*

Feb
24

mean that we are no longer useful to God. God is a God of "second chances." The study for today highlights Jonah's second chance to hear and then heed God's call to service. But note that God's requirements did not change; for Jonah to take advantage of God's second chance meant accepting God's terms. There is always hope for those willing to take that step.

Others in the Bible also illustrate this point. David was guilty of covetousness and adultery in his affair with Bathsheba. He then plotted the death of her husband in an attempt to cover up the sin. His Psalm of penitence (Psalm 51) still gives hope to those who may think that their sins have left them without hope.

Peter's three denials of Jesus followed his bold declaration that he would never do such a thing (Matthew 26:33-35). But Peter was restored to a place of useful service (John 21:15-19). He preached the first gospel sermon on the Day of Pentecost, wrote two of the epistles in the New Testament, and may have been the primary source used by Mark in the writing of his gospel.

And speaking of Mark (or John Mark)—the mention of his name brings to mind how he earned the disfavor of Paul for "bailing out" during Paul's first missionary journey (Acts 13:13). Paul therefore refused to allow John Mark to go with him on the second journey (Acts 15:36-38). But years later, when Paul was in prison in Rome, he instructed Timothy to bring Mark to him. "He is helpful to me in my ministry" (2 Timothy 4:11), Paul wrote.

God specializes in second chances. He was willing to forgive the entire city of Nineveh when the people turned to him in repentance, and today he desires to forgive all who will come to him through Jesus Christ.

B. LESSON BACKGROUND

The lesson text for today begins where last week's text ended. The fish that the Lord had prepared to swallow Jonah (Jonah 1:17) vomited him on to shore (2:10). We do not know how much time passed until the Lord's call came a second time to Jonah. We do know that Jonah responded quite differently when it did! However, we shall see in our study today that Jonah still harbored certain attitudes that needed to be corrected. We shall also observe God's efforts to accomplish that correction.

I. JONAH'S OBEDIENCE (JONAH 3:1-5, 10)

A. THE CALL (vv. 1, 2)

1, 2. Then the word of the LORD came to Jonah a second time: "Go to the great city of Nineveh and proclaim to it the message I give you."

The *second* call to *Jonah* is similar to the first one (Jonah 1:1). The *word of the Lord* included no rebuke for his reluctant prophet. He was simply to *go to the great city of Nineveh.*

The Lord's instructions to Jonah concerning his message were slightly different on this second occasion. This time Jonah was to *proclaim to it the message* that the Lord would give him. (Previously he was to "preach against" Nineveh, according to Jonah 1:2.) Preaching anything but the Lord's message is perilous to both the preacher and his audience.

B. THE CRUSADE (vv. 3, 4)

3. Jonah obeyed the word of the LORD and went to Nineveh. Now Nineveh was a very important city—a visit required three days.

This time Jonah *obeyed* and headed in the right direction, though apparently he still had some reservations about going, as we shall see. The trip would have been several hundred miles, depending on where Jonah was in Israel when he

WHAT DO YOU THINK?

The lesson writer says, "Preaching anything but the Lord's message is perilous to both the preacher and his audience." How can a listener be sure the preacher is preaching what the Lord wants him to say? What should a listener do if the preacher is not preaching the truth?

began. But any site on the Mediterranean coast, where the fish would have spit Jonah out, would have still been hundreds of miles from Nineveh. Obviously, then, making the journey was no small undertaking.

Nineveh is here described as *a very important city*. Some translations render the word for *important* as a reference to size. Archaeological excavations have revealed that Nineveh's inner wall had a length of almost eight miles. That may not sound large to us, but it was huge by ancient standards.

The statement that *a visit required three days* must not be taken as a reference to how long it would take Jonah to get there. A journey of hundreds of miles would have taken many days, even weeks. Instead, the phrase is another indication of the impressive size of Nineveh itself. Usually one of the following three interpretations of the phrase is suggested: (1) it would take three days to go either across or around the city; (2) it would take Jonah three days to preach in the various neighborhoods of the city; or (3) it would take three days to travel through *Nineveh* and the towns of the surrounding area. Greater Nineveh (which would have included those towns) covered approximately sixty miles in circumference.

4. On the first day, Jonah started into the city. He proclaimed: "Forty more days and Nineveh will be overturned."

On the first day Jonah entered Nineveh, which probably means that he had not been there an entire day when he began to deliver the Lord's message. In the Hebrew text, Jonah's preaching consists of only five words; in our English translation there are eight words: *Forty more days and Nineveh will be overturned*. These few words could have been sufficient to make quite an impact, but they probably represent a summary of Jonah's preaching. By themselves, they say nothing of why Nineveh would be overturned, or by whom. The fact that the people of Nineveh "believed God" (v. 5) and repented suggests Jonah included the fact that their sin was the reason for the impending doom and that the God of Heaven would shortly execute judgment. As noted in the previous lesson, some believe that Jonah's appearance (bleached or whitened from his time inside the fish) may have enhanced the power of his message. If so, Jonah must have explained how God had turned him around and sent him to Nineveh with this message.

It is interesting to speculate about Jonah's attitude as he preached. He had not wanted to go to Nineveh, and now he was preaching where he did not want to be. Classes on preaching usually emphasize that the message of God has warnings, but these are to be delivered so that the hearers know that both God and the preacher have a genuine love for them. Preachers often have been accused of trying to scare people into being good, but the warnings within God's message have always represented his loving concern for mankind. To what degree Jonah communicated this concern cannot be measured, but we know from the results that his preaching had an impact! The *forty days* mentioned by Jonah provided a time for the people of *Nineveh* to determine the type of response they would make to his message.

C. THE CONSEQUENCES (vv. 5, 10)

5. The Ninevites believed God. They declared a fast, and all of them, from the greatest to the least, put on sackcloth.

To some, the most amazing event recorded in the book of Jonah is how he was swallowed by a fish. But far more amazing is that Jonah's preaching sparked a citywide revival! Three responses on the part of *the Ninevites* are cited in this verse: they *believed God, declared a fast,* and *put on sackcloth*. These acts of repentance involved every citizen, *from the greatest to the least*—from the king down to the animals (vv. 6-8)!

WHAT DO YOU THINK?

Jonah did not want to go to Nineveh, but he was persuaded to do so for God. What are some things you would not do for pleasure, for money, or for anyone but God?

WHAT DO YOU THINK?

When the Ninevites repented of their sins, they showed their sincerity by fasting and wearing sackcloth. What actions today would indicate a proper attitude of repentance?

As was stated in the Background to last week's lesson, the year that Jonah went to Nineveh is not given in the Bible. Some place this event as early as 790 B.C., in the early years of the reign of King Jeroboam II of Israel (793-753 B.C.). It probably occurred sometime during that reign, but whether early or late we cannot be certain. Over a century later, Nahum, another prophet of God, would announce that Nineveh would be totally destroyed and that this time there would be no reprieve (Nahum 1:1, 2; 3:7, 18, 19). True to the prophet's word, an alliance composed mainly of Babylonians and Medes destroyed Nineveh completely in 612 B.C. For now, however, the people had delayed that hour of judgment.

THE CLOTHING OF REPENTANCE

Life was difficult for farm families during the Great Depression of the 1930s. Some companies that produced cattle feed put it in sacks that could be reused as dress material. Many a farm girl went to school wearing a homemade dress that had been made from feed sacks. Out of necessity, girls wore sackcloth!

Of course, the situation described in today's text is very different from that. The residents (and animals) of Nineveh wore garments made of rough, coarse material (perhaps goat's hair) as a sign of their repentance. Even the king participated in this citywide demonstration of a willingness to turn from sin to the Lord (Jonah 3:6).

In the Sermon on the Mount, Jesus taught that certain acts of worship are best done in private. For example, those who fast should give no outward indication that they are fasting (Matthew 6:16-18). And though Jesus did not mention repentance in his sermon, it too is something that should not be done so that we are "honored by men" (Matthew 6:2). The primary outward expression of repentance should be in the way we live, not in the way we look. We do not want men to praise us for our devotion; we want them to praise God for the changes he has made in our lives. We want to "clothe [ourselves] with the Lord Jesus Christ" (Romans 13:14). That is part of letting our light shine—not to draw attention to us, but to our Heavenly Father (Matthew 5:13-16).   —R. C. S.

What Kind of God Will Accept Sinners?

"a gracious God, and merciful, slow to anger, and of great kindness"

—Jonah 4:2

Note how the descriptions of God illustrate his grace, which Jonah took for granted. Do we take it for granted?

10. When God saw what they did and how they turned from their evil ways, he had compassion and did not bring upon them the destruction he had threatened.

As a result of the people's repentance, God *did not bring upon them the destruction he had threatened.* Because the people *turned away from their evil ways,* God withheld his hand of judgment. It is still true that God takes "no pleasure in the death of anyone" (Ezekiel 18:32). He is "not wanting anyone to perish, but everyone to come to repentance" (2 Peter 3:9).

II. JONAH'S OBJECTIONS (JONAH 4:1-5, 11)

A. JONAH'S COMPLAINTS (vv. 1-3)

1. But Jonah was greatly displeased and became angry.

Now the focus shifts from the people of Nineveh back to the interactions between Jonah and the Lord. The negative reactions of Jonah toward Nineveh's repentance were intense. The prophet was *greatly displeased and became angry,* though many prophets (and preachers today) would envy such success! Jonah's experiences with the storm, the pagan sailors, and the fish had encouraged him to go to Nineveh; but he was still far from God in his attitudes.

2. He prayed to the LORD, "O LORD, is this not what I said when I was still at home? That is why I was so quick to flee to Tarshish. I knew that you are a gracious and compassionate God, slow to anger and abounding in love, a God who relents from sending calamity.

There is one good thing that may be said about Jonah at this point: *he prayed* (though his language in this prayer differs greatly from his prayer in the sea).

WHAT DO YOU THINK?

Jonah's heart was not in his ministry. His displeasure at the success of the Ninevite revival demonstrates that clearly! How important is a preacher's attitude to the success of his preaching? What should you do if you discover your preacher has some bad attitudes?

Certainly he knew much about the ways of God. His description of God as gracious, merciful, slow to anger, and of great kindness is similar to that found in Exodus 34:6. Jonah himself, however, did not possess these attributes—at least not toward Assyria. He had his own set of values, and they were much different. He harbored an intense dislike for the people of Assyria, apparently believing that only Israel should receive God's mercy.

3. *"Now, O LORD, take away my life, for it is better for me to die than to live."*

In the depths of self-pity, Jonah expressed a desire for death. This was not an idle statement; it was a sincere prayer—just as sincere as his prayer in the sea. There, however, he had given thanks for the Lord's deliverance toward him personally; here he expresses scorn for that deliverance when shown toward the Assyrians. It is difficult to imagine that Jonah would view his circumstances as so depressing that death was preferred or that he would pray to that end. Yet even the Lord's servants can experience such despair; Elijah is another example (1 Kings 19:1-4).

B. THE LORD'S CORRECTION (v. 4)

4. *But the LORD replied, "Have you any right to be angry?"*

With a gentle question—again, consider the similarity to Elijah in 1 Kings 19:9—the Lord responded to the rash prayer and statement by Jonah. It is the response that a person in Jonah's situation often does not want to hear. It demands thought—reasoned thought, not merely emotional responses that center on self. One may recall God's question to angry Cain in Genesis 4:6.

LIVING IN ANGER

In Austria there is a village called Anger. It is a small place; however, if all the people whose lives are dominated by anger lived there, it would be (like Nineveh) a very large city! Of course, the word *anger* does not have the same meaning in Austria as it does here. It is an old German word meaning *meadow*. Still, it is a sad fact that many people do live their lives in anger. By doing so they spoil life for both themselves and others.

Thus the question that God put to Jonah needs to be put to all of us. The setting may be different, but the question is still valid: "Have you any right to be angry?" Sometimes, of course, the answer is "Yes." It would be strange indeed if a person never got angry. There are many injustices and cruelties in the world, to which we ought to respond with righteous indignation.

On the other hand, often the answer to God's question must be "No." Our reasons for anger can amount to nothing more than "molehills." James advised, "For man's anger does not bring about the righteous life that God desires" (James 1:20). We do serious spiritual damage to ourselves when we live in anger. We cannot think, speak, or act like Jesus when we are angry. And anger unchecked will feed on itself, becoming more intense and harmful in the process.

If you are living in anger, it is time to move out. —R. C. S.

C. JONAH'S CONCERN (v. 5)

5. *Jonah went out and sat down at a place east of the city. There he made himself a shelter, sat in its shade and waited to see what would happen to the city.*

Jonah did not answer the Lord's question (at least no verbal response is recorded). He simply *went out and sat down* to watch *what would happen* from a vantage point *east* of Nineveh. Apparently Jonah still held to some hope that Nineveh would be destroyed. Perhaps he took God's question in verse 4 as indicating that his judgment might yet fall upon the city.

HOW TO SAY IT

Assyria. Uh-SEAR-ee-uh.

Babylonians. Bab-uh-LOW-nee-uns.

Bathsheba. Bath-SHE-buh.

Elijah. Ee-LYE-juh.

Jeroboam. Jair-uh-BO-um.

Medes. Meeds.

Mediterranean. MED-uh-tuh-RAY-nee-un.

Nahum. NAY-hum.

Nineveh. NIN-uh-vuh.

Tarshish. TAR-shish.

The context indicates that this occurred during the summer, so while waiting, Jonah attempted to provide himself with some relief from the heat of the sun. He *made himself a shelter* so he could have a shaded area in which to sit.

Verses 6-10 provide additional details concerning this encounter between the prophet and the Lord. Apparently Jonah's booth did not offer sufficient relief from the heat, so overnight the Lord "provided a vine" that supplied extra protection and made Jonah "very happy." But the next day the Lord "provided a worm" to attack the plant, and it died. Note that the word "provided" was also used for the fish (Jonah 1:17), but there is a great difference in size between the fish and the worm. God is the sovereign ruler over "all creatures great and small." Without the protection of the vine, the heat of the sun (coupled with a hot east wind that the Lord again "provided") made Jonah miserable. Jonah again expressed his feelings by saying, "It would better for me to die than to live."

The confrontation between the Lord and Jonah then continued with another thoughtful question from the Lord. He asked Jonah if the prophet should really be that upset about losing a plant—upset enough to want to die. Jonah replied that he was justified to be that angry, "angry enough to die." The Lord knew what Jonah's reply would be, and he set him up for the real question that concludes the book. Verse 10 begins that question. There the Lord challenged Jonah to think about all the emotion that he had felt for a plant. He had not done anything to cause that plant to grow; it had arrived overnight, and it had perished in a night.

D. THE LORD'S CONCERN (v. 11)

11. "But Nineveh has more than a hundred and twenty thousand people who cannot tell their right hand from their left, and many cattle as well. Should I not be concerned about that great city?"

Here is the lesson of the book of Jonah in the proverbial nutshell. God loves all the people of the world. Jonah was concerned about only himself. God wanted to *spare* the people of *Nineveh*, while Jonah preferred death because of losing a plant. The destruction of Nineveh did not disturb his conscience at all.

The *one hundred and twenty thousand people who cannot tell their right hand from their left* is usually interpreted one of two ways. Some believe it indicates the number of young children in Nineveh—so young that they had not yet learned the difference between right and left. If so, then the population of Nineveh was perhaps around six hundred thousand. Others think that one hundred twenty thousand was the total population of Nineveh, and that spiritually they could not discern right (the right hand) from wrong (the left hand). In either case, the point is clear: God wanted to spare Nineveh.

The phrase *and many cattle as well* is interesting in that it may reflect how such animals depend on humans for receiving proper care. If the people in the city of Nineveh are destroyed, then human protection of these animals is removed.

CONCLUSION

Over the past three months, our lessons from Isaiah, Ruth, and Jonah have provided different ways to consider the theme that God is the "Light for All People." In a time when religious pluralism is emphasized and publicized, it is often awkward and unpopular to assert that there is only one God and one way to him. All roads do not lead to Heaven. Jesus is the one way to God: "There is no other name under heaven given to men by which we must be saved" (Acts 4:12).

If this is true (and it is), then it places a great responsibility upon all followers of Jesus. It is imperative that we live as the "light of the world" (Matthew 5:14), so that others may come to him who is the real light of the world (John 8:12).

WHAT DO YOU THINK?

Jonah was not the last of God's people to think more about himself than others. How can we cultivate a selfless attitude in Christians today so that they are more eager to reach out to the lost than they are to satisfy themselves?

PRAYER

Our Father in Heaven, lead us to develop the attitudes that we must have to defend the faith in a courageous way and to love others genuinely so that we may accomplish the task of reaching them for your Son. We ask in his name. Amen.

THOUGHT TO REMEMBER

"God is light; in him there is no darkness at all" (1 John 1:5).

Discovery Learning

This page contains an alternate lesson plan emphasizing learning activities. Classes desiring such student involvement will find these suggestions helpful. The next page is a reproducible activity page to further enhance discovery learning.

LEARNING GOALS

After this lesson each student will be able to:

1. Retell the story of Jonah's mission to Nineveh, including the people's repentance and Jonah's displeasure.

2. Contrast Jonah's anger at Nineveh's repentance with God's steadfast love for all people.

3. Suggest a specific means to demonstrate the mercy of God through some ministry of the church or in his or her relationship with another person.

INTO THE LESSON

Use one of these activities to introduce today's study:

Circle Response. Seat the class or small group in a circle. Go around the circle asking each person to complete the following statement. "I believe that the toughest people to share Christ with are. . . ." List the responses. Remind the class God had to tell Jonah twice to take his message to a tough audience. But Jonah's experience teaches us some valuable lessons.

Musical Reflections. Remind the class that God's will includes sharing our faith, a commission reflected in songs we sing. Ask the class members to "sing out" lines of songs or song titles that encourage us to share our faith. List these titles and lines. Remind the class that it is easier to sing and talk about this commission than it is to do it! Even Jonah found it tough to obey. But he and God teach us a valuable lesson in today's text.

INTO THE WORD

Use the background information and notes on Jonah 3:10 (see pp. 224, 226) to prepare a brief lecture on the setting for this event and on Nineveh's future. Next, use three students to read today's printed text. Give each student a photocopy of the text with his or her part highlighted. You will need someone to read the parts of the narrator, the Lord, and Jonah.

Examine the text in more detail with one of the following activities. Arrange the class in pairs or small groups. Ask each group to write on a poster words that would describe Jonah's nature and character. (Students may wish to reflect on last week's events for additional insights into Jonah's character.) After they have completed their lists, ask the teams or groups to circle two of Jonah's characteristics that they see as dominant in his life. Have a team member post the group's work, commenting on why the particular traits were chosen.

If your class members work better individually than in groups, distribute copies of the reproducible activity "Jonah's Report Card" from the next page. Allow a few minutes for students to complete the activity; then ask volunteers to report the grades they gave and to tell why.

Make the transition to the next activity by restating Jonah's dominant traits, emphasizing that the one good thing to mention about him was that Jonah prayed. He had a close enough relationship with God that he could talk to him freely.

Discuss with the class the following questions:

1. A huge revival took place in Nineveh. With what you know of the people there, does this surprise you? Why or why not?

2. Reread Jonah 4:1, 2. Sometimes Jonah is called "the pouting prophet." What do you think was the real reason for Jonah's pouting anger?

3. Why do you think Jonah asked God to take his life?

4. How did the Lord respond to Jonah's pouting anger? What does this teach you about him?

INTO LIFE

Ask each student to select the two song titles that best represent his or her response to God's call to share our faith. Read the following list. Then call for responses, asking why students chose the titles they did.

A. "The Fight Is On"

B. "I Cannot Tell"

C. "It Took a Miracle"

D. "I Am Praying for You"

E. "O for a Thousand Tongues"

F. "Softly and Tenderly"

G. "Where He Leads Me"

H. "I Am Weak But Thou Art Strong"

I. "One Day"

Distribute copies of the reproducible activity "Jonah and Me!" from the next page. Ask teams or small groups to follow the directions printed there. Ask students to report their answers. Focus the discussion on "Taking the Good News." Ask how the church is already doing this and for new ways to do it better. Then ask students to work alone and take a few minutes to jot a few notes about how they will respond or apply these principles to their lives. Ask them to consider adding names of people to their response. Close with a prayer for boldness in taking God's message to others.

Jonah's Report Card

What grades would you assign Jonah in his first cross-cultural mission assignment? Circle the grade you think best represents his accomplishment.

Effort	A	B	C	D	F
Ability to Follow Instructions	A	B	C	D	F
Sincerity	A	B	C	D	F
Enthusiasm	A	B	C	D	F
Personal Relationships	A	B	C	D	F

Jonah and Me!

Note the events or lessons from Jonah listed in the first column on the chart below. In the second column jot a few of the reasons you think God would choose to include this in the Bible. What principles does he want us to learn? In column 3 note what response you think God is expecting from you. Be specific.

Events/Lessons	Principles and Lessons Learned	My Response
God's Mercy and Compassion		
Second Chances (3:1)		
Jonah's Nature and Character		
Taking the Good News to Non-Jewish Nineveh		

Spring Quarter, 2002

The Power of the Gospel
(Romans, Galatians)

Special Features

Lessons

About These Lessons

The lessons of the previous quarter showed us that, even in the Old Testament, God demonstrated his concern for all people, not just the members of the Jewish race. In the present quarter we shall see how this concern translates into a gospel of grace. Paul's letters to the Romans and the Galatians state clearly and unmistakably that God's grace is for everyone, and that only by the grace of this gospel will anyone be saved!

Mar 3
Mar 10
Mar 17
Mar 24
Mar 31
Apr 7
Apr 14
Apr 21
Apr 28
May 5
May 12
May 19
May 26

Laws Are Not Enough

by John W. Wade

The past three decades have brought an appalling increase in crime rates across the country. In response we have passed new laws with tougher penalties and built more prisons to house the growing number of convicts. Still the crime and violence persist.

If we had studied history a bit more carefully, we would have realized that laws alone are not enough to maintain a stable and healthy society. The Israelites had the best laws in the ancient world—after all, the laws had come from God. But the Mosaic code did not solve all the problems that arose in the Jewish society. The law did bring some benefits for the Jews. For one thing, the law provided some definite standards for determining whether an act was right or wrong. Any society that does not set up such standards is likely to fall into anarchy, in which each person becomes his own police force and judge over his neighbors. Further, the law was a tutor or schoolmaster to bring the people to Christ. Most important of all, the law looked to the coming of God's Messiah, who would fulfill the law perfectly.

But there were weaknesses in the law. The most glaring was that it was "weakened by the [flesh]" (Romans 8:3; in this and several other verses the word for "flesh" is translated as "sinful nature"; "flesh" is a better translation). The law could identify and describe sin, but by itself it lacked the power to help overcome the sin in one's life. Further, if one broke one single commandment, he or she bore the guilt for the whole law. But the gospel offers the power to overcome all the weaknesses of the law. Under the law, salvation could come only through keeping all the commandments. In the gospel, however, God offered a new and better way. Salvation through the gospel was through grace by faith.

UNIT 1, JUSTIFIED BY FAITH

The **first lesson**, "God's Righteousness Revealed," provides the theological foundation for the rest of the lessons of the quarter. The key verse, Romans 1:17, affirms that the "righteous will live by faith." When Martin Luther understood the meaning of this verse, he was moved to challenge the Roman Catholic Church of his day, which made salvation by works a central part of its teaching. This lesson should challenge us to examine our own thinking and practices lest we subtly succumb to the temptation to base our salvation on good works rather than on faith.

Lesson two deals with "justification." This term is more likely to be heard among theologians than among ordinary church members, but we shouldn't allow that to turn us off. In a judicial sense, justification means to make or declare one just. God is our Supreme Judge, and under the terms of the law he would have to declare us guilty when we stand before him. But because of his infinite grace, he sent his Son to die for us, and if we are by faith willing to accept that grace, we will be justified.

In **lesson three** Paul anticipates objections that Jews may raise to the gospel basis for salvation through faith. Before God ever revealed the law on Mount Sinai, Abraham was justified by his faith, not his works. Paul was able to quote Genesis 15:6 as the basis for this claim.

Lesson four deals with "reconciliation," another term used by theologians. Our sins have opened a vast chasm between us and God that we on our own can never hope to span. But God has provided a way for us to cross that gulf. He has offered his Son, who died on the cross, as a bridge over which we may cross to enjoy God's wonderful blessings.

Lesson five gives us an opportunity to study the Easter story from a little different perspective. The first part of the lesson is based on John 20, which gives the historic setting for the resurrection. The remaining portion of the lesson is based on Romans 6. In these verses Paul shows the direct relationship of baptism to our Lord's death and resurrection. The act of baptism depicts the death, burial, and resurrection of Christ. The person who is being baptized has, through his or her faith and confession, died to the old man of sin, who is then buried in the watery grave of baptism, only to arise again to live a new life."

UNIT 2, LIVING BY FAITH

APRIL

Romans 8, which is the Scriptural basis for **lesson six**, has been acclaimed as one of the great chapters in the entire Bible, and justifiably so. Among other things, it deals with the problem of suffering. Although we may suffer grievously in this life, these sufferings "are not worth comparing with the glory" that awaits us in the future. The lesson concludes with Paul's assurance that nothing can separate us from the love of God, an assurance that can carry us through the many trying situations that we have to face in this life.

Lesson seven urges us to "Proclaim the Gospel." Earlier in his life, Paul had been an ardent foe of Christianity; he had pursued and persecuted Christians. Once he became a Christian, however, he was zealous to proclaim his newfound faith. His first concern was for his fellow Jews that they would also come to know the Savior, but the message of salvation is for all nations. That message must be proclaimed if all are to learn the good news of God's love. The task of sharing the good news is not assigned just to ministers or missionaries, but is laid upon all of us. Encourage your students to think of new ways that we can share the gospel.

Therefore is a key word. Paul uses it in **lesson eight** to move from theological issues to a practical application of these issues. When one becomes a Christian, a changed life is not incidental or optional. Paul puts it very starkly: "offer your bodies as living sacrifices." This kind of total commitment brings a transformation of lifestyle that keeps us from being conformed to the world.

Lesson nine continues this emphasis on living one's faith in the world. Paul addresses the problem of becoming judgmental of others who do not agree with our way of doing things. He does not suggest that we compromise the faith, but he insists that on issues that are not vital to the faith, we should learn to be tolerant of the views of others. He reminds us that ultimately we are all accountable to God and his standards.

UNIT 3, NO OTHER GOSPEL

MAY

The last four lessons of this quarter are based on texts taken from Paul's letter to the Galatians. The immediate occasion for Paul's writing this letter was a vital theological issue that arose when Judaizers upset the churches with their insistence that Gentiles must submit to the Mosaic law. Paul resisted this effort with some of the strongest language he used in any of his writings. If the Judaizers had prevailed, Christianity would have been reduced to just another Jewish sect and lost its appeal to the non-Jewish world.

In **lesson ten** Paul established his authority to speak to this issue. He was, first of all, an apostle, called by Jesus Christ and not by any human authority. He further affirmed that the gospel he preached had not been received from man but had come directly from Jesus Christ. After establishing his authority, he addressed the theological issue. He concluded by pointing out that if righteousness had come by the law, then "Christ died for nothing."

The title and emphasis of **lesson eleven** is the "Gospel of Adoption." Jewish people prided themselves on being children of Abraham, and they had come to believe that they were entitled to special blessings as a result. This led the Judaizers to insist that Gentiles be brought under the law so that they could qualify for these blessings. Paul pointed out that those who have been baptized into Christ have put on Christ, and in Christ racial and cultural differences are meaningless. All who have come into Christ have been adopted into the family of Abraham.

Freedom can be either a wonderful blessing or a serious threat. In **lesson twelve** Paul deals with this issue. Some took the position that since they were no longer under the law, they were freed from all restraints. He urges the Galatians to hold on to their freedom in Christ. At the same time, he points out that this freedom must not become an occasion to indulge the flesh, but should be used to benefit others. This lesson concludes with a timely admonition to avoid strife and bitterness.

Lesson thirteen closes this quarter by emphasizing the importance of life in the Spirit. Paul contrasts the behavior of one who acts simply to satisfy his or her fleshly desires with the "fruit of the Spirit." Just to read the two lists is to gain an immediate understanding of the opposite directions they lead. Realizing that no one can perfectly live up to the high standards set by the gospel, he urges brethren to assist and restore those who have been "caught in a sin." He concludes by reminding his readers of the law of the harvest—that we reap what we sow.

This series of lessons may stimulate your interest in the important doctrines that are at the heart of our Christian faith. As a result, you may want to study some of these issues in greater depth. We encourage you to visit your local Christian bookstore, where you will find many fine commentaries on Romans and Galatians that will help you in this study.

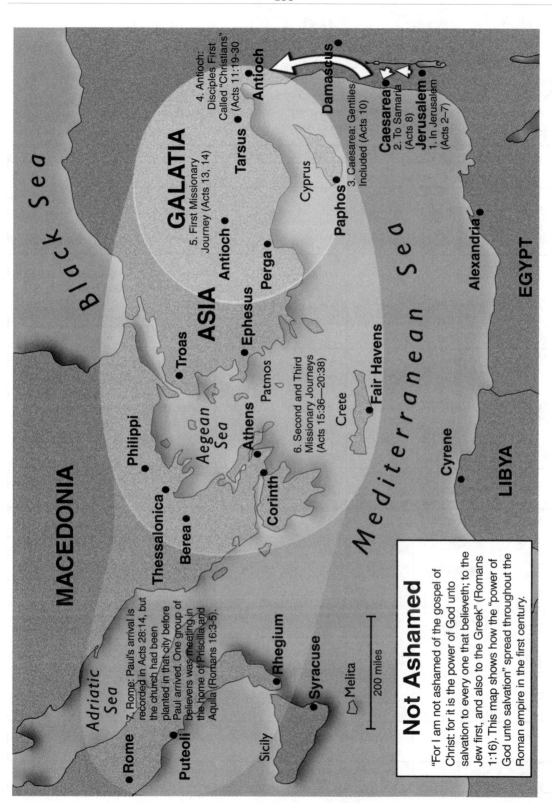

MACEDONIA

Black Sea

Adriatic Sea

Aegean Sea

• Rome

Puteoli

• Rhegium

• Syracuse

Sicily

◁ Melita

⊢————⊣
200 miles

• Philippi

Thessalonica •

Berea •

• Troas

• Athens

Corinth •

Patmos

Crete

• Fair Havens

Mediterranean Sea

Cyrene •

LIBYA

6. Second and Third
Missionary Journeys
(Acts 15:36—20:38)

ASIA

Ephesus •

Perga •

Antioch •

GALATIA

5. First Missionary
Journey (Acts 13, 14)

Cyprus

Paphos •

Tarsus •

Antioch •

4. Antioch:
Disciples First
Called "Christians"
(Acts 11:19-30)

Damascus •

Caesarea •

Jerusalem •

3. Caesarea: Gentiles
Included (Acts 10)

2. To Samaria
(Acts 8)

1. In Jerusalem
(Acts 2—7)

Alexandria •

EGYPT

7. Rome: Paul's arrival is
recorded in Acts 28:14, but
the church had been
planted in that city before
Paul arrived. One group of
believers was meeting in
the home of Priscilla and
Aquila (Romans 16:3-5).

Not Ashamed

"For I am not ashamed of the gospel of
Christ: for it is the power of God unto
salvation to every one that believeth; to the
Jew first, and also to the Greek" (Romans
1:16). This map shows how the "power of
God unto salvation" spread throughout the
Roman empire in the first century.

Peter and Paul in Antioch

In lesson 10, in a text from Galatians 2, we encounter an event in which Paul was compelled to confront Peter publicly in Antioch. The only information we have of this event is this mention by Paul; it is not mentioned in Acts. Therefore, it is not apparent when this event occurred. Careful comparisons between Acts and Galatians, however, can yield a close approximation of the timing of this event. The chart below will assist the student in knowing how to place the event into the chronological framework of Acts.

Event	Date	Biblical Reference	Comments
Saul's Conversion	34	Acts 9:1-19	
3 Years in Arabia	34-37	Galatians 1:17, 18	Acts makes no mention of this visit to Arabia, skipping over this three-year period to tell of Paul's (Saul's) reception in Jerusalem.
First Visit to Jerusalem	37	Acts 9:26-30; Galatians 1:18-20	Acts tells of the church's reaction to Saul's conversion. Paul focuses only on his purpose in coming. The short visit of 15 days is explained in Acts: the Jews tried to kill Paul, so he was sent to Tarsus.
Second Visit to Jerusalem	46	Acts 11:25-30	This visit, to deliver famine relief (Acts 11:29, 30), is not mentioned in Paul's letter to the Galatians. It must have been very brief, and Paul apparently thought it not worth noting. The next visit, for the Jerusalem Conference, was much more significant to Paul's point in Galatians.
First Missionary Journey	47-49	Acts 13, 14	Some or all of the churches in Galatia were established on this journey.
Third Visit to Jerusalem/ Jerusalem Conference	50	Acts 15; Galatians 2:1-10	Paul says he went to Jerusalem fourteen years after his first visit (Galatians 2:1). Counting both the beginning year (37) and the end gives us this date, which matches what we know of his later travels. Paul went "in response to a revelation" (Galatians 2:2), indicating that he went, not to learn from the apostles and elders, but to demonstrate the unity that existed among God's inspired messengers. This is consistent with his message in Galatians that the gospel he preached did not come from men, but from God (Galatians 1:11, 12).
Return to Antioch	50	Acts 15:30, 35	This must be when Peter came to Antioch (Galatians 2:11).
Paul Resumes His Missionary Journeys	50	Acts 15:36	Paul wrote to the Galatians probably from Macedonia in 57 or 58.

The Power of the Gospel
Unit 1: Justified by Faith
(Lessons 1-5)

GOD'S RIGHTEOUSNESS REVEALED

LESSON 1

WHY TEACH THIS LESSON?

People wait in great anticipation for something to be "revealed" to them. Sometimes this anticipation is one of excitement, as when the contents of a long expected birthday present are about to be made known. At other times this anticipation is one of dread, as when the results of an important medical test are expected. But one of the most important things to be revealed in all of human history is the *righteousness from God* in the gospel (Romans 1:17). And this is not something that we have to unwrap for ourselves—God has already done it for us. As we shall see, this gift is the central part of the gospel (the "good news"!).

Sadly, many have missed the message of this gift. Some choose to ignore the gift. Others, who misunderstand its true meaning, try to unwrap this gift by their own effort. Today's lesson ensures that we do not join the ranks of either group!

INTRODUCTION

A. "THE JUST SHALL LIVE BY FAITH"

As a young man Martin Luther had come to believe that God was a severe judge who meted out harsh punishment to all who did not measure up to his standards of righteousness. He also had been taught that God's wrath could be turned away by doing good works. But he realized that he had no way of measuring whether he had performed enough good works to appease God's anger. So for several years, as a young monk and Bible scholar, he struggled with this soul-wrenching conflict.

As a teacher at the University of Wittenberg, he began to study the book of Romans. As he studied Romans 1:17, the truth suddenly burst upon him as a shining light. One is not saved by good works but by faith: "The righteous will live by faith!" From that time on a dramatic change took place in his life, and he began to challenge many of the teachings of the Roman Catholic Church. Before long he was involved in heated controversy with the Roman Church that led to his expulsion and the beginning of the Protestant Reformation.

B. LESSON BACKGROUND

The epistle to the Romans is almost universally acknowledged as the work of the apostle Paul. We are first introduced to Paul at the stoning of Stephen, when he was known as Saul (Acts 7:58). Within a short time he earned a reputation as a persecutor of Christians. After venting his rage against Christians in Jerusalem, he set out for Damascus to hunt down Christians there. But on the road to that city he was confronted by the Lord, which led to his turning to Christ, being baptized, and being called to become an apostle to the Gentiles.

Later the Holy Spirit called Barnabas and Saul to become missionaries to the Gentiles. On their first journey Saul began to go by the name Paul (Acts 13:9).

DEVOTIONAL READING:
PSALM 34:1-8
BACKGROUND SCRIPTURE:
ROMANS 1
PRINTED TEXT:
ROMANS 1:1-17

LESSON AIMS

After this lesson each student will be able to:

1. Tell what Paul says about the substance of the gospel and his desire to visit the Christians in Rome.

2. Explain what it means for the gospel to reveal "the righteousness of God."

3. Express his or her own faith in Christ.

KEY VERSES:

I am not ashamed of the gospel, because it is the power of God for the salvation of everyone who believes: first for the Jew, then for the Gentile. For in the gospel a righteousness from God is revealed, a righteousness that is by faith from first to last.
—Romans 1:16, 17

LESSON 1 NOTES

Paul and Barnabas parted after this, and Paul made two other journeys accompanied by other companions. On the third of these journeys, he spent about three months at Corinth. It was here that he penned this letter in A.D. 56. The immediate occasion for his writing of the letter may have been his desire to carry on a ministry in the west with a stop in Rome on the way (Romans 15:23, 24).

While some late traditions attribute the founding of the church at Rome to Peter, there is no solid historic or Scriptural evidence to support this tradition. Among those who heard Peter at Pentecost were persons from Rome (Acts 2:10), and when they returned to Rome, it is reasonable to believe that they carried the gospel with them. Others who had been converted on Paul's missionary journeys later made their way to Rome and there found fellowship with the Christians already there. This is the reason that Paul knew so many people in the Roman church even before he had visited there.

Most scholars consider the Roman epistle to be Paul's greatest work. This letter is a profound theological thesis that deals with many aspects of the doctrine of salvation through Christ. But Paul is not just a scholar discussing theology in a remote cloistered retreat. The closing chapters of this letter deal with a number of practical issues touching on the daily lives of the saints.

I. PAUL'S GREETING (ROMANS 1:1-5)

A. HIS IDENTITY (v. 1)

1. Paul, a servant of Christ Jesus, called to be an apostle and set apart for the gospel of God—

It was a common practice for *Paul* and others of his day to introduce themselves at the beginning of a letter rather than at its close. Paul was no stranger to many persons in the Roman church. Paul had met these believers in other cities during his missionary journeys. But other Christians in the church there had never met Paul. For them, and as a reminder to his friends, Paul identifies himself as *a servant of Christ Jesus*. Literally, this word means a bond servant or slave. Paul had surrendered himself to Christ so completely that he was a slave. Specifically, he had been *called to be an apostle* to the Gentiles (Romans 11:13). He was *set apart* as a bearer of the good news to those who lived outside the Jewish religion (Acts 9:15).

B. HIS MESSAGE (vv. 2-4)

2. . . . the gospel he promised beforehand through his prophets in the Holy Scriptures.

For centuries Hebrew *prophets* had predicted that God would send a Messiah, an anointed One, to save his people. On Pentecost Peter boldly announced to his listeners that Jesus was that long-awaited Messiah (Acts 2:36).

3. . . . regarding his Son, who as to his human nature was a descendant of David.

The good news that Paul preached was about Jesus, the *Son* of God. The prophets had long foretold that the Messiah would be a *descendant of David*. Jesus fulfilled that requirement.

4. . . . and who through the Spirit of holiness was declared with power to be the Son of God by his resurrection from the dead: Jesus Christ our Lord.

On the human side, Jesus was of the lineage of David, but according to the *Spirit of holiness*, he was *the Son of God*. This was not just an assertion on Paul's part. His deity had been confirmed *with power*. In the New Testament the word *power* often means a show of miracles. On numerous occasions Jesus gave dramatic demonstration of his deity and affirmed his claims by his miracles. And while there were others who performed miracles, only Jesus authenticated his claims *by his resurrection from the dead.*

WHAT DO YOU THINK?

Paul identified himself as a "servant of Jesus Christ." The concept of servitude or slavery is repugnant to most people today. How, then, can we approach servanthood to Christ in a positive manner? What makes being a "servant of Jesus Christ" a good thing?

Visual for lesson 1. The map in the Adult Visuals *packet serves as a reminder of how the gospel spread in Paul's day.*

C. HIS CREDENTIALS (v. 5)

5. Through him and for his name's sake, we received grace and apostleship to call people from among all the Gentiles to the obedience that comes from faith.

The *apostleship* into which Paul was called was not something that he had worked for or earned in any special way. Rather, it came through *grace*, a gift from God. Paul's mission was to call *all the Gentiles*. Paul recognized that Jews were to receive the gospel first (Romans 1:16), but his special ministry was to the Gentiles. Most Gentiles never had known directly about God; as a result they were living in ignorance and disobedience. Paul's task was to lead them to faith in God and into *obedience* to him, to living lives of service and good works that demonstrated their obedience. Obedience is a logical consequence of faith, and any claim to faith that does not bring forth spiritual fruit is a sham (James 2:17-26).

II. PAUL'S READERS (ROMANS 1:6-13)

A. THEIR IDENTITY (vv. 6, 7a)

6, 7a. And you also are among those who are called to belong to Jesus Christ.
To all in Rome who are loved by God and called to be saints:

Although Paul had converted some Jews on his missionary journeys, the majority of his converts were Gentiles. It seems likely, then, that most of the Roman Christians were Gentiles. Yet Paul adds *to all in Rome*, thus including Jewish Christians who may have been there. All of them, Jews and Gentiles alike, were *called to be saints*. Today we often think of a saint as a person who lives on a higher spiritual plane than the rest of us. But that is not the meaning of the Greek word that is here translated "saints." Here it means persons who have been dedicated to God or set apart to his service. Thus every Christian is a saint.

A COMMUNITY SET APART FROM THE WORLD

In 1994, the new village of Vauban, Germany, was promoted as a utopia—with no need for fossil fuels to provide heat, light, or transportation. It was to be a community set apart from the "unenlightened" folks who depend on petroleum products for a luxurious standard of living. Solar power provided heat and light; narrow streets barred automobiles, which were seen as the primary symbol of the "old" way of doing things.

But compromise came soon. It turned out that many residents, who claimed not to own cars, actually did—and they were parking them illegally. So new parking lots were built on the perimeter of Vauban, where people willing to pay $17,000 for the privilege could park their cars. One of the original boosters for Vauban says that, just as in other European "auto-free" communities, "the idea always falls apart. People just can't get by without some access to a car." Vauban residents really aren't a "separated people"; they do not live in the utopia they had imagined.

Paul had once seen Judaism as the ideal faith, but Christ called him to a new way. He was separated—set apart—to be a leader in a new kind of community, one that eventually would produce a true utopia! The gospel message is that everyone can be a part of it if they are willing to commit themselves to Christ in the uncompromising obedience of faith.　　　　　　　　　　　　　　　　　　　　　　　—C. R. B.

B. HIS PRAYER FOR THEM (vv. 7b-9)

7b. Grace and peace to you from God our Father and from the Lord Jesus Christ.

Grace and *peace* comprise a standard greeting that Paul used in several of his other letters. By using these terms, he combined a Greek greeting (*grace*) with a Jewish greeting (*peace*), showing his ability to transcend ethnic and cultural barriers. He adds significance to the common terms, however, by declaring that grace and peace are gifts *from God our Father and from the Lord Jesus Christ*.

WHAT DO YOU THINK?

Do you think of yourself as a "saint"? Why or why not? What difference would it make in the church if everyone thought of every member as a saint?

DAILY BIBLE READINGS

Monday, Feb. 25—Hold to Sound Teaching (2 Timothy 1: 8-14)

Tuesday, Feb. 26—Teaching God's Righteousness (2 Timothy 2:1-13)

Wednesday, Feb. 27—The Lord Knows Who Are His (2 Timothy 2:14-22)

Thursday, Feb. 28—The Power of the Gospel (Romans 1:11-17)

Friday, Mar. 1—World Judged in Righteousness (Acts 17:22-31)

Saturday, Mar. 2—Judge Others and You Condemn Yourself (Romans 2:1-11)

Sunday, Mar. 3—Law Written on Their Hearts (Romans 2:12-16)

WHAT DO YOU THINK?

Paul said the faith of the church at Rome was "being reported all over the world." What is our church known for—either positively or negatively? Why? What would characterize a church today that was known for its faith?

8. First, I thank my God through Jesus Christ for all of you, because your faith is being reported all over the world.

Once he completed his greeting, Paul's first thought was a word of thanks to God for them. Specifically, he was thankful for their *faith* that had become known and talked about *all over the world.* Without all the modern means of communication that we enjoy today, Paul and others had learned of their faith. This says something about how extensively people traveled throughout the Roman Empire in the first century.

In the early centuries, the church at Rome played a predominant role in the history of Christianity in western Europe, but Paul never envisioned the ecclesiastical structure and control that the Roman church would come to demonstrate. The church's greatness in Paul's day was one of faithful example.

9, 10a. God, whom I serve with my whole heart in preaching the gospel of his Son, is my witness how constantly I remember you in my prayers at all times.

What a great prayer life Paul must have had! Not only did he pray for the church at Rome, but for those in Ephesus, Philippi, Colosse, and Thessalonica (Ephesians 1:16; Philippians 1:4; Colossians 1:3; 1 Thessalonians 1:2). He prayed for individuals, including Timothy and Philemon (2 Timothy 1:3; Philemon 4). To show his sincerity in praying for the Roman believers, Paul called upon *God* as his *witness.* (Note similar expressions in 2 Corinthians 1:23; Galatians 1:20; and Philippians 1:8.) Paul's example suggests that we today ought to remember in our *prayers* our brothers and sisters in Christ—both those we know and those in places we have not been.

C. HIS DESIRE TO VISIT THEM (vv. 10-13)

10b. . . . and I pray that now at last by God's will the way may be opened for me to come to you.

In verse 8 Paul offered a prayer of thanksgiving for the faith of the Romans. Here his prayer is a petition that he might be able to visit them. Apparently, he had harbored this desire for several years (Romans 15:22, 23). His prayer that *now at last* he might be able to visit Rome suggests he was even a bit frustrated that his long-standing desire had not been met. But his deep faith led him to trust *God's will* in this matter. Eventually God did honor Paul's desire and allow him to visit Rome. But ironically he came not as a triumphant missionary but in chains as a prisoner (Acts 28:15, 16, 20).

11. I long to see you so that I may impart to you some spiritual gift to make you strong.

It was not Paul's desire to visit Rome as a sight-seeing tourist. He wanted to see them so that he could give *some spiritual gift* to them. The word for *gift* is *charisma,* which is used in the New Testament to refer to either miraculous or non-miraculous gifts. In this case it probably means the miraculous gifts, such as were bestowed by Paul on the disciples in Ephesus (Acts 19:6) and by Peter and John on the Samaritans (Acts 8:17, 18). There is no record in the New Testament of non-miraculous gifts being given by the laying on of hands; these appear to have been given directly from God.

12. . . . that is, that you and I may be mutually encouraged by each other's faith.

Even as Paul desired to bring a gift to the Romans, he also expected to be blessed himself. This is a frequent result among those who share a mutual *faith.* When one brings a blessing to other Christians, the giver as well as the recipient is blessed.

13. I do not want you to be unaware, brothers, that I planned many times to come to you (but have been prevented from doing so until now) in order that I might have a harvest among you, just as I have had among the other Gentiles.

HOW TO SAY IT

Barnabas. BAR-nuh-bus.
Colosse. Ko-LAHSS-ee.
Ephesus. EF-uh-sus.
Habakkuk. Huh-BACK-kuk.
Philippi. fih-LIP-pie or FIL-ih-pie.
Thessalonica. THESS-uh-lo-
   NYE-kuh (th as in thin).
Wittenberg. WIT-ten-berg or
   VIT-ten-berg.

Some may have felt that he really wasn't serious in his desire to visit them. Now he assures them that he often planned to come to Rome but had *been prevented from doing so until now.* We are not told what factors may have kept him from coming. He may have been so heavily involved in successful evangelistic work in other places that he could not leave and go to Rome. The Holy Spirit may have kept him from going (see Acts 16:6, 7). Nor can we rule out the possibility that Satan may have been involved in keeping Paul from visiting Rome earlier.

The *fruit* Paul expected to have may be converts that he would win to the faith or spiritual growth the Roman saints would experience as a result of his teaching. Since Paul was specially called to be God's witness to the Gentiles, it was natural that he wanted to visit a church made up predominantly of Gentile Christians. The expression *as . . . among the other Gentiles* suggests that Paul saw the church at Rome as similar to the fields in which he had already labored, and that he expected the results to be similar.

III. PAUL'S DEBT (ROMANS 1:14-17)
A. HIS DEBT TO ALL (v. 14)
14. I am obligated both to Greeks and non-Greeks, both to the wise and the foolish.

The ancient *Greeks*, like many people even today, considered themselves superior to those who were not Greeks. In a similar way, the Jews divided people into two categories—Jews and Gentiles, and considered Gentiles to be inferior. For the Greeks, anyone who did not speak Greek was considered a barbarian. Of course, in Paul's time the Greek language was widely spoken around the Mediterranean. It is significant that Paul spoke Greek and the New Testament was written in Greek. Thus here Paul was not using *Greek* in an ethnic sense, but in a linguistic sense.

Paul's intent is to acknowledge that his debt to proclaim the gospel was to the whole human race, both Greek and barbarian. *Both to the wise and the foolish* is another way of saying the same thing—the debt is owed to everyone.

B. HIS READINESS TO PAY THAT DEBT (v. 15)
15. That is why I am so eager to preach the gospel also to you who are at Rome.

Every person who has ever lived has a debt to God as Creator. Further, every Christian has a debt to God as Savior. We cannot pay that debt, for salvation is a gift of grace. But since we are saved by grace, we have a debt to others who are yet in need of God's grace. We have an obligation to share the good news with them. Paul had a unique obligation *to preach the gospel* to all Gentiles, and in this case, to those *who are at Rome.*

C. HIS MEANS OF PAYING THAT DEBT (vv. 16, 17)
16. I am not ashamed of the gospel, because it is the power of God for the salvation of everyone who believes: first for the Jew, then for the Gentile.

Paul had committed his life totally, every breath he breathed, to *the gospel.* He was convinced that he would never have a reason to be ashamed of this commitment. He had good reason for his confidence: the gospel *is the power of God for . . . salvation.* The Greek word here translated *power* is the basis for such English words as *dynamic, dynamo,* and even *dynamite.* The dynamic power of the gospel is manifested in many ways, including the blasting down of barriers between Jew and *Gentile,* black and white, male and female (cf. Galatians 3:28). The power of the gospel to bring *salvation* has only one limitation—it comes only to those who believe.
17. For in the gospel a righteousness from God is revealed, a righteousness that is by faith from first to last, just as it is written: "The righteous will live by faith."

WHAT DO YOU THINK?

What would be the result if every believer shared Paul's sense of obligation to spread the gospel? Why doesn't every believer feel indebted to spread the gospel? How can we cultivate such an attitude?

VISUALS FOR THESE LESSONS

The small visual pictured in each lesson (e. g., page 238) is a small reproduction of a large, full-color poster included in the Adult Visuals packet for the Spring Quarter. The packet is available from your supplier. Order No. 392.

WHAT DO YOU THINK?

What do you think it means to live by faith? What attitudes and actions are characteristic of one who lives by faith?

PRAYER

Gracious Father, we thank you for offering to us the forgiveness of sins and the hope for eternal life through your Son, Jesus Christ. May we acknowledge our debt to you by seeking to serve you wherever you may call us. Through faith in Jesus Christ we pray. Amen.

THOUGHT TO REMEMBER

We are all debtors.

Later in the book of Romans, Paul contrasts salvation by works, as the Jews understood the law, with salvation by grace through *faith*, as the gospel presents it. Paul here adapts Habakkuk 2:4 as a basis for his position.

This *faith* that is necessary for salvation is not merely a mental action, an easy acknowledgment that one accepts the truth of a given statement. Saving faith leads one to obedience and good works—such a one *will live* by faith. This is not to say that we may earn salvation by works, but that real faith always produces good works. As James 2:26 states: "Faith without deeds is dead."

NEVER OUT OF DEBT

Most of us carry some debt, whether for a house, car, or other products. Eventually, we will be able to pay it off. But none will personally experience the kind of debt the Motorola Corporation incurred with their sixty-six Iridium communications satellites. The system was intended to provide worldwide wireless phone service. Instead, it put Motorola into bankruptcy, with debts of $4.4 *billion*—a debt the company could not pay.

Iridium was at the leading edge of technology when the system was conceived, but it took ten years to get the satellites into orbit. In that time improvements in ordinary cellular phones had advanced so far that the Iridium system was obsolete. So in March, 2000, the bankruptcy court gave the company permission to stop service and to let the satellites burn up in the earth's atmosphere.

Paul's debt was also great—greater, perhaps, because it was a spiritual debt. The former persecutor of the church now knew the Savior and felt compelled to try to repay his unpayable debt by telling everyone he could about the grace of God in Christ. It's a debt that every Christian owes, and we should be ready, as Paul was, to serve Christ in whatever way we are called to do so. It's a debt we never can fully repay.

—C. R. B.

CONCLUSION

A. WE ALSO ARE DEBTORS

Paul acknowledged that he was a debtor to both Greeks and barbarians to preach the gospel of salvation to them. He became a special missionary to carry the good news across the Roman Empire in the first century. This was a unique call that none of us today has received. But as Christians we are debtors to witness in whatever situation we may find ourselves. A few may be called to witness as missionaries or evangelists in cross-cultural situations. Others may be called to witness by public proclamation of the gospel as ministers and teachers. Most of us, however, will witness in less public situations in the office, the factory, or at school. Some may find their ministries in serving the sick, the poor, or the discouraged. Wherever we may be, let us never forget that we are debtors. But this debt is not an overwhelming burden that must be discharged slowly and painfully. Rather, paying this debt brings us a joy that this world cannot know.

B. FAITH IN A WORLD OF SKEPTICISM

Ours is an age of skepticism and doubt. On every hand we hear of those who reject the Christian faith and sneer at believers as "weaklings." But, of course, everyone lives by a faith of some kind or other. That faith may be in one's own intellect or physical strength, in money, or in some anti-Christian philosophy.

Since everyone lives by some kind of faith, the real issue is not faith as such but faith in what or whom. For Paul that was no problem: "The righteous will live by faith." He makes it quite clear that if we are to live righteous lives before God, it must begin with a faith in Jesus Christ, who died for our sins, and who was raised from the dead to give us hope for eternal life.

Discovery Learning

This page contains an alternate lesson plan emphasizing learning activities. Classes desiring such student involvement will find these suggestions helpful. The next page is a reproducible activity page to further enhance discovery learning.

LEARNING GOALS

After participating in this lesson, each student will be able to:

1. Tell what Paul says about the substance of the gospel and about his desire to visit the Christians in Rome.

2. Explain what it means for the gospel to reveal "the righteousness of God."

3. Express his or her own faith in Christ.

INTO THE LESSON

Purchase enough small envelopes for each member of your class (and a few extras for visitors and newcomers). Insert copies of this letter: "I am excited to be your teacher and leader for these lessons on Romans. Today we will explore Romans 1:1-17. I hope we all catch the excitement of the gospel." Sign it with your name. Use as your official title, "Teacher of the Gospel."

Have each class member write his or her own name on the outside of the envelope. After all finish, ask each one to open the envelope and read the letter. Ask the following questions:

"How do you feel about mail personally addressed to you?"; "What is your first thought when you read the phrase 'excitement of the gospel'?"; "Who among your friends should receive a letter like this one?"

INTO THE WORD

Develop a brief lecture on background and introductory material for Romans. Remind students that Paul had met many of the Roman Christians on his journeys. Incorporate Romans 1:1 into the lecture so students understand Paul's greeting and introduction.

Divide your class into groups of six or fewer. If you have more than two groups, assign the following to more than one group. Give each group a large white poster board. One person in each group serves as secretary.

Direct group one to read Romans 1:1-6, 16, and 17. They are to complete an acrostic of the word *gospel* with as many words, phrases, or ideas that describe the gospel in the text. Examples include: God's promise, Obedience to the faith, Spirit of holiness, Power of God, Eternal life, and Living by faith. (This activity is in the student book, *NIV® Bible Student.*) Tell the group to be ready to describe Paul's teaching of the gospel and his description of Jesus.

Group two will read Romans 1:7-15. They will list all the "I" messages given by Paul. For example, "I thank my God . . . for you all." This group will discuss what the desire of Paul seems to be.

Call the groups together and have them present their findings to the class. Discuss any difficult points using the lesson commentary for answers. Ask the following series of questions:

1. What do we learn about Jesus in the passage? (*He is the declared Son of God. He is Lord. Grace comes through him.*)

2. What do we learn about Paul in this passage? (*He is wholeheartedly involved in spreading the gospel. He is passionate about his message and ministry. He is eager to preach!*)

3. What is the gospel? (*The gospel is the good news that God has provided a way of salvation, for all people, through Jesus.*)

4. How does this gospel reveal "the righteousness of God"? (*Righteousness is being in a right standing with God. No human being can be right with God on his or her own merits. But God provides a way, through Jesus Christ and his righteousness, for us to be right with him. This "good news" had to be revealed.*)

INTO LIFE

Ask the class members to return to their small groups to discuss individuals who are excited about sharing the gospel with others. Perhaps they will recall missionary presentations, a co-worker's challenge, a neighbor's friendly persuasion, or a relative's concern. Encourage them to share what are the common denominators in each. Examples may include enthusiasm, perseverance, and knowledge of subject matter. (For this and the next activity, you may want to use the reproducible page that follows.)

Within their small groups, have students sit in pairs. Distribute envelopes and sheets of blank paper. Address each envelope to a friend he or she identified at the start of the lesson. Allow a few minutes for each to write a two-paragraph explanation of the gospel, its impact on the student's life, and the enthusiasm the student has to share this message. Ask for one or two volunteers to read their letters. (A similar activity is in the student book.)

Close the session by having the pairs pray for each other and the sharing of the gospel.

Eager to Tell Someone

Read Romans 1:1-17. Then answer these questions:

QUESTIONS ON PAUL

Why does Paul want to thank God?

How does Paul describe his feelings about being with the Romans?

What would be the result of his visit?

How does Paul feel about the gospel?

QUESTIONS ON THE GOSPEL

What is the content of the gospel Paul preaches?

How did God confirm the truth of the gospel?

What is the result of the gospel message being proclaimed?

How does the gospel reveal "a righteousness from God"?

Take It to Your Friend

Though many books have been written about communicating the gospel to others, most suggest that making and developing friendships is the best starting place for bringing others to Christ. Think of the friendships you have and their potential for sharing.

What is the name of one non-Christian friend?

How can you develop a deeper friendship with him or her?

What can you be praying for this person right now?

When can you next see this person?

What will you say concerning the gospel?

JUSTIFIED BY GOD'S GRACE

LESSON 2

WHY TEACH THIS LESSON?

Recent polls have indicated that a majority of professed Christians believe people can earn their way to Heaven by doing good works. We might expect this misconception on the part of unbelievers, from people who have not read the Bible and discovered its message of grace. But of "born-again Christians"?

Apparently, the message of justification by God's grace is one that needs repeating, even in the church. Today's lesson will give you an opportunity to do just that!

INTRODUCTION

A. I'VE BEEN REDEEMED

Many years ago an evangelist was traveling in a railway coach. As he rode along, he sang to himself the song, "I've Been Redeemed." Another passenger sitting nearby heard him and joined in the song. When the song was finished, the evangelist asked the stranger, "Have you indeed been redeemed?"

"Yes, praise the Lord," came the reply.

"How long ago were you redeemed?"

"Nearly two thousand years ago."

"Two thousand years ago!" echoed the evangelist in surprise.

"Yes, sir, the Lord purchased my redemption more than nineteen hundred years ago," was the reply, "but I am sorry to say that I spent years trying to earn it by good works. Only a few months ago did I finally learn that it was already mine through God's grace, if I were willing to accept it through faith."

The Scriptures do indeed tell us that we have redemption through Christ's blood if we are willing to accept it by faith. But many of us have missed the joys of that redemption because we have tried to earn it through good works.

B. LESSON BACKGROUND

You may find it helpful to review the Lesson Background from last week's lesson. This will give your students a better understanding of Paul and his ministry. Having been a zealous Jewish leader who persecuted Christians because they did not keep the law, Paul (then known as Saul) was completely changed at his conversion. He became the apostle to the Gentiles, spreading the gospel of salvation in Jesus Christ. This represented a radical shift in his theology. Before, as a Jewish scholar, he held that one could be saved by meticulously observing the law. As a Christian he recognized one could be saved only by God's loving grace through faith in Jesus Christ.

Paul appreciated this concept better than most of his contemporaries. Even within the church there were some, of Jewish background, who believed law-keeping remained essential to salvation. Some of these believers stirred up no little controversy in Antioch between Paul's first and second missionary journeys. The dispute led to the "Jerusalem Conference" described in Acts 15. Whether there were similar Jewish agitators in Rome or Paul merely wanted to avoid such a situation we do not know. In any event, Paul's clearest explanation of the issue is in the letter he wrote to the Romans, and is the subject of our text today.

DEVOTIONAL READING:
PSALM 33:13-22
BACKGROUND SCRIPTURE:
ROMANS 3
PRINTED TEXT:
ROMANS 3:1-4, 9, 10, 19-31

LESSON AIMS

After this lesson each student will be able to:

1. Contrast the way of law with justification by grace as Paul describes the difference in Romans 3.

2. Explain the importance of the doctrine of justification by grace.

3. Praise God for his grace and for the salvation that it makes available to us.

KEY VERSES

For all have sinned and fall short of the glory of God, and are justified freely by his grace through the redemption that came by Christ Jesus.
—Romans 3:23, 24

I. ADVANTAGES OF THE JEWS (ROMANS 3:1-4, 9, 10)

A. WORD OF GOD (vv. 1, 2)

1, 2. What advantage, then, is there in being a Jew, or what value is there in circumcision? Much in every way! First of all, they have been entrusted with the very words of God.

In the previous chapter Paul pointed out that God regards "circumcision of the heart" over that which is "merely outward and physical" (Romans 2:28, 29). In these verses he answers some of the objections he expects Jewish believers to raise. The most obvious question that they might raise is, *What advantage . . . is there in being a Jew?"* Paul's reply is that there is *much in every way!* The most important advantage is that they have been entrusted with *the very words of God.* God has revealed himself through nature, or what is called "general revelation," which helps us know God as Creator. As helpful as this is, it is not as important as "special revelation," the Scriptures. God revealed himself and his will to prophets who wrote down their revelations in what we know as the Old Testament. This allowed the Jews to know God as a loving Heavenly Father. Of all ancient peoples, only the Jews enjoyed this great privilege. Through the Scriptures, they also knew that God intended to send them a Messiah.

WHAT DO YOU THINK?

Paul said the chief advantage of the Jews was that they had the Word of God. Today we have the Word of God to an extent the ancient Hebrews never would have imagined. Each person can have his or her own copy for personal study at any time and at any place. What kind of obligation or responsibility do you think that advantage places on us? How can we faithfully execute that responsibility?

B. GOD'S FAITHFULNESS (vv. 3, 4)

3. What if some did not have faith? Will their lack of faith nullify God's faithfulness?

Although the Jews had the Scriptures, many of them did not accept them. At least, they did not accept them fully. Some of them might have claimed acceptance, but their behavior proved their unbelief. Indeed, in the past many had lived in open rebellion against God's laws. But their unfaithfulness did not invalidate God's ultimate plan for the human race any more than the unfaithfulness of many Christians cancels God's covenant of grace for Christians.

4. Not at all! Let God be true, and every man a liar. As it is written:

"So that you may be proved right when you speak and prevail when you judge."

Paul rejects the idea emphatically. God by his very nature cannot be unfaithful to his promises. It is impossible for God to lie in any way (Titus 1:2). *Let God be true.* Let everyone recognize that God is always true even if *every man* should prove to be *a liar.* Paul quotes the Septuagint version of Psalm 51:4. The application is that no matter how people may deny or doubt God, he will fulfill his promises.

C. ADVANTAGED, BUT NOT BETTER (vv. 9, 10)

9, 10. What shall we conclude then? Are we any better? Not at all! We have already made the charge that Jews and Gentiles alike are all under sin. As it is written:

"There is no one righteous, not even one."

This verse offers something of a problem. Who is the *we?* Is Paul here identifying himself with his fellow Jews or with Christians? He has previously spoken of the Jews in third person ("they," v. 2; "their," v. 3), so we might think the "we" refers to Christians. The following context, however, suggests that Paul has shifted his focus and that the "we" refers now to the Jews. He denies that *Jews* have any advantage over *Gentiles:* both stand *under* the condemnation of sin. To bolster his case, Paul paraphrases Ecclesiastes 7:20. (See also Psalm 14:1.) In the verses that follow (11-18) Paul gives more specific details about the universal sinfulness of man. It is not a pretty picture!

WHAT DO YOU THINK?

Contrast Paul's message that "there is no one righteous" with the popular self-esteem mantra that includes the idea that all personal behavior is to be accepted, and that "rightness" is relative. How can we inject the truth of Paul's statement into our culture?

SURELY WE'RE BETTER THAN THEY!

On Halloween night in "Christian" America nowadays, witches celebrate their paganism publicly. Really! One recent Halloween saw some two hundred of them holding a two-day pagan ritual at various memorials in Washington D.C. The purpose of the rally was to worship the "divinity" the pagans find in "trees, rocks, birds, animals, and people."

These folks come from all social classes and have varying preferences for what they should be called: Witches, Wiccans, Druids, even Radical Faeries. Most of them claim that they do not worship the devil, since "the devil is a Christian idea," as one of their spokesmen says. It is estimated that there are more than three hundred thousand pagans in America.

It's a bit hard for us Christians not to feel superior to these modern pagans, by whatever name they call themselves. After all, they have regressed to a paganism similar to that which existed two millennia ago when the church began. Doesn't our awareness of the true God make us better than they are? The apostle Paul would answer, "No, it doesn't! We are sinners just as they are. The only righteousness we have is that which Christ gives us." We are in the same position as Jewish Christians of the first century! Knowing Christ only makes us more blessed, not better, than the pagans around us.   —C. R. B.

II. RIGHTEOUSNESS OF GOD (ROMANS 3:19-26)

A. THE FUNCTION OF THE LAW (vv. 19, 20)

19. Now we know that whatever the law says, it says to those who are under the law, so that every mouth may be silenced and the whole world held accountable to God.

In the previous verses Paul used several quotations from Psalms and Proverbs to show how sinful people had become, even those who had the advantages of having received God's Word. To compound their wickedness, they had denied it or attempted to blame God for their guilt. Paul faces that issue squarely in this verse.

At first glance, *those who are under the law* might seem to refer specifically to those who follow the Mosaic law, the Jews. However, Paul's use of other Old Testament references indicates that he has something more in mind. Many scholars believe Paul's condemnation is even more inclusive, taking in the principle of law as well as the specific law of Moses. In the first chapter of Romans, for example, Paul makes a forceful denunciation of the sinfulness of Gentiles, insisting that they knew enough about God's will not to engage in these wicked acts (Romans 1:19, 20, 32; see also Romans 2:14, 15). With the phrase *that every mouth may be silenced,* Paul seems to be depicting a court scene in which the evidence against the accused parties is so overwhelming that they have no basis for speaking in their own defense. The court plays no favorites in this judgment, for all the world is *held accountable to God.*

20. Therefore no one will be declared righteous in his sight by observing the law; rather, through the law we become conscious of sin.

In theory, if one could fulfill the requirements of the law perfectly, he or she could stand before the divine Judge as justified. But, of course, no one can fulfill *the law* completely and thus earn salvation. One function of the law is to show us how sinful we are, to provide a measuring stick to evaluate our moral status. Had Paul ended his letter at this point, we would have been left in a desperately gloomy situation. Fortunately, the picture is not totally bleak. What follows offers hope.

B. THE FOUNDATION OF FAITH (vv. 21, 22a)

21. But now a righteousness from God, apart from law, has been made known, to which the Law and the Prophets testify.

Once he has established that human righteousness is impossible through works of the law, Paul turns to another source of *righteousness.* God knew from the beginning that no one would be able to fulfill his *law* perfectly. For that reason he prepared another way, a way that does not depend on the law, for people to be

WHAT DO YOU THINK?

The Jews depended on keeping the law to put them in good stead with God. On what do people today depend for salvation? Why?

justified. *Now* for the first time that plan is being revealed to the world. That plan awaited the coming of Christ before it could be revealed in full, but *the Law and the Prophets* had testified to it. Some passages of the Old Testament give only vague hints about the nature and work of the coming Messiah while others, especially several in Isaiah, are much more explicit. Taken together, all of these witnesses provide evidence for God's plan for salvation.

22a. *This righteousness from God comes through faith in Jesus Christ to all who believe.*

Paul continues to show the contrast between *righteousness* through good works and righteousness through God's grace. The first method simply won't do. If we violate even one apparently insignificant part of the law, we are guilty of violating the whole law and stand condemned (James 2:10). By contrast, the righteousness that God now offers is *through faith*. This is not some nebulous faith in faith itself or even faith in God. It is faith in *Jesus Christ*, God's only Son. This path of salvation is open to all regardless of race or ethnic background.

C. THE FAILURE OF ALL (vv. 22b, 23)

22b, 23. *There is no difference, for all have sinned and fall short of the glory of God.*

There is no difference at the judgment seat of God between Jew and Gentile. Whatever advantages Jews may have had as custodians of the Scriptures and as ancestors of Jesus Christ, these do not really matter. *All have sinned.* The burden of sin rests crushingly on the whole human race. Some hold that this refers to the original sin of Adam, as the old New England Primer had it: "In Adam's fall, We sinned all." But Paul's statement seems more inclusive than that. It means that every person who has ever lived and reached the age of accountability has violated God's law. Some have done it knowingly and deliberately, while others may have done it in ignorance. Yet the conclusion is the same: all have sinned!

In their sinning, all *fall short of the glory of God*. Scholars differ as to the precise meaning of *the glory of God*. Some hold that it refers to the glory that saints will share with God in eternity. Others take the view that the saints who live godly lives reflect God's glory, and thus bring glory to God in the eyes of the world. It seems more likely that it refers to the glory God himself displays because of his holiness. Sin, which is a "falling short" of the mark, separates us from that glory.

D. THE FREE GIFT OF GRACE (vv. 24-26)

24. . . . *and are justified freely by his grace through the redemption that came by Christ Jesus.*

This verse sends a brilliant beam of hope into the otherwise hopelessly gloomy situation stated in verse 23: "All have sinned!" Even after sin there is hope, there is the possibility of *redemption*. The word *justified* is a legal term that describes the status of an accused person in court. When one is justified, it does not necessarily mean that he or she is innocent. Rather, it means that in the eyes of the court that one will not have to pay the penalty for the crime. Christ has already paid the penalty by his death on the cross. This debt has been *freely* paid, and the only stipulation required of the condemned is that he or she accept it. That's what grace is all about. *Grace* is often defined as "unmerited favor," meaning that the recipient does not deserve it and cannot earn it. The only choice is to accept it or reject it.

"YOU'RE [NOT] A WINNER!"

Something for nothing seems to be a nearly universal human quest. Lotteries and gambling casinos in America and elsewhere prey upon people who are looking to get "lucky" and become wealthy without working for it.

WHAT DO YOU THINK?

What do you find significant in the lesson writer's note that faith in God is not enough, but that faith in Jesus Christ is what will save us?

[Consider Acts 4:12 in your discussion.]

Children . . .
. . . justified by grace
Sinners . . .

Visual for lessons 2 and 11. This poster illustrates the universal need for salvation, "for all have sinned." Post it as you discuss verse 23.

A more subtle form of this fever is fed by the sweepstakes letters that come in the mail. Elderly people especially fall victim to the artfully worded "come-ons" in those letters, with the result that their savings are jeopardized. An eighty-eight-year-old man in California made two trips to Florida to claim the eleven million dollars that he mistakenly believed he had won. His sad story is like that of scores of other people—often in failing mental health—who are taken in by the get-rich-quick pitch of the sweepstakes. They believe they have put the right sticker at the right spot on the right paper and placed it in the right envelope, so the prize must be theirs!

It's much like the temptation that so many of us fall prey to. We think, "I live by the Golden Rule and the Ten Commandments (for the most part), I go to church regularly, I give my offering, I care for my family, and I do my job pretty faithfully. So, God, I guess I deserve my reward, right?" But the answer is, "No, trying to keep the law only makes you a sinner. Salvation comes only through Christ."   —C. R. B.

25. God presented him as a sacrifice of atonement, through faith in his blood. He did this to demonstrate his justice, because in his forbearance he had left the sins committed beforehand unpunished—

In the Old Testament *atonement* was associated with the mercy seat in the Holy of Holies. There each year on the day of atonement the high priest sprinkled the *blood* of the sacrificial animal on the mercy seat to atone for the people's sins. In the New Testament this term takes on a fuller meaning. Christ is not just the place where the atonement takes place, and not merely the high priest who offers the sacrifice; he is the sacrifice that makes the atonement possible.

It may seem unfair that we, the guilty, go free while Christ, the innocent, bears the penalty. But this transaction shows us that God is a just Judge who demands an accounting for all *sins*, but he is also a loving Heavenly Father, who desires that all be saved.

26. . . . he did it to demonstrate his justice at the present time, so as to be just and the one who justifies those who have faith in Jesus.

In a sense God is faced with a divine dilemma. As a holy God, he cannot tolerate sin. At the same time, he is a loving God who wants to save everyone. In the human sense, this is an impossible contradiction, but for God all things are possible. He resolved the dilemma by offering his Son as the perfect sacrifice for sin. Thus God is both *just*—exacting the fair penalty for sin—and *the one who justifies those who have faith in Jesus.*

III. JUSTIFICATION (ROMANS 3:27-31)

A. NOTHING TO BOAST OF (v. 27)

27. Where, then, is boasting? It is excluded. On what principle? On that of observing the law? No, but on that of faith.

A system that provides for salvation through the performing of good works leaves itself open to the danger of pride. In Jesus' day the Jews considered the Pharisees to be the most pious people among them. They kept the *law* (and their additions to the law) with meticulous dedication. This gained them the plaudits of others and fed their pride. This was the reason that they so vigorously resisted Jesus when he challenged this whole system. But if justification is an unearned gift of God's grace received by *faith*, there is no basis for pride or *boasting*.

B. NOT BY DEEDS OF LAW (v. 28, 29)

28. For we maintain that a man is justified by faith apart from observing the law.

This verse succinctly sums up two approaches to salvation: God's way, which is by grace through *faith*, and the human way through *observing the law*. It is important to note that the faith mentioned here is not simply a mental assent to a

DAILY BIBLE READINGS

Monday, Mar. 4—*Grace Freely Bestowed (Ephesians 1:3-14)*

Tuesday, Mar. 5—*Called to Hope (Ephesians 1:15-22)*

Wednesday, Mar. 6—*Saved by Grace (Ephesians 2:1-10)*

Thursday, Mar. 7—*No Longer Strangers and Aliens (Ephesians 2:11-22)*

Friday, Mar. 8—*Under the Power of Sin (Romans 3:1-9)*

Saturday, Mar. 9—*The Law Brings Knowledge of Sin (Romans 3:10-20)*

Sunday, Mar. 10—*Justified by God's Grace (Romans 3:21-31)*

WHAT DO YOU THINK?

Paul said the doctrine of justification by faith left no room for pride or boasting. How does pride interfere with Christian living today?

We come to you, Father, in humble faith, recognizing that we are helpless to save ourselves by our works. Teach us to accept your marvelous grace, and fill us with a burning desire to share your love and your grace with those about us.

fact or a body of facts. It involves a commitment to Jesus Christ, which must result in submission to him, or it is less than saving faith. It is worth observing that on the first occasion after the ascension that the gospel was publicly proclaimed, faith—although it is clearly implied—is not specifically mentioned. Rather, repentance and baptism are stated as necessary prerequisites for "the forgiveness of . . . sins" (Acts 2:38).

29. Is God the God of Jews only? Is he not the God of Gentiles too? Yes, of Gentiles too,

Through their long history the Jewish people often succumbed to the temptation to look on God as belonging exclusively to them. Although they were chosen by God for a special mission, that mission was to bring the Messiah into the world, and the Messiah would bring a blessing to the whole world (Isaiah 42:6; 49:6). Paul's rhetorical questions merely state what always had been true.

C. JUSTIFIED BY FAITH (vv. 30, 31)

30, 31. . . . since there is only one God, who will justify the circumcised by faith and the uncircumcised through that same faith. Do we, then, nullify the law by this faith? Not at all! Rather, we uphold the law.

Both the *circumcised* (Jews) and the *uncircumcised* (Gentiles) are saved *through* the *same faith*. Some as a result might be led to believe *the law* was without value. Not so, Paul strongly affirms. Indeed, justification by faith serves to *uphold the law*. It confirms that the law, though powerless to provide salvation, still has value, for it made preparation for the gospel of grace. And even in the age of grace the law serves as a guide for those who have accepted God's gift of salvation.

CONCLUSION

The idea of salvation by works raises some serious practical as well as theological problems. One problem is trying to get a precise definition of just what constitutes saving works. The Jews had the law, but they soon began to define and redefine what the law meant in practical situations. For example, the law forbade working on the Sabbath, and certain things were specifically forbidden. But situations arose that were not covered. In Jesus' day the lawyers had defined walking more than about five-eighths of a mile on the Sabbath as work. They also charged Jesus with breaking the Sabbath because he performed miracles of healing on that day. In our drastically changed culture we would have to spend most of our time on nitpicky arguments trying to define the law.

Another problem that works salvation raises is trying to determine how many good works are essential. The Roman Catholic Church faced this issue prior to the Reformation in the practice of selling indulgences. It was this very issue that sent Luther on his reforming path. If, for example, one has to perform a hundred good deeds in order to be forgiven, how can he be certain that a hundred and one good deeds aren't required?

A third, and perhaps more serious, problem is that a way of salvation that is based upon good works is almost certain to lead to human pride. We take pride in the things we accomplish—the work we do, the family we rear successfully, the buildings we build, the bank accounts we accumulate. In our better moments we recognize that we were able to do these things only because God gave us the strength and intelligence necessary to do them. But still Satan is always there, tempting us to take credit for our accomplishments. The most effective temptation he can set before us is to convince us that we have earned our salvation by fulfilling the works of the law.

Plenteous grace with thee is found,
Grace to cover all my sin;
Let the healing streams abound;
Make and keep me pure within.
    —Charles Wesley

Discovery Learning

This page contains an alternate lesson plan emphasizing learning activities. Classes desiring such student involvement will find these suggestions helpful. The next page is a reproducible activity page to further enhance discovery learning.

LEARNING GOALS

After this lesson, each student will be able to:

1. Contrast the way of law with justification by grace as Paul describes the difference in Romans 3.

2. Explain the importance of the doctrine of justification by grace.

3. Praise God for his grace and for the salvation that it makes available to us.

INTO THE LESSON

Begin class by brainstorming excuses people have for not following Jesus. (*People may say, "I'm really not so bad." "There are other ways to God besides Jesus." "I know too many hypocrites." "All the church wants is my money!"*) Continue with the following questions.

"What are some ways people believe one can please God?" (*Answers may include being good, obeying the commandments, going to church, and loving others.*) Next ask, "What did the Jews believe was the way to please God?" (*Answers may include obeying the commandments, being born a Jew, and knowing the words of God.*)

Say, "Paul's writing in Romans 3 presents to us the New Testament's teaching on how to please God. Some accuse God of not being fair. Paul explains in our text today that God is more than fair!"

Distribute copies of the reproducible activity "God's Grace" from the next page. Have students complete the exercise to reveal the the only right way to "please God."

INTO THE WORD

Secure a large piece of butcher paper four feet wide by three feet high. Write "Law vs. Grace" at the top and attach it to the wall. Read the printed text. On the left side of the paper have the class list how a person is justified by law. On the right side, how a person is justified by grace.

Once you have completed the above exercise, divide the class into at least three groups with no more than six in a group. Assign the following.

Group 1. Distribute the following questions. (Use the lesson commentary with the indicated verses from Romans 3 for answers. Questions are included in the student workbook, *NIV® Bible Student.*)

1. What were some of the spiritual advantages the Jews enjoyed? (v. 2)

2. In what is God faithful? (vv. 3, 4)

3. How does Paul prove that all people need God's grace? (vv. 9, 10)

4. Why does the law silence every mouth? (v. 19)

5. What is the law's role? (v. 20)

6. What is the "righteousness from God, apart from law"? (vv. 21, 22)

Group 2. Distribute Bible dictionaries or study Bibles with dictionaries. Ask the group to prepare a short report on the meaning of the words *justification, redemption,* and *atonement.* These words are critical for understanding the implications of this passage of Scripture.

Group 3. Prepare an outline (from Romans 3:21-31) of how we are justified by faith without the works of the law. This outline should include the following:

JUSTIFICATION BY FAITH WITHOUT THE LAW

1. All have sinned and need to be justified. (v. 23)

2. Redemption comes through Jesus. (v. 24)

   a. He is the sacrifice. (v. 25)

   b. God demonstrates his justice. (vv. 25, 26)

3. There is no room for boasting about deserving justification. (v. 27)

4. God will justify all who demonstrate faith in Jesus. (vv. 29, 30)

5. The law can now be a guide for right living. (v. 31)

Display this outline during their presentation. Give each group eight to ten minutes. Each presentation should be about three minutes long.

INTO LIFE

Say, "Paul says that we all fall short of God's glory. We are all 'guilty as charged.' Our text also says we cannot be made right through any action of our own. God has chosen to deal with our sin and guilt by taking on himself the penalty and punishment due our sin. Through the sacrifice of Jesus, he freely forgives us. We can be considered as 'not guilty'!

Say, "For the next two to three minutes I want you to meditate on Romans 3:21-26, focusing on what we have said today about God's way and God's grace; then write a prayer of praise. If you need to talk about your personal salvation, please see me after class." Distribute blank cards or the reproducible activity "My Reaction" from the next page for students to use to record their prayers.

Close this session by asking two or three students to share prayers aloud. (Ask them privately in advance.)

God's Grace

Romans tells us that we are "justified by faith apart from observing the law." Cross out the letters from that quote in the following sequence of letters to make the message of Romans 3.

JUSRITGIFIEHTDBEYOFAUITSHAPNARETFRSSOMFOBSR

EROVINGMTHGELAOWD

__ __ __ __ __ __ __ __ __ __ __ __ __ __ __ __   __ __ __ __   __ __ __

—ROMANS 3:__ *

My Reaction

Write a paragraph about the impact that the message of grace is having on your life.

*Righteousness from God —Romans 3:21

SHARING IN THE PROMISE

LESSON 3

WHY TEACH THIS LESSON?

When we attempt to communicate Christian truth to unbelievers, certain types of words can give us trouble. One type is those specifically "religious" words that aren't really ever heard outside of church settings. Just two examples are "sanctification" and "atonement." When we matter-of-factly use such words when witnessing to our non-Christian acquaintances, we run the risk of "losing" them.

At the other end of the scale are biblical words that are so common in English that we run the risk of misunderstanding when Christian usage differs from secular usage. *Credit* and *credited* are part of just such a word group. One dictionary lists *credit* as having eight primary meanings as a noun and five as a verb. Counting secondary meanings and related words from the same root, there are at least twenty-seven understandings! People have good and bad *credit*. People have *credit* cards. Movies list *credits* at the end. A person is a *credit* to his or her profession. A person is *credited* with an invention—etc. But as we shall see shortly, *credited* is a word we dare not misunderstand when it comes to grasping the core of the Christian faith.

INTRODUCTION

A. WHEN YOU CAN'T SEE THE BOTTOM

One night several years ago we camped along the Green River in Utah. We noticed some people playing in the river, and since we had endured a long, hot day on the road, we donned our swimsuits and went down to the river. The river carried such a heavy load of silt that the water was opaque. I cautioned the children to stay on the bank while I tested the river for any deep places that could not be seen in the murky waters. The river proved to be quite shallow, and even after I was halfway across, the water was only waist deep. One of the girls jumped into the water to join me. "Come back," shouted Mother. "You can't see the bottom."

"I don't have to see the bottom," replied my daughter. "As long as I can see Daddy, I'll be all right."

That's what Abraham's faith was all about. He was able to walk with confidence even when he couldn't see what lay ahead because he trusted God.

B. LESSON BACKGROUND

Some of the Jews who read this Roman epistle may have had some problems with Paul's teaching that one could be justified by faith. To reassure them, Paul cited the example of Abraham. Every Jew was proud to call Abraham "father" (Matthew 3:9; John 8:39). The Jews knew that both Abraham and Sarah were past the age of having children when God promised Abraham he would make of him "a great nation" (Genesis 12:2). They believed they were the heirs of that promise, that Israel was that "great nation." Paul would not argue that point, but he would not limit the promise to those who were Abraham's children by genealogy. He expanded it to those who were Abraham's children because they exhibited a faith like that of Abraham.

DEVOTIONAL READING:
PSALM 32

BACKGROUND SCRIPTURE:
ROMANS 4

PRINTED TEXT:
ROMANS 4:1-5, 13-25

Mar
17

LESSON AIMS

After participating in this lesson, each student will be able to:

1. Tell how Abraham and those who follow his example are considered righteous on the basis of their faith.

2. Explain the significance of Abraham's example for both Jews and Gentiles.

3. Suggest some specific means for helping people to come to know how to share in the promise of being justified by faith.

KEY VERSE

Abraham believed God, and it was credited to him as righteousness.
—Romans 4:3

LESSON 3 NOTES

I. ABRAHAM'S EXAMPLE (ROMANS 4:1-5)

A. INTRODUCTION (vv. 1, 2)

1, 2. What then shall we say that Abraham, our forefather, discovered in this matter? If, in fact, Abraham was justified by works, he had something to boast about—but not before God.

As a Jew, Paul had a right to claim *Abraham* as his *forefather*. In so doing, he identified with his Jewish readers. Indeed, Abraham was the physical ancestor of all Jews. The question that Paul is asking is how Abraham would understand the basis of his justification.

Some Jews may have so revered Abraham that they believed he *was justified by works*. If he had lived a sinless life, then he would have had *something to boast about*. But the Scriptures tell us that he did not live a sinless life. For example, on two occasions he lied about his wife, Sarah (Genesis 12:10-20; 20:1-13). Thus on the basis of his life, he had no grounds to claim that he was justified before God.

B. BELIEVED GOD (v. 3)

3. What does the Scripture say? "Abraham believed God, and it was credited to him as righteousness."

To prove that *Abraham* was justified by faith and not by works, Paul goes to the best authority available—*the Scripture*. Genesis 15:6 says Abraham *"believed* the Lord; and he *credited to him as righteousness."* (See also Galatians 3:6; James 2:23.)

C. CREDITED WITH RIGHTEOUSNESS (vv. 4, 5)

4. Now when a man works, his wages are not credited to him as a gift, but as an obligation.

Paul here states an obvious fact. When a worker makes an agreement to work for wages, that person's wages are due when the assigned task is completed. The employer pays the agreed amount as wages earned, not as a gift. The parallel with salvation is obvious. If one were able to keep the law of God perfectly, that one would have earned salvation, and it would not be a gift. But since no one is able to keep the law in all its details, another way to salvation is necessary.

5. However, to the man who does not work but trusts God who justifies the wicked, his faith is credited as righteousness.

Since a person cannot gain salvation by good works (all the good works of a lifetime cannot atone for one sin), God offers hope through *faith* that can justify *the wicked*. One's faith in and of itself is not *righteousness*, but God through his grace accepts it as righteousness.

"IS THAT YOUR FINAL ANSWER?"

The most popular television program of the 1999–2000 season was *Who Wants to Be a Millionaire?* Who *hasn't* heard Regis Philbin say, "Is that your final answer?" Along with a handful of contestants who won large sums of money, the ABC Network also profited handsomely: thirty-second commercials on the program were netting ABC a half-million dollars each!

Similar offerings soon appeared on other networks, including the Fox network's appropriately named *Greed!* But *Millionaire* had staying power: in its second season it was still on four nights a week.

At first look, it may seem that Abraham was interested in a "get rich quick" scheme like *Millionaire's* participants were: come up with the right answers to a few questions and "Hey, I'm a millionaire!" But the difference is that after Abraham and Sarah tried to *work* out the promise on their own—and brought disaster on their family in the process—their "final answer" was to believe in the promises of God

WHAT DO YOU THINK?

On what grounds do some people today claim to be justified before God? How can we persuade such people that they are in need of God's grace for salvation?

Use this poster to illustrate verse 3. Discuss what it means to believe God as Abraham did.

and act accordingly. Ultimately, it was Abraham's faith that brought the priceless gift of righteousness. God's gift still comes through faith, not through our works, no matter how "good" we might think them to be.   —C. R. B.

II. ABRAHAM'S PROMISE (ROMANS 4:13-16)
A. BASED ON FAITH (vv. 13-15)
13. It was not through law that Abraham and his offspring received the promise that he would be heir of the world, but through the righteousness that comes by faith.

A central theme of this part of the Roman epistle is the contrast between justification by performing deeds of the *law* and justification *by faith*. Here Paul illustrates the theme with the example of *Abraham*.

Paul summarizes the promise to Abraham as that of being *heir of the world*. Genesis 12:2, 3 details what this inheritance involved: God would (1) make of Abraham a great nation, (2) grant him material blessings, (3) exalt his name, and (4) use him to bless all the families of the earth.

These blessings did not come *through law* either to Abraham or *his offspring*. Obviously Abraham could not have been justified by the Mosaic law because he lived hundreds of years before that law was received at Mt. Sinai. Even those who still considered the Mosaic law as essential to justification had to admit that Abraham had been justified without it. Instead, all of these blessings came through the *righteousness that comes by faith*.

And the promise was given to Abraham's offspring during Abraham's lifetime (Genesis 17:7, 8). So they also receive the promise apart from the law. These offspring include both Abraham's physical descendants and his spiritual descendants—that is, those who believe in Jesus Christ. (See verse 16 below.)

14. For if those who live by law are heirs, faith has no value and the promise is worthless.

If one could be justified *by law*, then *faith* would have nothing to do with it. If God justified only those who kept the law, no one would be justified, for no one has kept or does keep it. God's *promise* to Abraham, then, would be *worthless*.

15. … because law brings wrath. And where there is no law there is no transgression.

Generally speaking, the purpose of any law is to define what is right and what is wrong. *The law* also spells out the *wrath*, that is, the punishment for lawbreakers. That means everyone, for all have sinned (Romans 3:23). Abraham and others of his time could not transgress a law that did not yet exist, so they would not come under God's wrath for that reason. However, that does not mean they were safe from his wrath if they did wrong. "All who sin apart from the law will also perish apart from the law" (Romans 2:12). The only way of escape from wrath is Abraham's way. He believed in the Lord, and therefore the Lord credited him with righteousness even though he did not attain righteousness in his living (Genesis 15:6).

THE TEACHING FUNCTION OF LAW

The clean air movement began in Donora, Pennsylvania, in October of 1948. For five days that month, a yellowish blanket of acrid smoke from the town's steel mills and zinc works suffocated the town. One man who lived through it recalls spraining his ankle when he stepped off a curb because the smog was so bad he couldn't see his feet! More than 40 percent of the town's citizens were made ill and twenty people were killed by the pollution. The industrial revolution had brought jobs and prosperity to millions, and (at least until 1948) the smoke belching from the factories had seemed a small price to pay for the affluence people could now enjoy.

In 1950, partly because of Donora's brush with smoggy death, President Truman convened the first national conference to face the issue of air pollution. By

---

DAILY BIBLE READINGS

Monday, Mar. 11—*Your Descendants As the Stars (Genesis 15:1-6)*

Tuesday, Mar. 12—*Promise to Abraham and Descendants (Genesis 15:12-18)*

Wednesday, Mar. 13—*God Chose Our Ancestors (Acts 13:13-25)*

Thursday, Mar. 14—*Believers Set Free by Jesus (Acts 13:26-39)*

Friday, Mar. 15—*Continue Your Heritage (2 Timothy 3:10-17)*

Saturday, Mar. 16—*Abraham's Faith Reckoned as Righteousness (Romans 4:1-8)*

Sunday, Mar. 17—*Heirs Through Faith (Romans 4:13-25)*

WHAT DO YOU THINK?

The Bible presents faith as necessary for salvation. Some will ask, "But what of those who have not heard of the Lord? Is it fair that they perish?" How would you frame your answer to affirm that it is indeed "fair" for God to punish such people eternally?

1963, the first Clean Air Act was passed by Congress. That and subsequent laws have forced us to realize that we have been polluting our air, poisoning our streams, killing wildlife, and destroying the health of millions of human beings. The laws we have passed have educated us about the ethics of pollution. In similar fashion, God's law has taught us that we risk killing ourselves and others spiritually when we fail to give heed to the spiritual environment in which we live.   —C. R. B.

B. GROUNDED IN GRACE (v. 16)

16. Therefore, the promise comes by faith, so that it may be by grace and may be guaranteed to all Abraham's offspring—not only to those who are of the law but also to those who are of the faith of Abraham. He is the father of us all.

The law could educate people and bring them to an understanding of right and wrong, but once a person had broken even one small part of the law, the law was powerless to provide a remedy. But because the promise is *of faith* and not of the law, it can become available through *grace*. As a result, it is available *to all Abraham's offspring*. Grace goes beyond the scope of the law, that is, those who have tried to live according to the law. It is offered also to *those who are of the faith of Abraham*. Probably most Jews of that day believed that God's justification was offered only to the physical descendants of Abraham. Paul makes it clear that grace is offered not only to Jews but to Gentiles also, to those who have the faith of Abraham. Paul affirms this idea in Galatians 3:28, 29: "There is neither Jew nor Greek. . . . you are Abraham's seed, and heirs according to the promise."

III. ABRAHAM'S FAITH (ROMANS 4:17-22)

A. FAITH IN GOD (v. 17)

17. As it is written: "I have made you a father of many nations." He is our father in the sight of God, in whom he believed—the God who gives life to the dead and calls things that are not as though they were.

The passage Paul quotes here is Genesis 17:5. Abraham's only child at the time was Ishmael, and God said the promise would not be fulfilled through him (Genesis 17:19-21). Still, Abraham *believed*.

Paul cites two reasons Abraham could believe God's promise. First, God is the one *who gives life to the dead*. He knew God was able to give a son to Abraham and Sarah long after their normal bearing years were past (v. 18). This phrase also reminds the Christian of God's power to raise the dead—particularly, to raise Jesus from the dead. Because Jesus has been raised, we can by faith in him be called Abraham's children.

Second, God *calls things that are not as though they were*. This may have reference to God's creative ability, creating from nothing everything that is. Or it may have to do with his ability to know the future and to declare what will be with the same certainty as what already is. Actually, both are involved in God's promise to make Abraham the father of many nations. When God promised it, Abraham and Sarah had no children. But God would make it possible for them to give birth to a son, Isaac, and for people of faith to be children of Abraham as well.

B. FAITH WITH HOPE (v. 18)

18. Against all hope, Abraham in hope believed and so became the father of many nations, just as it had been said to him, "So shall your offspring be."

The dictionary defines *hope* as "desire accompanied by expectation." At their advanced ages, Sarah and Abraham had no logical basis for believing they would be the forebears *of many nations*, that their offspring would be as numerous as the stars (Genesis 15:5). And yet against all odds Abraham continued to believe.

C. STRONG IN FAITH (vv. 19, 20)

19. Without weakening in his faith, he faced the fact that his body was as good as dead—since he was about a hundred years old—and that Sarah's womb was also dead.

In Egypt Abraham lied to the pharaoh and said that Sarah was his sister, hoping to save his life by this strategy. This certainly seems to indicate that he had weakened *in his faith* at a critical moment. He was, in effect, taking control of the situation himself instead of trusting God to work things out.

Before we become too critical of Abraham, we need to examine our own efforts at rationalizing some of our actions and decisions. Have we ever told a little "white lie" in order to achieve some important good? Have we ever purchased an item that we wanted and then justified it as something that we needed?

The important thing to remember is that even though Abraham may have wavered in his faith occasionally, the overall judgment of the Scriptures is that he was a man of great faith (Hebrews 11:8-10). Even though he was *about a hundred years old* and *Sarah's womb* was *dead,* yet he never wavered in his fundamental conviction that God would fulfill his part of the covenant that he had made.

20. Yet he did not waver through unbelief regarding the promise of God, but was strengthened in his faith and gave glory to God,

The expression *he did not waver* suggests an image of a man carrying a heavy load up a long, steep trail with strong, steady strides. The reason he can make such progress is that he is strong in his *faith.* This in a way depicts the life of Abraham. When he became weary and temptations beset him, he was able to keep going because of his faith. In so doing, Abraham gives all of us an example to follow.

D. FULLY PERSUADED (vv. 21, 22)

21. . . . being fully persuaded that God had power to do what he had promised.

Abraham's confidence in the promises were grounded in his faith in Almighty God. That's where faith must begin. We who come to God "must believe that he exists and that he rewards those who earnestly seek him" (Hebrews 11:6).

22. This is why "it was credited to him as righteousness."

Decisions and actions have consequences. In Abraham's case his faith had both temporal and eternal consequences. Paul closes his discussion of the results of Abraham's faith by quoting from Genesis 15:6. Abraham's faith *was credited to him as righteousness.* Abraham was not righteous in an absolute sense—without sin. Rather, God was willing to accept Abraham's faith as a substitute for absolute righteousness. As spiritual descendants of Abraham, our faith in God and in Jesus Christ serves in a similar way.

IV. ABRAHAM'S SUCCESSORS: US (ROMANS 4:23-25)

A. RESULT OF OUR FAITH (vv. 23, 24a)

23, 24a. The words "it was credited to him" were written not for him alone, but also for us, to whom God will credit righteousness—

The Jews, of course, understood God's dealings with Abraham. But they needed additional teaching from Paul to understand that God's actions with Abraham became a model for his actions under the Christian covenant. Christians who came from either Jewish or Gentile backgrounds could accept and rejoice in this.

B. SUBSTANCE OF OUR FAITH (vv. 24b, 25)

24b, 25. . . . for us who believe in him who raised Jesus our Lord from the dead. He was delivered over to death for our sins and was raised to life for our justification.

WHAT DO YOU THINK?

Tell about a time when you were "weak in faith" and what you learned from the experience. Or tell of a time when you were "strong in faith." How did your faith sustain you?

WHAT DO YOU THINK?

Suppose some friend complained, "You Christians are always using those special 'code words' that nobody else understands! Just what do you mean by justification, anyway?" How would you respond?

PRAYER

We thank you, gracious Father, that through your Word you have given us the example of Abraham as a model for us. Help us to realize that even as he was justified by his faith, even so we must seek our justification through our faith in you and your Son, Jesus Christ. Amen.

THOUGHT TO REMEMBER

By faith Abraham "was looking forward to the city with foundations, whose architect and builder is God" (Hebrews 11:10).

Here Paul spells out the heart of the gospel message. Our faith is in God *who raised Jesus . . . from the dead.* This is the same God who brought life to Abraham and Sarah so that they could become forebears of "a great nation." Jesus, the Son of God, *was delivered* for our offenses. His *death* on the cross purchased our redemption. Through his resurrection we can be assured that we have been justified.

These basic items of faith are absolutely essential to the gospel. Without them there is no gospel.

CONCLUSION

A. WE COULDN'T PAY THE FINE

Several years ago before the Iron Curtain was removed, we were traveling in East Germany. On our last day there we were headed toward the West German border, which was only an hour or so away. We stopped at a rest center and went inside to use the rest rooms. When we returned to our car, a policeman was standing there in the process of writing out a ticket. He indicated that we were parked in a no parking zone. We could not understand why we were getting a ticket when there were no signs there to indicate that it was a no parking zone, and there were other cars parked there.

The policeman then demanded that we pay the fine right there to him. I tried to explain to him that since we were leaving East Germany, we had already spent all our East German currency. He then demanded that I let him look in my billfold. In my billfold I had Austrian, West German, and American currency but no East German money. This seemed to anger him even more. I couldn't understand exactly what he was saying, but I got the impression that he was going to take us to jail. With the tense political situation that then existed between East Germany and the West, that was a rather grim prospect.

The policeman then called to another officer, who was obviously his superior. When he came over, I was sure we were in real trouble. He spoke with the officer for a minute, and then he demanded to see our passports and visas. After he had looked these over, he took the ticket and smiled. Pointing us toward the highway, he then waved us on.

Now that's grace! We apparently had broken the law, and we couldn't pay our way out of the situation. Only through an officer's grace were we saved from a situation that could have been quite stressful.

This is rather like our situation when we stand before the Supreme Judge. We have broken his laws time and time again, and we have no way of paying our debt. But we don't have to pay our debt. It has already been paid for us by Christ's death on the cross. We are saved by grace!

B. FAITH VERSUS WORKS

Theologians have long debated the place of faith and works in God's plan of salvation. Paul insists that Abraham was justified by faith. James, on the other hand, asks, "Was not . . . Abraham considered righteous for what he did?" (James 2:21). Then he adds, "A person is justified by what he does and not by faith alone" (2:24). Martin Luther was so disturbed by the writings of James that he once referred to it as a "book of straw."

But there is really no contradiction between these two writers. Paul is writing about God's involvement in justification, which is his grace. James, on the other hand, is concerned about man's involvement. One may say he has faith, but if that faith does not lead him to act in a manner that demonstrates his faith, then that faith is dead (James 2:26). Yet the good works of a lifetime cannot wash away even one sin. That takes the blood of Christ. That's what grace is all about!

Discovery Learning

This page contains an alternate lesson plan emphasizing learning activities. Classes desiring such student involvement will find these suggestions helpful. The next page is a reproducible activity page to further enhance discovery learning.

LEARNING GOALS

After this lesson each student will be able to:

1. Tell how Abraham and those who follow his example are considered righteous on the basis of their faith.

2. Explain the significance of Abraham's example for both Jews and Gentiles.

3. Suggest some specific means for helping people to come to know how to share in the promise of being justified by faith.

INTO THE LESSON

Write this statement on the board: "Have it your way." Remind the class that several years ago a popular restaurant used this as an advertising slogan. Society today wants to have as many options available as possible. We want to do things our way. We want to be in control, whether we are choosing the options on a car or decorating a house. Ask your class to identify other situations where people want to "do it their way."

Allow two minutes for quick responses. Then challenge the students to think of some of the ways this principle is applied to our being acceptable to God. Have them think of different religions or even specific rule keeping. Lead into the Bible study by saying, "As we have just discussed, one of the most important areas in which this 'have-it-your-way' principle is lived out is in being acceptable to God. People will try many ways, each keeping the person in control of the relationship. Today we will see that God has his way of making us acceptable. That way is ancient, a principle shown true since the time of Abraham."

To show how this principle was important in the Old Testament, distribute copies of the reproducible activity page that follows. Give students six or eight minutes to complete the first activity, "By Faith."

INTO THE WORD

To provide some background information for today's lesson, divide your class into at least two groups of five or six people each. If you have a large class, make several groups and give duplicate assignments.

Group One will study Genesis 12:1-9; 15:1-7; 17:1-6; 21:1, 2. They are to prepare a brief report that will answer the following questions for each passage: Who initiated the contact/conversation? What was said? How did Abraham respond? What were the results? Have the students report by developing narratives or by developing short skits to depict these events.

Group Two will study Romans 4 to answer the question, "What arguments are given to prove that we are saved (justified, made righteous) by faith and not by works?" Give this group a large piece of poster board and some markers. The poster is to be divided into six sections marked as follows: vv. 1-3; vv. 4-8; vv. 9-12; vv. 13-15; vv. 16, 17; vv. 18-25. In each section students are to write answers based on the verses cited.

Allow ten minutes for research and five minutes each for presentation. Then briefly summarize the material and ask, "Why is Abraham's example important for the Jews and Gentiles?" In the discussion that follows note that the key to this question is Romans 4:23-25. Ask students to write a summary of this discussion on the reproducible page under the heading "The Difference."

INTO LIFE

Say to the class, "It is always a tendency of humans to want to have things their own way. It may be based on likes and dislikes or upon traditions. This can be true in how we follow God and seek to be accepted by him."

Ask, "Where are you in the matter have having things your way or accepting God's grace by believing?" Ask each student to mark the scale on the reproducible page ("Where Am I?") to assess his or her own faith.

Have the groups reconvene. Point them to Romans 3 and 4. Provide markers and blank sheets of paper. After reviewing the chapters, groups are to develop a tract that will communicate how a person is justified by faith. (A similar activity is included in *NIV® Bible Student.*)

As an example, provide the following outline:

1. We have a problem (Romans 3:23).

2. God answers our problem with Jesus' sacrifice (Romans 3:24, 25).

3. We must respond (Romans 3:25, 26).

4. Faith has always been God's means (Romans 4:2, 3, 13).

5. We, too, come to God as Abraham did (Romans 4:23-25).

Ask one or two groups to share the message of the tract. Conduct a brief brainstorm of ways individuals can share this message with others. Then ask each person to choose a way he or she will share the good news. Close with a prayer for strength to fulfill this challenge.

By Faith

Read Hebrews 11 and compile a list of those mentioned as living by faith. Using a concordance, document each person's story from the Old Testament.

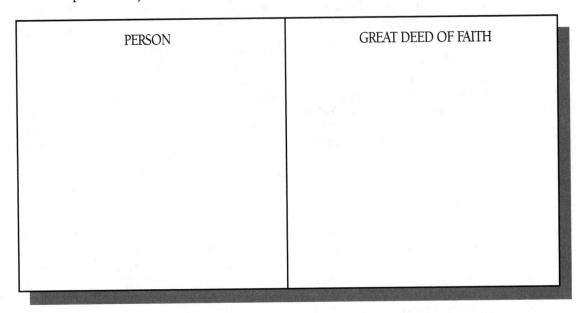

PERSON	GREAT DEED OF FAITH

The Difference

Write a short explanation of why it matters whether righteousness is a gift received from God or a prize to be earned.

Where Am I?

On the scale below, mark with an X where you are in your focus for salvation.

"Working"   "Believing"

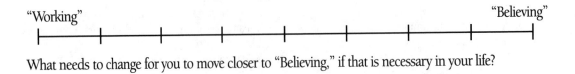

What needs to change for you to move closer to "Believing," if that is necessary in your life?

RECONCILED BY CHRIST'S DEATH

WHY TEACH THIS LESSON?

"Keep your eyes on the prize!" was the battle cry of the United States' Civil Rights Movement of the early 1960s. How difficult it must have been to *do* that in the face of overwhelming odds! Everywhere this movement's leadership looked, there seemed to be opposition—from a settled indifference on the one hand, to outright assassination on the other. But from a perspective of some three decades hence, those who endured that struggle will say, "It was worth it!"

Sometimes it takes a years-later perspective to render a positive judgment like this. Some undoubtedly gave up hope along the way, choosing to sit on the sidelines. In the Christian life as well, some will give up; the struggle just doesn't seem "worth it" anymore, given all that the world seems to offer (cf. 2 Timothy 4:10). Perhaps you or some of your students are at that point, wondering whether it really is worth it. Today as you consider what it means to be reconciled by Christ's death, use that message as encouragement to persevere. May the fact of that reconciliation help each of us "keep our eyes on the prize" of eternal life!

INTRODUCTION

A. WHILE WE WERE YET SINNERS

A pious English couple had only one son, but he was a fine Christian young man, the pride of their lives. When World War I began, he was called to the colors and soon found himself in the front lines in France. Within a few months his parents received the distressing news that their son had been killed in action. The only thing that softened their tragedy was the news that he had died heroically, saving the life of one of his comrades.

Some time later the man whose life had been saved returned to England on furlough, and the couple invited him to spend a few days with them. When he arrived at their home, they were shocked. He was obviously intoxicated, and his language was filled with profanities. Now the couples' agony was intensified, for it was clear that their son had given his life for a man who was crude and carnal.

For their daily devotions, the couple was reading from the book of Romans, and the next morning it so happened that they were reading from the fifth chapter. At verse 8, the husband paused. After a long silence he said quietly, "Now I begin to understand what this verse means."

B. LESSON BACKGROUND

For all of us the door to the past is closed forever and we can never open it. For some of us that is a very good thing, for the past holds painful memories of mistakes we made that pulled us away from God and his will for us. For some the past holds pleasant memories, but even pleasant memories are sometimes painful because we know that we cannot bring the "good old days" back and relive them.

DEVOTIONAL READING:
PSALM 25:1-11

BACKGROUND SCRIPTURE:
ROMANS 5

PRINTED TEXT:
ROMANS 5:1-11, 18-21

Mar
24

LESSON AIMS

After participating in this lesson, each student will be able to:

1. Summarize Paul's description of the blessings of being justified by faith.

2. Explain what it means to be "reconciled to God by the death of his Son" and "saved by his life."

3. Seek to be a messenger of reconciliation whenever and wherever one is needed this week.

KEY VERSE

Therefore, since we have been justified through faith, we have peace with God through our Lord Jesus Christ. —Romans 5:1

Just as the door to the past is closed, so also is the door to the future. None of us possesses a crystal ball that will give us the power to penetrate the darkness that shrouds the future.

Only the present is ours. Yet we dare not live just for the moment. The past has shaped us and will have an impact on how we make the decisions that will shape the future. But even the wisest and most pious of us cannot, on our own, face the future with complete assurance. An accident, an unexpected illness, the actions of a friend or an enemy, even some event in a remote part of the world may change our future dramatically.

In a world of uncertainties, two things we can know for certain. At some point days, weeks, months, or years from now, we will breathe our final breath. The other thing we can know for certain is that "while we were still sinners, Christ died for us." Our faith in that fact can give us the assurance to face whatever the future brings us.

I. BLESSINGS OF JUSTIFICATION (ROMANS 5:1-5)

A. PEACE WITH GOD (v. 1)

1. Therefore, since we have been justified through faith, we have peace with God through our Lord Jesus Christ.

Romans 4 closes with a succinct statement of the heart of the gospel message: Christ was crucified for our sins and "raised to life for our justification." Here as in other places, Paul uses the word *therefore* as a transition from a theological statement to the practical applications of that statement. One thing that follows from one's justification is *peace with God*. Our sins alienate us from God. We oppose his will for us and are at war with his kingdom. As long as we continue to oppose him, we cannot enjoy this peace. God's promise of peace is certain if we are willing to accept it. But even though we may understand this objectively in our minds, we may not always enjoy it emotionally in our hearts. We may have rebelled so long and so strongly that we find it difficult to accept his promise. Augustine (A.D. 354–430), who had long rebelled against God, observed that "our heart is not quiet until it rests" in God. If we are really to have peace, we must accept his promise both mentally and emotionally.

HOW TO SAY IT

Augustine. AW-gus-TEEN *or* Aw-GUS-tin.

B. ACCESS INTO GRACE (v. 2)

2. . . . through whom we have gained access by faith into this grace in which we now stand. And we rejoice in the hope of the glory of God.

Grace was linked with peace in the salutation of the letter (1:7) and has been mentioned three times since (3:24; 4:4, 16), the latter two drawing a clear distinction between *faith*/grace and works/law. Paul reaffirms here that faith, not works, provides the *access* to God's grace, by which we are heirs of the promise to Abraham (4:16).

As sinners, we fall short of *the glory of God* (Romans 3:23), but by grace we anticipate the time when that glory will be revealed in us (Romans 8:18). It is not surprising, then, that this grace leads the believer to *rejoice in . . . hope!*

C. ENDURANCE THROUGH TRIALS (vv. 3, 4)

3, 4. Not only so, but we also rejoice in our sufferings, because we know that suffering produces perseverance; perseverance, character; and character, hope.

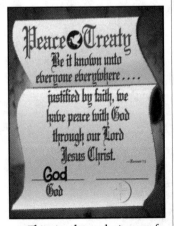

This visual uses the image of a "peace treaty" to illustrate verse 1, "We have peace with God."

While God has promised us peace, he does not guarantee that our lives will be free of problems. There is a danger that when we have difficult times, our faith may waver. Paul tries to prepare his readers for the trials that may come because they are Christians. Like Peter (1 Peter 4:12, 13) and James (James 1:2), Paul wants his readers to *rejoice* in such trials. But the word Paul uses here is emphatic; it is the same word that was used in Romans 4:2, where he says Abraham would have had cause to "boast" if his justification were based on works.

So, while Satan uses these *sufferings* to upset and weaken our faith, Paul urges us to rejoice or even "boast" about them. They can help us to gain spiritual strength. The word *perseverance* suggests endurance. One who has endured the fires of suffering knows that God will give him or her the strength to survive; such a one can meet these difficulties with calm assurance.

The word for *character* here carries the idea of being tested, like gold that has been through the refiner's fire to burn off the impurities. (The *New American Standard Bible* has "proven character.") In the same way, a person who has gone through the many trials of life has gained the discipline that allows the future to be viewed with *hope*. One who has felt the guiding hand of God through the deep shadows of life's disappointments has no apprehension about what the future may hold. Such a person knows that God will still be at his or her side.

D. LOVE OF GOD (vv. 5-8)

5. And hope does not disappoint us, because God has poured out his love into our hearts by the Holy Spirit, whom he has given us.

In times of testing, our *hope* will not leave us helpless and humiliated. The reason is that *God has poured out his love into our hearts*. While this refers to God's love that has been shown toward us, it does not mean God does not love us until we express our faith and find reconciliation with him. God's love is unconditional, as the following verses, and especially verse 8, make clear. But we do not realize the benefit of his love until we enter a relationship with him. The father of the prodigal son loved him even when he was in the far country, but he had to return to the father before he could enjoy that love (Luke 15:11-32).

The Holy Spirit is the means by which God pours out his love to us. The presence of the Holy Spirit is not promised alone to a few very special saints, but is a gift that everyone who repents and is baptized receives (Acts 2:38, 39).

6. You see, at just the right time, when we were still powerless, Christ died for the ungodly.

In the verses that follow, Paul contrasts the human situation before Christ came with that after he came. Before Christ came, we were *powerless*. Paul is not describing our physical condition but our spiritual situation. In the first chapter of Romans Paul describes in some detail the wicked state into which the human race had fallen. The worst part of man's condition was not his evil but the fact that he was utterly helpless to do anything to save himself. Even in their efforts to worship God men "exchanged the glory of the immortal God for images made to look like mortal man, and birds and animals and reptiles" (Romans 1:23). God then in his infinite wisdom and mercy sent his Son to die for all sinners, *the ungodly*.

7. Very rarely will anyone die for a righteous man, though for a good man someone might possibly dare to die.

Some see in this verse a contrast between a *righteous man* and a *good man*. In this view the *righteous man* describes a pious person who has a "holier-than-thou" attitude. He may be respected, but not greatly loved, and thus no one would be likely to die for him. A *good man*, on the other hand, is a moral person whose good deeds are well known and appreciated by many. As a result, people will "do anything" for him; someone might be willing even *to die* for him.

Others take the verse to present, not a contrast between two different types of persons, but two ways of saying the same thing. Either way, the idea is that it is a rare thing indeed to find a person who would be willing to die for another, and it

WHAT DO YOU THINK?

It is easy to compare ourselves with those who are guilty of gross crimes and to believe that we are "not so bad." In God's eyes, however, we are all sinners, and Christ died for sinners. In an age that recognizes few if any absolutes, how can we communicate the need to accept the gift of Christ's atoning death to those sinners who see themselves as "not so bad"?

is expected that it is some good quality in the person that would motivate one to make such a sacrifice. That contrasts sharply with Christ's sacrifice since he died for all—not just the good, righteous people but for the worst of sinners.

8. But God demonstrates his own love for us in this: While we were still sinners, Christ died for us.

We might picture a person standing on the shore of a river, trying to throw a life preserver to a person who is struggling in the water to save himself. But this would not accurately portray the situation presented in this verse. Rather, the rescuer jumps into the water to rescue the other person, who openly fights against the rescuer. As a result, the drowning person is saved, but the rescuer is drowned.

THE BLESSING THAT COMES THROUGH TRIALS

Christopher de Vinck is an English teacher. Each time he introduces his class to *The Miracle Worker,* the play about the blind and deaf Helen Keller, he tells the students about his brother Oliver. Oliver lived in his parents' home for thirty-three years, blind, deaf, legs twisted, and apparently with insufficient intelligence to learn anything.

His parents had been urged to put the baby in an institution, but they said, "No, we will take him home." Rather than focus on the difficulty associated with providing the level of care Oliver required, Oliver's parents focused on their blessings. Although Oliver was profoundly disabled, he was neither hyperactive nor wild, nor did he demand constant attention. Christopher says of him, "He was the most helpless human I ever met. But we were blessed with his presence, a true presence of peace." And when the time came for Christopher to choose a wife, her reaction to his helpless brother became the litmus test by which she was judged worthy of his love.

Oliver de Vinck was the means by which a whole family and their friends learned the meaning of our text today: through trials come patience, experience, and hope in the love of God that the Spirit makes known to us.   —C. R. B.

WHAT DO YOU THINK?

A good way to remember the meaning of the word justified is to think of it as "just as if I'd" never sinned. Imagine living a life without any history or without any regrets. If you could make a list of those events or circumstances in your life that you would like to put behind you, what would you include?

II. RESULTS OF JUSTIFICATION (ROMANS 5:9-11)

A. SAVED FROM WRATH (vv. 9, 10)

9. Since we have now been justified by his blood, how much more shall we be saved from God's wrath through him!

Christ died for sinners, but this was *much more* than a courageous act of love, Paul insists. Through *his blood* we are *justified.* The Scriptures tell us that "without the shedding of blood there is no forgiveness" of sins (Hebrews 9:22). The Old Testament tells us of the sacrifices made in the tabernacle and temple, all of which looked forward to Jesus Christ, who was the perfect sacrifice.

10. For if, when we were God's enemies, we were reconciled to him through the death of his Son, how much more, having been reconciled, shall we be saved through his life!

Justification addresses the problem of sin from a legal point of view and reconciliation from a personal point of view. In a lawsuit, a court may hand down a decision that meets the requirements of the law for justice. But there is still no reconciliation. Not until the two contestants shake hands as a sign of mutual respect can there be a reconciliation. God has extended his hand through the death of his Son. It is up to us to accept it.

WHAT DO YOU THINK?

Paul makes it clear that Jesus, alive and living forever, is still active in our salvation. What does this suggest to you about how to face trials? How do we use the power of Jesus' life in our lives?

But even that is not the whole story. *Much more* than this great reconciliation that was effected by Jesus' death is the benefit of his resurrection and continuing life. By that, Paul says, *shall we be saved.* Salvation is more than a matter of having our past sins erased by Jesus' atoning death. It is a relationship with a living Lord. And if Christ was willing to die for our sins when we were sinners (and he was), *how much more* will he do for us in this living salvation relationship we now enjoy with him!

B. Joy in God (v. 11)

11. Not only is this so, but we also rejoice in God through our Lord Jesus Christ, through whom we have now received reconciliation.

The immediate and obvious response to our realization that we have been justified and reconciled is joy *in God*. This joy is not just an exciting emotion that will soon pass. It is a deep, lasting sense of security that will carry us into eternity.

Dying for Those Who Are Evil

NBC TV commentator Tom Brokaw wrote *The Greatest Generation* (Random House, 1998). In it he tells of the commitment and sacrifice of a generation of Americans that grew up during the difficult days of the Great Depression and then were conscripted to fight World War II. The book has had an amazing effect. Brokaw says baby boomers who had rejected the values of their parents have told him that the book has given them "a new appreciation for the sacrifices and deprivations of their mothers and fathers." Men often tell him, "Thank you for writing. . . . I finally understand my father." One man says he read the book to his nearly blind father—a veteran of the war—and "it was the most meaningful father-son time we'd ever had." Untold thousands of that "greatest generation" died for the sake of loved ones back home and for the preservation of a homeland they would never see again.

The sacrifice these men and women made for their loved ones is not unlike the potential sacrifice Paul notes by some who might dare to die for the good. But Christ's love is different! He was willing to die for every tyrant and despot, enemies and not friends—the worst in all of us! We honor those willing to die for the good; we can only be amazed at the One who died for those who are evil.   —C. R. B.

III. GOAL OF JUSTIFICATION (ROMANS 5:18-21)

The closing verses of today's lesson deal with some theological issues that have been debated for centuries. From verse 12 on Paul compares and contrasts the effects of Adam's sin and Christ's sacrificial death. In every point the effect of Adam's sin is answered by Christ—and "much more" (vv. 15, 17).

A. Imputed Righteousness (vv. 18, 19)

18. Consequently, just as the result of one trespass was condemnation for all men, so also the result of one act of righteousness was justification that brings life for all men.

This verse brings to a climax a series of contrasts between Adam and Christ. Adam's act was a *trespass*; Christ's was an *act of righteousness*. Adam's act brought death; Christ's brings *life*. In one respect, however, their actions were the same—the effect of their actions came upon *all* who ever lived.

19. For just as through the disobedience of the one man the many were made sinners, so also through the obedience of the one man the many will be made righteous.

Here Paul explains how these two actions affect everyone. First, why did condemnation come upon "all men" as a result of Adam's offense? The answer is that the *many were made sinners.* (The word *many* is apparently equivalent to *all* from verse 18.) But in what sense are all *made sinners*? Everyone who comes into this world suffers consequences of Adam's sin. Just what are those consequences? As a minimum, they must include physical death (1 Corinthians 15:22). But do they include Adam's guilt?

Further, how does *justification that brings life* come to "all men"? Certainly it cannot mean that everyone will be saved. That would be contrary to what the Scripture says elsewhere. It does suggest that whatever consequence and guilt we inherit from Adam is erased in Christ. Death is annulled by resurrection, which happens to the righteous and the wicked alike (John 5:29). Guilt, to whatever extent it is inherited from Adam, is also taken away. Thus we are left

Daily Bible Readings

Monday, Mar. 18—Happy Are Those Who Are Forgiven (Psalm 32:1-5)

Tuesday, Mar. 19—By the Grace of God (1 Corinthians 15:1-11)

Wednesday, Mar. 20—Made Alive in Christ (1 Corinthians 15:20-28)

Thursday, Mar. 21—Justified by Faith (Romans 5:1-11)

Friday, Mar. 22—Free Gift of Righteousness (Romans 5:12-17)

Saturday, Mar. 23—Your King Arrives on a Donkey (Zechariah 9:9-13)

Sunday, Mar. 24—"Hosanna in the Highest Heaven!" (Matthew 21:1-11)

with accountability for our own sin, and not that of Adam. And this, too, is answered in Christ and is available to all (Romans 10:13).

B. ABUNDANT GRACE (v. 20)

20. The law was added so that the trespass might increase. But where sin increased, grace increased all the more.

Law, whether it refers to the law of Moses or law in the more general sense, serves at least one important function: it makes us aware of our sinfulness. As a result, our situation is exposed as hopeless. But no matter how desperate one's condition is as a result of *sin,* God's *grace* has provided a remedy. Just as sin is all-encompassing, so grace is just as extensive—and more powerful. Praise the Lord!

C. REIGNING GRACE (v. 21)

21. . . . so that, just as sin reigned in death, so also grace might reign through righteousness to bring eternal life through Jesus Christ our Lord.

The consequence of *sin* is *death*—both physical and spiritual—"for the wages of sin is death" (Romans 6:23). But the bright side of this contrast is that we have the hope of *eternal life through Jesus Christ.*

CONCLUSION

A. EXCITING PROMISES

At least two or three times a week we receive some exciting opportunities through the mail. We are promised a new car, a trip to Hawaii, or even a million dollars! On occasion we have been informed that we are already on the winner's list! All we have to do, we are told, is to write our name and address on a card and mail it in. Most of these are quickly disposed of without even being opened. Why? Because we know that the glowing promises are just that—promises, promises that have nothing to back them up. Yet many people have believed the promises and have been sadly disappointed when they have proven to be false. Periodically, governmental agencies take steps to curtail this kind of mail.

Yet in today's lesson we have studied promises that surpass any promises we have received through the mail. Even though we are sinners, we are promised justification. Even though we have been alienated from God, we are promised reconciliation. Even though we live under the curse of death, we are promised life.

How can we trust such promises? We trust them because we read about them in the Scriptures. We can trust them because God sent his own Son to die for us.

B. JOY AND PEACE

Years ago we sang a chorus that went something like this: "I have the joy, joy, joy, joy down in my heart, down in my heart, down in my heart to stay!" Another stanza, which was always a tongue twister for me, went "I have the peace that passeth understanding down in my heart!"

Joy and peace belong together. In the first verse of today's lesson we read that we are justified by faith. All of us were sinners, facing judgment, certain of being eternally condemned, and without any way of saving ourselves—helpless and hopeless. Yet by faith we are justified. That means that even though we are sinners, we do not have to pay the penalty for our iniquities. Christ has already paid the penalty on the cross. Thus we stand justified, which someone has explained as being "just as if I'd" never sinned.

Being justified means that we can enjoy a peace that the world doesn't even begin to understand. Because of that peace we can meet the problems of life with joy that springs from the confidence that justification brings.

Discovery Learning

*This page contains an alternate lesson plan emphasizing learning activities. Classes
desiring such student involvement will find these suggestions helpful. The next page
is a reproducible activity page to further enhance discovery learning.*

LEARNING GOALS

After this lesson each student will be able to:

1. Summarize Paul's description of the blessings of being justified by faith.

2. Explain what it means to be "reconciled to God by the death of his Son" and "saved by his life."

3. Seek to be a messenger of reconciliation whenever and wherever one is needed this week.

INTO THE LESSON

Tell the students, "Think of all the world peace accords since you were born. We will list them here." (Refer to a marker board or poster attached to the wall.) The class might list these, among others: Treaty of Versailles (1919, WWI); Yalta and Potsdam Conferences (1945, WWII); Korean Armistice (1953); Suez Canal Treaty (1956, Israel-Egypt); Paris Peace Talks (1973, Vietnam); Camp David (1978, Israel-Egypt); Oslo Agreements (1993, 1995, Israel-PLO); Dayton Peace Accords (1995, Bosnia); Wye Summit Agreement (1998, Israel-PLO).

After listing several accords, ask, "What comes to mind when you hear the word *peace?*" Allow time for responses; then ask, "Why is it so hard for the world to achieve peace?" After a few responses, note, "Today's lesson explores how to find peace with God. We will note what is essential for peace with God and with others."

INTO THE WORD

Before this week's lesson, recruit a class member to read today's text. Be sure that he or she has reviewed the text, paying close attention to punctuation. If you are not using student books, you may want to copy the text for learners' use.

Say, "Justification by faith brings many blessings for the Christian. Reread the text; then circle the blessings you can find." (You may find the puzzle on the reproducible page useful.) After the class has finished its work, call for volunteers to list these on your board.

Blessings include: peace with God (v. 1), access into grace (v. 2), hope (v. 2), character produced in our lives (vv. 3, 4), God's love in our hearts (v. 5), being saved from God's wrath (v. 9), and life in Christ (vv. 18, 19).

Develop a short lecture to help students understand the difference between justification and reconciliation. Draw on the information given in the commentary and from your own research on vv. 9-11.

Divide the class into groups of four to six members each. If you have more than two groups, number the groups. Each group is to read v. 10. The odd-numbered groups are to brainstorm the things God had to overcome for us to be reconciled to him while we were yet his enemies. (*These include our sin, death, and Satan's power.*) The even-numbered groups are to brainstorm what "more" God will do for us now that we are reconciled. (*These include give us real joy and give us eternal life.*)

Call the groups back together and compile your lists. Say, "As a result of Christ's death, we have been reconciled to God. Now that we are his friends, much more awaits us, as we have listed. God's work in our lives spurs us on to be messengers for him."

INTO LIFE

Write on the chalkboard "God is. . . ." Ask students to return to their groups and reread verses 1-11. Ask each group to create two or three bumper stickers from what these verses tell about God. (*Suggestions include "God is love," "God is my friend," "God is glorious," "God is the reconciler."*) Allow five minutes for this exercise.

Call the groups together, asking volunteers to share their bumper stickers. Ask, "Why is this an important image of God? How can we best communicate this truth to our neighbors and society? Where are some of the places this message needs most to be seen?"

Option. If possible, have on hand peel-and-stick labels with the letter R. Give one to each class member. Suggest that each student wear the label this week and be prepared to explain it to anyone who asks. The class may want to make a list of R's it could stand for: *reconciled, redeemed, rejoicing, resurrected.*

Option. Distribute copies of the reproducible activity "Messenger" from the next page. Students can use this "telegram" to summarize the gospel in concise fashion.

Since the group has mentioned some places where the message of reconciliation needs to be shared, close with a challenge for each to be a "reconciler" this week. Ask them to pray this prayer after you (a few words at a time). "Lord, this week help me to be your representative. Open my eyes to see the situations where you want your message proclaimed. Open my ears to hear the cries of those who need your presence. Open my mouth to speak your message. Open my arms to be an instrument of your love. In Christ Jesus, I pray. Amen."

Blessings

Read Romans 5:1-11, 18-21 and circle words you find from the text in the puzzle below. These words are used by Paul to show the blessings we receive by being justified by faith and some of our resulting behaviors. Find nine words or phrases.

```
R  F  G  O  E  D  A  H  O  P  E
O  E  N  L  A  B  C  I  L  L  F
D  A  C  P  E  A  C  E  X  O  I
S  C  G  O  H  Z  E  J  K  V  L
Q  B  O  P  N  C  S  M  L  E  L
D  Z  R  S  L  C  S  B  F  O  A
E  Y  A  I  Z  Y  I  X  W  F  N
V  X  F  D  F  J  M  L  N  G  R
A  E  R  E  J  O  I  C  E  O  E
S  V  G  E  H  Q  V  K  T  D  T
T  S  U  O  E  T  H  G  I  R  E
```

Messenger

Write a four-line telegram to your best friend explaining your excitement about the gospel and its message.

Dear Friend:

_____

_____

_____

Because of the gospel,

_____

MADE ALIVE IN CHRIST

LESSON 5

WHY TEACH THIS LESSON?

Centuries before the time of Christ, Greek philosophers developed the concept of *soma sema*—literally, "the body, a tomb." This idea proposes that a person's physical body is a type of prison in which the soul is trapped, waiting to be released when a person dies. The concept of a body's "resurrection" becomes, therefore, undesirable at best and nonsensical at worst. (Perhaps this belief is why the Greek philosophers at the Areopagus scoffed at Paul when he spoke of resurrection; see Acts 17:32.)

But how different is God's revealed truth from the fanciful inventions of man! The key distinction between these two viewpoints is that the truth of Christian teaching about our own future resurrection is based on an objective fact of history: Jesus' own resurrection. Because of that first Easter, Christians "may live a new life" (Romans 6:4) even as we await the great day of the resurrection of our own bodies (cf. 1 Corinthians 15:12-58). Today's lesson is about the importance of daily meeting the challenge of that new life in light of our baptism.

INTRODUCTION

A. HE'S DIFFERENT

A community drama club practiced many weeks in order to present a play for their friends and family members. The play they selected required so many characters that some of the club members had to play more than one part. One young man played a character who was killed in the first act. His little nephew was in the audience when this happened, and he cried out, "They killed Uncle Bobby! They killed Uncle Bobby!"

The young man appeared as another character in the next act. When he came on the stage, the nephew was perplexed for a moment, and he cried out once again, "Uncle Bobby's not dead! But he's different!"

Jesus used the imagery of the cross to describe his disciples' commitment to following him (Matthew 16:24). Paul used a similar figure when he said, "I have been crucified with Christ" (Galatians 2:20). Christian baptism pictures this same idea of a death for the follower of Jesus, and a new life as well. When a penitent believer is buried in Christian baptism, that one is not literally dead, but he or she rises from the water very different!

B. LESSON BACKGROUND

Today's lesson deals with the Easter theme, but it is handled in a somewhat unusual way. The resurrection account is presented first, as seen through the eyes of Mary Magdalene. At least six women bear the name Mary in the New Testament, three of whom play significant roles in the Gospel accounts—Mary the mother of Jesus, Mary the sister of Martha and Lazarus, and Mary Magdalene. "Magdalene" indicates that the latter Mary was from the town of Magdala, located southwest of Capernaum on the western shore of the Sea of Galilee. She is mentioned along with several other women who followed Jesus during his ministry. She must have felt a special debt to Jesus because he had healed her of evil spirits (Luke 8:2).

DEVOTIONAL READING:
ROMANS 6:12-23
BACKGROUND SCRIPTURE:
JOHN 20:1-18; ROMANS 6
PRINTED TEXT:
JOHN 20:1, 11-17; ROMANS 6:3-11

Mar
31

LESSON AIMS

After participating in this lesson, each student will be able to:

1. Describe the details surrounding the resurrected Christ's appearance to Mary Magdalene, and how Paul linked Christian baptism with Jesus' resurrection.

2. Explain the impact that being "raised with Christ" should have on a Christian's daily conduct.

3. Identify one behavior or attitude that needs to be put to death in order to demonstrate the "new life" that should characterize a believer.

KEY VERSE

We were therefore buried with him through baptism into death in order that, just as Christ was raised from the dead through the glory of the Father, we too may live a new life.   —Romans 6:4

LESSON 5 NOTES

Mary was among the women who went to the tomb early on that first resurrection day. During the dismay and turmoil that followed the discovery that the tomb was empty, Mary returned to the tomb. Standing outside, she began to weep, and as she wept the Lord appeared to her.

The second part of today's lesson deals with theological implications of the burial and resurrection of Jesus. In Romans 6 Paul points out some parallels between Christian baptism and the death, burial, and resurrection of Jesus.

I. JESUS' RESURRECTION AND MARY (JOHN 20:1, 11-17)

A. MARY'S DISCOVERY (v. 1)

1. Early on the first day of the week, while it was still dark, Mary Magdalene went to the tomb and saw that the stone had been removed from the entrance.

Jesus was crucified on Friday and his body was hastily buried by Joseph of Arimathea and Nicodemus before the beginning of the Sabbath. Then *early* on Sunday morning several women who had been followers of Jesus went to the tomb to make further preparations of his body (Luke 23:54–24:1). Apparently the work of Joseph and Nicodemus was inadequate for Jesus' final burial.

We don't know why *Mary* was the only woman mentioned by name in John's account. Perhaps it was because she plays a significant role later in this chapter.

As Mary and the other women approached *the tomb*, their chief concern was how they were going to roll away *the stone* that sealed its mouth (Mark 16:1-3). If Jesus' tomb was typical of that period, then the stone would have been massive, requiring several strong men using pry bars to move it. Imagine Mary's surprise as she approached the tomb to see that the stone already *had been removed*.

B. MARY'S GRIEF (vv. 11-13)

11. But Mary stood outside the tomb crying. As she wept, she bent over to look into the tomb.

The intervening verses, omitted from our lesson text for the sake of space, tell how Mary left *the tomb* and hurried to tell Peter and John that Jesus' body was missing. They both ran to the tomb to check out her story. The other women told the rest of the apostles what they had seen, but the apostles rejected the women's story as "nonsense" (Luke 24:11). After Peter and John had seen the empty tomb for themselves, they returned home.

In the meantime, Mary, who apparently had not been able to keep up with Peter and John, returned to the tomb alone. For a time she stood outside weeping, confused and distraught by the events of the morning. Finally she stooped down and peered into the empty tomb.

12. . . . and saw two angels in white, seated where Jesus' body had been, one at the head and the other at the foot.

But the tomb was no longer empty! *Two angels*, dressed *in white*, were sitting where the *body* of Jesus had lain. In that day, a sepulchre usually was used for several bodies, which were placed in niches cut into the wall. The central part of the sepulchre included a stone bench on which the body was laid for preparation for final internment in one of the niches. Apparently the angels were sitting on this stone bench.

13. They asked her, "Woman, why are you crying?"

"They have taken my Lord away," she said, "and I don't know where they have put him."

It seems strange that Mary was not frightened when she saw the angels. Perhaps because she was too concerned and fearful over finding the tomb empty. The angels open a conversation by asking, *"Woman, why are you crying?"*

WHAT DO YOU THINK?

One ploy skeptics use to try and discredit the the resurrection is to allege discrepancies in the Gospel accounts. Suppose a co-worker said to you, "Look, John says Mary came to the tomb of Jesus alone, but all the other Gospels say she was in a group of women. They can't all be right, so why should I believe any of them?" How would you answer?

HOW TO SAY IT

Areopagus. Air-ee-OP-uh-gus.
Arimathea. AIR-uh-muh-THEE-uh.
Capernaum. Kuh-PER-nay-um.
Galilee. GAL-uh-lee.
Magdala. MAG-duh-luh.
Magdalene. MAG-duh-leen or Mag-duh-LEE-nee.
Nicodemus. NICK-uh-DEE-mus.
Rabboni. Rab-O-nye.
sepulchre. SEP-ul-kur.

Nothing in Mary's response suggests she expected Jesus' resurrection. Mary said, *"They have taken my Lord away,"* but it is unclear who Mary thinks "they" might be. Did Jesus' enemies steal the body? Had Jesus' friends moved the body so that his enemies could not desecrate it? Mary did not know.

C. MARY'S PLEA (vv. 14, 15)

14. At this, she turned around and saw Jesus standing there, but she did not realize that it was Jesus.

Now *Jesus* enters the picture. When Mary *turned* away from the tomb and the angels, there stood Jesus. But why did she not recognize him? Of course, she was not expecting to see him; none of Jesus' followers anticipated his resurrection. Perhaps her tears may have hampered her vision, or it may be that she saw Jesus only from the corner of her eye. Later, when Jesus called her name, she "turned toward him" to face him (v. 16).

15. "Woman," he said, "why are you crying? Who is it you are looking for?"

Thinking he was the gardener, she said, "Sir, if you have carried him away, tell me where you have put him, and I will get him."

Even when Jesus asked two gentle questions, Mary still did not recognize him. The Greek word for *Sir* is sometimes translated "Lord" (as it is in v. 13), but it was also used as a general term of respect, and all modern versions translate it as such here. Jesus' questions, like that of the angels', are not for the purpose of gaining information—he actually knows why she is crying and whom she seeks—but are designed to start a conversation.

Supposing Jesus to be *the gardener,* she asks where he has taken the body. That she thinks that she would by herself be able to return the body to the tomb indicates that in her emotional state she is not thinking clearly.

D. MARY'S MASTER (vv. 16, 17)

16. Jesus said to her, "Mary."

She turned toward him and cried out in Aramaic, "Rabboni!" (which means Teacher).

Jesus now addresses her personally—*Mary*. This broke through the veil of her grief, and now she recognizes him. *Rabboni* is an Aramaic word that is similar to "rabbi," which means teacher. It is an intensified form of "rabbi," so it may be a more honorable title, or perhaps a more personal one. John translates the Aramaic term for his non-Jewish readers, but normally we would expect the Greek word he used to be translated as "teacher" in English.

17. Jesus said, "Do not hold on to me, for I have not yet returned to the Father. Go instead to my brothers and tell them, 'I am returning to my Father and your Father, to my God and your God.'"

Jesus' words, *Do not hold on to me,* are translated "Stop clinging to me" in the *New American Standard Bible*. Jesus had an urgent mission to reach many people in a limited time. He could not afford to be delayed by Mary at this time.

Jesus no longer addresses his followers as "servants" or even "disciples," but as *brothers*. They are entering into a new relationship. On the night he was betrayed, Jesus had indicated this change in status (see John 15:15).

Also, Jesus indicates that he was preparing to return, to ascend, to his *Father.* In the limited time he had remaining on this earth, he would be preparing his followers to carry on his work after he departed. Jesus' reference to *my Father and your Father . . . my God and your God* has a dual significance. First, it emphasizes the uniqueness of Jesus' relationship with his Father—no one is the Son of God in the same way Jesus is. Yet God is our Father as well (Galatians 3:26).

WHAT DO YOU THINK?

What does Mary's irrational suggestion that she would return the body of Jesus to the tomb suggest to you about what to expect from someone who is grieving the loss of a loved one? Can we expect to reason with such a one? What should be the basis of our discussion with someone in grief?

Today's visual illustrates the link between the resurrection of Christ and Christian baptism.

II. JESUS' RESURRECTION AND BAPTISM (ROMANS 6:3-11)

At first glance, one might conclude that a lesson dealing with Jesus' resurrection combined with a discussion about baptism seems a rather strange arrangement. But as we examine it more carefully, the connection seems quite appropriate. The resurrection of Christ is much more than the occasion for new clothes and a spring vacation. Its implications touch every aspect of our lives as Christians. Why then should it not be involved in the action that brings us into a saving relationship with our Lord and marks our entrance into his church?

A. BURIED WITH CHRIST (vv. 3, 4)

3. Or don't you know that all of us who were baptized into Christ Jesus were baptized into his death?

The Jews had several observances that pictured significant events from their past. For example, the Passover reenacted their deliverance from Egypt, and the Feast of Tabernacles reenacted the wilderness wandering. The church has two such pantomimes: baptism and the Lord's Supper. In the Lord's Supper, the loaf and the cup depict Jesus' suffering and death. (See 1 Corinthians 11:26.) In a similar way, the burial of a penitent believer in the waters of baptism gives us a picture of Jesus' death, burial, and resurrection.

Paul here sounds like a teacher gently chiding his students to lead them to a deeper understanding. His readers who were Christians would certainly remember their own physical baptism. In the New Testament there is no such thing as an unbaptized Christian. Now Paul wants to guide them into a fuller meaning of that initiatory rite. Those *who were baptized into Christ Jesus were baptized into his death.* That is, in baptism they were able to appropriate to themselves the benefits that his death brought. Of course, these blessings are the result of God's grace. It would be foreign to Paul's teaching that we have studied thus far to suppose that baptism was some kind of a good work that purchased or earned one's redemption.

4. We were therefore buried with him through baptism into death in order that, just as Christ was raised from the dead through the glory of the Father, we too may live a new life.

The verb phrase *were . . . buried* is past tense; it looks backward to their own *baptism* that had already happened. Paul uses this visual image to move on to another important point. The *death* here is not the death of Christ, but that of the believer. Of course, he is not talking about physical death. He is referring to their death to sin, an idea he introduces in verse 2 when he says, "We died to sin." Completing the visual, Paul argues that death to sin is followed by a resurrection into a walk in newness of life, or to *live a new life.* Baptism is nothing but an empty ritual unless it is followed by a life that is so dramatically changed that it can be appropriately termed a resurrection.

SYMBOLS

An automobile, at least in the United States, is much more than transportation. Very often it is a symbol—it says something significant about its owner. A Rolls-Royce, for example, tells us that its owner is very wealthy (or is trying to appear wealthy). The new electric and hybrid gasoline/electric cars that are coming on the market may symbolize a driver's concern for pure air (or perhaps just her interest in avant-garde technology).

Other types of cars speak of their owners' personalities and/or eccentricities. For example, there are the "art cars" that appear in a Houston, Texas, parade every year. A recent parade featured a grocery cart powered by a motorcycle engine, a Volkswagen "bug" welded upside down on top of another, a Pontiac with thousands of

WHAT DO YOU THINK?

What "new life" have you found as a Christian? What about your life is different from before? What is better? What is the most challenging aspect of this new life?

fuzzy tennis balls hot-glued to its surfaces. Such symbols are capricious conveyors of silliness. Other symbols state profound truths: a Buick Riviera vividly pictured the evils of drunk driving with its crumpled front end covered by the huge tree it had apparently run into.

Christian baptism is more than a symbol; it is an action. But the act of being buried in the "watery grave" and lifted from it speaks eloquently about what is happening to us. It says we have accepted Christ's claim on our lives. Our baptism ushers us into a new relationship with God and empowers our lives with new purpose and direction.   —C. R. B.

B. RAISED WITH CHRIST (vv. 5-7)

5. If we have been united with him like this in his death, we will certainly also be united with him in his resurrection.

United with him . . . in his death does not mean that we physically die with Christ. Paul is not suggesting that we are to be nailed to a cross as Jesus was. Rather, in repentance and baptism we figuratively die to our former life of sin. Just as Christ's *resurrection* began a new life, so our baptismal resurrection is into a new life.

6. For we know that our old self was crucified with him so that the body of sin might be done away with, that we should no longer be slaves to sin—

Our old self refers to the sinner's former life, unregenerate and in rebellion against God. This former way of life is crucified, a striking way of saying that it must be totally abandoned. The sinful thoughts, the sinful acts, the rebellion against God must all be left behind. We no longer serve *sin*, we are not bound to sin with shackles like a pitiful slave.

7. . . . because anyone who has died has been freed from sin.

This verse must not be taken to mean that one who has been baptized is able to live without *sin*. This is certainly not what Paul had in mind, and such an interpretation does not square with our own observations. We know from experience that we have not been able to resist every temptation of sin in our own lives. *Freed from sin* is more accurately translated "justified from sin" in the *American Standard Version* of 1901. This conveys the idea that Christ through his death has canceled the penalty for sin, a theme that Paul has dealt with in earlier lessons.

C. ALIVE WITH CHRIST (vv. 8-11)

8. Now if we died with Christ, we believe that we will also live with him.

Paul restates in different words the position he takes in verse 4. The words *we believe* should not be understood in the sense that this is just his personal opinion. This statement is the very heart of the gospel and a glorious affirmation of the Easter message.

9, 10. For we know that since Christ was raised from the dead, he cannot die again; death no longer has mastery over him. The death he died, he died to sin once for all; but the life he lives, he lives to God.

Christ died *once*, but death could hold him only briefly. Whatever power death held over him has been destroyed. Once he came from the tomb alive, there was no way that death could ever again lay a claim upon him. *He lives to God* in the sense that he now sits at the right hand of God in the heavenly throne room.

11. In the same way, count yourselves dead to sin but alive to God in Christ Jesus.

Today's lesson text responds to the challenge that Paul raised in Romans 6:1—"Shall we go on sinning so that grace may increase?" His answer is a resounding "By no means!" Then in the following verses he shows how that position is false. Verse 11 sums up his argument.

WHAT DO YOU THINK?

How would you respond if someone challenged you by saying, "If your 'old self,' as you put it, has been 'crucified,' how come you still sin? Or do you think you are now perfect?"

WHAT DO YOU THINK?

Paul says we are to count ourselves "dead to sin but alive to God in Christ Jesus." How will you do that? What kind of behavior characterizes one who is "alive to God"?

DEAD TO SIN; ALIVE WITH CHRIST

Wade Clark Roof is a chronicler of religious trends and a professor of religion at the University of California/Santa Barbara. In 1993 he wrote about how baby boomers were "remaking American religion," in his terms. Several years later, he visited the "boomers" again to see how their quest for spirituality was coming along.

Roof found "a grand game of religious musical chairs" going on. About 70 percent of the seekers in his first survey are now strong believers, and about the same number of strong believers in the first survey are now seekers or doubters! Perhaps Roof's most important observation is that "the real story of American religious life in this half-century is the rise of a new sovereign self that defines and sets limits on the very meaning of the divine." In simple terms, what that means is that people believe they can remake God in their own image.

Christian baptism proclaims a far different message: those who follow Christ are remade in his image. Being crucified and risen with Christ to a new way of life means that we are to be dead to this world's values and standards. Our spirituality is to be patterned after what God has revealed, not after the changing fads of human invention.
—C. R. B.

CONCLUSION

A. HE HAS RISEN!

As the women made their way to Jesus' tomb in the darkness of early morning, they had a problem. How could they possibly move the stone that covered the entrance to the tomb? Although they were troubled by it, there were solutions to the problem. Sooner or later enough people would come to the tomb so that together they could move the stone.

When they arrived at the tomb, they had another problem. The tomb was open, solving their original problem, but Jesus' body was missing. Several possible solutions to this mystery may have occurred to them—his enemies may have stolen the body or friends may have moved the body to protect it. In any event, before long the mystery would be solved.

And solved it was! But they could not have anticipated the solution to the problems they had worried about. The tomb was open and Jesus was not in the tomb, for he had risen.

Our lives are often like this. We worry and are concerned about many problems, and we try to come up with possible solutions to them. Many, many of our worries would evaporate if only we realized that Jesus has risen and is alive today and is still working in our lives.

B. WE HAVE RISEN!

Every Christian has gone through the process of dying, dying to sin, that is, and has risen to walk in a new life. In that process, the old man has been crucified and buried in the watery grave of baptism. The old man, whether a sinner or a saint in his own eyes, has been left behind.

As new creations in Christ, we no longer live in sin. That does not mean that we do not commit sins. Rather, it means that we no longer live in sinful rebellion against our Lord. It means that we will be more loving toward both friend and enemy. It means that we will be more generous, more concerned about others. It means that we will be eager to share with others the joys we know in Christ.

To live such a life is, from the human point of view, impossible. We are weak, we have problems, we become discouraged. But we don't have to fight these battles alone. We have a Savior who has risen and is with us as we strive to live as persons who have risen to a new life.

Discovery Learning

This page contains an alternate lesson plan emphasizing learning activities. Classes desiring such student involvement will find these suggestions helpful. The next page is a reproducible activity page to further enhance discovery learning.

LEARNING GOALS

After this lesson each student will be able to:

1. Describe the details surrounding the resurrected Christ's appearance to Mary Magdalene, and how Paul linked Christian baptism with Jesus' resurrection.

2. Explain the impact that being "raised with Christ" should have on a Christian's daily conduct.

3. Identify one behavior or attitude that needs to be put to death in order to demonstrate the "new life" that should characterize a believer.

INTO THE LESSON

Wrap a large (empty) box in brown paper. Display it prominently before the class. As members are seated, ask them to guess what might be in the box. Write their guesses on the chalkboard.

Ask for a volunteer to unwrap and open the box. As the person is opening the box, ask class members for words that describe the feelings a person has when opening a plain, paper-wrapped box. Feelings could be excitement, apprehension, fear, wonder, or others.

When the box is open, it will be seen to be empty. Show the box to the class. Ask for emotions that are expressed now: disappointment, shock, disbelief, surprise, and others. Say, "This activity reminds us that things are not always as they appear. Today we remember the empty tomb of Christ and how that event has changed history—and has changed our own lives, as well!"

INTO THE WORD

Develop a brief outline using the introductory remarks of the commentary. Both "He's Different" and the "Lesson Background" (page 269) will give you useful information. Have two volunteers read the Scripture texts: one for John 20:1, 11-17 and one for Romans 6:3-11.

Divide the class into at least three groups of no more than six individuals. If your class is larger, give the third assignment to the extra groups.

Group One is to prepare a skit to relate the details of John 20:1-17. Encourage the group to be creative. You may need to bring props to class, such as strips of cloth and white robes.

Group Two will need pens or pencils and copies of the reproducible activity "Details, Details" from the next page. This group will arrange the events of resurrection morning in chronological order.

Group Three will need pens or pencils and a handout as described below for this activity. They are to read Romans 6:3-11 and develop an interview with Paul on the resurrection significance of Christian baptism. The handout you provide will have the following interviewer's questions; the group will use the text to write Paul's answers.

Interviewer: Paul, how is the resurrection of Jesus connected to a person's being baptized? (Romans 6:3, 5)

Paul:

Interviewer: Who raised Jesus to life? Who raises us to life? How? (Romans 6:4)

Paul:

Interviewer: How are we different because we have new life? (Romans 6:6, 7)

Paul:

Interviewer: How should the Christian view sin and obedience to God? (Romans 6:7, 11)

Paul:

The lesson commentary is helpful for these answers. Let the Scriptures show the students the importance of their own baptism. Paul uses baptism as a "marker" for the Christian, a point from which he or she is committed to live a different life and lifestyle.

INTO LIFE

Say, "Because Christ has come into our lives, we are new. We no longer walk in our old ways. What are some of the behaviors or attitudes put to death by a Christian in his or her new life?" List the students' responses on the board or on a poster. Expect a variety of answers, such as jealousy, greed, lying, self-centeredness, and more.

Distribute copies of the reproducible activity "Put to Death" from the next page. Ask each student to choose one or more behaviors or attitudes that he or she needs to "put to death" and to write that on the activity page. (Students are not limited to the problem areas listed earlier. If some of them have problems with issues not listed, they should choose those. They will not have to reveal what they write.)

Ask the class to read in unison Romans 6:4-7. Then have each person write "Romans 6:4-7" over the area written on his or her page. Provide a wastebasket for each person to cast that sin away after tearing the page into pieces. Have a closing prayer and then have someone lead the class in singing the first stanza of "Amazing Grace."

Details, Details

From John 20:1, 11-17, number the following in order from first to last event. (Answer key at the bottom of the page.)

___ a. Jesus appears to Mary.
___ b. Mary speaks in Aramaic.
___ c. Mary cries.
___ d. Mary comes to the tomb in the dark.
___ e. The angels speak to Mary.
___ f. The disciples return home.
___ g. Jesus tells Mary to return to the brothers.
___ h. Jesus calls Mary by name.

Put to Death

Read Romans 6:3-11 and Colossians 2:9-15. On the tombstone below, write your name. On the cross, write some of your sins Christ has taken away.

Raised to Life!

How will you bring glory to God through your new life?

The Power of the Gospel
Unit 2: Living by Faith
(Lessons 6-9)

ANTICIPATE GOD'S GLORY

LESSON 6

WHY TEACH THIS LESSON?

The world in which we live is characterized by sharp class and economic "divides." On TV we can see wealthy people getting out of their limousines and walking past the homeless and destitute. Larry King, on his CNN talk show, recently asked a movie star what it was like to visit the squalor of a Balkan refugee camp in the morning, and (with the help of a jet airplane) be back at his luxury hotel suite in the afternoon; the individual candidly replied that the change was "surreal." Well-to-do Christians in the United States worry about how to put their children through college, while poverty-stricken Christians in other parts of the world worry about how to keep their children from being sold into slavery.

Both believers and unbelievers are well aware of such "divides." Sometimes the unbeliever will use this reality to question God's goodness or justice—or even his very existence. Today's lesson helps the believer avoid the trap of such futile thinking by encouraging us to direct our gaze toward that which is of ultimate importance: the future and the eternity it holds for us.

INTRODUCTION

A. SINKERS AND FLOATS

A fish net, in order to be useful, must be more than just a net. For one thing, along the bottom edge of the net must be weights or sinkers to hold the net down in the water. Otherwise the bottom edge would float to the top, making the net useless. The weights are like the tribulations that come into the life of a Christian. These keep the Christian humble and prevents him or her from drifting uselessly about.

A net must also have floats. These keep the net from sinking to the bottom where it would become entangled with debris, snagged, and torn. The floats correspond to Christian hope. Without hope the Christian would be dragged down by tribulations and despair. Thus both tribulations and hope are necessary for the successful and victorious Christian life.

B. LESSON BACKGROUND

The eighth chapter of Romans is one of the most popular chapters in the New Testament, and for good reason. First of all, it contains profound theological teachings. But perhaps even more important to the Romans when they received it was the hope it offered as they began to face persecutions. They had not yet felt the full impact of these persecutions as Christians in other areas had, but soon the rage of Nero would fall upon them. When that happened, they would need all the hope that was available to sustain them through those trials.

I. THE CHRISTIAN'S HOPE (ROMANS 8:18-28)

A. HOPE AND SUFFERING (v. 18)

18. I consider that our present sufferings are not worth comparing with the glory that will be revealed in us.

DEVOTIONAL READING:
ROMANS 8:1-11
BACKGROUND SCRIPTURE:
ROMANS 8
PRINTED TEXT:
ROMANS 8:18-28, 31b-34, 38, 39

LESSON AIMS

After participating in this lesson, students will be able to:

Apr
7

1. Summarize Paul's description in this text of a Christian's perspective on the future.

2. Contrast the believer's hope with conditions that might seem to challenge that hope.

3. Think of seemingly hopeless circumstances that they (or people they know) are facing, and affirm a renewed hope that Christ is working in those situations.

KEY VERSE

I consider that our present sufferings are not worth comparing with the glory that will be revealed in us. —Romans 8:18

LESSON 6 NOTES

Suffering is an inescapable fact of human existence. We see overwhelming evidence of it in our own lives and in the world around us. The fact of suffering in this life is probably the most perplexing problem that Christians have to deal with. If only the wicked suffered, there would be no problem, for we could explain it on the basis that they are getting their just deserts. But what about the suffering of the innocent, especially little babies and children? Job struggled with this problem, but could find no easy intellectual answer for it. He finally was forced to accept God's actions on faith, realizing that God in his infinite wisdom operates in areas and in ways beyond human understanding.

Paul does not attempt to deal with this problem on the theological or philosophical level. His purpose in this verse is to give his readers hope that sees beyond the present suffering. The *sufferings* of the *present*, though they are painful and discouraging, are nothing compared *with the glory that will be revealed*. In a feeble way, we see this in the training of an athlete, who undergoes intense agony in preparation for the contest. Long hours of practice, exhausting physical activities, and strict discipline are endured only because the athlete sees a victory in the future. But even an Olympic gold medal, bringing fame and fortune, is nothing compared with the future glory that awaits the victorious Christian.

B. HOPE FOR REDEMPTION (vv. 19-23)

19. The creation waits in eager expectation for the sons of God to be revealed.

Paul uses personification here to emphasize his point, giving to *the creation* the feelings and aspirations of mankind. Sin has brought suffering into the human world, but sin also has had an impact on nature around us.

The *eager expectation*, or anticipation, of the creation involves some kind of deliverance (v. 21). Some scholars take this to mean that the earth will not be destroyed in the event Peter describes (2 Peter 3:10-13), but merely purified. Others believe the "new heaven" and "new earth" (Revelation 21:1) will be a replacement of the current order of things, not only a recreation of the old. Whichever form the deliverance will take, it will happen in conjunction with God's glory being revealed in *the sons of God* (v. 18).

20. For the creation was subjected to frustration, not by its own choice, but by the will of the one who subjected it, in hope. . . .

One of the purposes of *the creation* was to provide a place for people to dwell in harmony with God. Sin disrupted this harmony, and creation was subjected to *frustration*, since its purpose is not being realized. Whether we take man as the one who *subjected* the creation to frustration (by his sin) or God (in response to sin), the effect is the same. But there is *hope*, as verse 21 describes.

21. . . . that the creation itself will be liberated from its bondage to decay and brought into the glorious freedom of the children of God.

The *bondage to decay* is Paul's description of the result of sin's entering the world. Corruption, death, and decay—and all that goes with them—are results of sin. At the resurrection, this bondage to death will end (Revelation 21:4). Of course, this liberty is only for *the children of God*; the wicked will endure the second death (Revelation 21:8).

22. We know that the whole creation has been groaning as in the pains of childbirth right up to the present time.

Paul continues his personification of *creation*. The creation's anticipation of the resurrection is as intense and as productive as a woman's labor pains. It looks forward, not only to the end of the pain, but to a wonderful new life. In this statement Paul seems to be alluding to one of the curses that came into the world as a result of the fall (Genesis 3:16).

WHAT DO YOU THINK?

How can we keep the view of victory at the forefront during suffering and difficulty, and how does our future outlook about God's goodness affect our present reaction to suffering?

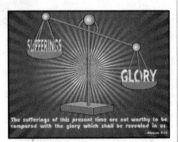

Visual for lesson 6. Today's visual illustrates today's Key Verse, Romans 8:18. Display it as you begin the lesson.

WHAT DO YOU THINK?

What, if any, is the connection between ecology and faith? How might the church's evangelistic efforts be affected by its views on environmental issues?

A "Downside" to Everything

How do you protect a city from disaster without messing up the environment? That is a dilemma faced by the citizens of Laguna Beach, California, where winter rains and mild spring weather promote a lush growth of weeds and brush in the coastal foothills, which then turns into tinder in the dry heat of summer and fall. In 1993 this dry growth became fuel for a wildfire that consumed 14,000 acres and destroyed 440 homes. Since the fire, the city has used goats—six hundred of them—to protect the city by eating up the vegetation that would otherwise cover a two-hundred- to three-hundred-foot-wide band of earth that surrounds the city.

The benefits are the removal of potential fuel for fires and economy. The goats do the job at about one-fifth the cost of having human crews do it. The problem is that the goats will eat anything! Whether a noxious weed or an endangered species of plant, it doesn't matter. Also, in the natural process of creating "fertilizer," they deposit weed seeds indiscriminately from one canyon to another, upsetting the natural ecological balance.

It seems that even our best efforts to "subdue" the earth often end up destroying some part of it and upsetting the balance of God's creation. The same is true in the moral world. Even when we try to do what is right, there are sometimes side effects that bring hurt and pain to others. It is true as Paul says: the whole creation *does* groan in pain to this very day because of our sins. —C. R. B.

23. Not only so, but we ourselves, who have the firstfruits of the Spirit, groan inwardly as we wait eagerly for our adoption as sons, the redemption of our bodies.

Even after the coming of Christ, we share in the suffering that was brought on the world as a result of Adam's sin. In the physical body, for example, we suffer many diseases and much pain. But this physical pain is nothing in comparison with the frustration and mental anguish we suffer because we are a part of the creation ruined by sin.

The idea of *firstfruits* was a prominent one in God's dealing with his people under the Old Covenant. When a crop was harvested, the first and best part of it was carefully kept and offered to God as a thank offering (Exodus 23:16-19; Leviticus 23:10). Paul uses the idea here to describe the Christian's relationship to the Holy *Spirit*. At baptism one receives the "gift of the Holy Spirit" (Acts 2:38). But this indwelling of the Holy Spirit is only a token of the blessings we shall know. In the meantime, we *groan inwardly as we wait* for the completion or our transformation, which is *the redemption of our bodies*. This refers to the resurrection, when this mortal body must put on immortality (1 Corinthians 15:53).

C. Hope and Patience (vv. 24, 25)

24. For in this hope we were saved. But hope that is seen is no hope at all. Who hopes for what he already has?

Since verse 18, Paul has been focusing on the believer's *hope* in salvation. We have hope of an end to suffering and revelation of glory (v. 18). Creation itself anticipates (or hopes for) that blessed event (v. 19). In fact, the creation's subjection to futility, at the time sin entered it, was done in hope of a deliverance from that futile state (vv. 20-22). We ourselves, having received the Holy Spirit as a "deposit" (Epheisians 1:14) of the blessings to come, share that same longing. This verse, then, sums up this line of thinking: *for in this hope we were saved!*

Having laid the foundation, Paul now builds on it an exhortation for patience. Obviously, what one already possesses he does not need to hope for. Even though we *were saved* (or have been saved), we do not yet possess our final salvation. There are yet trials to be faced patiently before that glory is revealed in us (v. 18).

What Do You Think?

How does the Christian's longing for God's adoption change with physical and/or spiritual maturity, and what effect do physical events have on that longing?

25. But if we hope for what we do not yet have, we wait for it patiently.

Patience is not a common virtue in a "hurry up" society. Even Christians, so often caught up in "business," fail to work at developing patience, even though it is part of the "fruit of the Spirit" (Galatians 5:22). Paul knew that Christians would soon be facing the wrath of the Roman government, and he urged them to suffer *patiently* through these persecutions, relying on their *hope* to sustain them. Most of us today do not face the kind of persecutions that those in the early church faced—though in many parts of the world religious persecution remains a fact of life. Whatever level of suffering we face, we need to display patience born of hope.

D. HOPE IN THE HOLY SPIRIT (vv. 26-28)

26, 27. In the same way, the Spirit helps us in our weakness. We do not know what we ought to pray for, but the Spirit himself intercedes for us with groans that words cannot express. And he who searches our hearts knows the mind of the Spirit, because the Spirit intercedes for the saints in accordance with God's will.

In this sin-tainted world we are weak; we are limited by the flesh. That is the reason we so earnestly yearn for the resurrection and our redemption bodies. We are so limited in the current order that we do not even know *what we ought to pray for.* Even in those situations in life that leave us without words to express our deepest desires, God has given us the Holy *Spirit,* who *intercedes for us* before God. Note that this passage does not say the Spirit takes our groans, as if we cannot express ourselves in words. It says the Spirit makes intercession *with groans*—it is the Spirit who groans before God to communicate what *words cannot express.* Of course, Jesus Christ is also our intercessor before God (Romans 8:34; 1 Timothy 2:5, 6), but the Spirit is our intercessor in the special matter of prayer.

28. And we know that in all things God works for the good of those who love him, who have been called according to his purpose.

Many people quote this as one of their favorite verses, and rightly so. Properly understood, the verse offers hope for the Christian in all kinds of situations. There are some differences among several modern versions in this verse. The differences deal with the subject of the verb *works.* The *King James Version* and some modern versions have *all things* as the subject, while other versions have *God* as the subject. Either way, it is clear that God is the one who *works for the good of those who love him.*

God is the absolute Sovereign of the universe and nothing can occur that lies outside his will. As a part of his permissive will, he has granted humanity some freedom. We have used this freedom in many tragic ways, even defying God. Our acts of rebellion often lead to suffering. Sometimes even good people make bad decisions that lead to suffering. God could prevent this suffering, but to do so he would have to deny human freedom. Even so, God can use the most arrogant rebellion or the most tragic mistakes to achieve his ultimate purposes.

We should not understand the words *for the good* to mean that the Christian is assured of material blessings or even joy and peace in all undertakings in this life. Across the centuries, Christians have suffered persecution and even martyrdom. But their suffering has led to the growth of Christianity and the preservation of the faith for modern believers. Only if we understand this verse in terms of God's ultimate purposes can we find comfort in it during our own trials. The *good* of verse 28 must be linked with the "glory" of verse 18.

IN HOPE OF SOMETHING GOOD

When smallpox was brought to the New World by Spanish explorers, it killed more than half the populations of Mexico and Haiti and killed thousands of the

WHAT DO YOU THINK?

When we can't adequately verbalize feelings to God, due to spiritual problems or discouragement, why should we continue to pray?

indigenous people of what is now the United States. Even into modern times, smallpox killed as many as 30 percent of those it affected, and survivors often were left with serious, permanent scarring. However, the process of vaccination—using a minute amount of the deadly virus to trigger the body into developing a natural immunity—led to eventual eradication of the disease. By intelligent use of a very bad organism, untold good came about. The last case of smallpox anywhere in the world was recorded in 1977, and most medical stocks of the virus and the vaccine have since been destroyed.

The two remaining known stocks of the virus—kept by the Russian and United States governments—were scheduled to be destroyed in 1999. However, this did not happen, partly in hope that the virus might someday be used to create vaccines against other, similar scourges of the human race. It may be that other, unknown good things can be developed from this deadly scourge. This is what God has promised us regarding all things in life: even in the midst of trial, God will provide *something* that is good and provides hope for his people.   —C. R. B.

II. THE CHRISTIAN'S SECURITY (ROMANS 8:31b-34, 38, 39)

A. GOD IS FOR US (vv. 31b, 32)

31b. If God is for us, who can be against us?

The word *if* does not express uncertainty. This verse would be better understood if it were translated "since *God is for us.*" Since God is indeed for us, *who can be against us?* Of course, there are many persons and forces that oppose Christianity. But this opposition cannot succeed. Paul's question may be paraphrased, "Who, with any hope of success, can be against us?" The obvious answer is "No one!"

32. He who did not spare his own Son, but gave him up for us all—how will he not also, along with him, graciously give us all things?

God has already shown that he will stop at nothing—not even the death of *his own Son*—to save us. We can be assured that he will continue to *give us all things* we need for continuing to walk with him.

B. CHRIST IS FOR US (vv. 33, 34)

33. Who will bring any charge against those whom God has chosen? It is God who justifies.

Verse 33 repeats the concept of verse 31 with the image of a courtroom scene. The enemies of the cross have brought charges against Christians. Of course, in some situations these charges are true. Christians have often sinned and not lived up to the high standards God has set for us. "All have sinned and fall short of the glory of God" (3:23). But our case is not hopeless; *it is God who justifies.* Since God, the "Supreme Court," as it were, has rendered a "not guilty" verdict, what lower court can bring any charges?

34. Who is he that condemns? Christ Jesus, who died—more than that, who was raised to life—is at the right hand of God and is also interceding for us.

Romans 8 began with the declaration, "Therefore, there is now no condemnation for those who are in Christ Jesus." Here Paul reaffirms that proposition, based on the work of *Christ,* who *is interceding for us.* We are immune from condemnation, not by our own goodness, but through Christ who *died* and *was raised to life.* He now stands *at the right hand of God,* pleading our case.

C. NOTHING CAN BEAT US (vv. 38, 39)

38, 39. For I am convinced that neither death nor life, neither angels nor demons, neither the present nor the future, nor any powers, neither height nor depth, nor

DAILY BIBLE READINGS

Monday, Apr. 1—The Greater Glory (2 Corinthians 3:1-11)

Tuesday, Apr. 2—Transformed From Glory to Glory (2 Corinthians 3:12-18)

Wednesday, Apr. 3—The Power Belongs to God (2 Corinthians 4:1-15)

Thursday, Apr. 4—Walk According to the Spirit (Romans 8:1-8)

Friday, Apr. 5—The Spirit Is Life (Romans 8:9-17)

Saturday, Apr. 6—Glory About to Be Revealed (Romans 8:18-30)

Sunday, Apr. 7—More Than Conquerors (Romans 8:31-39)

HOW TO SAY IT

intercession. IN-ter-SEH-shun.
Nero. NEE-ro or NIR-oh.
Tertullian. Tur-TULL-yun.

anything else in all creation, will be able to separate us from the love of God that is in Christ Jesus our Lord.

Paul concludes his argument with a ringing affirmation of his own faith, a faith that allowed him to face persecution and even death without flinching. He lists a variety of things that singly or together seek to *separate us from God's love.* Yet none of these things is able to stand between God and us.

Paul invites us to share with him in that faith. It is vital that we do so! It is true that no external power or entity can separate us from God's love. But we, like the prodigal son (Luke 15:11-32), can choose to walk away from the Father and to sever our relationship with him. (See Hebrews 10:19-39.)

CONCLUSION

A devout Christian farmer lived alongside a neighbor who was an outspoken unbeliever. The Christian always attended church Sunday morning, Sunday evening, and at midweek evening service. He refused to do any unnecessary work on Sunday.

His neighbor, on the other hand, paid no attention to Sunday or any other religious holidays, working whenever the weather was right. As a result, he was able to get his spring plowing and planting done earlier, and as a result his crops were ahead of those of his Christian neighbor. When the wheat harvest came, the unbeliever was able to get in his crop without any weather problems. The Christian, refusing to work on Sunday, lost part of his wheat crop because of rain. His soybeans and corn yielded less than the neighbor's, too, because the farmer had been late in planting them.

Later in November the two met in the local grain elevator where they were bringing their crops to sell. The unbeliever boasted of his bumper crops, and he sneered at the Christian: "Your God wasn't much help, was he? Without any help from God, I had much better crops than you did."

"Yes, you're right," admitted the Christian. "You had a better harvest than I did. But you must remember one thing: God doesn't balance the books in November."

Precisely! God balances the Lamb's book of life in eternity, not in November. But that may be a difficult truth to live with when we suffer persecution or lose out in the business world because of our trust in God.

Most of us have suffered very little for our Christian faith. In fact, in many situations we have enjoyed benefits and blessings, even material blessings, because we are Christians. But this has not always been true. In the early years of the church, Christians suffered imprisonment, exile, and even martyrdom at the hands of the pagan Roman government. And yet under these trying conditions the church continued to grow. The Christian writer Tertullian (c. A.D. 160–215) observed that "the blood of the martyrs is the seed of the church." When their blood was spilled, others sprang up to take their places.

Or think of that little band of Pilgrims who landed in Massachusetts in 1620. During that first terrible winter nearly half their number succumbed to hunger and disease. Yet they refused to give in to suffering, and those who survived gave thanks to God the following year for the meager blessings they had received. They recognized that the sufferings of the present were "not worth comparing with the glory" that God promised in the next life.

All of us are likely to experience suffering in this life, sometimes innocently and sometimes even because we are Christians. We can either react violently against it or we can accept it with a sense of triumph, trusting that God can use our response to it as an example for those who will come after us.

WHAT DO YOU THINK?

What impact on the church's heart for evangelism should take place when we realize that the only thing able to separate us from God is our own reluctance?

PRAYER

We pray, merciful Father, that we may escape suffering and disappointments in our life. But when suffering does come, grant us the strength to accept it courageously. May the verses we have studied today give us the courage we need in difficult times. In our Master's name we pray. Amen.

THOUGHT TO REMEMBER

"O God our help in ages past, Our hope for years to come, Our shelter from the stormy blast, And our eternal home."

—Isaac Watts

Discovery Learning

This page contains an alternate lesson plan emphasizing learning activities. Classes desiring such student involvement will find these suggestions helpful. The next page is a reproducible activity page to further enhance discovery learning.

LEARNING GOALS

After this lesson students will be able to:

1. Summarize Paul's description in this text of a Christian's perspective on the future.

2. Contrast the believer's hope with conditions that might seem to challenge that hope.

3. Think of seemingly hopeless circumstances that they (or people they know) are facing, and affirm a renewed hope that Christ is working in those situations.

INTO THE LESSON

Our introduction to this week's lesson will require research on your part, or you may assign this to a student who shows particular interest. Look for articles that make predictions for the future. Good sources may be a public library, the Internet, or the local newspaper. Many of these articles appear near the beginning of each year.

Bring several of these articles to class. Ask your students to form groups of three to five and read the articles. Ask, "What do these articles have in common?" (Most will recognize that they are predictive.) Ask, "What is their view of the future?" (Most of the articles will be about a better future that the author hopes will come true.) Ask, "How believable is each?" After a few responses, ask, "Why do the answers vary?" (Reasons may include the possibility of the prediction's happening, the believability or trustworthiness of the author, and the reputation of the newspaper or magazine.)

Say, "Each of those answers is important to us in evaluating the reliability of the view of the future. Each of us can be excited or discouraged by our outlook on the future." At this point, present the Lesson Background.

INTO THE WORD

Divide your class into groups of four to six students. You will need at least three groups. Otherwise, choose the activities you will use.

Give *Group One* sheets of blank 8-1/2" x 11" white paper, pencils, and colored markers. Ask them to read Romans 8:18-28, 31-39 and draw a four- or five-scene "cartoon" for verses 18-21, 22-25, 26-28, 31-34, 35-39. Stick figures and elementary drawings are great! (This is also in *NIV® Bible Student.*)

Group Two is to paraphrase the same sections of Scripture. Each person will need blank paper and a pen or pencil. Have the students rewrite the Scripture passages in their own words and understanding, but have them take care not to change Paul's original intent.

Group Three will answer the following questions concerning the text:

1. According to Paul, what has been the effect on the creation of mankind's sin?

2. How does the creation (as well as we ourselves) "groan" while waiting for the future?

3. What does the Spirit do for us?

4. How does verse 28 give confidence for the future?

5. What do verses 29 and 30 say about God's work on our behalf?

6. How did God show that he is unequivocally on our side?

7. How do verses 37-39 give us assurance?

Allow each group to give a brief description of its projects or findings. Place the "cartoons" around the room for the class to enjoy.

In addition to the activities listed above (or in place of one of them), distribute the reproducible page that follows and have the class/group members complete the first activity, "The Future."

INTO LIFE

Say: "While Paul gives us strong reasons for facing and anticipating the future, many things today threaten to rob us of that anticipation. Search these newspapers and magazines for articles that threaten us. Be ready to tell the class your concerns and how Romans 8 helps you."

Distribute newspapers or magazines you have collected. (Individuals will remain in their groups.) After a few minutes, ask each group member to tell the person on his or her left or right why this article is threatening and how Romans 8 helps one to overcome any fear of the future. After the groups share, ask for one or two volunteers to present their case to the class.

Be ready to share a difficult situation you or someone close to you is facing. After you have shared, repeat Romans 8:31, 37-39. Have the class members turn back to the person they did the neighbor-nudge with in the preceding exercise. Now they will share a circumstance and repeat the verses. After all have shared, distribute copies of the reproducible activity "Hold On!" from the next page (or refer students to it if they already have it). Allow time for students to respond; then have a volunteer close in prayer for the class.

The Future

Read Romans 8:18-39. When you fill in the blanks below, you will find the result of knowing Christ for your future.

1. Nothing can _____ us from the love of God (v. 39).
2. Those God _____ he also predestined (v. 29).
3. Jesus' place among brothers (v. 29).
4. Bible word for "process of buying back" (v. 23).
5. What God does in all things (v. 28).
6. The One who intercedes for us (v. 34).
7. How God brings us into his family (v. 23).
8. What the Spirit does for us in our weakness (v. 26).
9. What will be revealed in us (v. 18).
10. We are called according to God's _____ (v. 28).
11. What God does for his chosen one (v. 33).

1. ___ ___ ___ ___ | ___ ___ ___ ___
2. ___ ___ ___ | ___ ___ ___ ___
3. ___ ___ ___ ___ ___ ___ ___ |
4. ___ | ___ ___ ___ ___ ___ ___ ___
5. ___ | ___ ___ ___
6. ___ ___ ___ ___ ___ | ___ ___ ___
7. ___ | ___ ___ ___ ___ ___
8. ___ | ___ ___ ___
9. ___ ___ | ___ ___
10. | ___ ___ ___ ___ ___
11. ___ ___ ___ ___ ___ ___ | ___

Hold On!

Write below one of the reasons from this lesson that you can "hold on" for the future.

The Power of the Gospel

Unit 2: *Living by Faith*

(Lessons 6-9)

PROCLAIM THE GOSPEL

WHY TEACH THIS LESSON?

In the United States, about seventy-eight million people—more than one quarter of the population—were born between 1946 and 1964. As this "Baby Boomer generation" began to age, it came also to be known also as the "sandwich generation" because of three financial challenges: ensuring long-term care of aging parents, funding their own future retirements, and paying (or saving up) for the college education of their children. As Boomers began to take seriously their need to provide for their own retirements, "sandwich" became a painfully apt description as they began to feel the financial "bite" from the other two directions.

But where does support for proclaiming the gospel fit into this picture? This year, many will graduate from Bible college and seminary with a strong sense of God's call to some mission field, only to discover a "wall of indifference" when attempting to raise support from Boomers in local churches. Perhaps you will have some of these Boomers (and others) in your class today who need to rethink their personal financial priorities in light of this pressing need.

INTRODUCTION

A. THE O'S OF MISSIONS

The missionary imperative is at the heart of the Christian faith. As he closed his earthly ministry, Christ issued the Great Commission, sending his followers into the whole world with the gospel message. Paul in today's lesson text pays tribute to those who carry that message: "How beautiful are the feet of those who bring good news!" They may carry the good news across oceans to distant places in the world or across the street to their neighbors. These are the "GO" missionaries.

There are others who, for one reason or another, cannot go. We might not even think of them as missionaries at all. However, they are the "rope holders" for those who do go. Their financial and prayer support are essential to the "GO" missionaries. It would be appropriate to call them "CO" missionaries.

Unfortunately, there are some church members who are unwilling either to go as missionaries or to support missionaries. They either do not understand that those outside of Christ are lost without the gospel, or they do not understand the Great Commission. Such people might well be called "NO" missionaries. The imperative of the Great Commission demands that we move the "NO" missionaries into becoming "CO" missionaries, and that we continually challenge the "CO" missionaries into becoming "GO" missionaries.

B. LESSON BACKGROUND

In Romans 9 Paul discusses God's relations with Israel. Although God had blessed the Israelites and chosen them to become a blessing to all of mankind, they had often rebelled and turned away from him. God had endured their rebellion "with great patience," but he also warned through some of the prophets that he would offer his blessings to the Gentiles, and that only a remnant of Israel would be saved. The Jews had tried to attain righteousness through works of the law, not realizing that the law was weak toward the flesh and that the law looked

DEVOTIONAL READING:
ROMANS 11:1-6

BACKGROUND SCRIPTURE:
ROMANS 10

PRINTED TEXT:
ROMANS 10:1-17

LESSON AIMS

After this lesson each student will be able to:

1. Summarize the pattern of spreading the gospel as Paul explains it in Romans 10.

2. Tell why every Christian must consider himself or herself a "herald" of the good news.

3. Become more involved with the church's or the class's efforts to take the gospel to others, both locally and globally.

Apr
14

KEY VERSES

How can they believe in the one of whom they have not heard? And how can they hear without someone preaching to them? And how can they preach unless they are sent?
—Romans 10:14, 15

LESSON 7 NOTES

WHAT DO YOU THINK?

What significance do you see in Paul's combination of "heart's desire" and "prayer" regarding his burden for the unsaved?

forward to its fulfillment in Christ. Most of the Jews had rejected Christ; thus to them he became a "a stone that causes men to stumble and a rock that makes them fall" (Romans 9:33).

I. SALVATION FOR JEWS (ROMANS 10:1-4)

A. PAUL DESIRED IT (v. 1)

1. Brothers, my heart's desire and prayer to God for the Israelites is that they may be saved.

    Brothers is generic. It does not refer exclusively to men, but to fellow Christians. Some recent translations render it "brothers and sisters." In the previous chapter Paul discussed the plight of the Jews, or *Israelites*. Because they had hoped for salvation through works of the law, they had rejected the message of Christ. Those who continued to reject Christ would remain in their lost condition, but those who accepted God's grace in Jesus could yet *be saved*. Any Christian with unbelievers among his or her family has shared Paul's ardent *desire*.

B. THEY WERE MISSING IT (vv. 2, 3)

2. For I can testify about them that they are zealous for God, but their zeal is not based on knowledge.

    Paul was well qualified to testify about the *zeal* of the Jews. Only a few years before he wrote this letter, he had been one of the most *zealous* of them. His zeal had driven him to seek out and persecute Christians in Jerusalem and even led him to journey to Damascus to seek out Christians there. While there was no question about the Jews' zeal, it was *not based on knowledge*. Their zeal for the law caused them to close their minds to the fulfillment of the law—God's offer of salvation through the Lord Jesus Christ.

    One of the biggest problems of the church today is that many of its members lack zeal. They may attend church services regularly and even contribute financially to the work of the church, but they have no passion for the Lord's work. Another problem is the presence of people with misdirected zeal. Such people are adamant about music styles, time of services, or even the color of the carpeting, but they seem to be ignorant of the church's first priority: winning the lost to Jesus Christ. Occasionally, however, we meet a Christian who has both knowledge and zeal. How refreshing that is!

3. Since they did not know the righteousness that comes from God and sought to establish their own, they did not submit to God's righteousness.

    God's righteousness comes by accepting his gracious offer of salvation through his Son, Jesus Christ. At the time Paul wrote, most Jews probably had not heard the gospel. But some, especially among the leaders, had heard the good news and had deliberately rejected it.

    Through the long history of the church, many have substituted *their own* versions of *righteousness* for God's righteousness revealed in the Scriptures. Satan has tempted many of us to insist that our interpretation of the Scriptures represents God's true righteousness, and in our pride we try to force our views on others. The divided state of Christendom today bears painful testimony to the effectiveness of Satan's clever divisive tactic.

STILL SEARCHING

    Jewish people still keep the *Seder*—the Passover feast—as a means of remembering what God did for Israel when he freed them from Egyptian slavery. Christians recognize this feast as a meal that prophetically pointed to Christ—God's "Passover" for all peoples.

Religious Jews still zealously keep the feast, but strangely, so do many "secular" Jews. In a survey conducted recently in Los Angeles—which has a large Jewish population—one-fourth said that religion was of little or no significance in their lives. Two-thirds said they were not members of any synagogue, yet they keep the *Seder!* Rabbi Lawrence Goldmark, a rabbinical leader in Southern California, says of Jews who have no place for God in their lives, "Taking God out of Passover is like taking Jesus out of Easter—what are you left with?" What they are left with is a monument to their own attempts to be righteous. One unbeliever sees Passover this way: "The importance . . . is the effort and strength of people to overcome adversity by dint of their own talents and will." How tragic to miss God's redemption because of a zeal without knowledge! The same can be said of Christians whose mistaken pride in their good works causes them to miss the point of God's grace. —C. R. B.

C. CHRIST SECURED IT (v. 4)

4. Christ is the end of the law so that there may be righteousness for everyone who believes.

The word here translated *end* can mean either "fulfillment" or "termination." Each seems appropriate in this case. Jesus' critics on occasion accused him of breaking or destroying *the law*. His response was that he had not "come to abolish the Law or the Prophets," but "to fulfill them" (Matthew 5:17). The law set forth an absolute standard, which no one could live up to until Jesus came. His sinless life met every requirement of the law and thus fulfilled it.

Jesus also brought an *end* to the law (Colossians 2:14). At the heart of the law was the concept that one could gain salvation by good works. But no one could live up to the requirements of the law, nor could all the elaborate sacrifices required under the law atone for one single sin. All that these sacrifices could do was to look forward to the coming of the perfect sacrifice, Jesus Christ. Thus the death of Christ brought an end to the whole legalistic system of sacrifices for sins. Instead, our justification comes through faith in him.

II. GOD'S PLAN OF SALVATION (ROMANS 10:5-13)

A. NOT BY WORKS OF THE LAW (v. 5)

5. Moses describes in this way the righteousness that is by the law: "The man who does these things will live by them."

Paraphrasing Leviticus 18:5, Paul shows that one who chooses to live *by the law* must keep it perfectly. But since this is humanly impossible, the law, which served many valuable purposes, could not bring salvation from sins.

B. NOT BY MIGHTY DEEDS (vv. 6, 7)

6, 7. But the righteousness that is by faith says: "Do not say in your heart, 'Who will ascend into heaven?'" (that is, to bring Christ down) "or 'Who will descend into the deep?'" (that is, to bring Christ up from the dead).

Paul paraphrases Deuteronomy 30:11-14 and applies it to the gospel. Since the law looked to *righteousness* through works, some may have supposed that some mighty, heroic deed could accomplish what lesser deeds could not. This was not true under the law, and it certainly is not true under grace. There is an element of pride in the idea that one can somehow earn salvation. But there was no place for pride under the law, and there certainly is no place for it under grace.

C. BY FAITH (vv. 8-11)

8. But what does it say? "The word is near you; it is in your mouth and in your heart," that is, the word of faith we are proclaiming.

If salvation cannot be attained by storming the ramparts of Heaven or descending into the grave, how then may it be gained? The answer is surprisingly simple. It is as near as one's *mouth* and *heart*. *The word of faith*, when it is proclaimed by the mouth and taken into the heart, is the way of salvation. We are reminded of the experience of Elijah, who thought God would reveal himself in a mighty wind, or an earthquake, or in fire. Instead, God spoke to him through a "gentle whisper" (1 Kings 19:11, 12). In the same way, God's salvation comes to us, not through some awesome experience, but through the simple preaching of the gospel. The proclamation of the good news does not depend on a few high-powered proclaimers on a few special occasions, but can be shared every day by every Christian.

WHAT DO YOU THINK?

What are some examples of the saving power of God's Word preached by ordinary people? What responsibility do we have to join in that act of "preaching"?

9, 10. *That if you confess with your mouth, "Jesus is Lord," and believe in your heart that God raised him from the dead, you will be saved. For it is with your heart that you believe and are justified, and it is with your mouth that you confess and are saved.*

The word here translated *confess* means to agree with or to say the same thing. Of course, more than verbal agreement is involved here. The words that one uses in confessing the Lord Jesus must reflect the content of one's *heart* and mind.

In many congregations it is common for persons acknowledging their commitment to Christ to make a public confession. This is usually some version of Peter's confession at Caesarea Philippi: "You are the Christ, the Son of the living God" (Matthew 16:16). But the confession that Paul is talking about is much more than a one-time event. It incorporates our daily activities, our deeds confirming the profession of our mouths.

11. *As the Scripture says, "Anyone who trusts in him will never be put to shame."*

Paul quotes from Isaiah 28:16, a passage he had earlier referred to in Romans 9:33. For those who are moved by secular values, being a Christian is a mark of shame. Being a Christian puts restrictions on where one will go and what one will do, say, or think. One who takes a worldly view of life will not accept such limitations. Christians, who view life from the perspective of eternity, come to a very different conclusion. When a Christian stands before the Eternal Judge, he or she shall not be *put to shame*. A Christian has Jesus' assurance that "whoever acknowledges me before men, I will also acknowledge him before my Father in heaven" (Matthew 10:32). The only assurance that the unbeliever has is that he or she will be ashamed because that one has refused to accept the truth and has believed a lie instead.

WHAT DO YOU THINK?

What barriers must a Christian overcome in order to express publicly a belief in Jesus without being ashamed or embarrassed?

D. AVAILABLE TO ALL (vv. 12, 13)

12, 13. *For there is no difference between Jew and Gentile—the same Lord is Lord of all and richly blesses all who call on him, for, "Everyone who calls on the name of the Lord will be saved."*

Ancient people, like many today, divided humanity into two categories—"us" and "them." The Jews divided the entire population into two groups: *Jew* and *Gentile*. Paul uses the expression in that extended sense here. When Jesus sent his disciples out into the world, they were to "go and make disciples of all nations" (Matthew 28:19), to "preach the good news to all creation" (Mark 16:15).

WHAT DO YOU THINK?

How does an "us vs. them" mentality devalue the richness of the Lord's offer of salvation, and what can the church do to remove any hindrances to openly inviting and receiving all people in the name of Jesus?

Of course, there are differences in people—skin color, hair texture, language, customs, etc. But in the eyes of the Lord these differences do not matter, for *the same Lord is Lord of all*. All have sinned and all stand in need of God's grace. This marvelous grace is available to *everyone who calls on the name of the Lord*. This may refer to confessing him or it may refer to a prayer of petition.

III. GOOD NEWS OF SALVATION (ROMANS 10:14-17)

A. NEWS MUST BE TOLD (v. 14)

14. How, then, can they call on the one they have not believed in? And how can they believe in the one of whom they have not heard? And how can they hear without someone preaching to them?

In this verse and the one that follows, Paul uses a series of rhetorical questions to show that Christians have an obligation to carry the gospel to the whole world. The fact that "everyone who calls on the name of the Lord will be saved" carries a moral obligation, for it is quite obvious that no one will *call on* the name of the Lord if he or she does not *believe* in the Lord. And people cannot believe in the Lord if they have not *heard* of him. Finally, people cannot *hear* about Christ unless a preacher tells them about him.

The person described as a "preacher" in some versions (*someone preaching to them*) does not necessarily mean someone who stands behind a pulpit on Sunday morning. It refers to a herald, one who brings a message. Paul undoubtedly had in mind a flesh-and-blood messenger, whether a public speaker or a more personal messenger. Later on, the written Word became an effective messenger. Today we also rely on electronic media to carry the message. Regardless of our method, we must never forget that the message is more important than the messenger.

DIFFERENT WAYS TO PROCLAIM THE MESSAGE

Hubert Eaton's name is not as well known as that of his life's work: Forest Lawn. Eaton took an uninviting, twelve-acre cemetery and turned it into a complex of five memorial parks, exceeded as a cemetery tourist attraction only by Arlington National Cemetery.

The secret behind Eaton's success was his belief that the site of one's burial should be a beautiful place, one that speaks of resurrection and hope for eternal life. One of the most attractive features of Forest Lawn is the varied means of proclaiming the Christian message: exact reproductions of Michelangelo's marvelous statues—*David, Moses,* and *La Pietà*—are displayed in the parks, as is a stained-glass reproduction of da Vinci's painting of *The Last Supper.* Carefully staged presentations of two of the world's largest paintings depict Jesus' crucifixion and resurrection. Eaton's belief in the gospel message is readily apparent in his memorial parks.

There are no statistics on how many unbelievers have turned to Christ as a result of this method of "preaching" the good news. However, what it does say is that the gospel may be proclaimed by many different means and in even the most unlikely of places. Are we taking advantage of all our opportunities?   —C. R. B.

B. PREACHERS MUST BE SENT (v. 15)

15. And how can they preach unless they are sent? As it is written, "How beautiful are the feet of those who bring good news!"

Our word *missionary* comes from a Latin word meaning one who is *sent.* Most persons today who are engaged in missionary activities have been sent by a congregation, some kind of parachurch organization, or a denomination. Across the centuries men and women—travelers, businesspersons, even prisoners—have carried the gospel to others. But even though they were not officially sent, they were, in a very real sense, sent by our Lord. The Great Commission makes every one of us a messenger.

Isaiah 52:7, which Paul quotes, is a prophecy that originally looked forward to the Israelites' return from the Babylonian captivity. Isaiah praised the messengers as the heralds of a wonderful new day. He also saw beyond the return from Babylon to an even greater day. Thus, Paul applies this praise to the heralds of the good news of God's offer of salvation in Jesus Christ.

HOW TO SAY IT

Babylonian. Bab-ih-LOW-nee-un.

Caesarea Philippi. Sess-uh-REE-uh Fih-LIP-pie or FIL-ih-pie.

Damascus. Duh-MASS-kus.

Jerusalem. Jee-ROO-suh-lem.

mausoleums. MAW-zuh-LEE-umz.

Pentecost. PENT-ih-kost.

Seder. SAY-der.

WHAT DO YOU THINK?

How can congregations increase opportunities for people to join in the Biblical pattern of sending messengers so that others can hear the gospel and respond to God's offer of grace?

This poster illustrates missionaries in various fields. Discuss how your church is helping to send missionaries to preach.

C. MESSAGE MUST BE HEARD (vv. 16, 17)

16, 17. But not all the Israelites accepted the good news. For Isaiah says, "Lord, who has believed our message?" Consequently, faith comes from hearing the message, and the message is heard through the word of Christ.

God does not impose *faith* on people by some magical process; *hearing the message* is essential. Nor does God send the message by angels. The responsibility of spreading the word belongs to every Christian. People must hear the message to respond, and Christians must deliver the message in order for the lost to hear it.

Of course, not everyone who hears comes to faith. For many reasons some people reject *the good news* of the gospel. These include fear of change, social pressure, the unwillingness to give up a sinful lifestyle, personal greed, prejudices—and the list could be greatly extended. Our printed text began with Paul's noting his desire for Israel, that the Jews would cease their rejection of Christ and turn to him. But their resistance did not stop Paul from being faithful to his call to preach the gospel. And we, likewise, must be faithful to our own charge to share the good news.

CONCLUSION

A man noticed an ominous lump on his neck, so he immediately visited his physician, who took a sample for a biopsy. When the husband and his wife returned to the physician's office a few days later, the smile on the doctor's face when he greeted them told them that the news was good. The tumor was not malignant and could be readily treated. The wife immediately got on the telephone, calling the church and all her friends with the good news.

Good news travels fast—sometimes! On the Day of Pentecost in A.D. 30, the apostle Peter stood up and preached the first gospel sermon. Three thousand responded to this glorious good news and were baptized. Within a few days, many of these people left Jerusalem and returned to their homelands, carrying the good news with them. Churches sprang up all across the Roman Empire, and within three hundred years Christianity had become a legal religion. Hundreds of missionaries eventually carried the good news to pagan strongholds beyond the Empire. By A.D. 1000, much of Europe had become at least nominally Christianized.

About two hundred years ago, Protestants in Western Europe and North America experienced a revived interest in missions. In the past two hundred years thousands of missionaries have been sent out, carrying the gospel to Africa, Asia, and other areas, reaching into both the urban centers and the remote jungle villages. Thousands of "sent ones" still labor in mission fields around the world.

But the picture has changed. Western Europe, sadly, is now post-Christian. Only a small minority of the people regularly attends religious services. Europe's majestic cathedrals are but ornate mausoleums, testifying to a faith that is now dead. The good news is no longer good news there, and the United States seems headed in the same direction. Unless American Christians redouble efforts to share the good news, it may well be in another generation where Europe is today.

But the good news will not die that easily. Ironically, many of the lands that were once the recipients of missionary efforts have now become the senders of missionaries. Bearers of the good news are coming to Europe and the United States in growing numbers.

We often think of missionaries as those who go to remote and distant places to proclaim the gospel. Sometimes, however, there are ripe mission fields next door or just across the street. Let us carry the good news wherever and whenever we can, and let us spread it quickly!

PRAYER

Gracious God, thank you for sending us your Son. Teach us how to share the good news of his life, death, and resurrection, and give us the wisdom and courage to carry it to others as quickly as we can. In the name of our Savior we pray. Amen.

THOUGHT TO REMEMBER

We would not be Christians today if there had not been missionaries yesterday.

Discovery Learning

This page contains an alternate lesson plan emphasizing learning activities. Classes desiring such student involvement will find these suggestions helpful. The next page is a reproducible activity page to further enhance discovery learning.

LEARNING GOALS

After participating in this lesson, each student will be able to:

1. Summarize the pattern of spreading the gospel as Paul explains it in Romans 10.

2. Tell why every Christian must consider himself or herself a "herald" of the good news.

3. Become more involved with the church's or the class's efforts to take the gospel to others, both locally and globally.

INTO THE LESSON

Bring into class a gift-wrapped box. Inside place a gospel tract or a New Testament to represent the sharing of the good news. Display the box prominently.

Say, "Today I am conducting an unscientific poll. How many of you would rather receive gifts than give them?" Ask those who answer yes to move to the right side (Group 1). Next say, "I assume the others of you would rather give gifts than receive them." Move them to the left side of the room (Group 2). Ask for a representative from each group to give reasons for each answer.

Ask the members of Group 1 whether any of them has ever rejected a gift. Ask whether anyone in Group 2 has ever had their gift rejected. Ask both groups, "What does rejection of a gift say to the giver?" Expect an answer that indicates the person doesn't care for the gift, has no use for it, or might even be offended by it.

Say, "The lesson today explores how the gospel was spread, how the gift was given, and how we can participate in that spreading."

INTO THE WORD

Assign people to groups of four to six. Distribute the following outline and questions to each group. Say, "Paul seems to suggest a plan for taking the gospel to our communities. Fill in the details of this outline by answering the questions."

REACHING OTHERS FOR CHRIST

A. Show That You Care (Romans 10:1-5)

1. How does Paul show he is not anti-Semitic?
2. What good things does he say about the Israelites?
3. How did the Israelites go wrong?

B. Clearly Confess Christ (Romans 10:6-13)

1. How does Paul say we are saved?
2. What keeps us from being ashamed?

3. Why is this message for everyone?

C. Understand Your Commission (Romans 10:14-17)

1. With what questions does Paul challenge us to go?
2. How does Paul show the importance of the message and the messenger?
3. What words are used of the messenger?

After the groups have finished answering the questions, lead a brief discussion concerning difficulties encountered by those who carry the gospel, using the commentary for verses 14-17.

INTO LIFE

Summarize by saying, "Paul is challenging the church to continue its mission of carrying the gospel. Turn to Matthew 28:18-20 to see Jesus' words." After reading these verses, remind the class that nothing has changed. Using the comments for verse 14, lead the students to see that they are "heralds" of the good news. Using the lesson writer's ideas on effective messengers, brainstorm ways we can carry the gospel.

Challenge class members to participate in carrying the word with one of the following ideas:

Option 1: Create small outlines of a pair of feet on a four-inch-by-six-inch sheet of paper or note card. Make enough for every class member. Under this pair of feet write the title, "Beautiful Feet." Across the feet write, "I will carry the good news of the gospel to _____ this week." Ask each person to think of someone with whom he or she can share the good news and to write that name in the blank. Say, "Turn to the person beside you and pray for each other to be bold." This activity is in the student book, *NIV® Bible Student.*

Option 2: Contact your church's minister or missions committee. Ask for a list with addresses and phone numbers or e-mail addresses of missions and missionaries supported by your church. Bring envelopes, stationery (the reproducible page following can be used), and pens. Have each person select a mission or missionary to whom he or she will write a "beautiful feet" letter. The letter should encourage and thank the missionary.

After each has written, collect the envelopes for mailing. The class member should be asked to keep the name and make a commitment to pray for that mission or missionary for the rest of the month.

Close with prayer for the continued spreading of the gospel.

"How beautiful are the feet of those who bring good news!"
—*Romans 10:15*

April 14, 2002

Dear _____,

    Our Sunday school lesson today was from Romans 10:1-17. There was a lot of excitement as we considered ways to spread the gospel. I thought of your work.

Your Partner in Grace,

LIVE THE GOSPEL

LESSON 8

WHY TEACH THIS LESSON?

Occasionally, we hear of politicians or movie stars deciding to "reinvent" themselves. Such a reinvention is often deemed necessary after the politician loses an election or the movie star flops at the box office. The idea in either case is to remake a public image in order to recapture the favor of a fickle public. Stalled careers can then flourish again.

After we are saved, God, in a sense, wants to "reinvent" us into something new as we live out the gospel. This reinvention isn't for the purpose of gaining the public's favor—indeed, it may have just the opposite effect! Neither is it for the purpose of gaining God's favor—we already have that. We are reinvented (transformed) in order to be more like God himself.

Not everyone understands that, however. Many, perhaps even some of your students, feel like they have to reinvent themselves in order to be accepted by God. Today's lesson will give you a chance to "reinvent" that thinking.

INTRODUCTION

A. METAMORPHOSIS

With the coming of summer we often see trees plagued with crawling caterpillars that devour the foliage. But a caterpillar does not remain a caterpillar forever. After a period of time it forms a cocoon (called a chrysalis) and remains inside for about two weeks. Then it emerges as a butterfly that bears no resemblance to its earlier form. "Metamorphosis" is the name scientists give to the changes that make a crawling worm-like creature into a beautiful butterfly. That word comes from the Greek word that in Romans 12:2 is translated "transformed."

A line in one of our old hymns asks, "Would he devote that sacred head for such a worm as I?" Though we have crawled long in sin, we need not be worm-like creatures forever. Jesus did devote his head—his whole body—to our redemption. By his power and grace we can renew our minds, undergo a metamorphosis, and be transformed into the beautiful persons God designed us to be.

B. LESSON BACKGROUND

Many Christians seem to think theology (or doctrine) and Christian living are completely separate matters. Doctrine, they believe, is discussed and debated by scholarly theologians, but it is only remotely related to what happens in local churches and in the lives of individual Christians. Scholars help perpetuate this division by writing and speaking in technical jargon that seems like a foreign language. Some non-scholars also contribute to this gap by refusing to try to understand what the theologians are talking about.

The apostle Paul was a theologian and an impressive scholar, but he certainly did not believe that doctrine and practice ought to be separated. In the earlier chapters of the Roman epistle, Paul deals with a great deal of profound theology. But in chapter 12 (the basis for today's lesson) he turns to practical applications of his doctrinal statements. *Therefore* is a key word in Paul's writings. It often signals a move from the doctrinal to the practical. That is the case in today's lesson.

DEVOTIONAL READING:
ROMANS 12:4-8

BACKGROUND SCRIPTURE:
ROMANS 12

PRINTED TEXT:
ROMANS 12:1-3, 9-21

LESSON AIMS

After this lesson each student should:

1. Describe the "transformed" lifestyle Paul urges Christians to adopt.

2. Tell why it is essential that a Christian be transformed rather than conformed to the world.

3. Pinpoint an area of behavior where obedience to the Lord is lacking, and take action to be "pleasing to God" in this area.

Apr
21

KEY VERSE

Do not conform any longer to the pattern of this world, but be transformed by the renewing of your mind. Then you will be able to test and approve what God's will is—his good, pleasing and perfect will.   —Romans 12:2

As we study this lesson, it will be obvious that doctrine and practice belong together. If certain doctrines are true, then it follows that a definite attitude and a definite lifestyle should result. To separate doctrine and practice is foreign to the very nature of Christianity. We may not always agree on how the Scriptures apply to every life situation, but we must agree that the Scriptures are the standard by which we measure our lives.

I. GOD CALLS FOR HOLINESS (ROMANS 12:1-3)

Romans 12 covers several important issues for Christian living. What an impact the church would make on the world if every professing Christian took these teachings of Paul seriously. But it starts with personal surrender.

A. LIVING SACRIFICE (v. 1)

1. Therefore, I urge you, brothers, in view of God's mercy, to offer your bodies as living sacrifices, holy and pleasing to God—this is your spiritual act of worship.

As a divinely inspired apostle, Paul had the right to command his readers, but he chose not to do so. Instead, he makes an earnest appeal that they do as he asks because they want to, not because they have to. He reminds them of *God's mercy.* If they stopped for a moment to consider all God had done for them, they would not hesitate to do what Paul was asking them.

Paul's plea that they *offer* their *bodies as living sacrifices* would have a strong impact on Jewish Christians because of the sacrificial system that was at the heart of the Mosaic law. Christians who came from pagan backgrounds also would understand this because of the many sacrifices involved in pagan worship. But unlike these systems, this is a living, ongoing sacrifice. This sacrifice is *holy* in the sense that it is set apart to God. Just as the sacrificial animals under the Mosaic law were to be without blemish, so we are to present our bodies unmarred by sin.

The concluding clause in this verse is rendered differently in different versions. Where the *King James Version* has "reasonable service," the *New International Version* has *spiritual act of worship.* The reason is that Paul chose words with double meanings: "reasonable" and "spiritual" are both valid translations of the first; "service" and "worship" both properly translate the second. The idea goes beyond that of any single translation. This response to God's mercy is reasonable: it makes sense; it is rational. It is also spiritual: it recognizes that the body is more than flesh, more than an instrument of sensual function. It is also service: it serves God and people. And it is worship: whether in a formal worship setting or in daily living, the body is used to the glory of God.

WHAT DO YOU THINK?

What is "spiritual" about offering every part of ourselves wholly to God as living sacrifices? How does keeping God's mercy in view help us to see it that way?

B. TRANSFORMED (v. 2)

2. Do not conform any longer to the pattern of this world, but be transformed by the renewing of your mind. Then you will be able to test and approve what God's will is—his good, pleasing and perfect will.

The Phillips translation states this vividly: "Don't let the world around you squeeze you into its own mold." The world is not quietly inviting us to conform; it is trying to force conformity on us. In its advertising it screams a message of materialism and worldly pleasures. It passes laws that force Christians to acquiesce in its ungodly pursuits. The world is trying every way it can to force Christians to fit into its value system.

The *renewing of* the *mind* is consistent with the "reasonable" or rational aspect of the living sacrifice. Heart and mind are both important to conversion, and both remain important to Christian living. The mind is active as one reads and studies the Scriptures, through which the Holy Spirit guides our behavior.

Through the use of the mind we can evaluate and combat the pressures of the world that is trying to make us conform.

THE POWER TO SURVIVE AND WIN

Life seemed to be over for a twenty-four-year-old American athlete when, in 1996, he was struck with cancer. The cancer had spread to his lungs and brain, leaving him a 40 percent chance to live. Surgery and months of chemotherapy left him weak and nauseated.

But only three years later, in 1999, Lance Armstrong won the *Tour de France*, the most prestigious bicycle race in the world. And in 2000 he won again, decisively! The twenty-one-day race covered 2,255 miles—as great as the distance from Los Angeles to Atlanta, Georgia! Armstrong's average speed was nearly twenty-five miles per hour.

Those who saw the transformation from a beaten shell of a man into a two-time world champion just four years later spoke of Armstrong's athletic gifts, but also of his capacity to endure pain, his self-discipline, and his sense of purpose. In a bit of overstatement, a French rider said, "His mental powers are supernatural!"

This is similar to what the apostle Paul says about the means by which we may win our spiritual battles and be transformed into examples of God's goodwill: minds committed to God's noble purpose, willing to endure hardship to attain God's glorious prize.   —C. R. B.

C. HUMBLE (v. 3)

3. For by the grace given me I say to every one of you: Do not think of yourself more highly than you ought, but rather think of yourself with sober judgment, in accordance with the measure of faith God has given you.

Paul continues his emphasis on the mind by telling us how we are to *think.* We all experience that urge to be "number one." While we are not to think *more highly* of ourselves than we ought, we are not to think of ourselves too lowly, either. *Sober judgment* neither exalts nor debases. It recognizes personal weaknesses, but it also accounts for the fact that we have been created in God's image with all the potential that involves. Keeping such a view of oneself is not easy. But Paul reassures us that God has given each of us a *measure of faith* to help us in this evaluation.

II. GOD CALLS FOR LOVE (ROMANS 12:9-15)

In verses 4-8 Paul deals with various gifts that Christians enjoy. Just as the human body has many members, each with a different function, so the church, the body of Christ, has many members with various functions.

In verse 9 Paul introduces love, which every Christian should possess. The Greeks had several words for love, each with a different meaning or connotation. The word here is *agape,* which is an active, intelligent goodwill directed toward another without consideration of a response.

A. PURE (v. 9)

9. Love must be sincere. Hate what is evil; cling to what is good.

Love, like any other virtue, can be feigned—which is why it should *be sincere.* But true love always seeks to give more than it receives. This kind of love is not based on soft, unthinking sentimentality. It is discerning, rejecting *what is evil* and holding on to *what is good.* This means that sometimes real love must be "tough love," refusing to tolerate evil but confronting it squarely. It can mean hating sin but loving the sinner.

DAILY BIBLE READINGS

Monday, Apr. 15—Be Doers of the Word (James 1:19-27)

Tuesday, Apr. 16—Love Does Not Discriminate (James 2:1-13)

Wednesday, Apr. 17—Control the Tongue (James 3:1-12)

Thursday, Apr. 18—Gentleness Born of Wisdom (James 3:13-18)

Friday, Apr. 19—Patience and Endurance (James 5:7-12)

Saturday, Apr. 20—Do Not Conform; Be Transformed (Romans 12:1-8)

Sunday, Apr. 21—Marks of Christian Living (Romans 12:9-21)

WHAT DO YOU THINK?

Paul seems to link love with righteous living in verse 9. How do transformed people ensure that their love leads to righteous living?

WHAT DO YOU THINK?

What is the difference between "people who go to the same church" and "members of the same church family"? How will that difference affect areas Paul describes, such as our intensity, our sharing of resources, our willingness to associate with everyone, and our emotional involvement in the lives of others?

B. KIND (v. 10)

10. Be devoted to one another in brotherly love. Honor one another above yourselves.

In this one verse Paul uses two different words that come from the Greek word *phileo*. This is another of the Greeks' words for love, and is often applied to love among friends and family members. This normally involves mutual affection—give and take. Paul urges church members to show the same love among themselves that we expect to be shown toward members of one's own family.

The idea of honoring *one another* ahead of oneself sounds foreign to today's me-first culture. But it is altogether consistent with the attitude Jesus displayed in the upper room (John 13).

C. INDUSTRIOUS (v. 11)

11. Never be lacking in zeal, but keep your spiritual fervor, serving the Lord.

Love compels us to give our best effort for the Lord's kingdom. Such *spiritual fervor* transforms our role on church committees from simply doing a job to truly *serving the Lord*.

D. OPTIMISTIC (v. 12)

12. Be joyful in hope, patient in affliction, faithful in prayer.

Being *joyful*, even under adverse conditions, is frequently urged in the New Testament. Christians can rejoice in the midst of suffering because they take the long view of history. They know that ultimately the forces of truth will triumph. *Affliction* is temporary; the reward is eternal. In the meantime, believers give continuous diligence to *prayer*.

E. GENEROUS (vv. 13, 14)

13. Share with God's people who are in need. Practice hospitality.

Most of the industrialized nations of the world are enjoying a prosperity unknown at any other time in history. Yet in the midst of this unprecedented affluence, there are pockets of poverty. The admonition in this verse is to help *God's people*, or fellow Christians, who are in need (cf. Galatians 6:10). Yet we must not limit our charity and *hospitality* to fellow Christians. Nor should we limit it just to material things like food and clothing. Sometimes the poor need our guidance and encouragement more than they need material things.

14. Bless those who persecute you; bless and do not curse.

Love is not always "sugar and spice and everything nice." Sometimes it requires us to go contrary to human nature, to love our enemies and those who *persecute* us. Paul here reaffirms what Jesus taught in Matthew 5:44.

F. CONCERNED (v. 15)

15. Rejoice with those who rejoice; mourn with those who mourn.

When others *rejoice* because of some good fortune that they have received, we may find it difficult to rejoice with them because of jealousy. We may feel that we deserved the good fortune more than they did. We also sometimes have trouble mourning *with those who mourn* because we are afraid of becoming emotionally involved. We fear that such emotional involvement will make demands on our time and resources that we are not willing to give. Our growth toward Christian maturity may be measured in how well we learn to rejoice and weep with others.

III. GOD CALLS FOR PEACE (ROMANS 12:16-21)

Weeping with those who weep and rejoicing with those who rejoice sets the tone for harmony in our relationships.

This humorous poster points out the need for Christians to be different from the mold imposed by the world.

A. SEEK UNITY AND HUMILITY (v. 16)

16. Live in harmony with one another. Do not be proud, but be willing to associate with people of low position. Do not be conceited.

The first part of this verse follows naturally from the previous verse. Living *in harmony with one another* suggests an empathy that shares with others in their rejoicing and weeping. But its application goes further. Some think being of the same mind refers to agreement in matters of doctrine. That is an important point that is dealt with in other passages, but it does not seem to be Paul's point here. Rather, he is discussing harmonious relationships.

The *proud* take an interest in those things that make them appear superior to others. In our highly competitive society, we not only try to "keep up with the Joneses," we try to outdo them. We accumulate the status symbols that say to the world that we have the newest, the biggest, or the best.

Such a person looks down on other people, but Paul tells us to do just the opposite. *To associate with people of low position* is to join the lowly in their situation, to be one with them. Rather than looking down on others, we should join with the lowly as their equal. (See James 2:1-9.)

B. DO NOT SEEK REVENGE (vv. 17-19)

17. Do not repay anyone evil for evil. Be careful to do what is right in the eyes of everybody.

Whereas the earlier exhortations concerned relationships within the church, from here on Paul's focus is on how to respond to unbelievers—even enemies. The Old Testament law of "an eye for an eye and a tooth for a tooth" has been transcended by Christ's higher law—when you have been wronged, don't try to get even, but love your enemy.

Paul urges the saints to think ahead and *be careful* to live in such an honest and forthright way that their motives and actions are above reproach. In this way they will be less likely to incur anger, misunderstanding, or conflict.

18. If it is possible, as far as it depends on you, live at peace with everyone.

Paul recognizes that even those who *live* exemplary lives will not be able to avoid all conflicts. In fact, good people often incur wrath from the world because their godly lives expose the evil in the lives of sinners. It is not always *possible* to avoid conflict, but it is not necessary to incite conflict, either. We are responsible only for behaving in a proper manner ourselves; we cannot determine how others will respond.

19. Do not take revenge, my friends, but leave room for God's wrath, for it is written: "It is mine to avenge; I will repay," says the Lord.

This reaffirms what Paul stated in verse 17. There is a good reason a Christian should never seek personal *revenge*: vengeance belongs to *the Lord*. God in his own time and his own manner will reward the righteous and punish the wicked.

PUTTING THE PAST TO REST

Randolph McCoy accused Anderson "Devil Anse" Hatfield of stealing his pig. The year was 1878. McCoy's accusation was a reflection of years of ill will between the two clans over Civil War allegiances and business dealings. But this incident precipitated a series of vengeful acts. These acts of revenge comprise the essence of America's most legendary feud. Over the next dozen years a dozen Hatfields and McCoys were killed, some by ambush, some by lynching. The last to die was a Hatfield, who was hanged in 1890.

By then, most members of the two clans had had enough of violence and began to find ways to accommodate each other, if not *like* each other. But it took another

WHAT DO YOU THINK?

How do we "associate with people of low position" without being condescending? If it's an issue of swallowing our pride, how do we do that?

WHAT DO YOU THINK?

Paul says we are to be at peace with people "if it is possible." How can we tell when it is possible and when it is not?

HOW TO SAY IT

agape (Greek). Uh-GAH-pay.
chemotherapy. KEE-mo-THAIR-uh-pee.
chrysalis. KRIS-uh-liss.
metamorphosis. MET-tuh-MOR-fuh-suss.
Mosaic. Mo-ZAY-ik.
phileo (Greek). fil-LEH-oh.

century for a formal end of the feud to come. For many years, more thoughtful and decent members of both clans had found the tales of the feud to be a source of shame. They were embarrassed by the inability of their ancestors to get past the spirit of revenge and live at peace with members of the other clan.

And so, in June of 2000, the two clans gathered in Williamson, West Virginia, to visit the sites of the murders, offer prayer together, and put the past to rest.

These two clans are an excellent, yet tragic, example of what happens when we forget the teaching of today's lesson: that God's way for us is to overcome the evil of the past with the spirit of good. (And it shouldn't take us a hundred years to get around to it!)
—C. R. B.

C. OVERCOME EVIL WITH GOOD (vv. 20, 21)
20. On the contrary: "If your enemy is hungry, feed him; if he is thirsty, give him something to drink. In doing this, you will heap burning coals on his head."

In quoting Proverbs 25:21, 22, Paul shows us the Christian way to respond to our enemies. Give them food and *drink*—and clothing and shelter if they need it. The purpose of the *burning coals* is not to harm one's enemy, but in some way to help him. Perhaps the idea is that returning kindness for evil will have such an impact on the enemy's conscience that he will be led to repentance and reform.
21. Do not be overcome by evil, but overcome evil with good.

This verse sums up the paragraph. When we allow ourselves to seek revenge, we are playing the enemy's game. An old farmer put it this way: "If you try to wrestle a hog in a mud hole, you are sure to get muddy yourself."

CONCLUSION
The 4H organization is one hundred years old this year. It began as a "Boys and Girls Agricultural Club" meeting in the basement of the Clark County (Ohio) courthouse in January of 1902. Today it is popular all across the U.S., extending beyond the farms into the suburbs and inner cities as well. The four-leaf clover logo, with an H on each leaf, is familiar to many. The four H's stand for head, heart, hands, and health.

The name "4H" was not used, however, until 1918. In fact, the logo originally had only three leaves, for head, heart, and hands. This old logo, dating back to 1907 or 1908, could be applied to this passage in Romans, where Paul sets forth the 3H's of Christianity: HEAD—doctrines that are to be learned, HEART—changes that are to be made in attitudes, and HANDS—specific actions that should come as a result.

As Christians we apply our heads to read and study the Scriptures, the only adequate basis for our faith. God expects us to learn his Word so that we might not sin against him (Psalm 119:11). But more than the intellect, the head, is involved.

Our hearts (emotions, feelings, and wills) also must be involved. Unless this happens, all our Bible studies become cold, intellectual activities, unrelated to the real world in which we live.

To know the Scriptures and then to be moved by them to change our attitudes and our emotions is still not enough. We must be able to translate all of this into actions. Until our hands begin to practice what is in our heads and our hearts, our Christianity is a sham.

Paul does not suggest that following the Christian 3H's will be easy. Indeed, the application of Biblical truth to our daily lives faces formidable challenges in our times when the forces of the world are set against us. But the rewards are beyond measure. In this world we will know the peace that faithful service brings, and in the next world we are promised life eternal.

Discovery Learning

*This page contains an alternate lesson plan emphasizing learning activities. Classes
desiring such student involvement will find these suggestions helpful. The next page
is a reproducible activity page to further enhance discovery learning.*

LEARNING GOALS

After this lesson each student will be able to:

1. Describe the "transformed" lifestyle Paul urges Christians to adopt.

2. Tell why it is essential that a Christian be transformed rather than conformed to the world.

3. Pinpoint an area of behavior where obedience to the Lord is lacking, and take action to be "pleasing to God" in this area.

INTO THE LESSON

Place several large pieces of poster paper on the walls around the room, and have several colored markers near each poster. Say: "Several years ago there were toys called 'transformers.' Each of these toys was originally in one shape, a robot of sorts, but after being manipulated, the robot became something else: an airplane, a tank, a helicopter, etc. Step up to the posters and write what you would like to be transformed into, if it were possible."

After class members have taken a few minutes to write their choices, ask the group to give reasons for their answers. Then say, "From this activity it seems that each of us longs to be different, to be transformed. When you think of all the Christians you have met, who do you think has made the biggest transformation?"

Option. Use the reproducible activity "Transformation" from the next page to get students thinking about being transformed.

After a short discussion say, "Today we are studying Romans 12. Paul challenges us all to be transformed. Let's see how Christ wants us to change."

INTO THE WORD

Either during the week before class or a few minutes before you begin, recruit four readers for today. Have the Scripture read in these divisions: Romans 12:1-3, 9-13, 14-16, and 17-21. Follow the reading with a brief lecture using the Lesson Background section on page 293.

Divide your class into at least four groups of three to six. Give a copy of one of the four sections of Scripture that were read to each group. (If your class has more than twenty-four members, repeat some assignments.)

Group 1 (Romans 12:1-3) is to draw a "cartoon panel" that depicts the truth of this Scripture. To "prime the pump," you may want to challenge them to draw a picture of God's act of mercy (Jesus' sacrificial death).

Group 2 (Romans 12:9-13) is to develop a role play of an event or series of events in which the characteristics described are shown. Each of the short imperatives can lend itself to a brief scene of conflict or confrontation.

Group 3 (Romans 12:14-16) is to list the people or types of people Paul might be referring to if he were in our community today. Caution them to be careful not to insult or defame a group.

Group 4 (Romans 12:17-21) is to think of a recent news item or community happening where evil was evident. This group should agree on how a Christian should handle the situation, demonstrating the characteristics listed. Ask the group to decide how the final principle is a universal one: "Do not be overcome by evil, but overcome evil with good."

Call the groups together to present their findings. Then discuss the following two questions.

1. Which characteristic are you most apt to show?

2. Which characteristic are you least likely to show?

(Items from Group 3's assignment through these group discussion questions are included in the student book, *NIV® Bible Student.*)

INTO LIFE

Ask the students to move back to their original places. Distribute the following questions:

1. In what areas do you think Christians are conforming to the world? Which ones are obviously negative choices? Which ones really do not matter?

2. What is the result of a transformed life?

3. This week were you more "transformed" or "conformed"?

Say, "Often we live our lives playing to an audience, playing a role. We give our audience what they want. Here Paul tells us we are to live lives pleasing to God. He delineates the characteristics of godly living in Romans 12:9-21. Which characteristic or characteristics do you need to be developing? Write down the first two steps that you will take this week. Tell these two steps to the person sitting beside you."

Distribute copies of the reproducible activity "Relationship" from the next page. Have students complete the activity prayerfully. Then close in prayer for each person's strength to fulfill the pledge just made. You may want to use a "prayer circle" in which each one who wants to has an opportunity to pray audibly.

Transformation

Read the entire twelfth chapter of Romans. Then, on the worm below, write four or five ways Christians tend to "conform" to the world. On the butterfly write several of the characteristics cited in Romans 12:9-21.

"Worm   to   Butterfly."

Relationship

Think of the relationship in your life that most needs this lesson. Write a prayer expressing to God your need for forgiveness, understanding, and patience for this relationship. Ask God for the wisdom to implement a plan for improving this relationship.

Patient and Forgiving God,

The Power of the Gospel
Unit 2: Living by Faith
(Lessons 6-9)

LIVE UNTO THE LORD

LESSON 9

WHY TEACH THIS LESSON?

Several years ago, I became aware that a member of another church was involved in ongoing sexual immorality. A relative of mine was also a member of that church, and I suggested to her that the errant member was now subject to the corrective measures of church discipline as set forth in Scripture. Her vehement response was that we were to "judge not" (Matthew 7:1, *King James Version*)! Instead, she contended, we were to trust in the "love" of fellow church members to lead the erring one back into a holy life.

Her response reflects, at least partially, a cultural mindset that has enamored itself with the concept of "tolerance." Sadly, many churches have followed this path to the point that a misapplication of Matthew 7:1 supplants John 3:16 as their primary message! But the pendulum can swing to the other extreme as well: churches can become so intolerant on non-essential matters that their members continually sit in judgment on matters of opinion and conscience. Today's lesson will help your learners avoid both extremes.

INTRODUCTION
A. TO JUDGE OR NOT TO JUDGE

Paul's judgment against any who would preach a different gospel from the true gospel is unequivocal: "Let him be eternally condemned" (Galatians 1:8). Yet even so forthright a statement does not justify a quick denunciation or a public proclamation of the errant preacher's guilt. Paul's co-workers, Priscilla and Aquila, took a different approach, as we can read in Acts 18.

Apollos had come to town. He knew about Jesus, to a point. But he didn't know anything beyond John's baptism (vv. 24, 25). In other words, he did not know about the death, burial, and resurrection of Jesus. He didn't know the gospel! (See 1 Corinthians 15:1-4.) But rather than make a public spectacle, Priscilla and Aquila took the young preacher home with them. Probably over dinner they shared the gospel—they "explained to him the way of God more adequately [i.e., more completely]" (v. 26). As a result, Apollos was not condemned, but became a powerful preacher of the true gospel.

There is a time for judgment, for discernment, for careful analysis of the situation and determination of what to do in response. But that does not have to include being judgmental, condemning those with whom we have differences. We can discuss the issues in a godly manner and leave the judging to God.

B. LESSON BACKGROUND

In today's lesson Paul continues his emphasis on practical Christian living based on the doctrinal teachings in Romans 1–11. In chapter 12 he laid the basis for this by setting forth our relationship to God: we are to present our bodies "as living sacrifices" to God. In chapter 13 he discussed our relationship to civil government: we are to "submit . . . to the governing authorities." Now he turns to relationships between Christians. We are not to deal with our brothers and sisters (or even non-Christians, for that matter) with a judgmental attitude.

DEVOTIONAL READING:
ROMANS 14:14-23
BACKGROUND SCRIPTURE:
ROMANS 14:1–15:6
PRINTED TEXT:
ROMANS 14:1-13; 15:1, 2

LESSON AIMS

After studying this lesson, each student should:

1. Summarize what Paul says about the attitude with which a Christian should handle matters on which believers disagree.

2. Explain the significance of living unto the Lord in the context of getting along with others.

3. Suggest how a particular situation involving a disputable matter, either in the class or the church, could be handled in a way that will promote peace and will edify others.

Apr
28

KEY VERSE

Therefore let us stop passing judgment on one another. Instead, make up your mind not to put any stumbling block or obstacle in your brother's way.
—Romans 14:13

I. ACCEPT ONE ANOTHER (ROMANS 14:1-4)
A. RECEIVE THE WEAK BROTHER (vv. 1, 2)
1, 2. Accept him whose faith is weak, without passing judgment on disputable matters. One man's faith allows him to eat everything, but another man, whose faith is weak, eats only vegetables.

The expression *disputable matters* renders two Greek words that can mean "judgments" or "disputes," and "opinions" or "doubts," respectively. What Paul is prohibiting here is the apparent reception of one *whose faith is weak* for the purpose of then passing judgment on his or her opinions.

At issue here is the matter of Christian liberty. From the very beginning, Christians have had to make decisions about how their Christian faith applies in their culture. Since Christians have not always come to the same conclusions about these differences, disagreements and even conflicts have followed.

The one *whose faith is weak* takes a narrow view of freedom, interpreting Scripture in such a way as to limit liberty. This does not pose a problem as long as these limitations are applied only to one's own life. But when the person seeks to bind others to these restrictions, conflict is likely to follow.

Paul illustrates his point with a specific example: the eating of meat. Some people today choose a vegetarian diet for health reasons, but in Paul's day the issue was religious. Some Gentile Christians had come from pagan religions that involved animal sacrifices. Much of the meat sold in the market came from these sacrifices, and eating it seemed to these people to involve them in the paganism they had just left (cf. 1 Corinthians 8). Jewish Christians, who had been taught to avoid eating meat from unclean animals or from animals not killed according to the law of Moses, often refused to eat meat also.

B. ACCEPT THOSE GOD HAS RECEIVED (v. 3)
3. The man who eats everything must not look down on him who does not, and the man who does not eat everything must not condemn the man who does, for God has accepted him.

Eating meat or not eating meat was not a moral issue, but a matter of opinion. Since God accepts both groups, they are urged to accept one another. The strong, those who ate, were not to *look down on* those who did not. Those who did not eat were not to *condemn* those who did.

C. THE MASTER JUDGES HIS OWN SERVANTS (v. 4)
4. Who are you to judge someone else's servant? To his own master he stands or falls. And he will stand, for the Lord is able to make him stand.

A *master* has control over his servants, and outsiders have no right to interfere in matters between them. Since Christians are servants of God, we have no right to tell him how he should deal with his other servants. If a "weaker brother" seems to stumble, *the Lord is able to make him stand.*

II. LIVE UNTO THE LORD (ROMANS 14:5-9)
A. OBSERVE DAYS DIFFERENTLY (vv. 5, 6)
5. One man considers one day more sacred than another; another man considers every day alike. Each one should be fully convinced in his own mind.

Paul now introduces another issue that may have caused controversy for the church. Jewish Christians may have continued to keep the Sabbath and other days and feasts that they had observed under the law. Paul doesn't condemn this practice. Regardless of one's position, the important thing was that each *be fully convinced in his own mind.*

6. *He who regards one day as special, does so to the Lord. He who eats meat, eats to the Lord, for he gives thanks to God; and he who abstains, does so to the Lord and gives thanks to God.*

Some recognized *special* days to honor *the Lord.* Others honored the Lord by looking on every day as given by him. These positions must be held as matters of opinion and personal devotion. When persons try to force their views on others in a legalistic fashion, Paul makes it clear that this is a reversion to salvation by works rather than by grace. "Do not let anyone judge you by what you eat or drink, or with regard to a religious festival, a New Moon celebration or a Sabbath day" (Colossians 2:16). Rather, each one should focus on the Lord, giving *thanks,* instead of focusing on differences with other believers.

WHEN YOUR NEIGHBOR HAS A DIFFERENT VIEW

How much is a scenic view worth? That's probably not something that most of us have tried to quantify. But residents of Rancho Palos Verdes have. They have paid two million dollars or more for mansions with unobstructed views of the Ocean or the Los Angeles city lights. For them a scenic view can add as much as a hundred thousand dollars to property values! Some of them bought their homes when the downhill neighbors' trees were small, but these now full-grown trees are blocking their view! Which is worth more, an unobstructed view or beautiful trees?

The matter is taken seriously enough that the municipality has passed laws that allow residents to demand that their neighbors cut their trees if the trees have impinged on their view. Heated city council meetings have resulted in numerous angry exchanges and even a heart attack for one "downhill" defender of the property values that his trees provide.

The issue that Paul discusses in today's lesson did not involve property damages or monetary values. But it did have to do with the way a person looked at life, and it had great importance in terms of the quality of life within the Christian community in Rome.

When one member of the church in Rome chose not to see a matter of personal opinion from the perspective of others, the result was a loss of Christian spirit. The spirit that Paul urges upon us goes beyond mere forbearance. We are to find positive ways to set our fellow Christians at ease even when we are convinced they are wrong on these matters of opinion.
—C. R. B.

B. SERVE THE SAME LORD (vv. 7-9)

7, 8. *For none of us lives to himself alone and none of us dies to himself alone. If we live, we live to the Lord; and if we die, we die to the Lord. So, whether we live or die, we belong to the Lord.*

"No man is an Island, entire of itself," John Donne reminds us. We are by nature social creatures, and we find our greatest fulfillment in our associations with others. Because of this interrelationship, we need to learn to be tolerant of others. But Paul's statement goes beyond this. We also *live* and *die* before God. We belong to him in this life, but our servanthood does not end at death.

9. *For this very reason, Christ died and returned to life so that he might be the Lord of both the dead and the living.*

One of the central themes in Paul's writings is the death and resurrection of *Christ.* Here he comes back to it again and sets it forth as a basis for building loving, trusting, and generous relationships within the church. Because he is the *Lord of both the dead and the living,* he has the right to command our obedience. Part of the obedience that he demands is that we avoid making our opinions the standard by which we judge others.

DAILY BIBLE READINGS

Monday, Apr. 22—Act to Honor the Lord (Romans 14:1-6)

Tuesday, Apr. 23—We Are the Lord's (Romans 14:7-12)

Wednesday, Apr. 24—Do Not Cause Others to Stumble (Romans 14:13-23)

Thursday, Apr. 25—Build Up Your Neighbor (Romans 15:1-6)

Friday, Apr. 26—Gospel for Both Jews and Gentiles (Romans 15:7-13)

Saturday, Apr. 27—One Message: What Christ Accomplishes (Romans 15:14-21)

Sunday, Apr. 28—Paul's Ministry to Rome (Romans 15:22-33)

HOW TO SAY IT

amillennialism. AH-muh-LEN-ee-uhl-liz-um.

Apollos. Uh-PAHL-us.

Aquila. ACK-wih-luh.

Corinthian. Kor-IN-thee-un (TH as in THIN).

postmillennialism. POST-muh-LEN-ee-uhl-liz-um.

premillennialism. PRE-muh-LEN-ee-uhl-liz-um.

Priscilla. Prih-SIL-uh.

WHAT DO YOU THINK?

A believer who takes a more restricted view on an issue is tempted to label those with differing opinions as "liberals." The one with a more permissive view may label more restrictive Christians as "narrow-minded." How can Christians on both sides of an opinion take responsibility not to pass judgment on those with differing views?

Today's visual echoes Paul's admonition to stop passing judgment on one another. Display it as you discuss verse 13.

WHAT DO YOU THINK?

After all of Paul's admonitions not to judge, he says to "Make up your mind [literally, 'judge'] not to put any stumbling block or obstacle in your brother's way." Why is such an issue worthy of our "judgment"?

III. LET GOD BE THE JUDGE (ROMANS 14:10-13)

A. GIVE AN ACCOUNT OF YOURSELF (vv. 10-12)

10. You, then, why do you judge your brother? Or why do you look down on your brother? For we will all stand before God's judgment seat.

Paul addresses both sides of the dispute over the eating of meat. To the weaker brother, who ate no meat, he asks, *Why do you judge your brother?* By attempting to impose his rigid views on others, this weak brother was judging them, probably even accusing them of being sinners. To the stronger brother Paul asks, *Why do you look down on your brother?* Apparently the stronger believers ridiculed the views of the vegetarians, treating them as if they had no merit.

By asking these two questions, Paul reminds both parties that judging belongs to God, not to them. His words also remind us that *we will all stand before God's judgment seat.* We will all have to give an account before God. We do not dread that judgment in terms of our salvation, for we know we have an advocate, even Jesus Christ, who will plead our case before the Father. Still, it appears we will give an account for how we have treated our brothers and sisters.

11. It is written:

"'As surely as I live,' says the Lord, 'every knee will bow before me; every tongue will confess to God.'"

Paul cites Isaiah 45:23 as proof for his statement regarding the judgment. Bowing the *knee* is universally recognized as an act of submission. In that final scene, every person will submit to God, even those who had rejected him in this life. In the same way *every tongue will confess to God.* This will not be a confession of sins. It will be too late for that. It will be, rather, a recognition and acknowledgment that he is the Sovereign of the universe.

12. So then, each of us will give an account of himself to God.

These are sobering words for those who live in our times. We try to avoid personal responsibility for our mistakes and sins and blame others for our problems. But these excuses won't cut it on that final day.

B. PUT NO STUMBLING BLOCK IN ANOTHER'S PATH (v. 13)

13. Therefore let us stop passing judgment on one another. Instead, make up your mind not to put any stumbling block or obstacle in your brother's way.

To both sides in the dispute over the eating of meat Paul urges a moratorium on judging. The only way that such a moratorium will work is for both parties to observe it. Such an agreement must be based on mutual trust, respect, and love.

The latter part of the verse is directed toward the strong. They must act in such a way as to avoid putting a *stumbling block,* or an occasion to fall, in the path of another. Our Christian liberty allows us to engage in a wide range of activities that are not of themselves sinful. Yet we must not use that liberty in such a way that it causes another person to violate his or her conscience and fall into sin.

IV. SHOW CONCERN FOR OTHERS (ROMANS 15:1, 2)

A. HELP THE WEAK (v. 1)

1. We who are strong ought to bear with the failings of the weak and not to please ourselves.

Paul continues his discussion of the *strong* and *weak* Christians, focusing on the obligations of the strong. They are to *bear with the failings of the weak.* The word translated "to bear" is the same word used in Galatians 6:2 where Paul admonishes us to "carry each other's burdens." The strong not only tolerate the viewpoints of the weak, they expend themselves for the sake of these weaker believers.

Saving the Helpless

On April 12, 1999, Ivers Sims, an Atlanta construction worker, was operating a 250-foot-tall cantilevered crane that towered over the work site when a fire broke out below. Soon the crane itself was on fire, and Sims was trapped high above the ground. To escape the smoke and heat, he crawled out to the concrete counterweight on the crane's horizontal arm. His only hope for rescue was from above.

As the crane swayed in the gusting wind, a forest-fire-fighting helicopter was brought in as a means of saving him. The pilot directed his craft through the smoke and turbulence caused by the flames to a spot eighty feet above Sims. Even that far above the inferno, the heat was intense. Matt Mosely, a firefighter, risked his own life by dropping by cable to the swaying crane, then strapping Sims into a harness. Both men were then lowered safely to the ground away from the fire. The rescue was in the best of the fire-fighter tradition: those with the strength, skill, and training sometimes take extraordinary risks to save the helpless who otherwise might lose their lives.

What we are asked to do in terms of coming to the aid of weaker brothers and sisters is nowhere near as exciting and attention getting as the rescue of Ivers Sims. No one is likely to be called a hero for bearing the burdens of his neighbor. However, the task is no less important, since the spiritual life of another person may be at stake. In giving aid to others who are weaker than ourselves, rather than seeking our own pleasure and convenience, we are demonstrating that we have come to a true understanding of what the gospel of Christ is about. —C. R. B.

B. Edify One Another (v. 2)

2. Each of us should please his neighbor for his good, to build him up.

Each of us probably refers to the stronger Christian, thus continuing the discussion from the previous verse. In the same way, *neighbor* in this context should not be understood as including all one's neighbors but only fellow Christians. Obviously, there are some limits on how far one should go to please his fellow Christians. Paul spells out these limitations: *for his good, to build him up.* We are to please our neighbors only to the extent that our actions contribute to their spiritual maturity.

CONCLUSION

A. "In All Things Love"

"In matters of faith, unity; in matters of opinion, liberty; in all things love." Some groups have taken this statement as the basis for their relationships among themselves and with those outside their group. This statement summarizes what Paul teaches in today's lesson. If it were understood and followed, it could well bring unity and harmony within congregations and between denominations. As noble as this statement is, however, it does pose some problems. First of all, we have to define what we mean by "faith." It must include the central facts of the gospel: Jesus Christ is the divine Son of God; he lived on earth, died for our sins, and was raised from the dead; he ascended into Heaven and someday will return. These statements do not comprise "the faith" in its entirety, but they are certainly statements that must be considered essential.

Even these statements, however, have been the center of controversy. For example, while there is agreement that the Lord will return, there is considerable disagreement about the details. Indeed, disagreements over such concepts as premillennialism, postmillennialism, and amillennialism often have been heated, dividing congregations and even whole fellowships. The list of theological issues over which people have disagreed, debated, and even fought could go on almost without end.

What Do You Think?

How do we determine whether or not we are uplifting a fellow Christian "for his good, to build him up"?

PRAYER

Gracious God, we recognize that we live in a world that is becoming more complex with more situations in which Christians disagree among themselves. May today's lesson give us insights that help bring harmony to our discordant world.

Even as we judge others, let us never forget that each of us must stand before you in that final judgment. Through Jesus we pray. Amen.

When we begin to deal with matters of opinion, we run into similar problems. For example, few people would want to argue that the color we paint the walls in the church nursery is a matter of faith. Yet we have seen heated debates over just such issues. All of us have been conditioned by our culture to think in different ways and to approach matters with built-in prejudices. And we all have prejudices! Separating the essential elements of faith from matters of opinion has never been an easy task. But that task is now more difficult than ever because of the intermingling of cultures from all over the world. And these cultural differences are not just national or ethnic. Some of the most serious disagreements in our churches today are intergenerational.

An objective study of church history leads one to the easy conclusion that most of the divisions and conflicts in the church have come over matters of opinion and not of faith. That's where love comes in—or needs to. In one congregation, a young woman planned to hold her wedding reception in some of the church's classrooms. However, some in the church believed that 1 Corinthians 11:22 ("Don't you have homes to eat and drink in?") prohibited eating in the church building. When the bride and her family learned of this, they quietly and without making an issue of it rented a nearby hall for the reception. Love won out!

Women missionaries serving in some tropical jungle areas have another problem. There the nationals expect women to wear long skirts. Of course, slacks or jeans would make more sense, providing protection against insects and underbrush as they travel through the jungle. But because they love the people they serve and do not wish to offend them, they are willing to be guided by the sensitivities of the nationals.

Love, however, works both ways. The weaker brother or sister has a sensitive conscience that requires performing certain acts or prohibits engaging in other activities. This in itself is not a problem. The problem arises when he or she seeks to impose these duties or restrictions on others. In this kind of a situation they need to show love toward others by carefully examining their convictions. They need to ask themselves whether their convictions are based on Scripture or on cultural preferences.

Perhaps the most troubling source of discord among churches almost everywhere deals with styles of worship. Some prefer traditional styles; others want contemporary services. By now we all recognize that there is no easy solution to these so-called "worship wars." Yet in some congregations tolerant love is winning out, and solutions are being found.

B. JUDGING

"Do not judge, or you too will be judged," Jesus taught in the Sermon on the Mount (Matthew 7:1). Paul echoes these sentiments in today's lesson text. But we need to look more closely at what Jesus had in mind. He was condemning hypocritical, biased judgments—not all judgments. That is made evident only a few verses later when he warned against false prophets and affirmed that "by their fruit you will recognize them" (Matthew 7:15-20). Certainly a fruit inspector has to make some judgments. In the same way, Paul did not mean that Christians should never make any judgments. For instance, he insisted that the Corinthian church make some painful judgments about some of its sinful members: "Come out from them and be separate" (2 Corinthians 6:17).

Upon what basis, then, should we make judgments when we have to make them? The important thing is that we base our judgments on the Scriptures, not upon our personal feelings or biases. This is not an easy task, but it is one that we must accept if we are to have peace with our fellow Christians.

THOUGHT TO REMEMBER

"Blessed are the peacemakers: for they will be called sons of God" (Matthew 5:9).

Discovery Learning

This page contains an alternate lesson plan emphasizing learning activities. Classes desiring such student involvement will find these suggestions helpful. The next page is a reproducible activity page to further enhance discovery learning.

LEARNING GOALS

After participating in this lesson, each student will be able to:

1. Summarize what Paul says about the attitude with which a Christian should handle matters on which believers disagree.

2. Explain the significance of living unto the Lord in the context of getting along with others.

3. Suggest how a particular situation involving a disputable matter, either in the class or the church, could be handled in a way that will promote peace and will edify others.

INTO THE LESSON

Assign students to groups of four. Create a handout (or refer to the appropriate page in *NIV® Bible Student*) to have students answer these questions:

1. What movies should Christians never see?

2. What music should Christians never listen to?

3. What foods should Christians never eat?

4. What clothes should Christians never wear?

Collect the papers. On opposite walls of the classroom, mount two signs. Print "Agree" on one, "Disagree" on the other. Choose a few examples for each question. Read the example, then ask the individual class members to move to the sign that best represents their positions. Ask one or two members to defend each position taken.

Ask, "Who should determine such judgments?" Follow up with, "What arguments come because of such judgments?" Say, "Today's lesson is about handling controversy within the church. Paul gives us principles for getting along with others when there are disagreements."

INTO THE WORD

Remind students of Paul's purpose in the latter part of Romans. Read the "Lesson Background" (page 301). Paul's logical teachings are to have practical applications.

Form groups of six to eight. Use the "Issues and Attitudes" section of the reproducible page that follows, and ask each group to read through the passage and to circle "issues" and "attitudes" cited in the text. Each group should have a reporter. After a few minutes, call the groups together for reports.

Use an overhead transparency or a marker board to list the groups' findings. (**Issues** could include eating, drinking, and observing holy days. **Attitudes** may include accepting each other and building up each other.)

Ask, "Why did the Roman Christians have trouble with these issues?" and "Why does Paul say it is important to reflect these attitudes?" (Romans 15:7). People should be able to see the accepting nature of the church, so that God is praised. Say, "In your group, choose what you believe is the 'key verse' of this Scripture." Focus on Romans 14:13.

INTO LIFE

Call the class back into its original groups. Say, "Take your original list of 'nevers.' Using Romans 14 and 15, how would you help weaker Christians and stronger Christians maintain peace and unity? Be specific." Allow ten minutes for this discussion.

Option: Print the following two case studies. Distribute one to each half of the class. Discuss solutions in groups of four.

CASE ONE. The church has recently purchased a drum set to be used during worship. Several members have expressed reservations concerning the tempo of the music, the volume of the drums, and song selections. Others believe the drums should be used more often, along with other instruments. In fact, this group would like to see more new music used. How can the opposing parties apply the teaching of Romans 14 and 15?

CASE TWO. Your church has a large fellowship hall/gymnasium. Someone has proposed that, in order to reach out to new people, you should offer exercise classes, dance lessons, and classes on self-defense so that church members can invite non-Christian friends to introduce them to your building. Several people raised objections. How do you help these two groups apply Romans 14 and 15 to your church?

Whichever option is used, call the class together and ask for groups to share their insights. Be prepared to guide students to understand the principles of Romans 14 and 15. Helpful information is contained in the commentary on Romans 15:1, 2 and in the Conclusion.

Close by asking each member to reflect on the following. "What do you do that causes someone to think less of Christ?" Follow up with "What specific steps will you take this week to bear the burdens of someone?" Allow a few minutes for each person to write several things he or she will do. Lead the class in praying Romans 15:5, 6.

Issues and Attitudes

Assume that Paul has just sent you a letter concerning disputes in the church. Read this passage of Scripture—your letter!—and circle the words or phrases that are "issues." Then underline the words or phrases that are "attitudes."

ROMANS 14:1-13

1 Accept him whose faith is weak, without passing judgment on disputable matters.

2 One man's faith allows him to eat everything, but another man, whose faith is weak, eats only vegetables.

3 The man who eats everything must not look down on him who does not, and the man who does not eat everything must not condemn the man who does, for God has accepted him.

4 Who are you to judge someone else's servant? To his own master he stands or falls. And he will stand, for the Lord is able to make him stand.

5 One man considers one day more sacred than another; another man considers every day alike. Each one should be fully convinced in his own mind.

6 He who regards one day as special, does so to the Lord. He who eats meat, eats to the Lord, for he gives thanks to God; and he who abstains, does so to the Lord and gives thanks to God.

7 For none of us lives to himself alone and none of us dies to himself alone.

8 If we live, we live to the Lord; and if we die, we die to the Lord. So, whether we live or die, we belong to the Lord.

9 For this very reason, Christ died and returned to life so that he might be the Lord of both the dead and the living.

10 You, then, why do you judge your brother? Or why do you look down on your brother? For we will all stand before God's judgment seat.

11 It is written: "'As surely as I live,' says the Lord, 'every knee will bow before me; every tongue will confess to God.'"

12 So then, each of us will give an account of himself to God.

13 Therefore let us stop passing judgment on one another. Instead, make up your mind not to put any stumbling block or obstacle in your brother's way.

ROMANS 15:1, 2

1 We who are strong ought to bear with the failings of the weak and not to please ourselves.

2 Each of us should please his neighbor for his good, to build him up.

Hitting Home

Choose a situation in your congregation of believers that is potentially divisive. Write down the situation, and then choose the appropriate attitude(s) from those you underlined above. Ask God for help in developing the attitude(s).

GOSPEL OF FAITH

LESSON 10

WHY TEACH THIS LESSON?

In last week's lesson, Paul told us to "stop passing judgment on one another" (Romans 4:13). This week we hear him judge that certain people are to be "eternally condemned" (Galatians 1:8, 9)—what a switch!

Actually, it would be better to call this a matter of "discernment." Some things are not worth fighting over, and some things are. Opinions (last week's lesson) are not, but recognizing the exclusive truth of the gospel (this week) certainly is. This lesson will challenge you and your students not to take the gospel claims lightly.

INTRODUCTION

"I got my salvation the old-fashioned way: I earned it!" While few of us would ever be so bold as to say this openly, there is always the temptation to try to take matters into our own hands. Adam and Eve were impatient to share God's knowledge, so they ate the forbidden fruit. The people at Babel thought they could build their own tower to Heaven. Today, we may be tempted to think we can secure our own salvation by adding our acts of merit to the sacrifice of Christ.

Sometimes Christians, such as the believers in Galatia, turn from the gospel of faith to legalism. Legalism is the attitude of thinking we can earn salvation—and climb up the ladder of God's approval—by rigidly keeping a set of rules. Like the self-righteous Pharisee (Luke 18:11), we may even take pride in how much better we keep those rules than other people do. But the heart of the matter is this: do we trust Jesus or not? Are we saved by his blood or by our own goodness?

A. DANGERS OF LEGALISM

Even though Paul himself had planted the churches in Galatia (Acts 14), false teachers were able to come in and persuade the believers to turn back to the law for salvation. There were probably three things that made legalism so attractive to them—and us.

First, it seems so right. If rules like circumcision and Sabbath-keeping came from God, shouldn't they still be valid? Shouldn't we expect God to give his blessings on the people who keep those rules the best?

Second, it seems so innocent. What harm does it do to make just a few changes in the gospel? Perhaps we could even "help God out" by tacking on a few more requirements.

Third, it seems so easy. If I can get a surer claim on salvation by merely insisting on the rule of circumcision (or any other Old Testament law), why shouldn't I? At least with a rule like that I can know where I stand. It gives me a good feeling to have my salvation under my own control.

B. LESSON BACKGROUND

The lessons of this quarter have shown that faith in Christ is the heart of the gospel. We have been justified by faith rather than works of law, and we must live by that faith. But what if the gospel of faith is changed? What if the works of law in the Old Testament are combined with the gospel of faith in the New Testament? Is

DEVOTIONAL READING:
ACTS 13:26-39
BACKGROUND SCRIPTURE:
GALATIANS 1, 2
PRINTED TEXT:
GALATIANS 1:1, 2, 6-12; 2:15-21

LESSON AIMS

After participating in this lesson, each student will be able to:

1. Relate what Paul told the Galatians about the essence and the uniqueness of the gospel.

2. Contrast the true gospel with counterfeits both ancient and modern.

3. Examine one's life for any threats of legalism, and suggest a means by which to be guided by God's grace.

May
5

KEY VERSE

We, too, have put our faith in Christ Jesus that we may be justified by faith in Christ and not by observing the law.
—Galatians 2:16

it still the gospel? Will it still save? Paul had to confront this issue in Galatia, where some had deserted the original gospel for what they thought was a new and improved version. Alarmed that they were turning away from the truth, Paul sternly warned them that there is no other gospel.

I. GOD'S MESSENGER (GALATIANS 1:1, 2)

Paul wrote this epistle to the Galatian churches sometime after A.D. 50, following the Jerusalem Conference of Acts 15. This makes Galatians one of Paul's earliest letters.

A. THE WRITER (v. 1)

1. Paul, an apostle—sent not from men nor by man, but by Jesus Christ and God the Father, who raised him from the dead—

Paul begins by establishing his authority as *an apostle*. He is a man chosen and sent out *by Jesus Christ* himself. As apostles, Paul and the Twelve were given authority to be the Lord's spokesmen. The early church devoted themselves to what they taught (Acts 2:42). In Galatia, however, Paul's authority as an apostle was being challenged. Not only were certain people rejecting Paul as an apostle, they were rejecting, by extension, the apostolic gospel as well.

Paul stresses that his authority as an apostle comes from *God the Father*. The further note that God had *raised* Jesus *from the dead* underscores the fact that this is the same God who had accepted the sacrifice that Christ made at the cross. This was the very issue where the Galatians had lost their confidence, fearing that what Jesus did was not enough. All in all, this is a terse beginning to the letter, reflecting the seriousness of the situation in Galatia.

B. THE AUDIENCE (v. 2)

2. . . . and all the brothers with me,
   To the churches in Galatia.

Paul writes as a spokesman for the apostles and for *all the brothers* who knew the truth of the gospel. He does not stand alone as some kind of maverick preacher who puts his own personal spin on the gospel message.

The *churches in Galatia* were located in central Asia Minor (modern Turkey). Paul himself planted some of those churches on his first missionary journey, when he preached in Iconium, Lystra, and Derbe (Acts 13:51–14:24). While this area was located south of what was originally called Galatia, the Romans had combined both areas into a single province with that name.

II. GOD'S MESSAGE (GALATIANS 1:6-12)

After the salutation of verses 1-5, Paul dives right into discussing the problem. The absence of any praise for the Galatian churches in verses 1-5 is striking when compared to the salutations of his epistles to other churches.

WHAT DO YOU THINK?

Paul marveled that the Galatians would abandon the gospel for a code of legalism. What surprises you about people rejecting the gospel after they had once accepted it as true? How can the issues in question be addressed to call people back to the truth?

A. DANGEROUS COUNTERFEIT (v. 6)

6. I am astonished that you are so quickly deserting the one who called you by the grace of Christ and are turning to a different gospel—

Rather than his customary "I give thanks for you," Paul can only offer the sarcastic *I am astonished* to the churches of Galatia. It has been only a few years since they learned about Christ, and now they are *so quickly* turning away into false doctrine. They have been *called* to share in the wonderful *grace of Christ*, the undeserved favor and forgiveness of God. Now they are abandoning grace and turning to a counterfeit gospel: the gospel of legalism.

COUNTERFEITS

Back in the 1990s, the United States government began redesigning its paper money, starting with the hundred-dollar bill, then the fifty-dollar and twenty-dollar bills. In May of 2000, the ten-dollar and five-dollar bills were introduced. Many people did not like the new bills, saying, "They just don't look like real money—it's more like Monopoly® money!" Even though the new bills didn't seem like the "real thing" to some, there was a very important reason for the change.

With the advent of computers, the old bills had become too easy to counterfeit. Millions of counterfeit dollars were being foisted on an unsuspecting public each year. The new bills have several features that make them more difficult to counterfeit than the old ones: a special watermark that can be seen when the bill is held up to the light, a security thread that glows a different color under ultraviolet light, more detailed portraits, and ink that changes color when viewed from different angles.

So, whether Americans like it or not, the new money will stay. In this, many of us may be in a similar position to some of the Christians in Galatia. They *liked* the old way of "working" for their salvation, and Paul's gospel of God's grace was an idea they hadn't accepted because it didn't seem like *real* religion.

However, one of the problems with the old way was that it was too easy to counterfeit. One could go through the motions of being righteous without that righteousness being the "real thing." And that raises a question for us: What counterfeit approaches to Christian faith are we confronted with? —C. R. B.

B. TROUBLESOME FALSE TEACHERS (v. 7)

7. . . . *which is really no gospel at all. Evidently some people are throwing you into confusion and are trying to pervert the gospel of Christ.*

In verse 6, Paul spoke of "a different gospel." Here he is quick to add that the perverted gospel that the Galatians are accepting *is really no gospel at all.* The one true gospel does not come in a variety of flavors, shapes, and sizes; it cannot be altered to fit a person's own preferences.

Apparently, after Paul had left Galatia, false teachers had come in and had begun teaching that the Gentiles had to be circumcised and had to keep various other Old Testament laws in order to gain God's favor. Despite the clear pronouncement of the apostles at the Jerusalem Conference (Acts 15), these men insisted that all Christians had to live like Jews. They were trying to *pervert the gospel* by combining it improperly with precepts from the Old Testament law. (The name for those who taught this way is *Judaizers.*)

C. NO OTHER GOSPEL (vv. 8, 9)

8, 9. *But even if we or an angel from heaven should preach a gospel other than the one we preached to you, let him be eternally condemned! As we have already said, so now I say again: If anybody is preaching to you a gospel other than what you accepted, let him be eternally condemned!*

God determined what the *gospel* truth would be. He established the facts and set the terms of acceptance. No one—not even an apostle or *an angel from heaven*—has the right to overrule God.

The original gospel is the only true gospel. Whoever dares to preach a different gospel is God's enemy. Such a person is to be recognized as *eternally condemned* by God, which means that he or she is set aside as one whom God will destroy.

Paul repeats his warning to emphasize how serious the matter is. Whenever the gospel was preached, the Galatian believers needed to examine it to see whether it was the same as they had *accepted* from Paul in the beginning (cf. Revelation 22:18, 19). The original gospel is the inerrant standard.

DAILY BIBLE READINGS

Monday, Apr. 29—*Grace in Christ (1 John 2:1-6)*

Tuesday, Apr. 30—*Commandment of Love (1 John 2:7-17)*

Wednesday, May 1—*Living According to the Spirit (1 Corinthians 8)*

Thursday, May 2—*Everything for the Glory of God (1 Corinthians 10:23-31)*

Friday, May 3—*Commissioned Through Jesus Christ (Galatians 1:1-5)*

Saturday, May 4—*Gospel Is Not of Human Origin (Galatians 1:11-24)*

Sunday, May 5—*Salvation by Faith, Not Works (Galatians 2:15-21)*

WHAT DO YOU THINK?

Paul's condemnation of any who would preach another gospel is way out of step with current views of "tolerance" and acceptance of variant viewpoints. What charges are likely to be leveled against a person or church who takes a public stand for the one true gospel today? How can we answer these charges?

D. NO HUMAN ORIGIN (vv. 10-12)

10. Am I now trying to win the approval of men, or of God? Or am I trying to please men? If I were still trying to please men, I would not be a servant of Christ.

Paul may have been accused of omitting circumcision just to suit the Gentiles. His enemies could have said that he did not have the courage to make the Gentiles obey the Old Testament regulations. But Paul was not a man to fear confrontation. His bold message to the Galatians proved that he was not merely trying to *win the approval of* or *please men* rather than God. He knew that a servant must give an account of himself to his own master, not to others. And Paul was *a servant of Christ.*

11. I want you to know, brothers, that the gospel I preached is not something that man made up.

Paul's gospel was the true, original gospel. He could openly make known to them this fact. Just as his apostleship did not originate from any human source (v. 1), *the gospel* that Paul *preached* did not come from men either.

12. I did not receive it from any man, nor was I taught it; rather, I received it by revelation from Jesus Christ.

When Paul said the gospel was "not something that man made up" (v. 11), he meant it did not have a human source. When Paul says here that he did not receive the gospel *of man,* he means this divine message was not passed on to him by a human messenger. The *nor was I taught* clause that follows strengthens the fact that no human teacher brought Paul the gospel. Instead, the gospel had come directly to Paul *by revelation. Jesus Christ* himself laid open the truth to Paul.

Paul had seen the risen Christ on the road to Damascus (Acts 9:27), where his direct revelation began (cf. Galatians 2:2). When Paul proclaimed the gospel, he was speaking for Jesus. To prove that this was so, Paul later notes that there were no occasions in his early years when he could have learned the gospel from human sources (1:13-20).

III. GOD'S SALVATION (GALATIANS 2:15-21)

In Galatians 1:13–2:10 Paul continues his defense of his apostolic authority. Then, in 2:11-14, he notes how Peter had come to Antioch and had demonstrated acceptance of the Gentile Christians, even eating in their homes. (As a Jew he had been taught that Gentile homes and food were "unclean.") Then, when Jewish Christians from Jerusalem came to visit, Peter was suddenly afraid to be seen associating with the Gentile Christians. Paul, whose apostolic authority was second-to-none, confronted Peter with his wrongdoing.

A. JUSTIFIED BY FAITH (vv. 15, 16)

15. "We who are Jews by birth and not 'Gentile sinners' . . .

Paul points out that Peter himself had ceased to keep all the Jewish laws (v. 14), even though both he and Paul were *Jews by birth.* If even natural-born Jews no longer had to keep the regulations, why should the Gentiles who had become Christians have to keep them?

16. . . . know that a man is not justified by observing the law, but by faith in Jesus Christ. So we, too, have put our faith in Christ Jesus that we may be justified by faith in Christ and not by observing the law, because by observing the law no one will be justified.

This is one of the most important passages in this letter. Paul summarizes his three-fold stress to Peter that people are *not justified* (declared innocent in the sight of God) *by observing the law.* (This is the first time in the epistle—but certainly not the last—that Paul uses the words *justified* and *law.*)

WHAT DO YOU THINK?

What is the significance for us today that Paul received the gospel he preached by revelation? How does this fact apply to situations in which churches seek to change certain doctrines to be more "contemporary" or "politically correct"?

WHAT DO YOU THINK?

To accept the idea of being justified by faith, one must admit to being a sinner, one who needs to be justified. How might this concept, if better understood, refute the objections of those who accuse Christians of thinking they are better than other people? How can we make this point effectively?

The solution to the sinner's impossible predicament is not a new set of laws to keep. Paul reminded Peter that people are saved *by faith in Jesus Christ,* a truth stated three times here. Paul and Peter themselves had *put* their *faith in Christ Jesus,* trusting him and his sacrifice on the cross for their justification before God.

B. RETURNING TO SIN? (vv. 17, 18)

17. "If, while we seek to be justified in Christ, it becomes evident that we ourselves are sinners, does that mean that Christ promotes sin? Absolutely not!

Here Paul addresses a possible objection that might be raised: if people are saved by faith and not by keeping the law, won't this turn them loose to be worse *sinners?* And if so, wouldn't *Christ* then be to blame as one who *promotes sin? Absolutely not!* To be justified by faith does not mean that we have a license to sin (cf. Romans 6:15; Jude 4). Anyone who thinks salvation by faith makes one free to sin simply does not know the meaning of faith or follow the example of Christ.

It is inconceivable that Peter would have raised such an objection. Apparently, then, this is not part of what Paul said to Peter (even though many modern translations that use quotation marks include it). Perhaps Paul is mixing his words to Peter with commentary for the sake of his Galatian readers.

18. "If I rebuild what I destroyed, I prove that I am a lawbreaker.

To make his point, Paul puts himself in the place of the Galatians. What would happen if he rejected the principle of being justified by faith and tried to *rebuild* his record of good works and the framework of ritual laws? These were what he *destroyed* when he became a Christian. In such a case, the very best Paul could hope to accomplish would be to prove again that he was *a lawbreaker.*

C. CRUCIFIED WITH CHRIST (vv. 19, 20)

19. "For through the law I died to the law so that I might live for God.

The *law* itself had exposed Paul as a sinner and had pronounced the sentence of death: the soul that sins will die. But once Paul had *died to the law,* the law could do nothing more to him. When he was born again and given new life in Christ, he was free to *live for God.*

20. "I have been crucified with Christ and I no longer live, but Christ lives in me. The life I live in the body, I live by faith in the Son of God, who loved me and gave himself for me.

Paul repeats the same point of verse 19, but with more detail. When Christ died on the cross, he carried our sins and paid our penalty. When we put our full trust and confidence in him, we identify ourselves with him in that death. When we are *crucified with Christ,* we not only accept his death to pay the penalty for our sins, but we also agree to die to those sins (cf. Romans 6:2).

After Christ was crucified and buried, God gave him new life. Likewise, when we die with Christ and are buried with him, we are raised to new spiritual life. We *live,* and *Christ lives in* us. We still *live in the body,* but we walk by *faith* and live our lives for *the Son of God, who loved* us. It is only right that we should live for him, because he *gave himself for* us (cf. Romans 6:3, 4).

Use this poster to illustrate verse 20. Discuss what it means to be "crucified with Christ."

WHAT DO YOU THINK?

What are some ongoing evidences that one has been "crucified with Christ"? How is such a person different from those who have not been so united with Christ in his death?

LAW'S CONDEMNATION

Eighteen-year-old Daniel Altstadt was an Eagle Scout and a good student in 1975. But then he murdered his parents and sister with a hatchet. He also attacked his brother, leaving him paralyzed with a severed spinal cord. Then he set the house on fire. All of this was done apparently to collect insurance money. A jury convicted him of first-degree murder of his father and decided that he was insane by the time he killed his mother and sister and attacked his brother.

HOW TO SAY IT

Babel. BAY-bul.
Derbe. DER-be.
Galatia. Guh-LAY-shuh.
Iconium. Eye-KO-nee-um.
Judaizers. JOO-duh-IZE-ers.
Lystra. LISS-truh.
Pharisee. FAIR-ih-see.

PRAYER

Father, thank you for saving us through the death of Jesus on the cross. Help us cling to the cross for our salvation. Show us how to let Jesus live his life in us. In his name, Amen.

THOUGHT TO REMEMBER

The one true gospel is the gospel of faith.

Altstadt's attorney argued that the youth had snapped under the pressure of an overbearing and demanding father, whose laws for the family included even such things as how the children were to store their socks (toe-forward) in a drawer.

Twenty-five years later, Altstadt hanged himself in his prison cell. The laws laid down by his father had made him feel like an inferior person, and the laws of the state properly condemned him for his crime. He found no grace in either set of laws and could no longer live with himself.

The laws of our heavenly Father appropriately condemn us for our sinfulness, but fortunately for all of us, there is more to the story. The same God whose laws condemn us sent his Son to pay the penalty for us. What is demanded of us is that we willingly commit a form of spiritual "suicide." We are called upon to identify with Christ in his sacrificial death for us, so that we might also experience the new life that the risen Christ can give us. Giving up or even taking our own life cannot save us, but by willingly dying *to our sins,* we receive the gift of new life in Christ, a life no one can take away.

—C. R. B.

D. ACCEPTING GOD'S GRACE (v. 21)

21. *"I do not set aside the grace of God, for if righteousness could be gained through the law, Christ died for nothing!"*

Not even the finest saints of the Old Testament were able to live sinless lives. None of them ever made a perfect score on all the tests of life. If people had been able to achieve their own perfection, if *righteousness could* indeed *be gained through the law,* then there would have been no need for Jesus to die on the cross for them. If people could have saved themselves, then *Christ* would have *died for nothing.*

CONCLUSION

After Paul established churches in Galatia, certain people began to corrupt the truth of the gospel. These Judaizers wrongly taught that people couldn't become Christians without first becoming Jews. They insisted on circumcision, keeping the Sabbath, and various dietary laws. In short, they taught that the sacrifice of Jesus was inadequate and people had to add their own virtuous works to pay the price of salvation.

A. NO OTHER GOSPEL, THEN OR NOW

Just as the Judaizers came to Galatia and tried to pervert the gospel, other people through the centuries have tried to change the gospel of Jesus Christ. Sometimes they claim special visions; sometimes they claim visits from angels; sometimes they claim to be so intelligent that they no longer need the Bible to teach them God's truth.

The challenge for the church is to stand up for the truth of the gospel. Just as the Christians in the very beginning, we must continue steadfastly in the apostles' doctrine (Acts 2:42). When we hear religious teachers, we must always compare their message with the gospel preached by the apostles, the absolute and exclusive truth heard by the church in the beginning.

B. THE GOSPEL OF FAITH

The true gospel is the gospel of faith that cannot be combined with either legalism or license. We can put our trust in Jesus or we can put our trust in our own lawkeeping, but we cannot do both at the same time. And when we come to realize what Jesus did at the cross, when we acknowledge that sin is ugly and unacceptable to God, when we have our sins washed away by the precious blood of the Lamb, how could we even think of rushing back into our old defilement? To do so would make a mockery of the price he paid to set us free from that very sin!

Discovery Learning

This page contains an alternate lesson plan emphasizing learning activities. Classes desiring such student involvement will find these suggestions helpful. The next page is a reproducible activity page to further enhance discovery learning.

LEARNING GOALS

After participating in this lesson, each student will be able to:

1. Relate what Paul told the Galatians about the essence and the uniqueness of the gospel.

2. Contrast the true gospel with counterfeits both ancient and modern.

3. Examine one's life for any threats of legalism, and suggest a means by which to be guided by God's grace.

INTO THE LESSON

Bring to class a number of monetary bills from Monopoly® or other game sets. You could also make your own five-, ten-, twenty-, and hundred-dollar bills by cutting strips of green construction paper and putting the appropriate numbers on them. Divide your class into groups of four. Ask each group to examine the money and tell you whether it is real money. (Asking the question about a counterfeit assumes that there is a "real" bill.)

Ask one or two people in each group to place a real five- or ten-dollar bill in their hand. Now ask each group to list some differences between the counterfeits and the real. (*Answers may include size, feel, color, wording.*) Next ask, "What is the effect of using the real as opposed to using the counterfeit?" (*Possible answers include a person won't be arrested for using the real, and it's worth more.*)

After several have answered, share this: "The Treasury Department trains its agents to recognize counterfeit currency by having them diligently study authentic currency. Today, as we study Galatians 1 and 2, we will look for the marks of the real gospel as Paul teaches it."

INTO THE WORD

Your students need to understand the seriousness of Paul's concern in Galatians. Develop a short lecture from the material in the Introduction (page 309).

The following activity can be done with the whole class or in groups of five or six, depending on the time. Each will need a copy of the text. The reproducible page that follows has this text and a suggested activity. Have students follow the instructions to see Paul's concern about mixing the law and the gospel . If you use groups, assign the first Scripture passage, Galatians 1:1-12, to the odd-numbered groups; assign Galatians 2:12-21 to the even-numbered groups.

Say, "From the verses you have marked, we can see the characteristics Paul notes for the gospel. In your groups, list the characteristics given." On the chalkboard or on an overhead transparency make a list of the characteristics as developed by the groups. This will certainly include such attributes as *unique, revealed, true, impartial,* and *superior.* Your discussion also should include Paul's argument about how the gospel was given to Paul (by revelation, not invented or passed on to him by human agents).

Using this list and the information in the commentary, develop a brief lecture concerning the counterfeit gospel with which Paul contended. Include comments on the Judaizers and their challenge to incorporate more than God's design of the gospel.

INTO LIFE

After your lecture, ask the class to return to their groups. Have each group list two or three counterfeits to the gospel today. (*Their answers may include the formation of cults, the desire to be good enough for God, or a list of dos and don'ts to be a Christian.* See also the Conclusion in the lesson commentary, opposite page 314.) Help the class to recognize that we are talking about salvation issues, not about pursuing righteousness (as we learned in the book of Romans).

On strips of paper, print Galatians 2:16. Hand a strip to each member of the class. In their groups, individuals are to indicate ways in which we are tempted to justify ourselves by law. On the back of his or her strip, each class member is to write one or two ways. (*These may include keeping the Ten Commandments, tithing, attending church, or serving as a church officer.*) Ask the learners to write the international sign for "no" (a circle with a diagonal line within the circle) over the ways they have chosen. (*A similar activity is included in the student book, NIV® Bible Student.*)

Pass out index cards to each member. Have all print Galatians 2:20 on their cards. If there is time in class, encourage the students to begin the process of memorizing the verse. Challenge them to keep this verse in a prominent place for the next several days so that their lives are guided by the grace of God.

Close by having one person in each group pray for strength to live the life of faith. (Ask these members in advance if they will be willing to pray.)

True Gospel vs. Counterfeit Gospel

Read Galatians 1:1-12 and 2:12-21 given below. Put a ✔ beside any verse that relates to the true gospel. Put an ✗ beside any verse that describes the counterfeit gospel.

✔ or ✗   *GALATIANS 1:1-12*

1. Paul, an apostle—sent not from men nor by man, but by Jesus Christ and God the Father, who raised him from the dead—

2. and all the brothers with me, To the churches in Galatia:

3. Grace and peace to you from God our Father and the Lord Jesus Christ,

4. who gave himself for our sins to rescue us from the present evil age, according to the will of our God and Father,

5. to whom be glory for ever and ever. Amen.

6. I am astonished that you are so quickly deserting the one who called you by the grace of Christ and are turning to a different gospel—

7. which is really no gospel at all. Evidently some people are throwing you into confusion and are trying to pervert the gospel of Christ.

8. But even if we or an angel from heaven should preach a gospel other than the one we preached to you, let him be eternally condemned!

9. As we have already said, so now I say again: If anybody is preaching to you a gospel other than what you accepted, let him be eternally condemned!

10. Am I now trying to win the approval of men, or of God? Or am I trying to please men? If I were still trying to please men, I would not be a servant of Christ.

11. I want you to know, brothers, that the gospel I preached is not something that man made up.

12. I did not receive it from any man, nor was I taught it; rather, I received it by revelation from Jesus Christ.

GALATIANS 2:12-21

12. Before certain men came from James, he used to eat with the Gentiles. But when they arrived, he began to draw back and separate himself from the Gentiles because he was afraid of those who belonged to the circumcision group.

13. The other Jews joined him in his hypocrisy, so that by their hypocrisy even Barnabas was led astray.

14. When I saw that they were not acting in line with the truth of the gospel, I said to Peter in front of them all, "You are a Jew, yet you live like a Gentile and not like a Jew. How is it, then, that you force Gentiles to follow Jewish customs?

15. "We who are Jews by birth and not 'Gentile sinners'

16. Know that a man is not justified by observing the law, but by faith in Jesus Christ. So we, too, have put our faith in Christ Jesus that we may be justified by faith in Christ and not by observing the law, because by observing the law no one will be justified.

17. "If, while we seek to be justified in Christ, it becomes evident that we ourselves are sinners, does that mean that Christ promotes sin? Absolutely not!

18. If I rebuild what I destroyed, I prove that I am a lawbreaker.

19. For through the law I died to the law so that I might live for God.

20. I have been crucified with Christ and I no longer live, but Christ lives in me. The life I live in the body, I live by faith in the Son of God, who loved me and gave himself for me.

21. I do not set aside the grace of God, for if righteousness could be gained through the law, Christ died for nothing!"

GOSPEL OF ADOPTION

LESSON 11

WHY TEACH THIS LESSON?

As one who has an adoptive parent himself, I am always intrigued by stories of people who have grown up in loving, adoptive homes but choose, sometime later in life, to set out on quests to find their "real" parents. I myself have never been one who had a mind to do such a thing, believing fervently that my "real" parents were not my "natural" parents, but the ones who actually reared me.

Of course, many circumstances and emotions lie behind the decision to give a child up for adoption. Some natural parents are abusive and unfit to bring up children. Others, for a variety of reasons, believe the most loving thing they can do for their children is to put them in a position to be adopted by other parents more competent or better equipped for parenthood.

In our lesson today, Paul uses an adoption metaphor to describe our relationship to God. Our former condition was that of slaves—we were in an abusive situation. But God rescued us from that setting and adopted us as his own children and heirs. Use this lesson to help your students see our spiritual adoption in that light and to live with the confidence that God is now our "real" parent!

INTRODUCTION

A. WHO WILL INHERIT?

It is often said, "Where there's a will, there's a way." It is also said, "Where there's a will, there are relatives!" When it is time to divide a rich estate, long-lost friends and relatives often appear—seemingly from nowhere! Despite what the will says, they try to force each other out of the inheritance and claim it for themselves.

The Judaizers in Galatia were creating trouble for the church by teaching that some of the Christians could not inherit the blessings of God. They said that if a man were not circumcised, he was not eligible to be called a child of God. Trusting Jesus, they declared, was not enough. A man had to earn the right to his heavenly inheritance!

In the eyes of the false teachers, Gentile Christians were like unwanted orphans. Unless they submitted to circumcision and lived like Jews, they were not welcome in God's family. Paul had to step in and put a stop to such nonsense. As the appointed spokesman for the Lord, Paul became like a probate court. He had the authority to declare who was and who was not a legitimately recognized heir of God.

The irony of all this is that no one—Jew or Gentile—deserves to be in God's family or can earn the right to share in the inheritance. All of us were outsiders, strangers, rebels, and enemies. But God did not reject us as unwanted orphans; he had a plan for our salvation. From the time of Adam, God was preparing to accept and bless his people. The inheritance would not come through family bloodline or personal merit—it would come through Christ.

B. LESSON BACKGROUND

The lessons in this series have dealt with the power of the gospel, emphasizing the role of faith. Last week the scene shifted to Galatia, where Paul had planted churches on his first missionary journey. After he left, the truth of the gospel

DEVOTIONAL READING:
GALATIANS 4:21-31
BACKGROUND SCRIPTURE:
GALATIANS 3, 4
PRINTED TEXT:
GALATIANS 3:6-9, 23-29; 4:1-7

LESSON AIMS

After participating in this lesson, each student will be able to:

1. Explain the word pictures used by Paul in this passage to describe what Jesus has done for us.

2. Relate some of the blessings and responsibilities that come with being adopted into God's family.

3. Suggest a specific way in which a Christian's life can better reflect his or her standing as an adopted child of God.

May
12

KEY VERSE

You are all sons of God through faith in Christ Jesus.
—Galatians 3:26

began to be perverted by false teachers. They minimized the value of faith in Christ. They insisted that his sacrifice on the cross was not enough to pay the price for sin; people also had to earn approval by keeping the Old Testament laws. Today's lesson goes to the heart of this issue: Who will be approved to receive the blessings of God?

I. BLESSED WITH ABRAHAM (GALATIANS 3:6-9)

A. EXAMPLE OF FAITH (v. 6)

6. Consider Abraham: "He believed God, and it was credited to him as righteousness."

In the verses leading up to this statement, Paul began a series of arguments to show that the blessings of salvation do not come by works of law. The Holy Spirit, for example, did not come upon the believers in Galatia when they kept the law, but when they believed in Christ (v. 5).

Likewise, *Abraham* can be put on the side of faith, rather than on the side of works of law. When Abraham was an old man, God made him an incredible promise about future offspring and blessings. Against all reason, Abraham *believed God* and his faith *was credited to him as righteousness* (Genesis 15:6). He had the kind of faith that would obey the command to offer up his son Isaac. In this important historical precedent God showed that the people who would share his blessings were the people of faith, like Abraham.

B. FOLLOWING THE EXAMPLE (v. 7)

7. Understand, then, that those who believe are children of Abraham.

For nearly two thousand years the Jews had taken pride in the fact that they had descended from *Abraham* (cf. John 8:33, 39). Through Isaac, Jacob, and Jacob's twelve sons, the tribes of Israel had the blood of Abraham coursing through their veins. Some thought this alone made them favored by God.

The true *children of Abraham*, however, are *those who believe*. They are the people who believe God just as Abraham did. Even when God makes a promise that seems too good to be true, people who are like Abraham will trust what he says. When God says that the penalty for all our sins is covered by the blood of his Son, we have glad confidence that it is so.

C. BLESSED THROUGH FAITH (vv. 8, 9)

8. The Scripture foresaw that God would justify the Gentiles by faith, and announced the gospel in advance to Abraham: "All nations will be blessed through you."

God's plan from the beginning was to save the world *by faith*, not works. This was shown by God's statement in *the Scripture* that promised Abraham that *all nations* would *be blessed* in him. The Greek word for *nations* here is the same word rendered *the Gentiles* just before. It refers to people groups more than political boundaries. In fact, it is the root for our English word *ethnic*. It typically refers to any or all non-Jewish people groups.

God's promise to Abraham was a preview, a beautiful glimpse in advance, of the good news of salvation in Christ. In effect, this simple promise *announced the gospel in advance to Abraham* long before it ever came to pass. As Jesus told the Jews in Jerusalem, "Abraham rejoiced at the thought of seeing my day" (John 8:56).

9. So those who have faith are blessed along with Abraham, the man of faith.

There are two kinds of people who will one day stand before their final Judge. The first will try to stand on their own merit, trusting that they have done a good enough job of keeping the law and piling up good works. The others will be the

WHAT DO YOU THINK?

Paul's remark that the Gentile Galatians could be children of Abraham was a revolutionary concept. Who do you think found it more surprising, the Jews or the Gentiles? Why?

WHAT DO YOU THINK?

Paul said the promise to Abraham, "All peoples on earth will be blessed through you" (Genesis 12:3), was a prediction of the inclusion of Gentiles in God's plan of redemption. Why, then, do you think the Jews as a whole missed that? What significance do you think that has for us today?

people *of faith.* They will depend on the blood of Jesus shed on the cross to pay the penalty for their sins. When they put their faith in Jesus, they are doing the same as *Abraham, the man of faith,* and will be *blessed* by God with him.

A RICH LEGACY

Osgood, Indiana, is a rather unremarkable town. Fewer than two thousand people live within its two-and-a-half square miles. Among its citizens were two apparently common people, lifelong residents of Osgood—Gilmore Reynolds and his faithful wife, Goldie. They were frugal people, investing carefully and wisely in the stock market. Little did anyone guess what a blessing to their community this couple would become.

The Reynolds had no children, so they decided to help others when they could. From time to time, the town treasurer would receive a large check from the couple, but always with the stipulation that the gift was to be strictly anonymous (even the one hundred thousand dollars given for a new town hall).

Gilmore died in 1990, and Goldie in 1998. Their whole estate—twenty-three million dollars—was left to the town of Osgood. The gift exceeded the total assessed valuation of the whole town! So now, Osgood is being blessed by the marvelous gift of Gilmore and Goldie Reynolds.

Abraham may have seemed an unremarkable person to his neighbors back in Ur of Chaldees where he had grown up. But his faithful obedience to God resulted in great blessings to him. Even more so, his faithfulness was the basis of the fulfillment of a promise God had made when he called Abraham to follow wherever God would lead. The result is a blessing for all of us: the faith of that one man (and of his wife who went with him) has become the basis for people of every nation and era to inherit the riches of the kingdom of God.   —C. R. B.

II. UNITED WITH CHRIST (GALATIANS 3:23-29)

A. BROUGHT TO CHRIST (vv. 23-25)

23. Before this faith came, we were held prisoners by the law, locked up until faith should be revealed.

In the days of the Old Testament *before* God's people had *faith* in Christ, they were *held prisoners by the law.* They were *locked up* until a distant day of release. Though some of them caught a glimpse of what was coming, full knowledge of God's plan and *faith* in Christ would only *be revealed* later.

24, 25. So the law was put in charge to lead us to Christ that we might be justified by faith. Now that faith has come, we are no longer under the supervision of the law.

Paul compares the way God had used *the law* to a slave who was *put in charge* of the master's son. This slave was a male "nanny" of sorts, whose job was to watch over the child's behavior and to escort the child to and from school.

Just as the job of this slave was to take the children to the real teacher, the ultimate purpose of the law was *to lead us to Christ.* And when the minor child comes of age, the law is *no longer* in charge (see 4:1-7 below). Once the law had fulfilled its role in pointing to Christ, leading people to put their *faith* in him, its supervisory function ceased. Christians, then, whether Jewish or Gentile, are not under the law. The coming of Christ in the fullness of time (4:4) brings an end to the law's custodianship.

B. JOINED WITH CHRIST (vv. 26, 27)

26. You are all sons of God through faith in Christ Jesus,

It was a high privilege for the Gentiles to be counted as "children of Abraham" (v. 7). Now, an even higher status is announced for them. Whether their family

---

DAILY BIBLE READINGS

Monday, May 6—*One Body, One Bread (1 Corinthians 10:14-22)*

Tuesday, May 7—*All Gentiles Will Be Blessed (Galatians 3:1-9)*

Wednesday, May 8—*Receive the Promise by Faith (Galatians 3:10-14)*

Thursday, May 9—*Heirs According to the Promise (Galatians 3:19-29)*

Friday, May 10—*No Longer Slaves, but Heirs (Galatians 4:1-7)*

Saturday, May 11—*Do Not Turn Back (Galatians 4:8-16)*

Sunday, May 12—*Freedom in Christ (Galatians 4:17–5:1)*

Visual for lesson 11. This poster illustrates the one way for anyone to be justified: "by faith." Have it on display as you begin the lesson.

tree was made of Jews or Gentiles, they *all* were the *sons of God* as well. God was their father, and his parenthood was not established by any human bloodline, but by their *faith in Christ Jesus.*

27. . . . for all of you who were baptized into Christ have clothed yourselves with Christ.

At the first public preaching of the gospel after Jesus' ascension, the proclamation of the apostles was that people who believed in Jesus were to be baptized (Acts 2:38). The apostles certainly did not view having been *baptized* as a magic ritual or work of merit. Instead, baptism was the "point in time" when they *clothed* themselves *with Christ.* This new identity in him became more important than their own; his will replaced their will. Once they had been dressed in the filthy rags of their own unworthy deeds; now that they had put on Christ, they were clothed in the white robes of his righteousness (cf. Isaiah 61:10; Revelation 7:9).

C. EQUAL HEIRS IN CHRIST (v. 28, 29)

28. There is neither Jew nor Greek, slave nor free, male nor female, for you are all one in Christ Jesus.

In the Old Testament world of the Jews, the right to inherit was not given to Gentiles, to slaves, or to women. An ancient Jewish prayer even said, "Lord, I thank thee that Thou hast not made me a Gentile, or a slave, or a woman." But things change in Christ! When sinners repent and come into the family of God through faith and baptism (v. 27), nationalities, social standing (*slave* or *free*), and gender (*male* or *female*) do not matter. God welcomes all equally.

Keep in mind that God's family is not made up of "natural" children and "outsider" children. We are *all one in Christ Jesus* (cf. Romans 9:8). Whatever our color, our wealth, or our background, we all come into God's family on equal footing. Because God has welcomed us, we must welcome each other.

29. If you belong to Christ, then you are Abraham's seed, and heirs according to the promise.

Paul now slams the door shut on the Judaizers. They tried to require circumcision (and other legal observances) of those who wished to "join" them in being *Abraham's seed.* But those who are in Christ are part of that seed already and, by extension, *heirs* of eternal life.

III. ADOPTED BY GOD (GALATIANS 4:1-7)

A. A CHILD'S SITUATION (vv. 1, 2)

1. What I am saying is that as long as the heir is a child, he is no different from a slave, although he owns the whole estate.

The Gentiles in Galatia who have become Christians must not add circumcision to the gospel and thereby revert back to Judaism. The Jew of the Old Testament was like an infant in the family of God. He was potentially an *heir* but could not enjoy inheritance rights because he was not of age—he was *a child,* still under the watchful eye of his father's servant (3:24). A little child may one day grow up and become owner of *the whole estate,* but in the meantime he is no better than *a slave.*

2. He is subject to guardians and trustees until the time set by his father.

The child who is too young and immature to handle an inheritance will be placed under the care of *guardians and trustees.* Throughout his childhood he is at the bottom rung of the ladder of authority, since even the slaves in the household tell him what to do. The child will continue to be treated as a child, with no access to his inheritance, *until the time* comes which was *set by his father* for the child's coming of age.

WHAT DO YOU THINK?

What do you find most significant about the inclusive language of verse 28? Recognizing that this verse is concerned with acceptance into the body of Christ, and not with the specific roles of those who are in it, how should we demonstrate this truth?

B. A SLAVE'S SITUATION (v. 3)

3. So also, when we were children, we were in slavery under the basic principles of the world.

Looking back on his own Jewish ancestry, Paul described how he and his people were mere *children* in God's family. As children they could not obtain their inheritance; in fact, they were no better than slaves. They were enslaved by the law under the *basic principles* that differed little from *do*s and *don't*s anywhere in the pagan *world*.

To revert to Judaism was to become both an immature child and a slave. How could anyone in the Galatian churches want this? Why would they think that was progress?

C. ADOPTION (vv. 4, 5)

4. But when the time had fully come, God sent his Son, born of a woman, born under law.

God the Father had his timetable for the master plan of salvation. *When the time had fully come,* the stage was set for the gospel. Greece had provided a common language for the Mediterranean world; Rome had provided a time of peace and a good road system. Jewish synagogues and copies of the Old Testament in Greek were already found in all the major cities. The world was ready to hear—and to spread—the gospel.

Then *God sent his Son* to join the human race and die for our sins. Jesus was *born of a woman* and had to live *under* the *law.* Jesus stooped down to experience all the temptations and hardships that we face.

5. . . . to redeem those under law, that we might receive the full rights of sons.

Having lived a sinless life, Jesus could offer his life as a ransom *to redeem* lost sinners. He paid the price to buy out of bondage those who were still held *under law* (Mark 10:45). Jesus' death makes it possible for each of us to *receive the full rights of sons* in God's family. All Christians—including Gentiles, slaves, and females—are given the full inheritance rights that belong to *sons.*

If the Christians in Galatia turn back to keeping law in a futile attempt to earn God's favor, they are returning to slavery. After God has rescued them from spiritual poverty and has washed them clean in the blood of Christ, why should they be trying to sneak back to their old helpless existence? Instead, they should be grateful that God has welcomed them into his family.

A TOUCHING STORY OF ADOPTION

A wild mallard hen felt so much at home in the marina at Redondo Beach, California, that in two different years she chose the *Gypsea,* a sailboat moored there, for the site of her nest. She found a compartment on the deck that was to her liking, and there she hatched her clutch of seven eggs. When the father duck died after the ducklings were hatched, another drake adopted the family and patrolled the dock leading to the sailboat, keeping watch over his adopted family.

The owners of the Gypsea, Donald and Winifred Sudduth, also adopted the family of ducks. They accepted the inconvenience and cost of keeping the boat docked until the ducklings were mature enough to swim (or fly) away. Up to that point, the Sudduths provided food and a plastic washtub so the ducklings could eat and learn to swim.

We usually think of adoption as a relationship that exists between humans. As we have seen, it may exist between animals or between humans and animals. However, the most touching story of adoption ever told concerns God's reaching out to sinners. Although we were unworthy, God accepted the inconvenience of assuming care for any of us who is willing to become part of his family.

WHAT DO YOU THINK?

Paul said Jesus was born *"when the time had fully come."* How does God's timing give you comfort or reassurance today? Why?

HOW TO SAY IT

Abba. AB-buh.
Abraham. AY-bruh-ham.
Aramaic. AIR-uh-MAY-ik.
Judaizers. JOO-duh-IZE-ers.
Chaldees. KAL-deez.
Mediterranean. MED-uh-tuh-RAY-nee-un.
synagogue. SIN-uh-gog.
Ur. Er.

And yet, how insufficient a word *inconvenience* is to describe this action of adoption. This costly adoption was accomplished by Christ's willing sacrifice of his life so that all who wish may become a part of God's family. And we have full rights as heirs to all the heavenly blessings that our Father possesses!   —C. R. B.

D. INHERITANCE (vv. 6, 7)

6. Because you are sons, God sent the Spirit of his Son into our hearts, the Spirit who calls out, "Abba, Father."

God not only has sent forth his Son into the world (v. 4), he has also *sent the Spirit of his Son into our hearts.* The indwelling of the Holy Spirit in us is God's down payment, or first installment, of the inheritance we will receive in Heaven (see Ephesians 1:13, 14).

The Holy Spirit in our hearts becomes our link to the Father. The Spirit helps us when we pray (see Romans 8:26), enabling us even to address God as *Abba, Father* (also Romans 8:15). The word *Abba* is Aramaic (the native language of Palestine) and was what a child called his or her father in the intimacy of the family circle.

7. So you are no longer a slave, but a son; and since you are a son, God has made you also an heir.

Paul has used two different figures to illustrate what a person is like before coming to Christ. The Jews were like very young children; both Jews and Gentiles were like slaves. But in Christ a person is no longer *a slave,* but a *son* in God's family. Even more, the *son* is no longer a legally incompetent infant, but *an heir* of God.

CONCLUSION

A. WE ARE ADOPTED

Adoption is a wonderful thing. Loving parents open their arms to children who are unable to fend for themselves and have nowhere else to turn, providing the love and security of family. Some children are orphaned by war or famine. Other children need adoption because their parents cannot or will not provide for them. In our case, we were homeless by our own choice—we had chosen to abandon God. Homeless, helpless, enslaved by sin, we had no way to survive.

But God loved us in spite of ourselves. He set forth the gospel of adoption, the "good news" that Jesus has paid our debts and God has claimed us as his children. Though it is a humbling thing to realize, except for the grace of God we were unwanted and unwelcome.

God adopted us totally apart from any worth or value we could offer. We were not cuter or smarter than other orphans; we did nothing to earn his approval. He freely extended his goodwill to us at the cross. Whoever will join him there and accept his free offer of salvation in Christ can become his child forever.

B. WE WILL INHERIT

With adoption comes the right to inherit. Our loving Father has generously included us as heirs of eternal salvation. The promise made to Abraham also is extended to us, when we become his offspring through faith in Christ.

In Christ we already are beginning to enjoy the benefits of our inheritance. We no longer bear the load of past guilt. We are free from the fear that Satan will take us back to our former squalor and deprivation. The Holy Spirit now resides in our hearts as God's guarantee that he will follow through with all of our inheritance.

Finally, we will inherit eternal life in Heaven. In the Father's house are many mansions, plenty of dwelling places for all of us. Like little urchins who have slept in alleys and trash bins, our eyes will be wide with wonder at the beauty of our new home. Best of all, Heaven will bring us into the very presence of God.

WHAT DO YOU THINK?

What characteristics do you think should be evident in the lives of the children of God?

PRAYER

Abba, Father. Thank you for adopting us as your very own children and giving us an eternal inheritance in Heaven. Help us to be grateful for everything you have done for us.

THOUGHT TO REMEMBER

Because we have put on Christ, we are heirs of the promises of God.

Discovery Learning

This page contains an alternate lesson plan emphasizing learning activities. Classes desiring such student involvement will find these suggestions helpful. The next page is a reproducible activity page to further enhance discovery learning.

LEARNING GOALS

After this lesson each student will be able to:

1. Explain the word pictures used by Paul in this passage to describe what Jesus has done for us.

2. Relate some of the blessings and responsibilities that come with being adopted into God's family.

3. Suggest a specific way in which a Christian's life can better reflect his or her standing as an adopted child of God.

INTO THE LESSON

Distribute a sheet of ledger paper to each student. (A package can be bought at most office supply stores, or you can make a ledger sheet by making vertical lines on a sheet of regular ruled notebook paper.) At the top of the the sheet have the person write his or her name along with the heading, "Personal Ledger Sheet." (This activity is included in the student book, *NIV® Bible Student.*)

Have each person label four columns: "Items," "Expenses," "Credits," "Balance." Each person will then choose five monthly expenses to enter in the "Items" column, such as utilities, groceries, insurance, car expenses, and rent. The student should then enter monetary values in the next three columns for each item in such amounts that the balance is *negative.*

Have two volunteers tell their expenses and balances. After each one shares, say, "I give you a credit equal to one dollar over your expenses."

Ask the class, "What is necessary for the credit I offered to be effective?" (*Answers include the creditor's truthfulness and assets, the debtor's belief in the creditor, and the reputation of the creditor.*) Ask, "How would you feel if someone credited your account with an amount to clear your bills and debts?"

Say, "Today's study will show us how God has brought us into his family, canceling our debt, and setting us up to succeed as his child."

INTO THE WORD

Summarize the background for today's text (see page 317); then divide the class into groups of five or six participants. Give half the groups the "Group One" assignment; the other half "Group Two." Provide a large sheet of poster paper, pencils, and markers for each group. Answering the questions will help each group understand Jesus' work on our behalf.

Group One: Read Galatians 3:1-14, and answer the following questions. Create a "before and after" poster to depict what Jesus has done for us.

1. What was the basis of the Galatians' struggle? (*Seeking God's approval by performing God's law or believing his message.*)

2. How was Abraham considered righteous? (*By believing the message of God.*)

3. What did Jesus do for us to overcome the problem of our being unable to earn our right standing with God? (*He was hung on a tree to be our sacrifice, our curse, to satisfy God's justice.*)

Group Two: Read Galatians 3:23–4:7, and answer the following questions. Create a "before and after" poster to depict what Jesus has done for us.

1. How is the law like the overseers of children? (*The child needs to be taught, directed, and cared for. The law could do that for people.*)

2. How does Paul show that all are a part of Abraham's family? (*By being joined or belonging to Christ.*)

3. According to this text, who are sons of God? (*Those who have put on Christ, who through faith have been baptized into Christ.*)

Let each group explain its poster as they repeat the answers to the questions. Then distribute copies of the reproducible page that follows. Ask students to complete the first activity at this time.

INTO LIFE

Give these instructions: "Using your ledger sheet, this time fill in several lines of what you have done to fail God's standards. For example, under 'Items' you could write 'told a lie' or 'looked lustfully at a woman (or man) or a photograph of one.' After you have written several lines, write 'paid in full—Galatians 3, 4' across the lines. This represents what Christ has done for us."

Have the students brainstorm blessings and responsibilities of being adopted into God's family, such as being called *son*, having direct access to the Father, obeying the Father, and telling others the good news.

Have the students complete the second activity on the reproducible page. Then encourage each person to find a partner. The partners will then tell what they wrote—what they will do this week so that their lives will reflect their adoptive status with God. Ask the partners to pray silently for one another; then close in prayer.

Clothed with Christ

Read Isaiah 64:6 and Galatians 3:27. On the rags pictured here, write the things from which God has cleansed you. On the clean clothes, write some of the blessings of the new life.

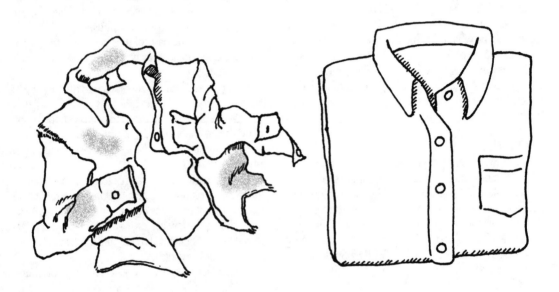

Prayer of Thanks

Fill in the "Adoption Proclamation" with your name. Then fill in the prayer below with some responsibility given to you by God as an adoptive child.

> Be it known unto all people everywhere that _____
> has been adopted by God to be his child forever in Christ.

Abba Father,

Thank you for adopting me into your family through Jesus. You have blessed me in many ways. This

week I pray that you will give me strength to _____

so that others may see that I am your child. Amen.

The Power of the Gospel

GOSPEL OF FREEDOM

LESSON 12

WHY TEACH THIS LESSON?

"Freedom isn't free!" We often hear this expression, usually as a sort of "battle cry" to arouse opposition against a perceived enemy that somehow threatens liberty. The phrase calls the hearer to be prepared to sacrifice something important or to accept a measure of risk in order to ensure that the threatened freedom isn't lost. As Memorial Day approaches, perhaps you will hear this phrase again.

But is it appropriate to apply this expression to the Christian faith? Yes and no. We answer "yes" in the sense that our freedom certainly wasn't free to God—it cost him the life of his Son to pay sin's penalty. But we also answer "no" in the sense that our spiritual freedom, and the future eternity in Heaven that it brings, is indeed free to us since we did nothing to earn it—and it's important not to *try* to earn it! Today, Paul reminds us of the consequences of losing sight of this fact.

INTRODUCTION

A. THREE DANGERS

On January 1, 1863, Abraham Lincoln issued the Emancipation Proclamation. By this decree he set free all the slaves of the Confederacy—at least in theory.

In actual fact, little was changed. Many of the slaves were not allowed to be told about the declaration. Even when they finally heard of it, they still were not free until the outcome of the Civil War was decided. After the war when the slaves actually were set free, many did not know how to use their newfound freedom. A few even returned to their former masters. They lived in the same slave quarters and worked like slaves in the same fields.

Freedom is of little value unless a person has learned how to claim it and keep it. Our freedom from the law has been provided by Jesus Christ, but it is not a freedom we can take for granted. There are at least three dangers that could cause us to forfeit the liberty that Christ purchased with his life's blood.

Danger #1: choosing to go back. When Christians agree to add circumcision to the requirements of the gospel and to be bound by other Old Testament laws, they are choosing to go back to the Old Covenant. When they think they have to earn God's favor by keeping such rules, they do not have enough faith in what Jesus did for them at the cross. When they try to justify themselves by works of law, they fall from the grace relationship they had in Christ.

Danger #2: being tricked into going back. Few Christians would knowingly choose to exchange their freedom in Christ for the chains of legalism. Many, however, have been tricked into thinking this is what God wants them to do. False teachers have persuaded them that God requires them to earn their salvation by good works, acts of penance, and blind obedience to their authority.

Danger #3: going back to a new slavery. A different kind of danger is the temptation to misuse the freedom of the gospel and become a slave to one's own flesh. If a person is set free from the law, but then is still trapped in his or her own sinful appetites, that person is even worse off than before!

The gospel frees us from both the condemnation of the law and the grip of sinful selfishness. Since this freedom came at a heavy price—the blood of

DEVOTIONAL READING:
1 JOHN 2:7-17
BACKGROUND SCRIPTURE:
GALATIANS 5:1-15
PRINTED TEXT:
GALATIANS 5:1-15

LESSON AIMS

After this lesson each student will be able to:

1. Explain how the gospel sets us free from the bondage to, and penalty of, the law.

2. Contrast Christian liberty with license.

3. Suggest some specific way to use Christian liberty to express love to some other person in the coming week.

KEY VERSE

You, my brothers, were called to be free. But do not use your freedom to indulge the sinful nature; rather, serve one another in love.

—Galatians 5:13

May
19

Jesus—we should treasure it and hold on to it. The goal of our freedom is not more sinning; the goal is faith working and serving through love.

B. LESSON BACKGROUND

The two preceding lessons have addressed the problem of legalism versus grace in Galatia. After Paul had planted churches in Galatia, Judaizers came in and convinced some of the Christians there that they needed to be circumcised and to keep the Old Testament laws in order to be saved. The good news of the gospel, however, is that we are saved by faith in Christ (Galatians 2:16).

I. DON'T GO BACK (GALATIANS 5:1-6)

A. STAND FAST (v. 1)

1. It is for freedom that Christ has set us free. Stand firm, then, and do not let yourselves be burdened again by a yoke of slavery.

Freedom must never be taken for granted. If people do not vigilantly guard their freedom, it will be taken from them. Similarly, Christians must *stand firm* in the liberty of the gospel of grace. *Christ* shed his blood as the ransom price for our sins; his death has *set us free* forever from the chains of the law.

Freedom in Christ is more than just one of the "extras" that Christians enjoy. It is a precious gift and a personal responsibility. If we appreciate what it cost Jesus to purchase our freedom, we will not easily surrender it. Instead, we will stand firm and not allow ourselves to become *burdened again by a yoke of slavery* to rules and rituals. We must not bow our necks again to that yoke (cf. Acts 15:10).

LIVING FREE OR RETURNING TO BONDAGE?

Maria Jeronimo died in June of 2000. She was considered by many to be the oldest woman in the world at the time of her death. She was not recognized as such by the *Guinness Book of Records,* since the publication demands a birth certificate or other irrefutable evidence. However, church records indicated that Jeronimo was 129 years old when she died.

Jeronimo was born a slave in Brazil. She was emancipated at the age of seventeen in 1888 when that nation became the last country in the Western Hemisphere to abolish slavery. But even as a free woman, Jeronimo continued to live in the same locale, doing the same kind of housemaid's work as she had done before she was freed.

Freedom did not erase the memories of slavery from Maria's mind. Even in her old age, she could recall life as a slave: the rapes, the frequent sicknesses, the families torn apart. Even after her mind faded in the last months of her life, her scarred back still bore testimony to the beatings she had received from her masters more than a century earlier. In her last interview (at age 127), she said she had only one wish left: "Now, I just want to see God." Maria Jeronimo was looking forward. She had reason not to want to go back.

When it comes to the slavery of sin, we carry with us the scars of our past. Strangely, many whom Christ has emancipated find themselves going back into the yoke of bondage instead of looking forward to the blessings and rewards of freedom that God has prepared for us.   —C. R. B.

B. REJECT CIRCUMCISION (vv. 2, 3)

2. Mark my words! I, Paul, tell you that if you let yourselves be circumcised, Christ will be of no value to you at all.

Paul emphasizes how important his point is by making a formal statement: *Mark my words!* In the earlier chapters of Galatians, he proved his authority to speak as an apostle. The gospel he preaches is the vital message they must heed. If they continue to compel believers to *be circumcised*, they are expressing a lack

WHAT DO YOU THINK?

Suppose a guest speaker in your church said, "The idea that we are 'free' in Christ is a mistake. Paul was overreacting to Pharisaic legalism! The truth is you must follow some rules to know you are living right. Let me tell you the three rules you must follow to be a good Christian and earn salvation." In the question and answer time that followed, what would you want to say?

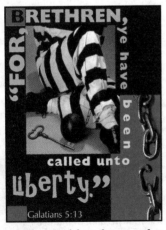

The visual for today reminds us of what a great blessing our freedom in Christ really is.

of faith in Christ. If they trust the law to save them, *Christ* will not be of any *value*, because they do not have confidence in him.

Paul's warning is not addressed to everyone who has ever been circumcised (cf. 1 Corinthians 7:18). Paul will plainly say that neither circumcision nor uncircumcision matters at all (Galatians 5:6). What is at issue here is the ongoing practice of the church to require the ritual as a step to salvation. This was a key point of dispute at the "Jerusalem Council" (cf. Acts 15:5, 10).

3. Again I declare to every man who lets himself be circumcised that he is obligated to obey the whole law.

Again Paul gives solemn testimony that one who accepts circumcision must face the enormity of the mistake he is making. If a man has put his faith in Christ but then agrees to *be circumcised*, he is returning to the Old Covenant. By accepting the badge of that covenant, he becomes *obligated to obey the whole law*.

The false promise of legalism is that, by keeping a few selected laws, one can earn "extra credit" with God. In fact, however, the moment we decide we need to add the merit of lawkeeping to the sacrifice of Christ, we are obligated to keep all the laws (James 2:10). Either we can be saved by depending on the cross of Jesus, or we can try (in vain) to save ourselves by lawkeeping.

C. DON'T FALL FROM GRACE (vv. 4, 5)

4. You who are trying to be justified by law have been alienated from Christ; you have fallen away from grace.

Christ becomes *alienated from* the person who does not trust him. He cannot save people who do not put their faith in him, nor can he save people who put their faith in him and then take it back.

The latter *have fallen away from grace*. Such a fall does not happen by accident, nor does it result from some moral failure. It happens when a person deliberately turns away from Jesus and depends on someone or something else for salvation. Such a person has lost confidence in Christ and is outside the grace of God.

5. But by faith we eagerly await through the Spirit the righteousness for which we hope.

Christians are a people of *hope*. That hope is a confident expectation. It is not based on any merit or goodness of our own, but on the *righteousness* of Christ that is imputed to us *by* our *faith* in him. *Through* the inner strength of God's Spirit (see Ephesians 3:16), we confidently *await* the goal of that hope: a declaration of "not guilty" on the Judgment Day.

D. PUT FAITH TO WORK (v. 6)

6. For in Christ Jesus neither circumcision nor uncircumcision has any value. The only thing that counts is faith expressing itself through love.

Paul would not have anyone think his standing with God to be based on a regulation that was part of the law that was nailed to the cross (Colossians 2:14). *Circumcision* has no power to save, and neither does *uncircumcision* (cf. 1 Corinthians 7:19). What matters, rather, is a person's present relationship with Christ.

The basis of that relationship is *faith* rather than law. But we must not think that real faith is merely an opinion about who Jesus is (cf. James 2:19). Real faith is always active faith, *expressing itself through*—or "being energized by"—*love*. Stated differently, "Faith without deeds is dead" (James 2:26).

II. DON'T BE MISLED (GALATIANS 5:7-12)

A. THOSE WHO MISLEAD (vv. 7-9)

7. You were running a good race. Who cut in on you and kept you from obeying the truth?

WHAT DO YOU THINK?

If we "eagerly await . . . righteousness," does that mean our righteousness now does not matter? Why or why not?

DAILY BIBLE READINGS

Monday, May 13—Lead the Life the Lord Assigns You (1 Corinthians 7:17-24)

Tuesday, May 14—Am I Not Free? (1 Corinthians 9:1-12)

Wednesday, May 15—Free, But a Slave to All (1 Corinthians 9:15-23)

Thursday, May 16—New Birth Into Living Hope (1 Peter 1:3-12)

Friday, May 17—God's Servants Are Free People (1 Peter 2:11-17)

Saturday, May 18—Free From Fear (1 Peter 3:13-22)

Sunday, May 19—You Were Called to Freedom (Galatians 5:4-15)

WHAT DO YOU THINK?

What kinds of hindrances threaten to act like yeast and "work through" the church of today and prevent her from obeying the truth of our freedom in Christ?

When Paul preached the gospel in Galatia on his first missionary journey, many people became Christians. Congregations were started, and soon Paul was able to appoint elders in every city (see Acts 14:23). The Galatian Christians were off to a good start and *were running a good race.*

Then something went wrong. Someone stepped in to hinder their progress in the gospel. Someone convinced them not to obey *the truth* that is in Jesus. Now Paul challenges them to identify and expose the false teachers.

8. That kind of persuasion does not come from the one who calls you.

This false *persuasion*, or way of thinking, did not come from God, who calls people to accept the gospel of grace. The Galatians should remember how God had called them through Paul's preaching, and how quickly they had turned away (Galatians 1:6). Then they should ask themselves why they had allowed anyone to lead them away from the salvation of the cross and take them back to the law.

BE CAREFUL WHAT YOU SWALLOW

An article by George Rector, a food column writer, in the *Saturday Evening Post* for September 5, 1936, recommended serving green salad in a wooden bowl. The article specified that the bowl was to be unvarnished, rubbed with a clove of garlic before the salad was placed in it, and never, *never* washed. Supposedly, this practice would "cure" the wood and each successive bowl of salad would be more delicious than the previous one.

So, for decades, hosts of American cooks followed Rector's advice, not knowing that they were victims of a hoax. Sometime in the 1960s, Rector admitted that he had invented the idea to give Americans some self-esteem in the preparation of food by (supposedly) doing it in the "French way." The French were considered by many Americans of that time (and this) to be the world's experts in the culinary arts. What Rector's readers did not know was that, instead of "curing" the wood, the salad dressing soaked into the pores of the wood, and since the bowls were never washed, they became saturated with rancid oil.

When those who are reputed to be experts lead us astray, there can be serious consequences for our health, whether physical or moral and spiritual. It was the latter kind of danger the Galatians found themselves in. By listening to false teachers, they were putting their souls at risk, turning away from faith in Christ to trust in works of the law. There are still teachers who would lead us astray. The moral of the story is that we should be careful of what we swallow, whether it is salad out of a rancid bowl or ideas from a false teacher. Both can hurt us.   —C. R. B.

9. "A little yeast works through the whole batch of dough."

A *little yeast* can be a good thing or a bad thing. In the parables of the kingdom of Heaven, Jesus used the illustration of yeast to show what great things can come from small beginnings (Matthew 13:33). But if the influence of the yeast is bad, like that of the Pharisees and Sadducees, it can cause great evil and must be avoided (Matthew 16:6). The yeast of the Judaizers in Galatia was threatening *the whole batch*, by corrupting doctrine in the entire church.

B. PENALTY FOR FALSE TEACHERS (v. 10)

10. I am confident in the Lord that you will take no other view. The one who is throwing you into confusion will pay the penalty, whoever he may be.

In spite of the attempts of the Judaizers to pervert the truth of the gospel, Paul expresses confidence in his converts in Galatia. He trusts them to agree with him about salvation by grace, and he is sure that they will not *take* any *other view.*

Every false teacher who troubles the church with false doctrine will *pay the penalty* from God. It does not matter if the person is rich or powerful; *whoever* is perverting the truth is under the curse of God (cf. Galatians 1:8, 9; Jude 12, 13). The sacred truth of the gospel of freedom must be preserved!

C. CONFLICT WITH FALSE TEACHERS (vv. 11, 12)

11. Brothers, if I am still preaching circumcision, why am I still being persecuted? In that case the offense of the cross has been abolished.

Some people claimed that Paul was inconsistent in his preaching. When he was among Jews, they said, he gladly enforced *circumcision* when it suited him. But when he was among Gentiles who might balk at such a command, he would change his message. In fact, however, Paul never required anyone to be circumcised as a matter of salvation.

Comparing the cases of Timothy and Titus is insightful. On one occasion, Paul had Timothy circumcised only because it was expedient in light of his future work in evangelizing Jews (Acts 16:3). But when certain "false brothers" demanded that Titus be circumcised as a matter of salvation, Paul refused. To have allowed it would have invalidated the message of grace (Galatians 2:3-5).

Paul shows the obvious error of the false charge: if he still preaches *circumcision*, why is he *still being persecuted* by the Jews? If Paul had preached a gospel that combined law and grace, the stumbling block or *offense of the cross* would have been removed. Jews would not object to Jesus or the gospel if it were on their own terms.

12. As for those agitators, I wish they would go the whole way and emasculate themselves!

Paul's wish *for those agitators* who harm the church is rather shocking. Instead of insisting on a partial cutting (circumcision), they should just go ahead and castrate themselves, as did the local priests who served the pagan goddess Cybele. One cannot mix the gospel with any other form of religion, whether pagan or Jewish. Perhaps if the false teachers considered their teachings in that ugly light, they would see the error of their way.

III. DON'T MISUSE FREEDOM (GALATIANS 5:13-15)

A. LOVE IS THE REASON FOR FREEDOM (v. 13)

13. You, my brothers, were called to be free. But do not use your freedom to indulge the sinful nature; rather, serve one another in love.

As *brothers* in Christ (see v. 11), Christians *were called to be free*. We have been invited to enjoy freedom from the demands of the law and from the guilt of sin. But after we have accepted this liberty, Satan still does not give up. He tempts us to exploit our liberty as an occasion *to indulge* the flesh (cf. Jude 4)—"flesh" is the literal translation of the word rendered *sinful nature* here. However, Christ did not give us freedom from the law so that we could be more sinful (cf. Romans 6:1, 2).

We have been given our freedom so that we can utilize liberty in love. Because we are motivated by *love,* and not because we are under compulsion by the law's demands, we can *serve one another.*

WHAT DO YOU THINK?

How do some people exploit Christian liberty? How can we be sure we are not guilty of doing so?

B. LOVE FULFILLS THE LAW (v. 14)

14. The entire law is summed up in a single command: "Love your neighbor as yourself."

Everything the *law* tried to compel people to do *is summed up* in a *single* statement: *Love your neighbor as* you love *yourself.* When a person loves his neighbor, he does not need to be told not to kill him. Neither does he need to be warned not to steal from him, lie to him, or take his wife away from him. Love covers all the situations better than any list of laws (cf. Luke 10:25-28; Romans 13:9).

Love is a better motivator than law for doing the right action. A husband who provides for his wife only because the law requires it will not be a very good husband. Sincere love will prompt him to do many things that law would not. In the same way, Christians who know the love of God should be motivated by that love to care about the needs of others (1 John 3:17). Just as we would not ignore our own need of food, clothing, or medicine, we should have the same concern for our neighbors.

The principle of loving others "as we love ourselves" is sometimes misunderstood to mean that we must first have an unhealthy preoccupation with our own needs, or that we should admire ourselves and find ways to boost our self-esteem. What it *does* mean is that we should care about meeting the needs of others, just as we naturally care about meeting our own needs.

C. LACK OF LOVE DESTROYS (v. 15)

15. *If you keep on biting and devouring each other, watch out or you will be destroyed by each other.*

If the members of the Christian community are not motivated by love, they may begin to act out of self-interest. Their backbiting and critical spirits will make them as dangerous as wild animals, *devouring each other.* When the law of the jungle replaces the law of love in the church, precious souls are always lost.

CONCLUSION

A. THE LOVE OF LIBERTY

On Liberty Island in New York Harbor stands the Statue of Liberty. A poem inscribed at its base says, in part, "Give me your tired, your poor, your huddled masses, yearning to breathe free." Many refugees from the chains of dictatorship or economic slavery have felt the thrill of freedom upon seeing Miss Liberty welcome them to the land of opportunity.

A more important statue of liberty stood at a place called Golgotha. It was the cross of Jesus Christ. Christ's death on that cross paid the price to set us free from the law, from the penalty of death, from the power of sin. The good news of what Jesus accomplished there is the heart of the gospel of freedom.

We show our love for Christ when we honor the freedom that he died to give us. The love of Christ and the love of liberty go hand in hand. We must stand fast in the freedom that he has secured for us and refuse to be bound by Old Testament law as our means of salvation.

B. THE LIBERTY OF LOVE

People love to define Christianity as a set of restrictions: "You're a Christian; you can't. . . ." In their minds, our relationship to Christ is a matter of being trapped, even enslaved, in a tangled web of "Thou shalt nots." But that isn't what Christianity really is.

Christianity is freedom. The power of love allows us to live in liberty. Because we love God and all his children, we don't need the law of Moses to keep us in line. We are merciful to our neighbors because we ourselves have received mercy; we naturally want to do the right thing. The world does not understand this freedom and ends up enslaved.

The gospel of freedom is the Emancipation Proclamation of Christ. He died to make us holy and free. Some have not yet heard the good news; others may not know that this war already has been won. Many seem not to know how to live in his freedom. But since we are "called to be free," let us obey the command to "stand firm" and not let ourselves "be burdened again by a yoke of slavery."

WHAT DO YOU THINK?

What are some practical methods by which you can show love to your neighbors in the coming week?

PRAYER

Our Father in Heaven, thank you for sending your Son to make us free. Teach us to honor that freedom, and help us to understand how to live as free citizens of your kingdom. In Jesus' name. Amen.

THOUGHT TO REMEMBER

Stand fast in freedom!

Discovery Learning

This page contains an alternate lesson plan emphasizing learning activities. Classes desiring such student involvement will find these suggestions helpful. The next page is a reproducible activity page to further enhance discovery learning.

LEARNING GOALS

After participating in this lesson, each student will be able to:

1. Explain how the gospel sets us free from the bondage to, and penalty of, the law.

2. Contrast Christian liberty with license.

3. Suggest some specific way to use Christian liberty to express love to some other person in the coming week.

INTO THE LESSON

Bring a picture or model of both the Statue of Liberty and a cross. Begin class by having students identify the statue; ask if they can quote the saying engraved on its base. (This quote is in the "Conclusion" section of the commentary.) Say, "Name some of the freedoms enjoyed by United States citizens." Record these responses.

Say, "In the late 1800s and early 1900s, immigrants arriving in New York by sea could see the Statue of Liberty. What do you suppose were their first impressions?" After responses, ask: "How would coming to the United States change their lives? What were they leaving behind? What would they lose if they went back?"

Next display the cross. Ask, "What freedoms does the cross represent?" Record these answers.

Say, "In the same way that the Statue of Liberty represents freedom in the United States, the cross represents freedom for the Christian. What feelings and thoughts do you have when you see the cross? What things have you left behind? What would you lose if you went back to your life before you became a Christian?" Say, "Today as we study Galatians 5, we will see Paul argue for us to keep on track with the gospel of grace."

INTO THE WORD

Develop a brief lecture using the Introduction from the commentary (page 325). Students will become aware of the struggles the Galatian Christians were facing. Your lecture will focus on the three dangers Paul articulates to the Galatians.

Give the following questions to each student. (They are also listed in *NIV® Bible Student.*) Divide the class into groups of four to six. Tell the groups to call for answers, beginning with the person whose birthday is closest to today and then moving to the left. The answers (from Galatians 5) are indicated with verse numbers.

1. What does Paul say happens if we slip from Christ's freedom? (*We take on a yoke of slavery, v. 1. Christ has no value for our lives, v. 2.*)

2. What is the outcome of trying to be justified by law? (*Grace is no longer the basis of our salvation, vv. 3, 4.*)

3. How do we share in Christ's righteousness? (*By faith, v. 5*)

4. What word pictures does Paul use to describe the concerns he has for the Galatians? (*Running a race, v. 7; a batch of dough, v. 9.*)

5. What is Paul's feeling about the outcome of his teaching? (*He is confident, v. 10.*)

6. Why is Paul so concerned about the false teachers? (*These teachers are upsetting the church, causing trouble and confusion, vv. 10-12.*)

7. Paul says we are "called to be free." From what are we set free? (*Obedience to the law as a means of salvation, v. 3; penalty of the law, v. 4.*)

8. What should be the attitude of Christians toward each other? (*Love our neighbor as ourselves, v. 14.*)

After each group has finished, discuss the answers. Ask the group to make a list of how the cross is an offense to the Judaizers. See the commentary for verse 11 and the Conclusion (pp. 329, 330).

INTO LIFE

Show the Statue of Liberty and the cross once more. Distribute copies of the reproducible page that follows. Ask the students to list responsibilities and/or guidelines for living that citizens of the United States make a part of their freedom; write these on or near the picture of the Statue of Liberty. (*Examples may include respecting property rights, obeying laws, and paying taxes.*) On or near the cross have students list responsibilities or guidelines for living that Christians follow. (*Examples include serving one another in love, resisting temptation, and worshiping God.*) Ask, "Why is liberty, in both cases, not a license to behave however you wish?"

Have students reread verses 6, 13-15. Encourage each person to design a business card (see the lower activity on the reproducible page). Next to the card, each student should list one or two people to whom he or she can express faith through love this week, along with two or three ways in which to express that loving service. Have the students turn to their neighbors and tell their examples. Each person should pray for the other.

Freedom's Responsibilities

Read Galatians 5:1-15. Over the Statue of Liberty image, list responsibilities that citizens have for living in their country, and over the image of the cross list responsibilities of citizens in God's kingdom.

Business Card

Design your own business card for your service that expresses your love for Jesus. This is a card you might use for introductions. You can develop a logo or a theme verse from Galatians 5:1-15. For example: "Broken Yoke Ministry" (from v. 1) with that broken-yoke image, or "Yeast Works" (from v. 9) with a bowl of dough overflowing its container. To the right, list some people and methods for employing such loving service.

PEOPLE TOWARD WHOM I CAN SHOW FAITH THROUGH LOVE

SPECIFIC WAYS TO SHOW LOVE

The Power of the Gospel
Unit 3: No Other Gospel
(Lessons 10-13)

GOSPEL OF LIFE BY THE SPIRIT

LESSON 13

WHY TEACH THIS LESSON?

"Empowerment" seems to be a favorite concept in the political arena these days. Groups of people who are deemed somehow to be the *haves* are said to be "empowered," while those who are the *have nots* are "disenfranchised." As useful (or annoying) as such terminology might be in the political arena, *empowerment by the Holy Spirit* is a key to making right choices in the Christian life.

This type of empowerment requires continuous cooperation on our parts. Unlike the "job hopping" between employers that many folks engage in, becoming a disciple of Christ involves a once-and-for-all-time decision. It is a death to the old way and a resurrection to new life; it is a rebirth.

But being a disciple involves being confronted with options and choices. Each day—in fact, several times each day—that initial decision to follow the Lord is challenged anew. If we are not diligent, we can easily make wrong choices. Today's lesson is about allowing the Spirit to strengthen us to choose the right and reject the wrong.

INTRODUCTION

A. THIS MEANS WAR!

In the history of every nation have been moments of crisis that plunged its people into armed conflict. "The shot heard 'round the world" precipitated the American Revolutionary War. Events like Napoleon's escape from exile, the sinking of the *Lusitania*, the invasion of Poland, and the attack on Pearl Harbor have caused people in various nations and periods of history to cry, "This means war!"

The Conflict. Wars come and wars go, but there is one conflict with eternal consequences: the struggle of our flesh against the Spirit. The flesh has no regard for what is moral or right—it just wants what it wants. The Holy Spirit, on the other hand, directs our spirits to reject the desires of our flesh when they are wrong. The flesh and the Spirit are thus at war, even in the lives of the finest Christians.

The Soldiers. In the war of flesh versus Spirit, people can enlist on whichever side they choose. Some choose to indulge their flesh, giving in to every appetite. The carnal results of their lives eventually become obvious; they reap what they sow. Others choose to be led by the Spirit. The fruit of the Spirit in their lives becomes a nine-fold thing of beauty. Sometimes, however, soldiers on the Spirit's side fall prey to the enemy. The Lord's army should not shoot its own wounded, but restore them. Working as a team, helping carry one another's burdens, the soldiers of the Spirit can win the victory.

The Victory. The winning side already has been determined. Even though the struggle may be hard, in due season we shall reap a rich reward if we do not give up. We who choose to walk with the Spirit will from the Spirit reap eternal life.

DEVOTIONAL READING:
COLOSSIANS 3:5-17

BACKGROUND SCRIPTURE:
GALATIANS 5:16–6:18

PRINTED TEXT:
GALATIANS 5:16-26; 6:1-9

LESSON AIMS

After this lesson each student will be able to:

1. List the qualities known as the "fruit of the Spirit," and contrast them with the works of the flesh.

2. Explain how the Spirit-led life reaches out to help those who are weaker.

3. Memorize the fruit of the Spirit, and choose one area in which he needs to submit to the Spirit rather than to the flesh.

KEY VERSE

Live by the Spirit, and you will not gratify the desires of the sinful nature. —Galatians 5:16

May
25

B. LESSON BACKGROUND

This unit of four lessons from Galatians has emphasized the one true gospel—the gospel of freedom from law as a way of salvation. The verses in this final lesson were written to warn the believers in Galatia not to turn their freedom into license. Salvation by faith does not mean that Christians are free to indulge their sinful desires. The sinful works of the flesh are still wrong, even when we are saved by grace. When we are led by the Spirit, we will replace the works of the flesh with the fruit of the Spirit. Then we will be truly free.

I. LUSTS OF THE FLESH (GALATIANS 5:16-21)

A. WHAT THE FLESH WANTS (vv. 16-18)

16. So I say, live by the Spirit, and you will not gratify the desires of the sinful nature.

Paul already has warned the Galatians not to use their freedom as an occasion to indulge their flesh (5:13, where, as here, the word is translated *sinful nature*). Instead, Christians must *live by the Spirit;* they are to let God's Spirit lead them in true freedom. When we follow the will of the Spirit, we *will not gratify the desires of our* flesh. We cannot obey the Spirit and give in to every desire of the flesh at the same time. As the next verse shows, these two courses are mutually exclusive.

17. For the sinful nature desires what is contrary to the Spirit, and the Spirit what is contrary to the sinful nature. They are in conflict with each other, so that you do not do what you want.

The flesh has *desires* that are *contrary to the Spirit.* While our physical appetites have their necessary and appropriate ways to be satisfied, these cravings can be dangerously amoral and selfish if uncontrolled. (It is this wrong satisfying of the flesh that is *sinful,* not the flesh itself.) Fleshly desires do not care if it is the wrong situation; they crave immediate fulfillment. When one's spirit tries to overrule the desires of the flesh, inner conflict begins. As Paul also wrote in Romans 7:18, 19, we cannot consistently *do what* we know we should because of our stubborn flesh.

18. But if you are led by the Spirit, you are not under law.

As long we try by our own power to control the lusts of our flesh, we will fail. The solution is not just to "try harder," for the demands of the law are overwhelming. The solution is to be *led by the Spirit* so we do not have to fight this battle alone. When we allow him to, God's Spirit begins putting a new set of desires in us. With God's Spirit leading and empowering us, we are *not under law.* The law could condemn us when we sinned, but it could do nothing to empower us to do any better.

WHAT DO YOU THINK?

If God's Spirit empowers us to live the Christian life, why is it so hard to do sometimes?

B. WHAT THE FLESH DOES (vv. 19-21)

19. The acts of the sinful nature are obvious: sexual immorality, impurity and debauchery.

Paul now gives the Galatian believers a sample listing of the *acts of the* flesh, even though such works should be *obvious* or "readily apparent" to the reader. They illustrate the kind of things the flesh will do when it is uncontrolled.

Sexual immorality is translated as "fornication" in other versions of the Bible (from the underlying Greek comes our word "pornography"). *Impurity* describes the kind of moral uncleanness that makes a person unfit to enter the presence of God. (The Old Testament had a large number of laws that taught this concept to the Jews.) *Debauchery* is total disregard for decency—in public or in private. Such sins can easily result when fleshly appetites are not restrained by the Spirit.

20. . . . idolatry and witchcraft; hatred, discord, jealousy, fits of rage, selfish ambition, dissensions, factions. . . .

Idolatry can be worshiping an idol or simply putting some part of one's own life ahead of God. (Covetousness is called idolatry in Colossians 3:5.) *Witchcraft* refers to the use of magic potions, spells, and incantations in an attempt to tap into supernatural powers. Those who practice such sorcery or "magic arts" are subject to eternal destruction (Revelation 21:8). The modern revival of pagan practices such as Wicca that involve such activities is sobering indeed.

The last seven vices in this verse could be called "social offenses." *Hatred* is the feeling of ill will and hostility toward one's enemies. *Discord* means strife, a fracturing of unity within a family or group. *Jealousy* is a feeling that results from guarding what one has against all others. Not all jealousy is evil—the Bible describes God himself as jealous (Exodus 20:5). Paul also cites what he calls "godly jealousy" (2 Corinthians 11:2). *Fits of rage* are explosions of anger. Anger itself is not the problem. There is such a thing as righteous anger (Mark 3:5; Romans 2:8, 9), but such anger is kept under control. What Paul condemns is out-of-control anger.

Selfish ambition is what leads people to try to pull others down so they can try to climb above them. *Dissensions,* sometimes translated "divisions" (Romans 16:17), are literally "acts of standing apart." *Factions* are acts of choosing up sides over pet doctrines. Those who cause divisions within the church are subject to being disfellowshipped (cf. Romans 16:17; Titus 3:10).

21. . . . and envy; drunkenness, orgies, and the like. I warn you, as I did before, that those who live like this will not inherit the kingdom of God.

While jealousy may not always be bad, *envy* is. Envy not only covets what the other person has, it would rejoice to see the other person lose it. *Drunkenness* is the intoxicated state that comes from indulgence in alcoholic beverages. *Orgies* are riotous parties featuring drinking and sexual immorality. Some translations have "carousing." As Paul has taught them *before,* people who do such things have no part in *the kingdom of God* (cf. 1 Corinthians 6:9, 10). This does not refer to the isolated lapse (cf. 1 John 1:9), but to willful, continuous sin.

II. MARKS OF THE SPIRIT (GALATIANS 5:22-26)

A. FRUIT OF THE SPIRIT (vv. 22, 23)

22. But the fruit of the Spirit is love, joy, peace, patience, kindness, goodness, faithfulness. . . .

The *fruit of the Spirit* is the harvest of virtues that is produced in the Spirit-filled life. While these characteristics are natural products of the Spirit, we must also actively cultivate them—each one is given as a command elsewhere in Scriptures. It is not enough to put aside the destructive works of the flesh; these must be replaced by something better.

Love is the primary Christian virtue. It does not count the cost or calculate the profit. Like God's own love, it is not restricted to recipients who are lovable. *Joy* is our spontaneous, happy response to life in Christ. It is not dependent on our circumstances, but triumphs over them. *Peace* is more than the absence of war; it is the sense of well-being that comes from knowing we have all we need in Christ. A rough Hebrew equivalent is the well-known *shalom.*

Patience is the ability to keep from losing our tempers with people. The Bible presents God himself as practicing patience (e.g., 1 Peter 3:20). *Kindness* is the sweet disposition that wants to serve the needs of people. *Goodness* involves both correct morals and a generous heart—it is more active than gentleness. *Faithfulness,* as used in this context, is about integrity in our dealings with one another and in being reliable (cf. Luke 16:10-12).

23. . . . gentleness and self-control. Against such things there is no law.

The world sometimes mistakes *gentleness* (sometimes translated "meekness") for weakness. The Christian, following the example of Jesus himself, is ready to yield his or her own rights for the good of others. *Self-control* is the ability of one's

WHAT DO YOU THINK?

Witchcraft is one of the works of the flesh cited by Paul. How seriously do you think people take this as a danger today? What, if any, additional precautions do you think people in general, and Christians in particular, need to take?

WHAT DO YOU THINK?

Why do you think Paul called these nine qualities the fruit (singular) of the Spirit instead of fruits (plural)? What significance do you see in that for applying these things to our lives?

Display today's visual as you begin to discuss the "fruit of the Spirit" (vv. 22, 23).

spirit to control one's flesh. It is not moderation in one's vices, but the kind of total self-control that is possible only when one is led by the Spirit. *Law* is designed to restrain evil, but there is no law or limitation on these virtues! When these are our pursuit, we are completely free.

B. LIFE IN THE SPIRIT (vv. 24-26)

24. Those who belong to Christ Jesus have crucified the sinful nature with its passions and desires.

When Paul uses the crucifixion image in Romans 6:6 and Galatians 2:20, the verb is passive. Here, those who belong to Christ have themselves done something: they *have crucified the sinful nature* (literally, "the flesh"). The flesh—try as it might—no longer controls the way they live. By the strength of God's Spirit, they master the old *passions and desires* that once brought guilt and shame.

25. Since we live by the Spirit, let us keep in step with the Spirit.

Since it is true that *we live by the Spirit* and the Spirit is the source of our life, then we should *keep in step with the Spirit.* If we claim to belong to God but ignore the lifestyle of the Spirit, our claim is conspicuously false (1 John 1:6). Real Christians not only "talk the talk," they also walk the walk and live the life.

26. Let us not become conceited, provoking and envying each other.

Self-centered people are like proud roosters that strut around trying to intimidate their rivals. People who are always *provoking* and *envying each other* are not full of the Spirit; they are full of themselves.

DISTINGUISHING SYMBOLS

Quick: what day do you think of when you hear the word *poinsettia?* Did anyone *not* think of Christmas? It seems that we see this flower almost everywhere in December. In Mexico, where the plant is native, seventeenth-century Franciscan priests found the rangy, wild poinsettias blooming naturally in December. It was an easy decision to use them as decorations in churches during the celebration of Christmas.

The Aztec Indians used the plant for medicinal purposes and as a source of red dye. Like other symbols of the season—such as the Christmas tree—the poinsettia has been adapted from secular usage to become a symbol of the Christmas season, as much so as wreaths, angels, and carols.

The plant is named after an American botanist Joel R. Poinsett. As American ambassador to Mexico in 1825–29, he discovered the plants there and had several sent to his home in South Carolina, where he found them to flourish as greenhouse plants. The plant has been developed over nearly a century into the variety of colors ranging from white to pink to mottled to the traditional red that we buy each Christmas. It is now a compact potted plant that graces homes, churches, and businesses throughout the world.

The virtues mentioned in our text are the distinguishing symbols of the Christian life. Just as the wild poinsettia plant has been carefully developed into a symbol of the season that speaks of the joy Christ brings, so the diligent Christian can develop these virtues into sublime "flowers" adorning the life led by the spirit.   —C. R. B.

III. SPIRITUAL LIFE (GALATIANS 6:1-9)

A. RESTORING THE FALLEN (v. 1)

1. Brothers, if someone is caught in a sin, you who are spiritual should restore him gently. But watch yourself, or you also may be tempted.

Sometimes in the battle between flesh and Spirit, sincere Christians fail. When a believer is *caught in a sin,* that person is not to be cast aside as a reject. Those who are recognized as *spiritual* leaders should go and try to *restore* that person. The spiritual rescuers must do their work *gently* and lovingly; they must not be heavy-handed or domineering. Rather, they should *watch* out for their own lives, realizing that they *also may be tempted.*

B. BEARING THE BURDENS (vv. 2-5)

2. Carry each other's burdens, and in this way you will fulfill the law of Christ.

Like soldiers in an army, "we are all in this thing together." We do not gloat or rejoice when we see a fellow soldier fall in battle; we realize that we are diminished by his fall. Therefore, we help each other when the going gets rough. We step in to *carry each other's burdens* whenever we see that the load has become heavier than a brother or sister can carry (Romans 15:1). In this way we carry out *the law of Christ:* "Love each other as I have loved you" (John 15:12; cf. v. 17).

3. If anyone thinks he is something when he is nothing, he deceives himself.

A foolish soldier, trying to be *something* great in bearing his or her own burden, might think that he or she can win the war alone. Such a soldier is always trying to go it alone. Actually, *he is nothing;* he simply *deceives himself.* Self-deceived, this person destroys the fabric of the community by an aloof, arrogant disdain for others.

4. Each one should test his own actions. Then he can take pride in himself, without comparing himself to somebody else.

The cure for arrogance and conceit is to take an honest assessment of ourselves. We should all *test* (examine) our *own actions*—the tasks the Lord gives us—and not try to take personal credit for what has been accomplished by the combined teamwork of many. When we have accurately pinpointed our own small contribution, we can feel the satisfaction of a job well done and *take pride in* ourselves. Then we will not be found boasting *somebody* else's work, as though it were our own.

5. . . . for each one should carry his own load.

There is no contradiction between verses 2 and 5. The word *burdens* in verse 2 comes from a Greek word that means "very heavy," but the *load* of verse 5 comes from a word that means "what can be carried," such as a backpack. Teamwork means that we help one another—we carry one another's burdens when those loads are too heavy to be carried alone. It also means we attend to our own assignments—*each one* should be expected to *carry his own load.*

DOING ONE'S DUTY

Vandenberg Air Force Base on the central California coast is a rocket launch test site for the United States government. That area of America's Pacific coast is also where the U.S. Navy experienced one of its most terrible peacetime disasters.

On the afternoon of September 8, 1923, fifteen U.S. destroyers were sailing in heavy fog from San Francisco to San Diego. All of the ships had been built just five years earlier at a cost of $1.5 million each. They were the best destroyer-class ships in the world. The commander of the squadron ordered the ships to follow his vessel, single file, at a distance of three hundred yards, and at a speed of twenty knots. Visibility was extremely limited, and the commander disagreed with the navigation signals given by Point Arguello. He thought they were many miles south and farther out to sea than their actual position. He gave the signal to turn east, and immediately his ship ran aground on the rocky shore, followed by eight of the others. Seven ships were total losses and were never even salvaged. Remarkably, only twenty-three out of eight hundred seamen lost their lives.

This tragedy may help us to understand Paul's instructions to carry each other's burdens and (just three verses later) to carry our own load. The vessels letting the commander carry their navigational burden in heavy fog found themselves prey to their commander's pride. The principle of working together does not absolve any

WHAT DO YOU THINK?
What is the importance of restoring fallen brothers and sisters and of carrying one another's burdens?

HOW TO SAY IT
Galatia. Guh-LAY-shuh.
shalom (Hebrew). shah-LOME.
Wicca. WIH-kuh.

of us from the responsibility to faithfully perform our own duty. To fail in that duty may bring terrible consequences to many of those who work with us.   —C. R. B.

C. SOWING TO THE SPIRIT (vv. 6-8)

6. Anyone who receives instruction in the word must share all good things with his instructor.

Anyone who receives instruction in the word has a responsibility he or she ought to carry (as in v. 5). Their teachers have a heavy burden (as in v. 2), being unable to support their families when they spend their lives teaching. Therefore, those who are taught should *share all good things with* their teachers. Jesus himself taught that the laborer is worthy of his support (Matthew 10:10); Paul said that those who preach the gospel have the right to live off their preaching (1 Corinthians 9:13-15), although he himself sometimes chose to earn his living as a tentmaker (Acts 18:3; cf. 2 Thessalonians 3:7-10).

7. Do not be deceived: God cannot be mocked. A man reaps what he sows.

We must *not be deceived* about what we sow—whether it be money or anything to do with our conduct. (See 2 Corinthians 9:6.) At issue is the final outcome of the warfare between our sinful nature and the Spirit.

8. The one who sows to please his sinful nature, from that nature will reap destruction; the one who sows to please the Spirit, from the Spirit will reap eternal life.

The person who invests all personal energy into making and keeping money *sows* to the selfish desires of *his sinful nature.* Like the rich fool in Luke 12:16-20, the self-indulgent miser will lose everything when life comes to an end. Furthermore, the person who lives life for carnal pleasure will *reap destruction,* often both now and in eternity (cf. Hosea 10:13). People who devote themselves to living for God, however, are planting for eternity. Their pocketbooks and their pleasures are in the hands of God. They sow *to please the Spirit.*

D. REAPING THE REWARD (v. 9)

9. Let us not become weary in doing good, for at the proper time we will reap a harvest if we do not give up.

All of us at times grow *weary in doing good.* Perhaps Paul switches to the first person *we* because he is fighting his own weariness. We try to do the right thing, but it goes unappreciated. We try to live moral lives, and the world laughs. While we struggle to make enough money to be able to contribute to the work of the Kingdom, the wicked prosper. Like the psalmist, we are envious of the foolish when we see the prosperity of the wicked (Psalm 73:3).

But there will be a day of reckoning. *At the proper time,* a time known only to God, *we will reap* our *harvest* (cf. John 4:35). Our lives will be filled with the fruit of the Spirit. Our eternity will stretch out before us in Heaven. We cannot give up, lose heart, or tire out. The prize for the winners is too great to lose.

CONCLUSION

The battle lines in the war of flesh *vs.* Spirit are sharply drawn. The battle that the Galatians faced is ours as well. With the leading of God's Spirit, we can win this war. In the process, we learn the meaning of true spirituality.

Wars are lost when combatants are unprepared. Anyone going into war untrained will likely end up as a casualty. If we expect to win the war of flesh *vs.* Spirit, we must know what we are fighting against, what we are fighting for, and how we expect to win. We fight against the selfish desires of our own flesh. We fight for a kind of life that is free in the Spirit. We expect to win because God's own Spirit is empowering us.

Discovery Learning

This page contains an alternate lesson plan emphasizing learning activities. Classes desiring such student involvement will find these suggestions helpful. The next page is a reproducible activity page to further enhance discovery learning.

LEARNING GOALS

After this lesson each student will be able to:

1. List the qualities known as the "fruit of the Spirit," and contrast them with the works of the flesh.

2. Explain how the Spirit-led life reaches out to help those who are weaker.

3. Memorize the fruit of the Spirit, and choose one area in which he needs to submit to the Spirit rather than to the flesh.

INTO THE LESSON

Have chairs arranged in groups of five as students enter the room. In each group set a bowl of different kinds of fruit that you have purchased this week. (Or you could use pictures of fruit.)

Say, "Let's suppose you are grocery shopping this week for fruit. What characteristics should you look for to know that the fruit is ripe? Take a couple of minutes to make a list." Provide the groups with pencils and the reproducible page that follows.

Call the groups together and ask them to give their responses. Then ask, "Why is it important to know what to look for?" (*Answers may include it will taste best, you can use it to prepare certain dishes, it looks good to present to others, and you will get your money's worth.*)

INTO THE WORD

Introduce the Bible study section by presenting a short lecture based on the Introduction section of the lesson (page 333). This lecture explains that Paul challenges the Galatians to live by the gospel of grace, but not license.

Divide the class into at least three groups. Provide paper, pencils, Bible dictionaries, word-study books, concordances, and/or handbooks for the groups.

Group One: Read Galatians 5:19-21. Assign to each student at least two of the words used in the text to describe works of the flesh. The student is to find the definition and pertinent information on each word to report to the class.

Group Two: Read Galatians 5:22-25. Assign at least two of the words listed as the fruit of the Spirit to each. The student is to find and report the definition and pertinent information on each.

Group Three: Read Galatians 6:1-9. This group is to develop a role play of a person who had been caught in a sin and who is being restored by the church. It will be important to identify the sin as well as appropriate Scriptures to use for the restoration.

Allow ten minutes for the groups to complete the activities. Then ask Groups One and Two for reports. During these reports, all the students should complete the "Fruit of Evil" and "Fruit of Good" sections of the reproducible activity page. (Information from the reports will help them to complete the activity.) Group Three should be given time to demonstrate its role play.

To help with discussion, use the following questions: How does the fruit of the Spirit overcome the "works of the flesh"? How does the teaching in verses 25 and 26 lead into the discussion of restoring an errant brother? What attitude should we have when restoring one who falls? What word picture does Paul use here to describe how a person's life will turn out?

INTO LIFE

Make the transition to application by saying, "Paul is challenging the Christian to show the fruit of the Spirit in his or her life. It should be evident to those around us that we are changed, allowing the Spirit to produce good fruit in our lives. Production of the fruit is to glorify God, not self; therefore, when a Christian slips, our task is not to condemn nor act superior, but to assist the one who has fallen so that his or her life can once again glorify God."

Have class members pair up with one another. This will be a time for an old-fashioned memorization drill. Each person is to make a list of the fruit of the Spirit, then drill his or her partner on the list.

The partners are to stay together for the closing activity. Ask each person to answer the following questions:

"Which acts of the flesh are dead in your life?" "Wounded?" "Alive?" "Which fruits of the Spirit are ripe in your life?" "Which are just beginning?" "Which will you seek to develop in your life, beginning this week?" (Encourage each student to complete the "Taking Action" activity from the reproducible page.)

Although answering these questions is difficult, encourage class members to be open. Have the pairs close in silent prayer.

As the teacher, thank the class for pursuing the study of Romans and Galatians for the past quarter. Remind them of the theme, "The Power of the Gospel." That power will save them, and the Holy Spirit will help them to keep the commitment just made. Pray for the class.

Fruit Market

What do you look for when you shop for fruit?

Why did you choose these characteristics/qualities?

Fruit of Evil

Read Galatians 5:19-21. Place each sinful act in the corresponding "basket."

Sexual Sins

Substance Sins

Spirit World Sins

Fruit of Good

Read Galatians 5:22-25. Define and describe each aspect of the fruit of the Spirit.

Love

Peace

Kindness

Faithfulness

Self-control

Joy

Patience

Goodness

Gentleness

Taking Action

This week I will allow the Holy Spirit to work on developing the fruit of

_____ in my life. I will ask both God and

_____ to hold me accountable.

Summer Quarter, 2002

Worship and Wisdom for Living

Special Features

Lessons

Unit 1: Songs for Faithful Living

Unit 2: Praise the Creator and Redeemer

Unit 3: Words for the Wise

About These Lessons

With this quarter's lessons, we transition from the doctrinally-focused studies of the spring to that of practical, "how to live" guidance. We must be careful not to separate the *doctrinal* from the *practical* too sharply, however, since the former provides the basis for the latter. Come and learn!

Jun 2

Jun 9

Jun 16

Jun 23

Jun 30

Jul 7

Jul 14

Jul 21

Jul 28

Aug 4

Aug 11

Aug 18

Aug 25

The Bible Cure

by Richard W. Baynes

Everyone wants to find cures for human ailments. Governments invest enormous amounts of resources attempting to improve longevity. Christians lift many prayers to God for the same purpose. But as we struggle with these concerns, we dare not overlook our most important source of comfort and "total person" healing: the Bible. Though it does not claim to be a manual of medicine, the Bible is a resource for good health. The late, great preacher Andrew Blackwood once suggested to his students a series of sermons from the Psalms to deal with various emotional ills. Since even a quick read of the Psalms reveals reliable prescriptions for certain mental-health complaints, many took his advice. The suggested sermons were dubbed "The Bible Cure Series."

JUNE

UNIT 1: SONGS FOR FAITHFUL LIVING

Lesson 1 could be called "The Bible Cure for Indecision." The instructions from Psalms 1 and 19 are true motivators in making right choices.

Lesson 2 might be called "The Bible Cure for the Blues." All Christians get "down in the dumps" occasionally, and Psalm 42 provides clear therapy.

Lesson 3 is "The Bible Cure for Fear." Millions have been—and continue to be—comforted by Psalms 23 and 121 when fear strikes.

Lesson 4, drawn from Psalms 82 and 113, is "The Bible Cure for Cynicism." A person controlled by cynicism isn't much use to God's kingdom.

Lesson 5 is "The Bible Cure for Generation Gaps," as we allow Psalm 78 to remind us how God's Word binds the youthful and the aged together.

JULY

UNIT 2: PRAISE THE CREATOR AND REDEEMER

In **Lesson 6**, Psalm 104 reminds us that God's creative power is motivation enough to elicit our eternal praise. As such, it is "The Bible Cure for Arrogance."

Lesson 7 emphasizes the superiority and honor that God has given to humans. The lesson texts thus serve as "The Bible Cure for an Inferiority Complex."

Lesson 8 brings us David's sweet spiritual relief—freedom and joy of forgiveness—as described in Psalm 32. It is "The Bible Cure for the Guilt-Ridden."

Lesson 9 invites all to worship with heart, soul, mind, and strength. In bringing all these together, we have "The Bible Cure for the Unfocused."

AUGUST

UNIT 3: WORDS FOR THE WISE

The previous nine lessons spoke to the needs (both actual and "felt") of Christians everywhere who yearn for direction, reassurance, and security. Our third unit of lessons for this quarter considers wisdom from Proverbs.

Lesson 10 centers on the chief topic of these sage sayings: wisdom itself. The thrust, simply put, is that God's wisdom is the wisdom that "works"!

Lesson 11 underscores the wisdom of avoiding evil. The result is walking in paths of righteousness, as we look toward our eternal home.

Lesson 12 considers the use of the tongue. Wise use of communication—oral or otherwise—is a virtue enabled by divine wisdom and right choices.

The final lesson in this quarter, **Lesson 13**, exhorts us to care for the needy. This was a prime concern of our Lord, and should be ours as well.

"Worship and Wisdom for Living" promises to be a profitable and practical quarter of study for adults who desire to mature in their faith by pursuing God's will.

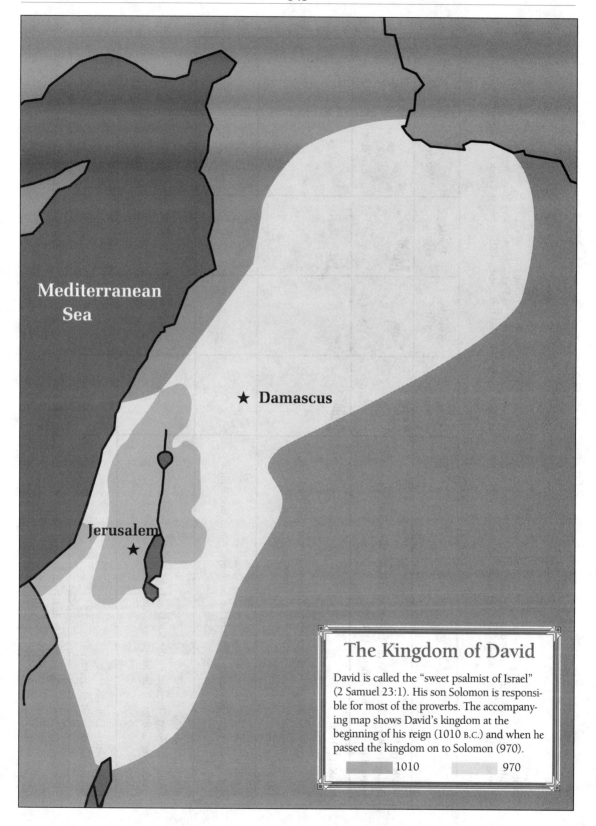

Mediterranean
Sea

★ Damascus

Jerusalem
★

The Kingdom of David

David is called the "sweet psalmist of Israel"
(2 Samuel 23:1). His son Solomon is responsible for most of the proverbs. The accompanying map shows David's kingdom at the
beginning of his reign (1010 B.C.) and when he
passed the kingdom on to Solomon (970).

1010   970

THE PSALMS

Beginning in the time of King David, the Psalms took about 700 years to come together as we have them now. Traditionally, they have been divided into five "books," each ending in a doxology (you can see these book divisions in all the major English translations of the Psalms).

Within these books can be found at least five "types" of Psalms, as this chart shows. (The notations "MANY," "Some," and "few" refer to the frequency of the five types within each of the five books.) The first nine lessons of this quarter are from the Psalms, and this chart will help you get your bearings in this very long book—the longest in the Bible!

	Complaint and/or Trust	Thanks-giving	Praise Hymns	Wisdom	Royal
BOOK I (1–41) *Ending doxology:* "Blessed be the Lord God of Israel from everlasting, to everlasting. Amen, and Amen" (41:13).	**MANY** Lesson 3	Some Lesson 8	**MANY** Lessons 1, 7	Some Lesson 1	Some
BOOK II (42–72) *Ending doxology:* "Blessed be the Lord God, the God of Israel, who only doeth wondrous things. And blessed be his glorious name for ever: and let the whole earth be filled with his glory. Amen, and Amen" (72:18, 19).	**MANY** Lesson 2	few	Some Lesson 9	few	few
BOOK III (73–89) *Ending doxology:* "Blessed be the Lord for evermore. Amen, and Amen" (89:52).	Some	few	Some Lessons 4, 5	few	few
BOOK IV (90–106) *Ending doxology:* "Blessed be the Lord God of Israel from everlasting to everlasting: and let all the people say, Amen. Praise ye the Lord" (106:48).	few	Some Lesson 7	**MANY** Lessons 6, 9	few	few
BOOK V (107–150) *Ending doxology:* all of chapter 150.	**MANY** Lesson 3	Some	**MANY** Lesson 4	Some	Some

The New Testament refers to the Psalms by name in Luke 20:42; 24:44 and Acts 1:20; 13:33. In Jesus' day, the Psalms were part of the "Writings" section of the Old Testament, as distinct from the "Law" and the "Prophets" (cf. Luke 24:44).

FOLLOW THE WAY OF THE RIGHTEOUS

LESSON 1

WHY TEACH THIS LESSON?

While "channel surfing" on my car radio several years ago, I came across a station that was announcing a "Highway to Hedonism" contest. Hedonism, a philosophy that goes back to a time before Christ, claims that *pleasure* is the main thing to be pursued in life. The "winner" of this particular contest would receive a certain luxurious (and immoral) vacation as a prize to that end.

Of course, we know the pursuit of pleasure is not really the way to find lasting happiness. Almost no one who gave the matter any thought would believe that it was. But the journey down that road seldom starts with thinking!

The road to ultimate happiness begins with recognizing that God has set eternity in our hearts (Ecclesiastes 3:11). When we focus on that fact, we are able to begin our journey along the path of the righteous. It is a path that avoids the empty philosophies of the godless in favor of that which brings us toward true—and eternal—happiness: our delight in the Word of God.

Today's lesson is a reminder to resist the allure of dead-end philosophies and hold to the purity of God's own revealed Word. Sure, your students know better than to buy into those empty philosophies—when they think about it. Today you will help them once again to think about it!

INTRODUCTION

A. "Is This the Way?"

A practical-joking preacher enjoyed pulling to the curb and asking unsuspecting pedestrians, "Can you tell me, is this the way?" The blank, puzzled look on the faces of those he joshed in this manner made him laugh as he pulled away out of earshot. This preacher was easily amused!

Jesus wasn't joshing his disciples when he announced, "I am going . . . to prepare a place for you." Thomas objected, "Lord, we don't know where you are going, so how can we know the way?" Jesus replied, "I am the way" (John 14:2-6). Unfortunately, too many people are unsuccessful in finding the right way because they don't know (or haven't decided) where they are going. They aren't sure of their destination, so any road will do.

"Where am I going?" must be answered before "Is this the way?" can make any sense. Once a person has decided to go to God, then the way is clear—revealed by the Scriptures. Divinely inspired instructions detail the route to righteousness, like a TripTik® to Heaven. Today's texts are good examples.

B. Lesson Background

If you had to "give up" thirty-eight of the thirty-nine Old Testament books, the one book you probably would choose to keep is the Psalms. More than one commentator has declared the Psalms to be the single most important book in the Old

Devotional Reading:
PSALM 19:1-6
Background Scripture:
PSALMS 1; 19
Printed Text:
PSALMS 1:1-6; 19:7-10

LESSON AIMS

After this lesson, each student will be able to:

1. Tell what today's texts say about the blessings and rewards of walking in the godly way.

2. Compare the psalmist's trust in the unchanging Word of God with the relativistic "standards" of contemporary society.

3. Suggest a plan of Bible reading and meditation that a believer can follow to become better acquainted with God's law.

KEY VERSE

The LORD watches over the way of the righteous, but the way of the wicked will perish.
—*Psalm 1:6*

LESSON 1 NOTES

Testament. As a window into the faith of ancient Israel, these "songs" still speak to us today since neither God nor human nature changes. And the communication to which they witness is a two-way street: not only does God speak to humanity to reveal his will, but humans also speak to God in prayer and praise.

Today we begin a nine-lesson series on the Psalms. What better place to begin than right at the beginning?

I. THE LORD'S PEOPLE (PSALM 1:1-6)

A. AVOID THE SINNERS' WAY (v. 1)

1. *Blessed is the man who does not walk in the counsel of the wicked or stand in the way of sinners or sit in the seat of mockers.*

The word *blessed* can mean "happy," but—as in the Beatitudes (Matthew 5:1-12)—it really means much more. We should understand it to suggest "fulfilled," "content," or "satisfied" in one's fellowship with God. Taken together, the three verbs *walk, stand,* and *sit* serve as an example of Hebrew parallelism, a technique used frequently in Scripture. Parallelism enlists two or more slightly different words or phrases to say virtually the same thing. This parallelism also holds for the terms *wicked, sinners,* and *mockers,* which are synonyms. Notice that the parallelism is negative, since this verse describes things that the godly are *not* to do. (A similar parallelism is found, in positive terms, in Deuteronomy 6:7.)

Avoiding *the counsel of the wicked, the way of sinners,* and *the seat of mockers* requires what might be called "discrimination" on the part of God's people, who must choose not to associate with certain types of people.

Discrimination is a difficult concept. Racial discrimination has blighted Western culture for centuries—and even the church has not been immune to it. Such discrimination has nothing to do with what this text is endorsing. On the other hand, to say that a person is a "discriminating" shopper is a compliment. Such a shopper will not be fooled by inferior merchandise presented as quality. True and lasting happiness in life is found by those who discriminate in the latter sense, as they learn to discern right from wrong, good from evil, throughout their lives. In this sense, discriminating people discipline themselves to become submissive and obedient to divine absolutes. They do not expose themselves any more than necessary to those who would lead them astray from those absolutes.

Those who choose not to discriminate in this way end up standing *in the way of sinners.* This is more than merely associating with non-believers; it implies a level of participation in wickedness. Joining *the mockers* in a scornful rejection of God's Word is ultimate folly, subjecting one's soul to terminal jeopardy. Even the way that seems right to us can lead to desperation and death (Proverbs 16:25). The happiest people on the planet are those who avoid and abstain from such evils.

B. DELIGHT IN GOD'S LAW (v. 2)

2. *But his delight is in the law of the* LORD, *and on his law he meditates day and night.*

Delight is the personal pleasure of a godly person when reading, studying, and applying to life the revealed truth of God. Such a person can gladly sing, "The B-I-B-L-E, yes, that's the book for me!"

Meditating on God's *law* should indeed be a delightful experience—a real pleasure. Actually, this law includes far more than the Ten Commandments and other statutes delivered through Moses. It embraces all of God's revelation, all of his truth. In providing this revelation, God has given us an inerrant "map" for our journey. Consulting it often and following its directions grants comfort and security on the way and ultimately brings us safely to our eternal destination.

WHAT DO YOU THINK?

If we had to produce a video illustrating the people in today's culture with whom Christians were not to walk or sit, who would be included? Did Jesus' practice of visiting and eating with sinners violate this admonition? Why or why not?

WHAT DO YOU THINK?

How would the average Christian's life change if he or she meditated more on biblical themes?

C. PRODUCE AND PROSPER (vv. 3-5)

3. He is like a tree planted by streams of water, which yields its fruit in season and whose leaf does not wither. Whatever he does prospers.

Photosynthesis is the natural process by which light generates life, growth, and productivity as it acts on carbon dioxide and *water*. Water is therefore one of the three ingredients in plants necessary to keep them green and growing. In a time when the vast majority of people were involved in agriculture in some way, the illustration of the *fruit*-bearing *tree* in this verse really hit home. Spiritual productivity and prosperity are promised to those committed and faithful to God's way, God's truth, and God's life. The prophet Jeremiah repeated this promise (Jeremiah 17:7, 8) to those who trust and hope in the Lord.

Meaning and hope are qualities of life for which everyone longs (again, cf. Ecclesiastes 3:11). Millions of people merely exist in "quiet desperation" because they are making no significant contribution to human society (or so they feel), and they possess no hope that the future will change that perception, which has become their reality.

But God is aware of all this. He knows our needs (including those slippery "felt needs"). And Scripture promises that he will supply all of our needs (Philippians 4:19). But for our part, an important obligation we have is to delight in his law; this is a key element in meeting our need to prosper spiritually.

4, 5. Not so the wicked! They are like chaff that the wind blows away. Therefore the wicked will not stand in the judgment, nor sinners in the assembly of the righteous.

The wicked are those whose attitudes and behavior do not identify them as children of God, as members of his family. In a creation sense, of course, all humans are God's children, but many do not believe that God exists, nor do they trust that God rewards those who seek him. Therefore, it is impossible for them to please him (Hebrews 11:6).

So, sadly, millions of people are simply spiritual *chaff*: throw-away refuse, unproductive plants in the garden of God. They will not find happiness or blessedness, nor will their excuses hold up *in the judgment*. They will be held accountable for their wickedness and judged for their iniquities. Their cases will not stand up in that final "court," nor will God consider them to be included in *the assembly of the righteous*—either as present for worship and fellowship on earth or in the final gathering before God in Heaven.

D. ENJOY GOD'S PROTECTION (v. 6)

6. For the LORD watches over the way of the righteous, but the way of the wicked will perish.

For the Lord watches over the way of the righteous. We can acknowledge the truth of this statement on an intellectual level, but when it comes right down to it, do we really live our lives with the continuous awareness that God is watching over us and our *way*—and that he has the power to help us on that way?

At one point in his ministry, the prophet Jeremiah affirmed God's sovereignty and that "nothing is too hard for you" (Jeremiah 32:17), but a bit later God repeats Jeremiah's affirmation right back to him in the form of a question (Jeremiah 32:27) as if to say, "Jeremiah, I've heard you say such-and-such about me, but do you *really* believe it?" The "blessed" person being described in this passage does indeed believe it and live it.

JUDGMENT COMES

For Bonnie and Clyde, earthly judgment came swiftly in a hail of bullets. For Al Capone, earthly judgment moved more slowly, but he eventually went to prison

---

WHAT DO YOU THINK?

Our current generation has been dubbed the "microwave generation" because we want everything "right now." In what ways does this impatience rob Christians of learning the lessons of Psalm 1?

WHAT DO YOU THINK?

Many Christians want troublesome sinners to be dealt with in a swift fashion (blown away like chaff in a windstorm). In what ways can Christians be disappointed if God does not carry out his judgment fast enough to suit their expectations?

VISUALS FOR THESE LESSONS

The small visual pictured in each lesson (e. g., page 348) is a small reproduction of a large, full-color poster included in the Adult Visuals packet for the Summer Quarter. The packet is available from your supplier. Order No. 492.

and died gradually of syphilis after his release. More recently, organized crime leader John Gotti received imprisonment.

Crooks are not the only ones who are forced to face the consequences of their actions. Anyone who violates God's law will face his condemnation. "For we must all appear before the judgment seat of Christ, that each one may receive what is due him for the things done while in the body, whether good or bad" (2 Corinthians 5:10).

Fear of divine condemnation is an appropriate motive to help us live righteously. Many young people make a genuine commitment to Christ motivated by the desire to avoid Hell. Many Christians say "No" to temptation because they do not want to face God's wrath. This need not be our only motive for righteous living. But when other reasons for following the Lord's guidance fail, this one is good enough. "The Lord watches over the way of the righteous, but the way of the wicked will perish" (Psalm 1:6).
—J. D. J.

II. THE LORD'S LAW (PSALM 19:7-10)

A. PERFECT AND SURE (v. 7)

7. The law of the LORD is perfect, reviving the soul. The statutes of the LORD are trustworthy, making wise the simple.

Now we turn to the results of meditating on *the law of the Lord*. Although this law is *perfect*, one cannot help but notice from the nightly news as well as many recent court cases that human law is not perfect, and that our justice system is not flawless. It can be disillusioning to see and hear the behind-the-scenes strategy sessions and plea-bargaining that go on prior to a trial.

Even so, the perfection of God's law reassures us that "the Judge of all the earth [will] do right" (Genesis 18:25). The perfection of God's revealed truth revives one's confidence in law and justice. It brings (or brings back) to one's soul convictions about sin, righteousness, and judgment (cf. John 16:8).

The Lord's *trustworthy statutes* give wisdom to those who are open to spiritual guidance. *Simple* does not refer to people with a low IQ (as in "simple minded"), but rather signifies something more like "inexperienced" (cf. Proverbs 1:4). Reading the Bible can be likened to digging for gems in a mine: some "gems" are very near the surface, and are easily accessible by the most inexperienced miner; other "gems" require deeper digging by the more experienced. But all "miners" can benefit from the search. Those who "hunger and thirst for righteousness" will be satisfied (Matthew 5:6). Psalm 19:1-6 notes what may be learned about God through nature. As useful as such knowledge is, the knowledge gained by studying *the law of the Lord* is much greater!

B. RIGHT AND PURE (v. 8)

8. The precepts of the LORD are right, giving joy to the heart. The commands of the LORD are radiant, giving light to the eyes.

The Hebrew parallelism noted in Psalm 1:1 is very strong here. The *law* and *statutes* of 19:7 are synonymous with the *precepts* and *commands*. Taken together, the picture that these four words paint is that all the words of God are important.

We must admit that human, earthly statutes do not always result in *giving joy to the heart*. A speed limit of twenty-five miles per hour in a residential area may seem unusually strict if we are in a hurry, particularly if the houses are set back a good distance from the road and the yards are safely fenced. But in our "right minds," we know that such laws are needed and reasonable, particularly when we think of our own neighborhoods! How much more should the rightness of God's statutes make our hearts rejoice.

This Psalm of David also reminds us that God's laws are enlightening. We know that idolatry, adultery, thievery, murder, and covetousness are wrong because, quite simply, God says so. The law of God is our great teacher. The apostle Paul notes that "through the law we become conscious of sin" (Romans 3:20).

Of particular interest here is that this enlightening comes through *the eyes.* Our eyes can be the conduit for much good as we use them to bring God's law to our awareness. But the eyes can also bring much harm to the soul if used, for example, to "read" pornography. David's most serious episode of sin began with the misuse of his eyes (2 Samuel 11:2). Perhaps as a result of this he vowed that he would "set before [his] eyes no vile thing" (Psalm 101:3). Jesus also had some important things to say about the eyes (Matthew 5:29; 6:22, 23).

C. CLEAN AND TRUE (v. 9)

9. The fear of the LORD is pure, enduring forever. The ordinances of the LORD are sure and altogether righteous.

This verse changes the parallel structure of the previous two verses. We find a description of human response to God rather than a synonym for law; *fear* in this context refers to reverential awe of God. But even with this departure from the parallel structure, there are interesting similarities to vv. 7, 8. First, *fear* is closely associated with God's Word or law elsewhere in Scripture (see Exodus 9:20 and Deuteronomy 28:58). Second, the parallel structure returns to a degree with the word *ordinances,* which brings back the specific idea of God's law. This word is found numerous times within Psalm 119.

Those who take seriously the Lord and his law react in a consistent, never-changing *(forever)* way. Since divine absolutes never change, so should our reception and obedience be unchanging. The living Word, Jesus Christ, is "the same yesterday and today and forever" (Hebrews 13:8), and he declared, "my words will never pass away" (Matthew 24:35). The unchangeableness (or "immutability") of God and of his Word satisfies the human desire for sameness and security.

ADDED INGREDIENTS

For someone who does not know how to cook, adding ingredients to a recipe feels adventuresome. What would pancakes taste like with Tabasco® sauce? How would cayenne pepper affect macaroni and cheese? We can do this with food. But adding new ingredients to our faith is not wise.

When someone preaches from God's Word each Sunday, you probably do not think much about it. You assume all preachers present God's truth accurately. However, this is not the case. Many preachers add ingredients to the gospel without hesitation.

Before the advent of cable TV, one preacher devoted his whole sermon to condemning people who let the devil into their homes. You could tell who they were, he said, because they have the devil's horns (TV antennas) on top of their houses. Another preacher changed his sermon topic when he saw a woman come to worship wearing slacks. He preached against evil, worldly women.

If the person in your church who preaches each week honestly communicates the Bible's truth, thank him. Let him know you appreciate his effort as he "correctly handles the word of truth" (2 Timothy 2:15).

In addition, beware that you do not unconsciously add ingredients to the gospel yourself. It is easy, for example, to superimpose popular "steps to success" from a self-help book on our faith. What might you have added unknowingly to God's recipe for Christianity? Remember: "Too many cooks spoil the broth."

—J. D. J.

WHAT DO YOU THINK?

In what ways can the Scripture "excite the senses"?

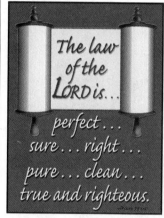

Display this poster from the Adult Visuals packet to introduce verses 7-10 of today's text.

HOW TO SAY IT

Beatitude. Bee-A-tuh-TOOD.
Hedonism. HEE-duh-nizm.
Jeremiah. Jair-uh-MY-uh.

PRAYER

Dear Lord, thank you for clear instructions in your Word about holy and happy living. Forgive us when we've been too proud to seek your help and ask your directions. Please walk beside us day by day on the Kingdom way and assist us when we stray. Rescue us when we are lost and lead us gently home. In the name of our savior Jesus Christ, amen.

D. RICH AND SWEET (v. 10)

10. They are more precious than gold, than much pure gold; they are sweeter than honey, than honey from the comb.

The psalmist uses figures here that appeal to human cravings for possessions and sense experiences. It comes quite naturally for us to desire wealth and to gratify our taste buds. Ownership and taste are two carnal drives that we can readily acknowledge. Described in this language, we are impressed by the indispensable value of the ordinances of God.

These observations, of course, now challenge us about our own perceptions. Is the Bible desirable and sweet to us? The answer will be revealed in our daily Bible-reading habits. It will also be found in our outrage and action (or lack of action!) over the contemporary court battles that threaten religious expression, such as prohibiting the display of the Ten Commandments in public schools and government buildings, etc.

Jesus described God's kingdom in terms similar to the figures of speech used here to describe God's Word. He compared the kingdom to "treasure hidden" and "fine pearls," which are to be desired to the point of sacrificing all else (Matthew 13:44-46). A Christian sense of values appraises spiritual commodities as invaluable. The Scriptures and the Lord's church are of inestimable eternal worth.

CONCLUSION

Contrary to a popular old song, life is not like a "mountain railroad"—at least in one respect. On a railroad, in the mountains or anywhere, the train follows a set of tracks in a predetermined direction. Passengers are not required to make choices regarding their route; they will simply go wherever the tracks take them. The only decision a train traveler must make is when to disembark.

Life, on the other hand, is packed with choices and decisions. It is more like driving a car than riding a train. We choose the road, the exits to take, the turns to make, the stops, the speed, the vehicles to pass, the yields, the merges—the number of decisions can be daunting.

Experienced auto travelers usually rely upon maps to plot their journey and upon manuals to operate their vehicles. Road signs help them find their way. Those on spiritual journeys, too, make their best progress when they consult a map and manual. Fortunately, Christians have been provided explicit directions for their spiritual journey. The Holy Bible is our guide (Psalm 119:105).

God's Word will keep us on the highway to Heaven, if we read it and heed it. Although the road is narrow (Matthew 7:14), the instructions are clear. Biblical precepts and precedents show us the right way to follow into the kingdom. Choosing the right route, making the right turns, passing the wrong exits, and not yielding to temptation—the whole TripTik® is written out for us. Roadside service even is available, for God is going with us, and he will not fail or forsake us (Deuteronomy 31:6).

A mystifying trait of travelers (especially of men, so it seems) is a reluctance to ask directions. Many would rather wander for an hour to find their destination than take five minutes to ask someone how to get there. But the Word of God stresses that if we ask and seek, we will find (Matthew 7:7). Asking requires humility and wisdom. It means you are admitting to being lost and not knowing the way. You are confessing helplessness: "I cannot find my way alone."

Such admissions and confessions are wise choices when one is lost. They are good for the soul, too, when you follow up by searching the Scriptures and by following Jesus, who is "the Way." God's inerrant Word is the map and manual for a successful journey into his presence.

THOUGHT TO REMEMBER

Before all else fails, read the Book!

Discovery Learning

This page contains an alternate lesson plan emphasizing learning activities. Classes desiring such student involvement will find these suggestions helpful. The next page is a reproducible activity page to further enhance discovery learning.

LEARNING GOALS

After participating in this lesson, each student will be able to:

1. Tell what today's texts say about the blessings and rewards of walking in the godly way.

2. Compare the psalmist's trust in the unchanging Word of God with the relativistic "standards" of contemporary society.

3. Suggest a plan of Bible reading and meditation that a believer can follow to become better acquainted with God's law.

INTO THE LESSON

OPTION: *Maze.* If you have flexible seating, a maze in your classroom can illustrate the need we have to trust in God's guidance. Ask for a volunteer to negotiate the maze of scattered chairs blindfolded. Ask for four volunteers to give guidance. Only one will give correct directions. The other three, (the wicked, the sinners, and the mockers of Psalm 1:1) give incorrect and distracting directions. Tell the walker he or she must listen carefully to the one voice only.

Make the transition by saying, "Many voices are giving directions to us in life, but only God's words are reliable and trustworthy."

OPTION: *Trip-Ticket.* Have your class design a trip-ticket to the tree of productivity and prosperity, a detailed map of the journey including construction sites and delays to avoid, plus scenic attractions and advice on how to get the most out of the trip.

For example, your trip-ticket might begin like this, "The journey to the tree of productivity and prosperity is a long journey through a variety of scenic country and city roads. If you should get lost, do not ask for directions or counsel from the ungodly." (This activity is in the *NIV® Bible Student.*)

The reproducible page has a puzzle maze on this same "difficult journey." Some will enjoy doing that.

Make the transition to Bible study by saying, "It is impossible to give directions to a place you have never visited if you do not have an accurate road map. In life we need an accurate map to find our desired destination."

INTO THE WORD

OPTION: *Choral Reading.* Psalms 1 and 19 both lend themselves to choral reading. Assign verses or phrases to be read by different voices. The purpose of a choral reading is to emphasize meaning and enhance enjoyment of the Psalm. For example, Psalm 1 might be assigned in this arrangement:

Blessed could be read by everyone. *Is the man*, by a man. *Who does not walk in the counsel of the wicked*, by a woman. *Or stand in the way of sinners*, by a duet of two voices. *Or sit in the seat of mockers*, by a trio of three voices. *But his delight*, by a strong, deep voice with an echoing chorus of delight that fades in volume. *Is in the law of the Lord*, by a female voice. *And on his law he meditates day and night*, by a strong, deep voice, with a fading echoing of *meditates..*

As you complete this, ask the class to enumerate the blessings and rewards of walking in a godly way. Discuss the difference between trusting in the Word of God and trusting—as many do—in the relativism of contemporary society.

OPTION: *Song.* Psalms were often written to be sung. Using Psalm 1 and Psalm 19 as models for content, write a song that honors and describes the Word of God. Tell your class the song does not have to rhyme. Select a simple, familiar melody. List ideas you want to include. Have a class member write ideas on a board or use an overhead projector. Encourage editing and rewriting. At the conclusion, ask the group to sing the song written, to the tune chosen. (This activity is included in the *NIV® Bible Student.*)

INTO LIFE

Bible Reading Plan. Following a daily Bible reading program is one way to make God's law one's delight. Many plans from a variety of sources are available. A plan for reading through the Bible in a year is included in some Bibles. Standard Publishing's quarterly *Devotions,* available at most Christian bookstores, includes a daily devotional thought based on a selected passage of Scripture related to this lesson series. (These are available also on the Standard Publishing web page at www.standardpub.com.) Daily plans on a single page are available through Bible societies or Christian bookstores. Make some available to your class members and ask members to commit themselves to a daily devotional and or Bible reading plan that will make God's Word their delight and meditation. (Directions for this are included in *NIV® Bible Student.*)

Maze

Start in the lower left corner of this maze and see if you can find your way to the Tree of Prosperity and Productivity without "stopping by" any of those who would keep you from your quest. How does this "trip" contrast significantly with a real life's journey?

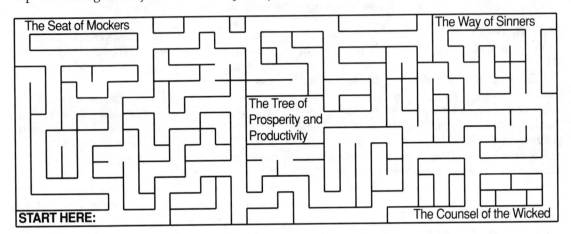

Word Search

Find these important words that refer to the Law of God for Psalm 19:7-9 in the following word search:

COMMANDS	PERFECT	RIGHT	FEAR	PRECEPTS	SIMPLE
WISE	HEART	PURE	SOUL	JOY	RADIANT
STATUTES	LAW	REVIVING	SURE	TRUSTWORTHY	

```
P  D  R  A  D  I  A  N  T  R  E  W  S
E  G  I  G  C  O  J  O  Y  F  R  I  I
R  U  G  W  P  R  E  C  E  P  T  S  M
F  I  H  S  D  D  C  D  S  U  R  E  P
E  S  T  C  P  I  O  E  S  R  S  E  L
C  O  M  M  A  N  D  S  A  E  I  W  E
T  U  E  F  E  A  R  O  S  E  L  A  W
K  L  T  R  U  S  T  W  O  R  T  H  Y
D  V  R  N  I  C  R  L  I  G  H  T  H
R  E  V  I  V  I  N  G  T  C  A  T  S
H  E  A  R  T  S  T  A  T  U  T  E  S
```

HOPE IN GOD

WHY TEACH THIS LESSON?

Tragedy and death seem to surround us—if not in our personal experiences then on the nightly news. Terrorism, tornadoes, and traffic accidents ceaselessly take their toll everywhere. And whenever people lose their lives through no fault of their own, the surviving loved ones respond in a predictable manner.

First, even devout believers often will cry out to God, "Why?" It is a natural human reaction, but no matter how many times it is asked, God does not give a direct answer. Only indirectly, in the pages of Scripture, can we discern God's answer.

Yet God is still on his throne, just as he has continued to be throughout all of human existence. (Remember that God did not directly answer Job's "why?" but rather asserted his divine sovereignty.) It is this third, never-changing fact that gave the ancient psalmist hope for the future despite his circumstances. And it is what each of your students will need to cling to in life's darkest hours.

INTRODUCTION

A. HOPE AT THE END OF YOUR ROPE

Sometimes hope seems in short supply. Far from home, alone among strangers, sleepless in the night—now there's a recipe for a big batch of hopelessness! Silence, darkness, humiliation, torment—these add to the despair. Perhaps you've been there, done that.

Maybe you recall a time when you were beaten up by a bully. Perhaps you've lost your way in a big city on a dark night, and some suspicious individuals followed you too closely while your gas gauge read empty. Or maybe you lost your job and came down with the flu on the same day that your car broke down and your teenage son was arrested for hacking into the private computer files of the IRS!

We've all had those days when things just seem to pile up. You know that hopeless feeling. You're at the end of your rope. The psalmist in today's text despaired under circumstances different from those above, but the anguish is familiar. Depression sets in, and there seems to be no hope or help. When the psalmist recalls, however, that God still exists and still rewards those who seek him, then praises and prayer witness to restored confidence, optimism, and faith.

B. LESSON BACKGROUND

The book of Psalms as a whole has traditionally been divided into five sub-books. Psalm 42 before us today begins "Book Two" of that five-part subset. This passage is a poetic conversation—a conversation that is sometimes between the writer and his own soul, and at other times is with God, who does not speak except through memories, his loving presence, and songs in the night. The psalmist alternately wallows in despair, then resists it; he complains, then switches to exaltation and self-encouragement.

The author of Psalm 42 is unknown to us, although the superscription says generally that this psalm is "of the sons of Korah" (in David's time the sons of Korah were musicians; see 1 Chronicles 6:22, 31, 32, 37). Whoever the author was, hope in God is what guided him through what John Bunyan in *Pilgrim's*

DEVOTIONAL READING:
PSALM 43
BACKGROUND SCRIPTURE:
PSALMS 42, 43
PRINTED TEXT:
PSALM 42:1-11

LESSON AIMS

After participating in this lesson, each student will be able to:

1. Summarize the psalmist's journey from being "cast down" to finding hope in God.

2. Define hope in the biblical sense.

3. Add an element of praise to personal devotional time that focuses more on God and less on personal circumstances.

KEY VERSE

Put your hope in God, for I will yet praise him, my Savior and my God.   —Psalm 42:11

Progress called the "Slough of Despond." It was the same kind of hope that kept the early Christian martyrs focused on their eternal goal despite their circumstances. And it is the kind of hope we still need today—a hope that will keep us moving toward eternity in Heaven.

I. CRAVING GOD (PSALM 42:1-6a)

A. INTENSE LONGING (vv. 1, 2)

1. *As the deer pants for streams of water, so my soul pants for you, O God.*

Unquenched thirst can be painful, debilitating—even fatal. When the *streams of water* are dry, *the deer* can die. Dehydration is the critical consequence of too little water. Most of us have seen animals as they "pant" in their search for water to slake their thirst. This is the psalmist's picture of his own search *for . . . God.*

The image is graphic, the yearning intense. The psalmist's *soul* is drying up. The word *soul* here is not just the spiritual part of his life; it refers to his whole being. If he remains separated from the divine fellowship of worship, if he does not find satisfying communion with God soon, his entire being will die—that is clearly his conviction. He is desperately thirsty for the living water that flows from divine/human encounters; this is the type of refreshment that proceeds only from God's presence, only from the Spirit's filling, only from his God's abiding truth.

2. *My soul thirsts for God, for the living God. When can I go and meet with God?*

I remember an occasion of unforgettable thirst. It was the summer of 1962, and I was a tourist in Egypt on an overnight train trip from Cairo to Luxor. The windows had to be open due to the horrendous heat, so great clouds of dust billowed in as the train raced through the desert. As I lay in my cramped berth, my throat became so dry I thought I might choke. My tongue seemed permanently stuck to the roof of my mouth. On the wall opposite the bunk was attached a carafe of water—warm, dusty, and who-knows-how-else contaminated. Despite the risk, however, I sucked it down in a chug-a-lug frenzy as if it might save my life. I still wonder at the thirst that could cause me to do such a thing!

The writer of this psalm sensed not a mere physical thirst like mine, but a "whole-being" thirst of great intensity. We can only speculate as to why he had been separated from venues and opportunities of worship and from the support and encouragement of other people of faith. But we can relate to the emptiness and longing he felt when he feared he was beyond the sphere of God's presence.

Remember that worship in the Old Testament era tended to be focused on the temple in Jerusalem, and separation from that place meant "no worship." (See "house of God" in v. 4 below.) Even as late as Jesus' day, a Samaritan woman, when speaking to Jesus, observed that while Samaritan worship focused on "this mountain," the Jews claimed that Jerusalem was the only proper place of worship (John 4:20).

Jesus' reply to that Samaritan woman makes it clear that location no longer limits worship and certainly never precludes God's presence. A realization that God is "everywhere" allows us to quench our thirst for him anywhere we happen to find ourselves—not just in a "church building." When the Samaritan woman had come to fill her vessel with water at Jacob's well near Sychar, Jesus offered her "living water . . . a spring of water welling up to eternal life" (John 4:10, 14). Christ promises that those who satisfy their souls with him will never thirst again.

Today, we are privileged to look back to the reality of fulfilled prophecy in Jesus and claim this truth for ourselves. The author of today's psalm, however, did not have this privilege. Although later in the text he will look forward in hope, his yearning could not draw upon the fulfilled prophecy of the Messiah's coming for comfort and strength; he could see only the dire straits of his present

WHAT DO YOU THINK?

What words do people use today to describe their longings for God? To what extent has the New Age trend to see many things as "spiritual experiences" blinded people so that they cannot recognize that they have a deep-seated longing for God?

circumstances, so he poured his heart out in song. Although today we, in contrast to the psalmist, have the clear fulfillment of the promised Messiah to look back to for assurance, sometimes our own circumstances can be so dismal that all we, too, can do is pour out our yearnings in song. In times like those, hymns such as "I Must Tell Jesus" become particularly meaningful.

In expressing his desire to *meet with God* (or "appear before God" in the *King James Version*), the psalmist is either articulating his need to worship or voicing a wish for death—it's hard to tell which. Psalm 84:7, part of a psalm also "of the sons of Korah," would support the worship idea in expressing the blessedness of everyone who "appears before God in Zion"; by association, "Zion" includes the temple, which was the focus of Israelite worship.

When we *meet with God* in worship, it is a foretaste of what eternity will be like. When Jesus returns, the righteous will be in his eternal presence (1 Thessalonians 2:19; 3:13; 4:17). On the other hand, the everlasting destruction of the unrighteous means, among other things, eternal banishment from his presence (2 Thessalonians 1:9).

B. PAINFUL TAUNTS (v. 3)
3. My tears have been my food day and night, while men say to me all day long, "Where is your God?"

The psalmist's perception of his separation from the presence of God causes the most profound grief (cf. Psalm 80:5). His suffering is magnified by the taunt of his enemies, *Where is your God?* This question perhaps causes the psalmist to ask himself in turn, "Where, indeed, *is* my God?" The question "Where is . . . ?" appears as a taunt several places in Scripture, and is used by both friends and enemies of God (e.g., Psalm 79:10; Joel 2:17; 1 Corinthians 1:20; 15:55).

How many Christians today actually shed *tears* when they have to miss public worship? Unfortunately, it doesn't mean that much to many, except in countries where people are deprived of that privilege and freedom. The one whose prayer we are studying today apparently was being persecuted for his faith, or at least being restricted from practicing it. Religious harassment and persecution is a tragic reality in many areas of the world today. The global Christian community is obligated to "Remember those in prison as if you were their fellow prisoners, and those who are mistreated as if you yourselves were suffering" (Hebrews 13:3).

C. PRECIOUS MEMORIES (v. 4)
4. These things I remember as I pour out my soul: how I used to go with the multitude, leading the procession to the house of God, with shouts of joy and thanksgiving among the festive throng.

The writer evidently has been prevented from enjoying worship and feast days in the temple as he formerly did. As already noted, the "why" is not clear. Given the taunt in verse 3, the situation likely involves some crisis where the psalmist is under the control of, or is imprisoned by, an enemy or foreign invader.

When distance, time, or other circumstances separate us from the experiences of the "good old days," our memories can still transport us to places and events that inspire and give peace. Reflecting on his worship activities and celebrations of the past—probably the *these things*—helped this poet tolerate his present troubles. In times of emotional distress and negative moods, people can encourage themselves by remembering who they are, how far they've come, and the many who have helped them on their way. Remembering good times with the church, good friends among Christians, and how our lives have been blessed by those relationships will lift our spirits and give us a more optimistic outlook.

WHAT DO YOU THINK?

The lesson writer notes that the psalmist's desire to "meet with God" may express a desire to worship or a desire for death. Suppose it is the latter. What does that suggest about the need for every Christian to listen carefully to the words and intentions of other Christians?

Hope thou in God: for I shall yet praise him, who is the health of my countenance, and my God.
—Psalm 42:11

Today's visual suggests various situations that produce despair and call for hope in God.

It is possible, of course, to become nostalgic to the point of merely feeling sorry for oneself. Some church members have been known to get into trouble in this regard when the church makes changes in matters of style or methods. They sink into "pity parties" as their familiar way of doing things is left behind. But in this rapidly changing world, life will never be exactly the same as it once was. Even so, it can be better. For those who dwell negatively on the past, the apostle Paul offers help: "Forgetting what is behind and straining toward what is ahead, I press on toward the goal to win the prize for which God has called me heavenward in Christ Jesus" (Philippians 3:13, 14).

D. HOPEFUL THOUGHTS (v. 5)

5, 6a. Why are you downcast, O my soul? Why so disturbed within me? Put your hope in God, for I will yet praise him, my Savior and my God.

Now we see the optimism and confidence of an overcomer! Having recalled pleasant memories of active worship and service in God's house, the psalmist seems to shake off his depression, question his doubts, and renew his commitment to trust and glorify God. It won't be the last time he must overcome discouragement, as we shall see in the next few verses, but for this moment, at least, he has experienced personal revival. He expresses a renewed passion for praising God. He has his head on straight, and he's ready to face the future.

Hope anticipates that God will act. When the psalmist's hope returns and God is acknowledged, faith comes alive. When faith is resurrected, believers long to *praise* the Lord. Then God "inhabits" (*King James Version*) or becomes "enthroned" on the praises (Psalm 22:3), and worshipers sense his presence. So a victorious cycle of hope and help increases faith that can overcome doubt and depression.

II. COMPLAINING TO GOD (PSALM 42:6b-11)

A. LONELINESS OF EXILE (vv. 6, 7)

6b. My soul is downcast within me; therefore I will remember you from the land of the Jordan, the heights of Hermon—from Mount Mizar.

The *therefore* demonstrates that the depressed poet has found an effective formula for beating the blues: remember the safe places, the supportive people, and the grand worship of yesteryear. Then he (and we) can praise God for the past, if not for the present.

The locales mentioned here are in the upper Jordan Valley, north of Jerusalem. They point to the sources of the Jordan River, thus the water imagery of verse 1 returns. Unable because of circumstances to attend the ceremonies of the Hebrews in the "Holy City," he does the next best thing: he vows to *remember* God where he now finds himself. Despite his despondent state, this faithful follower will not forget his God. Such an example is instructive for our own faithfulness.

7. Deep calls to deep in the roar of your waterfalls; all your waves and breakers have swept over me.

The poet's misery resurfaces here as the water imagery turns negative. He melodramatically describes the tragedies of his life as *all your waves and breakers*. The *roar* of the *waterfalls* isn't comforting—quite the opposite! Though it seems emotionally excessive, this is his perception and thus his reality. No one likes to have his problems minimized. No one should dispute the depths of the psalmist's grief. The next verse is evidence of yet another mood swing.

SECURE IN HIS STRENGTH

A framed photograph you may have seen in a Christian bookstore illustrates the reason for our hope in God. The picture shows a man standing at the back door of a lighthouse. Ten-foot waves are crashing against the structure, but the man is safe and dry in the doorway.

This psalm pictures waves and billows of trouble washing over us (verse 7). But again and again, the author turns for strength to God. He is our Rock (verse 9).

In the photograph, as in this psalm, the individual's sanctuary from the waves is something stronger than himself. He remains secure as long as he stays in its shelter. The Rock, the solid lighthouse, will protect him.

Unfortunately, we tend not to trust God's ability to shelter us. We often feel we must build our own addition to the protection he provides. "I trust God (plus my health insurance and IRA) to protect me." "I believe God (plus my skills and personality) will provide for me." We don't announce these heresies aloud. If we did, everyone, including ourselves, would see our faithlessness. But we continue to believe that God needs our help to get us successfully through life.

The lighthouse poster and this psalm call us to rest in God's strength. Trust him to handle the billows and waves. Remain in his protective shelter. This will give us another reason to praise him. —J. D. J.

B. GOD COMFORTS (V. 8)

8. By day the LORD directs his love, at night his song is with me—a prayer to the God of my life.

The psalmist's emotional venting vacillates wildly: first compliance, then praise, then bad news, later good news. The psalmist is up and down like a yo-yo—a problem with many Christians today. Sometimes life experiences put us on a roller coaster of mood swings. When that happens, we may become confused about our relationship with God. "Is he true? Have I drifted? Am I connected? Is he listening when I pray? Is it wrong to have questions? Is doubting a sin? Is pretending a transgression?"

Then a surge of faith may come, and once again we confess our trust in the Lord, much as the writer does in this verse. In our heart of hearts, we know God is loving and kind. When we're honest, we are certain that his providential care surrounds us both *by day* as well as *at night*—his care is available twenty-four hours a day, seven days a week. And we feel exhilarated to acknowledge his presence and power in our prayers. He never sleeps; he never changes; great is his faithfulness.

C. SAME SONG, SECOND VERSE (vv. 9-11)

9, 10. I say to God my Rock, "Why have you forgotten me? Why must I go about mourning, oppressed by the enemy?" My bones suffer mortal agony as my foes taunt me, saying to me all day long, "Where is your God?"

Not much is new here. With the same pen stroke, both blessing and cursing are scribed. Although God is addressed as *my Rock*, he seems to be silent. This silence probably compels the accusatory complaints: "Why don't you do something to rescue me, Lord? Can't you see I'm unhappy? *My foes* are stabbing me in the back—don't you care? And what shall I tell them when they ask *where* you are?"

Most Christians can relate to that prayer. In the midst of tragedy, humans have an insatiable desire to know *why*. Both Job and Jeremiah ask similar questions (see Job 13:24 and Jeremiah 12:1). In both instances, God did indeed answer their questions, but not in the way they really wanted!

And so it might be with our own questions to him. When we ask, we had better be prepared for (1) no answer at all (at least, not in this life), (2) a delayed answer, or (3) an answer not entirely to our liking. Remember that God is the One who is always able to see the "big picture" when we can't. Sometimes he will

HOW TO SAY IT

Corinthians. Kor-IN-thee-unz.
Hermonites. HER-mun-ites.
Jerusalem. Jee-ROO-suh-lem.
Jordan. JOR-dun.
Korah. KO-rah.
Mizar. MY-zar.
Philippians. Fih-LIP-ee-unz.
Samaritan. Suh-MARE-uh-tun.
Sychar. SIGH-kar.
Thessalonians. THESS-uh-LO-nee-unz.

WHAT DO YOU THINK?

Resisting the urge to give glib "advice," how would you counsel a struggling Christian to pray during a time of trouble? If the need gets worse, what changes would you expect to notice in the person's prayers?

WHAT DO YOU THINK?

The symptoms of depression usually include significant changes in sleeping and/or eating habits, indecisiveness, a negative outlook, a sense of worthlessness, and loss of interest in things that usually bring pleasure (cf. Elijah in 1 Kings 19). The presence of these symptoms in the psalmist's complaint suggests that he could have been suffering from at least a mild depressive episode. In what ways could fellow Christians help someone today in this emotional state?

WHAT DO YOU THINK?

In this psalm, the writer's mood seems to be on a "yo-yo." Some Christian helpers prefer that the person with the problem just "get over it." What does this psalm teach us about being good people helpers?

PRAYER

Dear Lord, thank you for the gift of hope. We praise you for your presence and your promises. Forgive us when we doubt your mercy or question your wisdom. Help us to remember your acts of kindness and deliverance. We promise to give you glory and honor. In Jesus' name, amen.

THOUGHT TO REMEMBER

When hope faces the Son, shadows fall behind.

allow us to see this "big picture" later when life turns around for us, showing us that he intended a temporary setback to result in a greater good.

When those times do come, we might end up thinking back on our complaints and accusations—frequently couched in the form of "why?" questions—with embarrassment. Unless we're careful with the questions we ask during tough times, we, like Job, might end up confessing "Surely I spoke of things I did not understand. . . . Therefore I despise myself and repent in dust and ashes" (Job 42:3, 6).

LOVED FOR LIFE

If you have been married for more than two months, you know about ups and downs in a relationship. You and your mate may love each other with all of your souls. You may be devoted with all of your hearts. However, this does not prevent you from becoming frustrated with each other and feeling estranged.

In tough times, you may wonder why your mate does not show more thoughtfulness toward you and seems uninterested in fulfilling your needs. Part of the problem is that your whole focus is on yourself. Shifting your focus can help heal the relationship.

We also get frustrated with God when we feel he is not meeting our needs. We whine in our prayers when he is (apparently) silent. A change from this self-centeredness can build a stronger relationship with God. Life is not primarily about us. "God . . . created all things. His intent was that now, through the church, the manifold wisdom of God should be made known to the rulers and authorities in the heavenly realms, according to his eternal purpose which he accomplished in Christ Jesus our Lord" (Ephesians 3:9-11).

The primary purpose of our lives is to display God's wisdom. When you feel frustrated with God, when you feel your Rock has forgotten you, shift your focus. Hold on to your faith. This will honor God and help you.   —J. D. J.

11. Why are you downcast, O my soul? Why so disturbed within me? Put your hope in God, for I will yet praise him, my Savior and my God.

This is the poet's refrain, repeated from verse 5 with only a minor change, and repeated again in Psalm 43:5. All readers are glad that the passage ends on this positive note. Of the "ups and downs" expressed, the "ups" are far more inspiring and reassuring.

When the psalmist spoke to himself, he used positive language and hopeful thoughts. With this approach, he was able to overcome doubts and fears. The same exercise will work today. "Whatever is true, whatever is noble, whatever is right, whatever is pure, whatever is lovely, whatever is admirable—if anything is excellent or praiseworthy—think about such things" (Philippians 4:8).

CONCLUSION

Faith is more than mere wishful thinking. "Things hoped for," in the context of godly faith, are certain to be received. It is a confidence that God exists, that Jesus died to save, and that Heaven is real—but it goes far beyond all of that. Faith trusts that God who has always told the truth is still telling the truth in the written Word that reveals the living Word. Belief and trust are generated by the hope born in a Christian's heart through the grace and knowledge of the Lord Jesus Christ.

Hope is substantive to faith because hope sees possibilities. Hope is visionary. Hope is a positive perception of the future. Hope is the essence of patience and prayer. Hope anticipates and predicts ultimate good because God's purposes will not be defeated. Hope always expects blessing. Hope always gives another chance.

Discovery Learning

This page contains an alternate lesson plan emphasizing learning activities. Classes desiring such student involvement will find these suggestions helpful. The next page is a reproducible activity page to further enhance discovery learning.

LEARNING GOALS

After participating in this lesson, each student will be able to:

1. Summarize the psalmist's journey from being "cast down" to finding hope in God.

2. Define *hope* in the biblical sense.

3. Add an element of praise to his or her devotional time, during which the individual focuses more on God and less on personal circumstances.

INTO THE LESSON

OPTION: *Neighbor Nudge.* Ask each person to turn to the person next to him and take thirty seconds to describe (1) a place where he or she always feels close to God or (2) a dark hour of the soul when he or she experienced doubts, depression, isolation, or abandonment.

Make the transition to the Bible study by saying, "Life is filled with emotional ups and downs. Sometimes our hearts are filled with praise for God. At other times we wonder where God is and why he appears not to be concerned about our plight. Today's passage gives us a biblical view of such fluctuations."

OPTION: *Case Study.* Ask a class member to read this case study to introduce today's lesson. (This is included in *NIV® Bible Student.*)

"Wanda has come to you for help. She says, 'I've been feeling so blue lately. I thought that since the children were grown, Jack and I would have more time for each other. But between his work and mine, that hasn't happened. I must work weekends, meaning I can't attend church. I really miss the Ladies Bible Class. My devotional life is practically non-existent. On some days I try to read my Bible and pray, but God seems so far away. Now don't preach at me—I feel bad enough already. Can you help me?'"

Read the transition statement in the activity above to lead into Bible study.

OPTION: *Picture Study.* Bring five pictures to class: (1) a picture of the interior or exterior of your church, (2) a picturesque scene of nature's splendor, (3) a picture of a mother and a baby, (4) a picture of someone playing golf or fishing, and (5) a group of people enjoying each other's company. They need to be large enough for class members to see. For a small class, full-page pictures from a magazine mounted on card stock would be appropriate. For larger classes, you could use projected

slides. Or you could make color transparencies if you have an overhead projector available. (Color pictures can be copied to transparency film at most copy service centers.) Ask a computer enthusiast for help—such a person will be delighted to share expertise.

Display the five pictures to open the class. Ask a class member to select the picture that makes him or her have hope in God and explain why.

INTO THE WORD

OPTION: *Marginal Markings.* The reproducible page has a copy of Psalm 42 with directions to mark it verse-by-verse based on how the reader responds to each truth. Give learners an opportunity to respond individually, and then let them share and discuss responses as a group.

OPTION: *Personalize and Paraphrase.* Provide paper and pens for class members to paraphrase today's text, expressing ideas and emotions of the text in their own words. Most today would not describe their desire to be with God by referring to a deer desiring water. We might say, "As a thirsty runner on a hot summer day longs for a cold drink, my heart desires you, O God."

Ask several class members to share their paraphrases with the entire class. Or in larger classes, you might have people share with those seated near them.

INTO LIFE

OPTION: *Debate.* Divide your class into two groups. Ask them to prepare to debate this proposition: "Being with people of hope is an important part of praise and worship." One side should be directed to affirm the statement, and the other side, to deny the statement.

OPTION: *Verse Memorization.* Challenge your class members to memorize a verse that would be helpful in times of need. Psalm 42:1 or 42:11 would both be good choices. Memorizing a verse as a group can be much more fun and easier to memorize than working alone. One technique is to write the verse on a board and have the class read through it a couple of times in unison. Then erase one or two words and repeat the verse together, filling in the blanks from memory. Continue this procedure until everything is erased, and your class will be pleasantly surprised to discover they have memorized the verse. Encourage daily devotional use of the verse for the coming week.

Marginal Markings

Read through Psalm 42:1-11 and make a mark in the margin beside each verse according to the following guidelines:

- Put a simple sad face beside any verse if you can identify with the sad feelings describing loneliness, isolation, depression, or abandonment in the verse.
- Put a **PTL!** (for "Praise the Lord!") beside any verse that causes you to well up with praise for God.
- Put an **"Amen!"** beside any verse that preaches at you with corrective instructions.
- Put a question mark (?) by any verse that raises a question that you would like discussed or answered.

Psalm 42

1As the deer pants for streams of water,

so my soul pants for you, O God.

2 My soul thirsts for God, for the living God.

When can I go and meet with God?

3 My tears have been my food day and night,

while men say to me all day long, "Where is your God?"

4 These things I remember as I pour out my soul:

how I used to go with the multitude,

leading the procession to the house of God,

with shouts of joy and thanksgiving among the festive throng.

5 Why are you downcast, O my soul?

Why so disturbed within me?

Put your hope in God, for I will yet praise him,

my Savior and 6 my God.

My soul is downcast within me;

therefore I will remember you from the land of the Jordan,

the heights of Hermon—from Mount Mizar.

7 Deep calls to deep in the roar of your waterfalls;

all your waves and breakers have swept over me.

8 By day the Lord directs his love,

at night his song is with me—a prayer to the God of my life.

9 I say to God my Rock, "Why have you forgotten me?

Why must I go about mourning, oppressed by the enemy?"

10 My bones suffer mortal agony

as my foes taunt me, saying to me all day long,

"Where is your God?"

11 Why are you downcast, O my soul? Why so disturbed within me?

Put your hope in God, for I will yet praise him, my Savior and my God.

FOLLOW THE LORD, OUR KEEPER

LESSON 3

Jun
16

WHY TEACH THIS LESSON?

"The proper role of government" is a never-ending topic of debate around the world. On one end of the spectrum are those who advocate extreme "collectivist" governments; in such cases, government becomes everyone's "keeper." At the other end of the spectrum are those who advocate pure "sink or swim" societies; in such cases, each individual becomes his or her own "keeper," without any governmental help or hindrance.

Christians should, of course, feel free to engage and debate these issues. In so doing, however, we must take care not to lose sight of the fact that it is the Lord who is our ultimate Keeper. Today's lesson focuses our attention on this very issue. In so doing, it helps us avoid the error of looking either to government or to our own self-sufficiency to meet those needs that are of ultimate importance in our lives.

INTRODUCTION

A. "WHO'S AFRAID . . . ?"

A "Big, Bad Wolf" of life is fear. Fear wears many names: worry, anxiety, doubt, timidity, indecision, alarm, shock, terror. It isn't readily recognized when it is called names like caution, care, and discretion.

Most children grow through a stage when they are "afraid of the dark." Of course, they are actually afraid of what they imagine to be in the dark. Adults, too, often fear the imaginary. But probably 95 percent of what we worry about never happens. Worry is a form of fear. No wonder Jesus teaches us not to worry (Matthew 6:34).

But although "big, bad wolves" often exist only in our imaginations, Scripture warns us to beware of wolves (false prophets) who come dressed "in sheep's clothing" (Matthew 7:15). And 1 Peter 5:8 cautions us that "the devil prowls around like a roaring lion looking for someone to devour." And ultimately, we are to "be afraid of the One who can destroy both soul and body in hell" (Matthew 10:28).

So, not all fear is neurotic and faithless. Sometimes it simply amounts to a healthy respect for real danger. And, of course, fear of the Lord is proper and positive reverence for our Creator and Sustainer.

Inappropriate fears are those that emotionally paralyze us so that we become ineffectual; they prevent going forward in faith and preclude bold witness. These are the fears that the apostle Paul had in mind when he wrote to Timothy, "God did not give us a spirit of timidity, but a spirit of power" (2 Timothy 1:7).

B. LESSON BACKGROUND

The texts selected for this lesson are classic examples of faith-filled testimonies in song, sung by those whose adventures with God had taught them not to be

DEVOTIONAL READING:
PSALM *80:1-3, 14-19*

BACKGROUND SCRIPTURE:
PSALMS *23; 80; 121*

PRINTED TEXT:
PSALMS *23:1-6; 121:1-8*

LESSON AIMS

After participating in this lesson, each student will be able to:

1. Compare God's care today to that of a shepherd in ancient times.

2. Contrast fear that is healthy with the kind of fear that reflects lack of faith in God.

3. Memorize portions of today's printed text for use during times when faith is in danger of being overpowered by fear.

KEY VERSE

I lift up my eyes to the hills—where does my help come from? My help comes from the LORD, the Maker of heaven and earth.
—Psalm 121:1, 2

Many citizens of the United States have grown accustomed to "looking to Capitol Hill" as a primary source of strength for solving problems both big and small. Is it easier or harder for American Christians to trust God (for short- or long-term solutions) as compared to Christians living in countries with weak or corrupt governments? Why?

afraid. They help replace fear with faith. They come from a time when life was much more difficult than it is now—physically if not spiritually. If the texts considered today inspired faith in those who lived in a time when one's health and "daily bread" were much more uncertain than they are now, how much more should these passages help us today in our own struggles!

I. PRAISING OUR SHEPHERD AND HOST (PSALM 23:1-6)

The shepherd metaphor, so often used in Scripture, is not as meaningful to us as to the writer and earliest readers of this poem. Their pastoral lives fitted them uniquely to understand such figures and illustrations. We can, however, be humbled by the psalmist's analogies of provision, protection, and guidance based upon any meager familiarity we may have with the herding of sheep. The host imagery that then follows should intensify our humility all the more.

A. REST AND RESTORATION (vv. 1-3)

1. *The Lord is my shepherd, I shall not be in want.*

The needs of sheep are comparatively simple—basic sustenance and protection. Having food, water, and rest, a sheep is content. A good *shepherd*, of course, also guides, protects, and dresses the wounds of the sheep he is tending.

Our God is a shepherd to us in all those ways and more. Human needs are more complex, since we are spiritual beings as well as physical, but God supplies all our needs "according to his glorious riches in Christ Jesus" (Philippians 4:19).

2. *He makes me lie down in green pastures, he leads me beside quiet waters,*

A shepherd's job is to find food and water for the sheep, something not always easy to do in dusty Palestine. But a good shepherd knows the best spots for pasture and water. And the water must be *quiet*, because sheep are afraid to drink from moving water, such as in creeks and rivers.

God knows we need food for our souls as well as for our bodies. He guides us to quiet places where spiritual sustenance is most readily available. Perhaps Jesus thought of this psalm when he spoke of "living water" (John 4:10). This kind of water is that by which God quenches the thirst of our souls; it becomes in us "a spring of water welling up to eternal life" (John 4:14). The deepest yearning of our hearts is completely satisfied when it is the Lord who gives us drink.

When God leads the psalmist to *lie down*, he is talking about rest. Rest—as important to good health as food and water—is for the soul as well as for the body. Surely that is the reason God created the Sabbath Day for his Old Testament people—one day out of seven when his people were to rest (Exodus 20:8-11). Spiritual renewal requires regular periods of freedom from duties, time for relaxing activities and for concentration on spiritual disciplines, such as worship and prayer. The Christian "Lord's Day" serves those same purposes.

3. *. . . he restores my soul. He guides me in paths of righteousness for his name's sake.*

The result of verse 2 is the restoration of *my soul*. Sheep need to lie down and rest as they eat, for proper digestion and revival of energy. A good shepherd insists on it; he makes the animals lie down. This "siesta" restores their strength, providing relief from the heat and hurts of travel over desert-like terrain. David experienced this rest-and-restoration therapy in his own soul. When spiritually fatigued, God restores passion to his faith and energy to his zeal.

Sheep need a shepherd not only to provide suitable times and places for rest, but to provide guidance along the *paths of righteousness*. Sheep will stray without a shepherd (cf. Mark 6:34). Without God's restoring guidance, David (and we) could not stay on the "straight and narrow" path of righteousness that leads to life.

FLYING BLIND

During the cold war, the United States Air Force's Strategic Air Command kept loaded B-52 bombers continuously "on alert," and an airborne command post flying every day, seven days per week, twenty-four hours per day.

The necessity of flying every day, in any weather, required the ability to land the airborne command post in any weather. In dense fog, Air Force flight controllers had to talk this large jet all the way down to the runway. The pilots had to listen carefully to the controllers, follow their directions exactly, and trust the controllers implicitly. Flying blind like that was not for the fainthearted.

In a very real sense, though, every person alive is flying blind. No one can see into the next year, the next week, even the next hour. People hurtle blindly into the future, hoping they can negotiate whatever obstacles or difficulties present themselves.

In Psalm 23, David assures us that the Lord, our Shepherd, is willing to serve as our air traffic controller. He will guide us in the paths of righteousness. Like a controller with a radar screen, he can see where we are headed and what lies ahead even though we cannot.

Like a pilot flying in fog, every person needs to listen carefully to this Controller, follow his directions exactly, and trust him implicitly. Those who do this will find that the Lord will guide them to a safe landing. Those who do not will crash and burn.

—J. D. J.

DAILY BIBLE READINGS

Monday, June 10—*Restore Us, O God (Psalm 80:1-7)*

Tuesday, June 11—*Have Regard for Your People (Psalm 80:8-19)*

Wednesday, June 12—*God: Our Refuge and Strength (Psalm 46:1-11)*

Thursday, June 13—*God Heard My Cry (Psalm 40:1-10)*

Friday, June 14—*Keep Me Safe Forever (Psalm 40:11-17)*

Saturday, June 15—*The Lord is My Shepherd (Psalm 23:1-6)*

Sunday, June 16—*The Lord Will Keep You (Psalm 121:1-8)*

B. PROTECTION AND PROVISION (v. 4)

4. Even though I walk through the valley of the shadow of death, I will fear no evil, for you are with me; your rod and your staff, they comfort me.

Palestinian shepherds often led their herds through dangerous spots, over steep trails bordered by sheer cliffs. Whether this refers to some particular *valley* or not, the implication of great risk is clear. Sometimes sheep do fall over the edges of trails and must be rescued by the shepherd with his crooked *staff*. Other times, predators attack the sheep, and the shepherd uses his *rod* (a short wooden pole, three or four feet in length) to fight them off.

We humans, too, face *the valley of . . . death* in our Christian pilgrimage. Our souls often seem in jeopardy, when discouragement, doubt, or temptation threaten to devour us. The Lord, however, is with us, protecting us with his "rod" and rescuing us with his "staff." As Paul reassures us, "God is faithful; he will not let you be tempted beyond what you can bear. But when you are tempted, he will also provide a way out so that you can stand up under it" (1 Corinthians 10:13). It is especially comforting to know, when we literally face death, that we are not alone.

FOXHOLE REALITY

A foxhole conversion can be nothing more than bargaining with God. "If You will get me out of this, Lord, I will be committed to you for the rest of my life." A promise like this is not likely to be kept. However, a face to face encounter with one's own death can change a person's sense of values. "I realized there were things more important than _____" (fill in the blank).

An encounter with death takes us to the core of our being. Amidst the darkness of this valley, David's core being felt comforted. Even at the threshold of the grave, David sensed God's reassuring presence.

A public television documentary several years ago followed two terminally ill hospital patients. Both patients' families were grief-stricken by the news that death was imminent. However, over the ensuing weeks, one family pulled together and found peace. The other family pulled apart and found nothing but pain. The first family had a living relationship with Christ; the second family did not.

You are terminal. Beyond insurance policies and a will, what are you doing to prepare yourself? David recommends you walk through this dark valley with the Lord. Then, you need fear no evil.   —J. D. J.

C. CARE NOW AND CARE LATER (vv. 5, 6)

5. You prepare a table before me in the presence of my enemies. You anoint my head with oil; my cup overflows.

David now departs from the shepherd imagery of verses 1-4. The new imagery is quite interesting: even as *enemies* threaten, the psalmist feels secure enough to anticipate a meal—a meal which has been prepared by the Lord himself. Since the Lord is the one preparing this meal, or *table,* he is the host of the banquet that the psalmist anticipates. Banquet imagery is found in several other passages in the Bible, including Isaiah 25:6-8; Matthew 8:11; Luke 14:15-24; 22:27; and Revelation 19:9, 17, 18. Jesus' own observance of the Passover Feast involved a table that now symbolizes the Lord's Table around which Christians gather to observe communion each Sunday (Mark 14:18; 1 Corinthians 10:21).

Also part of the banquet imagery is the anointing *with oil.* A good host at a banquet would anoint the heads of the honored guests (Luke 7:36, 46; cf. also Psalms 45:7; 92:10; 133:2). To be considered such a guest by the God of the universe and to be anointed by him is exciting to anticipate (again, cf. Matthew 8:11; Revelation 19:9)!

The third imagery here is that of a *cup* that *overflows.* This echoes the symbolism of care we have already seen in verses 1-4. Psalm 116:12, 13 depicts "the cup of salvation" as one of the benefits provided by the Lord (cf. 1 Corinthians 10:16).

6. Surely goodness and love will follow me all the days of my life, and I will dwell in the house of the LORD forever.

David now bursts forth with personal exultation and praise. The blessings of *goodness and love* will be enjoyed for life's little while on earth, then in the very eternal mansions of God without end.

II. FOLLOWING OUR KEEPER (PSALM 121:1-8)

A leader can be only as successful at leading as the followers are at following. Psalm 23 praises the Lord who leads like a shepherd and draws us to his banquet, while Psalm 121 sets forth the good things that happen when we submit to God as the one who watches over us. What might be called "followership" is important for godly living.

A. CALLING FOR HELP (vv. 1, 2)

1. I lift up my eyes to the hills—where does my help come from?

Israelite worshipers typically faced Jerusalem from wherever they were when they prayed. The use of the phrase *the hills* in this verse probably is a reference to the Holy City, as it is situated at high elevation on several hills surrounding Mt. Moriah, on which the temple was built (2 Chronicles 3:1). *Help* does not come literally from Jerusalem, but from God who inhabits the temple there.

2. My help comes from the LORD, the Maker of heaven and earth.

Old Testament worshipers often praised *the Lord* for his creation *of heaven and earth* (Psalms 115:15; 124:8; 134:3; 146:6; Isaiah 40:26). They got themselves into trouble, however, when they worshiped those created things rather than their Creator (2 Kings 17:16; 21:3-5; Jeremiah 19:13; Ezekiel 8:16; and others).

New Testament believers continue to worship their Creator (Romans 1:25). We have the additional blessing of having ourselves become a new creation (2 Corinthians 5:17), even as we look forward to God's final renewal of all things (Romans

---

WHAT DO YOU THINK?

The metaphors (symbols) used in Psalm 23 were very powerful for people in Old Testament times. If we wanted to update the metaphors (phrases like green pastures, quiet waters, rod, cup, etc.) of Psalm 23 in a meaningful effort to make the message more understandable to modern people, what symbols would we use? Why?

WHAT DO YOU THINK?

Some believers might take the phrase "goodness and love will follow me" as a promise that Christians will not have any troubles "all the days of my life." What would you say to someone who expressed such a belief?

I will lift up mine eyes unto the hills, from whence cometh my help. My help cometh from the LORD, which made heaven and earth.

Use this poster, which shows hills in Israel, to illustrate Psalm 121:1.

8:19; Revelation 21:1). The psalmist recognized that the One who had the power to create all things originally (Genesis 1:1) is also the One who could help him in his day-to-day life. Having experienced what it means to be a "new creation" in Christ, how much more should the modern believer trust God for those needs!

B. TRUSTING THE GUIDE (vv. 3-7)

3, 4. He will not let your foot slip—he who watches over you will not slumber; indeed, he who watches over Israel will neither slumber nor sleep.

When God is allowed to guide, followers reach their destination. Their feet will not *slip*—they make no missteps. Israel learned that while traveling from Egypt to the promised land. The ancient Israelites could see the pillar of cloud that directed their paths. And further proof that God was guiding them was the pillar of fire, which became evident at night (Exodus 13:21, 22). This was visible evidence that God was not sleeping. He was guiding.

We are not consistently good followers, but God is our faithful Guide. When we react with impatience as the ancient Israelites did, we are failing to trust him and we can easily lose our way or be led astray. Yet he continues to call us, always willing to lead and provide.

5, 6. The LORD watches over you—the LORD is your shade at your right hand; the sun will not harm you by day, nor the moon by night.

The assurance that *the Lord watches over* us stresses the protective nature of God. *Shade* and *right hand* are figures of speech for protection as well. The references to *sun* and *moon* mean that God's protection is never interrupted. His companionship and guarding are constant, as he helps and leads those who call upon him. God alone is the trustworthy guide for our lives. No matter what dangers of the day or night present themselves, God is still in control.

Human leaders had betrayed Israel for centuries. At Mt. Sinai, Aaron led them into idolatry, even as Moses was receiving the Ten Commandments on the mountaintop (Exodus 32). The judges who followed were fallible, and a minority of the numerous kings who ruled after the judges guided the people toward godliness. The nation of Israel learned the hard way that earthly leaders are not, as a whole, trustworthy. In their "right minds," at the right time, the Hebrew children confessed that they trusted only the Heavenly Father. The Lord is the one who consistently helps, guides, and protects. He alone is worthy of trust and obedience.

7. The LORD will keep you from all harm—he will watch over your life;

The psalmist shifts the focus from God's present protection to his future protection. But was ancient Israel indeed protected *from all harm?* Sometimes they suffered from drought and disease. They were attacked and besieged by the armies of political enemies. On a personal level, the Israelites were tempted and tried by all the usual afflictions and circumstances common to humanity. Finally, they were defeated and exiled to far-away countries. Foreigners frequently and permanently overran their homeland. Given the witness of Scripture as a whole, the promise of this verse must be seen as conditional (e.g., 2 Chronicles 7:14). When the ancient Israelites trusted and worshiped their God only, their lives did indeed prosper both physically and spiritually.

"Why do bad things happen to good people?" is an age-old question; the reverse "Why do good things happen to bad people?" is also asked (see both in Ecclesiastes 7:15). Jesus answered these questions when he explained that "He [your Father in Heaven] causes his sun to rise on the evil and the good, and sends rain on the righteous and the unrighteous" (Matthew 5:45). The laws of nature usually apply to all equally. Miracles of divine intervention sometimes happen, but God generally lets nature take its course.

WHAT DO YOU THINK?

In what way does the reminder that God made "heaven and earth" become helpful when trying to rely on Someone you cannot see or touch?

HOW TO SAY IT

Aaron. AIR-un.
Baal. BAY-ul.
Elijah. Ee-LYE-juh.
Israelites. IZ-ray-el-ites.
Jerusalem. Juh-ROO-suh-lem.
Jezebel. JEZ-uh-bel.
Moriah. Mo-RYE-uh.
Moses. MO-zes or MO-zez.
Sinai. SIGH-nye or SIGH-nay-eye.

Nevertheless, the righteous ultimately escape the eternal torments of Hell while the wicked do not. Christians are preserved for eternity. Considering the teaching of the Bible in its entirety, the promise of verse seven must be taken conditionally. In the New Testament era, only those who believe on Christ can claim this promise for eternity (John 3:16).

C. STAYING THE COURSE (v. 8)

8. . . . *the LORD will watch over your coming and going both now and forevermore.*

This is a song of the faithful. God is the eternal guardian of those who persevere in following him. A crucial part of being faithful and persevering is remaining holy (1 Peter 1:15, 16). The pursuit of holiness must persist until one's death or the return of Christ (cf. 1 Thessalonians 5:23).

As we pursue holiness and live our lives, it is reassuring to know that God looks after us in our entire *coming and going.* Modern society seems to be increasingly "busy." Families can become so busy that they don't know whether they are "coming or going." The danger is compounded by the fact that about one in six American families moves every year, with the average American moving 11.7 times in his or her lifetime.

When considered alongside the number of automobiles owned by each family, the mobility of contemporary society is mind-boggling. Families seem to be constantly on the move. Our comings and goings can seem like organized chaos at times. But God can track all that movement and busyness and still *watch over* the faithful. Our challenge is to keep all that busyness from distracting us to the point of not having the time to pause and offer the type of prayer the psalmist just has.

CONCLUSION

Franklin D. Roosevelt is remembered for having said, "The only thing we have to fear is fear itself." There are some reasons why that is true.

Fear clouds reality and produces irrational imaginations. Remember the experience of Elijah after he had killed all the prophets of Baal on Mt. Carmel? Wicked Jezebel threatened his life, and he fled in fear (1 Kings 19:3). In the wilderness, he sat beneath a juniper tree and prayed to die. He imagined that he was alone in standing for God. But God showed him that 7,000 Israelites remained faithful (1 Kings 19:18). Elijah was not killed in the desert by Jezebel, but much later was "taken up" to God in a whirlwind (2 Kings 2).

Fear can immobilize when faith is challenged. Many congregations have missed opportunities for progress and growth simply because they were afraid to venture with God. They might be afraid to change evangelistic strategies. Sometimes they fear significant changes in worship styles. Perhaps they are afraid to make commitments toward visionary goals. Whatever the case, fear often causes Christians to refuse to step through an open door. So they stand paralyzed and stagnate.

Fear inhibits trust in God. Many never speak of Christ and the church, even to friends and family, because they are afraid. They fear rejection, ridicule, and refutation. Others fail to give offerings to their church in proportion to their incomes because they are afraid they won't have enough money to maintain the lifestyle to which they've become accustomed. Fear often prevents us from obeying God.

An anonymous author noted that "Fear knocked at the door. Faith answered. No one was there." Replacing fear with faith is the key to living a life abundant with spiritual confidence, peace, optimism, and adventure.

Why not commit to memory a few of the verses considered in this lesson? A few to begin with are Psalm 23:1, 6 and Psalm 121:2, 8. Hide them in your heart and recite them whenever fear threatens to crush your faith.

WHAT DO YOU THINK?

Picture a missionary who has been on the mission field long enough that loneliness and culture shock are taking their toll. In comparing Psalm 23 with Psalm 121, which of these two would most likely be more helpful to him or her? Why?

PRAYER

Dear Lord, I trust you as my Good Shepherd. Thank you for supplying all of my needs and for protecting my soul. Again today, give me and mine just what we need. And show us ways we can help the less fortunate. In Jesus' name, Amen.

THOUGHT TO REMEMBER

Fear knocked at the door. Faith answered. No one was there.

Discovery Learning

This page contains an alternate lesson plan emphasizing learning activities. Classes desiring such student involvement will find these suggestions helpful. The next page is a reproducible activity page to further enhance discovery learning.

LEARNING GOALS

After participating in this lesson, each student will be able to:

1. Compare God's care today to that of a shepherd in ancient times.

2. Contrast fear that is healthy with the kind of fear that reflects lack of faith in God.

3. Memorize portions of today's printed text for use during times when faith is in danger of being overpowered by fear.

INTO THE LESSON

OPTION: *Neighbor Nudge.* Introduce this by saying, "Everyone has had an experience like a 'valley of the shadow of death.' It might be illness, death of a loved one, a debilitating condition or disease. Turn to the person next to you and in two minutes, tell him or her your 'valley of the shadow of death' experience. Tell how you felt—your fears, concerns, and worries."

At two minutes say, "Even if you are not finished, let your partner tell you about his or her 'valley of the shadow of death' experience."

Make the transition to the Bible study by saying, "Our journey through life often includes trips through the valley of the shadow of death. How do we feel in these situations? Do circumstances of life disable us with fear? Our text today includes two passages that describe the confident response of those who trust in God when life overwhelms us with fear."

OPTION: *Brainstorming.* Help your class make a list of things people fear. Do not stop to evaluate or comment. This allows one person's response to stimulate another's thinking. If you do not have a writing board in your classroom, mount a large sheet of newsprint or poster board on the wall. As class members call out answers like, "death," "darkness," or "heights," have a recorder write down the responses.

When you have a large list of fears, ask the class to rate them according to the intensity of the fear they inspire. On a scale of 1 to 5, 1 is mild concern and 5 is fear that paralyzes and prevents action. Read the list and ask class members to respond to each source of fear by holding up the number of fingers to indicate their rating.

Ask the class to identify the difference between healthy fear and the fear that arises because of a lack of faith.

INTO THE WORD

OPTION: *Paraphrase.* The pastoral analogy of a shepherd and his sheep that David uses is far from the experience of modern readers. Provide writing paper and pens for class members to use in paraphrasing Psalm 23. Encourage them to modernize and personalize it by using an analogy familiar to them. For example, one could use the analogy of a teacher and student or a patient and doctor. The student's Twenty-third Psalm might begin, "The Lord is my teacher. I shall not be ignorant. He makes me sit down in his classroom and pay attention. He guides me through his biblical library. When I am mentally exhausted, he restores my mind and soul. He leads me in a course of study that results in righteousness."

OPTION: *Draw or Illustrate.* Both of these passages abound with visual images and lend themselves to illustration. Provide your class members with colored markers and paper. Have them illustrate each verse or the passage. Ask class members to explain their drawings to those seated near them.

OPTION: *Crossword Puzzle.* Work collectively on the crossword puzzle that is included on the reproducible page following. This will encourage a close look at the text of Psalm 23.

INTO LIFE

OPTION: *Music.* After studying Psalm 121, conclude the class by listening to Jackie Grouche Farris's rendition of "My Help." Set the mood for this activity by altering the lighting. Make a focal setting with a picture or an open Bible displayed on a table with candles and flowers. The picture might be a pastoral scene with a shepherd and sheep or maybe the Good Shepherd.

OPTION: *Memorize and Meditate.* Both of these Psalms are filled with powerful concepts beautifully stated. Memorizing and meditating on these verses can be a faith-building experience. Guide you class by reading a phrase at a time and then pausing for class members to share personal insights. For example, your saying, "The Lord is my shepherd" might lead someone to say, "The Lord God himself, not some man, is my shepherd." Or, "My shepherd indicates that he has a personal interest in me and loves me." For "I shall not be in want" may elicit, "Why do I ever worry?"(This activity is included in *NIV® Bible Student.*)

Crossword Puzzle on Psalm 23

Use the clues given and the text of Psalm 23 to fill in this crossword puzzle.

ACROSS:

2. What the Lord does to my soul
4. What the Lord is to me
8. What follows me
10. How I travel
13. Jesus said to love these
14. More than a long time
15. What goodness does
16. What follows me, besides goodness
17. My relationship to heavenly mansions
18. What God does to my head
19. To make or get ready

DOWN:

1. What overflows
2. One thing that comforts me
3. An ungodly response to evil
4. Evidence of light
5. What is not to be feared
6. The color of lush pastures
7. What I walk on
9. What my cup does
11. From birth to death
12. My table is spread in God's _____

A Daily Reminder

Debilitating fear is a regular reality for far too many Christians. Psalm 121 is a powerful antidote for fear. Clip and display this copy of Psalm 121 on your morning mirror to "inoculate" yourself against fear.

Psalm 121

1 I lift up my eyes to the hills—
where does my help come from?
2 My help comes from the LORD,
the Maker of heaven and earth.

3 He will not let your foot slip—
he who watches over you will not slumber;
4 indeed, he who watches over Israel
will neither slumber nor sleep.

5 The LORD watches over you—
the LORD is your shade at your right hand;
6 the sun will not harm you by day,
nor the moon by night.

7 The LORD will keep you from all harm—
he will watch over your life;
8 the LORD will watch over your coming and going
both now and forevermore.

LOOK TO GOD FOR JUSTICE

LESSON 4

WHY TEACH THIS LESSON?

Recently, I was the victim of what I believe to be an injustice. I had hired a van line to move my household goods across the country, but when the time came to make delivery, their representative claimed that their large moving van couldn't maneuver down my particular street. As a result, I would have to pay several hundred dollars extra to have my stuff reloaded onto a smaller truck first. Over the next few months, however, I would see several eighteen-wheel moving vans from other companies maneuver successfully right by my residence. It seems to me that I was scammed.

But what can I do to right the wrong? A letter-writing campaign has not helped. Any attempt to have the issue decided by a small claims court will doubtlessly be met by a move by that large corporation's legal staff to shift the case to another court where I will have to hire my own (expensive) lawyer.

The only option I seem to have left is to live with the injustice. Even so, I know that two facts are inescapable: (1) in the great scheme of God's universe, this particular issue is pretty minor, and (2) God will correct all injustices on that great, final judgment day. Today's lesson serves two purposes. First, it will motivate your students to work toward correcting injustices wherever that is possible. And, second, for those injustices that cannot be corrected in this life—especially those that may involve your students directly—it will provide comfort as we await Jesus' return.

INTRODUCTION

A. LIFE ISN'T FAIR

Perhaps one of the most troubling realities for believers in God is the undeniable existence of inequities in human life. Why do the rich seem to get richer while the poor get poorer? Why do so many of the wicked prosper and so many of the righteous suffer? We saw this problem in our lesson last week, and we consider it again today (see Ecclesiastes 7:15).

So, after all we've learned in six thousand years of human history, why isn't life fairer? Why do the wheels of human justice often seem to turn so slowly at times? Why are the rights of perpetrators seemingly granted more importance than the rights of victims? Why are the wealthy, who can afford expensive lawyers, often able to elude justice and avoid prison sentences? The simple answer is that human justice is imperfect because humans themselves are imperfect. Humans make mistakes. Humans do what is "politically correct." Humans are sinners.

A more difficult question to answer is "Why does God himself continue to allow life to be so unfair?" Theologians have debated this issue for centuries. Some propose that God, although he is good, is not powerful enough to stop injustice. Others propose that God, although he is all-powerful, is not good. Volumes have been written that struggle with this problem. Some examples are *Why Do Bad Things Happen to Good People?* by Harold S. Kushner; *When God Doesn't Make Sense,* by James C. Dobson; *Disappointment With God,* by Philip Yancey; and *Dark Threads the Weaver Needs,* by Herbert Lockyer. Although the insights in

DEVOTIONAL READING:
PSALM 72:11-19

BACKGROUND SCRIPTURE:
PSALMS 72; 82; 113

PRINTED TEXT:
PSALMS 82:1-8; 113:5-9

Jun
23

LESSON AIMS

After participating in this lesson, each student will be able to:

1. Describe what today's Scriptures say about the kind of justice in which God is interested.

2. Explain how knowing that God is just provides encouragement in dealing with the seeming unfairness in a sinful world.

3. Suggest specific ways a believer or congregation can work for justice in the community.

KEY VERSE

Rise up, O God, judge the earth, for all the nations are your inheritance. —Psalm 82:8

such books might help, the "answers" they propose probably will never satisfy completely the universal doubts about life's inequities—especially to the one who is suffering injustice at the moment.

Even so, there is some comfort in simply acknowledging the truth that life is not fair! John the Baptist had his life unjustly taken (Mark 6:14-29). Jesus was killed in an act of judicial murder. And Jesus warns his own disciples that, "In this world you will have trouble" (John 16:33). Face it: we live in a fallen world.

Our ultimate comfort comes in the assurance that the "scales" will indeed be "balanced" by the Great Judge on the Last Day. Until that time, we rejoice that Jesus has "overcome the world" (John 16:33). God's indwelling Spirit empowers us to rise above circumstances, to tolerate suffering, to resist temptation, and to conquer despair. "Faith is the victory!"

The lesson texts for today underscore that kind of encouragement. Read and study with positive anticipation of God's presence and help.

B. Lesson Background

In the Old Testament God is very concerned with what today we would call "social justice." In many places he fervently stresses the importance of such justice (examples: Exodus 23:6; Deuteronomy 16:19, 20; 24:19; 27:19). In other places he rages against its lack (examples: Isaiah 1:21; 5:7, 22, 23; 10:1, 2; 59:4; Ezekiel 22:29; Malachi 3:5). Today's lesson is about this lack.

The superscription attributes Psalm 82 to Asaph, probably director of a guild of temple singers (1 Chronicles 6:39; 15:17; 2 Chronicles 5:12). It is both polemical (involving dispute) and imprecatory (invoking punishment on the wicked).

I. GOD CALLS FOR JUSTICE (PSALM 82:1-8)

A. God's Supremacy Unmatched (v. 1)

1. God presides in the great assembly; he gives judgment among the "gods."

God is depicted here as the "Judge of all judges." The two clauses offer parallel ideas: first, the God who *presides* is the same One who *gives judgment*; second, the *great assembly* where he stands is an assembly of all the so-called *gods* whom the nations worship (cf. Exodus 12:12; 15:11; 18:11; and Numbers 33:4).

B. Bad Judges Reproved (v. 2)

2. "How long will you defend the unjust and show partiality to the wicked? Selah

Having affirmed God's supremacy over all other "gods," the psalmist adopts God's voice, bringing serious accusation against their brand of justice. These "gods" have penalized the righteous and favored *the unjust*.

The meaning of *Selah* is not certain. It might be a device used in music composition comparable to our *Amen*.

C. Human Rights Upheld (vv. 3-5)

3, 4. Defend the cause of the weak and fatherless; maintain the rights of the poor and oppressed. Rescue the weak and needy; deliver them from the hand of the wicked.

The psalmist makes God's expectations clear with four imperatives: *defend, maintain the rights, rescue,* and *deliver*. Again, there is a certain parallelism in thought here, with *defend* and *maintain the rights* expressing the same idea. Similarly, *rescue* and *deliver* are synonyms. By extension, what God expects from the "gods" (who are really no gods at all; cf. Jeremiah 2:11; 1 Corinthians 8:4), he also expects of us as well.

What Do You Think?

Suppose a friend must make an appearance in court—and you have to be the judge. From today's lesson, how would you deal with the case? How would you try to imitate God?

What Do You Think?

Psalm 73 is the account of the intense spiritual struggle of an individual who could not understand why the wicked prospered and the righteous suffered at the hands of evil people. How can Psalm 73 and today's passages be an encouragement to those becoming disillusioned that the "wicked are winning"?

Many Old Testament passages stress God's concern for distressed groups such as the *weak* and *fatherless*. Just three examples are Deuteronomy 27:19; Isaiah 1:17; and Zechariah 7:9, 10. Such passages make it clear that God desires justice for all peoples; he does not show favoritism to the "upper class" (cf. James 2:1-9). The most defenseless people are to receive protection from exploitation.

WELCOME HOME

Emma Lazarus's poem adorns the base of the Statue of Liberty. In part it reads, "Give me your tired, your poor, your huddled masses yearning to breathe free, the wretched refuse of your teeming shore. Send these, the homeless, tempest-tossed to me. I lift my lamp beside the golden door!"

The Statue of Liberty has been a welcoming sight to hundreds of thousands of immigrants. Many of these people have left homelands devastated by war. Others have fled countries ravaged by famine. Some immigrants have been chased away from their birthplace because of violent prejudice. For all of these people, the Statue of Liberty has stood as a promise of a new life.

Church buildings ought to resemble the Statue of Liberty in people's minds: a welcome home for all who feel harassed and helpless. The compassion that seeks justice for the afflicted and needy ought to shine from our churches like Liberty's torch.

You probably know Christians who genuinely open their hearts and hands to people in need. You know brothers and sisters in Christ who often practice the gift of hospitality. You may even know believers who could match the good Samaritan's active compassion.

James instructed that "Religion that God our Father accepts as pure and faultless is this: to look after orphans and widows in their distress and to keep oneself from being polluted by the world" (James 1:27). What can you do this week to make your church a welcome home?   —J. D. J.

5. *"They know nothing, they understand nothing. They walk about in darkness; all the foundations of the earth are shaken.*

They points to the unjust "gods." Such gods—and, by extension, the nations that serve those fictitious gods—are self-condemned by what they don't *know* (cf. Isaiah 1:3) and by the *darkness* in which they *walk*. Being unenlightened, they refuse to comprehend and practice godly justice. The New Testament compares spiritual light to darkness in several places (e.g., Matthew 4:16; 6:23; 1 John 1:5-7).

The foundations of the earth is a figure of speech for the rule of the one true God who keeps everything in order. Left to the fake "gods," the foundations of the earth would be shaken. In other words, without God, darkness and chaos would result.

D. DIVINE JUDGMENT PREVAILS (vv. 6-8)

6, 7. *"I said, 'You are "gods"; you are all sons of the Most High.' But you will die like mere men; you will fall like every other ruler."*

The fate of the *gods* is now certain as the one true God sentences them to *die like mere men*. The mythology of one of ancient Israel's neighbors held such gods to be *sons of the Most High*. In condemning these gods, the one true God is affirming that it is impossible for them to indeed be his children (cf. Psalm 89:6-8). And if the nations that serve such gods reflect the injustice of those gods, those nations are condemned as well; this is the total picture of this "courtroom scene." We should further recall that God's judgment extends both to the world we can see and to the world we can't see (Matthew 25:41; 2 Peter 2:4; Jude 6, 7; Revelation 6:12-17; 20:10, 14, 15; 21:8). Jesus draws upon Psalm 82:6 in John 10:34.

In joining together the deaths of men with that of *rulers* in verse 7, the psalmist is using a literary technique known as "merism." In this technique, a writer places

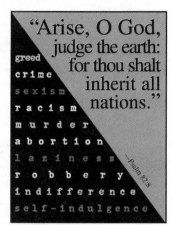

Use this visual from the Adult Visuals *packet to illustrate Psalm 82:8. Ask, "How do you think God will judge our nation for these evils?"*

two different ideas very close to each other to express completeness or totality. ("The young and the old" is an example.) So putting together men and rulers here signifies "everyone." (A similar example of merism can be seen in Psalm 105:14 which places "man" and "kings" together to mean "everyone you can think of.")

8. Rise up, O God, judge the earth, for all the nations are your inheritance.

The voice of this last verse switches from God to the singers of the psalm, petitioning God for immediate judgment. God will indeed *judge the earth*, exerting justice, righteousness, and equity. But we must remember that he does so "in his own time." Though we are impatient to see retribution fall upon the wicked and reward come to the godly, the timing of final judgment remains in the realm of divine prerogative. We trust that his ultimate will shall be done, just as he has promised. Jesus Christ will ultimately rule *all the nations* (Revelation 12:5).

II. GOD CHAMPIONS JUSTICE (PSALM 113:5-9)

A. GOD IS UNIQUE (vv. 5, 6)

5. Who is like the LORD our God, the One who sits enthroned on high?

The implied answer to the rhetorical question here is, "absolutely no one!" No one compares to *our God*.

But just how *on high* is our God? Despite the fact that we know that God is omnipresent (present everywhere), we generally think of his dwelling as "up," or as his "home on high." When Jesus taught us how to pray, he began, "Our Father in Heaven" (Matthew 6:9). We tend to think of Heaven as being somewhere above our heads, for Christ "ascended" to the Father's right hand. Yet God is Spirit, and spirits are not subject to the same limitations as those who have physical bodies. Spirits dwell on a plane of existence that is much greater than the reality with which we are familiar on earth. The next verse brings a different perspective to the whereabouts of God.

6. . . . who stoops down to look on the heavens and the earth?

God is not only transcendent (existing beyond the limits of our ordinary experience) but immanent (existing nearby) as well. "He is not far from each one of us. 'For in him we live and move and have our being'" (Acts 17:27, 28).

God stoops to care for all that he has created. He is no absentee landlord. He made us, and he keeps us. It matters to him what happens to us. He has not abandoned us; his presence protects us.

B. GOD RIGHTS HUMAN WRONGS (vv. 7-9)

7. He raises the poor from the dust and lifts the needy from the ash heap.

This is a quote from "Hannah's Song," found in 1 Samuel 2:8. It is a graphic picture of God rescuing his most needy children out of poverty, oppression, and social ostracism. It's a picture of the future, when God "will wipe every tear from their eyes. . . . for the old order of things has passed away" (Revelation 21:4).

But it is also a picture of God working through his servants now, as they labor in ministries around the world. Think of how God used Mother Teresa to minister to *the poor* in Calcutta. Remember David Livingstone (1813–1873), who gave himself totally to serving the physical and spiritual needs of primitive tribes in Africa.

In more recent times, God is working through dedicated missionaries in central India who remove cataracts from as many as one hundred patients per day in a small, understaffed eye clinic. The patients' children can attend a school also established by the missionaries, and hundreds of worshipers can gather in churches built in surrounding areas, too.

Mission personnel in Kenya are providing food, beds, showers, schooling, and Bible lessons for scores of "street children," some not yet even in their teens, who have no homes, no jobs—no future. God is raising up his poor and needy children. He's doing it through the compassion of Christians who have been commissioned to "go and make disciples of all nations."

"Religion that God our Father accepts as pure and faultless is this: to look after orphans and widows in their distress and to keep oneself from being polluted by the world" (James 1:27). God is full of mercy, and he wants his family to reflect his grace. Jesus taught that we are the "light" and "leaven" of the world, the "salt" of the earth. All those metaphors include the idea that God wants to use us to comfort, rescue, and save the needy—not just spiritually, but physically as well. We have been not only recruited, but also empowered for this great task. We are agents of God's love, by the strength of his Spirit.

GOD WILL PROVIDE

Horatio Alger, Jr. told the same story in dozens of settings. Whether in *Ragged Dick, Struggling Upward,* or *Wait and Win,* Alger always urged hard work and dedication on his readers. If you followed these moral principles, you were *Bound to Rise.*

Hard work and dedication to moral principles can improve people's lives. However, everyone needs help. Joseph, in the Old Testament, rose from slave to second in command over Egypt. David rose from shepherd boy to king. Esther rose from orphan to queen. Each of these people rose because they humbled themselves, and God worked in their lives.

"[The Lord] raises the poor from the dust and lifts the needy from the ash heap" (Psalm 113:7). Can you look back in your life and see where the Lord has raised you?

Our God is not a cosmic vending machine; you cannot order from him what you want. However, God tells us whom he raises up and for whom he will provide. "Humble yourselves before the Lord, and he will lift you up" (James 4:10). "Seek first his kingdom and his righteousness, and all these things will be given to you as well" (Matthew 6:33).

Here is both our promise and our challenge. Humbly trust the Lord and make him your priority. Then watch him lift you up.　　　　　　　　—J. D. J.

8. . . . he seats them with princes, with the princes of their people.

The psalmist sets forth a dramatic contrast. The poorest of the poor will one day share accommodations with the richest of the rich. God is going to balance all the inequities of the ages (cf. Luke 16:19-31). "Commoners" will sit with royalty. Reservations of the poor and afflicted will be upgraded to "First Class"! In Heaven, life will be fair.

Jesus promised, "In my Father's house are many rooms. . . . I am going there to prepare a place for you. And if I go and prepare a place for you, I will come back and take you to be with me that you also may be where I am" (John 14:2, 3). What a glorious future to anticipate (Revelation 21:1-8)!

9. He settles the barren woman in her home as a happy mother of children. Praise the LORD.

In 1 Samuel 1, Hannah, the wife of Elkanah, was unable to bear children. To be *a barren woman* was disgraceful in that place and time. Hannah wept tears of shame, and offered prayers to God "in bitterness of soul" (1:10). She was so serious about her request that she promised that if God granted her petition to bear a son, she would give that son "to the Lord for all the days of his life" (1:11). When Samuel was born to her and Elkanah, Hannah kept her promise. After Samuel was weaned, she delivered him to Eli, the priest at Shiloh. Samuel was dedicated to sacred service, to be mentored by Eli. The psalmist obviously had Hannah in mind as he reflected on how the Lord helps those who live, in one way or another, on the fringes of society.

WHAT DO YOU THINK?

Suppose it becomes evident that the poor (e.g., migrant workers) in a locality are being treated unfairly or partiality is being shown in the courts or at city hall. What, if any, God-given right or duty does the Christian have to become God's "colleague" to bring about justice and fairness? Try to support your views with Scripture.

WHAT DO YOU THINK?

Some people become cynical and say that God offers "barren promises." How can we help when a couple has prayed fervently for a child and it seems that God has not answered?

Dear Lord in Heaven, we thank you for all of life's privileges and challenges, but sometimes we don't understand your will. Show us somehow your divine intentions and what they mean for us here and now. And help us to accept your will, even when we don't understand it. In Jesus' name we pray, Amen.

CONCLUSION

If you want some advice on what is "fair" and what isn't, just ask any seven-year-old! In fact, you usually don't even have to ask. As all parents discover, their children are quick to point out perceived differences in treatment of siblings.

But if life were perfectly fair, everyone would get exactly what he or she deserved—all the time. But considering the reality of sin, Christians should be grateful that they are *not* getting what they actually deserve, namely, eternity in Hell! "All have sinned and fall short of the glory of God" (Romans 3:23), and "the wages of sin is death" (Romans 6:23).

But to excuse sinners from the fires of Hell—which is the punishment we deserve—leaves God open to the charge of being unjust. Sin must be punished in order for God to be just, and this is where the cross enters the picture. In taking our own punishment upon himself, God made Christ "who had no sin to be sin for us, so that in him we might become the righteousness of God" (2 Corinthians 5:21). This is how God can be, at the same time, both the one who is just and the one who justifies (Romans 3:26). To be "just" means that God, in perfect "fairness," lets no sin go unpunished. To be "the one who justifies" means that true believers will receive no penalty (even though they deserve it), because Jesus already has taken that penalty upon himself and paid it in full. This is called *grace*.

Now, in addition to fulfilling the Great Commission (Matthew 28:19, 20), God expects us to work for justice in the church and in the world (Matthew 25:35, 36; Luke 11:42; James 2:1-9). Motives are important, though, since we dare not think that we are earning God's favor by doing so (Isaiah 64:6; Ephesians 2:8, 9). Let us work for justice until he returns to judge the world in his own justice and righteousness (Acts 17:31).

Even as we look forward to that day, we probably will have to remind ourselves occasionally that although life may not seem "fair" at times, it certainly wasn't "fair" for Jesus to die at Calvary. But that's the requirement of grace: Jesus got what he did not deserve (death) so that we could get what we did not deserve (eternal life). In this respect, we should thank God for *not* being "fair"!

We also do well to remind ourselves that our own suffering is part of the human condition; it "comes with the territory" of the reality of sin. Our lives are subject to the "natural" and "scientific" laws that God ordained at creation and as a result of the fall. Germs cause infection in law-abiding citizens as well as in convicted criminals. Automobile accidents happen to both infants and drug dealers. Disease, old age, and death happen to all, no matter what their moral, ethical, and religious state might be. God "sends rain on the righteous and the unrighteous" (Matthew 5:45).

Some trials and troubles are not directly due to our "weakness in the flesh." Many fall victim to the sin of others (e.g., murder). That doesn't seem fair—and certainly isn't fair—at all. But such human wrongs are inevitable in a fallen world. It is not God who is causing this, but our own freewill actions. All citizens of an unredeemed society may suffer temporal consequences for the rebellious and disobedient behavior of even just a few. Even so, God did promise that he will never fail nor forsake us (Joshua 1:5). He did promise that our trials never would be more than we can bear (1 Corinthians 10:13). He did promise to work all things out for our good if we keep loving him (Romans 8:28). And he did promise to give us a "crown of life" if we are faithful unto death (Revelation 2:10).

The promise of this crown should cause us to realize that the unfair aspects and happenings of earthly life pale into insignificance when contrasted with eternal issues. "Murphy's Laws" have to do mostly with inconveniences and irritations. Think about it: what importance will common aggravations hold ten thousand years from now? As Richard Carlson's book reminds us, *Don't Sweat the Small Stuff!*

Life isn't fair, but God is still just.

Discovery Learning

This page contains an alternate lesson plan emphasizing learning activities. Classes desiring such student involvement will find these suggestions helpful. The next page is a reproducible activity page to further enhance discovery learning.

LEARNING GOALS

After participating in this lesson, each student will be able to:

1. Describe what today's Scriptures say about the kind of justice in which God is interested.

2. Explain how knowing that God is good provides encouragement in dealing with the seeming unfairness in a sinful world.

3. Suggest specific ways a believer or congregation can work for justice in the community.

INTO THE LESSON

OPTION: *Book Review.* Our lesson writer mentions several books that deal with the issues raised in this lesson—why bad things happen to good people. Check with your church or public library or local Christian bookstore for copies of such titles. Ask one or two class members to read and review one of these books for the class.

OPTION: *Role Play.* Ask two class members to role-play a conversation between two workers riding the bus to work and discussing how unjust our legal system is, particularly in highly publicized cases. In a role play, you set the tone and establish the attitude of each character but do not provide an exact script. You might suggest some timeless issues and problems, such as, "Justice seems to favor the rich and famous," or "The little guy gets lost in the bureaucracy."

Make the transition to the Bible study by saying, "The United States' Pledge of Allegiance to the Flag ends: 'with liberty and justice for all.' Is that true? Today's lesson text looks at the issue of justice and judicial issues. As we look at today's text, maybe we can resolve or better understand the reasons for injustices in life."

INTO THE WORD

OPTION: *Translation Study.* Bring several translations of the Old Testament to use in studying today's text. Get a sampling of the spectrum of translations. Include more literal translations, such as the *King James Version,* and freer translations, such as the *New English Bible.* Also have a paraphrase edition, such as *The Living Bible.*

Start the discussion of each verse by having a student read each translation.

OPTION: *Commentary Study.* Today's text lends itself well to a commentary study. In some places, it is not clear who is speaking, and a commentary is helpful in sorting out such issues and exploring various alternatives. Bring several commentaries to class. You may want to get recommendations from your preacher.

Divide the class into groups of two to four students. Have each group read each verse and the commentary entry. Then write an explanation of the verse to share with the rest of the class.

OPTION: *Choral Reading.* Today's text is dramatic in content and voice. Assign various parts to be read dramatically. (Use the reproducible page that follows to assign the parts.) In preparation, read and discuss each verse. Decide as a class whether it should be read by a male or female or by mixed voices. Should one person, a duet, trio, or the entire class read it? Some verses might include both. For example, Psalm 113:9 could have a woman read the first phrase and another woman read the second phrase. Then the entire class could join in and say, "Praise the Lord." Or Psalm 113:5 could begin with several voices echoing, "Who?" in a questioning tone. A male voice could say, "is like the Lord," with the entire class joining in with "our God." A female voice could render the last phrase, "who sits enthroned on high." Encourage class members to exaggerate tone and voice of each part to achieve a dramatic effect when heard by the group.

INTO LIFE

OPTION: *Personal Testimony.* Probably there are people in your class or church who have great testimonies about how they have triumphed over difficulties in life. Think about people who have faced cancer, disabilities, or injustices and have been victorious through Christ. Invite one of these people to visit and speak to your class and share the testimony of how God brought him or her through the times of trouble.

Ask him to tell what the difficulty was or is, and how God brought or is bringing him through it. What has been learned in the process? Have him conclude with a verse or passage that has been particularly helpful.

OPTION: *Prison/Justice Ministry.* A number of Christian organizations work in prison ministry and the justice system. Chuck Colson's "Prison Fellowship" is one. S. Lee Ladd's "Extended Hand Ministries" is another. Contact with such groups could provide helpful information to your class on a place and way to start. (Directions for this are included in *NIV® Bible Student.*)

Posters

The cynical sayings following would be humorous if they were not so often true. Why does the world seem to be bent toward difficulty and failure? What does today's text say about justice and fairness in life? Write a God-honoring alternative to each of these cynical sayings, such as, "If anything does go wrong, God will use it for my good and his glory." Add other samples of worldly wisdom and rephrase them to honor God.

If anything *can*
go wrong,
it will!

The later you leave,
the longer the trip
takes.

Psalm 113: A Choral Reading

Use this copy of Psalm 113 to plan a choral reading. A choral reading assigns parts to various individuals or groups depending on the content and tone of each verse or phrase. Write the names of the people or groups along the right margin and then read the chapter together.

Psalm 113	READERS
[1] Praise the LORD.	**EVERYONE**
Praise, O servants of the LORD, praise the name of the LORD. [2] Let the name of the LORD be praised, both now and forevermore. [3] From the rising of the sun to the place where it sets, the name of the LORD is to be praised.	
[4] The LORD is exalted over all the nations, his glory above the heavens. [5] Who is like the LORD our God, the One who sits enthroned on high, [6] who stoops down to look on the heavens and the earth? [7] He raises the poor from the dust and lifts the needy from the ash heap; [8] he seats them with princes, with the princes of their people. [9] He settles the barren woman in her home as a happy mother of children.	
Praise the LORD.	**EVERYONE**

TEACH THE WONDERS OF GOD

LESSON 5

WHY TEACH THIS LESSON?

A nationally known Christian evangelist and speaker was reflecting on the church of his childhood. During those formative years of his youth, this church was on the decline. Many years later, after this church had "died," this evangelist was looking through some of the church's records from its final years. He came across what might be called a brief "state of the church" evaluation written just before the church finally closed its doors. This evaluation had a mournful tone about it, noting that attendance continued to dwindle, and that the church's work for the year just completed was rather insignificant given the fact that "only a few children" had come forward to announce their decisions for Christ. This famous evangelist, whom God had used to point thousands to Christ, recognized himself as one of those children.

Does your church view the teaching of children the way this one did? As ancient Israel discovered again and again, God's people are always just one generation away from "losing it all." This is why children must be taught the truths of God. This is why your learners need this lesson today.

INTRODUCTION

A. "WHEN I WAS YOUR AGE . . . "

A grandson begs for stories about his parents, his uncles and aunts, his grandparents, and great-grandparents. He likes especially to hear humorous anecdotes of embarrassing incidents that have become family folklore. But he also listens with interest to more serious tales of historical happenings involving his ancestors' pasts that teach practical and profitable lessons.

He's only six years old, so he is still amused by his elders' reminiscences. Later, cynicism may set in, but we hope that he, and all of our grandchildren, will continue to listen with a degree of curiosity, at least, to how it was "when we were their age." Most of all, we want them to know about the heritage of faith we pass along from generation to generation. We know the importance of lessons and sermons they will hear at the church house, but we accept the fact that our personal teaching and example will be invaluable as well.

Sharing religious traditions and explaining their meaning to children is essential to developing faith. Youngsters need to know who they are and where they came from in more than a superficial sense. "My name is Chuck, and I'm from Michigan" is not nearly enough. One's identity is wrapped up in the roots of family trees. In the religious context, it is often shaped by the influence and dynamics of several generations, as well as by contemporary environments and events.

Telling "the story" keeps faith alive. It is essential for both the storyteller and the listener. Can you honestly sing the words of A. Catherine Hankey's (1834–1911) old hymn, "I love to tell the story . . . of Jesus and his glory, of

DEVOTIONAL READING:
PSALM 135:1-7
BACKGROUND SCRIPTURE:
PSALM 78:1-8
PRINTED TEXT:
PSALM 78:1-8

Jun
30

LESSON AIMS

After participating in this lesson, each student will be able to:

1. Tell what today's text says about the importance of teaching future generations the ways of the Lord.

2. Suggest some benefits that would come to society if God's Word were better known and followed.

3. State a specific way to help a young person know more about God.

KEY VERSE

We will tell the next generation the praiseworthy deeds of the LORD, his power, and the wonders he has done.   —Psalm 78:4

Jesus and his love"? Millions of children and adults need to hear it. Have you thought about who might need to hear it from you? Can you hear their plea?

> Tell me the story of Jesus,
> 　　Write on my heart every word;
> Tell me the story most precious,
> 　　Sweetest that ever was heard.
> 　　　　　—Fanny J. Crosby (1820–1915)

B. LESSON BACKGROUND

As we learned last week, Asaph was probably director of a guild of temple singers. His message today concerns the importance of keeping God's law alive. This psalm is a "wisdom poem," teaching that parents should instruct their children in truths of God, the foundation of their faith. The purpose of such instruction is clear: so that future generations will choose goodness over evil, and thereby be blessed rather than punished.

These final verses of this psalm express both negatively and positively the results that come with perpetuation of the prescribed historical perspective. Future generations will not forget and rebel; they will hope in God and obey him.

I. LEARNING FROM THE PAST (PSALM 78:1-3)

A. LISTEN AND LEARN (v. 1)

1. *O my people, hear my teaching; listen to the words of my mouth.*

As we will see later in verse 4, the larger context here is that of communication between generations. Each generation must tell of God to the next, but that telling is only half of the communication process. The other half is hearing. The older generation must not only tell—the younger generation must also hear.

Of equal importance to the telling-hearing process is the content of the communication: that content must be *my teaching* and *the words of my mouth.* (Compare this with the apostle Paul's warning in 2 Timothy 4:3, 4).

The urgent message here is to parents: share the heritage of religious faith with your offspring. Tell them about how you came to believe in God; tell them what you believe and why. Explain to them the meaning of religious rites and ceremonies. Involve them in memorials and observances. Inform them of God's expectations and how one's relationship to him is determined by one's attitude and actions. Illustrate the benefits of trust and obedience and the detriments of living in rebellion and sin. Relate both the faithfulness and the shortcomings of people from the past and emphasize the good and bad results, respectively.

In Christian families, children need to know about God and Jesus from their earliest stages of cognition. This is "home schooling" at its very best. Sunday school can be a wonderful help in this process, but it is no substitute for the "everyday school" as taught by parents and siblings. According to findings released in 1999 by Barna Research Ltd., children "between the ages of five and thirteen have a 32 percent probability of accepting Christ as their Savior"; however, the rate drops to only 4 percent for those between the ages of fourteen and eighteen, and 6 percent for adults ages nineteen and up. Given these sobering figures, can we afford to neglect the teaching of children?

B. PARABLES AND PROVERBS (vv. 2, 3)

2, 3. *I will open my mouth in parables, I will utter hidden things, things from of old—what we have heard and known, what our fathers have told us.*

Here is another example of Hebrew parallelism. *Parables* (a proverbial form of teaching) are the same as the *hidden things.* Note the use of the same terms (translated *proverb* and *riddle*) in Psalm 49:4. The writer is announcing his intention to teach, in proverbial form, the virtues of godly living and the vices of sinful living. He admits that the message is not new; in fact, he implies that his teaching possesses extra value because its source is ancient—the stories of ancestors.

Parables, of course, distinguished the teaching of Jesus (Matthew 13:34). In fact, Matthew cites Psalm 78:2 as being "fulfilled" while Jesus teaches in parables (13:35). Jesus used images and terms in those parables that would be understood by the general public. But although he taught in "laymen's language," many did not have "ears to hear" (Matthew 13:13-15; Acts 28:26, 27; cf. Ezekiel 20:49).

The *things from old* also must be repeated often. And conveying understanding is easier when using vivid images and stories—in a parabolic form that the psalmist predicts. "Word pictures" are an important part of the Old Testament narratives, and these may have touched the hearts of those who had returned from Babylonian captivity as Ezra and Nehemiah read and explained the Law to them (Nehemiah 8:8). These remnant Israelites actually stood near the "Water Gate" from morning until noon, listening to this reading (Nehemiah 8:3)! It's hard to imagine how they endured without padded pews, but apparently they had "ears to hear."

II. TEACHING FOR THE FUTURE (PSALM 78:4-8)

A. RELIGIOUS EDUCATION (v. 4)

4. We will not hide them from their children; we will tell the next generation the praiseworthy deeds of the LORD, his power, and the wonders he has done.

Israel was compelled by the urgency of the task as described in Deuteronomy 6:6-9: "These commandments that I give you today are to be upon your hearts. Impress them on your children. Talk about them when you sit at home and when you walk along the road, when you lie down and when you get up. Tie them as symbols on your hands and bind them on your foreheads. Write them on the doorframes of your houses and on your gates."

That seems a bit different from dropping the kids off at Sunday school and then going out for coffee! Not all parents take this responsibility seriously. Yet these instructions carry the weight of commands from God (cf. v. 1). It is absolutely imperative that biblical faith be passed along.

Perhaps some parents are reluctant to put this plan into action because they are ill prepared or "don't know enough." Remember, however, that the teacher usually learns more than the student in the teaching process. Prepare to share biblical faith by reviewing the material, reading, and studying the Scriptures. Pray for opportunities to tell what you remember. Most children occasionally ask hard questions; if you don't have an answer, promise you will try to find one. They probably already know you're not a genius, anyway! What they really need to know is that you are serious about your faith and the practice of your Christianity.

Remember that public schools do best when they concentrate on the basics: the "Three Rs" of Readin', 'Ritin', and 'Rithmetic. Similarly, the church will do its best when it helps parents stress to their children the three "Rs" of Repentance, Regeneration, and Righteousness. Three-dollar theological words can't be used with children, of course, but adolescents and older youth can be taught the concepts.

Important also to notice in this verse is the emphasis on positive lessons learned about God in history, as opposed to negative examples that could have been mentioned. *Praiseworthy deeds, power,* and *wonders* of the Lord are not to be hidden from the children. Hundreds of years after the Exodus, God still reminded the Israelites of that event (e.g., Isaiah 11:16; Jeremiah 7:22; Hebrews 11:22, 29).

WHAT DO YOU THINK?

Why is the use of parables such an effective method of teaching? How can children (and adults) be made more curious about God's truth through the use of parables and puzzles?

WHAT DO YOU THINK?

Occasionally one hears a cry that the educational systems need to provide more math and science majors to meet the demands of a highly technical society. But if it is true that "those who neglect the lessons of history are doomed to repeat them," should not modern culture also put a high priority on history majors to learn and teach correctly the lessons from the past?

WHAT DO YOU THINK?

In a sincere effort to help their children escape the entrapment of evil, many parents teach their children repeatedly the rules about right and wrong, but do not introduce them to the God whose very nature defines what is right and wrong. Does this explain why children often are not motivated to keep "arbitrarily established" adult rules? Why or why not?

Visual for lessons 5, 6. Display this poster as you consider verse 4. Discuss some creative ways of telling the next generation of God's works.

WHAT DO YOU THINK?

Old Testament parents could readily share their faith in what God had done and was doing. They learned this through the family because they had a "testimony in Jacob." They could share on a moment's notice "this is how God has influenced my family and my faith." How can a church help parents and church members develop their own natural "testimony in Jesus"?

WHAT DO YOU THINK?

Children go through "developmental stages" as they grow, and Christian parents usually receive little instruction on the most effective ways to teach about God and his truths in each stage. What can the church do to help parents upgrade their skills in this area?

FROM GENERATION TO GENERATION

What will be your most valuable contribution to the kingdom of God? For many Christians, our best ministry will be training our children or other young people to follow the Lord.

William Farel's encouragement of John Calvin advanced and expanded the sixteenth-century Reformation. Susanna Wesley's guidance of her sons John and Charles eventually affected hundreds of thousands of lives, as John founded Methodism in the eighteenth century and Charles wrote more than nine thousand hymns and poems. Thomas Campbell's influence on his son Alexander began an entire Christian movement in the nineteenth century.

Unfortunately, the opposite can occur as well. The sons of Eli from the time of the judges provide an example: "Eli's sons were wicked men; they had no regard for the Lord" (1 Samuel 2:12). Likewise, when Samuel began to age, "he appointed his sons as judges for Israel . . . . But his sons did not walk in his ways. They turned aside after dishonest gain and accepted bribes and perverted justice" (8:1, 3).

The development of godly young adults does not happen by accident. Children must be trained to know the Lord and to follow him from their hearts (cf. Proverbs 22:6). Timothy's grandmother Lois, his mother Eunice, and the apostle Paul all contributed to the formation of Timothy's faith and life of ministry. What can you do to guide your children, grandchildren, or young friends toward a life of service for the Lord? "These commandments that I give you today are to be upon your hearts. Impress them on your children. Talk about them when you sit at home and when you walk along the road, when you lie down and when you get up" (Deuteronomy 6:6, 7).   —J. D. J.

B. THE LAW OF THE LORD (v. 5)

5. He decreed statutes for Jacob and established the law in Israel, which he commanded our forefathers to teach their children.

A Cliffs Notes™ version of the Old Testament might read something like this: God chose a nation (*Israel*), gave them a *law* (Mosaic), and insisted that each generation be informed (Deuteronomy 6:6-9). That's an oversimplification, of course, but it does pretty well summarize the thrust of Asaph's message. *Jacob* stands for all the tribes of Israel—the law was for everyone.

Christians live under the New Covenant, of course, and not under this old law appointed for Israel. But Paul tells us the Old Testament provides instruction for New Testament disciples (1 Corinthians 10:11). It thus remains incumbent upon all readers to share and model the faith of their spiritual *forefathers*. Discipling future generations is not optional—it is God's will.

C. THE FUTURE FAITHFUL (vv. 6, 7)

6. . . . so the next generation would know them, even the children yet to be born, and they in turn would tell their children.

Faith often seems not to survive beyond the third generation. But if the instructions of this passage are carried out, many fewer descendants will be lost. Consider young Timothy, whose mother Eunice and grandmother Lois passed along their faith to him. They told "the story" to Timothy, the apostle Paul confirmed it, and then commissioned the young preacher to instruct others who will subsequently teach still others (2 Timothy 1:5; 2:2). The evangelistic implications multiply like compounding interest. Frank C. Laubach (1884–1970) fought illiteracy with his "each one teach one" technique. Think how soon all the world could hear the good news if each Christian taught just one more. What if each one taught three?!

7. Then they would put their trust in God and would not forget his deeds but would keep his commands.

Here's the purpose and motivation for telling the story of God's love and law: that future generations might, in the words of John H. Sammis (1846–1919), "trust and obey, for there's no other way to be happy in Jesus."

Some have been known to bring the charge of "manipulation" against Christian parents, accusing them of "indoctrinating" or "brainwashing" their children. But instructing children in the faith is not any more about manipulation than is instructing children about good nutrition and personal hygiene. Nor is such instruction merely to earn bragging rights for successful parenting. One does not pass the faith along so that conversations at family reunions will be less controversial.

Rather, we educate our descendants about God, his Word, and his church so that the generations to follow will have the privilege of knowing their Maker not only as Creator, but also as Lord and Savior. The abundance of their lives and their eternal destinies are at stake. Breaking the chain of discipling not only will jeopardize your own faith, but will very likely leave your kin with no witness, no testimony to God's grace. Such unfaithfulness has eternal consequences.

Making God's law and *works* known is a continuing process. It is not enough that children are taught once. They must be reminded again and again. (You don't tell them only once to clean their rooms, do you?) They will put *their trust in God* if they do *not forget his deeds* (Exodus 10:2; 12:26, 27; 13:8; cf. Deuteronomy 6:20-25). And they will not forget if we are faithful and persistent in telling "the story of unseen things above, of Jesus and his glory, of Jesus and his love. . . . The old, old story that I have loved so long."

D. PROFITING FROM BAD EXAMPLES (v. 8)

8. They would not be like their forefathers—a stubborn and rebellious generation, whose hearts were not loyal to God, whose spirits were not faithful to him.

Do you suppose that any of the ancient Israelites ever told a child, "Don't do as I do; do as I say!"? It is possible, even for parents who are careful to speak of religious values to children, to be far less faithful in their walk than in their talk. Probably the majority of Israelites were regular attendees at feast days, ceremonies, and formalities of their religion. But as this verse makes plain, the Israelites' *forefathers* were *stubborn, rebellious,* and inconsistent in performing the will of God; their *hearts* and their *spirits* was not in tune with God's (again we see Hebrew parallelism, with *hearts* and *spirits* meaning just about the same thing). Though he wanted to abide in them, they were not abiding in him. More than a dozen times in the Old Testament God calls the Israelites "stiff-necked" (e.g., 2 Chronicles 30:8).

By *not* being *faithful* they showed that their relationship to the Lord was only nominal. They went through the motions, but rebellious lifestyles betrayed their pretense. "These people . . . honor me with their lips, but their hearts are far from me" (Isaiah 29:13). Most Christians know, of course, that actions speak much louder than words. Our families see us when we aren't surrounded by church members. They observe our language and behavior in casual and careless moments, in stressful situations, and even when we think no one is paying attention. It becomes a question of "Will the real Christian please stand up?"

Asaph, like the prophet Isaiah, had the right message, but it likely was too late by itself to correct the rebellion of the "church of tomorrow." Sterner measures would be needed—these would come in 586 B.C. in the form of the Babylonian exile.

PATHS OF REMEMBRANCE

How can we keep from becoming a generation whose stubborn hearts are not right? The New Testament counsels, "We must pay more careful attention, therefore, to what we have heard, so that we do not drift away" (Hebrews 2:1).

HOW TO SAY IT
Asaph. AY-saff.
Ebenezer. EB-en-EE-zer.
Eunice. U-NYE-see or U-nis.
Isaiah. Eye-ZAY-uh.

God constructed the human brain to form "paths of remembrance." A computer will take approximately the same amount of time to bring up information stored in its memory or disk drive no matter how much or how little you use that information. The human brain, however, gets faster and better with use. Remembering how to tie your shoes took you a long time as a young child. Now, you can do it accurately and quickly without thinking.

The same holds true in the practice of your faith. The more you humble yourself before the Lord, the less likely it is that you will become stubborn. The more you implant God's word in your mind and heart, the less likely you are to drift away from it. The more you recognize and repent of daily self-centeredness and sin, the less likely it is that your heart will not be right.

Every day you have an opportunity to review some of God's works: the Exodus, David and Goliath, Daniel in the lion's den, etc. Every week you have an opportunity to commune with God, remembering the cross. Every hour you can set your hope on God and obey him. Build "paths of remembrance" into your brain to help you remain steadfast.

—J. D. J.

CONCLUSION

Occasionally, television executives come up with some programming that has more than a sound bite of "redeeming social value." The History Channel® is a positive example. That is, it can be helpful if viewers are perceptive in discerning the lessons to be learned from history and are conscientious in applying those lessons in order to influence today and tomorrow for good. The serious study of the past can be socially redemptive in the future.

Cases in point: reviewing the atrocities of the World War II "Holocaust" and the more recent Balkan "ethnic cleansings" that were inflicted on certain peoples can inspire determination that madmen never will be allowed to perpetrate such war crimes again. Seeing and hearing graphic reports of the Hiroshima bombing can, and should, weld the resolve of world powers against all future use of atomic and nuclear power to destroy. Documentaries of race riots, campus demonstrations, and cult-hostage situations might so sicken citizens that future episodes of civil disobedience will be precluded.

Are such results too much to hope for? God's messenger who wrote this lesson text was convinced that untarnished and unvarnished truth from the past would change the future for good.

Reviewing the sad results of ancient Israel's centuries-long rebellion against God's law should have influenced future descendants to trust and obey. What a travesty that God's law had to be periodically "rediscovered" (e.g., 2 Kings 23:2)! Knowing God's commandments and his history of blessing the faithful can inspire faithfulness among contemporary believers. Biblical history teaches the basic underlying lesson: righteousness works, corruption fails; morality wins, wickedness loses. These lessons need to be shared with all who come behind us. Our followers can avoid pitfalls, resist temptation, and "work out" their salvation (Philippians 2:12).

When Joshua led the Israelite nation into their promised land, God instructed him to leave a memorial "to the people of Israel forever" (Joshua 4:7) at the Jordan River. Later, Samuel erected an "Ebenezer" (or "stone of help") to remind the Israelites of the Lord's help (1 Samuel 7:12). Jesus instituted the Lord's Supper as an enduring reminder of his sacrifice (1 Corinthians 11:23-26). Will you be ready with answers when your children or grandchildren ask, "What is the meaning of baptism? . . . of this cup and bread? . . . of this nativity scene?" Be ready for the time when they ask. Better yet, tell them even before they ask.

Discovery Learning

This page contains an alternate lesson plan emphasizing learning activities. Classes desiring such student involvement will find these suggestions helpful. The next page is a reproducible activity page to further enhance discovery learning.

LEARNING GOALS

After participating in this lesson, each student will be able to:

1. Tell what today's text says about the importance of teaching future generations the ways of the Lord.

2. Suggest some benefits that would come to society if God's Word were better known and followed.

3. State a specific way to help a young person know more about God.

INTO THE LESSON

OPTION: *Listening Game.* Today's text begins with an admonition to listen carefully. To prepare for the lesson, have your class play the party game of "gossip," in which each person listens to a complex statement whispered to him or her and then whispers it to the next person as accurately as possible. Read this statement to the first person to start the game, "On June 23, 2002, we studied justice from Psalms 82 and 113. Today, June 30, 2002, we look at Psalm 78." Write the sentence on a poster or overhead transparency so that, at the end, you can show the class how well they listened.

Make the transition to Bible study by saying, "This party game shows how poor our listening skills usually are. Maybe that is why today's text begins with a call to listen carefully. Listening attentively is a foundational step for accurately passing on detailed information to others."

OPTION: *Hymn Study.* Provide copies of hymn books for each class member. Have them study the stanzas of hymns that capture the command of today's lesson, like "Tell Me the Old, Old Story" or "Wonderful Words of Life." Begin the class by singing a few selected stanzas. Recruit a class member to lead the singing and a musician to accompany.

Make the transition to the lesson by saying, "These hymns capture the command of today's lesson. Every generation is charged with the responsibility to pass faith on to the next generation. As we study Psalm 78:1-8, look for ideas included in these hymns." (This activity is included in NIV® Bible Student.)

INTO THE WORD

OPTION: *Illustrate the Passage.* Provide paper and pencils for your class members to illustrate the first eight verses of Psalm 78. The process of trying to present the truth of each verse in visual form will help your class understand the passage. Use the reproducible page segment entitled, "Illustrate a Verse."

OPTION: *Discussion Questions.* Copy the following questions for use with your class. Give two questions to each of four groups. Allow four to six minutes and then reassemble for answers to be shared. (This activity is included in NIV® Bible Student.)

Why does faith have to be verbalized to be passed on?

What parables have helped to form your faith?

Describe the special place that fathers have in the transmission of faith.

Describe the special place that mothers have in the transmission of faith.

Why would any parent hide the things God had done?

How many generations are mentioned in this passage?

What causes children to trust God?

What effect do stubborn and rebellious parents have on children?

What benefits would come to society if God's Word were better known and followed?

INTO LIFE

OPTION: *Brainstorm.* Have your class brainstorm for ways they can pass along their personal faith to children and grandchildren. Don't stop to evaluate ideas. Just write them as fast as possible and let class members feed on each other's ideas and creativity. Write the list large enough that everyone in the class can see it. When you have finished your list, have class members vote on the three best ideas. Suggest that each member select one of the ways and commit to implementing it.

OPTION: *Testimony.* Most churches have some people who are second, third, or fourth (or more) generation believers. Ask one of these people to visit your class and share a testimony of how this was accomplished and the blessing it has been to the family. Make sure you carefully explain the purpose of the testimony—to inspire and encourage your class members to tell diligently the next generation the praiseworthy deeds of God. Review Psalm 78 with your guest speaker to help her or him focus on this lesson's key truth and indicate how long you have allowed in your lesson plan for that person to speak.

Illustrate a Verse

Illustrate each verse from Psalm 78 in the space to the right of the verse. The illustration may be very simple—they need not be "masterpieces"! At the same time, if you have a particular talent for art and want to make them more detailed and involved, do so as an offering to the Lord!

Psalm 78

[1] O my people, hear my teaching;
listen to the words of my mouth.

[2] I will open my mouth in parables,
I will utter hidden things, things from of old—

[3] What we have heard and known,
what our fathers have told us.

[4] We will not hide them from their children;
we will tell the next generation
the praiseworthy deeds of the Lord,
his power, and the wonders he has done.

[5] He decreed statutes for Jacob
and established the law in Israel,
which he commanded our forefathers
to teach their children.

[6] So the next generation would know them,
even the children yet to be born,
and they in turn would tell their children.

[7] Then they would put their trust in God
and would not forget his deeds
but would keep his commands.

[8] They would not be like their forefathers—
a stubborn and rebellious generation,
whose hearts were not loyal to God,
whose spirits were not faithful to him.

Worship and Wisdom for Living
Unit 2: Praise the Creator and Redeemer
(Lessons 6-9)

WORSHIP THE CREATOR AND SUSTAINER

WHY TEACH THIS LESSON?

When a person accepts Christ as Savior, that is truly a great thing! To join the fellowship of the redeemed in that walk of faith results from what is without doubt the most important decision a person will ever make. Thus, we tend to think of the relationship to Jesus as our Redeemer as the beginning point of our relationship with him.

But as critically important as this relationship is, it is not the most foundational one. Long before Christ became our Redeemer, he was our Creator (Colossians 1:15-17). That fact has profound implications. For one, it means that Jesus-as-Creator holds the "certificate of ownership" to absolutely everything created. How amazing it is, therefore, to see people live their lives and do as they please as if they themselves owned their own bodies! How the world would change—and how your church might change—if every person began each day with the affirmation "I will live this day to please my Creator, because he owns it all and that makes me accountable to him."

INTRODUCTION

A. GOD'S RELATIONSHIP TO THE NATURAL WORLD

Devout people from many religions gather weekly (and sometimes daily) all over the world to worship God as they understand him. But their concepts of God are all different and often contradictory! Does God care? Jesus seems to think so when he declares that "the true worshipers will worship the Father in spirit and truth" (John 4:23). The passage we consider today offers us truth that is important for our worship of him. To worship God in truth surely includes a proper understanding of his relationship to us and our world.

B. LESSON BACKGROUND

With this week's lesson, we begin a new unit of study focusing on humanity's praise of the Creator and Redeemer. We will study what several psalms teach us about worshiping the Creator of life, about living as the crown of God's creation, about finding joy in forgiveness, and about all people praising God.

Psalm 104, for today's lesson, is a magnificent psalm of praise. Although we can't be sure, the historical setting probably involved the psalmist's own worship at the temple in Jerusalem. The psalmist reminds us here that God not only *creates*, but also actively *sustains* his creation. These truths should be part of our own worship.

I. GOD CARES FOR HIS CREATION (PSALM 104:24-30)

A key feature that sets this subsection apart from verses 31-35 to follow is its *direct address* to God. The psalmist talks to God directly, and we can, too!

DEVOTIONAL READING:
PSALM 65
BACKGROUND SCRIPTURE:
PSALMS 65; 104
PRINTED TEXT:
PSALM 104:24-35

Jul
7

LESSON AIMS

After participating in this lesson, each student will be able to:

1. List some of the ways God is glorified in his creation.

2. Tell how the psalmist says we should relate to God's creation and to him.

3. Praise God for his role as Creator and Sustainer of the universe.

KEY VERSE

How many are your works, O LORD! In wisdom you made them all; the earth is full of your creatures. —Psalm 104:24

LESSON 6 NOTES

A THE WISDOM OF GOD (v. 24)

24. How many are your works, O LORD! In wisdom you made them all; the earth is full of your creatures.

God's *wisdom* made possible all life and the forces of nature of which we know—and those we are yet to discover! The ancient Greeks knew only of four "elements": earth, air, fire, and water. Modern chemistry's "periodic table of the elements," however, contains over one hundred entries, with more presumably to come. In light of these impressive discoveries, humans often think themselves to be wise. But if humanity—which has yet to cure many diseases—is wise, then how much wiser must be the One who created all the intricacies of the universe in the first place!

On the timetable of human history, we have only recently begun to explore the wonders of outer space and the complexities of the life forms found in the depths of the oceans. God's wisdom in creating the universe is beyond our ability to comprehend fully. We look around and continually find new things to astonish and confound us. How sadly ironic to see humans congratulate themselves for their intellect in these matters, and yet ignore their Creator whose wisdom makes their own possible.

WHAT DO YOU THINK?

While there is a growing commitment to valuing and protecting our natural environment today, there seems to be a diminishing recognition that it is all the product of God's wisdom and work. Why do you think this is the case?

B. THE CREATURES OF THE SEA (vv. 25, 26)

25. There is the sea, vast and spacious, teeming with creatures beyond number—living things both large and small.

The psalmist has a sincere appreciation for the Mediterranean Sea, which stretches to the horizon. Although this is indeed an immense body of water, it hardly compares in size with the Atlantic or Pacific Oceans. Imagine how overwhelmed the psalmist might have been to have known of those immensely larger bodies of water!

The psalmist stands in awe of the varieties of life in *the sea*. But again, the psalmist's knowledge is limited compared with what we know today. In ancient times, there was no way to dive very deeply into any body of water. One could go down only as far as a single breath would allow. Our modern deep-sea research capabilities and discoveries would astound anyone living just two hundred years ago. In fact, they continue to astound even modern science, as new life forms are continually discovered and cataloged. Our increasingly sophisticated instruments of magnification make their contributions as well. Should not our greater knowledge lead to proportionately greater awe of the Creator?

26. There the ships go to and fro, and the leviathan, which you formed to frolic there.

The sea provides not only a habitat for God's creatures, but also a means of passage for human commerce. Both are sources of wonder and awe to the psalmist, especially since the ancient Jew was a landlubber for whom the sea held terror.

Of special interest here is the mention of *the leviathan*. This creature is also noted in Job 41:1; Psalm 74:14; and Isaiah 27:1, although no one really knows what a leviathan is (or was). From the psalmist's perspective, it may simply refer to a large marine creature, such as a whale. The psalmist's point is that it was God and no other who created this beast and gave it vast bodies of water to *frolic there*. We are thus impressed again by God's creative power and his desire to provide for his creation.

WHAT DO YOU THINK?

The more we learn about God's creation, the more we realize that all living things, including "both small and great beasts," have their place in the scheme of things. In a day when size, speed, volume, and the like seem to be the measure of worth, how can we learn to appreciate and value "both small and great"?

MAYBERRY SEA MONSTER

Andy Griffith's TV neighbors (especially Barney Fife) were terrorized by sightings of what appeared to be a huge water dinosaur in a local lake. Barney's antics, were hysterical as he "fished" for the monster using whole chickens for bait. The episode concluded with the discovery that the lake creature was merely a fake—carved from wood and used by the owner of a resort restaurant to create publicity for his business.

HOW TO SAY IT

leviathan. luh-VYE-uh-thun.

Human nature is fascinated by "believe it or not" reports of new and unusual discoveries. The mystery of unknown elements of creation is intriguing. Perhaps the psalmist actually had never seen "leviathan," but reports of large sea creatures surely had drifted inland. Since he already believed in a God great enough to create such beings, his mind was open to new evidence.

Barney Fife was hardly a credible witness, but the God-breathed testimony of Holy Scripture is reliable. Even centuries ago, the Spirit convinced believers of the limitless power of God to create mighty whales as well as aquatic microbes (and everything in between). "Is any thing too hard for the Lord?" (Genesis 18:14).   —R. W. B.

C. THE ONGOING PROVISION OF GOD (vv. 27-30)

27. These all look to you to give them their food at the proper time.

The psalmist depicts the creatures of the sea as almost helpless. They wait on God to feed them and take care of them. While we might not think of God as personally arranging every daily feeding schedule for the animals and fish, there is a sense in which he is very much in control of these processes. God placed within these creatures instincts that drive them to certain places at certain times. For some, those instincts will lead them to find food. For others, those instincts lead them to be food. (Most know this as the food chain.) God can personally override these instincts anytime he wishes, as he did in the case of the giant fish that swallowed Jonah.

Some may ask, "But how is God caring for some creatures when he provides them to be food for others?" This concern arises because humans tend to look at members of the animal kingdom in terms of a hierarchy of "values." Cute, furry animals seem to draw our compassion, while insects are swatted!

But in God's plan insects can be food for some animals (such as bats) just as certain mammals and fish can be food for others (such as seal pups for killer whales). On certain occasions when humans have removed predators from an environment, the result has been overpopulation and starvation of the prey remaining. God has worked out the various orders of creation according to his own priorities and values, not ours.

28. When you give it to them, they gather it up; when you open your hand, they are satisfied with good things.

The hunting instincts in sea (and other) creatures are innate—God made them that way. Some varieties of whales exhale underwater, and their food is trapped in the bubbles that float to the surface. The whales then surface and eat. God provides the food and the whales gather it in.

Humanistic scientists see this as the result of evolutionary processes at work. But these folks are never able to explain all the in-between steps that would have to occur for the whale to reach this final point in its "evolution." The psalmist, on the other hand, chooses to recognize God's care for his creation, and marvel at the fact.

29. When you hide your face, they are terrified; when you take away their breath, they die and return to the dust.

Every creature is dependent on God. Their (and our) continued existence is due to forces of nature that God has put in place and continues to control. Suppose God were to withdraw the moon and other forces that control the ocean tides and currents. How many life forms would perish as a result? These forces of nature, created and continually sustained by God, demonstrate his presence. And when God withdraws his presence, either personally or through the forces of nature he controls, creatures suffer or die. This includes humans (cf. Psalm 30:7).

When reading this passage, the Christian also recalls the spiritual renewal that is available only in Jesus. "Therefore if anyone is in Christ, he is a new creation; the old has gone, the new has come!" (2 Corinthians 5:17).

DAILY BIBLE READINGS

Monday, July 1—*Creator With Steadfast Love (Psalm 136:1-9)*

Tuesday, July 2—*Sustainer of Land and People (Psalm 147:1-11)*

Wednesday, July 3—*Mortals Sustained by Eternal God (Psalm 103:15-22)*

Thursday, July 4—*God Has Established the World (Psalm 93:1-5)*

Friday, July 5—*God Set the Earth's Foundations (Psalm 104:1-9)*

Saturday, July 6—*Sustainer of Life (Psalm 104:10-23)*

Sunday, July 7—*God Creates and Sustains (Psalm 65:1-13)*

WHAT DO YOU THINK?

Verses 27-29 suggest that there is interdependency in the universe that is part of God's creative intention. What are some of the evidences of this life-sustaining interdependency? Using 2 Corinthians 8:14, how can this same principle of interdependency apply in our personal relationships?

Visual for lessons 5, 6. Display again the poster from last week. Discuss some of the "manifold works" of God your students have admired.

30. When you send your Spirit, they are created, and you renew the face of the earth.

Without God there is no life. In noting the role of God's Spirit in creating sea creatures, the psalmist is perhaps recalling Genesis 1:2: "And the Spirit of God moved upon the face of the waters." But alongside the fact of creation the psalmist adds another idea: renewal. Renewal can be thought of as God's "recreating" things.

Interestingly, the Old Testament places these "create" and "renew" ideas alongside each other in several other places as well. One example is Psalm 51:10 which says, "Create in me a pure heart, O God, and renew a steadfast spirit within me." As new creations themselves, Christians look forward to the day when the old creation is renewed (Revelation 21:4, 5).

CYCLES OF LIFE

A few years ago, some criticized the popular film *The Lion King* for alleged New Age overtones. (For example, did Elton John's song "The Circle of Life" teach reincarnation?) Other movie fans preferred simply to enjoy the fable and music without analyzing the message.

There are, of course, cycles to life. Both flora and fauna demonstrate the fact. Grass, leaves, and flowers "die" in the fall and "come alive" again in the spring. Many animals and humans die each year, and many more are born. "The wind blows to the south and turns to the north; round and round it goes, ever returning on its course. All streams flow into the sea, yet the sea is never full. To the place the streams come from, there they return again" (Ecclesiastes 1:6, 7). And "there is . . . a season for every activity under heaven" (Ecclesiastes 3:1).

"What goes around comes around," the saying goes. It seems clear, yet mysterious. There is evident design in the universe, and God is the awesome architect. The cycles and passages of life are part of his grand plan. All that man has discovered, God invented. It is he who enhances our existence with his wise and gracious gifts of natural law. It is he who maintains order and sustains life in his creation. It is he who has made us, and he who gives "life to the full."
—R. W. B.

II. GOD'S GLORY ENDURES FOREVER (PSALM 104:31, 32)

The psalmist now shifts away from addressing God directly. The focus moves from creation and sustenance to glory and power.

A. GOD REJOICES IN THE GLORY OF HIS CREATION (v. 31)

31. May the glory of the LORD endure forever; may the LORD rejoice in his works.

Humanistic thinkers have attempted to have God declared dead or irrelevant. They have failed. There are more Christians in the world today than ever before. Human reason or decision cannot diminish the glory of God.

An interesting exercise is to look at some of these attempts and see how they have failed. Some thought, for example, that the space program would eliminate the need to rely on God, as humans on their own would eventually be able to unlock the mysteries of the universe and explain everything in humanistic ways.

Instead, the opposite has happened. Every answer gained seems to spawn two more questions. The intricacies of the universe defy humanistic explanations that exclude the concept of creation (otherwise known as "intelligent design"). Take some time and look at the breathtaking images that have come back from the Hubble space telescope (You can find these easily on the Internet.) "The heavens declare the glory of God" (Psalm 19:1).

B. GOD CONTINUES TO REVEAL HIMSELF (v. 32)

32. . . . he who looks at the earth, and it trembles, who touches the mountains, and they smoke.

WHAT DO YOU THINK?

It seems incredible that some continue to insist that our solar system is a fortuitous cosmic consequence. In what ways does our world bring glory to God as Designer and Creator?

God continues to offer us evidence of his existence through earthquakes and other forces of nature. Human beings, who often consider themselves to be too intelligent and sophisticated to believe in supernatural forces, have "produced" some mighty powers of their own, such as nuclear energy. These efforts, of course, are nothing more than the harnessing of forces that God himself already has created.

Even given our efforts to harness such forces, the results pale in comparison to the energy and force produced naturally by an earthquake or a volcano. The eruption of Mount Saint Helens in 1980, for example, released energy equivalent to five hundred atomic bombs of the type dropped on Hiroshima. A single solar flare (of which the psalmist knew nothing!) releases energy equivalent to millions of one-hundred-megaton hydrogen bombs. A discovery such as this should lead to even greater awe of the Creator than the psalmist demonstrated.

III. PRAISE FOR THE CREATOR (PSALM 104:33-35)

In our final subsection, we find the psalmist singing, meditating, and expressing a specific desire. The psalmist seems to be overcome with emotion.

A. PRAISE EXPRESSED IN SINGING (v. 33)

33. *I will sing to the LORD all my life; I will sing praise to my God as long as I live.*

When we consider the wonders of God, the proper reaction is to break forth in praise, which will often take the form of singing. (The word *psalm* itself can be used to designate song or instrumental music.) The psalmist expresses a lifelong commitment to sing praises to God.

Sadly, some people never sing to God. In church, this may be due at times to embarrassment at having an untrained singing voice. (In such cases, the local church could offer encouragement and even basic voice training where appropriate.) At other times, stubbornness may be the reason. In this case, the words of the old hymn "We're Marching to Zion" might come to mind: "Let those refuse to sing Who never knew our God." Although it is up to God to judge motives in such cases, one cannot help but wonder about those who are able to sing but refuse to do so.

The psalmist's expressive style conveys a very personal relationship with God, calling him *my God*. That small possessive adjective "my" speaks volumes! The psalmist does not feel that God is distant or unapproachable. The God who created the universe and set in motion all the processes and forces we know and experience is also a very personal God. He is personally interested in each of us. The psalmist recognizes that fact and responds to it. Notice that the psalmist's commitment to lifelong praise-through-song is not an "as long as everything is going well" commitment.

B. PRAISE EXPRESSED IN MEDITATION (v. 34)

34. *May my meditation be pleasing to him, as I rejoice in the LORD.*

The psalmist is committed to *meditation* as well as praise-through-song. When Joshua took the mantle of leadership following the death of Moses, the Lord told him to meditate on his word (Joshua 1:8). The Psalms themselves open by noting the importance of meditation (Psalm 1:2). There are many other references in the Psalms on the importance of meditating on God, his Word, and his works (see Psalm 19:14; 63:6; 77:12; 119:97, 99; and 143:5).

Meditating on the Scriptures seems to be a "lost art." Most people think they are just too busy. In a fast food, instant gratification culture, we have become unaccustomed to meditating, pondering, or thinking for extended periods of time. Many seem to have a need to hear the drone of a TV in the background at all times—even "muting" the sound during commercials is unknown in most households! The

WHAT DO YOU THINK?

Isaiah tells us that all of nature bursts forth in song and praise to the Lord (Isaiah 55:12). Why then, if all these created things seem to honor their Creator, is it so difficult for us, the crown of God's creation, to burst forth in spontaneous expressions of praise and adoration (vv. 33, 34)?

excesses of the Information Age and an entertainment-oriented culture tempt people away from private time with God. When one becomes used to thinking in "sound bites," meditation becomes "too much work." Undoubtedly, much of our unhappiness can be traced to a lack of time or effort in meditating on the Word of God.

The psalmist, however, finds meditation to be *sweet*. This unique time to reflect on God—perhaps in solitude, perhaps during worship with others—makes the psalmist *rejoice in the Lord*. We might discover the psalmist's joy for ourselves if we minimized the time we spend pursuing entertainment in order to create more time to meditate upon God and his Word.

C. PRAISE EXPRESSED IN A DESIRE FOR HARMONY (v. 35)

35. But may sinners vanish from the earth and the wicked be no more. Praise the LORD, O my soul. Praise the LORD.

Suddenly, a "negative wish" presents itself. The desire expressed here, at first glance, seems to shatter the sweet gentleness of this Psalm. How can the one who offered unrestrained praise to God express, in the same breath, such animosity toward humanity, the crown of God's creation?

In expressing a desire for the destruction of sinners, the psalmist longs for God's creation to be restored to its original, sinless purity. The apostle Paul notes that all of creation has been in disharmony since sin entered the world (Romans 8:22). The psalmist's desire for the removal of sinners reflects what God had already done once in the flood (Genesis 6–8) and promises to do again on the last day (Revelation 20).

But why has God waited so long to bring about this renewed harmony? Why does he continue to permit humanity to go on sinning and spoiling his creation? The answer is that God is waiting for people to answer the call of the gospel. God "is patient with you, not wanting anyone to perish, but everyone to come to repentance" (2 Peter 3:9). Even so, "the day of the Lord will come" (2 Peter 3:10). In his time, God will answer the prayer of the psalmist. God's patience and the promised restoration of his creation should cause all that know him to say *Praise the Lord* (untranslated, "Hallelujah").

CONCLUSION

Many today do not believe in creation, preferring instead to suppose that life "evolved" through random chance and "natural selection." Others, who might accept the concept of creation and believe in the existence of a Creator, deny that that Creator continually cares for his creation and intervenes on its behalf. The latter is part of a philosophy known as "Deism"; several founding fathers of the U.S., including Thomas Jefferson and Benjamin Franklin, were influenced by this belief system.

A persistent viewpoint in ancient and Eastern religions is that "god" is not distinct from creation, but is actually part of it. This philosophy has been called "pantheism" (literally, "everything is god"), but more foundational is an idea known as "pagan monism." Under this philosophy, we are ultimately not to see "boundary lines" between anything. Thus, we are "god" and "god" is us—there is to be no distinction or dividing line. This philosophy is supposed to apply to other aspects within creation. For example, we are told to see no difference between humans and animals, or even between the sexes themselves (cf. Genesis 1:27; Deuteronomy 22:5).

But in a few short lines, the psalmist challenges all of these lies. As we noted in the Introduction, centuries after the Psalms were written Jesus would contend for the importance of truth-in-worship (John 4:23). The truths of Psalm 104 deserve to be engraved on our hearts as we worship. The rightness of the psalmist's attitude rings clearly down through the centuries. It is an attitude that should (and could) be ours as well.

Discovery Learning

This page contains an alternate lesson plan emphasizing learning activities. Classes desiring such student involvement will find these suggestions helpful. The next page is a reproducible activity page to further enhance discovery learning.

LEARNING GOALS

After this lesson each student will be able to:

1. List some ways God is glorified in his creation.

2. Tell how the psalmist says we should relate to God's creation and to him.

3. Praise God for his role as Creator and Sustainer of the universe.

INTO THE LESSON

OPTION: *Creation Collage.* The psalmist looked at the created world and broke out in praise to God, the Creator. Bring a stack of old magazines with colorful photographs of the beauty of the world. Ask your class to tear or cut out pictures that show the glory of God through his creation. Provide large sheets of newsprint or poster board onto which these pictures can be glued or taped. This can be set up ahead of time and can begin when the first person enters the classroom.

Make the transition to Bible study by saying, "We have looked for pictures that show the glory of God in his creation. Our study today is from Psalm 104; the psalmist looks at the creatures of the sea and breaks forth in praise to the Creator. Let's read of what we have done with pictures."

OPTION: *Hymn Study.* Provide a hymnbook for each person in your class. If you are not a good song leader, ask for help. Explain what your goals are for the activity. Select some hymns that focus on creation and the glory it brings to the Creator, such as "How Great Thou Art" and "For the Beauty of the Earth." Begin by having members turn to these hymns and analyze what the creation tells us about the Creator. Sing the verses especially appropriate for today's lesson: stanza one of "For the Beauty of the Earth," stanzas one and two of "How Great Thou Art." (This activity is in *NIV® Bible Student.*)

INTO THE WORD

OPTION: *Research.* Assign a class member to research the leviathan the psalmist mentions in Psalm 104:26. (See also Job 41:1, Psalm 74:14, and Isaiah 27:1.) A little work in commentaries or the Internet will yield interesting results. (This activity is in *NIV® Bible Student.*)

OPTION: *Praise and Worship.* Have the students work together or in small groups to analyze Psalm 104, noting how the psalmist describes God's attributes and his works. Use the reproducible page that follows.

OPTION: *Outline.* Provide class members with pens and paper for outlining the passage. This is a good Bible study activity because readers have to examine the text carefully to find basic ideas and how the theme is developed. Have your class work in groups of three or four. After they have completed the outline, have them share their outline with the class. You might excerpt and show them the lesson writer's outline.

INTO LIFE

OPTION: *Poetry Writing.* Haiku is a type of Japanese poetry consisting of three lines of five, seven, and five syllables respectively. The topic is usually a subject from the natural world. Haiku has no rhyme or meter requirements. Here is an example.

> The sea at springtime.
> All day it rises and falls,
> Yes, rises and falls.

Show and read this one to your class, and then encourage them to write a haiku based on ideas from Psalm 104:24-35. You can lead your class in writing a haiku one line at a time. Ask your class to give you a five-syllable phrase on the topic of "the sea." For example, they might suggest, "The Lord made the sea." Then ask for a seven-syllable line. Conclude by asking for another five-syllable line. Write their suggestions where all can see them. Then edit as necessary.

OPTION: *Write a Song.* Psalm 104:33 shows that singing praise to God is the proper response after pondering the wonder of his Creation. Lead your class to write a song of praise based on this passage. Use a familiar melody, maybe one from the songs suggested in the hymn study that introduced this lesson. Then use ideas from the text and adjust the wording to fit the meter of the melody. For example, using the melody from "How Great Thou Art," one might write the following verse based on Psalm 104:20-35.

> O Lord, my God.
> Your works, they are unnumbered.
> In wisdom you have made them one and all.
> There is the sea, it is so vast and spacious;
> Teeming with life, with creatures large and small.

OPTION: *Praise Reminder.* Distribute copies of the lower section of the reproducible page. Ask students to complete the activity to provide a reminder for them to praise God each day.

God as Creator and Sustainer

Psalm 104 gives praise to God as the Creator and Sustainer of the universe. Caught up in the ecstasy of worship, the psalmist alternates between addressing God and describing him. The pronouns *you* and *he* divide the sections. Look at the whole psalm and label each section of verses with a *Y* (for *you*) or an *H* (for *he*).

v. 1	vv. 2-5	vv. 6-9	vv. 10-19	vv. 20-30	vv. 31-36

The psalmist enumerates God's Awesome Deeds and Wonderful Attributes. List five of each, as selected from the psalm. (These again can be related to the *you* and *he* passages; deeds are generally introduced with *he*, attributes, with *you*.)

AWESOME DEEDS   WONDERFUL ATTRIBUTES

_____   _____

_____   _____

_____   _____

_____   _____

_____   _____

If you had written this psalm, what other deeds and attributes of God might you have included?

_____   _____

_____   _____

Praise the Creator and Sustainer

Psalm 104 begins and ends with the joyous exclamation: "Praise the Lord, O my soul!" As a constant reminder to verbalize your praise this week, clip this box, tape it end to end (letters out), and set it on dashboard, desk, or dresser. (The letters, of course, are the first letters of "Praise the Lord, O my soul!")

P	T	L	O	M	S

Worship and Wisdom for Living
Unit 2: Praise the Creator and Redeemer
(Lessons 6-9)

LIVE AS THE CROWN OF CREATION

LESSON 7

WHY TEACH THIS LESSON?

In a Bible study in the book of Job years ago, we came to 9:9, where Job mentions three distinct constellations of stars: the Bear, Orion, and the Pleiades. I asked the class how many would be able to go outside later, look up into the night sky, and identify those same three groupings. I don't recall a single hand going up! Here before us in our text was a man, having lived some thirty-five centuries before, who was able to do something that we "moderns" could not. Job's ability in this area was not trivial, since it helped him remain humble before the one who is the Maker of all things.

Remembering our proper place in the created order is a special challenge today. The theory of evolution and our ever-expanding knowledge base tempt us to think more highly of ourselves than we ought (cf. Romans 12:3). Today's lesson will help your learners to address that problem.

INTRODUCTION

A. "A SHORT, EXQUISITE LYRIC"

C. S. Lewis (1898–1963) possessed one of the sharpest intellects of the twentieth century. Chair of Medieval and Renaissance Literature at Cambridge, he was a prolific writer of science fiction, fantasy, poetry, and prose. His works have been hailed as some of the finest literary products of all time. C. S. Lewis was an intellectual giant who found no satisfaction in the atheistic philosophies of his time. C. S. Lewis became a Christian.

Among Lewis's many works is a book entitled *Reflections on the Psalms*. In it he refers to Psalm 8 as a "short, exquisite lyric." As Lewis came to appreciate this Psalm's depth of insight into the natures of God and mankind, so may we as well. Our own appreciation of Psalm 8 will then help us meet the challenge of Psalm 100 to "shout for joy to the Lord." Today, it's "all about praise" as we explore Psalms 8 and 100. To offer praise to our Creator: what could be more basic?

B. LESSON BACKGROUND

King David, who lived about a thousand years before Christ, wrote Psalm 8. We are not entirely sure of its historical context; its address "to the chief musician" is tantalizingly brief. One conjecture is that this Psalm came to David while he was still a shepherd, and he wrote it down later for his musician after becoming king. Lying on his back under the open sky with his flock of sheep, the young David may have marveled at the arrangement of stars splashed upon the ebony canvas of the heavens above. He may have pondered his own apparent insignificance within the vastness of creation. Such thoughts may have inspired him to write the psalm.

The author of Psalm 100, on the other hand, is unknown. The author may have composed it for the specific purpose of leading people to worship. This

DEVOTIONAL READING:
PSALM 144:3-9

BACKGROUND SCRIPTURE:
PSALMS 8; 100

PRINTED TEXT:
PSALM 8:1-9; 100:1-5

Jul 14

LESSON AIMS

After this lesson each student will be able to:

1. Summarize God's position with regard to creation, his work in creation, and our place in that creation.

2. Understand his or her obligation to praise the Creator.

3. Praise God from a prepared heart for his goodness, mercy, and truthfulness as Creator.

KEY VERSE

What is man that you are mindful of him, the son of man that you care for him?
—Psalm 8:4

possibility certainly suits its title: "A Call to Praise the Lord." Perhaps you will recognize it as a call to worship or as part of a praise chorus that has been used in your own church on occasion.

I. THE MAJESTY OF GOD (PSALM 8:1-3)

Praise that is acceptable to God has its foundation in understanding his position with regard to our own. David is about to teach us what he knows in this regard.

A. GOD'S EXCELLENT NAME (v. 1a)

1a. O LORD, our Lord, how majestic is your name in all the earth!

Psalm 8 begins with a celebration of God's *name*. Notice the appearance of *Lord* twice. The first (seen with small capital letters as "LORD") is literally "Yahweh," a name so holy that the Israelites stopped using it, fearing that they would accidentally commit some blasphemy. The second word translated as *Lord* is literally "Adonai," which means something like "governor" or "ruler." So translated in terms of how the original reader would have understood it, the meaning is something like "O Yahweh, our governor."

In this brief phrase, then, David has addressed God by a very holy name (which he calls "majestic" in the phrase to follow), and has recognized one of God's most important functions. By implication, David is humbling himself as one who is to be governed.

B. GOD'S REVEALED GLORY (v. 1b)

1b. You have set your glory above the heavens.

This half-verse can be understood in two ways. First, there is a sense in which God's *glory* is revealed through that which we view around us. Although David's view of *the heavens* was not as complete as ours, he beheld God's *glory* nonetheless. As David looked into the night sky without the aid of a telescope, could he have had any inkling of the distance to those stars? Could he have imagined the size of a star, or even what a star actually was? To him, a star was a mysterious twinkling point of light in a dark sky. Yet even with that limited perception, David recognized the glory of God in creating such wonders.

A second way of understanding this half-verse focuses on the word *above*. To those who lived in the ancient world, what was visible in the night sky may have been merely a "preview" of what was above even that. The ancient mind may have sensed that there was a greater realm of glory known to God, but invisible to mankind. In either sense, God's creative power, even if incompletely revealed, compels us to recognize his glory.

C. UNSOLICITED PRAISE FOR GOD (v. 2)

2. From the lips of children and infants you have ordained praise because of your enemies, to silence the foe and the avenger.

Persuasive testimony comes from unlikely sources! At Jesus' triumphal entry into Jerusalem, *children* greet him with shouts of "Hosanna to the Son of David" (Matthew 21:15). This acclamation irritated the chief priests and scribes. When they complained to Jesus about what the children were proclaiming, he quoted the first half of Psalm 8:2 to them (Matthew 21:16). Upon hearing this response, these "experts" in the law could hardly miss the unspoken jab from the second half of Psalm 8:2: Jesus was implying that they themselves were the *enemies* of God.

Earlier Jesus had taught that those who would come to him needed to do so in the manner of a child approaching someone he or she instinctively knew to be superior (Matthew 18:1-4). That admonition calls for self-humility.

WHAT DO YOU THINK?

Children seem to have no difficulty at all acknowledging the majesty and glory of God. Why is it that we are often so reluctant to express such spontaneous adoration of him?

D. VISIBLE TESTIMONY ABOUT GOD (v. 3)

3. *When I consider your heavens, the work of your fingers, the moon and the stars, which you have set in place. . . .*

David's mind turns again to the testimony of God he has witnessed in the night sky. Its splendor should remind the reader of its Source. Unfortunately, the Israelite people got themselves into serious trouble at this very point. Early in their history, just before entering the promised land, Moses had warned them specifically not to bow down in worship of the created heavenly bodies (Deuteronomy 4:19). Yet some eight hundred years later, they will find themselves cast into exile because of doing just that (cf. Jeremiah 7:18; 8:2; 44:17-30; Ezekiel 8:16; Acts 7:42, 43). How ironic that such a majestic part of creation should have led God's people closer to him, but instead they allowed it to have the opposite effect!

II. THE POSITION OF HUMANITY (PSALM 8:4-9)

It is the magnificence of the night sky (v. 3) that leads David to contemplate his own apparent insignificance (v. 4).

A. A HUMBLE QUESTION (v. 4)

4. *. . . what is man that you are mindful of him, the son of man that you care for him?*

Many Bible scholars believe that this verse may have two "layers" of interpretation: David, in speaking of *man* in the strictly human sense, may at the same time be speaking prophetically of the Messiah who is to come. Note the phrase *son of man*, which Jesus will later use to describe himself in the Gospels (cf. also Daniel 7:13). On the other hand, this phrase is also used extensively in the book of Ezekiel to refer to that prophet's frailty and mortality.

The writer of Hebrews quotes from this section of Psalm 8 in a context which many commentators and translators believe applies to Jesus. Others think, however, that Psalm 8:4-6 as used in Hebrews 2:6-8 applies to mortals instead—so we see the two "layers" of interpretation in the New Testament as well. For deeper study, compare the translations of the *King James Version* and the *New International Version* to that of the *New Revised Standard Version* at this point.

B. A CONFIDENT ANSWER (v. 5)

5. *You made him a little lower than the heavenly beings and crowned him with glory and honor.*

If David's question in verse 4 was full of humility, then his answer in verse 5 is full of confidence. God created us to be *a little lower* than angelic beings for a time. Remember that the Bible describes only humans as being created in God's image (Genesis 1:26, 27). Ultimately, we will sit in judgment on angels (1 Corinthians 6:3).

The second part of verse 5 also speaks to humanity's place in God's created order, surely an important issue if we are to have a Biblical view of mankind. To be *crowned . . . with glory and honor* reflects the result of being created in the image of God (again, Genesis 1:26, 27). Our greatest attribute was not attained by our own effort; it was a gift from the Creator.

C. A CAREFUL DESCRIPTION (vv. 6-8)

6. *You made him ruler over the works of your hands; you put everything under his feet.*

Again, is this referring to humans only, or to humans as well as the coming Messiah in two "layers" of meaning? Assuming that it refers "at least" to humans,

What is man that you are mindful of him, the son of man that you care for him?

Visual for lesson 7. Use this poster to illustrate God's care for all people of every race.

this verse reveals great privilege and great responsibility. God set the world and the forces of nature in place, then he put us in charge of his creation (Genesis 1:26).

However, the entrance of sin into the world upset this ideal plan of God. Now humans must struggle constantly with nature to earn a living (cf. Genesis 3:17-19). We look forward to the day when the ideal of Psalm 8:6 and Genesis 1:26 will be restored (see Revelation 21:4, 5). While we wait expectantly for that day, we should note that Psalm 8:6 has implications for ecology and stewardship of resources.

7. . . . all flocks and herds, and the beasts of the field.

David gives a more detailed description of mankind's responsibility. Interestingly, the first group he mentions is *flocks*. Perhaps David still had the heart of a shepherd.

Some contemporary movements have attempted to make animals equal to human beings in value. This is not biblical. Animals were not created in God's image. They do not possess an eternal spirit, as humans do.

8. . . . the birds of the air, and the fish of the sea, all that swim the paths of the seas.

The description moves from land-bound creatures to those of *the air* and *the sea*. The picture is now complete: humanity's dominion is (or, ideally, should be) extended to all earthly creatures. This dominion, of course, is not a license for abuse or cruelty.

Christians should have a proper perspective concerning their ideal position in God's created order. Particularly questionable is the theory of evolution, which places us in a position of being no more than the most highly developed member of the animal kingdom. As wonderful as it might be to think of one's self solely as the top of that heap, such a "status" cannot compare with the Biblical fact of being created in the very image of God. Humankind is the crowning achievement of creation precisely because we alone are created in God's image.

WHALES OR SOULS?

Bumper stickers can be thought provoking. One admonished, "Forget whales; save souls!" Obviously, the owner was making a statement about the sometimes twisted priorities of ecologists. The extinction of whales is a legitimate concern, and humans who prey upon them for greed or sport should be restricted and restrained by law. But inordinate expenditures of money, time, and effort to "save" mere mammals of the sea must be viewed as excessive when contrasted with the usually meager investments made for world evangelism.

It's a matter of perspective. Christians consider human life to be of greater value than animal life. Despite his shortcomings, Captain Ahab is worth more than Moby Dick. Mankind is superior to the animals, for we alone are made in God's image.

Godly people should pursue a balanced viewpoint on environmental issues. Clean air and water, preservation of natural resources, and protection of threatened species—all of these causes are worthy to a degree. Our primary concern, however, must be the welfare and eternal destiny of *Homo sapiens*. Saving whales may be a *good* thing, but saving souls is the *best* thing.   —R. W. B.

D. A POTENT REMINDER (v. 9)

9. O LORD, our Lord, how majestic is your name in all the earth!

David repeats the phrase with which he opens the psalm. These two identical phrases thus form "bookends" that reinforce a straightforward theme: God is so wonderful that the excellence of his *name* extends to the entire *earth*! The second use of David's exclamation becomes more profound than the first, though, when we think of all he has had to say in verses 2-8. While we're thinking about the excellence of God's name, we should note God's concern that his name not be used carelessly or disrespectfully (Exodus 20:7).

III. THE PRAISE WE OFFER GOD (PSALM 100:1-5)

Psalm 8 humbles us, preparing us to offer the praise encouraged by Psalm 100.

A. JOYFUL AND GLAD (vv. 1, 2)

1. Shout for joy to the LORD, all the earth.

God calls *all* people to praise him. This praise should come from our lips naturally; it should not be coerced. We will see why when we consider verse 3 below.

Interestingly, this praise is to come from *all the earth*, not just Israel. (Psalms 98:4 and 117:1 are similar.) But in many lands the true God is unknown. In lands where the Son is not recognized as one with the Father, God is known only partially (John 10:30). How shall these lands praise him? The answer is in Romans 10:14.

2. Worship the LORD with gladness; come before him with joyful songs.

Serving *with gladness* does not mean serving with a giddy silliness, which is devoid of reason and propriety. It means, rather, that we willingly and wholeheartedly offer ourselves to God, without reluctance or hesitation. There is no "I wish I didn't have to do this" in the psalmist's heart.

Remember, to *worship the Lord with gladness* and to *come before him with joyful songs*, for worship are privileges the Creator has granted, not a monotonous obligation. Do we view worship as a privilege, or are we mainly just "going through the motions" while we think of where we're going to eat lunch after church is over?

B. HUMBLE AND MEEK (v. 3)

3. Know that the LORD is God. It is he who made us, and we are his; we are his people, the sheep of his pasture.

The people who came to worship were to do so in the proper spirit: the spirit of humility and meekness. That spirit comes when we recognize who *God* is and who *we are*. God is the Creator and we are not!

That may sound a bit "obvious." But it must not be obvious to everyone since the Bible offers several examples of people who get themselves into trouble when they try to elevate themselves to positions that belong only to him. Eve accepted Satan's temptation to eat the forbidden fruit upon hearing his promise that "you will be like God" (Genesis 3:5). Herod Agrippa I allowed others to see him as a "god" and paid the price (Acts 12:22, 23). The tower of Babel was an attempt by humans to become more than they ought (Genesis 11:1-9); modern science has the potential of leading us down a similar path unless we exercise care. We avoid these dangers when in humility we recognize that God is the Creator and we are not. This includes recognizing that we have many limitations, we are guilty of past sin, and we will continually be plagued by sin throughout this life.

A proper understanding of the natures of God and mankind is fundamental to our worship of God. It also is necessary for us to understand our proper role in serving God and to appreciate God's desire to have a relationship with us. And along with that understanding is the recognition that the *pasture*—the place in which we have our existence—is also his, and he has put us in it.

C. PREPARED AND REASONED (vv. 4, 5)

4. Enter his gates with thanksgiving and his courts with praise; give thanks to him and praise his name.

This verse recalls the layout of ancient Jerusalem and its temple. The city itself was walled on all sides for protection, and entrance was only through a limited number of *gates*. Within those walls was the temple, the focal point of ancient Israel's worship after its construction by Solomon. The temple consisted of, among other things, a series of *courts*. People would gather for worship in these courts.

WHAT DO YOU THINK?

Psalm 100 invites us to "come before" the Lord, and to do so with "gladness" and "singing." In what sense is this a part of our worship?

(Access to some courts was restricted, based on a person's status.) Even nearly ten centuries after its initial construction, the rebuilt temple of Jesus' day still served as the focus of Israelite worship (see Mark 13:1; John 2:13-17; and 4:20).

Note that the psalmist challenges the reader to enter *with*—meaning "already having"—a spirit of *thanksgiving* and *praise*. In other words, the psalmist's challenge is to "be prepared" to bless God's name when arriving at the place for worship.

This wasn't necessarily easy, as the psalmist's world was full of pressures that would distract from being prepared for worship. Trips to Jerusalem could be time-consuming and dangerous. Bringing an animal to sacrifice each time could be an expensive proposition. Leaving part of the family behind to watch the farm was something to think about. Even so, the psalmist desires the reader to be ready to worship. After all, if a person arrives at the place of worship having a negative spirit because he or she is dwelling on all the time and trouble it took to get there, then what would be the point of even coming?

WORSHIP WARS

Volumes already have been written concerning the ongoing conflicts in the church at large (and in nearly every local congregation) over the subjective issue of worship styles. It mostly boils down to disagreements as to personal preferences—nothing as important as "thus saith the Lord." The breaches in Christianity, however, seem to have dichotomized disciples into the younger contemporary camp and the older traditional camp. Can these diversities be reconciled without splitting churches?

Some feel that the senior saints (supposedly more mature) should forfeit their hymns and formality in the interest of unity and outreach. Others are adamant that the "Boomers and X'ers" should put aside their secular and sensational proclivities and give sober, objective praise to God with optimum decency and order.

Will these "worship wars" ever end? Some congregations have achieved at least temporary armistice by bending and blending their style of worship to please most folks in both camps. Other local bodies offer different styles at different hours (even different days) to give appeasing options to opposing groups.

Some sort of compromise seems to be necessary. Whatever it takes, we must keep "the main thing" (honoring God) "the main thing."   —R. W. B.

5. For the LORD is good and his love endures forever; his faithfulness continues through all generations.

The psalmist closes by setting forth three reasons why we are to worship with thanksgiving. Imagine what it would be like to worship a fickle god: sometimes he is *good*, sometimes he is not; his *love* runs hot and cold, depending on his whim; his truthfulness cannot always be counted on. Such were the "gods" of the surrounding peoples in the psalmist's day. But the God we serve, who promises to take the true believers home for all eternity (John 14:1-4), is not that way. He is the perfect "promise keeper"!

CONCLUSION

We all have seen the unbridled enthusiasm of fans at sporting events. Sadly, enthusiasm to praise our Creator is often absent from our worship services. Although it is right that we do things "in a fitting and orderly way" (1 Corinthians 14:40), that need not translate into that which is lifeless and dreary. Will your praise be enthusiastic this week?

We also see that offering praise that really "means something"—both to God and to us—is more complicated than we may have first thought. We are also now more aware of where Satan's points of attack may come as he tries to distract us from meaningful praise. Advance preparation for worship should be a key.

Discovery Learning

This page contains an alternate lesson plan emphasizing learning activities. Classes desiring such student involvement will find these suggestions helpful. The next page is a reproducible activity page to further enhance discovery learning.

LEARNING GOALS

After participating in this lesson, each student will be able to:

1. Summarize God's position with regard to creation, his work in creation, and our place in that creation.

2. Understand his or her obligation to praise the Creator.

3. Praise God from a prepared heart for his goodness, mercy, and truthfulness as Creator.

INTO THE LESSON

OPTION: *Singing*. Begin your class today by having members sing Psalm 8. Michael W. Smith has written a widely-recognized version. Play a tape or CD and have the class sing along. Include the enthusiastic clapping!

OPTION: *Debate*. Have your class prepare a debate on the nature of God and the nature of man. On one side, the universe could be described as formed by chance and natural elements. The other side would contend that God created the universe. In regard to man, one side would declare that man is created in the image of God and thereby endowed with dignity and honor. The opposing side could take either of two extremes: they could portray man as the accidental result of meaningless evolution and therefore an inconsequential blob of protoplasm. Or they could pursue the opinion that man is god-like among the products of evolution and his decisions are all that there is. (Material on the reproducible page can be useful in this.)

INTO THE WORD

OPTION: *Discussion Questions*. Lead your class in a discussion by asking the following questions:

What is God's name that is so majestic? (8:1)

How does the praise of children and infants silence enemies? (8:2)

What do the heavens tell us about God's power? (8:3)

Why is God concerned about mankind? (8:4)

What difference does it make if it is "God"—as in some translations— instead of "heavenly beings"? (8:5)

What is an appropriate view of creation, since God has given us "dominion" over it? (8:6-8)

What do these verses suggest, if anything, in regard to testing new products on animals prior to human use? (8:6-8)

Why is our worship not more typified by "shouts of joy"? (100:1)

What songs help you to connect gladness and singing? (100:2)

What does 100:3 say about the so-called "self-made man"?

How are thanksgiving and praise connected? (100:4)

Why are God's love and faithfulness described as "forever"? (100:5)

OPTION: *Illustration*. Ask class members to illustrate each verse, or suggest that they attempt a drawing that would capture the essence of the chapter. The images in both chapters are graphic and visual. For example, Psalm 8:1 could show "I AM" written in billowy, glowing clouds shining with the glory of God. Verse 2 might show children at Jesus' triumphal entry praising God with palm fronds and shouting "Hosanna!" Provide un-lined paper and markers for each class member. Or you might do a mural by taping white table cover paper to a wall and use colored markers. Assign different verses to each learner and let them work in the correct sequence.

INTO LIFE

OPTION: *Write a Prayer*. The content of Psalm 8:1, 2 should move the reader to prayerful response. Ask your class members to write a prayer in response to each verse. Read each verse and then discuss its application in daily life. Express that concept in a personalized prayer. For example, these two verses could inspire these words, "My Lord, your name and character are majestic and glorious above all things you have made. With childlike adoration I offer you the praise of my lips. May my praise silence your enemies who refuse to honor your name." (The directions for this activity are included in NIV® Bible Student.)

OPTION: *Responsive Reading*. Have your class members create a responsive reading based on these two familiar chapters. One technique is to have a repeated refrain after each verse, such as "His love endures forever" in Psalm 136. The most obvious refrain for Psalm 8 is the first verse, used also as a refrain at the end of the chapter. Have a leader read the chapter with the class repeating verse one after each verse. For Psalm 100, the phrase, "For the Lord is good" from verse 5, expresses a central truth of the chapter. (The directions for this activity are included in NIV® Bible Student.)

The Nature of God/The Nature of Man

THE NATURE OF GOD

Write a short statement of what each of these verses tells you about the nature of God.

Genesis 1:1 _____

Genesis 21:33 _____

Exodus 3:13, 14 _____

Exodus 34:5 _____

Deuteronomy 6:4 _____

1 Samuel 7:26 _____

Matthew 5:48 _____

Romans 1:20 _____

2 Corinthians 1:3 _____

2 Thessalonians 1:6 _____

1 Timothy 1:17 _____

THE NATURE OF MAN

The Bible is the only reliable source for truly understanding the nature of man. Man's tendency is to go to one extreme or the other. Some hold that man is better than he actually is; others claim that he is worse than he really is. Paul warns us in Romans 12:3 that one should "not think of yourself more _____ than you ought, but rather think of yourself with _____ judgment." In fact, each truth about man's nature is held in balance by a corresponding truth. Man is endowed with incredible dignity because men and women are created "in the _____ of _____" (Genesis 1:26, 27). The heart is also "_____ above all things and beyond _____" (Jeremiah 17:9). Every baby is born so pure and innocent that Jesus could say that unless you "become like _____ _____, you will never enter the _____ of _____" (Matthew 18:2). Yet he also says that "There is _____ _____ righteous, not even _____; . . . all have turned away [and] have . . . become _____" (Romans 3:11, 12). Man is so free that _____ may come and take the free gift of the water of life (Revelation 22:17), yet at the same time men are "_____ of depravity—for a man is a _____ to whatever has mastered him" (2 Peter 2:19).

How would you summarize the nature of man?

Worship and Wisdom for Living

Unit 2: Praise the Creator and Redeemer
(Lessons 6-9)

FIND JOY IN FORGIVENESS

LESSON 8

WHY TEACH THIS LESSON?

At times we're all amazed by the cleverness of TV commercials. Some of the best are those that take faddish ideas or modes of expression and apply them to the product they're trying to sell. A few years ago, one such commercial featured a nearly empty bottle of ketchup (or, if you prefer, catsup). All around the inside of the bottle one could see little leftover "clusters" of ketchup sticking here and there. Then the announcer was heard to say, "Why does some of the ketchup always stick to the sides? Because that ketchup has *issues.*"

I don't know if that commercial resulted in more ketchup sales, but it did remind me of how we humans tend to "rename" things for various reasons. This can be dangerous in the Christian life: if someone tries to excuse personal sins as being merely "issues," the eternal consequences can be devastating. Today's lesson can start (or keep) us on the road to recognizing sin for what it really is (cf. Romans 7:13). Only when that happens first are we able truly to repent and begin to experience the joy of God's forgiveness.

INTRODUCTION

A. AUGUSTINE'S FAVORITE PSALM

Augustine of Hippo (A.D. 354–430) is a well-known figure in church history. After spending his early years as a reprobate, he turned to Christ and found the joy of new life in him. Psalm 32 is said to have been Augustine's favorite Psalm. Perhaps he felt a kinship with David, whose sins had been so egregious. Perhaps he was simply delighted with the testimony of one whose life in many ways mirrored his own.

Augustine supposedly had Psalm 32 inscribed on the wall beside his bed as he approached his death. He apparently wanted to remember the greatness and wonder of a God who is full of compassion for sinners.

B. LESSON BACKGROUND

Psalm 32 is one of the seven "penitential psalms" (the other six are Psalms 6, 38, 51, 102, 130, and 143). This psalm comes alive when read in light of the third of those other six, namely Psalm 51. There we find David's hymn of repentance over the Bathsheba incident (cf. 2 Samuel 11). David's anguish is almost palpable as you read that Psalm. You feel that his sorrow for his sin has brought him to the point of physical pain. In Psalm 32 we find David's instructions about forgiveness. He learned a powerful lesson about the horror of guilt and the joy of forgiveness. In Psalm 51:13, he promised God that he would help change other people's lives by instructing them about his forgiveness. He fulfilled that promise as he penned the words of Psalm 32.

I. THE ONE WHO IS BLESSED (PSALM 32:1, 2)

A. SINS FORGIVEN AND COVERED (v. 1)

1. Blessed is he whose transgressions are forgiven, whose sins are covered.

Psalm 1 begins with these words: "Blessed is the man who does not walk in the counsel of the wicked or stand in the way of sinners or sit in the seat of mockers."

DEVOTIONAL READING:
PSALM 51:1-12
BACKGROUND SCRIPTURE:
PSALMS 32; 51
PRINTED TEXT:
PSALM 32:1-11

LESSON AIMS

After this lesson, each student will be able to:

1. Summarize what David says in Psalm 32 about the blessing of confessing sin, experiencing God's forgiveness, and seeking God's counsel.

2. Contrast the condition of one who is forgiven with the miserable state of the one who tries to hide his or her sin.

3. Specify someone who needs to hear the message of forgiveness, and tell that person what God has done in Jesus.

Jul 21

KEY VERSE

Blessed is he whose transgressions are forgiven, whose sins are covered. —Psalm 32:1

LESSON 8 NOTES

Display this poster as you begin. Ask, "Do you think Christians appreciate the blessing of forgiveness? Why or why not?"

look up Hebrew

WHAT DO YOU THINK?

Being "blessed" results in a sense of well-being and happiness. If David is right that the person whose sins are forgiven is the truly happy person, then why isn't forgiveness what most people are seeking in their "pursuit of happiness"?

WHAT DO YOU THINK?

If God's part in our forgiveness is not counting our sins against us, what is our part, if anything?

[Include passages such as Acts 2:38 and Romans 10:9-11 in your discussion.]

spirit

Body   spirit

How many of us can take honest inventory of our lives and feel *blessed* because we have lived out the instruction of that verse? Most of us would readily admit that we have fallen far short of those ideals. The opening verse of Psalm 32 brings the promise of blessing to the person who has completely failed to measure up to the precepts of Psalm 1. As one who himself had experienced forgiveness from grievous sin, the depth of David's joyous proclamation must not be understated. It is a blessing to know that our sins *are forgiven!* The blessing of God is not withheld from us because we fail in our human attempts to live up to his standards.

God forgives our *transgressions*. The Hebrew word carries the idea of disloyalty or rebellion. Although we sin against people and hurt others by our sin, we must remember that sin is ultimately rebellion against God's ideal for our lives and is thus an affront to him.   *missing the mark*

The Hebrew word for *sins* here includes the idea of missing God's will. Although we will never reach the goal of godly perfection in this life in following his will, this does not excuse us from trying (cf. Matthew 5:48). The joyous news that David proclaimed was that God forgives us even when we miss or rebel against his will.

The thought behind the word for being *forgiven* is to have something "lifted off," "removed," or "carried away." David used a potent word picture in Psalm 103:12: "As far as the east is from the west, so far has he [God] removed our transgressions from us." God did not simply set our sin aside. He moved it so far away that it is out of our sight and his.

David also rejoices that our sins have been *covered*. When something is covered, it is not visible. We do not notice it. We can be right next to something covered and not know it is there. That is how God deals with our sin. He covers it.

B. "THIS WON'T COUNT AGAINST YOU" (v. 2)

2. Blessed is the man whose sin the LORD does not count against him and in whose spirit is no deceit.

Taken with verse 1, this verse again demonstrates the Hebrew parallelism that we've seen in other places in the Psalms. The three different Hebrew words translated in verses 1 and 2 as *transgressions, sins,* and *sin* are synonyms. Likewise, the Hebrew verbs for *forgiven, covered,* and *not count against* are synonyms. *Not count against* is an accounting term; it suggests God will not place our sins against our "account." The apostle Paul quotes these verses in Romans 4:7, 8. He, too, felt the wonder of God's mercy in not counting his sin against him. Paul had been a murderous persecutor of Christians. After his experiences on the road to, and in the city of, Damascus, he found the joy of not having his sins counted against him.

When we know that our sins do not count against us, we can live without deceit. We can be honest about ourselves, just as David was. We do not have to try to fool anyone by pretending to be someone we're not. People do not like phonies, nor does God (cf. Matthew 23). The person who has been forgiven does not have to be a phony anymore.

II. THE ONE WHO IS MISERABLE (PSALM 32:3, 4)

A. THE POWER OF UNCONFESSED SIN (v. 3)

3. When I kept silent, my bones wasted away through my groaning all day long.

Sin that is unconfessed and unforgiven ravages the body and the spirit. This verse may refer to David's feelings between the time of his adultery with Bathsheba and arranging for Uriah's death and the time of his confrontation by Nathan and subsequent confession of sin.

Medical science has confirmed the harm done to the body by unresolved issues. Guilt leads to stress and depression. Guilt can result in a person taking his or her own life. Although we are bombarded with worldly ways to relieve stress and rid our-selves of guilt, we, like David, know that the only true resolution to the problem of guilt is to find forgiveness. Only then will one find relief from the daylong *groaning*.

B. THE POWER OF CONSCIENCE (v. 4)

4. For day and night your hand was heavy upon me; my strength was sapped as in the heat of summer. Selah.

The part of the Mediterranean world in which David lived had two seasons: a wet (rainy) season and a dry season. As the unconfessed sin of verse 3 takes its toll, to David it is like moving from that wet season to the *heat of summer.*

God gave us a great gift in the form of our conscience. While some may be igno-rant of certain specific laws, all people share an instinctive knowledge of right and wrong (cf. Romans 2:14-15). That is part of being created in God's image. We dare not ignore that instinct! To do so is to sap oneself of spiritual strength, to have God turn our productive moisture into a dreary, lifeless dryness (cf. Ezekiel 37:1, 2).

Paul wrote of the abandonment of conscience in Romans 1:18-32. He warns against disregarding both conscience and instinctive knowledge of God. He de-scribes those who have disregarded God's desires in truly horrifying terms.

The use of *Selah* is interesting. While it is found in many places in the Old Tes-tament, no one really knows what it means. Here it appears to draw special at-tention to what had just been written. It seems to say to the reader, "Stop and take special notice of this!" Today we might boldface and italicize the passage. In Hebrew, the ancients may have used the word *Selah* to highlight the importance of what had been written.

III. THE ONE WHOSE BURDENS ARE LIFTED (PSALM 32:5)

A. MAN CONFESSES (v. 5a)

5a. Then I acknowledged my sin to you and did not cover up my iniquity. I said, "I will confess my transgressions to the LORD."

The same three Hebrew words for sin in verses 1 and 2 occur here again in verse 5. Alongside these we now see three parallel verbs translated *acknowledged, did not cover up,* and *confess.* Unquestionably, David did not want anyone to share his misery. If you know a cure for a dread disease, you share it with others. David certainly knew the cure for guilt, and he was eager to share it with all who suf-fered from the anxiety that guilt produces.

A dramatic turning point in David's life came when Nathan confronted him with his *sin* (2 Samuel 12:1-14). David could have reacted in several ways. He could have denied the charge brought by Nathan. He could have threatened Nathan or had him put to death. He could have waffled and minimized his sin as his predecessor King Saul was known to have done (1 Samuel 15:20, 21, 24). He could have been so ashamed that he committed suicide. But by God's grace, none of those things occurred.

Whether this half-verse refers to the Bathsheba incident or not, David was one who admitted his guilt and confessed his sin to the Lord. Perhaps this is the reason the Lord could foresee that David would be "a man after his own heart" (1 Samuel 13:14; cf. 1 Kings 15:3, 5). Sin must be confessed before God can deal with us.

The apostle John wrote to Christians that, "If we *confess* our sins, he is faithful and just and will forgive us our sins and purify us from all unrighteousness" (1 John 1:9). While it is very tempting to focus entirely on God's forgiveness in this verse, one must remember the conditional phrase "if we confess" at the be-ginning of the verse. While God's grace is the source of forgiveness, confession is seen here as an activating agent of that grace.

WHAT DO YOU THINK?

In addition to the failure to receive God's forgiveness, what are some of the other conse-quences of unconfessed sin?

WHAT DO YOU THINK?

Since God demands repen-tance/confession in granting for-giveness, can we withhold our forgiveness of one who has wronged us unless that person first repents? Why or why not?

[Use Luke 17:3, 4 to frame your answer.]

grace = sin (handwritten)

B. GOD FORGIVES (v. 5b)

5b. . . . and you forgave the guilt of my sin. Selah.

rest on — siliano — musical note (handwritten)

A sign outside a church read, "God is in the forgiveness business." What a great message for a community to see! We confess our sins. Jesus pleads our case before the Father. The Father is faithful to forgive us.

David painted a powerful picture of God. He is not some tolerant old uncle who sees our sins, then winks and grins. He is not a sadistic ogre who cannot wait to throw people into the pit of Hell. He is a just God who takes sin seriously. He is also a loving Father who desperately wants us to spend eternity with him. We must acknowledge our sin to him. He, being more gracious and loving than we can imagine, is eager to hear our confession and to forgive us.

Jesus told a parable about a loving father who waited anxiously to receive his son back from a life of sin (Luke 15:11-32). The son came home and confessed his sins to his father, and his father was so overjoyed at his return that he immediately reinstated his son and threw a big party to welcome him home. The father in that parable represents God. He wants us to come home.

CAN YOU SAY, "I'M SORRY"?

Judges are facing criminals these days who show no remorse for their crimes. Many of these felons are young first offenders. A teenage girl doesn't shed a tear as she hears her sentence for clubbing her mother to death with a bat. A young man, charged with multiple counts of kidnapping and rape, hardly blinks an eye in the courtroom.

What has happened to conscience and penitent sorrow? One would think these social predators would at least be sorry that they were caught in their wrongdoing. David could be thankful for the "heavy hand of God" that produced the godly sorrow that brought him to repentance. For when he finally confessed his sin with genuine remorse, he experienced the forgiveness that gives spiritual peace.

Judges are more inclined to soften a sentence when the convict demonstrates a contrite spirit. As David wrote, "A broken and contrite heart, O God, you will not despise" (Psalm 51:17).

Is there unconfessed sin in your life? Are you able to say, "I'm sorry"—and mean it? "If we confess our sins, he is faithful and will forgive us our sins" (1 John 1:9).   —R. W. B.

IV. THE ONE WHO TRUSTS IN THE LORD (PSALM 32:6-11)

A. FINDS A HIDING PLACE (vv. 6, 7)

6. Therefore let everyone who is godly pray to you while you may be found; surely when the mighty waters rise, they will not reach him.

David wrote of danger and safety. There is a danger in waiting too long to acknowledge sin and seek forgiveness. Three centuries after David penned Psalm 32, the prophet Isaiah warned the people of Judah: "Seek the Lord while he may be found; call on him while he is near" (Isaiah 55:6). The message here is simple. God is sovereign. He can turn away from us at any moment he chooses. Do not place a false trust in the hope that God will forever keep open the door of salvation. There will come a day when he will call all people to be judged. If forgiveness has not been appropriated by then, it will be too late.

7. You are my hiding place; you will protect me from trouble and surround me with songs of deliverance. Selah.

Augustus M. Toplady (1740–1778) wrote the famous hymn "Rock of Ages." The words echo David's instruction: "Rock of Ages, cleft for me; let me hide myself in thee." In the swirling storms of life, God is our _hiding place_, our refuge, our

HOW TO SAY IT

Augustine. AW-gus-TEEN or Aw-GUS-tin.

Bathsheba. Bath-SHE-buh.

Nathan. NAY-thun (TH as in THIN).

Selah (Hebrew). SEE-luh.

Uriah. Yu-RYE-uh.

safe harbor. If verses 3, 4 of our lesson text describe David hiding *from* God; then verse 7 describes David hiding *in* God.

Those who truly follow the Lord experience a certain sense of safety. Part of that safety is in avoiding certain practices that we know would displease the Lord and that can also be very dangerous and harmful. Alcoholism, drug addiction, premarital sex, and homosexual acts are potent examples.

God surrounds us *with songs of deliverance*. The Israelites sang a song of deliverance after they crossed the Red Sea (Exodus 15:1-21). They escaped the perils of drowning and of capture by the Egyptian army. They had a lot to sing about! Those who are delivered from captivity to sin and its guilt have much to sing about, too.

B. LEARNS FROM THE LORD (vv. 8, 9)

8. I will instruct you and teach you in the way you should go; I will counsel you and watch over you.

David was compelled to teach others the difficult lesson he had learned about trying to hide sin. He had promised God that he would teach others his ways (Psalm 51:13). It has been said that "experience" is what you learn from your own mistakes, while "wisdom" is what you learn from someone else's! Certainly the old saw "Experience is the best teacher" cannot be true, because it requires that someone take "the test" before it provides "the lesson."

David is one who learned about unconfessed sin by his own experience, but he certainly did not want others to repeat it. If the reader will accept God's instruction, he or she will not have to learn the hard way by experience.

God uses many avenues of communication to *counsel* or *teach* us. We have his written Word to enrich us (2 Timothy 3:16, 17). God also expects us to learn from him by learning from others with more experience, maturity, and discernment (2 Timothy 2:2). Every parent wants to teach his or her children to make wise decisions and thus avoid some of the bumps and bruises of life. Parents have the responsibility of teaching their children to know and love the Lord (Ephesians 6:4). Those who trust the Lord have learned that life is a continuing spiritual adventure. The older generation is to pass on its knowledge and experience in trusting the Lord to those who are not as spiritually mature (Titus 2:3-5).

9. Do not be like the horse or the mule, which have no understanding but must be controlled by bit and bridle or they will not come to you.

David issued a warning about pride and stubbornness. Learning demands humility and a willingness to be led. David had earned a Ph.D. in humility. At one time in his life he had arrogantly disobeyed God's commands about murder and adultery, and it cost him dearly. He did not want others to pay such a penalty. David had been like an animal out of control. Arrogance causes people to act like wild beasts, trying not to be accountable to anyone but themselves. Hosea 4:16 compares the rebellious Israelites to "a stubborn heifer."

C. IS SURROUNDED BY LOVE (v. 10)

10. Many are the woes of the wicked, but the Lord's unfailing love surrounds the man who trusts in him.

Sometimes it seems that good people suffer and *the wicked* prosper, and that may be true on occasion (cf. Ecclesiastes 8:14). Those who observe the human condition would, however, generally conclude that wicked people most often get their just reward. For instance, many wicked people have become wealthy, but their wickedness has kept them from having true friends or people who genuinely love them. People who live sexually immoral lives may appear to be having more "fun" than others, but they also usually suffer from more disease, etc.

WHAT DO YOU THINK?

Why do you think it is important for us to think of God as our "hiding place" and the only One who can really protect us from "continuing in sin" (Romans 6:1)?

[handwritten: movement from hiding from God to hiding in God]

Our Loving Heavenly Father, we thank you for being in the forgiveness business. May our lives be filled with praise because of your power to remove our sin by means of the cross of Christ, and your mercy in not counting that sin against us. Help us to tell others of your love and your desire to forgive them. In Jesus' mighty name, amen.

But the person who trusts in the Lord finds himself or herself surrounded by love and mercy. That person does not feel an occasional twinge of love. Such a person is overwhelmed and inundated by love! God's love and mercy keep coming like the ocean waves lapping onto the sandy shore. There is no end. It just keeps coming and coming and coming.

D. IS FILLED WITH PRAISE (v. 11)

11. Rejoice in the LORD and be glad, you righteous; sing, all you who are upright in heart!

David had experienced the heights and the depths of a relationship with God. When he had been victorious over his enemies, he danced before the Lord (2 Samuel 6:14). When David's child died, he was in such despair that his servants thought he might do something desperate (2 Samuel 12:18). Exactly when this psalm was written in relation to those two incidents, we do not know. But the one declared by God to be after his "own heart" (Acts 13:22) would certainly be one to know what it meant to be *upright in heart*.

The result is joy. One key to this joy is never to permit Satan to assail you with your past. The person who has accepted God's remedy for sin in Jesus is new in Christ. The old has gone; the new has come (2 Corinthians 5:17).

HAPPY ARE THE FORGIVEN

Rejoice, ye pure in heart;
   Rejoice, give thanks and sing.
Your festal banner wave on high,
   The cross of Christ your King.
    —Edward H. Plumptre (1821–1891)

David found happiness ("blessedness") in seeking and finding God's forgiveness. Guilt had gone; peace had come. What a relief and release when he became accountable to God! Freedom from pangs of conscience, freedom from fear of punishment, freedom from personal shame—those were reasons for his uninhibited rejoicing.

Even so, David's forgiveness was "Old Covenant" forgiveness. It looked forward to Jesus Christ, whom he didn't know. Jesus' ministry would be "superior to theirs as the covenant of which he is mediator is superior to the old one" (Hebrews 8:6). Christ promised, "I will forgive their wickedness and will remember their sins no more" (Hebrews 8:12).

We have a personal Savior who made a superior and permanent sacrifice, and who continues to intercede for us (Hebrews 7:25). Is that good news? "Happiness is the Lord!"   —R. W. B.

CONCLUSION

Many years ago a teenage girl was being swept to the brink of Niagara Falls. She was in the grip of certain death. Some people on Goat Island saw her and leaned through a protective railing to grab hold of her arm just before she was carried over the edge by the strong current. They pulled her to shore and saved her life.

Every day we see people whose lives are in immediate peril. Their sin has crushed them. They have given up on themselves, thinking they are beyond hope. They need to hear the joyous words of a forgiven sinner. They need to hear Psalm 32. Share David's testimony. Share the message of the cross and forgiveness of sin. Share God's love and yours. Snatch them from the brink of hopelessness. Share God's longing to forgive them. As Fanny Crosby (1820–1915) put it in one of her hymns, "Tell them of Jesus the mighty to save."

God is in the forgiveness business. No one else can do what he can do!

Discovery Learning

This page contains an alternate lesson plan emphasizing learning activities. Classes desiring such student involvement will find these suggestions helpful. The next page is a reproducible activity page to further enhance discovery learning.

LEARNING GOALS

After participating in this lesson, each student will be able to:

1. Summarize what David says in Psalm 32 about the blessing of confessing sin, experiencing God's forgiveness, and seeking God's counsel.

2. Contrast the condition of one who is forgiven with the miserable state of the one who tries to hide his or her sin.

3. Specify someone who needs to hear the message of forgiveness, and tell that person what God has done in Jesus.

INTO THE LESSON

OPTION: *Agree-Disagree.* Read each of the following statements and ask your class to indicate whether they agree or disagree. Any who agree should raise a hand, pointing to the ceiling with the index finger. Any who disagree should raise a hand with five fingers spread. Tell them you will read each statement twice, count to three, and then they should raise their signs without checking friends' responses first. (This activity is included in *NIV® Bible Student.*)

1. Many adults suffer from guilt.
2. Living with guilt damages one's health.
3. Some adults refuse to accept forgiveness.
4. Some have trouble forgiving themselves.
5. Most adults rejoice in their forgiveness.
6. Adults tend to cover up what they do wrong.
7. God will always forgive our sins.

Make the transition to the Bible study by saying, "These statements have raised questions about forgiveness. Let's see if our text today answers our questions."

OPTION: *Discussion Starters.* Reproduce the four Discussion Starters below for your class members. (This is included in *NIV® Bible Student.*)

(1) By your personal standards, which of the following is the grossest sin: cheating on income tax; having premarital/extramarital sex; selling pornography; cutting shady business deals; child abuse?

(2) Whom would you have most trouble forgiving: a crooked politician; an adulterer; Nazi war criminal; a drug dealer; a rapist?

(3) Why do more people confess their sins to a bartender than to someone else? It's easier to talk when you're drinking; bartenders are more understanding; people are more at home in a bar; bartenders never judge their confessors;everybody in a bar has failed. (My other explanation: _____.)

(4) What do you do when you fail: crawl in a hole; try to be extra good; confess it to God and move on; talk to a minister about it; shrug it off?

INTO THE WORD

OPTION: *Circle Response.* Use a circle response as a means of guiding the discussion of Psalm 32:1-11. Seat your class in circles of four to eight people. Have each verse read, and then ask each person to make a short statement about the verse. Go around the circle and each person speaks once before anyone speaks a second time. This will help to draw out quieter learners.

OPTION: *Guest Lecturers.* Ask four class members to prepare mini-lectures on a part of today's text: vv. 1, 2; vv. 3-5; vv. 6, 7; and vv. 8-11.

OPTION: *Crossword Puzzle.* The crossword puzzle on the reproducible page will allow a close look at the text. Either work on it collectively, or let individuals work and then share responses.

INTO LIFE

OPTION: *Write a Witnessing Letter.* Provide paper and pens for your class members to write a witnessing letter to someone who needs to know God's forgiveness. Prepare for the writing by using these directions:

Name three people you know who need to experience God's forgiveness.

Which one would be most responsive to a letter from you about forgiveness?

What should be the tone of your letter?

What ideas from today's text should be included?

Provide everything necessary, so that the project can be completed and ready for mailing by the end of the class. (This is included in *NIV® Bible Student.*)

OPTION: *Personal Testimony.* Ask class members to prepare personal testimonies about their experience of God's forgiveness, beginning by explaining the negative results of sin in their lives—guilt, anxiety, fear, and confusion. Then have them describe how they came to be aware of the availability of forgiveness. What events led to "the change"? Conclude by sharing the joy and peace of full forgiveness in Christ. (This is included in *NIV® Bible Student.*)

Crossword Puzzle

Use Psalm 32 to respond to the clues for this puzzle.

ACROSS:
   1. These songs surround me (v. 7).
   3. The Lord's kind of love (v. 10).
   6. Synonym for sins (v. 1).
   8. What God's hand is (v. 4).
   9. Being _____ caused bones to waste (v. 3).
   12. Did not cover this (v. 5).
   13. An animal with no under-standing (v. 9).

DOWN:
   1. None in this man's spirit (v. 2)
   2. The description of the forgiven (v. 1)
   4. Synonym for transgressions (v. 1).
   5. These have many woes (v. 10).
   7. What God does for me with his songs (v. 7).
   9. What is covered (v. 1)
   10. This is unfailing (v. 10).
   11. An animal with no understanding (v. 9).

Personal Motto

Choose a verse from Psalm 32 and write a motto for this next week of Christian living. For example, from verse 9: "Don't be muleheaded when it comes to God's teaching!"

My verse: Psalm 32:_____

My motto:

Worship and Wisdom for Living
Unit 2: Praise the Creator and Redeemer
(Lessons 6-9)

LET ALL PEOPLES PRAISE GOD

LESSON 9

WHY TEACH THIS LESSON?

In a sermon one Sunday, I offered the people a challenge for their prayer lives: for the next week, every single time that they prayed, they were not ask God for *anything*—they were not to remind him of any needs, offer any prayers for the sick, or ask for his blessing in any way. Instead, they were to offer only prayers of praise. They were to praise him for who he is, for specific things that he had already done for them and others, and for what he has promised to do.

I followed this challenge with a warning that this could be one of their most difficult spiritual challenges ever, because most of us simply aren't used to praying that way. In our prayer lives over the years, we have grown accustomed to brushing right through the praise part and going right to the "requests"! The next week, one lady confirmed my suspicion. With a look of dismay on her face, she told me that after a less than a minute of superficial praise, she simply had nothing left to say to God in her prayers. This was a person who needed help in learning how and why to praise God deeply and profoundly. She was a person not unlike many of your learners. Today's lesson will address that need.

INTRODUCTION

A. SPECIAL PRIVILEGE, SPECIAL RESPONSIBILITY

Children seldom recognize the link between privilege and responsibility. As we mature, however, we learn just how strong that link becomes. The privilege of being married and sharing life with the one we love comes with the awesome responsibility of sacrificial love. Some wedding vows express that commitment "in joy and in sorrow, in prosperity and in adversity."

In employment, bosses have greater privileges, but they also bear more responsibility. Even children can learn this important lesson. The privilege of having a pet brings the responsibility of feeding, walking, and grooming that pet. The privilege of driving an automobile brings the responsibility of obeying traffic laws.

The Jews were a people chosen for a special privilege. Their forefather, Abraham, had been very special to God, and he chose to bless all of Abraham's progeny because of his faith (Genesis 17:1-8). Specifically, God had said to Abraham, "I will establish my . . . everlasting covenant between me and you . . . for the generations to come" (v. 7). God had firmly reestablished that covenant relationship after the Hebrew children were led out of bondage in Egypt. During their sojourn in the desert, God told Moses to tell the people, "If you obey me fully . . . , then out of all nations you will be my treasured possession. Although the whole earth is mine, you will be for me a kingdom of priests and a holy nation" (Exodus 19:5, 6; cf. 1 Peter 2:4, 5).

What a privilege to be a "treasured possession" unto God! But along with this special privilege came a special responsibility: they were to be a "kingdom of

DEVOTIONAL READING:
PSALM 97:6-12
BACKGROUND SCRIPTURE:
PSALMS 67; 96
PRINTED TEXT:
PSALMS 67:1-5; 96:1-9

LESSON AIMS

After participating in this lesson, each student will be able to:

1. Tell what these psalms say about the need for the entire world to praise God.

2. Explain how meeting this need is an important part of the church's mission.

3. Memorize a verse of praise from today's text.

Jul
28

KEY VERSE

May the peoples praise you, O God; may all the peoples praise you. —Psalm 67:3

priests." A priest is someone who represents God to the people and represents the people to God—a mediator or "go-between," if you will. Sadly, the Israelites focused solely on being God's *treasured possession*. In so doing, they failed to understand that they were to usher in his Messiah who would, in turn, commission his disciples to be his emissaries to *all* the nations of the earth, not just the Israelites (Isaiah 42:6; 49:6; Matthew 28:19, 20; Acts 13:47).

B. LESSON BACKGROUND

One significant difference between the Old and New Testaments is a distinction in missionary emphasis. The New Testament requires Christians to take the gospel to "all nations," but there is no similar command for Old Testament Israel. In fact, just the opposite seems to be true when we note that the ancient Israelites were not to mix with foreign peoples at all (Leviticus 20:24-26; Deuteronomy 7:3; 1 Kings 11:2; Nehemiah 13:23-27; etc.). Indeed, the idea of Israelite separation occurs about 260 times in the Old Testament. We see this "separation attitude" in the first-century disciples, who seem quite surprised that God had extended the offer of salvation to the Gentiles (Acts 11:18). The occasion of a foreigner converting to Judaism seems to have been relatively rare (cf. 1 Kings 8:41-43).

Even so, today's texts stress over and over that it is *all* nations and *all* peoples who are to praise the Lord. Other Old Testament texts stress this idea as well. In several contexts, we see this as ungodly nations that have no choice but to acknowledge that some miracle or wonder could have come from the one true God only, however grudging such an admission might be (e.g., Exodus 7:5; 14:4, 18; Leviticus 26:45; 1 Samuel 17:46; Ezekiel 20:41; 28:25; 36:23). In other contexts, this praise from "all nations" is a prediction of an ideal, future state of affairs that is not likely actually to occur until the second coming of Christ (Psalms 22:27; 47:9; 57:5; 64:9; 65:8; 66:1-7; 86:9; 98:2, 3; 99:2, 3; 102:15; Habakkuk 2:14).

The frequent references to praise from all nations and peoples in today's texts also reflect this ideal, as-yet-unrealized future. God wants all peoples to know him, love him, and praise him for who he is and what he has done.

I. PRAISE GOD FOR WHAT HE HAS DONE AND WILL DO (PSALM 67:1-5)

A. GOD HAS SHOWN HIMSELF TO ALL PEOPLE (vv. 1-3)

1. *May God be gracious to us and bless us and make his face shine upon us,* Selah.

The psalm begins with a familiar prayer. During the Exodus, God had told Moses to tell his brother Aaron, who would become the great high priest of Israel, to pronounce a blessing upon the people: "The Lord bless you and keep you; the Lord make his face shine upon you and be gracious to you; the Lord turn his face toward you and give you peace" (Numbers 6:24-26). This blessing was thus very familiar to the Israelites. It is also quoted, in part, in Psalms 4:6; 29:11; 31:16; and 80:3, 7, 19.

On the other hand, there are also numerous times in the Old Testament when God is said to have hidden his face from the people (e.g., Psalm 13:1; 30:7; Isaiah 59:2). When God "hides his face," he is not playing "hide 'n' seek" games. The people of God knew when they were disobedient to God. That disobedience produced feelings of alienation and estrangement. He seemed to be "hiding" from them.

The desire to have God shine his face upon them reflects the ancient idea that the facial expression of a king revealed that king's pleasure or displeasure, approval or disapproval. As such, this phrase did not necessarily express a desire for God to bless them in any material sense. It was the simple expression of a desire to have God's approval, and to feel close to him again.

WHAT DO YOU THINK?

There are moments in life when God seems to be distant. His face doesn't seem to be shining on us. What are some possible reasons we may have these times of doubt and uncertainty?

2. . . . that your ways may be known on earth, your salvation among all nations.

The psalmist got it right. The Israelites were not to be blessed because they deserved the blessings of God. They were to be blessed so that God's *salvation* would be demonstrated *among all nations.* The particular Hebrew word translated as *salvation* is very profound. It deals not just with "deliverance" or "victory," but also, in a broader sense, with God's sovereign kingship. God wanted to reveal himself to all the people of the world through his special relationship with the Hebrew people, his sovereignty and his kingship. The Israelites were to model for the world the kind of life that has the one true God at its center. God's blessings to and through the Israelites were to be so obvious that the whole world would notice (Psalm 46:10). These blessings would find ultimate expression in the Messiah, who would come to all peoples through the Israelite nation.

3. May the peoples praise you, O God; may all the peoples praise you.

When people see how great God is, *praise* is the natural response! God did not desire the praise of the Jews only. He desired the praise of *all the peoples* of the earth. God chose to bless the Jews so that they could express his greatness to all people. Through Israel would come "a light for the Gentiles" so that all people could come to know God and be saved by him (Isaiah 49:6; cf. Acts 13:47).

WHAT DO YOU THINK?

Why do you think God's people so often fail to understand the purpose of his blessings?

B. GOD WILL RULE ALL PEOPLE RIGHTEOUSLY (vv. 4, 5)

4. May the nations be glad and sing for joy, for you rule the peoples justly and guide the nations of the earth. Selah.

When people see how wonderfully God rules and reigns, they will praise him. Sadly, many people in our day have a very secular view of God. They either see him as a Santa in the sky who is there to bless us without asking anything from us, or they see him as some vengeful, vicious, vindictive ogre who cannot wait to send people to eternal damnation. But both ideas are wrong.

When God is enthroned on the human heart, he rules with wisdom, power, and compassion. A central concept of the Christian life is that because of God's grace through the death of Christ, we do *not* get what we actually deserve (namely, Hell), and we *do* get what we do not deserve (namely, Heaven)! People have a choice to make in how they want to relate to God as their king. Those without Christ relate to him as the Holy Lawgiver, who will punish them justly in his wrath. Those with Christ, on the other hand, relate to him as a God of grace and love. Such people are quick to offer generous praise to him, and they look forward to the time when Jesus will rule *the nations* fully and finally (Psalm 2:9; Revelation 19:15).

5. May the peoples praise you, O God; may all the peoples praise you.

This is a repetition of verse 3. The repetition highlights the importance of the thought. God's righteous reign should cause all who know him to *praise* him. This does not mean that absolutely every person from every nation will actually praise God—at least, not in this life. But that fact does not stop the psalmist from *desiring* that all praise God. The apostle Paul affirms that in the judgment, "every knee shall bow" and "every tongue shall give praise to God" (Romans 14:10, 11, *New American Standard Bible*).

WHAT DO YOU THINK?

What is the greatest danger for any people or nation who have been abundantly blessed by God?

II. PRAISE GOD FOR WHO HE IS (PSALM 96:1-6)

A. HE IS THE SOURCE OF SALVATION (vv. 1, 2)

1. Sing to the LORD a new song; sing to the LORD, all the earth.

Psalm 96 is formed, in part, from 1 Chronicles 16. That text includes the joyous *song* of David on a festive occasion in Israel's history. The ark of the covenant, having been captured by the Philistines, was returned and held by the family of Abinadab in Kirjath Jearim (1 Samuel 6:21; 7:1). When it was ultimately returned

Use this poster to illustrate Psalm 67:3. It shows people singing to praise God. Ask the class to suggest other ways to praise him.

to Jerusalem, David broke forth in praise to God (1 Chronicles 16:7-36). The middle verses of David's song (vv. 23-30) are recorded in Psalm 96:1-6. Other portions of David's song are repeated in Psalms 105 and 106.

The emphasis of David's Psalm is in singing praise to God. The imperative *sing* is repeated, signifying its importance. *All the earth* is to sing. Praise to God is not to be limited to one locale or one nation; neither is praise to be expressed merely through the familiar old songs we grew up with. We are to sing *a new song* because every day we recognize new facets to the wonder and majesty of God.

NO BUCKET TO CARRY MY TUNE!

Not everyone is blessed with a singing voice. Some can't "carry a tune in a bucket." A few don't even have a bucket! Inability to sing is a serious handicap in a worship assembly. Repeated admonitions in Scripture teach us to make vocal music in praise to God. What's the tone-deaf worshiper to do? Usually we tell such a person simply to make a "joyful noise." But the people seated next to that person in church may not find much joy in that noise!

Those who cannot sing can hum quietly, only mouth the words, or just read the lyrics silently as the congregation sings. Better yet, the church can offer basic singing classes to benefit even the tone-deaf.

But what about those who have no song in their hearts? That makes worship much more difficult. If you have no gratitude, joy, or hope to move you to sing in worship, there is hardly any way for you to participate with integrity.

On the other hand, your mood and your motives don't change the purpose of the worship assembly. Your despondency does not alter the truths that are being celebrated. Your joylessness cannot evict God's presence from praise.

When you don't feel like singing, sing anyway. The very action of participation can cheer your soul. Expression makes an impression. And God can make your worship real—even something you feel.   —R. W. B.

2. Sing to the LORD, praise his name; proclaim his salvation day after day.

The imperative *sing* is again repeated, but this time praise is linked to proclamation. The exact nature of *his salvation* in this context is uncertain, but it may be intended to include God's acts of creation as well as redemption (cf. vv. 11-13; Psalm 136:4-25).

To *proclaim* (or "show") is also an important concept in the New Testament. For instance, through our observance of the Lord's Supper we "proclaim the Lord's death until he comes" (1 Corinthians 11:26). Paul later says to the Corinthians that as a result of his ministry they "show that [they] are a letter from Christ" (2 Corinthians 3:3). Just a bit later, his encouragement to them is that they have a "treasure in jars of clay to show that this all-surpassing power is from God" (4:7). Such "proclaiming" or "showing" demonstrates that our witness is not hidden (cf. Matthew 5:14-16).

B. HE IS THE WORKER OF WONDERS (v. 3)

3. Declare his glory among the nations, his marvelous deeds among all peoples.

All peoples should glorify God once they recognize the *deeds* he has performed. The Jews could give many examples to *the nations* (Gentiles) of the miracles (*marvelous deeds*) that God had performed on their behalf. He had divided the Red Sea, made the seabed dry so that they could cross, and then destroyed the pursuing Egyptian army. He had miraculously provided the Jews with food (manna) during their long sojourn in the desert. God had stopped the flooding Jordan River so that his people could cross into the land he had promised them. Miraculous victory was given at Jericho. The Israelites certainly were not lacking in examples of

God's ability to work wonders on their behalf. Miracles cause us to recognize God (John 20:30, 31). They also cause us to praise God (Mark 2:12).

C. HE IS THE ONE TRUE GOD (vv. 4-6)

4. For great is the LORD and most worthy of praise; he is to be feared above all gods.

The one true God is *great* and deserves great *praise* from all people. He should be *feared* more than any other *gods*. Why? As we will learn in the next verse, the other "gods" are idols—mere statues people have made with their hands. They are a fiction; they do not represent any real supernatural being.

Some people have a problem with the concept of "fearing" God. Moses had instructed the Hebrew people to fear God (Deuteronomy 6:13; 10:12; 31:12). Fearing God is the beginning of wisdom (Psalm 111:10; Proverbs 9:10), and teaches wisdom (Proverbs 15:33). Fearing God causes us to avoid evil (Proverbs 16:6). Fearing God leads to life (Proverbs 19:23). Isaiah prophesied that even the Messiah would fear the Lord (Isaiah 11:3). The word *fear* includes the concepts of respect and reverence, but we should not dilute the significance of fear too much. Remember what Jesus said: "Do not be afraid of those who kill the body and after that can do no more. But I will show you whom you should fear: Fear him who, after the killing of the body, has power to throw you into hell" (Luke 12:4, 5).

5. For all the gods of the nations are idols, but the LORD made the heavens.

There are no other *gods* in the sense of actual, supernatural beings (Jeremiah 2:11). People made *idols* to worship. They were carved wood or chiseled stone. The only real God had commanded that no such images be worshiped (Exodus 20:4, 5). These were the products of human hands. Isaiah mocked the idea of a person worshiping something he had made with his own hands (Isaiah 44:9-20).

6. Splendor and majesty are before him; strength and glory are in his sanctuary.

The psalmist considered certain attributes of God. Since no other gods were real, the Lord alone has *strength and glory*. God's acts of creation (v. 5) mean that as Creator, he alone is splendid and majestic (Psalm 104:1-3).

In Western culture, such an exclusive view of God is not politically correct. We are encouraged to believe that all religions contain truth (relative to the believers of each religion) and should be accepted as true, as long as the adherents of those religions are "sincere." We are encouraged to embrace religious diversity as a strength of modern civilization. To believe the Bible's exclusive statements about Jesus—that he is the only way to God (John 14:6)—is to be intolerant and narrow-minded (cf. Luke 13:24). Those who are vocal in their belief that Jesus' name is the only name by which we can be saved (Acts 4:12) can find themselves accused of bigotry and even hatred. Few people seem to be interested in the truth of the claim. But the claim is, indeed, true, and the disciple of Jesus must not be ashamed to believe and declare it (Mark 8:38).

BEAUTIFUL SANCTUARIES

Have you seen the Crystal Cathedral? Even on television it is awesome! Famous churches usually have beautiful sanctuaries. The design and decor of a worship center can impose considerable influence on the mood and expressions of worshipers.

Some of the largest churches, however, have rather plain buildings, with conservative decorating and furnishings. They depend on lighting, sound, and programming to beautify their worship. Verse 6 of our text says the "strength and beauty" of God's sanctuary are reflected by his "honor and majesty" (*King James Version*).

What makes a sanctuary? Isn't it the presence of God and the praise of his people? Thousands of Christians in Africa and India worship in the open air. Those outdoor spaces become beautiful sanctuaries, as sincere songs are sung, as holy Communion is observed, and as the inspired Word is proclaimed.

HOW TO SAY IT

Abinadab. Uh-BIN-uh-dab.
Abraham. AY-bruh-ham.
Kirjath Jearim. Keer-jath JEER-um.

WHAT DO YOU THINK?

In comparing the "gods of the nations" with the Lord, the psalmist identifies them as "idols" while he affirms that "the Lord made the heavens." What kind of "idols" are people and nations still worshiping today?

The usually small chapels in hospitals can become unusually beautiful sanctuaries as the effectual, fervent (often desperate) prayers of worried "waiters" are offered there. People sometimes gather in gymnasiums, stadiums, campgrounds, or amphitheaters for worship. And wherever authentic worship happens, those places are transformed into beautiful sanctuaries. —R. W. B.

III. GIVE GOD WHAT IS DUE HIM (PSALM 96:7-9)

A. PRAISE FOR HIS POWER (v. 7)

7. Ascribe to the LORD, O families of nations, ascribe to the LORD glory and strength.

All *families of nations* are called to recognize the *glory and strength* of God. Interestingly, Psalm 29:1 calls for angels (the "mighty ones") to offer the same acclamation.

B. OFFERINGS FOR HIS GLORY (v. 8)

8. Ascribe to the LORD the glory due his name; bring an offering and come into his courts.

We don't come before God with silent lips; neither should we come before him with empty hands. The Old Testament system included many types of offerings that the Israelites were to *bring* to God. Today we often think of *offering* as a time in the worship service when we give our gifts of money to God. For the New Testament era, however, this concept of "offering" is far too limited. Romans 12:1, 2 describes the main offering God desires: he wants us to offer ourselves as living sacrifices to him.

C. REVERENCE FOR HIS MAJESTY (v. 9)

9. Worship the LORD in the splendor of his holiness; tremble before him, all the earth.

When we *worship* God, we should do so with humility and reverence. When we worship, we should be offering God our best. Sadly, many of the world's most blessed people seem to take God for granted. We do not tremble in the presence of God. Many do not even manage to stay awake during a church service! We may sing "How Majestic Is Thy Name," but end up mouthing mere words (cf. Isaiah 29:13).

Often it is people in "less advanced" cultures who seem to offer more genuine praise to God. Perhaps they are not embarrassed to be believers. Maybe they are simply more sensitive to their own frailty. Perhaps they are not so overawed with their own accomplishments that they still have room in their lives for awe for God. A heightened sense of self destroys the ability to recognize and appreciate the wonder and majesty of God.

The blindness of the Jews to the wonder and majesty of God caused many of them to reject Jesus as the Messiah (cf. Matthew 23:16-22). He did not fit their preconceived notions of what the Messiah would be. Even when performing the miracle of a resurrection right before their very eyes, some would not believe (John 11:45). They failed to recognize that God was calling all people to himself through his Son. He wanted to offer salvation to all people, and he wanted all people to worship him (cf. John 20:28-31).

CONCLUSION

Imagine that you had found a cure for cancer: would you keep that news to yourself? Of course not! You would share your cure with anyone who had cancer. God has a cure for man's longing for fellowship with him. He chose the Hebrew people to be his conduit to the world. They shared a special privilege and bore a special responsibility (Romans 3:1, 2). Sadly, they failed to understand their unique position. They failed to grasp the message (Acts 13:46). God loves all people. He wants all people to be saved (2 Peter 3:9). He wants all people to praise him!

Discovery Learning

This page contains an alternate lesson plan emphasizing learning activities. Classes desiring such student involvement will find these suggestions helpful. The next page is a reproducible activity page to further enhance discovery learning.

LEARNING GOALS

After this lesson each student will be able to:

1. Tell what these psalms say about the need for the entire world to praise God.

2. Explain how meeting this need is an important part of the church's mission.

3. Memorize a verse of praise from today's text.

INTO THE LESSON

OPTION: *Hymn Study.* The lesson writer gives three reasons God should be praised: for what he has done; for who he is; and because it is due to him. Bring hymn books for each class member to look for hymns that develop each of the three ideas. For example, the verses of "How Great Thou Art" praise God for what he has done; the chorus exalts God for who he is, while "Majesty" gives God the praise he is due. Display these three ideas on a transparency or poster so that all class members can see it.

OPTION: *Praise List.* Use the reproducible activity "Psalm 96 and Praise" from the next page to explore these same three reasons for praising God.

OPTION: *Make an Acrostic.* Have your class make an acrostic about worship using words that are in the text, such as, *sanctuary*, *majesty*, or *holiness*. While the word making the acrostic is usually formed by the first letters of each word, *sanctuary*, *majesty*, or *holiness* can connect the other words in cross word style like this:

Selah	Marvelous	Homage
Ascribe	Adoration	Obeisance
Name	Jesus	Lord
Courts	Exalt	Invoke
Tremble	Sing	Natural
Ubiquitous	Tremble	Elohim
Adoration	Yahweh	Shekinah
Reverence		Selah
Yahweh		

INTO THE WORD

OPTION: *Worship Lesson.* In addition to any activity or activities you use to explore the text, use the reproducible activity "Worship Wisdom" from the next page to provide some background on the meaning of worship.

OPTION: *Rewrite a Psalm.* Psalm 96 is addressed to people, encouraging them to worship. Ask the class to rewrite Psalm 96 so that it addresses God. For example:

Lord, I sing to you a new song;
I join the whole earth in singing to you.
I sing to you, Lord, and praise your name.
I proclaim every day that you have saved me.
I declare your glory among the nations
And your marvelous deeds among all peoples."

Provide pens and paper. Ask members to share their psalms with the class. Lead a brief discussion on why the whole world should praise the Lord.

OPTION: *Choral Reading.* Today's text begs to be read dramatically. In preparation for this choral reading, read and discuss each verse of Psalm 67:1-5 and Psalm 96:1-9. Decide as a class whether it should be read by a male, female, or mixed voices, and assign parts. Should one person, a duet, trio, or the entire class read it?

INTO LIFE

OPTION: *Plan a Worship Hour.* Both of today's psalms are "calls to worship." Using the text, ask your class to plan a worship hour for your church.

For example, Psalm 96:1-3 suggests a robust song service with a new song being introduced. Verses 4-6 might lead to a sermon on the character and attributes of God. Verses 7, 8 imply a testimony time sharing what God has done. An offering is mentioned in verse 8. The service could close with a time of prayer, and Psalm 67 could be prayed as a benediction. Submit your results to whoever plans the worship hour at your church.

OPTION: *Write a Letter.* Psalm 67 and 96 encourage people to worship. Every church has some members and acquaintances who are away from home for school, military service, or work. Be ready with addresses, envelopes, stationery, and stamps. Ask your class to use these chapters as a basis for encouraging someone to worship and praise God. This simple Bible school activity might be God's means for keeping a young believer on the high road of worship.

OPTION: *Memorize a Verse.* Challenge your class members to memorize a verse that would be helpful in preparing for worship. Any verse from Psalm 96 would be a good choice. One group technique is to have the class sit in a circle and read through it two or three times in unison. Then go around the circle and have each person read one word. Have both the first and last person give the reference for the verse.

Psalm 96 and Praise

Psalm 96 gives us three reasons for praising God: we should praise God for who he is, for what he has done, and because he is worthy of our praise. See how many words or phrases you can find and write them in the appropriate column. Include the verse reference. An example is given for each column.

WHO HE IS:	WHAT HE HAS DONE:	HE IS WORTHY:
He is great, v. 4.	He made the heavens, v. 5.	Glory is due his name, v. 8.

Worship Wisdom

Most Christians have an idea of what worship is, but some have not studied what the Bible teaches. Look up each of these verses and write a one-line summary of what each teaches about worship.

Exodus 34:14 _____

Deuteronomy 12:5-7 _____

Psalm 29:2 _____

Psalm 99:5 _____

Psalm 99:9 _____

Psalm 100:2 _____

Isaiah 29:13 _____

Zechariah 14:17, 18 _____

Matthew 4:9, 10 _____

John 4:21, 23, 24 _____

Romans 12:1 _____

1 Corinthians 14:19 _____

Revelation 14:7 _____

These references may give you additional insights: 1 Samuel 1:3; Job 1:20; Psalm 86:9, 10; Psalm 102:22; Psalm 132:7; Jeremiah 7:2; Matthew 2:2; Hebrews 12:28; Revelation 4:10; Revelation 15:4.
How are you doing in relationship to these biblical criteria for worship? What do you need to do better?

Worship and Wisdom for Living
Unit 3: *Words for the Wise*
(Lessons 10-13)

EMBRACE WISDOM

LESSON 10

WHY TEACH THIS LESSON?

Many years ago, I had a high school English teacher who, in a certain instance, revealed her frustration with teaching. I recall her saying with a look of resignation that the school had set before us a "banquet" of knowledge and wisdom, but that very few of us seemed interested in attending that feast.

She was right. At the time, however, I didn't know it—thinking her observation to be rather laughable. I, along with most of my fellow students, was merely focused on passing the next test any way possible in order to get that diploma so I could get on with life. Unfortunately, this attitude follows many people throughout their adult lives. "The next big thing" captures their attention to the point that they're always focused on achieving "it" while larger issues of true wisdom—godly wisdom—go unnoticed. Today's lesson will help your learners break through this "tyranny of the urgent" and get (or stay) on the road to gaining the type of wisdom that is of eternal significance.

INTRODUCTION

A. FINDING WISDOM

Diogenes, a Greek philosopher who lived from about 412 to 323 B.C., led a simple life and often resorted to bizarre behavior to gain attention. Alexander the Great tolerated his eccentricities and learned to respect the old man.

On one occasion, Alexander saw Diogenes carefully examining a large pile of human bones. Having come to expect such curious behavior, Alexander retained his composure and asked Diogenes why in the world he was doing this.

"Sir, I am searching for the bones of your father," came the reply, "but I can't distinguish those of your father from those of his slaves." Diogenes seems to have realized that the "paths of glory lead but to the grave" and that wisdom is "better than the merchandise of silver, and the gain thereof than fine gold" (Proverbs 3:14, *King James Version*).

B. LESSON BACKGROUND

Scholars refer to certain portions of the Old Testament as "Wisdom Literature." Although wisdom literature may be found at various places in the Old Testament, most of it is centered in the books of Job, Psalms, Proverbs, and Ecclesiastes. The main emphasis of wisdom literature is to impart moral values and provide information that will allow a person to live a godly life.

Solomon, for example, prayed at the beginning of his reign for "a discerning heart" that he might rule his people justly and prudently (1 Kings 3:9). God granted Solomon his desire, and before long he had gained a reputation for his wisdom. The life of Solomon also shows that wisdom is not necessarily a permanent endowment, for later in his life he made decisions that were anything but wise. The book of Proverbs is attributed to "Solomon son of David, king of Israel" (Proverbs 1:1). While Solomon may have written some of the individual proverbs, most scholars believe that the book as we know it today is a collection of wise sayings that was assembled over a long period of time.

DEVOTIONAL READING:
PROVERBS 3:1-8
BACKGROUND SCRIPTURE:
PROVERBS 3, 4
PRINTED TEXT:
PROVERBS 3:13-18; 4:1-9

LESSON AIMS

After participating in this lesson, each student will be able to:

1. Describe the value and importance of getting wisdom and of passing it on.

2. Contrast God's wisdom with that of the world.

3. Suggest an area of one's relationship with God where his or her wisdom needs to be applied more consistently.

Aug
4

KEY VERSE

Blessed is the man who finds wisdom, the man who gains understanding.   —Proverbs 3:13

As for literary form, Proverbs is cast as poetry. Poetry takes various sub-forms. *Epic* poetry, such as the *Iliad* and the *Odyssey*, tells of heroes and legends. *Lyric* poetry is intended to be sung, and the book of Psalms offers good examples of this. *Didactic* poetry is designed to teach, and that is what we find in the book of Proverbs.

I. THE VALUE OF WISDOM (PROVERBS 3:13-18)

A. For Its Inherent Qualities (vv. 13-15)

13. Blessed is the man who finds wisdom, the man who gains understanding.

The setting for the third chapter is a father making an appeal to heed parental advice (cf. 3:1). The first verse in our printed text depicts one who is actively seeking *wisdom*. Wisdom is not usually acquired by accident, nor is it gained without some effort. We may note also that it does not come suddenly. Even for our Lord it was a developmental process. Luke 2:52 notes that "Jesus grew in wisdom and stature."

In this verse we are not told how or where the person should seek for wisdom, but common sense tells us that some activities and some places are more likely than others to prove fruitful in this quest. One is not likely, for example, to find wisdom when most of his or her energy is directed toward seeking pleasure. Nor is one likely to find wisdom in a place notorious for carnal or intemperate living.

Although the demands in the search for wisdom are rigorous, the result is worth the effort, for it brings happiness. This suggests Jesus' parables of the lost sheep, lost coin, and lost son. When they were found, great rejoicing resulted. In this verse wisdom and *understanding* are practically synonymous.

But remember that the mere gaining of knowledge does not necessarily lead to wisdom. Learning how to understand factual information and how to use it appropriately leads to the wisdom that is desired.

14. . . . for she is more profitable than silver and yields better returns than gold.

The profit that results from gaining wisdom is far better than the profit one might realize by gaining only *silver* and *gold*. In the mythical story of King Midas, everything the king touched turned to gold. It seemed like a dream come true; but when he touched his daughter and she turned to gold, the king learned how worthless that yellow metal really was. King Solomon himself learned a similar lesson. He accumulated large stores of silver and gold, but concluded with the dismal lament that it was all "meaningless" (Ecclesiastes 2:11).

WISDOM OR KNOWLEDGE

A few years ago, Caroline Sutton wrote a book entitled, *How Do They Do That?* The book answers all sorts of questions, such as "How do homing pigeons find their way home?" "How do they get the lead into a pencil?" "How do they make pictures big enough to put on billboards?" And, of course, "How do astronauts relieve themselves in outer space?"

It's amazing that there really are people who know the answers to questions like these. Maybe you're one of them.

The world is filled with smart people who have accumulated knowledge. Ours is the most educated generation in history. According to the *PrayerNet Newsletter* of July 18, 1997, the sum total of all human knowledge doubles about every twenty-two months. *Executive Book Summaries* reports more information was generated in the last thirty years than in the previous five thousand. More than four thousand books are published every day. The *New York Times* includes more information in a single day than a resident of seventeenth-century London was likely to encounter in a lifetime.

We're pretty smart, but are we wise? There is a difference between knowledge and wisdom. It's possible to accumulate tons of information about the world, but to know nothing about living. That's the reason wisdom is so valuable. Wisdom helps us use what we know. Wisdom guides us to a successful life, not just one filled with facts.   —J. A. M.

15. *She is more precious than rubies; nothing you desire can compare with her.*

In poetry of this period it was a common practice to personify qualities and attributes. Here wisdom is personified as a woman, a technique used in other places in Proverbs. *Rubies* may refer to the well-known gemstone or it may refer to a rare and valuable form of red coral. Either way, the point is that wisdom is more valuable than these items used in jewelry. In some of the mines, slaves were used to do the actual work of mining. If a slave found a precious stone of a certain size, he would be granted his freedom. Certainly few things could be more valuable or desired than freedom. Yet even this did not compare with the value of wisdom.

B. FOR THE BLESSINGS IT BRINGS (vv. 16-18)
16. *Long life is in her right hand; in her left hand are riches and honor.*

Every culture has a set of values by which it determines what things are most important. In ancient Israel, belief in a life after death was not so widely or firmly held as it is among Christians today. As a result, the Israelites thought a *long life* to be greatly desirable. One thing wisdom promised was a long life. We can readily understand this. Even in those ancient days when little was known about medicine, wisdom would lead one to realize that a lifestyle based on carousing and excessive drinking would shorten one's life. Further, wisdom would lead one to avoid situations that were needlessly dangerous and to avoid personal confrontations that could lead to violence. Today, a wise person will take advantage of all the advances made in medical science. We now know that proper diet, exercise, and regular physical checkups can prolong life.

Wisdom also offers *riches and honor*. One who manages personal resources wisely is more likely to provide adequately for family needs and eventual retirement. One who, like the prodigal son, wastes resources in "wild living" is not likely to be able to do either. When wisdom leads one to follow a life committed to honesty and humble service, that person will be honored even without seeking recognition.

As Solomon began his reign, he asked God for wisdom to rule wisely. God granted this prayer and then went far beyond it, promising "riches and honor" as well. God also promised to lengthen his days if he obeyed God's (1 Kings 3:13, 14).

17. *Her ways are pleasant ways, and all her paths are peace.*

We should not understand this to mean that one who lives wisely will avoid all suffering and hardships. Indeed, in verses 11 and 12, just preceding our lesson text, we are told not to despise the "Lord's discipline and do not resent his rebuke, because the Lord disciplines those he loves." As Christians we recognize that the road of life may be rough at times, but we also know that the destination is worth whatever we have to endure to get there.

One example is marriage. Even with wisdom on the part of both partners, the best of marriages is not always characterized by *pleasant ways* or *paths* of *peace*. But how much worse would that marriage be when one or both partners act unwisely!

18. *She is a tree of life to those who embrace her; those who lay hold of her will be blessed.*

The expression *tree of life* is used metaphorically to refer to the pleasures and satisfactions of life. But we cannot avoid the larger implications of this expression found in Genesis 2:9; 3:22; and Revelation 22:2, 14, where this phrase clearly refers to eternal life. The reader is encouraged to *lay hold of* the tree of life, which represents wisdom. This must be an ongoing experience, for they must retain *her*.

WHAT DO YOU THINK?

It would seem that length of years would inevitably result in greater wisdom, but this doesn't always seem to be the case. Why?

In other words, gaining wisdom is not a once-and-for-all experience; it must be a continuous process throughout life.

II. OUR ATTITUDE TOWARD WISDOM (PROVERBS 4:1-9)

A. Wisdom Received (vv. 1-3)

1. Listen, my sons, to a father's instruction; pay attention and gain understanding.

In ancient Israel, the father bore the major responsibility for the spiritual training of the children. Without any formal schools, this training took place in the home and in the daily work in the fields and pastures (Deuteronomy 6:3-9).

While the father had the responsibility for bringing his children up in the way they should walk, he, along with the mother, deserved the respect of the children. The Fifth Commandment required children to honor their parents, and the penalty was severe for those who openly rebelled against their parents—death by stoning (Deuteronomy 21:18-21). Thus, when the *sons* are told to *listen* to the *instruction* of a father, this admonition was not to be taken lightly.

2. I give you sound learning, so do not forsake my teaching.

The *teaching* is synonymous with *sound learning*. It is *sound* first of all because it came originally from God. The Ten Commandments given to Moses on Mount Sinai and supplemented by later revelations formed the basis for all doctrine.

3. When I was a boy in my father's house, still tender, and an only child of my mother. . . .

The teacher reflects on his own childhood when he learned from his own father the teachings he now wishes to pass on to his son. Combined with *tender* love and care from his *mother*, one sees here the solid framework of love that always should surround parental teaching. An authoritarian stance by parents that lacks love is almost certain to lead to rebellion on the part of the child. On the other hand, this does not mean giving in to the child's every whim. This is not really love at all. Sometimes parents have to display "tough love" that makes demands and expects obedience. To do otherwise is to cheat the child out of the proper training that he or she deserves.

PASS IT ALONG

Proverbs 4:1 makes it clear that sharing wisdom is an intergenerational responsibility. Wisdom is to be passed along from parent to child. The late actor Jimmy Stewart used to tell how his father helped him connect with the wisdom and strength of the Bible.

When the United States entered World War II, Stewart enlisted in the Army Air Corps. When he deployed overseas, Stewart's father, Alex, wanted to encourage his son but was overcome with emotion. Instead he wrote a note. Jimmy later read the words his father had been unable to say aloud. He passed along this wisdom:

"My dear Jim boy. Soon after you read this letter, you will be on your way to the worst sort of danger. Jim, I'm banking on the enclosed copy of the 91st Psalm. The thing that takes the place of fear and worry is the promise of these words. I am staking my faith in these words. I feel sure that God will lead you through this mad experience. I can say no more. I only continue to pray. Goodbye, my dear. God bless you and keep you. I love you more than I can tell you. Dad."

Alex Stewart was a veteran of the Spanish-American War. He knew from experience the comforting power of Psalm 91:3-5: "Surely he will save you from the fowler's snare . . . under his wings you will find refuge. . . . You will not fear the terror of night, nor the arrow that flies by day."

Jimmy Stewart returned home a decorated hero of twenty combat missions. He learned from his father the wisdom of trusting the God whom Psalm 91:2 describes as a refuge and fortress.   —J. A. M.

B. WISDOM RETAINED (vv. 4-6)

4. . . . he taught me and said, "Lay hold of my words with all your heart; keep my commands and you will live.

When a baby enters the world, his or her mind is, except for a few rudimentary things, a blank. Immediately, however, the mind begins to absorb and respond to the stimuli that affect it. What happens to the child as he or she grows and matures depends upon the kind of stimuli received. Psychologists who work with children are unanimous in their belief that the "zero to three" years are crucial in forming a child's character and personality. (That is one good reason a church should be very concerned about the quality of programs it has in its nursery and preschool departments.)

In this verse, the writer is reflecting on his own learning experience as a child. In his own case, it seems obvious that his father had taken his responsibilities seriously. It is not enough for the father to be a good teacher, however. The student must also *keep* that which is *taught*. To help his son retain his teaching, the father undoubtedly drew upon his own experiences, telling how obedience to God's *commands* had brought happiness. But at the same time it is likely that he shared with his son some of his misdeeds that led to painful consequences. These anecdotes would help the son remember the lessons the father taught.

5. "Get wisdom, get understanding; do not forget my words or swerve from them.

Learning is not a passive activity in which the teacher does all the work and the student sits through it like an inert lump. The imperative to *get wisdom* implies activity—seeking or buying—that involves a cost to the student. The same idea is expressed later in Proverbs 23:23: "Buy the truth and do not sell it; get wisdom, discipline and understanding."

The teacher is experienced enough to know that sometimes the student rebels against the truth, thus the warning not to *swerve from* his *words*. Sometimes the rebellion occurs because the ideas are new or strange to the one being taught, or because the ideas require the student to do something he or she doesn't want to do (or to avoid something he or she does want to do). A wise teacher will anticipate such reactions and be prepared for them.

6. "Do not forsake wisdom, and she will protect you; love her, and she will watch over you.

This verse is a good example of "synonymous parallelism," a literary device common to Hebrew poetry. In this device the truth stated in the first line is then repeated in different words in the second line. In addition to its poetic value, the repetition reinforces the stated truth.

C. WISDOM EXALTED (vv. 7-9)

7. "Wisdom is supreme; therefore get wisdom. Though it cost all you have, get understanding.

Most of us, consciously or not, have a list of priorities that divides important things from those of lesser importance. This verse illustrates just such a list and at the top of it is *wisdom*, which is the principal thing. No matter how many other things a person may become involved in, getting *understanding* ought to be at the top of the list. In fact, one who gains wisdom and understanding is more likely to be able to gain the other things he or she seeks.

8. "Esteem her, and she will exalt you; embrace her, and she will honor you.

Not only are the children to seek wisdom and cling to it, they are to *esteem* it. Some young people sneer at learning, and if one of their number excels academically, he or she may be rejected as a "nerd." But this verse rejects such an attitude. One who esteems wisdom will in turn be exalted.

HOW TO SAY IT

Diogenes. Die-AH-jin-ees.
Ecclesiastes. Ik-LEEZ-ee-AS-teez.

This poster illustrates Proverbs 4:7. Contrast the wisdom found in these settings with godly wisdom.

WHAT DO YOU THINK?

What should be the primary purpose of education, whether Christian or secular?

WHAT DO YOU THINK?

Why is wisdom not highly esteemed and eagerly embraced by society today?

9. "She will set a garland of grace on your head and present you with a crown of splendor."

The reward of *a garland of grace* does not necessarily mean a *crown* such as a king might wear, but rather refers figuratively to any honor or blessing that comes as a result of pursuing wisdom. ("Crown" in the New Testament is used to designate eternal life; however, that does not seem to be the point here.)

CONCLUSION

A. WISDOM FOR WHAT?

The advantages of wisdom are many and varied. Employers prize the wisdom of a worker that goes beyond the skills needed to perform a job. Teachers appreciate the student whose wisdom carries him or her beyond the pages of the textbook. Churches earnestly seek wise leaders who can guide the congregation in the many decisions it must make.

But as important as wisdom is in all these areas, the wisdom that leads us to God is most important. While the book of Proverbs deals with many everyday forms of wisdom, its central emphasis is upon the wisdom that brings us to God and helps us to grow in our spiritual stature.

The psalmist writes, "The fear of the Lord is the beginning of wisdom" (111:10), and Proverbs 9:10 echoes this idea. Thus our concern must be to acquire not just wisdom, but wisdom that leads us to God (cf. 1 Corinthians 1:18-25).

B. WISDOM IS INTERGENERATIONAL

In secular as well as Christian education, we hear a great deal about the important part that parents play in the education of their children. But even as we voice this emphasis, we should not overlook the part that grandparents can play in helping their grandchildren gain wisdom (cf. 2 Timothy 1:5). Grandparents are good for many things. If they live nearby, they are convenient baby-sitters. Then at Christmastime and at birthdays they can be generous givers. Of course, sometimes they may spoil the grandchildren, but that is a reasonable price to pay for all the help and wisdom they can bring.

I was fortunate to live in a three-generation household. When my grandfather died, we moved in with grandmother. When it became necessary for my mother to work outside the home, my grandmother watched over us during our growing-up years. In her quiet, humble, pious way she made a lasting impression on me, my siblings, and our cousins. One of the lasting images that we have is of her falling asleep each night in her favorite rocking chair as she read her Bible. In good times or bad, her usual response was to quote a Bible verse or a wise old saying. Today I find myself doing the same thing for my own children and grandchildren. Grandmother did not live to see the full impact of the wisdom she passed on to succeeding generations. Today six of her grandchildren and great-grandchildren are engaged in "full-time Christian service," and several others are involved actively in local churches.

This lesson emphasizes embracing wisdom. For one to embrace wisdom, he or she must come into contact with it. That is not as simple or as easy as it was in previous generations. For one thing, teaching biblical wisdom is rarely possible in public schools. Further, many parents are not equipped for this task. And many have not come to realize how important it is to begin this teaching while our children are infants. Another serious obstacle to this kind of teaching is that we are immersed in a media sea that offers all kinds of alternatives to biblical wisdom. All this means that we as parents, grandparents, and young people must embrace wisdom, and share with others the joys and blessings of following God's wisdom.

Discovery Learning

This page contains an alternate lesson plan emphasizing learning activities. Classes desiring such student involvement will find these suggestions helpful. The next page is a reproducible activity page to further enhance discovery learning.

LEARNING GOALS

After participating in this lesson, each student will be able to:

1. Describe the value and importance of getting wisdom and of passing it on.

2. Contrast God's wisdom with that of the world.

3. Suggest an area of one's relationship with God where his wisdom needs to be applied more consistently.

INTO THE LESSON

OPTION: *Sentence Completion.* Write "Wisdom is . . ." on the board or on a poster. Go around the class and have each person complete the sentence. Then make the transition to the Bible study by saying, "We have heard some good ideas about what wisdom is. How will our answers measure up with what the Bible teaches? Today's lesson will help us do that!"

OPTION: Video Interview. Every church has someone interested in and knowledgeable about video equipment. Ask such a person or a group to prepare a man-on-the-street video to introduce this lesson. They should ask people to complete the two sentences "Wisdom is . . ." and "Understanding is . . . ." They could interview people after church or go to a mall or busy street corner to get a sampling.

INTO THE WORD

OPTION: *Chart List.* Have class members complete a chart list showing blessings and benefits from gaining wisdom and understanding. The chart could be duplicated for each student or by drawing it on the board or a transparency. Results might look like this:

BLESSINGS AND BENEFITS OF WISDOM

3:13	Blessing
3:14	Better returns than silver or gold
3:15	Value beyond that of rubies
3:16	Long life, riches, and honor
3:17	Pleasantness and peace
3:18	Tree of life
4:4	Life
4:6	Being protected and kept
4:8	Being exalted and honored
4:9	A garland of grace and a crown of splendor

OPTION: *Write a Biblical Definition.* Challenge your class to write a biblical definition for wisdom. Bring several concordances to class and have your students look up references to the words *wisdom* and *wise* in Proverbs and other Bible books to help them define the words. (The reproducible page that follows carries a similar activity.)

OPTION: *Marginal Markings.* Ask your class members to read through Proverbs 3:13-18 and 4:1-9 and make a mark in the margin beside each verse according to these guidelines. Write *"Ouch!"* beside any verse that convicts you of a sin or shortcoming. Put a *PTL!* for "Praise the Lord" beside any verse that makes you want to praise God. Put an *"Amen!"* beside any verse that preaches at you with corrective instructions. Put a question mark beside any verse that raises a question you would like to have discussed. You may want to reproduce the text on a handout for each class member.

After class members have completed their markings, ask, "What verse did you mark with a question mark?" Discuss the verse and then ask for another. Then ask for verses marked with other marks. (The instructions for this activity are included in *NIV® Bible Student.*)

INTO LIFE

OPTION: *Plan a Speech.* Many adult classes have grandparents vitally concerned about passing wisdom and understanding to their progeny. Young adults could look ahead to what they would want to say to grandchildren about wisdom and understanding. Make this a discussion activity rather than writing out the speech. What definitions would be important to include? What verses would you want them to memorize? What false ideas should they avoid? If they do not have biblical wisdom and understanding, what results? What rewards should they anticipate? (Directions for this activity are included in *NIV® Bible Student.*)

OPTION: *Write an Article.* Parents of young children have a staggering responsibility. Write a letter of encouragement to parents of young children for your church newsletter or bulletin. What ideas from today's text should you include? Is there a verse parents should memorize for motivation and mission? Conclude with a call for prayer on behalf of parents.

Some class members might rather personalize this article in the form of a letter to a specific parent or set of parents. If you take this direction, provide stationery and envelopes.

Wisdom and the Word

Wisdom is a dynamic word with rich insights hidden in its biblical usage. Wisdom is never just an intellectual concept of the mind but always focuses on practical responses to life situations. A good biblical definition is, "Wisdom is looking at life from God's perspective and responding to life's situations as Jesus responded or would respond." Write a practical application for your life from each of these Bible references about wisdom. The last one is done as an example for you.

Job 28:28 _____

Psalm 111:10 _____

Proverbs 11:2 _____

Proverbs 13:10 _____

Proverbs 14:6 _____

Proverbs 14:8 _____

Proverbs 15:33 _____

Proverbs 19:11 _____

Proverbs 21:11 _____

Proverbs 29:15 _____

Ecclesiastes 2:26 _____

Isaiah 11:2 _____

Matthew 11:19 _____

Acts 6:3 _____

Acts 6:10 _____

James 1:5 _____

James 3:13-17   Wisdom is based in character, not in intellect or the mind.

Blessed is the man who finds wisdom, the man who gains understanding.
—Proverbs 3:13

Worship and Wisdom for Living
Unit 3: Words for the Wise
(Lessons 10-13)

RUN FROM EVIL

LESSON 11

WHY TEACH THIS LESSON?

Early in 2001, one of the four major television networks in the U.S. aired a salacious series called *Temptation Island*. The idea was to see who among four unmarried couples could resist the temptation to cheat on his or her "significant other" when thrown together with other attractive and seductive singles. Since all those participating in the show were cloistered on a remote Caribbean island, there wasn't really anywhere to run from this evil—even if anyone had wanted to.

As artificial as this particular situation was, many Christians today do indeed fall (or jump) into temptation—sexual and otherwise—on a regular basis. How sobering this is, since a life that is pleasing to God is to be characterized by just the opposite! With eternal life at stake, today can be the day your students start to learn the importance of running from evil.

INTRODUCTION

A. TURNING THE DECREES TO THE WALL

Under their great leader Pericles (495–429 B.C.), ancient Athens built an extensive empire around the Aegean Sea. To govern other cities that had become a part of this empire, Pericles from time to time issued decrees, which were inscribed on plaques and displayed in a prominent place in each city. On one occasion an ambassador came to Pericles asking that a certain decree be changed and the plaque be removed.

"I am sorry," replied Pericles, "but I cannot do that. We have a law that once a decree has been posted, the plaque carrying the decree cannot be removed."

"But," argued the ambassador, "we are not asking for you to remove the plaque. Just turn it around to face the wall so that we won't have to see it."

That sounds very much like the attitudes many today take toward sin. Although we've retained God's laws, those laws are "turned around" so that one is no longer a criminal or even a sinner, but is merely "socially maladjusted." A couple living in open adultery is demonstrating an "alternate lifestyle." Those who murder unborn babies talk about a woman's right to "privacy" or to "control her own body"; they are called "pro-choice," not "anti-life."

But the writer of the verses used as our lesson text would have none of these elusive euphemisms. He asserted that certain sins were "detestable" to the Lord. It may not be "politically correct" to use such forceful language, but it certainly is biblically correct. There is no place in the Scriptures that allows us to turn divine decrees to the wall and thus ignore them.

B. LESSON BACKGROUND

As in last week's lesson, the format today is that of a parent giving sound advice to his son. In the previous lesson the emphasis was on gaining wisdom as a means of avoiding sin and the troubles it brings. Today's lesson emphasizes the importance of guarding against certain sins. The lesson title, "Run From Evil," is appropriate for this kind of emphasis, and reminds us of Paul's advice to Timothy to "flee the evil desires of youth" (2 Timothy 2:22).

DEVOTIONAL READING:
PROVERBS 6:6-15

BACKGROUND SCRIPTURE:
PROVERBS 6

PRINTED TEXT:
PROVERBS 6:16-28

LESSON AIMS

After participating in this lesson, each student will be able to:

1. List the warnings about evil that are found in today's text.

2. Tell why the warnings against the specific sins mentioned in the text are especially necessary today.

3. Develop a strategy for dealing with one or more of the temptations cited in today's text.

Aug
11

KEY VERSE

My son, keep your father's commands and do not forsake your mother's teaching. Bind them upon your heart forever; fasten them around your neck.
—Proverbs 6:20, 21

I. CATALOG OF DETESTABLE SINS (PROVERBS 6:16-19)

The list of sins found in the opening verses of the lesson text is not intended to be exhaustive, but it is representative of a wide range of sins that plagued society at the time these verses were written. During the Middle Ages, the church had a list of "seven deadly sins"—pride, anger, envy, sexual impurity, gluttony, laziness, and greed. The sins listed in today's lesson could be called "Israel's seven deadly sins." If we were to draw up a list of sins that especially threaten our society, our list might be somewhat different, but all of the sins listed here are certainly prevalent today.

A. PRIDE, LYING, VIOLENCE (vv. 16, 17)

16. There are six things the LORD hates, seven that are detestable to him.

The "numerical ladder" of *six things . . . seven* is a literary device used to attract attention (cf. Job 5:19). It hints that the list that is about to be set forth is not necessarily exhaustive—that is, there are not just seven things that God hates. Rather, the list is suggestive of the kind of things that God hates.

17. . . . haughty eyes, a lying tongue, hands that shed innocent blood . . .

Some scholars suggest that the writer mentions the sins of verses 17 and 18 in relation to parts of the human body, going from the head to the feet—*eyes, tongue, hands,* heart, and feet. Others have noted that the first five sins (vv. 17, 18) deal with general moral character, while the last two (v. 19) apply to a legal or judicial setting.

A *haughty* look reveals a proud and arrogant heart. It shows disdain for others, but worst of all it shows an attitude of contempt toward God. Several Scriptures indicate that God deals severely with this sin. God will "bring low those whose eyes are haughty" (Psalm 18:27); "God opposes the proud but gives grace to the humble" (James 4:6). Job requests God to "look at every proud man and bring him low" (Job 40:11).

A *lying tongue.* Lying is the deliberate telling or withholding of information so as to misrepresent certain facts and thus deceive the listener. Lying is such a severe offense that Ananias and Sapphira were struck dead for misrepresenting their contribution to the church (Acts 5:1-11). "All liars" are subject to eternal punishment (Revelation 21:8).

Hands that shed innocent blood. We live in a violent society, making this warning against violence much needed. Psychologists, sociologists, legislators, and religious leaders have all addressed this issue with little to show for their efforts to date. Shedding innocent blood can occur in many contexts—in the home, in the schools, in the womb against the unborn, etc. Violence is widely portrayed and even glorified on our movie and television screens. Many remedies for reducing violence have been proposed, but no remedy is better than changing the anger and hatred that control many people's lives into love. That's what the gospel is designed to do.

B. A WICKED HEART, EAGERNESS TO SIN (v. 18)

18. . . . a heart that devises wicked schemes, feet that are quick to rush into evil . . .

All of us at times struggle with *wicked schemes* or evil thoughts. The condemnation in this verse is of those who nourish thoughts in their minds and plot wicked things. Martin Luther (1483–1536) once observed that while we can't keep eagles from soaring above our heads, we can keep them from building nests in our hair. Those who devise "wicked schemes" not only permit, but also encourage the eagles of sin to build nests in their hair.

Feet, for their part, also can be directed in a variety of ways. They can walk slowly, deliberately, and carefully; they can be *quick,* stumbling, and purposeless; or they can be some combination of these. The idea here is probably that of premeditated, rapid movement toward evil. The Lord considers such behavior an "abomination."

This poster illustrates verses 16-19. Ask, "How can we be as aggressive in avoiding evil as runners are in keeping fit?"

C. FALSE WITNESS, SOWER OF DISCORD (v. 19)

19. . . . a false witness who pours out lies and a man who stirs up dissension among brothers.

Some scholars believe that the final two detestable sins have the tone of a judicial setting. Lying in the general sense already has been condemned in verse 17. Bearing *false witness* refers to lying in a court while under oath (cf. Exodus 20:16). Whether one is in court as the accused or as the accuser, lying under oath is destructive of the whole justice system. We refer to this as perjury, and our laws are designed to deal firmly with it (cf. 1 Timothy 1:10).

One who *stirs up dissension among brothers* subverts the harmony of a group or church, creating a hindrance to achieving goals. While some of the sins previously condemned affect only individuals, discord can disrupt the work of the entire group (Titus 1:11), which makes it a very dangerous sin, indeed. In the New Testament, church members are subject to discipline—even to the point of being disfellowshipped—for three reasons: doctrinal defection (e.g., 1 Timothy 1:3, 20), moral defection (e.g., 1 Corinthians 5:11), and divisiveness (e.g., Titus 3:10). Divisiveness is the same as stirring up dissension.

WHAT DO YOU THINK?

What might be the underlying motivations of one who "stirs up dissension" among fellow Christians?

Most of us have heard the phrase that we are to "hate the sin, but love the sinner." That's good advice, especially since we are to reach out to those very sinners with the saving gospel of Jesus Christ. But the section of verses just studied is one of the clearest examples in the Bible of God actually *hating the sinner personally.* This speaks to the holiness of God.

HAVE WE LOST OUR SENSE?

Have we lost our good sense? Paul Harvey observed that "The world is jiving us. We call dirty pictures art. We build shrines to Elvis. We get our truth from tabloids and our religion from Shirley MacLaine."

Robert Welsh says, "The world is a giant insane asylum run by the worst of its inmates." We live in a world that needs, but often rejects, the wisdom of God.

When Sam Wyche was head coach of the Cincinnati Bengals, he once was fined thirty thousand dollars for not permitting a female reporter into the men's locker room. But when a player for the New England Patriots sexually exposed himself to a female reporter in his locker room, he was fined only twelve thousand dollars. Does that make sense?

It is illegal in Florida to gamble in a game of cards, but I've waited in line behind a man who spent one hundred dollars gambling on the state lottery at the local convenience store. Does that make sense?

A person can be heavily fined for cruelty to animals. But in each of the United States it is legal to destroy the life of an unborn human being. Does that make sense?

There are scores of examples of how we seem to have lost our good sense. Perhaps that would be interesting only if it were not dangerous. When wisdom is absent, society is threatened. We are called to be wise. Wisdom is the ability to see life from God's perspective. That means we learn to hate what God hates: the sinful behaviors that threaten our society.   —J. A. M.

II. KEEPING PARENTAL COMMANDMENTS (PROVERBS 6:20-23)

In this next section we move from the *what* to the *who, why,* and *how.*

A. KEEP THEM CONTINUALLY (vv. 20, 21)

20. My son, keep your father's commands and do not forsake your mother's teaching.

The admonition is from the father to the *son,* as at the beginning of chapter 6. In ancient Israel, the father had the greatest responsibility for the proper upbringing of his children. But the law did not minimize the importance of the mothers in this duty. The children were required to obey the *mother* just as much as they were to obey the father (cf. Exodus 20:12). In fact, as our society is presently structured, mothers have a greater impact on the lives of their children than do most fathers (cf. 2 Timothy 1:5).

21. Bind them upon your heart forever; fasten them around your neck.

One cannot keep the commandments by just an occasional observance of them. They must be lodged permanently in one's mind and conscience. To ensure that this happens, we must discuss them with others, be involved in study groups, and listen to sermons regularly. Some may complain that they never hear anything new in lessons or in sermons, and in a sense they are right. The Lord's commandments are certainly not new, but we still need to hear them over and over again, lest Satan find a way to dislodge them from our hearts.

The phrase *fasten them around your neck* recalls Deuteronomy 6:8 and 11:18. The idea is surely a figure of speech, and the Pharisees got it wrong when they thought that a literal application of such passages would win God's favor (cf. Matthew 23:5).

B. KEEP THEM WHEREVER YOU GO (v. 22)

22. When you walk, they will guide you; when you sleep, they will watch over you; when you awake, they will speak to you.

This same order—walking, sleeping, and awaking—is found in Deuteronomy 6:7. Keeping the Lord's commandments is not a part-time, one-day-a-week task. It is a "24/7/365" job. In our busy lives, we may find it difficult to stop in order to go through some ritualistic activities to ensure that we are keeping the Lord's commandments. That's really not the point of this verse. The important thing is that in all our thoughts and our relations with others we demonstrate that we understand how God wants us to behave.

C. KEEP THEM TO BRING LIGHT AND LIFE (v. 23)

23. For these commands are a lamp, this teaching is a light, and the corrections of discipline are the way to life.

Most of us have had the experience of walking through a room at night with all the lights out. Even a familiar room may be hazardous because of toys or clothing left on the floor. Yet some people try to make their way through the rooms of *life* without any spiritual *light* at all. To make the situation even more dangerous, they often have to travel through strange rooms where they have never been before. How much safer they would be if they just allowed the light of God's laws to light their way. "Your word is a lamp to my feet and a light for my path" (Psalm 119:105).

III. WARNING AGAINST ADULTERY (PROVERBS 6:24-28)

Now the writer combines a *what* with a *why* concerning one of the most devastating of all sins.

A. AVOID EVIL WOMEN (v. 24)

24. . . . keeping you from the immoral woman, from the smooth tongue of the wayward wife.

This specific warning logically follows the teachings of the previous verses that urge the son to keep the commandments of the father and mother. The warning against adultery or other forms of illicit sex are found in other places in the book of Proverbs (5:3-23; 7:6-27). We may conclude from these and other passages that sexual sins were a common problem in ancient Israel. We know that they are a serious problem in modern times as well. The *wayward wife* (or "strange woman" in the *King James Version*) describes a prostitute in other places in Proverbs; here it also can refer to a married woman who seeks to entice a man other than her husband in order to engage in adultery.

One obvious way to escape sexual temptations is to steer clear of people and situations where such temptations are likely to arise. "Bad company corrupts good character" (1 Corinthians 15:33). If feet are to run swiftly (Proverbs 6:18), then let them be used to flee such a temptation (1 Corinthians 6:18)!

B. AVOID LUST (vv. 25)

25. Do not lust in your heart after her beauty or let her captivate you with her eyes.

Before *lust* results in the actual act of adultery, it grows in the *heart*. Modern culture crassly flaunts sexuality for commercial reasons, intending to plant certain desires within the person—desires that result in reaching for one's wallet. We see this technique used to sell everything from automobiles to clothing to food to jewelry to cosmetics. Pornography itself is readily available on the Internet and on newsstands.

With all of these temptations surrounding us, it is more difficult than ever to protect ourselves from the unhealthy lusts that arise from natural human desires. But unless we do protect ourselves, we will not be able to view the people who are the objects of our lusts as being created in the image of God and in need of eternal life. They will simply be objects to be used and cast aside. Jesus cautioned against the lust of the eyes and heart (Matthew 5:28).

EYE CONTROL

In 1 John 2:16, the apostle John describes the power of the lust of the eyes. We must manage what we see. Job said, "I made a covenant with my eyes not to look lustfully at a girl. . . . if my heart has been led by my eyes, . . . then may others eat what I have sown, and may my crops be uprooted" (Job 31:1, 7, 8). Job recognized in his day that the heart follows the eyes; the same holds true today. One key to conquering lust is to make a covenant with your eyes. Job determined *in advance* to guard himself in the area of sexual temptation by making a pact with his eyes not to gaze at a woman who might tempt him.

A study by Michigan State University reported that teenage girls will witness fifteen hundred hours of sexual acts before graduating. (Teenage boys will see one hundred hours less because they don't watch soap operas.) Approximately 94 percent of all sex acts on television are between people who are not married.

In 1998, Americans rented 686 million sexually explicit, hard-core videos. (That's about two-and-one-half for each and every American citizen!) The U.S. adult cable and satellite industries are a multi-billion dollar business. *On Command Corporation* and *LodgeNet Entertainment Corporation* provide movies for over 1.5 million hotel rooms. More than half of their pay-per-view business comes from pornography. Such temptations were not available to Job!

Our eyes are under attack. If you are serious about this area of your life, you're going to have to monitor your media intake. David declares, "I will set before my eyes no vile thing" (Psalm 101:3). Are you exercising eye control?   —J. A. M.

C. AVOID THE CONSEQUENCES (vv. 26-28)

26. . . . for the prostitute reduces you to a loaf of bread, and the adulteress preys upon your very life.

The phrase *the prostitute reduces you to a loaf of bread* suggests that one who engages in adultery may be brought to poverty (cf. Luke 15:13). While this may not always be literally true in the monetary sense, we all know cases where it was true

HOW TO SAY IT

Abomination. A-bom-ih-NAY-shun.

Aegean. A-JEE-un.

Pericles. PAIR-ih-kleez.

WHAT DO YOU THINK?

Why do you think that persons who get involved in the kind of immoral behavior the writer identifies in verses 24-26 so often fail to take account of the consequences?

WHAT DO YOU THINK?

Why is the battle against sin the one we so often lose?

PRAYER

Heavenly Father, we thank you for the wonderful help and direction you have given us through the Scriptures. We thank you also for your love—a love that receives us back when we sin, sets our feet on the right path, and shows us the way we should go. In the Savior's name we pray. Amen.

THOUGHT TO REMEMBER

Fear God, and keep his commandments:
for this is the whole duty of man.
—Ecclesiastes 12:13

in other ways—situations where adultery shattered families, destroyed marriages, and ruined ministries. The penalties for adultery are not limited to the physical life, but extend to eternal life as well (1 Corinthians 6:9, 10; Revelation 21:8).

27, 28. Can a man scoop fire into his lap without his clothes being burned? Can a man walk on hot coals without his feet being scorched?

To clinch his argument against adultery, the writer asks two rhetorical questions. The answer to both is obvious and inescapable.

A few years ago, a segment on the television news magazine *20/20* demonstrated how easy it was to tread on hot coals and actually *not* be burned. But the test subjects were moving quite fast across those hot coals! They weren't merely out for a stroll, as this text implies. Both of the experiences depicted in this verse would be extremely painful, even life-threatening in some circumstances—just as adultery will be.

CONCLUSION

A. ON YOUR MARK! GET SET! GO!

These are the words that a runner hears at the start of a footrace. But one will not hear these words in the most important race of all: the race to escape evil. There are some interesting parallels between a footrace and the race of life. A person who wants to run a successful footrace must spend a great deal of time and energy training for the event. In the same way, if we are to escape evil, we must train by learning the Scriptures and learning how to apply them to life situations.

In a footrace, a runner wears only the clothing that will aid in the run. To carry any extra weight will slow the runner down. The writer of Hebrews expresses a similar idea: "Let us throw off everything that hinders and the sin that so easily entangles" (12:1). In the race of life we dare not allow the weight of sin to encumber and distract us. We run in order to get the prize of eternal life (1 Corinthians 9:24).

But as we attempt to escape from evil, we often need places of refuge and protection. We can find that shelter in God: "For you have been my refuge, a strong tower against the foe" (Psalm 61:3). We can also find in the church help and support from fellow Christians, who are also involved in the race of life. Fleeing *from* sin is not enough. After Paul warns Timothy to "flee the evil desires of youth," he adds that he must move *toward* "righteousness, faith, love and peace"; young Timothy will find these things "with those who call on the Lord out of a pure heart" (2 Timothy 2:22). We also find those noble things in God and in his church.

B. IS THERE HOPE?

All of us at one time or another have failed to heed the good counsel of parents or teachers. Is there any hope for us when we have made a mess of our lives? Is it possible for God to take a life shattered by sin and put the pieces back together again? Thank the Lord, there is hope. All of us have been wounded by sin, but God can apply the healing "balm of Gilead" that can restore us. Even though the scars may remain, we can still be used by him.

Where it is possible, we must make restitution for our misdeeds. If we have hurt others, we need to try to repair the damage. If we have rejected the good counsel of parents and teachers, it would be helpful to go to them and thank them for the help they tried to give and admit our mistake for not heeding it (cf. Matthew 5:23, 24).

In the parable of the prodigal son (Luke 15:11-23), Jesus gave us a wonderful picture of the attitude to have when we come to ourselves as the prodigal did. He also showed us the loving Father, standing and waiting, ready to receive us with open arms.

Discovery Learning

This page contains an alternate lesson plan emphasizing learning activities. Classes desiring such student involvement will find these suggestions helpful. The next page is a reproducible activity page to further enhance discovery learning.

LEARNING GOALS

After this lesson each student will be able to:

1. List the warnings about evil that are found in today's text.

2. Tell why the warnings against the specific sins mentioned in the text are especially necessary today.

3. Develop a strategy for dealing with one or more of the temptations cited in today's text.

INTO THE LESSON

Lead your class in a brainstorming session to list the most offensive sins—from God's perspective. Make the list without lengthy discussion. Write this phrase on the chalkboard: "The Most Detestable Sins." As class members enter, ask them to help you make a list. When you have an extensive list, ask them which ones you should put a star beside because they are worse than the others. Finally, ask which one you should underline because it is the worst of all.

OPTION: *Collage.* Bring a stack of old catalogs and magazines to class. Ask class members to tear or cut out pictures of things they would like to have and pictures that would represent sins they would like to avoid.

Have your class members arrange their pictures on a poster with a vertical line dividing it into two parts: "Things I Would Like to Have" and "Things I Would Like to Avoid."

If you are unable to collect magazines, a similar activity can be done using the reproducible activity "Have or Have Not!" from the next page.

Make the transition to Bible study by noting that Satan is ever tempting us with attractive things that, in the end, prove deadly. Other people seem to enjoy them, but the discerning one knows the danger. Our text today will help us discern between what we may pursue and what we should flee!

INTO THE WORD

OPTION: *Compare and Contrast.* Compare and contrast the list of sins in today's text with lists of sins in other places in Scripture. A catalog of sins is found in these three New Testament passages: Romans 1:29-31; Galatians 5:19-21; and 1 Corinthians 6:9, 10. List these sins in parallel columns on a handout as well as on the chalkboard or an overhead projector transparency. What terms appear in all three lists? Circle those. Are there any that appear only here? Underline those. Is there significance to the order of the listings?

OPTION: *Research.* Many class members have Bibles with a center reference column, but some do not know how to use it. Others simply don't have them. Bring to class several Bibles that have a center reference column. Check your church library, ask your preacher for help, or call class members and ask them to bring Bibles with center reference column to class.

Introduce the activity by saying, "Today's text has a list of sins to avoid. The words will not be hard to understand, but it will be hard to put the principles into practice. Sometimes looking at other passages that use the same terms or ideas can help us to understand and apply the truth we are studying. Let's read each verse; and then we will look up all of the references in the center reference column and summarize what we find."

INTO LIFE

OPTION: *Evaluation and Confession.* Ask your learners, either collectively or individually, to list the sins that appear in today's text. Then ask each one to place a mark beside each sin according to these instructions: "Put an F beside each verse that names a sin where you have fallen short and need Forgiveness. Put an S beside any verse that names a sin where you are struggling and need the Lord's Strength. Put a V beside any verse where you are walking in the Lord's Victory."

Ask your class to form prayer partners. Encourage members to confess to their prayer partner any sin for which they need forgiveness. Then their prayer partner should read 1 John 1:9 and assure them of God's forgiveness. Then they should pray for each other in those areas where they are struggling.

OPTION: *A Call for Sexual Purity.* Proverbs 6:25-28 gives a strong warning against sexual immorality. Have your class write a call for sexual purity; for example, "Today I take a public stand for sexual purity. The Bible is clear in warning about the dangers of sexual sins, and I pledge myself to purity before God. I will stay away from anyone who would compromise my stand. I will be wary of anyone who flatters me. I will guard my eyes from looking lustfully at any other person)."

OPTION: *Hatred for Sin.* Ask your learners to end this class by giving personal and private attention to the "Hatred for Sin" section of the following reproducible page.

Have or Have Not!

Imagine your favorite store has sent you a catalog of every item it carries in stock. By some good fortune you actually have time to sit down and thumb through it and dream of having many of the items pictured. Which ones would you really like to have if money were no object? List those under "Have" below.

Of course, there are some things that you believe have no place in your home—you wouldn't take them as a gift! List some of those under the "Have Not!" column, along with a brief note of why you don't want it.

HAVE   HAVE NOT!

Hatred for Sin

The writer of today's text, by the Spirit's guidance, indicates that God hates sin. The *New International Version* uses the word *detestable* to express his holy attitude. Other versions use such strong words as *abomination, cannot stand, cannot tolerate,* and *loathes.* If you were to label your own attitude toward sin, what would that one word be? Fill in your name on the first line following; put the verb that best reflects your attitude on the second line:

sin!

_____   _____
Name   Verb

Put a check mark (✔) before each of the following actions you have taken to demonstrate your attitude toward sin.

I have . . .

❑ written a public official regarding a sinful law.

❑ picketed a business catering to evil desires.

❑ left a conversation group involved in evil talk (of any sort).

❑ communicated with a media source regarding its programming.

❑ cried over the devastating effects of sinful activity.

❑ boycotted a store for its merchandising sinful items.

❑ removed yourself from a potentially lustful circumstance.

❑ other: _____

Which do you need to do?

Worship and Wisdom for Living
Unit 3: Words for the Wise
(Lessons 10-13)

WATCH WHAT YOU SAY

LESSON 12

WHY TEACH THIS LESSON?

Sometimes "talk is cheap," but sometimes it is extremely powerful. Some people's skill in the use of the spoken word makes it a valuable tool for change. Adolf Hitler was one such speaker. It was his inflamatory rhetoric that set in motion a chain of events that resulted in World War II and its fifty million-plus casualties.

To the contrary, some speakers can use the spoken word for positive change. Dr. Martin Luther King, Jr., was an extraordinary speaker. His motivational style was instrumental in launching the Civil Rights Movement of the 1960s.

But most of your learners today won't need to be reminded of the power of the tongue—they've already experienced it (for good and ill) in their own lives. What they will need, however, is some help in controlling and directing the tongue. That's where this lesson comes in!

INTRODUCTION
A. PEARLS

People respond differently to good counsel. In the Sermon on the Mount, Jesus spoke of the danger of casting pearls before swine. When swine see a person throwing something out before them, they come expecting to be fed. But if one should throw pearls to them rather than the corn they are expecting, they will "trample them under their feet, and then turn and tear you to pieces" (Matthew 7:6). Of course, Jesus was not giving information about hog farming. he was talking about using discretion in instructing people. Some people will not only reject godly counsel, but will also turn on the one who offers it to them.

On another occasion, Jesus told a parable about the kingdom of Heaven involving a man who discovered a valuable pearl. Once he realized the value of his discovery, he sold all that he had to buy the pearl (Matthew 13:46). But not all will realize the value of what they have found. Even today, some people are like this man while some are not.

In these two situations, the offer/discovery of the pearls results in surprisingly different reactions. The differing responses reveal the differing characters of the hearers.

B. LESSON BACKGROUND

The first nine chapters of Proverbs are made up of discourses on vices and virtues. These discourses are laid out rather logically. However, with chapter 10 there begins what one scholar calls "a collection of pithy sayings seemingly without editorial arrangement." That seems to be the case with the texts for today's lesson. While several of these sayings deal with the use or abuse of the tongue, other sayings are interspersed with them in a way that seems to depart from this pattern.

Proverbs 10:1 begins, "The proverbs of Solomon: A wise son brings joy to his father, but a foolish son grief to his mother." Here we have a picture of a father offering advice to his son. Sessions between parents and children often do not follow any logical pattern and may even seem rambling and disconnected. But that's the way it happens in real life. If we understand that and put ourselves into

DEVOTIONAL READING:
PROVERBS 16:16-30

BACKGROUND SCRIPTURE:
PROVERBS 15–17

PRINTED TEXT:
PROVERBS 15:1-4, 7, 8; 17:4-10

LESSON AIMS

After participating in this lesson, each student will be able to:

1. Summarize the benefits of wise speech and the dangers of foolish speech.

2. Tell what makes wise speech wise and foolish speech foolish.

3. Suggest some specific means of keeping one's speech wise and helpful.

Aug
18

KEY VERSE

A gentle answer turns away wrath, but a harsh word stirs up anger. —Proverbs 15:1

the situation, what follows makes a lot of sense. Above all else, today's lesson conveys a great deal of good advice—for both children and parents.

I. CONTROLLING OUR SPEECH (PROVERBS 15:1-4)
A. SOFT SPEECH (v. 1)
1. A gentle answer turns away wrath, but a harsh word stirs up anger.

Perhaps no verse of Scripture has been so often underused as this one. Jesus' teaching embodied the same idea when he advised us to turn the other cheek when someone strikes us (Luke 6:29). We might speak of holding our tongue as a certain way of turning the other cheek. Even though we don't always heed this good advice, we know that it works. All of us have seen or been involved in heated controversy and watched as *a gentle answer* acts as a fire extinguisher to put out the flames of anger.

We know just as certainly that *a harsh word stirs up anger.* How often domestic arguments turn into anger and even violence just because each party wants to get in the last angry word or insult. Even as I write this, a football star sits in jail charged with murder. A discussion following the Super Bowl led to heated words and then to violence. The result was two men lying on the pavement, stabbed to death. In the Chicago area in the mid-1990s, an off-duty sheriff's deputy and an off-duty Chicago police officer were providing security for a social event. During a conversation, both pulled their handguns and emptied them into each other at very close range.

The issues that these folks were arguing about couldn't have been that important! At any point short of violence, a gentle answer could have prevented tragedy.

James tells us that the tongue is a hard member to control. "All kinds of animals . . . are being tamed, . . . but no man can tame the tongue" (James 3:7, 8). Even if we didn't have this Scriptural warning about how difficult the tongue is to tame, we would know this from experience. All of us on occasion have said things, sometimes thoughtlessly, sometimes angrily, that we wished we could take back.

WORDS HAVE POWER
The book of Proverbs makes it clear that words have power. Life and death is in our speech. With our words we bless and curse, build and destroy. As surely as God's spoken Word created reality, our words shape our environment.

In an article in *U.S. News & World Report,* July 21, 1994, Joannie Schroff pointed out that the way newlyweds speak to one another is one important predictive factor of their marital success. One study found that newlyweds who ended up staying married would be critical about each other in only five comments out of one hundred times they spoke to each other. Among those who later divorced, ten of every one hundred remarks was a put-down. By the time ten years of marriage had rolled by, the pairs who were headed for divorce were insulting each other five times more often than the other couples.

For a marriage to survive, husbands and wives should learn to keep their negativity under control, to use words to keep the conflict manageable. Otherwise, the hostility escalates to the point that their mental state and physiological condition make it impossible to process any new information. Efforts to communicate then become futile.

God's ancient wisdom says, "A gentle answer turns away wrath, but a harsh word stirs up anger." That's true at home and wherever people talk to one another.
—J. A. M.

B. WISE SPEECH (v. 2)
2. The tongue of the wise commends knowledge, but the mouth of the fool gushes folly.

Elsewhere in Proverbs the writer has pointed out the difference between *knowledge* and wisdom. In our modern electronic culture, knowledge is readily

Use this poster to illustrate Proverbs 15:1. Ask learners to tell of times they have seen the truth of this verse demonstrated.

available to almost anyone who turns on a computer. But having information available is not the same as understanding what this information means or how it should be used. Wisdom is the ability to employ knowledge in a useful way that will help others and please God.

Fools are not necessarily those who are ignorant. Indeed, a fool may be well educated and able to score very high on an IQ test. Yet such a one *gushes folly* if his or her intellectual prowess is not put to some good purpose. A few years ago, Americans were shocked by the exploits of the "Unabomber." Although he probably had the IQ of a genius, he lacked wisdom, using his intelligence to maim and kill the innocent. The person who says there is no God is a fool no matter what his or her IQ, or how many degrees he or she may hold (Psalm 14:1).

C. Watched Speech (v. 3)
3. The eyes of the Lord are everywhere, keeping watch on the wicked and the good.

Since we are talking about speech, we might expect the writer to speak of the "ears of the Lord," but here he is stressing God's omnipresence. What God can see, he can certainly hear. No corner is so remote nor whisper so quiet that God does not see and hear. What God sees and hears he also judges (cf. Matthew 12:36).

D. Wholesome Speech (v. 4)
4. The tongue that brings healing is a tree of life, but a deceitful tongue crushes the spirit.

A tongue that brings healing speaks words of praise to God and words of joy and encouragement to others. Lives that are enhanced by such words will be more useful in the Lord's kingdom.

A deceitful tongue, on the other hand, is destructive of the spirits of others. Today on television and in the movies we hear language that was once confined to the gutter and would never be heard in polite society, much less in a Christian gathering. "Sitcoms" are filled with the kind of slashing sarcasm that creates humor by demeaning and dehumanizing others. Even the kidding and teasing we do with others is often painful to its victims.

II. VIRTUES AND VICES OF THE TONGUE (PROVERBS 15:7, 8)
A. Speech of the Wise and the Foolish (v. 7)
7. The lips of the wise spread knowledge; not so the hearts of fools.

The *wise* are respected, not because they have *knowledge,* but because they know how to use it wisely. A wise person is also respected for not being a know-it-all who displays knowledge to bolster an ego. The wise person is respected for knowing when to speak and when to remain silent (cf. Ecclesiastes 3:7). An old Quaker proverb cautions, "Do not speak unless you can improve on silence."

But *the hearts of fools* will lead them to a very different kind of speech. Those whose hearts are full of envy and pride will be betrayed by their tongues. Deceitful people may fool others for a time, but sooner or later their own tongues will trap them. Following the foolish counsel of foolish people can be devastating (1 Kings 12:13-15).

B. Speech of the Wicked and the Upright (v. 8)
8. The Lord detests the sacrifice of the wicked, but the prayer of the upright pleases him.

In this context, *sacrifice* refers not just to offerings made in formal worship, but also to prayers. *The wicked* may pray pious prayers but these prayers are

WHAT DO YOU THINK?

The words we speak carry tremendous potential for either good or ill. How can we be sure that our words have a positive rather than a negative effect in the lives of others?

WHAT DO YOU THINK?

People value freedom of speech. Can you think of ways in which this freedom is sometimes misused and abused?

detestable to *the Lord*. The King in Shakespeare's *Hamlet* (Act III, Scene III) expresses the idea well:

> My words fly up, my thoughts remain below.
> Words without thoughts never to heaven go.

God "hears" every prayer, but he doesn't necessarily "listen" to every prayer (Isaiah 1:15; Lamentations 3:44). He views the prayers of the the hypocrite to be just that. Jesus dealt with this problem when he contrasted the prayers of the Pharisee and the tax collector (Luke 18:9-14).

On the other hand, God delights in *the prayer of the upright* (cf. James 5:16). Some prayers are uttered in public, others in private. The most sincere prayers of all are those that are offered from the depths of our hearts.

III. SUNDRY ADVICE (PROVERBS 17:4-10)

A. LISTENING TO LIARS (v. 4)

4. A wicked man listens to evil lips; a liar pays attention to a malicious tongue.

The author now moves to other topics that in one way or another involve speech. We all know that good people sometimes are misled by those who are *evil*. Indeed, good people tend to be more trusting of others and thus often fall victim to the schemes of con men. But that is not the point the writer is making in this verse.

The thrust of the message here is captured in the axiom, "Birds of a feather flock together." People who are bent on doing *wicked* deeds will listen to liars and will themselves turn to lying to further their own evil schemes. Further, they will lie to escape their guilt when they are challenged.

This is another example of Hebrew parallelism. To listen *to evil lips* is synonymous with paying *attention to a malicious tongue*. This may refer to the gossip that many people engage in. The *liar* often makes the gossip worse by "enhancing" the stories as he or she repeats them.

INTEGRITY

Years ago, the old TV game show *Truth or Consequences* challenged people to tell the truth or face the consequences. The results were often funny. Centuries ago Jesus called the church at Pergamum (also known as "Pergamos") to be true or to face the consequences (Revelation 2:12-16).

Christ's call, however, is no game. The results of compromise are never funny. Jesus expects us to put away lying and be true, to live with Christlike integrity in every circumstance.

Integrity, even in the face of adversity, is not all that common. A recent U.S. president tarnished his presidency by his poor choices and subsequent lies. For him, false lips became an art form, and many around him seemed intent on helping him cover up his lies. And while it seemed that most people considered the matter a minor one, not worthy of severe reprimand, his party's next presidential candidate blamed him and the scandals associated with him for his own inability to win the election.

A few years ago a man went to a large Christian bookstore looking to find any books written on living a life of integrity and honesty, free from lies. He found a few scattered references, but no entire book addressing the topic. Finally, he asked the clerk for help and indicated that he couldn't find any books on how to live a life of integrity or how to be a person known for truth. She said, "That's strange, we have a whole wall of them." She smiled and pointed to a wall of Bibles.

The wholeness, the integrity, we seek is found in God's truth. So, will we look to the words of Jesus and live them, or we will face the consequences instead?—J. A. M.

WHAT DO YOU THINK?

Proverbs 15:7, 8 identifies the connection between character and communication. How can the words we use be an indicator of our character?

[Consider Matthew 12:34 and other verses in your discussion.].

WHAT DO YOU THINK?

It's interesting how people tend to gravitate to their own "kind." Why do you think this is true?

B. THE HARD-HEARTED (v. 5)

5. He who mocks the poor shows contempt for their Maker; whoever gloats over disaster will not go unpunished.

Poverty has been a curse of every civilization in history. Poverty has many causes—crop failure, ill health, political oppression, bad decisions, ignorance, laziness, etc. Though many solutions to poverty have been suggested and tried, no society has yet been able to eliminate poverty. Even as the United States now enjoys the greatest prosperity any nation in history has ever known, it still has pockets of extreme poverty (cf. Mark 14:7).

This verse does not suggest any solutions to the problems of poverty. Rather, it deals with the attitudes of those who are not poor. The reason for the condemnation of one who *shows contempt for the poor* is that every person, regardless of financial status, is created in the image of God and deserves to be respected.

It is hard to imagine anyone so perverse as to gloat over the disasters that others suffer. God will deal with such a one; he *will not go unpunished.*

C. THE JOY OF CHILDREN (v. 6)

6. Children's children are a crown to the aged, and parents are the pride of their children.

In ancient Israel, a family that included many children and grandchildren was considered a blessing (cf. Psalm 127:3-5). In an age that didn't have such things as Social Security, a large family ensured that older people would be cared for in their advanced years. But, just as important, a large family made for stability in society and within the family itself. Grandchildren are *a crown to the aged;* that is, they are a source of joy and honor. For older people, few joys are greater than that of watching their grandchildren mature into responsible citizens.

In the same way, *parents* become a source of joy and honor for their children and grandchildren. Unfortunately, modern society is missing out on much of this. In the United States, the old "extended family" has long since given way to the "nuclear family." A highly mobile society and changing values have helped undermine these wonderful relationships, and modern civilization suffers as a result.

D. SPEECH REVEALS CHARACTER (v. 7)

7. Arrogant lips are unsuited to a fool—how much worse lying lips to a ruler!

Every culture develops a system of classes. In some it is a vague recognition of a poor class, middle class, and upper class. In others it is a more complicated and rigid arrangement, such as India's caste system. Each class is likely to develop its own distinctive dress, speech, and behavioral patterns. Each class is expected to conform to its own patterns. The Hebrew word translated as *arrogant* can also be rendered as "eloquent" (as in the footnote in the *New International Version*) or "excellent" (as in the *King James Version*); in the writer's day, *a fool* was not expected to converse with such *lips.* This may have involved such things as grammar, accents, and content of the speech.

In the same way, certain speech and behaviors were expected of rulers. *A ruler* was not expected to speak with *lying lips.* It is unfortunate that we don't have the same high standards for our rulers today. The truth is, we have come to expect politicians to lie to us. This in turn may say something about our own values.

E. THE VALUE OF "GIFTS" (v. 8)

8. A bribe is a charm to the one who gives it; wherever he turns, he succeeds.

Here and in other modern versions, *bribe* makes more sense than the *King James Version's* word "gift" in this context because a bribe is a form of speech (compare

DAILY BIBLE READINGS

Monday, Aug. 12—*Mouths That Destroy Neighbors (Proverbs 11:9-14)*

Tuesday, Aug. 13—*Transgressions of the Lips (Proverbs 12:13-22)*

Wednesday, Aug. 14—*Foolish and Gracious Words (Proverbs 15:12-14, 23-30)*

Thursday, Aug. 15—*Pleasant Words Are Like a Honeycomb (Proverbs 16:21-29)*

Friday, Aug. 16—*Stop Before Quarreling Begins (Proverbs 17:14-20)*

Saturday, Aug. 17—*Tongue's Power: Life and Death (Proverbs 18:6-8, 19-21)*

Sunday, Aug. 18—*Lips Informed by Knowledge (Proverbs 20:15-22)*

HOW TO SAY IT

Pergamos. PER-guh-muss.

Pergamum. PER-guh-mum.

PRAYER

Almighty God, we thank you for the wonderful blessing of speech. Teach us how to use that gift in such a way that your name will be honored and that those to whom we speak will be blessed. In Jesus' name. Amen.

the *King James Version* with the *New International Version* at Exodus 23:8 and Deuteronomy 16:19). The latter part of this verse is satire, in that the giver of bribes *succeeds* in the sense that such a person receives favors in return for the bribe. Bribery has been a problem in every culture, and, unfortunately, is still an accepted practice in many places today. Even where bribery is illegal, giving and receiving gifts and favors often become a "legal" way to bring about the same result.

F. FORGIVING AND REVEALING SPEECH (v. 9)

9. He who covers over an offense promotes love, but whoever repeats the matter separates close friends.

He who covers over an offense is not the one who is guilty of wrongdoing and is trying to cover the matter to avoid detection. This phrase describes one who is willing to forgive and forget a wrong that has been done by another person. The transgression may be something done against this one personally or against someone else. Either way, this person is seeking or promoting love by working to minimize the offense and to bring about reconciliation.

Whoever repeats a matter is a gossip. This one will not cover the offense, but will broadcast and embellish it. As a result, a minor oversight may be portrayed as a deliberate snub. *Close friends* are divided when they might have been able to work out their differences.

G. SPEECH THAT CORRECTS (v. 10)

10. A rebuke impresses a man of discernment more than a hundred lashes a fool.

One way to distinguish between a person *of discernment* and *a fool* is to note how one responds to a *rebuke*. A wise person will accept criticism and change accordingly. A fool stubbornly refuses to change behavior even when beaten severely—*a hundred lashes*. None of us enjoys being corrected, especially in public. Our egos become involved, and when that happens, we are likely to become defensive, even when the criticism is justified. And we have to recognize that at times criticism is not always fair, and even when it is fair it may be stated unkindly and harshly. But the wise person will learn to deal with even this kind of criticism.

CONCLUSION

Among other things, humans are superior to animals in the fact that we can *talk*. (Although animals do have rudimentary ways of communicating with one another, they cannot carry on conversations.) Our ability to communicate is increasingly enhanced by all kinds of electronic gadgets, whether for good or for evil.

This means that we must be more careful than ever about what we say (and write). Here are a few suggestions that may help us use our speech—whether by tongue or by E-mail—more effectively for the Lord.

1. Don't talk too much. If we do, sooner or later we are likely to say some things that are stupid, false, or hurtful to others. Even God doesn't like to hear someone babble on and on (Matthew 6:7).

2. Don't put your tongue in motion until your brain is in gear (cf. Proverbs 13:3).

3. Don't speak hastily when you are filled with anger or hatred (Proverbs 15:1). Try counting to ten—or a hundred—first.

4. Don't be a gossip (Proverbs 11:13; 18:8).

5. Don't use foul language or "trash talk" that seems so popular in many circles today. This is specifically condemned in Ephesians 5:4.

6. Speak to edify (Proverbs 25:11), especially with the message of the gospel.

7. Be an encourager. A few kind words can lift a discouraged person (Acts 4:36).

8. Carry on every conversation as if Jesus were listening—which he is.

THOUGHT TO REMEMBER

"May the words of my mouth and the meditation of my heart be pleasing in your sight, O Lord."   —Psalm 19:14

Discovery Learning

This page contains an alternate lesson plan emphasizing learning activities. Classes desiring such student involvement will find these suggestions helpful. The next page is a reproducible activity page to further enhance discovery learning.

LEARNING GOALS

After participating in this lesson, each student will be able to:

1. Summarize the benefits of wise speech and the dangers of foolish speech.

2. Tell what makes wise speech wise and foolish speech foolish.

3. Suggest some specific means of keeping one's speech wise and helpful.

INTO THE LESSON

OPTION: *Sentence Completion.* Today's text has much to say about the misuse of tongue and words. Complete these sentences without looking at Proverbs. (This activity is included in *NIV® Bible Student.*)

A gentle answer turns away _____ (15:1).

A harsh word stirs_____ (15:1).

The mouth of the fool gushes _____ (15:2).

The tongue that brings healing is a _____ (15:4).

He who mocks the poor shows contempt for ___ (17:5).

He who covers an offense _____ (17:9).

OPTION: *Skit.* Ask members of your class to prepare a skit featuring concerned parents giving final words of advice to a young adult leaving home for college, the military, or a job in another city. Set the tone of the conversation rather than spelling out specific lines. Both parents are deeply concerned. They can hardly wait for their partner to finish a sentence before they jump in with another admonition. The young adult leaving home could vacillate between "Yes, Mom. I know, Mom. Okay, Mom," and "Can I still bring laundry home?"

Make the transition to the Bible study by saying, "Concerned parents are anxious to give their final words of advice to a young adult leaving home. Such sessions are not well organized, rehearsed speeches but rambling shots at a variety of topics. This section of Proverbs is like that. Where earlier sections dealt with connected thoughts or a logical progression of ideas, today's text lacks any cohesive unity. It is random bits of good advice and warnings."

INTO THE WORD

OPTION: *Small Group Study.* Divide your class into six small groups for study and discussion. Distribute copies of the reproducible activity "Look in the Book" from the next page, and assign each group one of the sets of verses cited there. Each group should assign a recorder to write down their insights in the space provided and to report to the rest of the class. They should read their verses three times before discussion begins. Then each person must make at least one comment before anyone can make a second comment. Have commentaries available, if necessary.

OPTION: *Translation Study.* Bring a variety of translations of the Old Testament for your class members to use in studying today's text. Try to get a sampling of the spectrum of translations and paraphrases. Start the discussion of each verse by having a student read a translation or paraphrase.

OPTION: *Draw Cartoons.* Many turn to the comics when they open the newspaper. A cartoon can be useful in illustrating biblical truth. Ask your class to draw cartoons that will explain and illustrate each verse in today's text. For example, Proverbs 17:6 almost begs to show grandparents gloating with pride over their grandchildren and youngsters boasting of their father's strength. Or Proverbs 17:10 depicts a young man listening intently while his father shakes a finger correcting him. The adjacent frame would portray a man bent over receiving a beating but all the while covering his ears so he cannot hear the correcting advice. (The directions for this activity are included in *NIV® Bible Student.*)

INTO LIFE

OPTION: *Write a Letter.* Most churches have young adults away from home temporarily for college, the military, or work. Encourage class members to write letters including the advice from today's text. Discuss the tone of the letter, the topics to be addressed, and how personal to be. Provide all supplies needed (The directions for this activity are included in *NIV® Bible Student.*)

OPTION: *Tongue Tamers.* Today's text is filled with verses that warn about the misuse of the tongue and words. Select three verses that could be used as "tongue tamers" to memorize and meditate upon. For example, Proverbs 15:1, 2 and 4 would make a fine trio of "tongue tamers." (The directions for this activity are included in *NIV® Bible Student.*)

OPTION. *Case Study.* The case studies in "Gentle or Harsh" on the reproducible page can be a helpful application activity and could be done in the class group.

Look in the Book

Look up ther following passages (or the passages assigned for a group activity). Record your thoughts on the meaning of each.

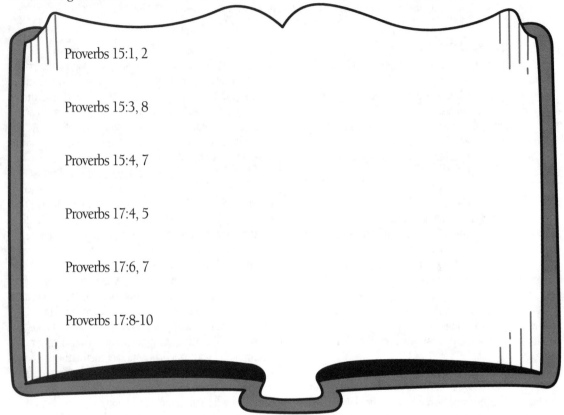

Proverbs 15:1, 2

Proverbs 15:3, 8

Proverbs 15:4, 7

Proverbs 17:4, 5

Proverbs 17:6, 7

Proverbs 17:8-10

Gentle or Harsh

For each of the following situations, what would be the "gentle answer" that "turns away wrath"? What would be the "harsh word" that "stirs up anger"?

A neighbor catches you in the driveway as you arrive home from work, and says, "Your leaves are all blowing over into my yard!"

A coworker consistently arrives late for work, causing you to wait for tasks of mutual responsibility. Today, the associate is forty-five minutes late and comes in saying, "Are you waiting for me?"

Your spouse has approached you on Saturday and said, "I have quite a list of things you need to do today."

Your boss has not got a project finished but has blamed you and your associates. His boss comes by and confronts you with the problem.

Worship and Wisdom for Living
Unit 3: Words for the Wise
(Lessons 10-13)

CARE FOR THE POOR

LESSON 13

WHY TEACH THIS LESSON?

Who can forget the story of Robin Hood and his band of merry men? Those legendary figures of twelfth-century England supposedly robbed from the rich and gave to the poor. But as one humorist noted, "It doesn't take a lot of brains to do it that way. Who in their right mind would rob from the poor? They don't have anything!"

We may smile at that, but there is nothing humorous about poverty. And while many solutions to this problem have been tried over the ages—including various forms of this "Robin Hood strategy"—nothing has really worked in a permanent or long lasting way. Is the situation hopeless?

Today's lesson will give you and your learners a chance to reassess that issue. What does the Bible say? Where is its focus? And do we share the same concerns?

INTRODUCTION

A. GOD LOVES THE POOR

Every society in the history of the world has had its share of poverty. Even today, one can find very definite pockets of poverty within the borders of the world's most affluent nations. Thus far no society has found a way to solve this problem.

But this failure is not for lack of effort. On March 16, 1964, U.S. President Lyndon B. Johnson introduced to the U.S. Congress his "Proposal for a Nationwide War on the Sources of Poverty," which led to a massive effort to reduce or even eliminate poverty. The U.S. spent billions of dollars on this "war" with little positive results to show for the effort. Instead, the country created a bureaucracy that institutionalized the very problem it was trying to eliminate, creating a dependency class in the process. By general consent, both major political parties in the U.S. agree that the effort was a failure. So now what?

Today's lesson emphasizes the Christian's personal responsibility in response to poverty. One problem is that those of us who live in affluent suburbs are safely insulated from the poor and rarely see a poor person unless we are accosted by a beggar in the central city; this results in an "out of sight, out of mind" mentality. Another problem is that many Christians are very cautious about "doing more harm than good" while in the process of feeding and clothing the poor (cf. 2 Thessalonians 3:10).

If we are to help the poor, most of us, as a first order of business, will have to get out of our "comfort zones" and go to where the poor are. Perhaps your church already has a program that works with the poor. Some churches cooperate with other churches in such programs. Either way, these programs almost always need volunteers. If your congregation is not presently involved in a program that addresses some of the problems of poverty, perhaps you and your class could investigate some opportunities to do so.

B. LESSON BACKGROUND

Today's lesson is the final one in this unit that deals with wisdom from Proverbs. All of these lessons have emphasized various aspects of Christian living

DEVOTIONAL READING:
PROVERBS 19:1-8
BACKGROUND SCRIPTURE:
PROVERBS 19:17; 22:1-4, 8, 9, 16, 22, 23; 23:10, 11
PRINTED TEXT:
PROVERBS 19:17; 22:1-4, 8, 9, 16, 22, 23; 23:10, 11

LESSON AIMS

After participating in this lesson, each student will be able to:

1. Give several reasons, both practical and theological, why the believer should help those who are poor.

2. List reasons that Christians sometimes give for not helping the poor, and examine each in light of today's Scriptures.

3. Get involved in some effort, either individually or with others, to provide tangible relief to those who are disadvantaged in some way.

KEY VERSE

He who is kind to the poor lends to the LORD, and he will reward him for what he has done.
—Proverbs 19:17

Aug
25

The Adult Visuals *packet contains this real-life illustration of the message of verse 17.*

WHAT DO YOU THINK?

What are some of the reasons Christians need to be more concerned and helpful with regard to the needs of the poor? Use Genesis 1:27, 28 and Proverbs 22:2 to frame your answer.

rather than theological issues. These studies may encourage you and your students to do further study in this helpful book. Such a study will not necessarily reveal any new truths, but these truths are often couched in catchy language that make them easier to remember and to share with others.

I. GOD'S CONCERN FOR THE POOR (PROVERBS 19:17; 22:1-4)

A. KINDNESS TO THE POOR (v. 17)

17. He who is kind to the poor lends to the LORD, and he will reward him for what he has done.

The economy of ancient Israel was largely agricultural, but the nation was not blessed with an abundance of rich soil. Further, the rainfall in good years was just barely enough to grow a crop. If the land did get enough rain for a good crop, it could be devoured by an invasion of locusts. Most of the farmers had only a small plot of ground to till, and even if they had a good crop year, few of them had adequate facilities to store the crops over a two- or three-year period. In addition, they sometimes faced the danger of foreign invaders who would steal their crops (cf. Judges 6:3, 4).

All this adds up to a rather pessimistic picture for the typical Israelite. When bad times hit for whatever reason, the ancient Jew had to turn to friends and other family members for help. An appeal might be made to wealthier neighbors for a loan because there were no lending agencies or a benevolent government to help. While the Old Testament laws prohibited the charging of interest on loans to fellow Israelites (Exodus 22:25; Leviticus 25:35-37), unscrupulous people found ways around these laws. As a result, people who did not repay their loans ended up losing their land (cf. Mark 12:40), and, in extreme cases, even their freedom.

The situation of the poor did not have to be so desperate, however. The wealthy were encouraged to *be kind to the poor*—extending kindness in the form of a loan or an outright gift. They were to look upon this act of kindness as if it were extended *to the Lord*. The Lord would then *reward him for what he has done*. The suggestion is that the Lord's favor would be more valuable than any money actually lent.

B. A GOOD NAME AND RICHES (v. 1)

1. A good name is more desirable than great riches; to be esteemed is better than silver or gold.

This verse is another good example of Hebrew parallelism, the poetic device that makes a statement in the first part of the verse and then repeats the idea in different words in the second part. While the word *good* is not in the Hebrew text, it is clearly implied in the context and most translations include it.

One who hoards wealth does not have *a good name*; a miser will probably have no pity on the poor (19:17). *Riches* may buy luxuries and pleasures, but they cannot obtain what a good name offers. *Silver* and *gold* may buy companions, but they can never win real friends. This verse does not oppose wealth as such, but when a person sells his or her good name for riches, the price is always too high.

Some people have done such evil in their lives that their very names have become synonymous with evil. (Judas and Hitler are two examples.) A few years ago, the History Channel® noted the case of a baby boy who, at the insistence of his grandfather, was given at birth the same name as the notorious outlaw Jesse James. As the child moved into adulthood, he lived up to (or, rather, "down to") his namesake—he became a hardened criminal, noting that his name had caused him nothing but trouble.

On the other hand, some people have the good fortune of having been born into a family that has established a good name for itself across two or three generations. A person born into such a family has a responsibility to maintain this noble family reputation. All of us, and especially young people, need to be reminded that one bad decision, one misstep, can destroy a good name, and it may take years to recover what has been lost.

C. GOD MADE THE RICH AND POOR (v. 2)

2. Rich and poor have this in common: The LORD is the Maker of them all.

The distinctions we make because of externals such as *rich and poor* are ultimately artificial. Those who have forfeited their good names or who have taken advantage of the poor to gain wealth are reminded that all of us are created by *the Lord*. The rich and the poor do not live in two separate worlds, but meet together in the *common* pursuits of life. And when this life is over, the grave erases all the artificial distinctions we create. Thomas Gray reminds us that the "paths of glory lead but to the grave."

D. ACTIONS OF THE PRUDENT (v. 3)

3. A prudent man sees danger and takes refuge, but the simple keep going and suffer for it.

The *prudent man* is one who anticipates problems and avoids them. When this type of person sees a storm approaching, taking cover becomes a priority. This type of person may have gained wisdom from painful experience, or may have gained it from observing others (which is usually the better way).

The simple (that is, the foolish) always seem to learn the hard way—if they learn at all. They may ignorantly pursue an unwise financial course, such as pursuing "can't lose" investments, and end up being part of the poor we just talked about. Or they may reject good advice and arrogantly plunge into situations that are dangerous. Family and society may attempt to erect "foolproof" barriers that will protect the simple, but such folk often find ways around or over these restrictions. Decisions and actions have consequences, and those who make unwise decisions will *suffer for it*. Sometimes they suffer because of the laws of nature, such as when they drive an automobile recklessly. At other times they suffer from the legal system—ours or God's—when they are involved in criminal or sinful activity.

E. TWO GRACES AND THEIR REWARD (v. 4)

4. Humility and the fear of the LORD bring wealth and honor and life.

Humility is frequently extolled in the Scriptures as a virtue, but it is rare indeed in a modern, self-centered culture. *Humility and the fear of the Lord* are logically expressed together. A humble person readily acknowledges personal weaknesses and thus turns to the Lord. At the same time, one who fears the Lord also recognizes such weaknesses and does not dare attempt to stand on his or her own strength (cf. James 4:10).

The rewards for such behavior *are wealth and honor and life*. We should not take this to mean that the humble person will always enjoy material wealth. Indeed, a humble person may walk the paths of poverty. But humility enables one to appreciate what little he or she does have and thus, in a very real sense, be rich (cf. Luke 6:20).

WHAT DO YOU THINK?

Why are some Christians reluctant to be involved in a significant ministry to the poor?

WHAT DO YOU THINK?

The poor often seem to be significantly disadvantaged when faced with legal concerns, whether civil or criminal. What can we do to help them at these times?

HUMILITY

A chief executive officer (CEO) of a Fortune 500 company visited his doctor. The news wasn't good—the businessman had a terminal disease. Knowing that his time on earth was coming to an end, he started thinking, "What is the most important principle I can teach my associates?" He really cared about those who worked closely with him.

He called together his vice presidents for a special luncheon meeting to brief them on his health and the future of the company. Before he started the meeting, a disagreement arose among them as to which man carried the most weight. To them, authority was equated with position.

The CEO now knew what he needed to teach the men. He interrupted the discussion and told them about his health, and how he expected the company to be run after his death.

Then he did a very strange thing. He sent for a shoeshine kit that he kept in his office and proceeded to shine their shoes! The room was silent—no one knew what to say. When he came to the man most likely to succeed him, that man refused the shine, saying it was beneath the dignity of the CEO to do such a thing.

The CEO replied, "If you won't let me shine your shoes, then clean out your desk—you're outta here." Because the man greatly respected his boss, he told him to do whatever he wanted.

The wise CEO passed on an invaluable life lesson: "When you stoop to serve, you raise your level of authority" (cf. John 13:1-17).   —J. A. M.

II. SOWING AND REAPING (PROVERBS 22:8, 9)

A. SOWING INIQUITY (v. 8)

8. He who sows wickedness reaps trouble, and the rod of his fury will be destroyed.

Both in the physical world and in the moral realm, the law of the harvest is absolute. If one plants corn in a garden, a corn crop will grow. But if thistles are planted, the result is a crop of thistles.

In the same way, God rewards those who live lives pleasing to him. A person *who sows wickedness*, however, will reap *trouble*. Some commentators see *the rod of his fury* as God's wrath on the evildoer. But since this rod *will be destroyed*, it is much more likely that it refers to the evildoer's persecution of others. The evildoer's rod will be destroyed, and his persecution of others will ultimately cease.

GARDEN-VARIETY WISDOM

I grew up where farming was the predominant activity and where every family had a garden. Every summer day found me helping my mother in the garden. For years I thought my mother was growing tomatoes, corn, and green beans. Only later did I realize my mother's primary crop was me. In the garden I discovered the laws of the harvest.

Harvest principle #1: You reap what you sow. This is the principle of *investment*. Proverbs 22:8, 9 makes this clear: Sow evil and reap a harvest of trouble. Sow blessings and you will reap blessings as surely as one who plants tomatoes reaps tomatoes.

Harvest principle #2: You reap after you sow. This is the principle of *interval*. The productive farmer is patient. The crop that is planted today does not yield its fruit tomorrow. Neither evildoers nor the righteous reap the harvest of their behavior at the end of every day, but harvest day will come.

Harvest principle #3: You reap more than you sow. This is the principle of *increase*. Every gardener understands this. A farmer who plants two bushels of wheat can anticipate reaping sixty-seven bushels, a 33:1 return! Three bushels of oats usually produce seventy-nine bushels at harvest time, an increase of 2,630 percent. Plant seven and a half pounds of corn, and you can expect an average yield of one hundred twenty bushels at harvest. A farmer in Illinois regularly receives back seven hundred grains of corn for every grain he plants. What an amazing return!

God calls us to be wise and understand these harvest principles. Evaluate your life. What are you sowing? Is this wise? What kind of harvest can you expect?   —J. A. M.

DAILY BIBLE READINGS

Monday, Aug. 19—Plight of the Poor (Proverbs 19:1-8)

Tuesday, Aug. 20—The Lord Pleads the Poor's Case (Proverbs 22:7-9, 16, 22, 23)

Wednesday, Aug. 21—Give to the Poor (Proverbs 28:20-27)

Thursday, Aug. 22—Defend Rights of the Poor (Proverbs 31:4-9)

Friday, Aug. 23—Do Not Withhold Good (Proverbs 3:27-35)

Saturday, Aug. 24—Generous Persons Will Be Enriched (Proverbs 11:17, 18, 24-28)

Sunday, Aug. 25—Happiness: Kindness to the Poor (Proverbs 14:20-22, 31-34)

B. BLESSINGS OF THE GENEROUS (v. 9)

9. A generous man will himself be blessed, for he shares his food with the poor.

The *generous* person contrasts sharply with someone who is stingy (Proverbs 23:6; 28:22). The former looks for opportunities to share blessings with others, going out of his or her way to find those who need help. This verse suggests that the generous person provides *food* for others even when it means taking from his or her own supply.

III. GOD PROTECTS HIS PEOPLE (PROVERBS 22:16, 22, 23; 23:10, 11)

A. FROM OPPRESSORS (v. 16)

16. He who oppresses the poor to increase his wealth and he who gives gifts to the rich—both come to poverty.

Every society has oppressors who take advantage of others to enrich themselves. This is just as true today as it was in ancient times—maybe even more so. Oppressors come in many sizes and shapes. Some may be military dictators, who seize power by force and squeeze everything they can from the people they rule in order to support their lavish lifestyles.

More familiar to most of us are those who sell shoddy goods or overcharge their customers. When a natural disaster strikes, we see such "vultures" swarm into the disaster area, taking advantage of people who have been left destitute by hurricanes or floods. And what about companies that import goods from countries that use child labor to produce products that we gladly buy because they are less expensive than goods produced here at home? The list could go on, but we can see that this verse is just as applicable today as when it was written. We have our share of oppressors today; the only difference is that they are more sophisticated than they were in Bible times.

The oppressors may seem to prosper for a time. But justice will be done. The twentieth century has seen the violent end of some brutal dictators—Hitler, Mussolini, and Ceausescu are examples. But those who are able to avoid justice in this life eventually will stand before the Eternal Judge, where complete justice will be meted out.

God has promised to protect *the poor* from oppressors. But how would you answer an unbeliever who says, "Why isn't your God rescuing such-and-such people from their grinding poverty?" Gideon asked a similar question in Judges 6:13, and the answer in the very next verse was "Go . . . and save Israel. . . . Am I not sending you?"

B. FROM ROBBERS (vv. 22, 23)

22, 23. Do not exploit the poor because they are poor and do not crush the needy in court, for the LORD will take up their case and will plunder those who plunder them.

The opening lines of these two verses hearken back to verse 16. *The poor,* with what little they do have, are ready targets for robbers because their poverty leaves them in a weakened condition, both socially and physically. The poor are usually not very well organized. The rich ignore them and their problems and, in fact, may even contribute to their problems by oppressing them and charging interest on loans. Governments frequently ignore their pleas for help because the poor don't have many friends in high places and don't make many campaign contributions. These same conditions exist today in the slum areas of large cities.

The poor could appeal for justice from judges presiding in *court,* which was ordinarily held at the city gate in ancient times. But justice here was not always fair.

How To Say It

Ahab. AY-hab.

Ceausescu (Romanian). Chow-CHESS-cue.

Naboth. NAY-bawth.

Hosea. Ho-ZAY-uh.

Isaiah. Eye-ZAY-uh.

Jeremiah. Jair-uh-MY-uh.

Jezebel. JEZ-uh-bel.

WHAT DO YOU THINK?

These proverbs speak of the benefit that comes to those who are humble, reverent, and generous. What is there about these qualities that blesses us?

WHAT DO YOU THINK?

What are some specific ways that your local church or you personally might "care for the poor" of other needy persons?

PRAYER

Father, we pray for the sick, the hungry, and the helpless of the world. But we also pray for ourselves that we may open our hearts to them. Save us from "compassion fatigue," which results in our doing nothing. In Jesus' name, amen.

THOUGHT TO REMEMBER

"Blessed are the merciful, for they will be shown mercy"
—Matthew 5:7.

When King Ahab wanted Naboth's vineyard, the powerful Jezebel arranged with the elders and nobles to bring false witness against Naboth. He was condemned, taken outside the city, and stoned (1 Kings 21:1-14).

C. FROM LAND GRABBERS (vv. 10, 11)

10, 11. Do not move an ancient boundary stone or encroach on the fields of the fatherless, for their Defender is strong; he will take up their case against you.

Fertile soil was scarce in ancient Israel, and it was important for a family to hold on to whatever land it had. In a day when accurate surveying tools and precise records of land ownership did not exist, people had to depend on identifiable landmarks to indicate boundary lines, such as large rocks, outcroppings of stone, or trees. Some of these could be moved or changed in such a way that one could steal land from a neighbor. *The fatherless* (orphans)—especially young children—would be quite vulnerable to this kind of activity. With no older person around to remember where the landmarks originally had been, an evil person could readily take advantage.

But their situation was not hopeless. Even though they had no human defenders, *their Defender is strong*. This Defender, of course, was God. One important instance when he ended up pleading *their case* was the punishment meted out in the form of exile (Isaiah 1:23-25; 10:1-4; Jeremiah 5:27-29; Hosea 5:10).

CONCLUSION

When we were children, we were urged to clean our plates at mealtime because the "starving children in India" had no food at all, let alone any food to waste. There are still starving children in India and many other places in the world. The problem is getting worse, not better, and because of the media we are made more aware of them. Perhaps forty thousand children die of starvation every day worldwide.

There are many reasons for world hunger. Some things, such as floods, hurricanes, and drought, are beyond human control. Insects, which eat a very large percentage of the world's food supply each year, are only partially within our control. In other situations, political and military upheavals have created starvation and poverty in areas that could support themselves. Some governments intentionally use hunger as a "weapon" against factions of their own populations. Sometimes starvation and malnutrition occur because people do not know how to use the resources they have available. The extent of the need is so great that frequently only governmental and large private relief agencies, such as the International Disaster Emergency Service (IDES), can be of real help. We rejoice that such agencies are in place and that we can contribute to them financially.

But we don't have to travel overseas to find the needy. They are all about us, especially in our larger cities. Many churches support missions in the inner cities to feed, clothe, and teach the homeless. These missions always need contributions of food, clothing, and money. But they especially need volunteers. It is not easy work, and at times it is even frightening, but God gives a special blessing to those who do this task.

Remember: you don't have to get a passport, a visa, and learn a foreign language to help. The needy are all about us. For example, one man serves as a financial counselor with a group that shows people how to manage their money so that they can escape poverty. A woman serves with an agency that counsels unwed pregnant women, helping them arrange for their babies to be adopted or for the mothers to become responsible single mothers. Yes, the impoverished "Lazarus" may be at your gate. Don't be "the rich man" who ignored him!

Discovery Learning

This page contains an alternate lesson plan emphasizing learning activities. Classes desiring such student involvement will find these suggestions helpful. The next page is a reproducible activity page to further enhance discovery learning.

LEARNING GOALS

After this lesson each student will be able to:

1. Give several reasons, both practical and theological, why the believer should help those who are poor.

2. List reasons that Christians sometimes give for not helping the poor, and examine each in light of today's Scriptures.

3. Get involved in some effort, either individually or with others, to provide tangible relief to some who are disadvantaged in some way.

INTO THE LESSON

OPTION: *Debate*. Early in the week ask two people from your class to debate the resolution: "The poor are poor because they are the victims of the greed and callousness of the rich." Allow each person two to three minutes to present his case. Then make the transition to the Bible study by saying, "Our debaters have raised some interesting and controversial points about poverty. Let's look to the Word of God to get God's perspective on the poor."

OPTION: *Agree-Disagree Quiz*. Begin your class today with this Agree-Disagree Quiz. The statements are designed to be somewhat controversial. The purpose is to get people to say, "But the Bible says . . . ." When people ask you for the "right" answers, turn the question back with, "What do you think?"

1. People are usually poor because of their own laziness, foolishness, or inability to handle money.

2. God has a special concern for the poor.

3. The church has an obligation to meet the needs of the poor.

4. The government has a responsibility to meet needs of the poor.

5. Neither the church nor the government can solve the problem of poverty.

Use a transition statement like the one in the debate option above to move to the Bible study portion of the lesson.

INTO THE WORD

OPTION: *Personalized Paraphrase*. Guide your class in writing a personalized paraphrase of today's text. Personalize the passage by inserting personal pronouns, such as *I, me,* and *my.* Paraphrase by putting the ideas of the text in your own words.

For example, Proverbs 19:17 might be personalized and paraphrased to read, "When I show pity by giving to the poor, I am actually lending my money to the Lord; and he will no doubt pay back my loan!"

OPTION: *True-False Quiz*. Have your class write a true-false quiz about God's view of poverty and the poor. Each verse could easily generate several questions. For example, Proverbs 19:17 suggests these affirmations:

1. If I give money to a beggar, God will give back to me whatever I give to the poor.

2. One cannot show pity without a financial involvement.

3. Giving money indiscriminately to the poor is neither wise or godly.

4. Having pity on the poor means giving them money.

5. Giving money to the poor is wasting your money.

(Directions for this activity are in *NIV® Bible Student.*)

OPTION: *Reproducible Page*. Distribute copies of the activity "Making a Choice" from the next page and have students follow the directions there. Discuss each point.

OPTION: *Make a Poster*. Each verse in today's lesson could stand alone and make good sense. Therefore, each would make a good poster to decorate your classroom or provide a focal center for the "Into Life" section of the lesson. Provide poster board and brightly-colored markers. Ask class members to letter posters to present the truths of today's text graphically.

INTO LIFE

OPTION: *Partner With a City Congregation*. Probably someone in your class is acquainted with an urban congregation in need of help that your class could provide. Ask for volunteers to look for an urban church involved with serving the poor that you could become a partner with in providing prayer support, funds, equipment, and short-term workers. (The directions for this activity are included in *NIV® Bible Student.*)

OPTION: *Sponsor a Child*. Many Sunday school classes or individual class members have the resources to sponsor a third-world child or others in need through some missionary benevolent agency. Ask for volunteers to form a search committee to gather information. Start by checking with missionaries that your church supports. (The directions for this activity are included in *NIV® Bible Student.*) A related activity is included under the "Making a Difference" segment of the reproducible page.

Making a Choice

What one does with the financial blessings and opportunities God gives him is a choice of great consequence. For each of the following multiple-choice questions, make the biblical choice, based on today's text.

__1. He who is kind to the poor (A) is a fool, (B) is creating dependency, (C) will be loved, (D) lends to the Lord.

__2. A good name is more desirable than (A) great riches, (B) a wardrobe of fine clothes, (C) a gold ring, (D) a quiet household.

__3. Rich and poor have one thing in common: (A) they both want more money; (B) they both die; (C) the Lord is the Maker of both; (D) money corrupts both.

__4. A generous man will himself be (A) poor one day, (B) judged by God, (C) admired by all, (D) blessed.

__5. He who gives gifts to the rich will (A) gain an influential friend, (B) have a hole in his money bag, (C) come to poverty, (D) receive honor among the wealthy.

__6. If one crushes the needy in court, (A) judges won't care; (B) the Lord will take the case of the poor; (C) he will be reviled in his village; (D) he will lose much sleep.

__7. To encroach on the fields of the fatherless will result in the encroacher (A) being stoned, (B) meeting the poor's Defender, God, (C) being praised for his shrewdness, (D) risking the wrath of their mother.

Making a Difference

What Christian service agencies that minister to the poor and needy do you know? (Your church's budget may include some.) Write each here.

(If you cannot name any, how can you discover such agencies? To whom can you go for such information?)

James, led by the Spirit, says, "Suppose a brother or sister is without clothes and daily food. If one of you says to him, 'Go, I wish you well; keep warm and well fed,' but does nothing about his physical needs, what good is it?" (James 2:15, 16)

The question comes to each who knows of needs among God's children: "Am I good for nothing?" Use the space below to write a statement of commitment (between you and God) to provide tangible help for someone who is in need.